Fodor's

FIRST New EDITION

China

D1102806

The complete guide, thoroughly up to date

Packed with details that will make your trip

The must-see sights, off and on the beaten path

What to see, what to skip

Mix-and-match vacation itineraries

City strolls, countryside adventures

Smart lodging and dining options

Essential local do's and taboos

Transportation tips, distances and directions

Key contacts, savvy travel tips

When to go, what to pack

Clear, accurate, easy-to-use maps

Books to read, videos to watch, background essays

Fodor's Travel Publications, Inc.
New York • Toronto • London • Sydney • Auckland
www.fodors.com/

Fodor's China

EDITOR: Nancy van Itallie

Editorial Contributors: Jan Alexander, Anya Bernstein, Colin B. Cowles, Shann Davies, Nigel Fisher, Nancy Hearst, Christina Knight, Christopher Knowles, David Murphy, Jennifer Paull, Bill Smith, Dinah Spritzer, Marshall Schwartzmann, Saul Thomas, Lily Tung, Deborah Washburn, George Wehrfritz, Angela Yuan

Editorial Production: Linda K. Schmidt, Melissa Klurman

Maps: David Lindroth, *cartographer;* Steven K. Amsterdam, *map editor*

Design: Fabrizio La Rocca, *art director;* Guido Caroti, *associate art director;* Jolie Novak, *photo editor*

Production/Manufacturing: Mike Costa

Cover Photograph: Dennis Cox/ChinaStock

Copyright

First Edition

ISBN 0–679–03459–5

Special Sales

Fodor's Travel Publications are available at special discounts for bulk purchases for sales promotions or premiums. Special editions, including personalized covers, excerpts of existing guides, and corporate imprints, can be created in large quantities for special needs. For more information, contact your local bookseller or write to Special Markets, Fodor's Travel Publications, 201 East 50th Street, New York, NY 10022. Inquiries from Canada should be directed to your local Canadian bookseller or sent to Random House of Canada, Ltd., Marketing Department, 2775 Matheson Blvd. E, Mississauga, Ontario L4W 4P7. Inquiries from the United Kingdom should be sent to Fodor's Travel Publications, 20 Vauxhall Bridge Road, London, England SW1V 2SA.

PRINTED IN THE UNITED STATES OF AMERICA

10 9 8 7 6 5 4 3 2 1

CONTENTS

ON THE ROAD WITH FODOR'S

WE'RE ALWAYS THRILLED to get letters from readers, especially one like this:

It took us an hour to decide what book to buy and we now know we picked the best one. Your book was wonderful, easy to follow, very accurate, and good on pointing out eating places, informal as well as formal. When we saw other people using your book, we would look at each other and smile.

Our editors and writers are deeply committed to making every Fodor's guide "the best one"—not only accurate but always charming, brimming with sound recommendations and solid ideas, right on the mark in describing restaurants and hotels, and full of fascinating facts that make you view what you've traveled to see in a rich new light.

About Our Writers

Our success in achieving our goals—and in helping to make your trip the best of all possible vacations—is a credit to the hard work of our extraordinary writers.

Jan Alexander, who wrote Chapters 8 and 11 (Hong Kong and Western China) and the essay "Doing Business in China," has lived on and off in Hong Kong since 1992. She has written for *Newsweek, Money,* and the *Wall Street Journal,* specializing in business and not-for-the-faint-hearted travel stories.

Anya Bernstein, who wrote Chapter 5, East Central China, graduated from Columbia College in 1996 and spent the following year in China at the Johns Hopkins–Nanjing University Center for Chinese and American Studies, in Nanjing. She is working on her doctorate.

Colin B. Cowles, who wrote the Books and Films and Vocabulary sections, is director of program operations at China Institute in America, in New York City. Mr. Cowles has lived in Xian and in Nanjing and traveled throughout China. He is fluent in Mandarin and frequently runs travel workshops at China Institute.

Shann Davies, who wrote Chapter 6, Guangdong, is a veteran travel writer who has lived in Asia for many years. Now a long-time resident of Hong Kong, she has traveled extensively around China. She is the author of the annual *China Welcomes You* book, the *Official Guide to China,* and magazines such as *Guangdong Citylife.*

Nigel Fisher, the peripatetic writer and knowledgeable publisher of "Voyager International," a newsletter on world travel, wrote Chapter 12, Tibet. His particular interests are in telling his readers about art, about good places to stay, and about the most delicious food. He is currently living in Thailand.

Nancy Hearst, who wrote "China at a Glance: A Chronology," in Chapter 13, is librarian at the Fairbank Center for East Asian Research, Harvard University.

Christopher Knowles, who wrote Chapters 7 and 9 (Southeastern China and West Central China), is the author of books on England, Italy, Russia, China, and Japan. For many years a tour guide specializing in train tours through the former Soviet Union, Mongolia, China, and the Orient Express and Silk Road routes, he has been a regular visitor to China since 1981.

Bill Smith, who wrote Chapter 10, The Mongolias, and the nightlife section of Chapter 2, Beijing, studied philosophy (BA) and sociology (MA) at Leeds and London universities. He is now a freelance writer whose work has appeared in publications in Britain and the United States. He has traveled extensively in China since his first visit in 1988, after which he began studying Chinese language and culture. He has lived in Beijing since 1996.

Saul Thomas, who helped prepare Chapter 5, East Central China, has studied and traveled in China and Taiwan for 2½ years. He is currently working toward a master's degree in modern Chinese history at Nanjing University. In the future, he hopes to enter a PhD program in the United States focusing on current Chinese culture and politics.

Lily Tung, a native Californian, wrote Chapter 4, Shanghai. She has lived in Shanghai on and off since 1991 when she first traveled to China to study the language. She has written for the *Wall Street Journal, South China Morning Post, Newsweek,* and *Asian Business Magazine.* She is currently the editor of the magazine *Shanghai Talk* and a correspondent for PRI's "The World."

George Wehrfritz and **Diana Garrett** collaborated on Chapter 2, Beijing. The pair moved to Taiwan in 1985, married there two years later, and have lived in Asia ever since. George co-authored *Southwest China Off the Beaten Track,* a backpacker's guide to China's remote southwest, published in 1988. He is currently *Newsweek* magazine's Beijing bureau chief. In Taiwan, Diana wrote and edited travel articles for *Verve,* EVA Air's inflight magazine. She currently does poverty alleviation work in Beijing.

Angie Yuan, who wrote Chapter 1, Destination China, recieved an MFA from the University of Arizona and is currently in the process of writing her first collection of poetry. She spent a year teaching English in Shanghai after finishing her graduate work and now edits the English News Program for the Shanghai International Broadcasting Station.

We'd also like to thank Shen Mao Mao of Haida Tours in Nanjing and Stewart Shen of the Guilin Shanhu Travel Service for their valuable help in gathering information for the book.

New This Year

We'e extremely proud of this all-new edition of *Fodor's China.* Our writers and editors have worked very hard to compile this guide so that your trip to China can be an adventurous, exciting, and enjoyable one.

We're also proud to announce that the American Society of Travel Agents has endorsed Fodor's as its guidebook of choice. ASTA is the world's largest and most influential travel trade association, operating in more than 170 countries, with 27,000 members pledged to adhere to a strict code of ethics reflecting the Society's motto, "Integrity in Travel." ASTA shares Fodor's devotion to providing smart, honest travel information and advice to travelers, and we've long recommended that our readers consult ASTA member agents for the experience and professionalism they bring to the table.

On the Web, check out Fodor's site (www.fodors.com/) for information on major destinations around the world and travel-savvy interactive features. The Web site also lists the 85-plus radio stations nationwide that carry the Fodor's Travel Show, a live call-in program that airs every weekend. Tune in to hear guests discuss their wonderful adventures—or call in to get answers for your most pressing travel questions.

How to Use This Book

Organization

Up front is the **Gold Guide,** an easy-to-use section divided alphabetically by topic. Under each listing you'll find tips and information that will help you accomplish what you need to in China. You'll also find addresses and telephone numbers of organizations and companies that offer destination-related services and detailed information and publications.

The first chapter in the guide, Destination: China, helps get you in the mood for your trip. New and Noteworthy cues you in on trends and happenings, What's Where gets you oriented, Pleasures and Pastimes describes the activities and sights that really make China unique, Fodor's Choice showcases our top picks, and Festivals and Seasonal Events alerts you to special events you'll want to seek out.

Chapters in *Fodor's China* are arranged by major city or region, starting with Beijing and moving on to the northeastern provinces and then south and westward through the country to Tibet. Each city chapter begins with an Exploring section subdivided by neighborhood; each subsection recommends a walking or driving tour and lists sights in alphabetical order. Each regional chapter is divided by province; within each province, towns are covered in logical geographical order, and attractive stretches of road and minor points of interest between them are indicated by the designation *En Route.* Within town sections, all restaurants and lodgings are grouped together.

To help you decide what to visit in the time you have, all chapters begin with recommended itineraries; you can mix and match those from several chapters to create a complete vacation. The A-to-Z section that ends all province sections covers getting there and getting around. It also provides helpful contacts and resources.

At the end of the book, in Portraits, you'll find a useful chronology of Chinese history and a wonderful essay on doing business in China, followed by suggestions for any pretrip research you want to do, from recommended reading to movies on tape with China as a backdrop.

Icons and Symbols

★ Our special recommendations
✗ Restaurant
🏠 Lodging establishment
✗🏠 Lodging establishment whose restaurant warrants a special trip
⚠ Campgrounds
☺ Good for kids (rubber duckie)
☞ Sends you to another section of the guide for more information
✉ Address
☎ Telephone number
FAX Fax number
☉ Opening and closing times
🎫 Admission prices (those we give apply to adults; substantially reduced fees are almost always available for children, students, and senior citizens)

Numbers in white and black circles—② and ❷, for example—that appear on the maps, in the margins, and within the tours correspond to one another.

Dining and Lodging

The restaurants and lodgings we list are the cream of the crop in each price range. Price charts appear in the Pleasures and Pastimes section that follows each chapter introduction.

Hotel Facilities

We always list the facilities that are available—but we don't specify whether they cost extra: When pricing accommodations, always ask what's included. In addition, assume that all rooms have private baths unless otherwise noted.

Assume that hotels operate on the **European Plan** (EP, with no meals) unless we note that they use the **Continental Plan** (CP, with a Continental breakfast daily).

Restaurant Reservations and Dress Codes

Reservations are always a good idea; we note only when they're essential or when they are not accepted. Book as far ahead as you can, and reconfirm when you get to town. Unless otherwise noted, the restaurants listed are open daily for lunch and dinner. We mention dress only when men are required to wear a jacket or a jacket and tie. Look for an overview of local habits in the Gold Guide and in the Pleasures and Pastimes section that follows each chapter introduction.

Credit Cards

The following abbreviations are used: **AE**, American Express; **DC**, Diners Club; **MC**, MasterCard; and **V**, Visa.

Don't Forget to Write

You can use this book in the confidence that all prices and opening times are based on information supplied to us at press time; Fodor's cannot accept responsibility for any errors. Time inevitably brings changes, so always confirm information when it matters—especially if you're making a detour to visit a specific place. In addition, when making reservations be sure to mention if you have a disability or are traveling with children, if you prefer a private bath or a certain type of bed, or if you have specific dietary needs or other concerns.

Were the restaurants we recommended as described? Did our hotel picks exceed your expectations? Did you find a museum we recommended a waste of time? If you have complaints, we'll look into them and revise our entries when the facts warrant it. If you've discovered a special place that we haven't included, we'll pass the information along to our correspondents and have them check it out. So send us your feedback, positive *and* negative: email us at editors@fodors.com (specifying the name of the book on the subject line) or write the China editor at Fodor's, 201 East 50th Street, New York, New York 10022. Have a wonderful trip!

Karen Cure
Editorial Director

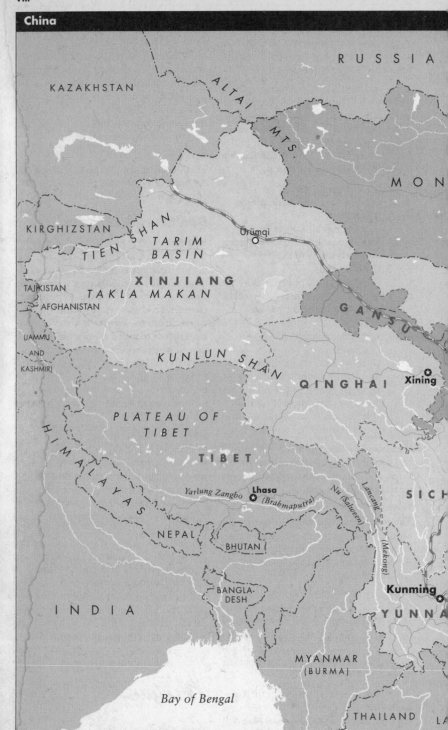

China

RUSSIA

KAZAKHSTAN

ALTAI MTS.

MON

Ürümqi

TIEN SHAN

TARIM BASIN

XINJIANG

TAKLA MAKAN

KIRGHIZSTAN

TAJIKISTAN

AFGHANISTAN

(JAMMU AND KASHMIR)

KUNLUN SHAN

GANSU

QINGHAI

Xining

PLATEAU OF TIBET

TIBET

HIMALAYAS

Yarlung Zangbo

Lhasa (Brahmaputra)

Nu (Salween)

Lancang (Mekong)

SICH

NEPAL

BHUTAN

BANGLA-DESH

INDIA

Kunming

YUNNA

MYANMAR (BURMA)

Bay of Bengal

THAILAND

LA

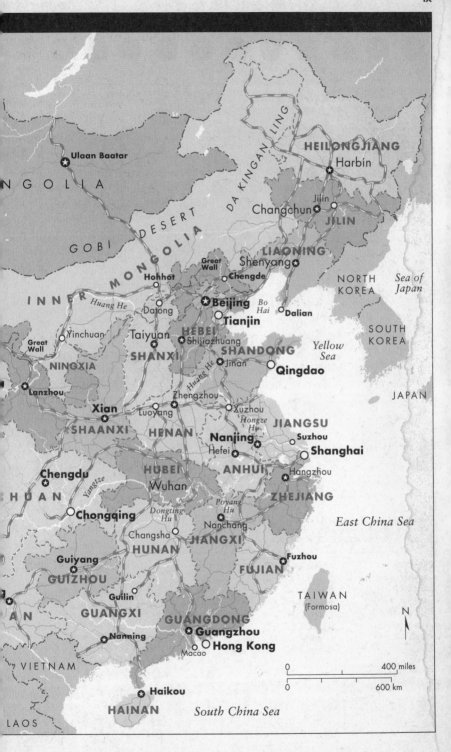

World Time Zones

MONDAY
SUNDAY

International Date Line

+12 +13 -9

-10

-11 -10

+11

+12

-7

-8

-6

-5 -4

-3:30

-5

-4

-10

-3

-3

-4

-3

-3

Numbers below vertical bands relate each zone to Greenwich Mean Time (0 hrs.).
Local times frequently differ from these general indications,
as indicated by light-face numbers on map.

+11	+12	-11	-10	-9	-8	-7	-6	-5	-4	-3	-2

Algiers, **29**
Anchorage, **3**
Athens, **41**
Auckland, **1**
Baghdad, **46**
Bangkok, **50**
Beijing, **54**

Berlin, **34**
Bogotá, **19**
Budapest, **37**
Buenos Aires, **24**
Caracas, **22**
Chicago, **9**
Copenhagen, **33**
Dallas, **10**

Delhi, **48**
Denver, **8**
Djakarta, **53**
Dublin, **26**
Edmonton, **7**
Hong Kong, **56**
Honolulu, **2**

Istanbul, **40**
Jerusalem, **42**
Johannesburg, **44**
Lima, **20**
Lisbon, **28**
London
(Greenwich), **27**
Los Angeles, **6**
Madrid, **38**
Manila, **57**

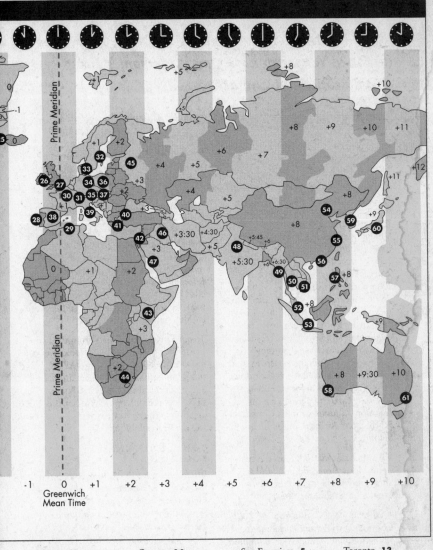

SMART TRAVEL TIPS A TO Z

Basic Information on Traveling in China, Savvy Tips to Make Your Trip Easier, and Companies and Organizations to Contact

A
AIR TRAVEL

MAJOR AIRLINE OR LOW-COST CARRIER?

Most people choose a flight based on price, yet there are other issues to consider. Major airlines offer the greatest number of departures; smaller airlines—including regional, low-cost and no-frill airlines—usually have a more limited number of flights daily. Major airlines have frequent-flyer partners, which allow you to credit mileage earned on one airline to your account with another. Low-cost airlines offer a definite price advantage and fewer restrictions, such as advance-purchase requirements. Safety-wise, low-cost carriers as a group have a good history, but **check the safety record before booking** any low-cost carrier; call the Federal Aviation Administration's Consumer Hotline (☞ Airline Complaints, *below*).

Various Asian national airlines also fly to Hong Kong, Beijing, and Shanghai via their capital cities, usually at reasonable rates.

➤ MAJOR AIRLINES: **Asiana** (☎ 800/227–4262) to Beijing and Shanghai via Seoul on a local carrier. **Canadian** (☎ 800/426–7000) to Beijing via Vancouver or Toronto. **Korean Air** (☎ 800/438–5000) to Beijing via Seoul. **Northwest** (☎ 800/225–2525) to Beijing. **United** (☎ 800/241–6522) to Beijing via Tokyo.

➤ SMALLER AIRLINES: **China Eastern** (☎ 818/583–1500) to Beijing and Shanghai.

GET THE LOWEST FARE

The least-expensive airfares to China are priced for round-trip travel. Major airlines usually require that you **book far in advance and stay at least seven days** and no more than 30 to get the lowest fares. Ask about "ultrasaver" fares, which are the cheapest; they must be booked 90 days in advance and are nonrefundable. A little more expensive are "supersaver" fares, which require only a 30-day advance purchase. Remember that penalties for refunds or scheduling changes are stiffer for international tickets, usually about $150. International flights are also sensitive to the season: **plan to fly in the off-season** for the cheapest fares. If your destination or home city has more than one gateway, **compare prices to and from different airports.** Also price flights scheduled for off-peak hours, which may be significantly less expensive.

To save money on flights from the United Kingdom and back, **look into an APEX or Super-PEX ticket.** APEX tickets must be booked in advance and have certain restrictions. Super-PEX tickets can be purchased at the airport on the day of departure—subject to availability.

DON'T STOP UNLESS YOU MUST

When you book, **look for nonstop flights** and **remember that "direct" flights stop at least once.** International flights on a country's flag carrier are almost always nonstop; U.S. airlines often fly direct. Try to **avoid connecting flights,** which require a change of plane. Two airlines may jointly operate a connecting flight, so ask if your airline operates every segment—you may find that your preferred carrier flies you only part of the way.

USE AN AGENT

Travel agents, especially those who specialize in finding the lowest fares (☞ Discounts & Deals, *below*), can be especially helpful for booking plane tickets. When you're quoted a price, **ask your agent if the price is likely to get any lower.** Good agents know the seasonal fluctuations of airfares and can usually anticipate a sale or fare war. However, waiting can be risky: The fare could go *up* as seats become scarce, and you may wait so long that your preferred flight sells out. A wait-and-see strategy works best if your plans are flexible, but if you must arrive and depart on certain dates, don't delay.

CHECK WITH CONSOLIDATORS

Consolidators buy tickets for scheduled flights at reduced rates from the airlines and then sell them at prices that beat the best fare available directly from the airlines, usually without advance restrictions. Sometimes you can even get your money back if you need to return the ticket. Carefully read the fine print detailing penalties for changes and cancellations, and **confirm your consolidator reservation with the airline.**

➤ CONSOLIDATORS: **United States Air Consolidators Association** (✉ 925 L St., Suite 220, Sacramento, CA 95814, ☎ 916/441–4166, FAX 916/441–3520).

Airlines routinely overbook planes, knowing that not everyone with a ticket will show up; but sometimes everyone does. When that happens, airlines ask for volunteers to give up their seats. In return these volunteers usually get a certificate for a free flight and are rebooked on the next flight out. If there are not enough volunteers, the airline must choose who will be denied boarding. The first to be bumped are passengers who checked in late and those flying on discounted tickets, **so get to the gate and check in as early as possible,** especially during peak periods.

Always **bring a photo ID to the airport.** You may be asked to show it before you are allowed to check in.

ENJOY THE FLIGHT

For more legroom, **request an emergency-aisle seat;** don't however, sit in the row in front of the emergency aisle or in front of a bulkhead, where seats may not recline.

If you don't like airline food, **ask for special meals when booking.** These can be vegetarian, low-cholesterol, or kosher, for example.

Some carriers have prohibited smoking throughout their systems; others allow smoking only on certain routes or even certain departures from that route, so **contact your carrier regarding its smoking policy.**

COMPLAIN IF NECESSARY

If your baggage goes astray or your flight goes awry, complain right away. Most carriers require that you file a claim immediately.

➤ AIRLINE COMPLAINTS: U.S. Department of Transportation **Aviation Consumer Protection Division** (✉ C-75, Room 4107, Washington, DC 20590, ☎ 202/366–2220). **Federal Aviation Administration (FAA) Consumer Hotline** (☎ 800/322–7873).

WITHIN CHINA

Within mainland China, all carriers are regional subsidiaries of the **Civil Aviation Administration of China (CAAC).** Reservations and ticket purchases can be made in the U.S. through the **U.S.-China Travel Service,** which has offices in Los Angeles and San Francisco; in Hong Kong at the **China National Aviation Corporation** office or **Air-China Travel Ltd.;** or in China through local **China Travel Service** (CTS) offices (☞ *individual city and regional chapters for addresses*).

The service on China's regional carriers has improved somewhat since the national airline, CAAC, was broken up into regional carriers. Flights between major cities generally offer first-class or business-class seating. The food is at best unremarkable. You can ask for vegetarian meals, but don't count on getting what you ordered. Generally, the best that can be said is that they get you where you're going.

➤ RESERVATIONS: **U.S.-China Travel Service** (U.S.: ☎ 800/332–2831 in the U.S.; Hong Kong: ✉ 34th floor, United Centre; 95 Queensway; Admiralty, ☎ 852/2861–0288). **Air-China Travel Ltd.** (✉ Room 1604, Wheelock House, 20 Pedder St., Central, Hong Kong, ☎ 852/2801–9111).

AIRPORTS

The major airports are Beijing Airport, Hong Kong's Kai Tak International Airport, and Shanghai Hongqiao International Airport.

Flying time to Hong Kong or Beijing is between 20 and 24 hours from New York, including a stopover on the West Coast or in Tokyo; 17 to 20 hours from Chicago; and 13 hours direct from Los Angeles or San Francisco.

➤ AIRPORT INFORMATION: Beijing Capital International Airport (☎ 010/6456–3604). Kai Tak International Airport (☎ 852/2769–7531). Shanghai Hongqiao International Airport (☎ 021/6298–8918).

B

BUS TRAVEL

There are public buses in every city, to almost every destination. The fare is usually about 20 fen. The best way to use public buses in a Chinese city is to **ask the hotel concierge which one to take to a specific destination.** However, if you don't speak Mandarin, you're likely to get lost.

In **Hong Kong,** buses travel all over Hong Kong Island and into the New Territories. The **Hong Kong Tourist Association** (HKTA) Visitor Information Centers at Star Ferry, Tsim Sha Tsui, and Jardin House, Central, have bus maps. Fares run from HK$3 to $HK30.

➤ INFORMATION: **Hong Kong Tourist Association** (HKTA) information hot line (☎ 852/2807–1199).

BUSINESS HOURS

Banks, offices, government departments, and police stations (known as Public Security Bureaus or PSB) are open Monday to Saturday. Most open between 8 and 9 AM, close for lunch from noon to 2 PM, and reopen until 5 or 6. Many branches of the Bank of China, China International Travel Service (CITS), and stores catering to foreigners are open Sunday morning. Some close on Wednesday afternoon. Museums are open 9 to 4 six days a week. They are usually closed on Monday.

Stores in Hong Kong generally open at 10. Outside Central, some shops stay open until 7:30 or 9:30 PM. Most are open on Sunday.

All businesses are closed on Chinese New Year and other major holidays.

C

CAMERAS, CAMCORDERS, AND COMPUTERS

Always **keep your film, tape, or computer disks out of the sun.** Carry an extra supply of batteries, and **be prepared to turn on your camera, camcorder, or laptop** to prove to security personnel that the device is real. Always **ask for hand inspection of film,** which becomes clouded after successive exposures to airport x-ray machines, and **keep videotapes and computer disks away from metal detectors.**

➤ PHOTO HELP: Kodak Information Center (☎ 800/242–2424). *Kodak Guide to Shooting Great Travel Pictures,* available in bookstores or from Fodor's Travel Publications (☎ 800/533–6478; $16.50 plus $4 shipping).

CUSTOMS

Before departing, **register your foreign-made camera or laptop with U.S. Customs** (☞ Customs & Duties, *below*). If your equipment is U.S.-made, call the consulate of the country you'll be visiting to find out whether the device should be registered with local customs upon arrival.

CAR RENTAL

Car rentals are not recommended and generally not available in China. Some local rentals are now possible in Beijing and Shanghai, but only for driving within the city. It is possible, however, to hire a car with a driver for the day, and the costs in most Chinese cities are reasonable. In China, check with your hotel concierge or local CITS/CTS office about car hires. Many hotels also have bicycles for rent at very inexpensive day rates.

In Hong Kong, the only major car rental company is **Avis.** Rates begin at $100 a day and $400 a week for an economy car with unlimited mileage.

➤ MAJOR AGENCIES: **Avis** (☎ 800/331–1084; in Canada ☎ 800/879–2847).

NEED INSURANCE?

When driving a rented car you are generally responsible for any damage to or loss of the vehicle. You also are liable for any property damage or personal injury that you may cause while driving. Before you rent, **see what coverage you already have** under the terms of your personal auto insurance policy and credit cards.

BEWARE SURCHARGES

To avoid a hefty refueling fee, **fill the tank just before you turn in the car,** but be aware that gas stations near the rental outlet may overcharge.

MEET THE REQUIREMENTS

In China your own driver's license is not acceptable. An International Driver's Permit is a good idea; it's available from the American or Canadian automobile association, or, in the United Kingdom, from the Automobile Association or Royal Automobile Club.

CHILDREN AND TRAVEL

CHILDREN IN CHINA

The Chinese are fond of children, and foreign children are likely to receive a great deal of attention. The cities have parks, zoos, and frequent performances involving acrobats, jugglers, and puppets. Most large international hotels in Hong Kong, Beijing, and Shanghai have baby-sitting services and may even offer special activities, but services may not be on a level with those in the West. In addition, travel can be rugged, familiar foods hard to find, and there are health risks and sanitation problems. It is not advisable to take children on trips outside the major cities.

Be sure to plan ahead and **involve your youngsters** as you outline your trip. When packing, include things to keep them busy en route. On sightseeing days try to schedule activities of special interest to your children. If you are hiring a car, you can probably **arrange for a car seat** when you reserve in Beijing or Shanghai; look into bringing your own if you'll be driving in other parts of the country.

Most hotels in China allow children under a certain age to stay in their parents' room at no extra charge, but others charge them as extra adults; be sure to **ask about the cutoff age for children's discounts.**

➤ LOCAL INFORMATION: Check with the CTS office in most cities for activities or tours. In Hong Kong, check with the **HKTA** (☎ 852/2807–1199) for scheduled activities for children. *The Great Hong Kong Dragon Adventure*, an illustrated book about a dragon that flies children from place to place, is available at HKTA Visitor Information Centers.

FLYING

As a general rule, infants under two not occupying a seat fly at greatly reduced fares and occasionally for free. If your children are two or older **ask about children's airfares.**

In general the adult baggage allowance applies to children paying half or more of the adult fare. When booking, **ask about carry-on allowances for those traveling with infants.** In general, for babies charged 10% of the adult fare you are allowed one carry-on bag and a collapsible stroller, which may have to be checked; you may be limited to less if the flight is full.

According to the FAA it's a good idea to use safety seats aloft for children weighing less than 40 pounds. Airlines, however, can set their own policies: U.S. carriers allow FAA-approved models but usually require that you buy a ticket, even if your child would otherwise ride free, since the seats must be strapped into regular seats. Airline rules vary regarding their use, so it's important to **check your airline's policy about using safety seats during takeoff and landing.** Safety seats cannot obstruct any of the other passengers in the row, so get an appropriate seat assignment as early as possible.

When making your reservation, **request children's meals or a free-standing bassinet** if you need them; the latter are available only to those seated at the bulkhead, where there's enough legroom. Remember, however, that bulkhead seats may not have their own overhead bins, and there's no storage space in front of you—a major inconvenience.

CONSUMER PROTECTION

Credit cards have become a common method of payment in China for hotels, airline transportation, and major purchases at international stores. Whenever possible, **pay with a major credit card** so you can cancel payment if there's a problem, provided that you can supply documentation. This is a good practice whether you're buying travel arrangements before your trip or shopping at your destination.

Finally, if you're buying a package or tour, always **consider travel insurance** that includes default coverage (☞ Insurance, *below*).

CUSTOMS AND DUTIES

When shopping, **keep receipts** for all of your purchases. Upon reentering the country, **be ready to show customs officials what you've bought.** If you feel a duty is incorrect, appeal the assessment. If you object to the way your clearance was handled, get the inspector's badge number. In either case, first ask to see a supervisor, then write to the port director at the address listed on your receipt. Send a copy of the receipt and other appropriate documentation. If you still don't get satisfaction, you can take your case to customs headquarters in Washington.

ENTERING CHINA

You will receive a short customs form either in the airplane or in the terminal on landing. If you are bringing in over US$10,000 in cash, you will have to register it. You are not allowed to bring in live animals, fresh produce, or printed matter deemed seditious or pornographic. The former is very broadly defined, of course, and would include anything that criticizes the Chinese government. They do not usually inspect your personal baggage for improper reading matter, but it could happen. It's best, for example, not to bring a book by a Chinese dissident with you. Customs inspection is usually fast and painless, unless of course you're suspected of bringing in the above-mentioned items.

On leaving, you are not allowed to take out Chinese antiques over 150 years old and deemed valuable to the country.

ENTERING THE U.S.

U.S. Customs forbid the importation of ivory and bootlegged goods. Customs officials at home might search your bags if they suspect you of bringing back bootlegged CDs, videos, software, or designer goods for sale in the U.S.

You may bring home $400 worth of foreign goods duty-free if you've been out of the country for at least 48 hours and haven't already used the $400 allowance or any part of it in the past 30 days.

Travelers 21 and older may bring back 1 liter of alcohol duty-free. In addition, regardless of your age, you are allowed 200 cigarettes and 100 non-Cuban cigars. (At press time, a federal rule restricting tobacco access to persons 18 years and older did not apply to importation.) Antiques, which the U.S. Customs Service defines as objects more than 100 years old, enter duty-free, as do original works of art done entirely by hand, including paintings, drawings, and sculptures.

You may also send packages home duty-free: up to $200 worth of goods for personal use, with a limit of one parcel per addressee per day (and no alcohol or tobacco products or perfume worth more than $5); label the package PERSONAL USE, and attach a list of its contents and their retail value. Do not label the package UNSOLICITED GIFT, or your duty-free exemption will drop to $100. Mailed items do not affect your duty-free allowance on your return.

➤ INFORMATION: **U.S. Customs Service** (Inquiries, ✉ Box 7407, Washington, DC 20044, ☎ 202/927–6724; complaints, Office of Regulations and Rulings, 1301 Constitution Ave. NW, Washington, DC 20229; registration of equipment, ✉ Resource Management, 1301 Constitution Ave. NW, Washington DC, 20229, ☎ 202/927–0540).

ENTERING CANADA

If you've been out of Canada for at least seven days you may bring in C$500 worth of goods duty-free. If you've been away for fewer than seven days but more than 48 hours, the duty-free allowance drops to C$200; if your trip lasts 24–48 hours, the allowance is C$50. You may not pool allowances with family members. Goods claimed under the C$500 exemption may follow you by mail; those claimed under the lesser exemptions must accompany you.

Alcohol and tobacco products may be included in the seven-day and 48-hour exemptions but not in the 24-hour exemption. If you meet the age requirements of the province or territory through which you reenter Canada you may bring in, duty-free, 1.14 liters (40 imperial ounces) of wine or liquor *or* 24 12-ounce cans or bottles of beer or ale. If you are 16 or older you may bring in, duty-free, 200 cigarettes and 50 cigars; these items must accompany you.

You may send an unlimited number of gifts worth up to C$60 each duty-free to Canada. Label the package UNSOLICITED GIFT—VALUE UNDER $60. Alcohol and tobacco are excluded.

➤ INFORMATION: **Revenue Canada** (✉ 2265 St. Laurent Blvd. S, Ottawa, Ontario K1G 4K3, ☎ 613/993–0534, 800/461–9999 in Canada).

ENTERING THE U.K.

From countries outside the EU, including China, you may import, duty-free, 200 cigarettes or 50 cigars; 1 liter of spirits or 2 liters of fortified or sparkling wine or liqueurs; 2 liters of still table wine; 60 milliliters of perfume; 250 milliliters of toilet water; plus £136 worth of other goods, including gifts and souvenirs.

➤ INFORMATION: **HM Customs and Excise** (✉ Dorset House, Stamford St., London SE1 9NG, ☎ 0171/202–4227).

D

DISABILITIES AND
ACCESSIBILITY

ACCESS IN CHINA

There are few special facilities for people with disabilities, except in five-star hotels. Public toilets may be particularly problematic, as most are squatters, and buses, which are generally crowded, will be difficult to board. In most restaurants, museums, and other public spaces, people will be helpful and respectful to visitors with disabilities.

The Hong Kong Tourist Association has *A Guide for Physically Handicapped Visitors in Hong Kong,* which lists places with special facilities for people with disabilities and the best

access to hotels, shopping centers, government offices, consulates, restaurants, and churches.

TIPS AND HINTS

When discussing accessibility with an operator or reservationist, **ask hard questions.** Are there any stairs, inside *or* out? Are there grab bars next to the toilet *and* in the shower/tub? How wide is the doorway to the room? To the bathroom? For the most extensive facilities meeting the latest legal specifications, **opt for newer accommodations,** which are more likely to have been designed with access in mind. Older buildings or ships may offer more limited facilities. Be sure to **discuss your needs before booking.**

➤ COMPLAINTS: **Disability Rights Section** (✉ U.S. Department of Justice, Box 66738, Washington, DC 20035–6738, ☎ 202/514–0301 or 800/514–0301, ℻ 202/307–1198, TTY 202/514–0383 or 800/514–0383) for general complaints. **Aviation Consumer Protection Division** (☞ Air Travel, *above*) for airline-related problems. **Civil Rights Office** (✉ U.S. Department of Transportation, Departmental Office of Civil Rights, S-30, 400 7th St. SW, Room 10215, Washington, DC 20590, ☎ 202/366–4648) for problems with surface transportation.

TRAVEL AGENCIES AND TOUR OPERATORS

The Americans with Disabilities Act requires that travel firms serve the needs of all travelers. That said, you should note that some agencies and operators specialize in making travel arrangements for individuals and groups with disabilities.

➤ TRAVELERS WITH MOBILITY PROBLEMS: **Access Adventures** (✉ 206 Chestnut Ridge Rd., Rochester, NY 14624, ☎ 716/889–9096), run by a former physical-rehabilitation counselor. **Accessible Journeys** (✉ 35 W. Sellers Ave., Ridley Park, PA 19078, ☎ 610/521–0339 or 800/846–4537, ℻ 610/521–6959), for escorted tours exclusively for travelers with mobility impairments. **CareVacations** (✉ 5019 49th Ave., Suite 102, Leduc, Alberta T9E 6T5, ☎ 403/986–6404, 800/648–1116 in Canada) has group tours and is especially helpful with cruise vacations. **Hinsdale Travel**

Service (✉ 201 E. Ogden Ave., Suite 100, Hinsdale, IL 60521, ☎ 630/325–1335) is a travel agency that benefits from the advice of wheelchair traveler Janice Perkins. **Wheelchair Journeys** (✉ 16979 Redmond Way, Redmond, WA 98052, ☎ 425/885–2210 or 800/313–4751) is for general travel arrangements.

DISCOUNTS AND DEALS

Be a smart shopper and **compare all your options before making a choice.** A plane ticket bought with a promotional coupon may not be cheaper than the least expensive fare from a discount ticket agency. For high-price travel purchases, such as packages or tours, keep in mind that what you get is just as important as what you save. Just because something is cheap doesn't mean it's a bargain.

LOOK IN YOUR WALLET

When you use your credit card to make travel purchases you may get free travel-accident insurance, collision damage insurance, and medical or legal assistance, depending on the card and the bank that issued it. American Express, MasterCard, and Visa provide one or more of these services, so **get a copy of your credit card's travel benefits policy.** If you are a member of the American Automobile Association (AAA) or an oil-company-sponsored road-assistance plan, always **ask hotel or car rental reservationists about auto club discounts.** Some clubs offer additional discounts on tours, cruises, or admission to attractions. And don't forget that auto-club membership entitles you to free maps and trip-planning services.

DIAL FOR DOLLARS

To save money, **look into "1-800" discount reservations services,** which use their buying power to get a better price on hotels, airline tickets, even car rentals. Always ask about special packages or corporate rates.

When shopping for the best deal on hotels and car rentals **look for guaranteed exchange rates,** which protect you against a falling dollar. With your rate locked in you won't pay more even if the price goes up in the local currency.

➤ AIRLINE TICKETS: ☎ 800/FLY–4–LESS.

➤ HOTEL ROOMS: **Steigenberger Reservation Service** (☎ 800/223–5652). **Travel Interlink** (☎ 800/888–5898).

SAVE ON COMBOS

Packages and guided tours can both save you money, but don't confuse the two. When you buy a package your travel remains independent, just as though you had planned and booked the trip yourself. Fly/drive packages, which combine airfare and car rental, are often a good deal.

JOIN A CLUB?

Many companies sell discounts in the form of travel clubs and coupon books, but these cost money. You must use participating advertisers to get a deal, and only after you recoup the initial membership cost or book price do you begin to save. If you plan to use the club or coupons frequently you may save considerably. Before signing up, find out what discounts you get for free.

➤ DISCOUNT CLUBS: **Entertainment Travel Editions** (✉ 2125 Butterfield Rd., Troy, MI 48084, ☎ 800/445–4137; $23–$48, depending on destination). **Great American Traveler** (✉ Box 27965, Salt Lake City, UT 84127, ☎ 800/548–2812; $49.95 per year). **Moment's Notice Discount Travel Club** (✉ 7301 New Utrecht Ave., Brooklyn, NY 11204, ☎ 718/234–6295; $25 per year, single or family). **Privilege Card International** (✉ 237 E. Front St., Youngstown, OH 44503, ☎ 330/746–5211 or 800/236–9732; $74.95 per year). **Sears' Mature Outlook** (✉ Box 9390, Des Moines, IA 50306, ☎ 800/336–6330; $14.95 per year). **Travelers Advantage** (✉ CUC Travel Service, 3033 S. Parker Rd., Suite 1000, Aurora, CO 80014, ☎ 800/548–1116 or 800/648–4037; $49 per year, single or family). **Worldwide Discount Travel Club** (✉ 1674 Meridian Ave., Miami Beach, FL 33139, ☎ 305/534–2082; $50 per year family, $40 single).

E

ELECTRICITY

To use your U.S.-purchased electric powered equipment, **bring a converter and several different adapters.** The electrical current in China is 220 volts, 50 cycles alternating current

(AC); a few wall outlets take American-style plugs, with two flat parallel prongs, but may not take the converter's one oversized prong, used for grounding, now in general use in the U.S. Most wall outlets take three-pronged plugs with round prongs, sometimes with two different sizes in the same room. Check the adapter's packaging to see whether it can be used in China.

In Hong Kong wall outlets use British-style three-pronged plugs. Sizes and shapes vary, so it is best to buy special adapters there, which will fit two-pronged American appliances or adapters.

If your appliances are dual-voltage, you'll need only an adapter. Don't use 110-volt outlets, marked FOR SHAVERS ONLY, for high-wattage appliances such as blow-dryers. Most laptops operate equally well on 110 and 220 volts and so require only an adapter. It is a good idea to invest in a surge protector for use with 220 volt outlets, as electricity in China can fluctuate.

G
GAY AND LESBIAN TRAVEL

While China has opened to many outside customs, it is still a conservative country when it comes to open sexual behavior. Couples, whether heterosexual or homosexual, are advised not to engage in outward displays of affection. Homosexuality is not illegal but is considered highly improper. There is a growing underground gay scene in Shanghai and other major cities, but discretion is always the safest policy.

➤ LOCAL RESOURCES: In Hong Kong, *Contacts,* a magazine covering the local gay scene, is available for HK$35 at the boutique **Fetish Fashion** (✉ 29 Hollywood Rd., Central, ☎ 852/2544-1155, ☉ Tues.–Sun. 11–7). **Propaganda** (✉ 30–32 Wyndham St., Central, ☎ 852/2868–1316) is the largest gay and lesbian bar in Hong Kong. **Petticoat Lane** (✉ 2 Tun Wo Lane, Mid-Levels, ☎ 852/2973–0642) is a popular restaurant with a large, though by no means exclusive, gay clientele. Hong Kong **AIDS Hotline** (☎ 852/2780–2211).

➤ GAY- AND LESBIAN-FRIENDLY TRAVEL AGENCIES: **Advance Damron** (✉ 1 Greenway Plaza, Suite 800, Houston, TX 77046, ☎ 713/850–1140 or 800/695–0880, FAX 713/888–1010). **Club Travel** (✉ 8739 Santa Monica Blvd., West Hollywood, CA 90069, ☎ 310/358–2200 or 800/429–8747, FAX 310/358–2222). **Islanders/Kennedy Travel** (✉ 183 W. 10th St., New York, NY 10014, ☎ 212/242–3222 or 800/988–1181, FAX 212/929–8530). **Now Voyager** (✉ 4406 18th St., San Francisco, CA 94114, ☎ 415/626–1169 or 800/255–6951, FAX 415/626–8626). **Yellowbrick Road** (✉ 1500 W. Balmoral Ave., Chicago, IL 60640, ☎ 773/561–1800 or 800/642–2488, FAX 773/561–4497). **Skylink Women's Travel** (✉ 3577 Moorland Ave., Santa Rosa, CA 95407, ☎ 707/585–8355 or 800/225–5759, FAX 707/584–5637), serving lesbian travelers.

H
HEALTH

In China you can find an English speaking doctor in most major cities. The best place to start is with your hotel concierge, then the local Public Security Bureau. The major cities have modern hospitals, but if you become seriously ill or are injured, it is best to try to get flown home, or at least to Hong Kong, as quickly as possible. Check for medevac coverage with your health insurer before you go.

In Hong Kong, English-speaking doctors are widely available. Hotels have lists of accredited doctors and can arrange for a doctor to visit your hotel room. Otherwise, consult the nearest government hospital. Check the Government section of the business telephone directory under Medical and Health Department for a list.

STAYING WELL

In China the major health risk is traveler's diarrhea, caused by eating contaminated fruit or vegetables or drinking contaminated water. So **watch what you eat.** Stay away from ice, uncooked food, and unpasteurized milk and milk products, and **drink only bottled water** or water that has been boiled for at least 20 minutes. Bottled water is widely available in the major cities of China. If you're going to rural areas, bring water purification tablets. Mild cases may respond to Imodium (known generically as loperamide) or Pepto-Bismol (not as strong), both of which can be purchased over the counter. **Do NOT buy prescription drugs in China,** as the quality control is unreliable. Ask your doctor for an antidiarrheal prescription to take with you. Drink plenty of purified water or tea—chamomile is a good folk remedy. In severe cases, rehydrate yourself with a salt-sugar solution (½ teaspoon salt and 4 tablespoons sugar per quart of water).

Pneumonia and influenza are also common among travelers returning from China; many health professionals recommend inoculations for both before you leave. Be sure you're well rested and healthy to start with.

According to the National Centers for Disease Control (CDC) there is a limited risk of hepatitis A and B, typhoid, polio, malaria, tuberculosis, dengue fever, tetanus, and rabies in small cities and rural areas. In most urban or easily accessible areas you need not worry. However, if you plan to visit remote regions or stay for more than six weeks, **check with the CDC's International Travelers Hotline.** In areas where malaria and dengue, both of which are carried by mosquitoes, are prevalent, use mosquito nets, wear clothing that covers the body, apply repellent containing DEET, and use spray for flying insects in living and sleeping areas. Also **consider taking antimalarial pills.** There is no vaccine that combats dengue.

➤ HEALTH WARNINGS: **National Centers for Disease Control** (✉ CDC, National Center for Infectious Diseases, Division of Quarantine, Traveler's Health Section, 1600 Clifton Rd., M/S E-03, Atlanta, GA 30333, ☎ 404/332–4559, FAX 404/332–4565).

MEDICAL PLANS

No one plans to get sick while traveling, but it happens, so **consider signing up with a medical assistance company.** Members get doctor referrals, emergency evacuation or repatriation, 24- hour telephone hot lines for medical consultation, cash for emergencies, and other personal and legal assistance. Coverage varies by plan, so **review the benefits carefully.**

➤ MEDICAL-ASSISTANCE COMPANIES: **International SOS Assistance** (✉ Box 11568, Philadelphia, PA 19116, ☎ 215/244–1500 or 800/523–8930; ✉ 1255 University St., Suite 420, Montréal, Québec H3B 3B6, ☎ 514/874–7674 or 800/363–0263; ✉ 7 Old Lodge Pl., St. Margarets, Twickenham TW1 1RQ, England, ☎ 0181/744–0033). **MEDEX Assistance Corporation** (✉ Box 5375, Timonium, MD 21094-5375, ☎ 410/453–6300 or 800/537–2029). **Traveler's Emergency Network** (✉ 3100 Tower Blvd., Suite 1000B, Durham, NC 27707, ☎ 919/490–6055 or 800/275–4836, FAX 919/493–8262). **TravMed** (✉ Box 5375, Timonium, MD 21094, ☎ 410/453–6380 or 800/732–5309). **Worldwide Assistance Services** (✉ 1133 15th St. NW, Suite 400, Washington, DC 20005, ☎ 202/331–1609 or 800/821–2828, FAX 202/828–5896).

HOLIDAYS

National holidays include January 1 (New Year's Day), two days in late February–early March (Chinese New Year, also called Spring Festival, based on lunar calendar), March 8 (International Working Women's Day), May 1 (International Labor Day), May 4 (Youth Day), June 1 (Children's Day), July 1 (Anniversary of the Founding of the Communist Party of China; in Hong Kong, the anniversary of the establishment of the Special Administrative Region), August 1 (Anniversary of the Founding of the Chinese PLA), October 1 (National Day—founding of the Peoples Republic of China in 1949).

I

INSURANCE

Travel insurance is the best way to **protect yourself against financial loss.** The most useful policies are trip-cancellation-and-interruption, default, medical, and comprehensive insurance.

Without insurance you will lose all or most of your money if you cancel your trip, regardless of the reason. It's essential that you **buy trip-cancellation-and-interruption insurance,** particularly if your airline ticket, cruise, or package tour is nonrefundable and cannot be changed. When considering how much coverage you need, look for a policy that will cover the cost of your trip plus the nondiscounted price of a one-way airline ticket, should you need to return home early. Also **consider default or bankruptcy insurance,** which protects you against a supplier's failure to deliver.

Medicare generally does not cover health-care costs outside the United States, nor do many privately issued policies. If your own policy does not cover you outside the United States, **consider buying supplemental medical coverage.** Remember that travel health insurance is different from a medical-assistance plan (☞ Health, *above*).

Citizens of the United Kingdom can buy an annual travel-insurance policy valid for most vacations during the year in which it's purchased. If you are pregnant or have a preexisting medical condition, make sure you're covered.

If you have purchased an expensive vacation, particularly one that involves travel abroad, comprehensive insurance is a must. **Look for comprehensive policies that include trip-delay insurance,** which will protect you in the event that weather problems cause you to miss your flight, tour, or cruise. A few insurers sell waivers for preexisting medical conditions. Companies that offer both features include Access America, Carefree Travel, Travel Insured International, and Travel Guard (☞ *below*).

Always **buy travel insurance directly from the insurance company**; if you buy it from a travel agency or tour operator that goes out of business you probably will not be covered for the agency or operator's default, a major risk. Before you make any purchase, **review your existing health and home-owner's policies** to find out whether they cover expenses incurred while traveling.

➤ TRAVEL INSURERS: In the U.S., **Access America** (✉ 6600 W. Broad St., Richmond, VA 23230, ☎ 804/285–3300 or 800/284–8300), **Carefree Travel Insurance** (✉ Box 9366, 100 Garden City Plaza, Garden City, NY 11530, ☎ 516/294–0220 or 800/323–3149), **Near Travel Services** (✉ Box 1339, Calumet City, IL 60409, ☎ 708/868–6700 or 800/654–6700), **Travel Guard International** (✉ 1145 Clark St., Stevens Point, WI 54481,

☎ 715/345–0505 or 800/826–1300), **Travel Insured International** (✉ Box 280568, East Hartford, CT 06128–0568, ☎ 860/528–7663 or 800/243–3174), **Travelex Insurance Services** (✉ 11717 Burt St., Suite 202, Omaha, NE 68154-1500, ☎ 402/445–8637 or 800/228–9792, FAX 800/867–9531), **Wallach & Company** (✉ 107 W. Federal St., Box 480, Middleburg, VA 20118, ☎ 540/687–3166 or 800/237–6615). In Canada, **Mutual of Omaha** (✉ Travel Division, 500 University Ave., Toronto, Ontario M5G 1V8, ☎ 416/598–4083, 800/268–8825 in Canada). In the U.K., **Association of British Insurers** (✉ 51 Gresham St., London EC2V 7HQ, ☎ 0171/600–3333).

L

LANGUAGE

The national language of China is Mandarin, known in China as Putonghua. Nearly everyone speaks Mandarin, but many also speak a local dialect that uses the same characters as Mandarin but whose pronunciation can vary greatly. In Hong Kong, the main language spoken is Cantonese.

All of the Chinese languages are tonal. Each syllable has a different meaning depending on the pitch or musical inflection the speaker gives it. To give an example, in Mandarin the syllable *ma* can mean mother, horse, curse, or hemp plant or be a particle denoting a question, depending on the tone used. Since 1949, the government has revamped the teaching of Mandarin, introducing a simplified phonetic system known as pinyin, which uses the Roman alphabet to indicate the pronunciations of the myriad Chinese characters. Names of sites in this book are given in pinyin with English translations.

It is difficult for foreigners to speak Chinese, and even harder to be understood. However, the Chinese will appreciate your making the effort to speak a few phrases understood almost everywhere. Try "Hello"—"Ni hao" (nee how); "Thank you"—"Xie xie" (hsyeh, hsyeh); and "Good-bye"—"Zaijian" (tsigh djyan).

You can usually find someone who speaks English in the major cities.

There are English signs almost everywhere in Hong Kong, but these are rare in the rest of China. It is difficult to get around China on your own without speaking the language. If you are not planning to go with a tour group, you can go from city to city and hire a local English-speaking guide from the CTS office at each stop.

LODGING

Major cities in China all have luxury hotels. Except for Hong Kong, Beijing, Shanghai, and Guangzhou, the service even in the best hotels might not measure up to international standards. They will, however, have English speakers on staff, business centers, laundry service, foreign currency exchange, and a concierge who can arrange tours and transportation. Many also have exercise facilities and restaurants.

Always bring your passport when checking into a hotel. The reception desk clerk will have to see it and record the number before you can be given a room.

APARTMENT AND VILLA RENTALS

Although furnished rentals are not common in China, **Property Rentals International** has condo rentals in Hong Kong and Beijing. These can save you money, but some rentals are luxury properties, economical only when your party is large.

➤ RENTAL AGENTS: **Property Rentals International** (✉ 1008 Mansfield Crossing Rd., Richmond, VA 23236, ☎ 804/378–6054 or 800/220–3332, FAX 804/379–2073).

M

MAIL

Post offices are open 8 AM to 6 PM Monday through Saturday. Public post offices are generally crowded, but large hotels have postal services open all day Monday through Saturday, and Sundays 8 to noon.

Postal codes in China are very specific, as they designate areas equivalent to city blocks, and can be useful for finding a building.

RATES

A postcard to the U.S. costs Y1.60. A letter, up to 20 grams, costs Y2.20.

RECEIVING MAIL

Long-term guests can receive mail at their hotels. Otherwise, the best place to receive mail is at the American Express office. Hong Kong and most major Chinese cities have American Express offices with client mail service. Be sure to bring your American Express card, as the staff will not give you the mail without seeing it.

MONEY

The Chinese currency is officially called the renminbi (RMB; People's Money). You can change money at most Bank of China branches, or at the front desk of your hotel. China is in the process of converting to hard currency, i.e., making the renminbi fully convertible with foreign money. Currently you cannot change RMB back into foreign currency, except at banks in Hong Kong. If you are not leaving China through Hong Kong, change only as much money as you will need for the duration of your stay.

The Bank of China issues RMB bills in denominations of 2, 5, 10, 50, 100, 500, and 1,000 yuan. Yuan are commonly referred to as kuai; the abbreviation is Y. The exchange rates are approximately Y8.28 = $1, Y5.96 = 1C$, Y5.81 = 1$ Australian, Y13.53 = £1.

Hong Kong, as a special autonomous entity, has its own convertible currency, the Hong Kong dollar ($) and the cent. There are bills of 1,000, 500, 100, 50, 20, and 10 dollars. Coins are 10, 5, 2, and 1 dollar and 50, 20, and 10 cents. At press time exchange rates for the Hong Kong dollar were approximately HK $7.75 = US $1; HK $5.45 = 1C$; HK $5.20 = 1$ Australian; HK $12.75 = £1.

The official currency unit in Macau is the pataca, which is divided into 100 avos. Bills come in 500, 100, 50, 10, and 5 pataca denominations; coins are 5 and 1 patacas and 50, 20, and 10 avos. The pataca is pegged to the Hong Kong dollar. At press time there were 8 patacas to the Hong Kong dollar. Be sure to change your patacas before you leave Macao.

ATMS

ATMs using the Cirrus and Plus networks can be found in Hong

Kong, Beijing, Shanghai, and other major cities.

Before leaving home, **make sure that your credit cards have been programmed for ATM use in China.** Note that Discover is accepted mostly in the United States. Local bank cards often do not work overseas or may access only your checking account; **ask your bank about a MasterCard/Cirrus or Visa debit card,** which works like a bank card but can be used at any ATM displaying a MasterCard/Cirrus or Visa logo. These cards, too, may tap only your checking account; check with your bank about their policy.

➤ ATM LOCATIONS: **Cirrus** (☎ 800/424–7787). A list of **Plus** locations is available at your local bank.

COSTS

Costs vary widely from city to city and depending on whether the establishment caters to locals or foreigners. Standard museum entrance fees range between $3.50 and $6. A soft drink costs about $1.25. A bottle of beer costs $1.25. A dumpling costs about $1.25; a slice of pizza costs about $6.

CURRENCY EXCHANGE

For the most favorable rates, **change money at banks.** Although fees charged for ATM transactions may be higher abroad than at home, Cirrus and Plus exchange rates are excellent, because they are based on wholesale rates offered only by major banks. You won't do as well at exchange booths in airports or rail and bus stations, in hotels, in restaurants, or in stores, although you may find their hours more convenient.

Note: You cannot obtain Chinese currency outside of China, and you cannot exchange it back into foreign currency outside of China. This situation will change when RMB becomes fully convertible.

➤ EXCHANGE SERVICES: **International Currency Express** (☎ 888/842–0880 on the East Coast or 888/278–6628 on the West Coast for telephone orders). **Thomas Cook Currency Services** (☎ 800/287–7362 for telephone orders and retail locations).

TRAVELER'S CHECKS

As China has so few ATMs, your best bet is to take traveler's checks. **Take cash if your trip includes rural areas** and small towns, traveler's checks to cities. If your checks are lost or stolen, they can usually be replaced within 24 hours. To ensure a speedy refund, buy your checks yourself (don't ask someone else to make the purchase). When making a claim for stolen or lost checks, the person who bought the checks should make the call.

P
PACKING FOR CHINA

Although the Chinese have become more fashion conscious in the past few years, informal attire is still appropriate for most occasions. The streets are dusty, so you may prefer to bring older clothes and shoes. Sturdy, comfortable walking shoes are a must. Summers are very hot and winters very cold in most of China, so pack accordingly. Avoid bringing clothes that need dry cleaning. You will find it much easier to get around if you travel light, with no more than two or three changes of clothes. Most hotels have reliable overnight laundry and pressing services, so you can have your clothes washed frequently.

For Hong Kong, bring new, fashionable clothes, or plan on buying some there. Eyeglasses, film, pantyhose, sundries, and over-the-counter medicines are widely available in Hong Kong, but such items are harder to find in the rest of China. Be sure to pack the following essentials for China: alarm clock, contraceptives, dental floss, deodorant, mosquito repellant, shampoo, shaving cream and razors, sunglasses, sun screen, tampons, toothbrush, and toothpaste.

If you're planning a longer trip, or will be using local tour guides, bring a few inexpensive items from America as gifts. American cigarettes are popular in China, but if you don't wish to promote smoking, bring candy, T-shirts, or small cosmetic items, such as lipstick and nail polish, or postcards of rural American scenes. Do not give American magazines and books as gifts, as this could be considered propaganda and get your Chinese friends into trouble.

Other useful items to have in China are a flashlight with extra batteries, English-language books and magazines, and a money belt. Bring a pen knife to peel fruit and, if you're going to smaller cities and rural areas, water purification tablets.

Bring an extra pair of eyeglasses or contact lenses in your carry-on luggage, and if you have a health problem, **pack enough medication** to last the entire trip or have your doctor write you a prescription using the drug's generic name, because brand names vary from country to country. It's important that you **don't put prescription drugs or valuables in luggage to be checked**: it might go astray. To avoid problems with customs officials, carry medications in the original packaging. Also, don't forget the addresses of offices that handle refunds of lost traveler's checks.

LUGGAGE

In general, you are entitled to check two bags on flights within the United States and on international flights leaving the United States. A third piece may be brought on board, but it must fit easily under the seat in front of you or in the overhead compartment.

If you are flying between two foreign destinations, note that baggage allowances may be determined not by piece but by weight—generally 88 pounds (40 kilograms) in first class, 66 pounds (30 kilograms) in business class, and 44 pounds (20 kilograms) in economy. If your flight between two cities abroad *connects* with your transatlantic or transpacific flight, the piece method still applies.

Airline liability for baggage is limited to $1,250 per person on flights within the United States. On international flights it amounts to $9.07 per pound or $20 per kilogram for checked baggage (roughly $635 per 70-pound bag) and $400 per passenger for unchecked baggage. Insurance for losses exceeding these amounts can be bought from the airline at check-in for about $10 per $1,000 of coverage; note that this coverage excludes a rather extensive list of items, which is shown on your airline ticket.

Before departure, **itemize your bags' contents** and their worth, and label the bags with your name, address, and phone number. (If you use your home address, cover it so that potential thieves can't see it readily.) Inside each bag, **pack a copy of your itinerary.** At check-in, **make sure that each bag is correctly tagged** with the destination airport's three-letter code. If your bags arrive damaged or fail to arrive at all, file a written report with the airline before leaving the airport.

PASSPORTS & VISAS

Once your travel plans are confirmed, **check the expiration date of your passport.** It's also a good idea to **make photocopies of the data page**; leave one copy with someone at home and keep another with you, separated from your passport. If you lose your passport, promptly call the nearest embassy or consulate and the local police; having copies of the data page and of your birth certificate can speed replacement.

GETTING A VISA

It takes about a week to get a visa in the U.S. See your travel agent or contact the **Consulate General of the People's Republic of China** (⊠ Visa Office; 520 12th Avenue; New York, NY 10036; ☎ 212/330–7409). Travel agents in Hong Kong can issue visas to visit China. Costs range from about $35 for a visa issued within two working days to $50 for a visa issued overnight. **Note:** The visa application will ask your occupation. The official Chinese do not like journalists or anyone who works in publishing or media. Americans and Canadians in these professions routinely state "teacher" under "Occupation." U.K. passports state the bearer's occupation, and this can be problematic for anyone in the "wrong" line of work. Several years ago a British journalist on holiday in Beijing was detained for a day because of his occupation. Before you go, contact the Consulate of the People's Republic of China to see how strict the current mood is.

U.S. CITIZENS

All U.S. citizens, even infants, need a valid passport with a tourist visa stamped in it to enter China for stays of up to 90 days. For Hong Kong, you need only a valid passport.

➤ INFORMATION: **Office of Passport Services** (☎ 202/647–0518).

CANADIANS

You need a valid passport with a tourist visa stamped in it to enter

China for stays of up to 90 days. For Hong Kong, you need only a valid passport.

➤ INFORMATION: **Passport Office** (☎ 819/994–3500 or 800/567–6868).

U.K. CITIZENS

Citizens of the United Kingdom need a valid passport with a tourist visa stamped in it to enter China for stays of up to 90 days. For Hong Kong, you need only a valid passport.

➤ INFORMATION: **London Passport Office** (☎ 0990/21010) for fees and documentation requirements and to request an emergency passport.

S

SAFETY

There is little violent crime against tourists in China, partly because the penalties are severe for those who are caught; execution is the most common. Sexual harassment and rape of foreign women are relatively rare, but there are cases. Women out alone at night are particularly vulnerable. There have been reports of serious sexual harassment in Xinjiang, a Muslim area.

Pickpocketing, however, is a growing problem. Keep valuables in a money belt or locked in a hotel safe. A general rule of thumb is **don't wear anything that will stand out**: i.e., revealing or flashy clothes, expensive jewelry. If nothing else, you may be harassed by people politely asking if you will trade clothes or give them your watch!

The traffic in Chinese cities is usually heavy and just as out-of-control as it looks. Be very careful when crossing streets or riding a bicycle.

Respiratory problems may be aggravated by the polluted air in China's cities. Some residents and visitors alike find that wearing a surgical mask helps.

SENIOR CITIZEN TRAVEL

To qualify for age-related discounts, **mention your senior citizen status up front** when booking hotel reservations (not when checking out) and before you're seated in restaurants (not when paying the bill). Note that discounts may be limited to certain menus,

days, or hours. When renting a car, **ask about promotional car rental discounts,** which can be cheaper than senior-citizen rates.

➤ ADVENTURE TRAVEL: **Overseas Adventure Travel** (✉ Grand Circle Corporation, 625 Mt. Auburn St., Cambridge, MA 02138, ☎ 617/876–0533 or 800/221–0814, FAX 617/876–0455).

➤ EDUCATIONAL TRAVEL PROGRAMS: **Elderhostel** (✉ 75 Federal St., 3rd floor, Boston, MA 02110, ☎ 617/426–8056). **Interhostel** (✉ University of New Hampshire, 6 Garrison Ave., Durham, NH 03824, ☎ 603/862–1147 or 800/733–9753, FAX 603/862–1113). **Folkways Institute** (✉ 14600 Southeast Aldridge Rd., Portland, OR 97236-6518, ☎ 503/658–6600, FAX 503/658–8672).

SHOPPING

With the exception of Hong Kong (☞ Shopping *in* Chapter 8), China has few things to buy other than souvenirs, Chinese medicines, and tea. There are shops specializing in jade, old Chinese porcelain, and antique furniture, but remember when shopping that forgery runs rampant. Stick to **Friendship Stores** (formerly emporia selling luxury goods for foreigners only, now more like an upscale department store chain) and shops attached to international hotels for some assurance of getting what you pay for. These shops usually have fairly good selections of Chinese carpets, which can also be a good buy.

With antiques, an item over 100 years old will have an official red wax seal attached, but this is not a guarantee of authenticity. The Chinese government has cleared only certain antiques for sale to foreigners. Save the bill of sale to show customs when you leave the country, or the antique will be confiscated.

Post offices in hotels usually have interesting Chinese stamps for sale. Ask about designs that were issued during the Cultural Revolution.

Around the tourist centers, you will find street merchants selling an array of cloisonné and jade jewelry, old Chinese coins (usually fake), fans, tea sets, chops (stone stamps that can be carved with your name in Chinese), embroidered silk robes and pillowcases, and other souvenirs. You can often bargain for these items. Areas frequented by tourists also abound with stores and street vendors selling art: scrolls, woodblock prints, paper cuttings, and some contemporary oils. Prices can be as low as Y250 for something produced by a youngster selling his or her own work. Most of this is not of value, but buy what you like.

STUDENTS

To save money, **look into deals available through student-oriented travel agencies.** To qualify you'll need a bona fide student ID card. Members of international student groups are also eligible.

➤ STUDENT IDs AND SERVICES: **Council on International Educational Exchange** (✉ CIEE, 205 E. 42nd St., 14th floor, New York, NY 10017, ☎ 212/822–2600 or 888/268–6245, FAX 212/822–2699), for mail orders only, in the United States. **Travel Cuts** (✉ 187 College St., Toronto, Ontario M5T 1P7, ☎ 416/979–2406 or 800/667–2887) in Canada.

➤ HOSTELING: **Hostelling International—American Youth Hostels** (✉ 733 15th St. NW, Suite 840, Washington, DC 20005, ☎ 202/783–6161, FAX 202/783–6171). **Hostelling International—Canada** (✉ 400-205 Catherine St., Ottawa, Ontario K2P 1C3, ☎ 613/237–7884, FAX 613/237–7868). **Youth Hostel Association of England and Wales** (✉ Trevelyan House, 8 St. Stephen's Hill, St. Albans, Hertfordshire AL1 2DY, ☎ 01727/855215 or 01727/845047, FAX 01727/844126). Membership in the U.S., $25; in Canada, C$26.75; in the U.K., £9.30).

T

TAXES

There is no sales tax. Hotels have a room tariff of 10% for service charges plus 5% tax. Domestic airport departure tax is Y50 and international is Y90, cash only. Hong Kong's airport tax is HK$100.

TELEPHONES

The country code for China is 86; for Hong Kong, 852. To dial China direct from the U.S. or Canada, you must know the city code. Some important city codes are: Beijing, 10; Guangzhou, 20; Shanghai, 21. When dialing from within the country, add 0 before the city code.

CALLING HOME

Before you go, **find out the local access codes** for your destinations. AT&T, MCI, and Sprint long-distance services make calling home relatively convenient, but you may find the local access number blocked in many hotel rooms. First ask the hotel operator to connect you. If the hotel operator balks, ask for an international operator, or dial the international operator yourself. One way to improve your odds of getting connected to your long-distance carrier is to travel with more than one company's calling card (a hotel may block Sprint, for example, but not MCI). If all else fails, call your phone company collect in the United States or call from a pay phone in the hotel lobby.

➤ TO OBTAIN ACCESS CODES: **AT&T USADirect** (☎ 800/874–4000). **MCI Call USA** (☎ 800/444–4444). **Sprint Express** (☎ 800/793–1153).

OPERATORS & INFORMATION

It is hard to find English-speaking operators in China, except through International Directory Assistance (dial 115). You can dial overseas direct from many hotel room and business center telephones. The international access code in China is 00. Hotels usually add a 30% surcharge to long-distance calls.

In Hong Kong, dial 1081 for assistance from English-speaking operators. To dial overseas direct, the international access code is 001.

PAY PHONES

Most hotels have phone booths where you can place domestic and overseas long distance calls. You pay a deposit of about Y200 and receive a card with the number of the phone booth. A computer times the call and processes a receipt, which you pay at the end. Post offices have telecommunications centers where you can buy cards in denominations of Y20, Y50, and Y100 to make long distance calls.

TIPPING

Tipping used to be unheard of, but now the custom is taking hold. In restaurants, tip about 3% of the bill. A 10% service charge is added in most restaurants in Hong Kong. Tip bellboys and room service waiters Y10 to Y20, or US$1–$2. (U.S. dollars are always appreciated as tips.) It is not necessary to tip taxi drivers, although you might let them keep small change. In Hong Kong, taxi drivers charge you HK$5 per piece of baggage that they handle.

CTS tour guides are not allowed to accept tips. You can give guides and drivers small gifts. They often appreciate American cigarettes, but you also can offer American candy or T-shirts. Female guides might prefer a lipstick or nail polish.

TOUR OPERATORS

If you don't want to take any chances, book a tour through one of the many tour operators in the United States or Great Britain, with an American or English guide in charge.

Buying a prepackaged tour or independent vacation can make your trip to China less expensive and more hassle-free. Because everything is prearranged, you'll spend less time planning.

Operators that handle several hundred thousand travelers per year can use their purchasing power to give you a good price. Their high volume may also indicate financial stability. But some small companies provide more personalized service; because they tend to specialize, they may also be more knowledgeable about a given area.

A GOOD DEAL?

The more your package or tour includes, the better you can predict the ultimate cost of your vacation. Make sure you know exactly what is covered, and **beware of hidden costs.** Are taxes, tips, and service charges included? Transfers and baggage handling? Entertainment and excursions? These can add up.

If the package or tour you are considering is priced lower than in your wildest dreams, **be skeptical.** Also, **make sure your travel agent knows the accommodations** and other services. Ask about the hotel's location, room size, beds, and whether it has a pool, room service, or programs for children, if you care about these. Has your agent been there in person or sent others you can contact?

BUYER BEWARE

Each year consumers are stranded or lose their money when tour operators—even very large ones with excellent reputations—go out of business. So **check out the operator.** Find out how long the company has been in business, and ask several agents about its reputation. **Don't book unless the firm has a consumer protection program.**

Members of the National Tour Association and United States Tour Operators Association are required to set aside funds to cover your payments and travel arrangements in case the company defaults. Nonmembers may carry insurance instead. Look for the details, and for the name of an underwriter with a solid reputation, in the operator's brochure. Note: When it comes to tour operators, **don't trust escrow accounts.** Although the Department of Transportation watches over charter-flight operators, no regulatory body prevents tour operators from raiding the till. You may want to protect yourself by buying travel insurance that includes a tour-operator default provision. For more information, *see* Insurance, *above.*

It's also a good idea to choose a company that participates in the American Society of Travel Agents' Tour Operator Program (TOP). This gives you a forum if there are any disputes between you and your tour operator; ASTA will act as mediator.

➤ TOUR-OPERATOR RECOMMENDATIONS: **American Society of Travel Agents** (☞ Travel Agencies, *below*). **National Tour Association** (✉ NTA, 546 E. Main St., Lexington, KY 40508, ☎ 606/226–4444 or 800/755–8687). **United States Tour Operators Association** (✉ USTOA, 342 Madison Ave., Suite 1522, New York, NY 10173, ☎ 212/599–6599, FAX 212/599–6744).

USING AN AGENT

Travel agents are excellent resources. In fact, large operators accept bookings made only through travel agents. But it's a good idea to **collect brochures from several agencies,** because some agents' suggestions may be influenced by relationships with tour and package firms that reward them for volume sales. If you have a special interest, **find an agent with expertise in that area**; ASTA (☞ Travel Agencies, *below*) has a database of specialists worldwide. Do some homework on your own, too—local tourism boards can provide information about lesser known and small-niche operators, some of which may sell only direct.

SINGLE TRAVELERS

Prices for packages and tours are usually quoted per person, based on two sharing a room. If traveling solo, you may be required to pay the full double-occupancy rate. Some operators eliminate this surcharge if you agree to be matched with a roommate of the same sex, even if one is not found by departure time.

GROUP TOURS

Among companies that sell tours to China, the following are nationally known, have a proven reputation, and offer plenty of options. The classifications used below represent different price categories, and you'll probably encounter these terms when talking to a travel agent or tour operator. The key difference is usually in accommodations, which run from budget to better, and better-yet to best.

➤ SUPER-DELUXE: **Abercrombie & Kent** (✉ 1520 Kensington Rd., Oak Brook, IL 60521-2141, ☎ 630/954–2944 or 800/323–7308, FAX 630/954–3324). **Travcoa** (✉ Box 2630, 2350 S.E. Bristol St., Newport Beach, CA 92660, ☎ 714/476–2800 or 800/992–2003, FAX 714/476–2538).

➤ DELUXE: **Globus** (✉ 5301 S. Federal Circle, Littleton, CO 80123-2980, ☎ 303/797–2800 or 800/221–0090, FAX 303/347–2080). **Maupintour** (✉ 1515 St. Andrews Dr., Lawrence, KS 66047, ☎ 913/843–1211 or 800/255–4266, FAX 913/843–8351). **Tauck Tours** (✉ Box 5027, 276 Post Rd. W, Westport, CT 06881-5027, ☎ 203/226–6911 or 800/468–2825, FAX 203/221–6828).

➤ FIRST-CLASS: **Collette Tours** (✉ 162 Middle St., Pawtucket, RI 02860, ☎ 401/728–3805 or 800/832–4656, FAX 401/728–1380). **Orient Flexi-Pax Tours** (✉ 630 Third Ave., New York,

NY 10017, ☎ 212/692–9550 or 800/545–5540, FAX 212/661–1618). **Pacific Bestour** (✉ 228 Rivervale Rd., River Vale, NJ 07675, ☎ 201/664- -8778 or 800/688–3288, FAX 201/722–0829). **Pacific Delight Tours** (✉ 132 Madison Ave., New York, NY 10016, ☎ 212/684–7707 or 800/221–7179, FAX 212/532–3406). **United Vacations** (☎ 800/328- 6877).

➤ BUDGET: **Cosmos** (☞ Globus, *above*).

PACKAGES

Like group tours, independent vacation packages are available from major tour operators and airlines. The companies listed below offer vacation packages in a broad price range.

➤ AIR/HOTEL: **Brendan Tours** (✉ 15137 Califa St., Van Nuys, CA 91411, ☎ 818/785–9696 or 800/421–8446, FAX 818/902–9876). **Cameron Tours** (✉ 6249 N. Kensington St., McLean, VA 22101, ☎ 800/648–4635). **Orient Flexi-Pax Tours** (☞ Groups, *above*). **Pacific Bestour** (☞ Groups, *above*). **Pacific Delight Tours** (☞ Groups, *above*). **United Vacations** (☞ Groups, *above*).

THEME TRIPS

➤ CUSTOMIZED PACKAGES: **Cameron Tours** (☞ Air/Hotel, *above*). **Pacific Experience** (✉ 185 Spring St., Newport, RI 02840, ☎ 800/279–3639, FAX 203/618-0121).

➤ BICYCLING: **Backroads** (✉ 801 Cedar St., Berkeley, CA 94710-1800, ☎ 510/527–1555 or 800/462–2848, FAX 510/527–1444).

➤ JEWISH CULTURE: **American Jewish Congress** (✉ 15 E. 84th St., New York, NY 10028, ☎ 212/879–4588 or 800/221–4694).

➤ LEARNING VACATIONS: **Distant Horizons** (✉ 350 Elm Ave., Long Beach, CA 90802, ☎ 310/983–8828 or 800/333–1240, FAX 310/983–8833). **Smithsonian Study Tours and Seminars** (✉ 1100 Jefferson Dr. SW, Room 3045, MRC 702, Washington, DC 20560, ☎ 202/357–4700, FAX 202/633–9250).

TRAIN TRAVEL

Train tickets usually have to be purchased in the city of origin. If you do not speak Mandarin it will be difficult to negotiate the ticket windows at the train station, so buy tickets from the local CTS office or ask your hotel concierge to make the arrangements. It is best to make train reservations at least a day or two in advance, if possible. Although China's classless society has all but disappeared, the train system offers a glimpse of old-fashioned socialist euphemisms. Instead of first class and second class accommodations, passengers choose hard seat or soft seat, and for overnight journeys, hard sleeper or soft sleeper.

Trains are always crowded, so arrive at the station two hours before departure. In Hong Kong there will be a queue to get on the train; on the mainland, it's every passenger for him/herself.

TRAVEL AGENCIES

A good travel agent puts your needs first. Look for an agency that has been in business at least five years, emphasizes customer service, and has someone on staff who specializes in your destination. In addition, **make sure the agency belongs to the American Society of Travel Agents** (ASTA). If your travel agency is also acting as your tour operator, *see* Buyer Beware in Tour Operators, *above*).

➤ LOCAL AGENT REFERRALS: **American Society of Travel Agents** (ASTA, ☎ 800/965–2782 24-hr hotline, FAX 703/684–8319). **Alliance of Canadian Travel Associations** (✉ Suite 201, 1729 Bank St., Ottawa, Ontario K1V 7Z5, ☎ 613/521–0474, FAX 613/521–0805). **Association of British Travel Agents** (✉ 55–57 Newman St., London W1P 4AH, ☎ 0171/637–2444, FAX 0171/637–0713).

➤ IN HONG KONG: **Phoenix Travel** (✉ Milton Mansions, 96 Nathan Road, Room 6B; Tsim Sha Tsui, Kowloon, ☎ 852/2722–7378, FAX 852/2369–8884).

TRAVEL GEAR

Travel catalogs specialize in useful items, such as compact alarm clocks and travel irons, that can **save space when packing.** They also offer dual-voltage appliances, currency converters, and foreign-language phrase books.

➤ MAIL-ORDER CATALOGS: **Magellan's** (☎ 800/962–4943, FAX 805/568–5406). **Orvis Travel** (☎ 800/541–3541, FAX 540/343–7053). **TravelSmith** (☎ 800/950–1600, FAX 800/950–1656).

U

U.S. GOVERNMENT

The U.S. government can be an excellent source of inexpensive travel information. When planning your trip, **find out what government materials are available.**

➤ ADVISORIES: **U.S. Department of State** (✉ Overseas Citizens Services Office, Room 4811 N.S., Washington, DC 20520); enclose a self-addressed, stamped envelope. Interactive hot line (☎ 202/647–5225, FAX 202/647–3000). Computer bulletin board (☎ 301/946–4400).

➤ PAMPHLETS: **Consumer Information Center** (✉ Consumer Information Catalogue, Pueblo, CO 81009, ☎ 719/948–3334) for a free catalog that includes travel titles.

V

VISITOR INFORMATION

For general information before you go, including information about tours, insurance, and safety, call or visit the National Tourist Office in New York City, Los Angeles, London, or Sydney.

Within China, China International Travel Service (CITS) and China Travel Service (CTS) are under the same government ministry. Local offices, catering to sightseeing around the area (and to visitors from other mainland cities), are called CTS. CITS offices can book international flights.

➤ CHINA NATIONAL TOURIST OFFICE: **New York:** ✉ 350 5th Avenue, Ste. 6413, New York, NY 10118, ☎ 212/760–9700, FAX 212/760–8809. **Los Angeles:** ✉ 333 W. Broadway, Ste. 201, Glendale, CA 91204, ☎ 818/545–7504, FAX 818/545–7506. **U.K.:** ✉ 4 Glentworth St., London NW1, ☎ 0171/935–9427, FAX 0171/487–5842.

➤ CHINA INTERNATIONAL TRAVEL SERVICE (CITS): **U.S.:** ✉ 2 Mott St.,

THE GOLD GUIDE / SMART TRAVEL TIPS

New York, NY 10002, ☎ 212/608–1212. **Canada:** ⊠ 556 W. Broadway, Vancouver, BC V5Z 1E9, ☎ 604/872–8787, ℻ 604/873–2823.

W
WHEN TO GO

Summer is the peak tourist season, and hotels and transportation can be very crowded. Book early—several months in advance if possible—for summer travel. The weather can be scorching in the summer in most of China. The weather will be better and the crowds not quite as dense in late spring and early fall, although be prepared for rain. Winter is bitterly cold and not conducive to travel in most of China. Avoid traveling around Chinese New Year, as much of China shuts down and the Chinese themselves travel, making reservations into and out of China virtually impossible to get.

CLIMATE

What follows are average daily maximum and minimum temperatures in cities in various parts of China.

BEIJING

Jan.	34F	1C	May	81F	27C	Sept.	79F	26C
	14	–10		55	13		57	14
Feb.	39F	4C	June	88F	31C	Oct.	68F	20C
	18	–8		64	18		43	6
Mar.	52F	11C	July	88F	31C	Nov.	48F	9C
	30	–1		70	21		28	–2
Apr.	70F	21C	Aug.	86F	30C	Dec.	37F	3C
	45	7		68	20		18	–8

SHANGHAI

Jan.	46F	8C	May	77F	25C	Sept.	82F	28C
	33	1		59	15		66	19
Feb.	47F	8C	June	82F	28C	Oct.	74F	23C
	34	1		67	19		57	14
Mar.	55F	13C	July	90F	32C	Nov.	63F	17C
	40	4		74	23		45	7
Apr.	66F	19C	Aug.	90F	32C	Dec.	53F	12C
	50	10		74	23		36	2

HONG KONG

Jan.	64F	18C	May	82F	28C	Sept.	85F	29C
	45	13		74	23		77	25
Feb.	63F	17C	June	85F	29C	Oct.	81F	27C
	55	13		78	26		73	23
Mar.	67F	19C	July	87F	31C	Nov.	74F	23C
	60	16		78	26		65	18
Apr.	75F	24C	Aug.	87F	31C	Dec.	68F	20C
	67	19		78	26		59	15

ÜRÜMQI

Jan.	13F	–11C	May	72F	22C	Sept.	69F	21C
	–7	–22		47	8		47	8
Feb.	17F	–8C	June	78F	26C	Oct.	50F	10C
	–3	–19		54	12		31	–1
Mar.	31F	–1C	July	82F	28C	Nov.	30F	–1C
	12	–11		58	14		13	–11
Apr.	60F	16C	Aug.	80F	27C	Dec.	17F	–8C
	36	2		56	13		8	–13

➤ FORECASTS: **Weather Channel Connection** (☎ 900/932–8437), 95¢ per minute from a touch-tone phone.

1 Destination: China

CHINA'S DANCE

WALKING DOWN A street in Suzhou, a city over 2,500 years old with its walls still intact, I came across an advertisement for cellular phones taped to an old shop window: A young Chinese woman holds a phone to her ear as she stands on the Great Wall, the long structure twisting off into the distance behind her. "Get Connected," says the ad. "This is the new China."

Bamboo scaffolding and gleaming department stores, construction cranes looming over wooden villages, KFC and chopsticks, yak herders and cell phone abusers within miles of each other, communism and capitalism co-existing—China has more paradoxes than it does dialects. To visit China now is to witness a country revolutionizing itself in the cities and struggling to stay alive in the countryside. Wracked with ambiguity as it transforms rapidly from a socialist to a market economy, China is perched, it seems, at the edge of the world at the turn of the millennium.

While the West has focused its attention on human rights and continues to see China through the lens of Tiananmen, the country itself has imploded into a thousand perplexities. While it is true that the more time one spends in China the more the country takes on an elusive sheen, the experience of living day to day, traveling from the markets to the elevated highways, from the desert to the city, along rivers and before incredible mountain ranges will undoubtedly stay with the visitor forever.

Beginning with the Xia dynasty and ending with the Qing, China has seen as many dynastic cycles spanning hundreds of years as the United States has seen presidents. Though the museums house some incredible artifacts and the Xian terra-cotta soldiers remain one of China's most famous attractions, much of China's cultural history and art were destroyed or transported swiftly to Taiwan during the Cultural Revolution. Nevertheless, from Mao's years of social reconstruction to the resilient character of Deng Xiao Ping and his re-

form of the economy, what is fascinating about China today is the juxtaposition of the old and the new.

The third-largest country in the world, holding the world's largest population, China is chiefly challenged by questions of cohesiveness, centrality—how to bring a country speaking hundreds of different dialects together under one rule. Beginning with the Zhou dynasty (1100–771 BC), China held its government together based on the idea of the Mandate of Heaven. Essentially, heaven granted power to those who were chosen *by* heaven to rule. The Mandate was later modified to include heaven's demonstration of its disapproval of evil rulers through natural disasters like droughts and earthquakes, disease and flood. An element of fate was incorporated into the mandate, as it was believed that heaven would not grant validity to a rebellion unless that rebellion was successful.

Today, as communism becomes a theoretical name for a system that is beginning to incorporate capitalism, the mandate of heaven has been called into question. Were Mao and communism another manifestation of heaven's will? Some Chinese scholars believe Mao was the founder of the first peasant dynasty. Others theorize that the cult of personalities like Deng Xiao Ping and now Jiang Zemin has undermined the socialist foundation Mao set forth. Whatever the case, it is clear that as the country continues to modernize, especially with Hong Kong under its belt, communism appears to be taking a very back seat to an undefined foreground, neither capitalism in a Western sense nor Communism as in the years of Mao. The Chinese government has found itself in an awkward situation. If it tries to clamp down, it will surely lose in the race for modernization. If it allows modernization to continue, its control is inevitably weakened. Who can say what heaven will grant next?

Ranging from the Three Gorges Dam, a colossal project that will uproot 2 million people, to the perpetual construction of skyscrapers crowding the cities' skylines, the Chinese landscape is changing faster than any other the 20th century has witnessed. In some respects, it's as if the people had been plucked from their traditional homes and transported 100 years into a future where families struggle to uphold loyalty in an environment that tries to rip it apart. Foreign companies and joint ventures are asking single men and women to climb a corporate ladder on a speeded-up schedule; eating habits have changed from family style to a quick bite from McDonald's; grocery stores have begun to replace outdoor markets; bars and discos stay open all night. The country has become more modern, but what does that mean to a nation that looks back on over 5,000 years of history?

THE ANCIENT PHILOSOPHY of Confucianism laid a foundation for Chinese ethics and morals that still survives today, teaching respect, selflessness, obedience, and a sense of community. Unlike Americans, who prize their individuality and independence, the Chinese believe it is important to stay within and abide by a community that is usually filial. Shame is considered a much graver emotion than guilt: It is in the eyes of those whom they love and respect that the Chinese judge themselves. As a new generation works the corporate life in cities away from home, how this undeniably Chinese characteristic will be affected is the subject of much debate, though emotional conflict seems inevitable.

The Chinese believe that no matter where you were born, where you live, what you speak as your native tongue, if you have Chinese ancestry, you are still Chinese. A Chinese-American teacher's students at Fudan University insisted that she was more Chinese than American despite the fact that she spoke no Mandarin and had never been in China before meeting them. Michael Chang, the American tennis player, is viewed as a national hero in China. It is a sense of pride over their emergence into the world economy combined with a deep sense of race that holds the country tentatively together. *Just Say No,* a book written by a young Chinese and on the bestseller list here for over a year, celebrates a sense of neo-nationalism, suggesting that China should isolate itself from the rest of the world

in the race to become the most powerful country.

Paradoxically, China is busy buying up Western products, from French fries to Hollywood action movies. Nike is cool. Madonna is hip. It's exactly this external desire for Western style combined with an internal nationalism that makes China capable of living comfortably in irony. The Chinese have so internalized their landscape that, for example, the TV tower in Shanghai is for them comparable to the Jade Buddha Temple down the street as a site not to be missed; advertisements in subway stations are celebrated as a new form of artistic expression; the elderly happily practice tai chi to the beat of rock music; women wear revealing blouses unaware of their sexual allure.

Over 70% of the mainland population lives along the eastern seaboard, leaving the westernmost provinces barren and nearly vacant. A major reason for these demographics is that only 20% of China's land is arable. In the 1970s, peasants' lifestyles improved as a result of Deng Xiao Ping's policy of allowing profit after government quotas had been met, but small plots of land and an ever-increasing population meant that the new policy only marginally solved the problem. People still flock to the cities, creating a large homeless population. Although China appears to be overhauling itself, many of the smaller cities and villages are still living the way they did 100 years ago. As in other countries, there is a profound division between the growing middle class and unemployed farm workers.

Excursions to small towns reveal just how much China relies on basic human power. Farm laborers stand up with their tools and wave as a train passes, herds of sheep carry goods down dirt roads into the village center, local buses are crowded full of men and women carrying raw animal furs. Even in the cities, one sees a surplus of men working with hammer and nail to build a skyscraper. Perhaps these images will disappear in a few years, but for now they reveal a country in the throes of revolution still holding quite tightly to tradition.

Many Chinese speak of the Tang Dynasty as one of the few great periods in which art flourished. The Buddhist thinker Xuan Zang and poets such as Li Bai and

Du Fu lived during this dynasty. Chinese landscape paintings from this period of a solitary man living at the base of a spectacular mountain suggest that for the Chinese, time and space overwhelm and uplift the human spirit. The paintings and the poetry offer no single vantage point but are meant to surround the participant. As these themes exemplify the traditional Chinese way of life in the Tang and later dynasties, one wonders if there are new themes, perhaps new vantage points being created today.

A new aesthetic may be in the making in terms of modern art, but China appears not to have had a flowering of art for many hundreds of years. Some artists were intimidated in the days of the Hundred Flowers and the Tiananmen Massacre when intellectuals and artists spoke their minds and were duly punished. Unfortunately, many of China's young artists have turned commercial, working in television and advertising. Chinese painters in Beijing and Shanghai have incorporated Western influences, especially American abstract expressionism, with what one critic calls "a definitive Chinese stroke," but pieces are sold to an entirely foreign market. Though Chinese films have found their own style in international cinema, it is perhaps the need to explain a history that has gone unexplained for so many years that keeps Chinese filmmakers from feeling imaginatively free.

It's a paradox, then, for the traveler to view what has survived 5,000 years of history—what artists have left us—and know that art today is having a difficult time both being expressed and being heard. Equally, though, one could argue that art is being expressed but not heard, perhaps not even recognized. One thinks of the first time Cubism was introduced to the public at large, shocking viewers. China bears a bit of this aesthetic today, for what is new, as Picasso said, will always appear ugly simply because it has not yet been defined. And so out of a cloud of ambiguity comes China's dance that is both old and new, rich and poor, roaring and shy and may carry with it a vision that could teach us not about modern China but about a post-modern world still undefined.

—Angela Yuan

NEW AND NOTEWORTHY

Chinese tourism itself is extremely new. Only recently have local Chinese had the money and mobility to travel in their own country and actually see the landmarks their government has raved about for so many years. Whether a place is worth raving about is an unexplored issue with the Chinese; what matters is whether or not it is "famous."

Often the best moments are the ones you invent on your own, not what the hotel or CITS recommends. The consequence of making up your own itinerary is that you have to traverse a very cryptic and archaic route, one where the roads may not be paved, the train does not show up, hotels are not where they are supposed to be, and PLA officers creep out of nowhere. There is little peace, little comfort, and incredible mark-ups for foreigners. Nevertheless, the 10-hour hard-seat ride on the train where a woman waves to you with a chicken while a man sings Western pop tunes in Chinese proves that the real fun is in the getting there. It's best to keep an open mind and an adventurous spirit.

A glimpse of China's minority cultures in newly opened remote regions reveals a China dramatically different from that seen in the major cities. Many of these regions are difficult to reach—either a special travel visa is required or roads and buses are extremely poor. But the flip side is that these regions—Xinjiang, Northern Sichuan, Southern Gansu, Qinghai, Yunnan, and Tibet—are truly magical and, for the most part, untainted by the western world.

The Three Gorges Dam, scheduled for completion in the year 2008, will flood out many towns and villages along the banks of the Yellow River. The river basin scenery that inspired hundreds of Chinese artists and painters, as well as the rare monkeys and other animals, will be sacrificed for an artificial lake over 480 km (300 mi) long. Close to 2 million people will be uprooted from lifelong homes, and though officials say that a new Three Gorges River cruise will replace the old, it is too early to know what, exactly, that would entail.

WHAT'S WHERE

China will reveal herself to the traveler who wants to see it all—snowcapped mountain ranges, cities packed full of bicycles and mopeds, Tibetan monasteries perched on hills, crystal blue rivers, creeks full of raw sewage, markets selling dried rats, charming friendly people who shout hello wherever you go, people who never look at you in the face, people who say anything not to lose face. China is a country to be understood on many levels.

China slopes from west to east, creating three general tiers of land. Some of the world's highest mountain ranges (the highest point being Everest's 29,000 ft on the border of Tibet and Nepal) are found in the Northwest and characterize the first tier; the majority of China is made up of plateaus of roughly 3,000 to 6,000 feet, the country's second tier. Last, the plains and lowlands harbor over two-thirds of the population and the industrial community.

As you navigate in China, remember the Chinese words for directions: North = Bei; South = Nan; West = Xi; East = Dong; Middle = Zhong. Street signs in cities are marked in both Chinese characters and pinyin.

Beijing

Red flags blowing over Tiananmen, the Summer Palace at dusk, the Great Wall seen from space, the endless steps and red tiled roofs of the Forbidden City—Beijing and the surrounding area are firmly rooted in grandeur. The Liao, Jin, Yuan, Ming, and Qing dynasties all chose it as their capital, for close to 2,000 years of imperial presence. The Chinese view the whole city as a historical and cultural museum, as much of China's past has been demolished elsewhere. Although the wide avenues and huge blocks create a sterile feel, they embody the image those in control want to project; they're laid out so that the individual feels small in comparison to "order."

East Central China

The East Central provinces are the most heavily populated and industrialized regions in the country. They are also home to some of China's most heavily visited spots. The Yangzi River flows through much of this mainly lowland region, carv-

ing the famous Three Gorges in Hubei before it spills into the sea at Shanghai's port. Nearby Suzhou, with its meditative gardens, and Hangzhou, with its serene lake, are often paired as "Heaven and Earth" by the Chinese and are famous for attracting China's most illustrious poets and painters. The Huangshan range are officially China's most beautiful mountains, with not only amazing and rare views but an incredible number of people to go with them. The Qing and Song dynasties developed much of the region, investing cities such as Nanjing in Jiangsu province and Kaifeng in Henan with historical and cultural merit. The terra-cotta soldiers are the chief attraction in Xian, although the city is home to other historic sights and pockets of delightful Muslim character.

Guangzhou

The Chinese have a saying: In Beijing one talks, in Shanghai one shops, in Guangzhou one eats. The infamous Qing Ping market demonstrates how well this proverb reflects reality. From insects to dogs to indistinguishable rodents both live and dried, it appears the Cantonese (Guangdong people) eat anything and everything. The Cantonese tend to associate themselves with neighboring Hong Kong rather than faraway Beijing, sharing the same dialect, Cantonese food specialties, and money-making ventures. Indeed, Guangzhou and the affluent region of Guangdong province have seriously tested Deng Xiao Ping's mandate in 1990: "To get rich is glorious." There's a frenzy and chaos to the city, a buzz and energy like no other.

Hong Kong

With all the political hype surrounding Hong Kong and forebodings for the future, the city is still land-filling, hotel-expanding, bridge-laying, business-dealing, and world-class–shopping as always. Take the tram up to Victoria Peak and witness a city below that can inspire awe the way the Grand Canyon does. Equally amazing are the blue waters and small islands surrounding the city. Cheung Chau, Lantau, and Lamma islands are speckled with fishing villages and lovely hiking areas. Hong Kong is expensive compared to China.

The Mongolias

The Mongols invaded and conquered China on horseback in the 13th century and today Mongolian children still learn to ride horses at the age of four or five. Racing, archery, and wrestling make up the annual Naadam Festival in Ulaan Baatar, the most heavily populated city, where the surrounding grasslands fill up with riders in brightly colored dress. Bordering Siberia, Mongolia's huge territory (600,000 sq mi) covers diverse geography ranging from the Gobi Desert to the pristine lake of Xowsgol to the Altai Mountain Range and is home to a variety of cultural and historical museums as well as a few monasteries that survived the Stalinist purge. Inner Mongolia, often confused with Mongolia, is part of China; here the Mongolian way of life continues, though modernization seems to be hitting fast.

Northeastern China

China's Northern treaty ports—Qingdao, Tianjin, and Dalian—offer a counterpoint to nearby Beijing as major cities. Colonial architecture ornaments small neighborhoods in and around these ports. One can even glimpse a fairly blue ocean over the rooftops. Harbin's winter ice festival draws visitors bundled up in −30° C weather to Heilongjiang—China's northernmost province. Just south is Jilin, home to the best Chinese ski resorts as well as China's largest nature reserve, where one can hike through thick forests up into the mountains to stand before a giant crater lake.

Shanghai

Infamous in the 1920s for its gambling, prostitution, gangsters, and opium dens, Shanghai is beginning to regain some of the reputation it lost after the Cultural Revolution. As one of the most Westernized cities in China, excluding Hong Kong, Shanghai is on the cutting edge of China's race for modernization. It's full of underground clubs, high-class restaurants, and upscale boutiques. Almost a quarter of the world's construction cranes are located in this city of 14 million; often it feels like half of those are on the street you happen to be walking down. On the other hand, architectural remnants of a strong colonial past survive along the charming, winding, bustling streets that make this city undeniably and intimately Chinese.

Southeastern China

Appearing as if they were sandcastles dropped from the sky, the karst rock formations of Guangxi province are among China's most spectacular landscapes. As Guilin has become more industrial and crowded, Yangshuo has become notable for banana cakes, diluted coffee, and bicycle rides down empty roads. Other parts of southeastern China contain both affluent cities and towns backed by big businesses and industry—a result of being the region closest to Taiwan—and remote countrysides populated with herding communities, small villages, and minorities. Jingdezhen is historically China's first and main producer of ceramics and porcelain; today it still turns out reproductions of ancient work of unnervingly high quality. The cities of Shaoshan and Changsha, birthplaces of many Communist leaders, including Mao himself, draw steady streams of pilgrims.

Tibet

Tibet, hung from the Himalayas, was considered one of the most magical places in the world before the Chinese invasion of 1950. Though the autonomous region still holds a lofty place in Western imagination, Tibet has been largely stripped of its freedom and identity as a thriving Buddhist region. Nevertheless, Tibet remains a country of colorful people strengthened and characterized by the rugged terrain. The Potala Palace in Llhasa, which only a handful of foreigners laid eyes on before the 1980s, stretches up its one thousand rooms to the sky.

West Central China

From Chengdu to Chongqing locals gather in tea houses by day, dine on the spiciest food in China, and play mahjongg long into the night—a relaxing way of life that has become tradition in Sichuan. In Gansu province, yaks run aplenty in the charming, ethnically Tibetan town of Xiahe nestled in the mountains and surrounded by grasslands. Ningxia is home to a large Hui population, beautiful sand dunes, and Western Xia tombs among herds of goat and sheep. Just north of Vietnam and bordering Burma and Laos lies the ethnically diverse province of Yunnan, home to the Dai, Bai, Yi, and Naxi minorities. Backpackers relax in the ancient town of Dali below spectacular mountains before heading north to Lijiang and hiking through the waterfalls and valleys of Tiger Leaping Gorge. The Dai minority inhabits the tropical area of Xishuangbanna, earning its name from the Thai, where sparkling waters and jungle-like flora evoke a bit of Southeast Asia inside China.

Western China

Sip Uighur tea while watching camels carry in goods from across the desert. Stroll through a bustling Sunday bazaar full of traders, embroidered hats, hand-carved knives, books, and Muslim snacks. The famed Silk Road ran through here. Though the region has lost some of the charm of the late 19th century (one can fly from Turpan to Kashgar instead of walk for five weeks through the desert), it is still quite a sweltering experience. The Uighur minority populates much of the region and is currently at odds with the Han Chinese who make Ürümqi and other eastern cities within Xinjiang their home.

PLEASURES AND PASTIMES

Antiques Markets

Chairman Mao alarm clocks, calligraphy scrolls, porcelain, jade pieces, valuable coins, old Chinese locks, and a great number of fake antiques are spread carefully on tables that line the streets of most Chinese cities on a weekly, sometimes daily basis. Ask around for the date and time of the antiques market in your area and be aware of ripoffs when you arrive. If you are seriously searching for antiques, it's best to get a local who speaks English to bargain for you while you wait unseen for the right price.

Bicycling

Most cities and popular tourist towns offer bicycle rentals for an average of a dollar a day. Mounting a Flying Pigeon and cruising down wide, tree-shaded bike lanes with the locals is an experience not to be missed.

Dining

Dining in China is best enjoyed in large groups so you can sample a variety of dishes. Usually the menus are divided into appetizers, meats, vegetables, seafoods, soups, and so on. It's best to order from each category so that you dine in the true Chinese style—dishes at your elbows, across the table, in front of you, stacked up, and sometimes even on the ledge behind to make room for the next round. Although each province and indeed each city in China has a distinctive way of cooking and eating, there are generally four regional categories of food found across the country.

Northern or Mandarin cuisine is characterized by fine cutting and pure seasoning, providing dishes with strong garlic, ginger, and onion flavors. Beijing duck served with pancakes and hoisin sauce and Mongolian hot pot are also native to this region. An abundance of steamed bread (mantou) and flat pancakes are sold on the street and make good snacks.

Southern or Cantonese cooking is famous for dim sum, an eating experience found in Hong Kong, Guangdong province, and some larger cities with an overseas contingent. Bite-size dumplings, wontons, rice noodle dishes, sesame seed buns filled with bean paste, and a variety of other tasty snacks are pushed around on carts for patrons to choose from. Cantonese cooking tends to be the lightest and least oily of the four categories, though snake, turtle, monkey, rabbit, and a host of other animal and reptile specialties find their way into the menus.

Eastern and most notably Shanghainese food is notorious for its heavy use of oil, though the freshest seafood, from hairy crabs to snails to shark's fin soup, are served in this region. Chicken and seafood dishes are simmered, boiled, or braised in their own juices, enhancing the natural flavors. Some wonderful *baozis* (steamed white bread) filled with either vegetables, pork, or black bean paste are sold on the streets of most cities and towns scattered throughout the region.

The spiciest of the four categories, Sichuan cooking loves to use that Chinese peppercorn and will keep you slugging back bottles of purified water. Chengdu is famous for its snacks, a variety of small dishes both hot and cold, served all day. Tea-smoked duck, marinated for over 24 hours, peels right off the bone and melts in the mouth. Sichuan hot pot restaurants have become so popular that they are popping up as far away as Beijing.

Early Morning

At six in the morning, no matter where you are in China, everyone is up and outside buying their daily vegetables, fruits, meats, eggs, and noodles in the local market. Vendors are out steaming, frying, boiling, and selling breakfast snacks to people on their way to work. Men and women practice tai chi in parks, along rivers, and in some unlikely places—the steps of a movie theater, an empty alley, the side entrance of a hotel—whenever the sun rises. Early morning in China is when the cities, towns, and villages come alive and should be experienced as much as possible, as every place has a different way of doing "business."

Hiking

Although the activity is unpopular with locals, China rewards the hiker with natural preserves, national parks, and sacred mountains. Songhuahu in Jilin, the Tiger Leaping Gorge, Emeishan, Huangshan, the Guilin-Yangshou area, Xinjiang—practically every province has something to offer.

Tea Houses

Along West Lake in Hanghzhou, inside Chengdu's parks, on the fourth floor of a department store, on cobblestone streets, in subway stations, and along China's many rivers—tea houses are to China as cafés are to France. Relax, chat, and meditate over a pot of Oolong while sampling dried fruit snacks.

Wandering

Wandering and sometimes getting lost in China will reveal an inner logic to the city or town you are visiting. Here is where you get to experience China without a frame of propaganda around it. Encounter charming alleyways that twist behind major streets, hidden outdoor markets, friendly, responsive locals gesturing unintelligible messages, dramatic shifts from poverty to riches, and wild displays of the new and old.

FODOR'S CHOICE

Hotels

★ **Grand Hotel, Nanjing, Jiangsu,** has a rooftop restaurant, excellent Japanese food, and a Chinese medical center ($$$$, Ch. 5).

★ **Peninsula, Hong Kong,** is simply one of the best and most famous hotels in the world, full of good taste and old-world style as well as all the latest conveniences ($$$$, Ch. 8).

★ **Beijing Hotel, Beijing,** the capital's oldest, has hosted such luminaries as Field Marshal Montgomery, Noel Coward, and Zhou Enlai ($$$, Ch. 2).

★ **Ningwozhuang Guesthouse, Lanzhou, Gansu,** is an old-fashioned villa set in beautiful gardens ($$$, Ch. 9).

★ **Heping Fandian, Shanghai,** also known as the Peace Hotel, is an Art Deco masterpiece right on the Bund ($$, Ch. 4).

★ **Karakorum Yurt Camp, Karakorum, Mongolia,** set in open grassland, offers the chance to stay in a real yurt without having to rough it too much ($$, Ch. 10).

★ **Qingdao Ying Bingguan, Qingdao, Shandong,** built in 1903 as the residence of the governor-general of the German colony of Qingdao, is surrounded by gardens ($, Ch. 3).

★ **Victory, Guangzhou, Guangdong,** a budget hotel composed of former colonial guesthouses, stands on Shamian island among restored old mansions ($, Ch. 6).

Man-made Wonders

★ **Bingling Si Shiku, Gansu,** or Thousand Buddha Temple and Caves, are filled with Buddhist wall paintings and statuary from the 10th through 17th centuries (Ch. 9).

★ **Changcheng (The Great Wall), Beijing,** built by successive dynasties over two millennia, is a collection of many defensive installations that extends some 2,500 mi from the East China Sea to Central Asia (Ch. 2).

★ **Dunhuang, Gansu,** a small oasis town, is the place to visit the extraordinary Mogao Ku (Mogao Grottoes), caves painted by Buddhists from the 4th through the 10th centuries (Ch 9).

✴ **Longmen Shiku, Luoyang, Henan,** the Dragon Gate Grottoes, are filled with thousands of Buddhist figures carved over several centuries (Ch. 5).

✴ **Mingshisan Ling, Beijing,** the Ming Tombs, in a valley northeast of Beijing, is the final resting place for 13 of the 16 Ming emperors; the approach is along a spirit way lined with weeping willow trees and imperial advisers, elephants, camels, horses, and other animals all carved of stone (Ch. 2).

✴ **Qin Shihuang Ling, Xian, Shaanxi,** the tomb of the first Qin emperor, from the 3rd century BC, stands near an army of thousands of life-size terra-cotta soldiers with individual faces, buried as Qin's garrison in the afterlife and now being unearthed by archaeologists (Ch. 5).

✴ **Victoria Peak, Hong Kong,** known as Tai Ping Shan, or Mountain of Great Peace, in Chinese, offers a breathtaking panorama of sea, islands, and city on a clear day, as well as parklands for walking or hiking (Ch. 8).

✴ **Wangshi Yuan, Suzhou, Jiangsu,** the Master of the Nets Garden, the finest in this city of gardens, was originally laid out in the 12th century (Ch. 5).

✴ **Yuyuan, Shanghai,** a garden built in the 16th century, creates an atmosphere of peace amidst the clamor of the city, with rocks, trees, dragon walls, bridges, and pavilions (Ch. 4).

Museums

✴ **Gansu Sheng Bowuguan, Lanzhou, Gansu,** the Gansu Provincial Museum, though old-fashioned, has some excellent exhibits on the Silk Road, especially pottery, porcelain, and bronzes (Ch. 9).

✴ **Hubei Sheng Bowuguan, Wuhan, Hubei,** the Hubei Provincial Museum, contains Mao memorabilia and a fine collection of antiquities from 5th-century BC tombs (Ch. 5).

✴ **Nan Yue Wang Mu, Guangzhou, Guangdong,** the Museum and Tomb of the Southern Yue Kings, displays a priceless collection of funerary objects from a 2nd-century BC tomb discovered in 1983 (Ch. 6).

✴ **Shaanxi Lishi Bowuguan, Xian, Shaanxi,** Shaanxi Historical Museum, opened in 1992, exhibits artifacts from the Paleolithic Age to 200 BC (Ch. 5).

✴ **Shanghai Bowuguan, Shanghai,** an exquisitely displayed collection of Chinese art and artifacts, opened in 1996 (Ch. 4).

✴ **Zhongguo Lishi Bowuguan, Beijing,** the Museum of Chinese History, is one of the world's best troves of Chinese art (Ch. 2).

Natural Wonders

✴ **Changbaishan, Jilin,** the Changbaishan Nature Reserve, has mountainous forests, hiking, and hot springs (Ch. 3).

✴ **Hengshang Shan, Hengyang, Hunan,** is one of China's five holy mountains (Ch. 7).

✴ **Huangshan, Hefei, Anhui,** a misty, pine and rock-covered mountain with peaks that have inspired emperors and artists for centuries, is networked with paths and stairways (Ch. 5).

✴ **Li Jiang, Guilin, Guangxi,** the Li River, is lined with evocative, tree-covered karst mountains jutting up above both shores; the boat ride to Yangshuo is spectacular (Ch. 7).

✴ **Tianchi, Xinjiang,** one of the prettiest lakes in China, with clear, clear water, is surrounded by mountains (Ch. 11).

✴ **Wuyi Shan Fengjingqu, Fujian,** Wuyi Mountain Natural Reserve, has dramatic scenery with peaks, waterfalls, bamboo groves, and tea bushes (Ch. 7).

Palaces

✴ **Forbidden City (Imperial Palace), Beijing,** was home to 24 emperors and two dynasties for 500 years; the 200-acre compound is filled with halls, courtyards, and lesser buildings all stained imperial vermilion decorated with gold on the outside and furnished with exquisite screens, thrones, paintings, and more (Ch. 2).

✴ **Potala, Lhasa, Tibet,** built in the 17th century on the foundation of the 7th-century original, was until the 20th century the world's tallest building and served as the spiritual and political headquarters of Tibet's theocracy (Ch. 12).

★ **Yiheyuan (Summer Palace), Beijing,** built in the mid-18th century, is a garden retreat on the northwest fringe of the city where imperial families escaped summer heat in airy pavilions among trees and man-made lakes and aboard a marble boat (Ch. 2).

Restaurants

★ **Dingshan Meishi Cheng, Nanjing, Jiangsu,** with traditional latticework on the windows, serves excellent local Huainan cuisine ($$$$, Ch. 5).

★ **Fortune Garden, Beijing,** the city's foremost Cantonese restaurant, serves dishes such as roast suckling pig ($$$$, Ch. 2).

★ **All Seasons, Guangzhou, Guangdong,** prepares cuisines from Shanghai, Beijing, Sichuan, and Taiwan in a coolly elegant setting ($$$, Ch. 6).

★ **Indochine 1929, Hong Kong,** in Central on Hong Kong Island, evokes the atmosphere of French Indochina of the 1930s in decor, service, and fare ($$$, Ch. 8).

★ **Tangle Gong, Xian, Shaanxi,** specializes in authentic Tang dynasty imperial cuisine ($$$, Ch. 5).

★ **Li Family Restaurant, Beijing,** in a tiny, informal space, serves imperial dishes whose recipes were handed down from a forebear in the Qing court ($$, Ch.2).

★ **Mao Lin Huo Guo Cheng, Hohhot, Inner Mongolia,** is the place to go for excellent hotpots ($$, Ch. 10).

★ **Meilongzhen, Shanghai,** dating from 1938, serves outstanding Sichuanese food in traditional surroundings ($$, Ch. 4).

★ **Caigenxiang, Guangzhou, Guangdong,** is a joy for vegetarians, with 200 dishes and 100 snacks to choose from ($, Ch. 6).

Temples and Monasteries

★ **Gandan Khiid, Ulaan Baatar, Mongolia,** houses a Tibetan Buddhist monastery and temples in buildings covered with golden roofs (Ch. 10).

★ **Ganden, Lhasa, Tibet,** an enormous monastery established in 1409 that became the foremost center of the Gelugpa sect of Tibetan Buddhism, draws pilgrims paying homage to its sacred sites and relics (Ch. 12).

★ **Jokhang, Lhasa, Tibet,** the most sacred building in Tibet, is a temple built in the 7th century that continues to attract worshipers (Ch. 12).

★ **Laboleng Si, Xiahe, Gansu,** Labrang Monastery, one of the two great Lamaist temples outside Tibet, was founded in 1710 and holds religious festivals several times a year (Ch. 9).

★ **Linggu Si, Nanjing, Jiangsu,** the Spirit Valley Temple, is entered through a 14th-century beamless hall—made entirely of brick (Ch. 5).

★ **Liu Rong Si Hua Ta, Guangzhou, Guangdong,** the Six Banyan Temple, is a landmark in the city with its trompe l'oeil 184-foot tall pagoda and colorful, carved roofs (Ch. 6).

★ **Tiantan (Temple of Heaven), Beijing,** holds the round altar where the emperor conducted sacrifices on the summer and winter solstices and the blue-roofed Hall of Prayer for Good Harvests (Ch. 2).

★ **Wenshu Yuan, Chengdu, Sichuan,** dating from the Tang dynasty, the Buddhist monastery has buildings with exquisite carvings (Ch. 9).

★ **Yufo Si, Shanghai,** the Jade Buddha Temple, contains a 6½-ft-high statue of Buddha carved from white jade, as well as precious paintings and scriptures (Ch. 4).

FESTIVALS AND SEASONAL EVENTS

China has only three official holidays a year: Spring Festival or Chinese New Year, National Day, and International Labor Day, for a grand total of five days off. These are high travel times for the Chinese, especially during Chinese New Year, and it's best to avoid them if at all possible.

Many of the most colorful festivals are celebrated by the minorities, particularly in the region of Yunnan, an added bonus if your visit coincides with festival times.

The majority of China's holidays and festivals are calculated according to the lunar calendar and can vary as much as a few weeks from year to year. Check your lunar calendar for dates more specific than those below.

DEC. 25/JAN. 1➤ **Christmas and New Year's Day** are becoming an excuse for the Chinese to exchange cards, buy decorations (made in China) and eat out banquet-style. In the big cities, Christmas makes itself known by a ubiquitous paper Santa that is taped to almost every store. Some employees get a day off on New Year's.

JAN./FEB.➤ **Harbin's Ice Festival**, a tour de force of bigger-than-life ice sculptures of animals, landmarks, and legendary figures is held from the

beginning of January to late February. Although it can be as cold as −30°C, many visitors come to Zhaolin Park to check out the best ice festival China has to offer.

FEB.➤ **Chinese New Year,** China's most celebrated and important holiday, follows the lunar calendar and falls in early to mid-February. Also called Spring Festival, it gives the Chinese an official three-day holiday to visit family and relatives, eat special meals, and throw firecrackers to celebrate the New Year and its respective Chinese zodiac animal. Students and teachers get up to four weeks off, and many others consider that the festival runs as long as a month. It is a particularly crowded time to travel in China, as workers and students use their time off to go to and from home. Many offices and services reduce their hours or close altogether. Tickets and hotels may be unavailable for as much as a week.

FEB./MAR.➤ Following a lunar calendar, the **Tibetan New Year** is celebrated in Tibet, Gansu, and Northern Sichuan provinces with processions, prayer assemblies, and yak butter sculptures and lamps.

FEB./MAR.➤ The **Spring Lantern Festival** marks the end of Chinese New Year on the 15th day of the first moon. Colorful paper lanterns are carried through the streets, sometimes accompanied by dragon dances.

APR.➤ The Dai Minority in the Xishuangbanna region of Yunnan celebrate their own Lunar New Year, the **Water Splashing Festival,** usually in mid-April. Legend has it that the Dai people were subjected to demons by an evil ruler until one of his consorts lopped off his head with a single hair from his head. This produced an overflow of blood, which is now celebrated as the washing away of one's sins of the previous year. Minorities in colorful dress come from all over the region to enjoy three days of revelry with activities ranging from boat races on the river to buffalo slaughter.

APR.➤ Also in Yunnan, the **Third Moon Fair** (15th to 21st day of the 3rd moon, usually April), attracts people to Dali from all over the province to celebrate a legendary sighting of the Buddhist Goddess of Mercy, Guanyin.

APR. 5➤ Not so much a holiday as a day of worship, **Qing Ming** (clean and bright), or Remembrance of the Dead, gathers relatives at the graves of the deceased to clean the surface and leave fresh flowers.

MAY 1➤ **International Labor Day** is another busy travel time, especially if the holiday falls near a weekend.

MAY 4➤ **Youth Day,** though no longer a publicly celebrated holiday, commemorates the first mass student movement in 1919, which has come to symbolize a rejection of traditional, political and religious ideas.

MAY➤ In Dali of Yunnan province, **The Three Temples Festival** on the 23rd to the 25th day of the fourth moon is celebrated with walks to local temples and general merry-making.

MAY➤ The **Birthday of Tun Hau,** Goddess of the Sea, is celebrated most heartily in Sai Kung in Kowloon, where fishermen decorate their boats and gather at temples to pray for good catches for the coming year.

SUMMER

JUNE➤ **The Dragon Boat Festival,** on the fifth day of the fifth moon, celebrates the national hero Qu Yuan, who drowned himself in the 3rd century in protest against the corrupt emperor. Legend has it that people attempted to rescue him by throwing rice dumplings wrapped in bamboo leaves into the sea and frightening fish away by beating drums. Today crews in narrow dragon boats race to the beat of heavy drums and rice wrapped in bamboo leaves is festively consumed.

JULY 1➤ Perhaps **July 1st** will go down in history as the day China ended 150 years of shame and looked to the future with Hong Kong under its wing. Stay tuned for what turns up on both the island and the mainland—a memorial day or a celebration?

JULY➤ **The Torch Festival** is celebrated in the towns of Lijiang and Dali in Yunnan on the 24th day of the sixth moon.

MID-JULY–MID-AUG➤ Mongolia and Inner Mongolia celebrate the **Naadam Festival** in late summer. The Festival centers around equestrian activities including racing, wrestling, and hunting. Mongolia celebrates the festival a month earlier in accordance with their 1921 revolution. Hohhot, in Inner Mongolia, attracts people from all over the region who arrive on horseback during festival time.

AUTUMN

SEPT. 8➤ **Confucius's Birthday** may be overlooked in other parts of China, but there are celebrations aplenty in Qufu, his birthplace.

OCT. 1➤ **National Day** celebrates the founding of the People's Republic of China. Tiananmen Square fills up with flowers, entertainment, and a hefty crowd of visitors on this official holiday.

OCT.➤ **Mid-Autumn Festival** is celebrated on the 15th day of the 8th moon, which generally falls in early October. The Chinese spend this time gazing at the full moon and exchanging tasty moon cakes filled with meat, bean paste, sugar, and other delectable surprises.

OCT./NOV.➤ For 10 days the Xishuangbanna region of Yunnan shoots off rockets to celebrate **The Tan Ta Festival.** Special ceremonies take place in local temples in the area.

2 Beijing

Wide-eyed Chinese tourists converge on Tiananmen Square each day at dawn to watch a military honor guard raise China's flag. As full-dress soldiers march forth from the vast Forbidden City, these visitors, who usually number in the hundreds, begin to take pictures. They jockey for spots beneath the fluttering banner. They pose before the Gate of Heavenly Peace, its huge Chairman Mao portrait gazing benignly from atop the imperial doorway. This same shot, snapped by countless pilgrims, adorns family albums across the Middle Kingdom.

By George
Wehrfritz and
Diana Garrett

THE DAILY PHOTOGRAPHIC RITUAL, the giddy throng gathered beneath the Forbidden City's ancient vermilion edifice, illustrates Beijing's position—unrivaled to this day—at the center of the Chinese universe. In spite of devastating urban renewal, modern Beijing continues to convey an imperial grandeur. But the city is more than a relic or a feudal ghost. New temples to communism—the Great Hall of the People, Chairman Mao's Mausoleum—convey the monumental power that still resides within the city's secret courtyards. If China is a dragon, Beijing is its beating heart.

Beijing's historic, cultural, and political preeminence dates back nearly six centuries. In 1406, Emperor Yongle relocated the Ming court to this Northern Capital in a bid to secure the frontier from marauding nomadic herdsmen. He mobilized 200,000 corvee laborers to construct his palace, a maze of interlinking halls, gates, and courtyards now known as the Forbidden City. Ming planners dug moats and canals, plotted Beijing's sweeping roadway grid and, in 1553, constructed a massive new city wall to protect their thriving capital. The Ming also built their (or any) empire's grandest public works project: the Great Wall of China. In ruins, it still traverses the rugged mountains north of Beijing. But wall-building drained Ming coffers and, in the end, failed to prevent Manchu horsemen from taking the capital—and China—in 1644.

This foreign dynasty, the Qing, inherited the Ming palaces, built their own retreats (most notably, the Summer Palace on Kunming Lake), and perpetuated feudalism in China for another 267 years. In its decline, the Qing proved impotent to stop humiliating foreign encroachment. It lost the first Opium War to Great Britain in 1842 (and was forced to cede Hong Kong "in perpetuity" as a result). In 1860, a combined British and French force stormed Beijing and razed the Old Summer Palace, carting away priceless antiquities. After the Qing crumbled in 1911, its successor, Sun Yatsen's Nationalists, struggled to consolidate power. Beijing became a cauldron of social activism. On May 4, 1919, students marched on Tiananmen Square to protest humiliations in Versailles, where allied commanders negotiating an end to World War I gave Germany's extra-territorial holdings in China to Japan, not Sun's infant republic. Patriotism intensified. In 1937, Japanese imperial armies stormed across Beijing's Marco Polo Bridge to launch a brutal eight-year occupation. Civil war followed close on the heels of Tokyo's 1945 surrender, and raged until the Communist victory. Chairman Mao himself declared the founding of a new nation, the People's Republic of China, from the rostrum atop the Gate of Heavenly Peace on October 1, 1949.

Like Emperor Yongle, Mao built a capital that conformed to his own vision. New, Soviet-inspired institutions rose up around—even in— Tiananmen Square. Beijing's city wall, the grandest rampart of its kind in China, was demolished to make way for a ring road. Temples were looted, torn down, closed, or turned into factories during the 1966– 76 Cultural Revolution. In the countryside, large sections of the Great Wall disappeared—pilfered by peasants brick by brick for use in nearby villages.

In recent years, old Peking has suffered most from prosperity. Many ancient neighborhoods, replete with traditional courtyard homes lining narrow *hutong,* or alleys, have been bulldozed. In their place, a new city of dreary apartment blocks and glitzy commercial developments has risen to house and entertain a citizenry more interested in indoor plumbing than protecting Beijing's heritage. Preservationism has begun to take hold, albeit slowly, although the Chinese ideogram CHAI, meaning "to pull down," remains a common sight in Beijing's historic neighborhoods.

Beijing's 12 million residents are a compelling mix of old and new. Early morning *taiqi* (tai chi) enthusiasts, bearded old men with caged songbirds, and amateur Peking Opera crooners still frequent the city's many charming parks. Cyclists, most pedaling cumbersome, jet-black Flying Pigeons clog the roadways. But few wear padded blue Mao jackets these days, and they all must share the city's broad thoroughfares with trendy Chinese yuppies and their private cars. Beijing traffic has gone from non-existent to nightmarish in less than a decade, adding auto emissions to the city's factory-darkened skies and sparking the newest threat to social order—road rage.

Outsiders, or *waidiren,* are the newcomers to Beijing's human landscape. Migrants from the impoverished hinterland, they typically work construction, clean houses, run pedicabs, or collect garbage. Look for them selling fruit (or tasty baked yams) on street corners, sleeping at train stations, or loitering in department store electronics departments to catch a glimpse of television.

Manifest "reform and openness" notwithstanding, Beijing still carries a political charge. It is the seat of China's bloated national bureaucracy, a self-described "dictatorship of the proletariat" that has yet to relinquish its political monopoly. In 1989, student protesters in Tiananmen Square tried—and failed—to topple this old order. The government's brutal response, carried live on CNN, remains etched in global memory. To this day, secret police mingle with tourists and kite-fliers on the square, ready to haul away all those so brave or foolish as to distribute a leaflet or unfurl a banner.

Mao-style propaganda campaigns remain a common mechanism for engineering proper behavior. Slogans that preach unity among China's national minorities, patriotism, and love for the People's Liberation Army decorate the city. Provincial leaders, who manage increasingly independent regional economies, have all but abandoned such ideological measures; in Beijing they still flourish. The result is an ironic mix of new prosperity and throwback politics: socialist mantras emblazoned on electronic billboards hung at shopping arcades that sell Gucci and Big Macs.

Pleasures and Pastimes

Biking
Beijing's pleasures are best sampled off the subway and out of taxis. In other words, walk (☞ Walking, *below*) or pedal. Rent bikes (available at many hotels) and take an impromptu sightseeing tour. Beijing is flat, and bike lanes exist on most main roads. Pedaling among the city's cyclists isn't as challenging as it looks; keep it slow and ring your bell often. Punctured tire? Not to worry, curb-side repairmen line most streets. Remember to park (and lock) your bike only in designated areas. Most bike parking lots have attendants and cost Y0.10.

Dining
China's economic boom has revolutionized dining in Beijing. Gone are the shabby, state-run restaurants, driven out of business (or into the care of new management) by private establishments that cater to China's emerging middle class. It is now possible to enjoy a hearty Cantonese or Sichuanese meal for under $5 per person—or to spend $100 or more per head on a lavish imperial-style banquet. Hamburgers (or

sushi, lasagna, and burritos) are available at numerous new eateries that target tourists, expatriates, and Chinese yuppies. Tips in hotel restaurants are included in the bill.

Peking Duck and other local specialties remain popular. New eateries offer regional delights like spicy Sichuan tofu, Cantonese dim sum, Shanghai steamed fish, Xinjiang kabob—even Tibetan yak penis soup. One popular restaurant has commandeered a former palace. Several dumpling shops offer dining under the stars in restored courtyard homes. The newest culinary trend, Cultural Revolution theme restaurants, summon Chairman Mao's ghost with such famine-inspired delicacies as leaves, grass, and fried cicadas. Enjoy.

CATEGORY	COST*
$$$$	over $25
$$$	$15–$25
$$	$7–$15
$	under $7

Per person for a standard three course meal; no tax or tips included.

Lodging

China's 1949 Communist victory closed the doors on the opulent accommodation once available to visiting foreigners in Beijing and elsewhere. Functional concrete boxes served the needs of the few "fellow travelers" admitted into the People's Republic of China in the 1950s and '60s. By the late '70s, China's lack of high-quality hotels had become a distinct embarrassment, to which opening to foreign investment was the only answer. Two decades later, a multitude of polished marble palaces await your dollars with attentive service; improved amenities, like business centers, health clubs, Chinese/Western restaurants, nightclubs, karaoke, beauty salons, and conference/banqueting facilities; and rising prices. Glitz and Western comfort, rather than history and character, are the main selling points for Beijing's near-identical hotels. If you're looking for Chinese-style accommodation enhanced by gardens and rockeries, consider the Bamboo Garden and the Lusongyuan and Youhao guesthouses (☞ Lodging, *below*).

As traffic conditions worsen, more business travelers are choosing hotels closer to their interests. The more distant hotels, such as the Lido, Friendship, Shangri-La, and Fragrant Hills, all offer shuttle bus service into the city center (Friendship Store, Beijing Hotel, Lufthansa Centre). Booking a few months in advance is always advisable, but the current glut of accommodation means room availability is rarely a problem, whatever the season.

CATEGORY	COST*
$$$$	over $250
$$$	$150–$250
$$	$55–150
$	under $55

Prices are per night for a standard double room, including taxes.

Opera

MTV culture has taken root in every Chinese city. But only in Beijing is it still possible to see authentic Peking Opera. Tragedy, warfare, palace intrigue—this is the stuff of the capital's traditional stage. Operas range from slothful to acrobatic; voices soar to near-shrill heights for female roles and sink to throaty baritones of generals and emperors. Costumes and make-up are without exception extravagant. Shortened performances catering to tourists are held at the Li Yuan Ju Chang theater in Liulichang. Full operas, and Beijing's enthusiastic opera crowd, can be seen several times each week at the Jing Guang Hui Guang opera hall.

Shopping

Modern supermarkets stock a wide range of imported food and drink, as well as most toiletries. Numerous "old goods markets" peddle everything from Chairman Mao kitsch to antique porcelain, jewelry, and furniture—plus a full selection of fakes. The Sunday flea market at Panjiayuan is the first stop for many portable antiques (wood carvings, statues, jade, old tile, and so on) entering Beijing from the countryside. Vendors, especially in the market's open-air rear section, are usually peasants who've journeyed to Beijing to sell items collected in their village. Antique rugs and furniture are perhaps Beijing's best bargain. A few dealers will arrange to ship larger items overseas.

Walking

Never bypass an intriguing alleyway. Strolls into the *hutong* frequently reveal ancient neighborhoods: mud-and-timber homes; courtyards full of children, chickens, and mountains of cabbage and coal; alleys so narrow that pedestrians can't pass two abreast. This is old Peking. See it before it vanishes.

EXPLORING BEIJING

Beijing rewards the explorer. Most temples and palaces have gardens and lesser courtyards that are seldom visited. Be curious. Even at the height of the summer tourist rush, the Forbidden City's peripheral courtyards offer ample breathing room, even seclusion. The Temple of Heaven's vast grounds are a pleasure year-round—and enchanting during a snowstorm.

While the Forbidden City and Tiananmen Square represent the heart of Beijing from imperial and tourist perspectives, the capital lacks a definitive "downtown" area in terms of shopping (bar Wangfujing, perhaps) or business, as commercial and entertainment districts have arisen all over.

Outside the city, budget time for hiking. Explore the Ming Tombs on foot and picnic in the ruins (a tradition among Beijing's expatriate community since the 1920s). Most upscale hotels offer elegant boxed lunches. If you've hired a car to the Great Wall, consider venturing a bit farther into the countryside where farming villages await. Don't be surprised when a peasant invites you into his home for a rest and some tea.

Numbers in the text correspond to numbers in the margin and on the Beijing, Forbidden City, and Side Trips from Beijing maps.

Great Itineraries

IF YOU HAVE 3 DAYS

Begin day one at the dawn flag-raising ceremony in **Tiananmen Square.** Stroll past the Monument to the People's Heroes, circle **Chairman Mao's mausoleum** and then head for the nearby ✕ **Grand Hotel** for coffee or breakfast. At 8:30 AM, walk through the **Gate of Heavenly Peace** and spend the morning at the **Forbidden City.** Take the audio tour, which offers an entertaining south-to-north narration. Depart through the Gate of Obedience and Purity (the north gate) and walk west to **Beihai Park** for lunch at the food stalls. Explore the park. Arrive at the North Gate before 1:30 PM for a half-day hutong tour, a guided pedicab ride through a maze-like neighborhood to the **Drum Tower.** Have dinner at the ✕ **Quanjude Peking Duck Restaurant** south of Tiananmen Square. On day two, visit the **Temple of Heaven,** the **Lama Temple** and perhaps the **National Art Gallery** or **Museum of the Chinese People's Revolution.** Allow time for shopping at **Beijing Curio City, Silk Alley,** and the **Yihong Carpet Fac-**

tory. For dinner, eat Sichuanese at ✕ **Ritan Park.** Set aside day three for a trip to the **Ming Tombs** and the **Great Wall** at Mutianyu, where a Japanese gondola offers a dramatic ride to the summit. Bring a brown bag lunch. Weather permitting, enjoy an outdoor dinner at the ✕ **Golden Cat,** Beijing's premier dumpling restaurant.

IF YOU HAVE 4 OR MORE DAYS

For the first two days follow the itinerary above. On day three, hire a car and visit the **Great Wall** at Simatai, where long unrestored strands ascend steep crags. Be prepared for no-handrails hiking, tough climbs, and unparalleled vistas. On day four, hire a car and visit the spectacular **Eastern Qing Tombs,** where a "spirit way" lined with carved stone animals and unrestored temple-like grave sites rest in a beautiful rural setting. Bring a lunch and wear walking shoes. The drive takes five hours round-trip, so depart early. For an enjoyable day trip closer to Beijing, walk around Kunming Lake at the rambling **Summer Palace,** then spend a few hours at the nearby **Old Summer Palace,** now an intriguing ruin. Plan an evening to experience **Peking Opera,** and another to relax at a club in the Sanlitun diplomatic quarter.

Tiananmen Square to Liulichang Antiques Market

The fame and symbolism of China's heart, Tiananmen, the Gate of Heavenly Peace, have been potent for generations of Chinese, but the events of June 1989 have left it forever etched into world consciousness. South of the square, a district of antiques shops and bookstores shows another side of Chinese culture.

A Good Walk

Start at the Renmin Yingxiong Jinianbei (Monument to the People's Heroes) in **Tiananmen Guangchang** ①. Look to either side of the square for the monuments to the new dynasty—the individual is meant to be dwarfed by their scale. To the west lies the **Renmin Dahuitang** ②, home to China's "parliament," the National People's Congress. The equally solid building opposite is host to the **Zhongguo Geming Lishi Bowuguan** and the **Zhongguo Lishi Bowuguan** ③.

Southward, straight ahead, between two banks of heroic sculptures, is the **Maozhuxi Jiniantang** ④. As you leave Chairman Mao's tomb, ahead stands **Qianmen** (Front Gate), the colloquial name for the **Zhengyangmen** ⑤, from the top of which you can see views of the city. Back at street level, the transition from imperial to "Chinese" city is apparent. The Qianmen area remains as bustling as ever. Head down Qianmen Dajie, the large road leading south, for about 30 yards before turning right (west) and sharply left (south) down a parallel north–south avenue, Zhu Bao Jie (Jewelry Market Street). The old Beijing Silk Shop at No. 5 will confirm you are on the right track. Here, in the **Dazhalan** ⑥ area, amid the silk and fur bargains of the '90s, continue traditions of commerce and entertainment stretching back to the Ming.

To escape the bustle into the calm of residential Beijing, take the second alley to your right, Langfang Ertiao (65 ft in on the left is a three-story house with carved decorative panels). You will see a number of such former inns and shops as you proceed west to the Meishijie (Coal Market St.) crossing, where you should head diagonally over to the Qudeng (Fetch Light) Hutong.

Follow Qudeng Hutong past traditional courtyard houses marked by wooden doorways, auspicious couplets, lintel beams (the more beams, the more important the original inhabitant), and stone door gods. At its end, veer right then left and onto Tiaozhou (Broom) Hutong. At its close, turn left again down Yanshou Ji (Long Life Street) and the eastern end of **Liulichang Jie** ⑦ will soon be apparent. Nanxinhua Jie divides Liulichang in two. From here you can visit the **Guangfu Tang Yi Shu Bowuguan** ⑧.

TIMING

Allow three hours for the walk, longer if the museums arrest you and if serious antique/curio browsing is anticipated in Liulichang.

Sights to See

❻ **Dazhalan** (Large Wicker Gate). Popularly known for a gate that was lowered each night in Ming times to enforce a curfew, this district of close-packed lanes crowded with flags and sideboards was filled with a cacophony of merchants, eateries, wine shops, theaters, tea houses, and pleasure houses staffed by Beijing's finest courtesans. Palace officials (and the occasional emperor in disguise) would escape here for a few hours' respite from the suffocating imperial maze. ⊠ *Zhubaoshi Jie, near Qianmen.*

❽ **Guangfu Tang Yi Shu Bowuguan** (Guangfu Classical Art Museum). This private museum contains a fine collection of imperial porcelain and furniture. The proprietor, Ma Yaodo, is a recognized authority on Chinese antiques. He offers occasional seminars (with English translation) on identifying and understanding traditional Chinese porcelain and furniture. Call to make reservations. ⊠ *53 Liulichang Xi Jie, Xuanwu District,* ☎ *010/6317–5059.* 🎫 *Y20.* ☾ *Daily 9:30–4.*

❼ **Liulichang Jie** (Glazed Tile Factory Street). The Ming factory that gives the street its name, and the Forbidden City its yellow top, was destroyed by the Qing, but renovation has restored the many book, arts, and antiques shops that crowded here in early Qing times. Be sure to visit the **Zhongguo Shu Dian** (China Bookstore; ⊠ opposite no. 115) and the most famous shop on the street, the **Rongbaozhai** (⊠ 19 Liulichang Xijie), which sells paintings, antiques, and calligraphy materials.

NEED A BREAK?   You can get a cup of tea upstairs at the **Boguge** teahouse (⊠ 136 Liulichang DongJie), next to the stone pedestrian bridge.

❹ **Maozhuxi Jiniantang** (Chairman Mao Zedong Memorial Hall). Begun in November 1976, it was ready to receive China's embalmed leader by August 1977, and opened to the public on September 9, the first anniversary of Mao's death. Sentries will assure that your communion with the Great Helmsman is brief—into a spacious lobby dominated by a marble Mao statue, and then to the Hall of Reverence where he lies in state, wrapped in a Chinese flag inside a crystal coffin that is lowered each night into a subterranean freezer. In a bid to limit Mao's deification, a second-story museum to Zhou Enlai, Zhu De, and Liu Shaoqi (whom Mao persecuted to death during the Cultural Revolution) was added in 1983. The hall is closed for renovation until sometime in 1998. Its builders willfully ignored the square's geomancy, for the mausoleum faces north, boldly contradicting centuries of imperial ritual. Once it reopens in 1998, check your belongings at the eastern side and then join the queue for a glimpse of Mao's embalmed body. Out back, reverence turns to tack: hawkers push the new "Maomorabilia" spawned by Mao's centennial in 1993. For genuine Cultural Revolution souvenirs, wait until Liulichang (☞ *above*). ⊠ *Tiananmen Sq., Chongmen District,* ☎ *010/6513–2277.* 🎫 *Free.* ☾ *Not available at press time.*

❷ **Renmin Dahuitang** (Great Hall of the People). This solid edifice owes its Stalinist weight to the last years of the Sino-Soviet pact. Its floor space (205,712 sq yd) exceeds that of the Forbidden City. It was built

Beijing

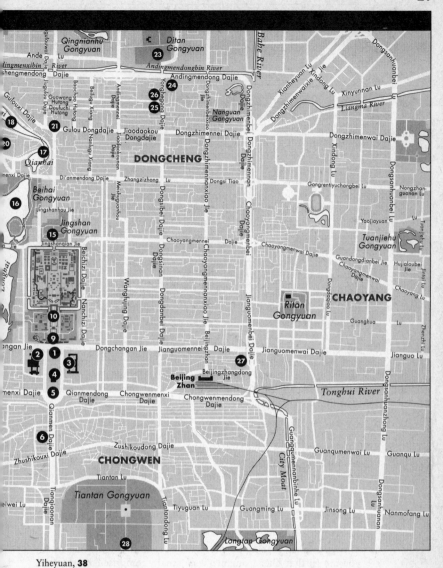

by 14,000 volunteers who worked round-the-clock for eight months. China's legislature meets in the aptly named Ten Thousand People Assembly Hall, beneath a panoply of 500 star lights revolving around a giant red star. Thirty-one reception rooms are distinguished by the arts and crafts of the provinces they represent. ⌧ *West side of Tiananmen Square, Xuanwu District,* ☎ *010/6309–6156.* ⌦ *Y30.* ⊙ *Daily 8:30– 3 (call ahead to confirm that it's open).*

❶ Tiananmen Guangchang (Tiananmen Square). The facts are bald: the world's largest public square, the heart of modern China. The square owes little to the grand imperial designs of the Yuan, Ming, and Qing— and everything to the successor dynasty of Mao Zedong. Turn your back on the entrance to the Forbidden City, the Gate of Heavenly Peace, and the wonders of Feudalism. Looking south, across the proletarian panorama, is the Great Helmsman's tomb. The old Imperial Way once stretched south from the Forbidden City. Where photo booths now hustle for customers once stood quarters for the Imperial Guard and rice and wood stores for the imperial kitchen. Fires and demolition resulted in the beginnings of the square during the Republican era. The young protesters who assembled here in the 1919 May Fourth Movement established an honorable tradition of patriotic dissent.

At the square's center stands the tallest monument in China, the **Renmin Yingxiong Jinianbei** (Monument to the People's Heroes), 125 ft of granite obelisk remembering those who died for the revolution. Exhortations from Chairman Mao and Premier Zhou Enlai decorate it; eight marble reliefs line the base with scenes of revolution from 1840 to 1949. Constructed from 1952 to 1958, the monument marks the formal passing of old Peking. For here stood the outer palace gate of the imperial city, the south gate of three in a concave defensive wall guarding the palaces beyond.

As you leave the terrace southward, imagine mass Soviet-style parades with 600,000 marchers. At the height of the Cultural Revolution in 1967, hundreds of thousands of Red Guards crowded the square for Maoist mass. Chanting Mao's name and waving his Little Red Book, they surged for a distant glimpse of the "sun that never sets," watching from atop the Tiananmen. Grand events aside, Tiananmen is truly a people's square, alive with local kite-fliers and wide-eyed tourists from out of town. ⌧ *Bounded by Changan Jie on north and Xuanwumen Jie on south, Chongmen District.*

❺ Zhengyangmen (Facing the Sun Gate). From its top looking south, you can see that Zhengyangmen was actually comprised of two gates, for the **Tian Lou** (Arrow Tower) in front was, until 1915, connected to it by a defensive half-moon wall. The central gates in both opened only for the emperors' biannual trips to sacrifice at the Temple of Heaven to the south. Do not miss the evocative photo exhibition of old Peking. Thirsty? Try some tea atop Zhengyangmen before heading up the Arrow Tower for views of the clock tower of old Qianmen Railway Station, now the Railway Workers Cultural Palace. ⌧ *Xuanwumen Jie.*

❸ Zhongguo Gemin Lishi Bowuguan (Museum of the Chinese Revolution). Exhibits convey China's official revolutionary history. The material, which includes rare photographs, documents, maps, and various medals awarded to "revolutionary martyrs," begins with the party's gestation during the May Fourth Movement (1919) and ends with the 1949 Communist victory. Explanations are in Chinese and English. All bags must be checked (Y1) before you enter. ⌧ *North end of building on east side of Tiananmen Square, Chongmen District,* ☎ *010/6526– 3355.* ⌦ *Y2.* ⊙ *Tues.–Sun. 8:30–5.*

❸ **Zhongguo Lishi Bowuguan** (Museum of Chinese History). An exten-
★ sive array of art and antiquities depicting China's cultural history is
on display here. The collection, much of it borrowed from provincial
museums, ranks among the world's best troves of Chinese art. Items
include 3,000-year-old Shang oracle bones, priceless Zhou bronzes, Tang
tomb relics, and imperial porcelains. Exhibitions are labeled in Chinese only. Bags must be checked (Y1) before you enter. ✉ *South end
of building on east side of Tiananmen Square, Chongmen District,* ☏
010/6512–8986. ✆ *Y10.* ☉ *Tues.–Sun. 8:30–4:30.*

The Forbidden City

★ It was from here that 24 emperors and two dynasties ruled the Middle Kingdom for more than 500 years. Built on nearly 200 acres at the
heart of the Northern Capital, the Zijin Cheng's (Gugong Bowuyuan
or Forbidden City) stately vermilion walls towered above old Peking
and humbled everything in their view. Moats and gigantic timber doors
protected each "son of heaven." Shiny double-eaved roofs, glazed imperial yellow, marked the vast complex as the royal court's exclusive
dominion. Inside, ornate decor displayed China's most exquisite arti-
sanship—ceilings covered with turquoise and blue dragons, walls
draped with scrolls holding priceless calligraphy or lined with intricate
cloisonné screens, thrones padded in delicate silks, floors of glass-
smooth marble. Miraculously, the palace survived fire and war and Imperial China's final collapse—the grandest symbol of a fallen empire.

Equally miraculous is how quickly the Forbidden City rose. The third
Ming emperor, Yongle, oversaw 200,000 workers who built the complex in just 14 years, finishing in 1420. Yongle relocated the Ming capital to Beijing to strengthen China's vulnerable northern frontier, and
Ming and Qing emperors ruled from inside the palace walls until the
dynastic system crumbled in 1911.

The Forbidden City embodies architectural principles first devised
three millennia ago in the Shang dynasty. Each main hall faces southward, toward the sun, and looks upon a courtyard flanked by lesser
buildings. This symmetry of courtyards within courtyards repeats itself along a north–south axis that bisects the imperial palace. This line
is visible in the form of a broad walkway paved in marble and reserved
for the emperor's sedan chair. All but the sovereign—even court ministers, the empress, and favored concubines—trod on pathways and
passed through doors set to either side of this Imperial Way.

A Good Walk

Enter the Forbidden City through the **Tiananmen** ①, easily identified
by its massive Chairman Mao portrait that overlooks Tiananmen
Square (☞ Tiananmen Square to Liulichang, *above*). Northward beyond the **Wumen** ②, where the Emperor made announcements, lies the
outer palace, comprised of three halls used for high public functions.
The first is the **Taihedian** ③, next is the **Zhonghedian** ④, and after this
you reach the **Baohedian** ⑤. For a break from the Forbidden City's grand
central halls, turn right beyond the Hall of Preserving Harmony to visit
smaller peripheral palaces—once home to imperial relatives, attendants,
and eunuchs, and the scene of much palace intrigue. Next comes the
Hall of Jewelry ⑥. Continue northward to Qanlong's Garden and the
Concubine Well. Return via a narrow north–south passage that runs
to the west of these courtyards. On the way is the **Hall of Clocks and
Watches** ⑦. Walk northward from the nine-dragon carving and through
the **Qianqingmen** ⑧ to enter the **Inner,** or private, **Palace** ⑨ where the
imperial family resided. Beyond the palace are the rocks, pebbles, and

Forbidden City

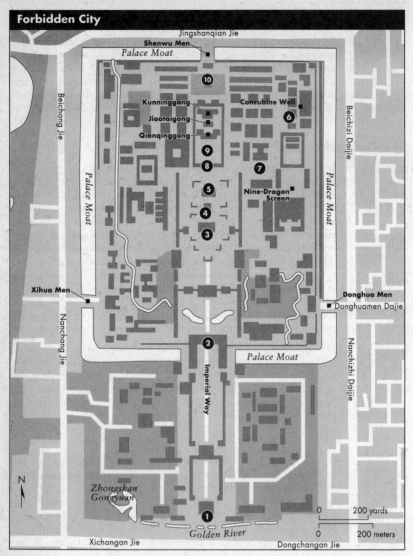

Baohedian, **5**
Nei Ting, **9**
Qianqingmen, **8**
Taihedian, **3**
Tiananmen, **1**
Wumen, **2**
Yuhuayuan, **10**
Zhenbaoguan, **6**
Zhongbiaoguan, **7**
Zhonghedian, **4**

greenery of the **Yuhuayuan** ⑩. From here you can go back southward to the Meridian Gate.

TIMING

The walk through main halls, best done by audio tour, takes about two hours. Allow two more hours to explore side halls and gardens.

Sights to See

❺ **Baohedian** (Hall of Preserving Harmony). Here emperors administered the highest civil service examinations. Candidates were selected from across China and if successful would serve the imperial court. Behind the hall, a 200-ton marble relief of nine dragons adorns the descending staircase. It is the palace's most treasured stone carving.

❾ **Nei Ting** (Inner Palace). Here, the Emperor and his family carried on the rituals of their daily lives. The **Qianqinggong** (Hall of Heavenly Purity) holds another imperial throne, the **Jiaotaidian** (Hall of Union) was the venue for the empress's annual birthday party, and royal couples consummated their marriages in the **Kunninggong** (Palace of Earthly Peace).

❽ **Qianqingmen** (Gate of Heavenly Purity). Even the emperor's most trusted ministers never passed beyond this gate; they gathered outside at dawn, by tradition, ready to report to their sovereign.

❸ **Taihedian** (Hall of Supreme Harmony). The building is fronted by a broad flagstone courtyard, the largest open area in the complex. Bronze vats, once kept brimming with water to fight fires, ring this vast expanse. The hall sits atop three stone tiers with an elaborate drainage system that channels rainwater through 1,100 carved dragons. On the top tier outside the hall, bronze cranes symbolize longevity, and an imperial sundial and grain measures invite bumper harvests. Inside, cloisonné cranes flank a massive throne beneath grand timber pillars decorated with golden dragons. Above the imperial chair hangs a heavy bronze ball—put there to crush any pretender to the throne. The hall was used in royal birthdays, weddings, and Lunar New Year ceremonies.

❶ **Tiananmen** (Gate of Heavenly Peace). This imposing structure was the traditional rostrum for the reading of imperial edicts. The Great Helmsman himself used it to establish the People's Republic of China on October 1, 1949, and again to review millions of Red Guards during the ultra-leftist Cultural Revolution. Ascend the gate for a dramatic vantage on Tiananmen Square. Bags must be checked prior to entry and visitors are required to pass through a metal detector. ⊠ *Changan Jie at Tiananmen Guangchang.* ☜ *Y30.* ☼ *Daily 8:30–5.*

❷ **Wumen** (Meridian Gate). At this U-shaped doorway the emperor reviewed his armies and announced yearly planting schedules. Before entering, you can buy tickets to the Forbidden City and rent the accompanying Acoustiguide audio tour at the ticket office in the outer courtyard. ⊠ *Forbidden City.* ☜ *Y55; audio tour, Y30.* ☼ *Daily 8:30–4.*

❿ **Yuhuayuan** (Imperial Gardens). Beyond the private palaces at the Forbidden City's northern perimeter stand ancient cypress trees, stone mosaic pathways, and a rock garden. You can exit the palace at the north through the park's **Gate of Obedience and Purity.**

❻ **Zhenbaoguan** (Hall of Jewelry). Actually a series of halls, it has breathtaking examples of imperial ornamentation. In the first room find imperial candle-holders, wine vessels, tea servings and—in the center—a 5-ft tall golden pagoda commissioned by Qing Emperor Qian Long in honor of his mother. A cabinet on one wall contains the 25 imperial seals, China's equivalent of the crown jewels in their embodiment of royal authority. Jade bracelets and rings, golden hair pins, and ornamental coral fill the second hall; and carved jade landscapes a third. ☎ *Y 5.*

7 Zhongbiaoguan (Hall of Clocks and Watches). Here you'll find a collection of water clocks and early mechanical time pieces from Europe and China. Clocks astride elephants, implanted in ceramic trees, borne by a herd of goats, and mounted in a pagoda are among this collection's many rewards. Don't miss the temple clock, with its robed monks that emerged hourly (one imagines) to clap gongs. ☎ *Y5.*

4 Zhonghedian (Hall of Complete Harmony). In this more modest building emperors granted audiences or held banquets. It housed the royal plow, with which the emperor himself would turn a furrow to commence spring planting.

NEED A
BREAK?

A small snack bar, **Fast Food** (✉ north end of vendors' row), offers noodles, set lunches, cola, and canned coffee from Japan.

The Muslim Quarter

Southeast of Liulichang is the lively Niu Jie (Ox Street) and its famous mosque. Ethnic Hui—Han Chinese whose ancestors converted to Islam—comprise most of the area's faithful. Their enclave, which occupies one of Beijing's oldest neighborhoods, has kept its traditional flavor despite ongoing urban renewal. Nearby is the extensive Buddhist Temple of the Source of Law, buried deep in a quintessential Beijing hutong, so far spared the demolition gangs of progress.

A Good Walk

Begin at the **Niu Jie Qingzhenshi** ⑪. From the mosque walk northward along the narrow Niu Jie (Ox Street), the center of commerce in the enclave. Turn right at the **Niu Jie Qingzhen Shiping Xiaoshichang** ⑫, which lines Shuru Hutong, a narrow alley extending into the residential district. Follow it west as it meanders past typical Beijing courtyards, obscured by tall gray walls. As in most alleys, doorway stone and wood carvings bespeak the neighborhood's great age and history. Continue down the alleyway until it meets Xiaozi Hutong (the first cross-street), some 500 yards east of Ox Street. Turn right and follow the alley past a large construction site on the left and more traditional courtyard homes.

Take the first left onto Fayuansi Qian Jie, which leads to the **Fayuansi** ⑬, on the left, which has an outstanding collection of bronze Buddha images. Continue eastward on Fayuansi Qian Jie until it ends at Qijing Hutong (Seven Well Alley). Turn right, cross Nanheng Xilu, and continue southward on Mengba Hutong. On the right, past a typical stretch of new high rise apartments, find **Wanshou Gongyuan** ⑭. Exit through the south gate and turn right on Baizhifang Dongjie (White Paper Lane East). Continue westward and turn right at Youannei Dajie, which becomes Niu Jie one block north.

TIMING

This walk takes about three hours, allowing for time in the mosque and temple. Exploring alleys in this neighborhood, especially those running west from Niu Jie, is always rewarding.

Sights to See

13 Fayuansi (Source of Law Temple). The Chinese Buddhist Theoretical Institute houses and trains monks at this temple. Visitors can observe them at practice and at play—robed students kicking soccer balls in a side courtyard; elderly practitioners chanting mantras in the main prayer halls. Before lunch, the smells of vegetarian stir-fry tease the nose. The dining hall reveals simple wooden tables set with cloth-wrapped bowls and chopsticks. Dating from the 7th century but last rebuilt in 1442, the temple holds a fine collection of Ming and Qing statues, including a "sleeping Buddha" and an unusual grouping of copper-cast Buddhas seated on a thousand-petal lotus. ⊠ *7 Fayuan Si Qianjie, Xuanwu District,* ☎ *010/6303–4171.* 🎫 *Y10.* ☼ *Thurs.–Tues. 8:30–11 and 1:30–4.*

⑫ **Niu Jie Qingzhen Shiping Xiaoshichang** (Ox Street Muslim Food Market). Identified by a painted metal arch over the entry, the market is filled with food vendors. Tiny restaurants serve Muslim dishes, including steamed meat buns, beef noodles, and a variety of baked breads. Shops offer tea from across China. Butchers selling beef products cater to local shoppers. ⊠ *Niu Jie, Xuanwu District.*

⑪ **Niu Jie Qingzhenshi** (Ox Street Mosque). Built during the Northern Song dynasty in 996, Beijing's oldest and largest mosque sits at the center of the city's Muslim quarter. From the outside, it looks decidedly Chinese, with a Chinese-style tile roof adorning its front gate. Note the free-standing wall built opposite the mosque's main entrance. It is a "spirit wall" erected to prevent ghosts, which are not believed to navigate tight corners, from passing into the mosque. Today, the main gate is kept closed. Enter the mosque on the alley just to the south. Inside, arches and posts are inscribed with Koranic verse, and a Tower for Viewing the Moon allows imams to measure the beginning and end of Ramadan, Islam's month of fasting and prayer. Visitors must wash themselves and remove their shoes before entering the main prayer hall. Women are confined to a rear prayer hall. At the rear of the complex is a minaret from where a muezzin calls the faithful to prayer. ⊠ *88 Niu Jie, Xuanwu District.* 🎫 *Y10.* ☼ *Daily 8–sunset.*

⑭ **Wanshou Gongyuan** (Wanshou Park). Enter through the east gate and wander. Though smaller than Beijing's more famous parks, this one offers an attractive lawn and inviting shaded benches. ⊠ *Between Mengba Hutong and Baizhifang Dongjie, Xuanwu District.* 🎫 *Y0.20.*

North and East of the Forbidden City

This busy neighborhood harbors numerous historic buildings, monuments, and parks.

A Good Walk and Cab Ride

Start just north of the Forbidden City at **Meishan** ⑮. From here you can walk through the greenery of **Beihai Gongyuan** ⑯, **Qianhai Gongyuan** ⑰ and **Houhai Gongyuan** ⑱. Outside the park, visit the traditional courtyard of the **Song Qing-ling Guzhu** ⑲. Next, take a cab to **Gongwangfu** ⑳ to see how imperial relatives lived. Walk or take a cab to the **Gulou** ㉑ and the nearby bell tower. Take a cab again to get to the **Gudai Qianbi Zhanlanguan** ㉒ to see rare Chinese coins. From here, ride a cab to the **Ditan Gongyuan** ㉓. Walk on to the **Yonghegong** ㉔, **Kongzimiao** ㉕, and **Guozijian** ㉖.

TIMING

If you want to do this all at once, it will take you a full day. The neighborhood is ideal for bike exploration (☞ Old Beijing by Bicycle, *below*).

Sights to See

⑯ **Beihai Gongyuan** (North Lake Park). The lake is central Beijing's largest and most beautiful public waterway. It lies immediately north of Zhongnanhai, the tightly guarded residential compound reserved for China's senior leaders, and is easily recognized by its imposing white Tibetan stupa (pagoda) perched on a hill. Near the south gate is the **Tuan Cheng** (Round City). It contains a white jade Buddha said to have been sent from Burma to Qing Emperor Qian Long and an enormous jade bowl given to Kublai Khan. Nearby, the well-restored **Yongan Si** (Temple of Eternal Peace) contains a variety of Buddhas and other sacred images. Climb to the stupa from Yongan Temple. Once there, you can pay an extra Y1 to ascend the Buddha-bedecked **Shangyin Tang** (Shangyin Hall) for a view into forbidden Zhongnanhai.

Amusement park rides line the east edge of the lake. Kiosks stock assorted snacks. On summer weekends, the lake teems with paddle boats. In the winter, it is Beijing's most popular ice-skating rink. The **Wu Long Ting** (Five Dragon Pavilion) on Beihai's northwest shore was built in 1602 by a Ming dynasty emperor who liked to fish and view the moon. The halls north of it were added later. Among the restaurants in the park is **Fangshan,** an elegant establishment open since the Qing dynasty. ⊠ *South Gate, Weijin Lu, Xicheng District.* 🖅 *Y10, extra fees for some sites.* ☉ *Daily 9–dusk.*

❷❸ **Ditan Gongyuan** (Temple of Earth Park). In the 16th-century park are the square altar where emperors once made sacrifices to the earth god and the Hall of Deities. ⊠ *Yonghegong Jie, just north of Second Ring Rd., Dongcheng District.*

❷⓿ **Gongwangfu** (Prince Gong's Palace). This grand compound sits in a neighborhood once reserved for imperial relatives. Built during the Ming dynasty, it fell to Prince Gong, brother of Qing Emperor Xianfeng and later an adviser to Empress Dowager Cixi. Some literary scholars contend that this was the setting described in *The Dream of the Red Chamber,* China's best-known classic novel. With nine courtyards joined by covered walkways, it was once one of Beijing's most lavish residences. The largest hall, now a banquet room, offers summer Peking Opera and afternoon tea to guests on guided hutong tours (☞ Beijing A to Z, *below*). ⊠ *Qianhai Xi Jie, Xicheng District.* 🖅 *Y5.* ☉ *9–5.*

❷❷ **Gudai Qianbi Zhanlanguan** (Museum of Antique Currency). This museum in a tiny courtyard house showcases a small but impressive selection of rare Chinese coins. Explanations are in Chinese only. Also in the courtyard are coin and curio dealers. ⊠ *Deshengmen Tower south buildings, Bei'erhuan Jie, Xicheng District,* ☎ *010/6201–8073.* 🖅 *Y4.* ☉ *Daily 9–5.*

❷❶ **Gulou** (The Drum Tower). Until the late 1920s, the 24 drums once housed in this tower were Beijing's timepiece. Sadly, all but one of these huge drums have been destroyed, and the survivor is in serious need of renovation. Kublai Khan built the first drum tower on this site in 1272. You can climb to the top of the present tower, which dates from the Ming dynasty. Old photos of Beijing's hutong line the walls beyond the drum; there's also a scale model of a traditional courtyard house. The nearby **Zhonglou** (Bell Tower), built in 1747, offers worthwhile views from the top of a long, narrow staircase. ⊠ *North end of Dianmen Dajie, Dongcheng District.* ☉ *Daily 9–4:30.*

❷❻ **Guozijian** (Imperial Academy). Once the highest academic institution in China, it was established as a school for boys in 1306 and evolved into a think tank devoted to the Confucian classics. Scholars studied here to prepare for imperial exams. ⊠ *Guozijian Lu next to Temple of Confucius, Dongcheng District.* 🖅 *Free.* ☉ *Daily 9–4:30.*

❷❺ **Kongzi Miao** (Temple of Confucius). This austere temple, which honors China's greatest sage, has endured close to eight centuries of additions and restorations. Stelae and ancient musical instruments are the temple's main attractions. The Great Accomplishment Hall houses the sage's funeral tablet and shrine, flanked by copper-colored statues depicting China's wisest Confucian scholars. A selection of unique musical instruments, played only on the sage's birthday, gathers dust in the building's gloom. A forest of stone stelae, carved in the mid 1700s to record the Thirteen Classics, philosophical works attributed to him, lines the west side of the grounds. ⊠ *Guozijian Lu at Yunghegong Lu near Lama Temple, Dongcheng District.* ☞ *Y10.* ☽ *Daily 9–4:30.*

⑮ Meishan (Coal Hill). This modest man-made peak, named for an imperial coal supply supposedly buried beneath it, is the mound of earth excavated during construction of the Forbidden City's moats. Climb a winding stone staircase past peach and apple trees to Wanchun Pavilion, the park's highest point. It overlooks the Forbidden City to the south and the Bell and Drum Towers to the north. Chongzhen, the last Ming emperor, is said to have hanged himself on Coal Hill as his dynasty collapsed in 1644. ⊠ *Jingshanqian Dajie at Forbidden City, Dongcheng District.* ☞ *Y0.30.* ☽ *Daily 9–4:30.*

⑰ ⑱ Qianhai Gongyuan and Houhai Gongyuan (Qianhai and Houhai Parks). The parks surrounding these two lakes are popular for their markets. Near Qianhai's southwest entrance antiques shops line the alley leading from Beihai Park's north gate. Another curio market, on Houhai's western shore, is reached by walking (or biking) along Qianhai's eastern shore to a bridge that leads to Houhai. Visit early on weekend mornings to view the produce and dry goods market at Houhai's northern end. ⊠ *North side of Dianmen Xi Lu, north of Bei hai Lake. Xicheng District.*

⑲ Song Qing-ling Guzhu (Soong Ching-ling's Former Residence). Soong Ching-ling (1893–1981) was the wife of Sun Yat-sen, the Nationalist revolutionary who founded the Republic of China in 1911. Unlike her younger sister, Soong Meiling, who married Nationalist strongman Chiang Kai-shek, Ching-ling sided with the Chinese Communists in 1949 and was hailed as a key supporter of the revolution. Her former residential compound is a wonderful example of traditional courtyard architecture. A small museum documents her eventful life and work in support of impoverished women and children. Exhibits are labeled in English. ⊠ *46 Houhai Beiyan, Xicheng District,* ☎ *010/6403–5997 or 10/6404–4205.* ☞ *Y10.* ☽ *Daily 9–4:30.*

★ ㉔ Yonghegong (Lama Temple). This Yellow Hat Tibetan lamasary is Beijing's most celebrated temple. Its five main halls and numerous galleries are hung with finely detailed tanka paintings and decorated with beautifully carved or cast Buddha images—guarded by young lamas who encourage boisterous visitors to remember their manners. Originally a palace for Prince Yongzheng, it was transformed into a temple after he became the Qing's third emperor in 1725. The temple flourished under Yongzheng's successor, Emperor Qianlong, housing some 1,500 resident monks. Unlike most "feudal" sites in Beijing, the Lama Temple survived the 1966–76 Cultural Revolution unscathed.

You walk past trinket stands with clattering windchimes to reach the temple's five main halls. The Hall of Heavenly Kings has statues of Maitreya, the future Buddha, and Weitou, China's guardian of Buddhism. In the courtyard beyond, a pond with a bronze mandala represents a Buddhist paradise. In the Hall of Harmony sit Buddhas of the Past, Present, and Future. Note the exquisite silk tanka of White Tara—the embodiment of compassion—hanging from the west wall. The Hall of Eternal Blessing contains images of the Medicine and

OLD PEKING BY BICYCLE

Michael von Itallie

THE BEST WAY to explore old Peking is by bicycle. The ride between Ditan Park and Coal Hill includes some of the city's most famous sights and finest hutong.

Begin at **Ditan Gongyuan** (Temple of Earth Park), just north of the Second Ring Road on Yonghegong Jie. Park your bike in the lot outside the south gate and take a quick walk. Next, ride south along Yonghegong Jie until you come to the main entrance of **Yonghegong** (Lama Temple), Beijing's largest and most ornate Tibetan Buddhist temple.

Running west, across the street from the temple's main gate, is Guozijian Jie. Shops near the intersection sell Buddhist statues, incense, texts (in Chinese) and tapes of traditional Chinese Buddhist music. Browse them before riding west to **Kongzi Miao** (Temple of Confucius), and the neighboring **Guozijian** (Imperial Academy). The arches spanning Guozijian Jie are the only ones of their kind remaining in Beijing.

Follow Guozijian Jie west until it empties onto Andingmennei Dajie. Enter this busy road with care (there is no traffic signal) and ride south to Guloudong Dajie, another major thoroughfare. Turn right (west), and ride to the **Gulou** (Drum Tower).

From the Drum Tower detour through the alleys just north to the **Zhonglou** (Bell Tower). A market of tiny noodle stalls and restaurants links the two landmarks. Stop for a snack.

Retrace your route south to Dianmenwai Dajie (the road running south from the Drum Tower), turning onto Yandai Jie, the first lane on the right. A brass historical marker explains that makers of long-stemmed pipes once lined the lane's narrow way. Sadly, much of the area is slated for reconstruction.

Wind northward on Yandai Jie past public baths, tiny restaurants, and crumbling traditional courtyard houses toward Houhai Park. Turn left onto Xiaoqiaoli Hutong and find the arched bridge that separates **Houhai** and **Qianhai** lakes. Follow the trail along Houhai's north shore, traveling west toward **Song Qingling Guzhu** (Soong Ching-ling's Former Residence). Circle the lake until you arrive at Deshengmennei Dajie. Follow it south to the second alley, turning east (left) onto Yangfang Hutong, which leads back to the arched bridge.

Park your bike in the first alley off Yangfang Hutong, Dongming Hutong, and walk toward the lake. At the footpath and market that hugs its banks, turn left and walk about 100 meters to find a tiny lane lined with antiques and curio shops.

After bargain-hunting, ride along Yangfang Hutong past the stone bridge and follow Qianhai Lake's west bank. Sip a soda, beer or hot cup of tea at the teahouse pavilion on the lake. Continue along the lane to Qianhai Xijie, then turn left (south). Nearby, but difficult to find, is **Gongwangfu** (Prince Gong's Palace), between Qianhai Xijie and the lake. Look for a brass plaque.

Allow half a day for this ride, longer if you expect to linger at the sights or explore the parks on foot.

Longevity Buddhas. Beyond, courtyard galleries display numerous statues depicting Tibetan deities and dharma guardians, some passionately entwined with consorts.

A large statue of Tsongkapa (1357–1490), founder of the Gelugpa or Yellow Hat Sect, sits in the Hall of the Wheel of Law. Resident monks practice here on low benches and cushions. A rare sand mandala is preserved under glass on the west side of the building. The temple's tallest building, the **Wanfuge** (Pavilion of Ten Thousand Fortunes), houses a breathtaking 85-ft Maitreya Buddha carved from a single sandalwood block. White and gold blessing scarves drape the statue, which wears a massive string of prayer beads. ✉ *12 Yonghegong Dajie, Beixingqiao, Dongcheng District,* ☎ *010/6404–3769.* 🎫 *Y10.* ⊙ *Tues.–Sun. 9–4.*

The Observatory and the Temple of Heaven

East and southeast of the city center are two ancient sites that reveal much about imperial traditions and beliefs.

A Good Drive
Start at the **Guguanxiangtai** ㉗, where the wide central avenue—called Jiangguonenwai Dajie here—meets the eastern leg of the Second Ring Road. From the Ancient Observatory, take a taxi, following the Second Ring Road south and then west to Chongwenmenwai Dajie and turning south to Tiantandong Lu and west on Yungdingmen Dajie to the south gate of the **Tiantan** ㉘, one of the most important historic sites in Beijing.

TIMING
Allow three hours for this tour.

Sights to See
㉗ **Guguanxiangtai** (Ancient Observatory). To China's imperial rulers, interpreting the heavens was the better part of keeping power. Celestial phenomena like eclipses and comets were believed to portend change, and if left unheeded might cost an emperor his legitimacy—or Mandate of Heaven. The instruments in this ancient observatory, established in 1422 atop the city wall's **Jianguomen** (Jianguo Gate), were among an emperor's most valuable possessions. Many of the bronze devices on display were gifts from Jesuit missionaries who arrived in Beijing in 1601 and shortly thereafter ensconced themselves as the Ming Court's resident star-gazers. Rare documents and a replica of a Ming dynasty star map are on display inside. ✉ *2 Dongbiaobei Hutong, Jianguomenwai Dajie, Chaoyang District,* ☎ *010/6524–2202.* 🎫 *Y10.* ⊙ *Tues.–Sun. 9–11, 1–5:30.*

★ ㉘ **Tiantan** (Temple of Heaven). One of Beijing's grand attractions, the Temple of Heaven is contemporary to the Forbidden City. Ming Emperor Yongle built it as a venue for imperial sacrifices conducted on the winter and summer solstices. The temple grounds, double the size of Yongle's palace, were designed in strict accordance with numerology and fengshui. The four gates mark the four points on the compass. The park is semi-circular on the north end and square on the south—the curve corresponding to heaven's supposed shape, the square to earth's.

Beyond the south gate rests the **Huanqiutan** (Round Altar), a three-tiered prayer platform. Nearby, the **Huangqiong Yu** (Imperial Vault of Heaven) is surrounded by the **Echo Wall,** where a whisper supposedly can be heard across the courtyard's 213-ft expanse. On the courtyard's step are three echo stones able to rebound hand claps one, two, or three times. Extreme quiet is needed to hear the effect.

A raised walkway, the Bridge of Vermilion Stairs, leads northward to the **Qiniandian** (Hall of Prayer for Good Harvests), the temple's hallmark structure. This magnificent blue-roofed wooden tower, originally built in 1420, burned to the ground in 1889 and was immediately rebuilt using Ming architectural methods (and timber imported from Oregon). The building's design is based on the calendar: 4 center pillars represent the seasons, the next 12 pillars represent months, and 12 outer pillars signify the parts of a day. Together, these 28 poles support the structure without nails. A carved dragon swirling down from the ceiling represents the emperor, or "son of heaven."

The **Zhaigong** (Hall of Abstinence), on the western edge of the grounds, is not of particular interest. But for Y1 you can climb the bell tower and ring the bell for good luck. Its chimes once served notice that the emperor approached to worship or had completed the rites and would depart. ⊠ *Yungdingmen Dajie (South Gate), Chongwen District.* ☎ *010/6702–2617.* ☞ *Y50.* ☉ *Daily 8–5:30.*

Western Beijing

Western Beijing, a vast industrial suburb, was once the domain of monks, nuns, and imperial hunting parties. Beijing's oldest temples dot the forested hills just west of the city. The Qing-era summer palace is the city's grandest park.

A Good Drive

Hire a car for a day and visit the temples in the following order; don't miss the summer palaces even if you must forgo another site for them: **Baiyunguan** ㉙, **Zhongguo Meishuguan** ㉚, **Baitasi** ㉛, **Dianshi Fasheta** ㉜, **Wanshousi** ㉝, **Beijing Dongwuyuan** ㉞, **Beijing Tianwenguan** ㉟, **Wutasi** ㊱, **Dazhongsi** ㊲, **Yiheyuan** ㊳, **Yuanmingyuan** ㊴, **Wofosi** ㊵, **Biyunsi** ㊶, and **Xiangshan Gongyuan** ㊷.

TIMING
This tour will take a full day with a brown-bag lunch.

Sights to See

㉛ **Baitasi** (Temple of the White Pagoda). This 13th-century Tibetan stupa, the largest of its kind in China, dates from Kublai Khan's reign and owes its beauty to a Nepalese architect (name lost to history) who built it to honor Sakyamuni Buddha. Once hidden within the structure were Buddha statues, sacred texts and other holy relics. Many of the statues are now on display in glass cases in the **Miaoying** temple, at the foot of the stupa. A local Qi Gong association also runs a traditional clinic on the premises. The stupa, under renovation in 1997, is scheduled for reopening in 1998. ⊠ *Fuchenmennei Dajie near Zhaodengyu Lu; turn right at first alley east of stupa, Xicheng District.* ☞ *Y10.* ☉ *Daily 9–4:30.*

㉙ **Baiyunguan** (White Clouds Taoist Temple). This working Taoist temple propagates China's only indigenous religion. Monks wearing blue cotton coats and black satin hats roam the grounds in silence. More than a hundred of them now live at the monastery, which also houses the official All-China Taoist Association. Believers bow and burn incense to their favorite deities, wander the back gardens in search of a Qi Gong master, or rub the bellies of the temple's three monkey statues for good fortune.

In the first courtyard, under the span of an arched bridge, hang two large brass bells. Ringing them with a well-tossed coin is said to bring wealth. In the main courtyards, the **Shrine Hall for Seven Perfect Beings** is lined with meditation cushions and low desks. Nearby is a museum of Taoist history (explanations in Chinese). In the western courtyard, the temple's oldest structure is a shrine housing the **60-Year**

Protector. Here, the faithful locate the deity that corresponds to their birth year, bow to it, and light incense, then scribble their names, or even a poem, on the wooden statue's red cloth cloak as a reminder of their dedication. A trinket stall in the front courtyard sells pictures of each protector deity. Also in the west courtyard is a shrine to Taoist sage Wen Ceng, depicted in a 10-ft-tall bronze statue just outside the shrine's main entrance. Students flock here to rub Wen Ceng's belly for good fortune on their college entrance exams. ⊠ *Lianhuachidong Lu, near Xibianmen Bridge, Xuanwu District.* ☞ *Y5.* ◷ *Daily 9–4:30.*

34 **Beijing Dongwuyuan** (Beijing Zoo). In spite of the zoo's tree-lined paths, ponds, and manicured lawns, its inhabitants live a sad existence. Iron bars and cramped enclosures are the norm. Chinese visitors, unschooled in proper zoo behavior, routinely shout at the unhappy captives or pelt them with treats wrapped in plastic. Children have even been known to shoot at the animals with pellet guns. It's not worth a visit, even for travelers who haven't seen a Giant Panda. ⊠ *Xizhimenwai Dajie, Xicheng District,* ☎ *010/6831–4411.* ☞ *Y3.* ◷ *Daily 7:30–5:30; Panda Hall, daily 8–5.*

35 **Beijing Tianwenguan** (Beijing Planetarium). This impressive, if slightly grubby, planetarium is a favored field-trip destination for Beijing area students. Programs change frequently. Call in advance to check schedules and reserve seats. ⊠ *138 Xizhimenwai Dajie at Beijing Zoo, Xicheng District,* ☎ *010/6831–2517 or 010/6835–3003.* ☞ *Y12 per show.* ◷ *Daily 9–5.*

41 **Biyunsi** (Temple of Azure Clouds). Once the home of a Yuan dynasty official, the site was converted into a Buddhist temple in 1331 and enlarged during the 16th and 17th centuries by imperial eunuchs who hoped to be buried here. The temple's five main courtyards ascend a slope in Xiangshan (Fragrant Hills) Park. Although severely damaged during the Cultural Revolution, the complex has been attentively restored. The main attraction is the Indian-influenced Vajra Throne Pagoda. Lining its walls and five pagodas are the most gracefully carved stone-relief Buddhas and bodhisattvas in the Beijing area. The pagoda once housed the remains of Nationalist China's founding father, Dr. Sun Yat-sen, who lay in state here from 1925 to 1929, when his mausoleum was completed in Nanjing. A hall in one of the temple's western courtyards houses about 500 life-size wood and gilt arhats—each sitting or standing in a gloomy glass case. ⊠ *Xiangshan Gongyuan, Haidian District,* ☎ *010/6259–1205.* ☞ *Park, Y3; temple, Y10.* ◷ *Daily 7:30–4:30.*

37 **Dazhongsi** (Big Bell Temple). A two-story bell cast with the texts of over 100 Buddhist scriptures is the temple's focus. Believed to date from Emperor Yongle's reign, this 46-ton relic is recognized as a national treasure. The temple also houses the **Ancient Bell Museum,** a collection of bells from various dynasties and styles. ⊠ *1A Beisanhuanxi Lu, Haidian District,* ☎ *010/6255–0843.* ☞ *Y10.* ◷ *Daily 8:30–4:30.*

32 **Dianshi Fasheta** (Central Radio and Television Tower). On a clear day, this needle-like tower offers an inspiring perspective on eastern Beijing and beyond. An outdoor viewing platform hangs 1,325 ft above the ground. Elevators take visitors there first, then down a few floors to an indoor deck where drinks and snacks are served. Another two levels down is a Chinese restaurant with simple set meals. This tower rests on the foundation of the Altar of the Moon, a Ming dynasty sacrificial temple. ⊠ *11 Xisanhuanzhong Lu, Haidian District,* ☎ *010/ 6845–0715, 10/6843–7755, ext. 377.* ☞ *Y50 includes a soda; bags must be checked before entering.* ◷ *Daily 8:30 AM–10 PM.*

�33 Wanshousi (Temple of Longevity). A Ming empress built this temple to honor her son in 1578. Qing Emperor Qianlong later restored it as a birthday present to his mother. From then until the fall of the Qing, it served as a rest stop for imperial processions traveling by boat to the Summer Palace and Western Hills. Today Wanshou Temple is managed by the Beijing Art Museum and houses a small but exquisite collection of Buddha images. The Buddhas in the main halls include Sakyamuni sitting on a thousand-petal, thousand-buddha bronze throne, and dusty Ming-period Buddhas. ⊠ *Xisanhuan Lu, Haidian District,* ☎ *010/6841–3380, 10/6841–9391.* 🎟 *Y20, includes admission to all museum exhibits.* ⊙ *Daily 9–4:30.*

㊵ Wofosi (Temple of the Sleeping Buddha). Although the temple was damaged during the Cultural Revolution and poorly renovated afterward, the Sleeping Buddha remains. An English-language description explains that the casting of the beautiful bronze, in 1321, "enslaved 7,000 people." It goes on to say that the work "demonstrates the prominent art achievements of the Chinese people." The temple is inside the **Beijing Botanical Gardens**; stroll north from the entrance through the neatly manicured grounds. ⊠ *Xiagshan Lu, 2 km/1 mi northeast of Xiangshan Park. Haidian District.* 🎟 *Gardens, Y4; temple, Y2.* ⊙ *Daily 8–5.*

㊱ Wutasi (Five-Pagoda Temple). Hidden behind trees and set amid carved stones, the temple's five pagodas betray obvious Indian influences. Indeed, the Five-Pagoda Temple was built from an Indian model in the early 1400s. Elaborate carvings of curvaceous female bodhisattvas, Tibetan snow lions, and hundreds of buddhas decorate the pagodas. Also on the grounds: the **Beijing Shike Yishu Bowuguan** (Beijing Art Museum of Stone Carvings), with its collection of some 1,000 stelae and stone carvings. ⊠ *24 Wuta Si, Baishiqiao, Haidian District,* ☎ *010/6217–3836.* 🎟 *Y2.5 includes admission to museum and pagodas.* ⊙ *Daily 8:30–4:30.*

㊷ Xiangshan Gongyuan (Fragrant Hills Park). This hillside park west of Beijing was once an imperial retreat and hunting ground. From the eastern gate, you can hike to the summit on a trail dotted with shady pavilions and small temples. If you're short on time, you can ride a cable car to the top. Avoid weekends if crowds are not to your liking. ⊠ *Fragrant/Western Hills, Haidian District,* ☎ *010/6259–1155.* 🎟 *Y3; cable car, Y50.* ⊙ *Daily 6 AM–7 PM daily.*

★ ㊳ Yiheyuan (The Summer Palace). This expansive, park-like imperial retreat dates from the Yuan dynasty, when engineers channeled spring water to create a series of man-made lakes. It was not until the Qing that the Summer Palace took on its present form. In 1750, Emperor Qianlong commissioned the retreat to mark his mother's 60th birthday. Construction of palaces, pavilions, bridges, and numerous covered pathways on the shores of Kunming Lake continued for 15 years. The resort suffered heavy damage when Anglo-French forces plundered, then burned, many of the palaces in 1860. Renovation commenced in 1885 using funds diverted from China's naval budget. Empress Dowager Cixi retired to the Summer Palace in 1889, and seven years later imprisoned her nephew, Emperor Guangxu, on the palace grounds and reclaimed control of the government. She controlled China from the Summer Palace until her death in 1908.

Enter the palace grounds through the **Donggongmen** (East Palace Gate). Inside, a grand courtyard leads to the **Renshoudian** (Hall of Benevolent Longevity), where Cixi held court. Just beyond, next to the lake, the **Yulantang** (Hall of Jade Ripples) was where Cixi kept the hapless

Guangxu under guard while she ran China in his name. Cixi's own residence, the **Leshoutang** (Hall of Joyful Longevity), sits just to the north and affords a fine view of Kunming Lake. The residence is furnished and decorated as Cixi left it. Just east of this hall, Cixi's private **theater**, constructed for her 60th birthday at a cost of 700,000 taels of silver, is not to be missed. The **Long Corridor** skirts Kunming Lake's northern shoreline for 2,388 ft until it reaches the **marble boat**, an elaborate two-deck pavilion built of finely carved stone and stained glass. Above the Long Corridor on **Longevity Hill**, intersecting pathways lead to numerous pavilions and several Buddhist prayer halls. Below, Kunming Lake extends southward for 3 km (2 mi), ringed by tree-lined dikes, arched stone bridges, and numerous gazebos. In summer, you can explore the lake by paddle boat (inexpensive rentals available at several spots along the shore). In winter, walk—or skate—on the ice. While the palace area along Kunming Lake's north shore is usually crowded, the less-traveled southern shore near Humpbacked Bridge is an ideal picnic spot. ⊠ *12 km (7½ mi) northwest of downtown Beijing, Haidian District.* ⌨ *Y30; additional fees at some exhibits.* ⊙ *Daily 7–7.*

★ ㊴ **Yuanmingyuan** (Old Summer Palace). Once a grand collection of Chinese and European-inspired palaces, the complex was looted and systematically blown up in 1860 by British and French soldiers commanded by Lord Elgin. The emperor's summer retreat from the 15th century to 1860, the Western-style buildings—patterned after Versailles in France—were added during the Qing dynasty and designed by Jesuits. Beijing has chosen to preserve the vast ruin as a "monument to China's national humiliation." Beijing students take frequent field trips to the site, and (encouraged by their teachers, no doubt) scrawl patriotic slogans on the rubble. A large lake, ideal for summer boating or winter ice skating, lies at the center of the palace grounds. ⊠ *Qinghuan Xi Lu, Haidian District,* ☎ *010/6255–1488.* ⌨ *Y5; extra for some sites.* ⊙ *Daily 7–7.*

㉚ **Zhongguo Meishuguan** (China Arts and Crafts Museum). Ceramics, stone carvings, lacquerware, and other traditional craft items are on display in this small museum sponsored by the China National Arts and Crafts Corporation (the official exporter of Chinese crafts). The museum is on the fifth floor of the Parkson Department Store. ⊠ *101 Fuxingmennei Dajie, Xuanwu District,* ☎ *010/6601–3377.* ⌨ *Y15.* ⊙ *Daily 9–5.*

DINING

Beijing has come onto the radar scope of global food franchises. The following sit-down Western restaurants are now open in Beijing: Chili's (⊠ 10 Yabao Lu, ☎ 010/65922–5184); Hard Rock Café (⊠ 8 Dongsanhuan Bei Lu, ☎ 010/6501–6688, ext. 2571); and T.G.I. Fridays (⊠ 19 Dongsanhuan Bei Lu, ☎ 010/6416–2272).

What to Wear

Casual attire is acceptable in most Beijing restaurants.

American

$$ ✕ **Frank's Place (Wanlong Jiuba).** The decor and bar make Frank's look like the set for the hit American sitcom "Cheers." In addition to great hamburgers, the menu includes chili, fried chicken, and Philly cheese steaks. ⊠ *Gongrentiyuguan Dong Lu across from Worker's Stadium, Chaoyang District,* ☎ *010/6507–2617. Reservations not accepted. AE, MC, V.*

$$ ✕ **Johnny's Coffee.** Beijing's first micro-roastery, Johnny's Coffee opened its doors in 1996 to rave reviews among gourmet coffee fans in the capital. Drinks include authentic espressos, cappuccinos, and lattes—served in a trendy coffeehouse setting popular with the hip university crowd. Bagels, muffins, and fruit juice are also available. ⊠ *Beisanhuan Dong Lu, Chaoyang District,* ☎ *010/6461–0827. Reservations not accepted. No credit cards.*

Chinese

$$$$ ✕ **Fortune Garden.** Arguably Beijing's best Cantonese restaurant, For-
★   tune Garden offers all the southern favorites: roast suckling pig, boneless duck, a selection of steamed dim-sum, and fresh vegetables stir-fried in oyster sauce. ⊠ *Palace Hotel, 8 Jinyu Hutong, Wangfujing, Dongcheng District,* ☎ *010/6512–8899. AE, V.*

$$$$ ✕ **Four Seasons.** Located at the Jianguo Hotel, the Four Seasons offers a delicious two-person Peking duck set meal plus a full menu of traditional Chinese dishes. The decor is elegant but understated. Tables are set with silver, fine china, and white linen. Nightly performances of traditional Chinese string music augment the intimate atmosphere. ⊠ *Jianguo Hotel, 3 Jianguomenwai Dajie, Chaoyang District,* ☎ *010/ 6500–2233. AE, DC, MC, V.*

$$$–$$$$ ✕ **Fangshan.** In a traditional courtyard villa on the shore of Beihai Lake you can sample China's imperial cuisine. Established in 1925 by three royal chefs, Fangshan serves dishes once prepared for Qing emperors based on recipes garnered from across China. Each of the 11 intimate dining rooms is adorned with calligraphy and antique furniture. The extensive menu includes a variety of fish, vegetable, and meat dishes—including mainstays like sweet-and-sour pork—plus several delicious soups. Fangshan is best known for its filled pastries and steamed breads—traditional snack foods developed to satisfy Empress Dowager Cixi's notorious sweet tooth. You can also order one of the banquet-style set meals. They range in price from Y150 per person for a satisfying, if somewhat ordinary, menu to Y1,000 or more for a truly exotic feast. ⊠ *Beihai Gongyuan (enter through the east gate, cross the stone bridge, and bear right), Xicheng District,* ☎ *010/6401– 1879. Reservations essential. AE, DC, MC, V.*

$$ ✕ **Li Family Restaurant.** This tiny eatery is in such demand that it some-
★   times takes weeks to book a table. The restaurant's imperial dishes are prepared and served by members of the Li family in a cozy, informal atmosphere. Li Li established the restaurant in 1985 (after flunking her college entrance exams) using recipes handed down from her great-grandfather, once a steward for the Qing court. Since then, her renditions of China's culinary classics, like deep-fried scallops, Gongbao chicken, and Mandarin (sweet-and-sour) fish, have won the family business national media exposure and a reputation as one of China's top restaurants. ⊠ *11 Yangfang Hutong, Denei Dajie, Xicheng District,* ☎ *010/ 6618–0107. Reservations essential. No credit cards.*

$$ ✕ **Quanjude Kaoyadian.** This legendary establishment has served succulent Peking duck since 1852. Nationalized after the 1949 Communist revolution, it survived collectivization and since has opened several branches across Beijing. Each serves the same traditional feast: cold duck tongue, sautéed webs, sliced livers and gizzards to start; a main course of roast duck, to be dipped in a fermented brown bean sauce and wrapped with scallions in a tortilla-like flour pancake, and duck soup to finish. The palatial "Big Duck," just south of Tiananmen Square, offers four garishly decorated floors with private rooms. The more intimate "Sick Duck," named for its proximity to the Capital Hospital, is in Wangfujing. ⊠ *Big Duck: 32 Qianmen Dajie,*

Chongmen District, ☎ 010/6511–2418. *AE, DC, MC, V;* ✉ *Sick Duck: 13 Shuaifuyuan, Dongcheng District,* ☎ 010/6525–3310. *AE, DC, MC, V.*

$$ ✕ **Sunflower Village.** This restaurant exploits a peculiar fondness many middle-aged Chinese have for the formative experience of their youth: the 1966–76 Great Proletarian Cultural Revolution. Decorated with murals of Chairman Mao, Sunflower Village seeks to emulate the rustic atmosphere of a rural commune. Its food recalls the fare dished out to millions of urban Red Guards sent by Mao to "learn from the peasants" in the countryside. Menu items range from stir-fried corn and pine nuts, tasty *wotou* (steamed cornbread), to various fresh grasses (challenging) or fried cicada larvae (yuck). More standard northern dishes, like braised tofu, hotpot, or stewed fatty pork, are also offered for those less interested in authenticity than a hearty meal. ✉ *51 Wanquanhe Lu, Haidian District,* ☎ 010/6256–2967. *No credit cards.*

$$ ✕ **Tianshi.** The chefs at this Taiwan-managed Buddhist vegetarian restaurant have mastered the art of concocting faux-meat dishes from soybean and other vegetarian ingredients. Even dedicated carnivores will recognize the tea-marinated "duck," crisp-fried "chicken" and sweet-and-sour Mandarin "fish." The look and taste is extraordinary. Tianshi also serves a wide variety of teas and even alcohol-free beer and an assortment of (non-dairy) fruit shakes. Upstairs, the main dining hall's decor melds fake Ionic columns with real modern art to create a trendy, pop feel. A ground-floor cafeteria offers inexpensive lunch platters, muffins, and donuts. It's open daily from 8 AM to midnight. ✉ *57 Dungshikou Dajie, Dongcheng District,* ☎ 010/6524–2349. *AE, DC, MC, V.*

$$ ✕ **Tibet Shambala.** "A Taste of Tibet in the Heart of Beijing" promises the menu. It should read "the only" taste of Tibet in a city of 12 million. Diners sit in small white-washed rooms draped with banners and Buddhist tanka paintings. A sample from the menu: *momos* (yak dumplings); *tsampa* (oat powder, to be washed down with yak butter tea); lama noodles (noodle soup with lamb, onions, turnips and coriander); yak penis with caterpillar fungus (no explanation required). ✉ *301 Xinjiang Xiao Lu, Baishiqao, Haidian District,* ☎ 010/6842–2631. *Reservations not accepted. No credit cards.*

$$ ✕ **Uncle Afanti Gourmet City.** Beijing's largest and best-known Xinjiang Muslim restaurant, Afanti offers a variety of Xinjiang kabob, hotpot, baked flatbread, and handmade noodles. Nightly Uighur dance performances augment the Central Asian atmosphere. ✉ *166 Chaonei Dajie, Dongcheng District,* ☎ 010/6525–1071, *or* 010/6525–5551 *ext. 3055. AE, V.*

$ ✕ **Duyichu Dumpling Restaurant.** History has it that this Shandong-style dumpling house won fame when Qing Emperor Qianlong stopped in on his way back to the Forbidden City after a rural inspection tour. A plaque hanging on the wall, and allegedly in Qianlong's own hand, attests to the restaurant's flavorful fare. Today the Duyichu's large, raucous dining hall is decidedly proletarian. But the dumplings and assorted Shandong dishes still command applause. Expect to wait for a seat during the dinner rush. Customers share large round tables. ✉ *36 Qianmen Dajie, Chongmen Dictrict,* ☎ 010/6511–2093, 010/6511–2094. *Reservations not accepted. No credit cards.*

$ ✕ **Golden Cat.** *Jiaozi* (dumplings) are the specialty of this informal eatery located in a courtyard house near Yuanjiehu Park. Some 30 varieties adorn the menu and are sold by the *liang* (one liang equals five dumplings). During fair weather sit in the courtyard, where the atmosphere is far superior to that in the cramped (and somewhat grimy) indoor dining rooms. The restaurant is open 24 hours. ✉ *North of the east gate of Tuanjiehu Gongyuan, Chaoyang District,* ☎ 010/6598–5011. *Reservations not accepted. No credit cards.*

Beijing Dining and Lodging

Dining

Asian Star Spicy Restaurant, **55**
Borom Piman, **57**
Duyichu Dumpling Restaurant, **15**
Fangshan, **11**
Fortune Garden, **26**
Four Seasons, **43**
Frank's Place, **42**
Golden Cat, **56**
Gongdelin, **14**
Guangdong Special Diner, **38**

Johnny's Coffee, **39**
Li Family Restaurant, **10**
Metro Café, **36**
Moscow Café, **7**
Paulaner Brauhaus, **53**
Quanjude Kaoyadian (Big Duck), **16, 24**
Red Basil, **47**
Ritan Park Restaurant, **35**
Roma Ristorante Italiano, **26**
Saigon Inn, **30**
Sansi Lang, **52**

Sichuan Hometown Restaurant, **37**
Sunflower Village, **2**
Tianshi, **23**
Tibet Shambala, **4**
Uncle Afanti Gourmet City, **29**
Zum Fass, **41**

Lodging

Beifang Hotel, **27**
Beijing Asia Hotel, **33**
Beijing Hilton Hotel, **51**
Beijing Hotel, **21**
Beijing International Hotel, **28**
Beijing New Century Hotel, **6**
China World Hotel, **45**

$ ✕ **Gongdelin.** This state-run vegetarian restaurant serves an array of soybean-based faux-meat dishes, as well as steamed and stir-fried vegetables. The two-floor dining area is bright, bustling, and somewhat dirty. But the fare is a treat. ✉ *158 Qianmen Nandajie, Chongmen District, no ☎. Reservations not accepted. No credit cards.*

$ ✕ **Guangdong Special Diner.** Across the street from the Sichuan Hometown Restaurant (☞ *below*), the Guangdong Special Diner is popular among locals and foreign diplomats alike. The predominantly Cantonese menu offers a less fiery assortment of soups, steamed dishes, and stir-fry. ✉ *Yonganxili Produce Market, 1 alley south of Jianguomen wai Dajie, opposite Friendship Store, Chaoyang District, ☎ 010/6500–7185. Reservations not accepted. No credit cards.*

$ ✕ **Ritan Park Restaurant.** Occupying a courtyard at the southwest corner of Ritan Park, it has seating either indoors (inside a garishly painted ceremonial hall) or in the courtyard (weather permitting) by a pond. This restaurant is especially popular with tour groups and expatriates because of its proximity to shopping, embassies, and diplomatic housing compounds. Sichuan dishes—like Mapo tofu and Gongbao chicken—dominate the menu. Steamed dumplings are also popular. ✉ *Southwest corner of Ritan Gongyuan, Chaoyang District, ☎ 010/6500–4984. No credit cards.*

$ ✕ **Sichuan Hometown Restaurant.** This bargain eatery typifies the small, private restaurants that have sprung up in recent years across Beijing. The food is (as the name implies) hometown Sichuan—hearty fare from China's most populated province that goes heavy on the spices (images of three succulent red peppers adorn the manager's business card). The restaurant offers indoor seating in a narrow dining hall as well as tables on the alley, by day a thriving fruit market. ✉ *Southeast of Friendship Store at Yonganxili Produce Market, Chaoyang District, ☎ 010/6595–7688. Reservations not accepted. No credit cards.*

European

$$$$ ✕ **Roma Ristorante Italiano.** The Roma's authentic northern Italian cuisine is legendary in Beijing. The menu offers a wide selection of antipasto, plus main courses that include lasagne, lamb, and succulent pan-fried sea bass. Roma's Sunday champagne brunch is a mainstay on the Beijing expatriate scene. ✉ *Palace Hotel, 8 Jinyu Hutong, Wangfujing, Dongcheng District, ☎ 010/6512–8899. AE, V.*

$$$ ✕ **Paulaner Brauhaus.** This Munich-style micro-brewery has authentic German cuisine in a festive, pub-like setting. ✉ *Kempinski Hotel, west wing, 50 Liangmaqiao Lu, Chaoyang District, ☎ 010/6465–3388, ext. 5731. AE, MC, V.*

$$ ✕ **Metro Café.** This café-style restaurant offers a standard assortment of Italian pastas. While service is inconsistent, the food is usually very good and the outdoor tables are wonderful (if you can get one) on mild evenings. ✉ *6 Gongrentiyuguan Xilu, Chaoyang District, ☎ 010/ 6501–3377 ext. 7706. AE, V.*

$$ ✕ **Moscow Café.** In times past, the Moscow Café, built in the 1950s, was Beijing's best Western restaurant. Its massive Stalinesque ballroom and Russian menu attracted the city's Communist elite, intellectuals, and east bloc foreign residents. Today, the neon-lit ballroom is gaudy and threadbare. But a side wing still serves passable braised beef, chicken Kiev, oxtail casserole, borscht, and other Russian dishes. ✉ *135 Xizhimenwai Dajie, Xicheng District, ☎ 010/6835–4454. Reservations not accepted. No credit cards.*

$$ ✕ **Zum Fass.** This Swiss-German restaurant and bar is a lunchtime mainstay among diplomats in Beijing. The menu offers standard Swiss-German fare such as pork knuckles, spit-roast chicken, sauerkraut, and

onion soup. ⊠ *10 Beixiaojie, Chaoyang District,* ☎ *010/6462–9666. AE, MC, DC, V.*

Japanese

$$ ✗ **Sansi Lang.** This affordable sushi bar could pass muster with any Japanese salary man. The menu offers sushi, sashimi, tempura, cold soba noodles, and a variety of delicious set meals. Seating is in booths or, upstairs, in private tatami rooms. ⊠ *52 Liangjiu Lu, Liangmaqiao, opposite Kempinski Hotel, Chaoyang District,* ☎ *010/6464–5030. No credit cards.*

Southeast Asian

$$$$ ✗ **Red Basil.** Understated Thai accents adorn the Red Basil's dining area, which is elegantly furnished in hardwood and leather. But the clientele, both expatriates and well-heeled Chinese, come for the food. House favorites include spicy glass noodles with shrimp and, in a bow to Beijing, a rich Thai red curry with Beijing roasted duck. The attentive staff will suggest dishes, which range on the spicy scale from mild to three-alarm fire. ⊠ *Sanhuan Beilu, Chaoyang District (south of San Yuan Bridge),* ☎ *010/6460–2342. AE, MC, V.*

$$$ ✗ **Borom Piman.** Guests must part with their shoes in the entry hall to accommodate traditional Thai floor seating around low tables. The food at Borom Piman, too, is traditional, with Thai curries, crab cakes, glass noodles, and spicy hot prawn soup, all of which make for superior dining. ⊠ *Holiday Inn Lido Hotel, Jichang Lu, Jiangtai Lu, Chaoyang District,* ☎ *010/6437–6688, ext. 2899. AE, MC, V.*

$$–$$$ ✗ **Asian Star Spicy Restaurant.** Asian Star's management imported chefs from Thailand, India, and Indonesia to offer an eclectic, not to mention authentic, menu. Thai braised chicken, Indonesian fried rice, and deep-fried shrimp cakes—the flavors are true. Hot dishes are rated with chili illustrations, but even a mild curried chicken is best accompanied by ice water or a yogurt lassi. Batik-patterned walls and a giant mural of Hong Kong's skyline brighten the decor. ⊠ *26 Dongsanhuan Bei Lu, Chaoyang District,* ☎ *010/6591–6716, or 010/6591–6717. AE, DC, MC, V.*

$$–$$$ ✗ **Saigon Inn.** Decorated in green and rose, this restaurant is elegant and expansive. The menu lists such Vietnamese mainstays as spring rolls, braised beef noodles, chicken salad, and tasty steamed prawns. Affordable set lunches are a hit with the business crowd. ⊠ *Gloria Plaza Hotel, 2 Jianguomennan Dajie, Chaoyang District,* ☎ *010/6515–8855 ext. 3355. AE, DC, MC, V.*

LODGING

International-Style Hotels

$$$$ 🏨 **Beijing Hilton Hotel.** This new Hilton is northeast of Beijing's imperial grid pattern, an area now studded with high-rises, bars, and restaurants. The hotel is comfortably elegant. Two of its popular eateries are a Japanese restaurant with top-notch sushi and the excellent Louisiana, serving Cajun cuisine. ⊠ *1 Dongfang Lu, Dongsanhuan Beilu, Chaoyang District, 100027,* ☎ *010/6466–2288,* 🖷 *010/6465–3052. 363 rooms, 24 suites. 6 restaurants, bar, pool, sauna, bicycles, dance club, car rental. AE, DC, MC, V.*

$$$$ 🏨 **China World Hotel.** One of the finest hotels in Beijing, the China
★ World is Shangri-La's flagship China hotel and part of the prestigious China World Trade Center, home to many offices, luxury apartments, and premium retail outlets. The conference and banqueting facilities are the preferred choice for large-scale receptions and presentations.

There is an executive floor. The hotel stands just east of the tall Trade Centre Tower, which serves as a landmark on the Jianguomen and Third Ring Road junction. The restaurants cover most cuisines. ✉ *1 Jianguomenwai Dajie, Chaoyang District, 100004,* ☎ *010/6505–2266,* FAX *010/6505–3167. 700 rooms, 56 suites. 20 restaurants, 2 bars, deli, beauty salon, massage, health club, dance club, car rental. AE, DC, MC, V.*

$$$$ 🏨 **Grand Hotel.** Added to the Beijing Hotel (☞ *below*) in 1955, it is freshly furnished and independently (Taiwan) managed. The large atrium off the lobby announces this as a more luxurious option than its older neighbor. Even if you don't stay here, try to make it to the top-floor terrace for sunset drinks overlooking the yellow roofs of the Forbidden City. There are both Western and Chinese restaurants. ✉ *35 Dongchangan Jie, Dongcheng District,* ☎ *010/6201–0033,* FAX *010/6202–9893. 217 rooms, 40 suites. 5 restaurants, pool, sauna, health club, bicycles, car rental. AE, DC, MC, V.*

$$$$ 🏨 **Great Wall Sheraton Hotel.** To match the name, a section of wall was built just outside the hotel. One of China's first joint-venture operations (1983), it stands on the Third Ring Road, near the Sanlitun embassy area. The hotel provides solid comfort, an executive floor, good conference and banquet facilities, a ballroom, a theater, and a Chinese garden. In the ground-floor tea house, jazz is performed every weekday evening; on weekends you can listen to piano and Chinese music. The health center is small but thorough. One of the restaurants serves French cuisine. ✉ *10 Dongsanhua Beilu, Chaoyang District,* ☎ *010/ 6353–8899,* FAX *010/6353–9189. 800 rooms, 200 suites. 4 restaurants, bar, pool, sauna, health club, dance club. AE, DC, MC, V.*

$$$$ 🏨 **Kunlun Hotel.** Near the Kempinski and the Hilton, but inside the Ring Road, this 28-story hotel topped by a revolving restaurant resembles a joint-venture hotel, yet is actually a domestic enterprise set up in 1986 and managed by Shanghai's Jingjiang Group. Impressive presentation and a full range of facilities make up for occasional lapses in service. A magnificent Chinese landscape painting greets you in the spacious lobby; on the second floor, one of Beijing's best hotel discos, the Glass House, attracts trendy locals and foreign students. The restaurants offer both Chinese and Western food. ✉ *2 Xinyuan Nanlu, Chaoyang District, 100004,* ☎ *010/6500–3388,* FAX *010/6500–3228. 1,000 rooms, 50 suites. 9 restaurants, bar, pool, sauna, exercise room, bicycles, car rental. AE, DC, MC, V.*

$$$$ 🏨 **Palace Hotel.** This luxurious and elegant hotel, in the downtown Wangfujing area, is jointly run by Hong Kong's Peninsula Group and the People's Liberation Army. A waterfall cascades down the spacious lobby, which is decorated with fine Chinese antiques. The large ballroom on the second floor has seen many prestigious events. Premium retail outlets include Louis Vitton and Davidoff. Beware traffic snarls around rush hour. The restaurants cover Chinese, Italian, and German food. ✉ *8 Jinyu Hutong, Wangfujing, Dongcheng District, 100006,* ☎ *010/6512–8899,* FAX *010/6512–9050. 511 rooms, 20 suites. 5 restaurants, bar, deli, pool, beauty salon, sauna, tennis court, health club, dance club, car rental. AE, DC, MC, V.*

$$$$ 🏨 **Shangri-La Hotel.** A vast joint-venture high-rise, it escapes with surprising elegance intact. The function rooms and ballroom are among the largest in the city. There is an executive floor. Comfortable rooms and good dining make the Shangri-La a worthwhile choice, though its location on the western Third Ring Road, beyond the zoo, may prove time-consuming for most tourist sites. There are Chinese and Japanese restaurants, as well as an excellent French restaurant. ✉ *29 Zizhuyuan Lu, Haidian District, 100081,* ☎ *010/6841–2211,* FAX *010/6841–8002. 764 rooms, 30 suites. 4 restaurants, bar, pool, beauty salon, health club, dance club, car rental. AC, DC, MC, V.*

$$$
★ 🏨 **Beijing Hotel.** The forerunner of them all, the Beijing Hotel is the capital's oldest, born in 1900 as the Hotel de Pekin. Within sight of Tiananmen Square, it has housed countless foreign delegations, missions, and friends of China such as Field Marshal Montgomery from Britain and American leftist writer Edgar Snow. Room 1735 still bears a sign indicating where China's longtime Premier Zhou Enlai stayed and worked. Tourists have been welcome here only in recent years, but the standards of service and comfort are catching up quickly. The central section, renovated in 1982, retains the strongest air of old-fashioned splendor. The western wing—the Grand Hotel (☞ *above*)—was added in 1955 and the eastern wing in 1974. ✉ *33 Dongchangan Jie, Dongcheng District,* ☎ *010/6513–7766,* FAX *010/6513–7842. 850 rooms, 100 suites. 5 restaurants, bar, pool, sauna, health club. AE, DC, MC, V.*

$$$ 🏨 **Beijing New Century Hotel.** This 32-story highrise is a joint-venture hotel with Japan, located in north Beijing's Haidian district, near the Capital Gymnasium. The restaurants offer Chinese, Japanese, and Western food. ✉ *6 Shoudu Tiyuguan Nanlu, Haidian District,* ☎ *010/6849–2001,* FAX *010/6849–1002. 700 rooms, 24 suites. 10 restaurants, bar, pool, sauna, exercise room, car rental. AE, DC, MC, V.*

$$$ 🏨 **Gloria Plaza Hotel.** In a good location just behind the Changfugong (☞ *above*) and CVIK (☞ *below*), this is a well-managed, Hong Kong-run hotel owned by China's Ceroils group. It has good facilities for banquets and functions and excellent Vietnamese fare on the second floor. ✉ *2 Jiangguomen Nandajie, Chaoyang District, 100022,* ☎ *010/6515–8855,* FAX *010/6515–8533. 423 rooms, 20 suites. 5 restaurants, bar, pool, sauna, exercise room, dance club, car rental. AE, DC, MC, V.*

$$$ 🏨 **Holiday Inn Crowne Plaza.** The third and perhaps best of Beijing's Holiday Inns is near the Wangfujing shopping area. Its Chinese name—International Art Crown Plaza—reveals one of the hotel's main features—an art gallery where paintings, often modern, are exhibited year-round. On the second floor is an art salon where Western classical and traditional Chinese music are performed. Restaurants include one Western establishment. ✉ *48 Wangfujing Dajie, Dongfeng District, 100006,* ☎ *010/6513–3388,* FAX *010/6513–2513. 500 rooms, 50 suites. 5 restaurants, bar, pool, sauna, bicycles, car rental. AE, DC, MC, V.*

$$$ 🏨 **Holiday Inn Lido Hotel.** North of the city close to the airport, the Lido has perhaps the fullest range of sporting, leisure, and entertainment facilities in Beijing. It caters to the expanding number of expat residential apartments and international schools in the compound. Completed in 1986, the hotel offered the capital's earliest Western supermarket and delicatessen. The wide variety of restaurants includes Chinese, Thai, German, Indian, Mexican, and American food. ✉ *Jichang Lu, at Jiangtai Lu, Chaoyang District, 100004,* ☎ *010/6437–6688,* FAX *010/6437–6237. 800 rooms, 10 suites. 8 restaurants, bar, pool, beauty salon, massage, sauna, exercise room, dance club. AE, DC, MC, V.*

$$$ 🏨 **Jianguo Hotel.** Despite its '50s patriotic name ("build the country"), this is a joint venture with the United States, established in 1982 as China's first JV hotel. The Jianguo has maintained its friendly and cozy feel. Wonderfully central, and close to the diplomatic compounds and southern embassy area, the hotel is a favorite of journalists and frequent visitors to Beijing. Nearly half of the rooms have balconies overlooking busy Jianwai Dajie. Western classical music, including opera, is performed every Sunday morning in the lobby. Justine's is probably the best Western (French) restaurant in Beijing. Other restaurants serve Chinese food as well. ✉ *5 Jianguomenwai Dajie, Chaoyang District, 100020,* ☎ *010/6500–2233,* FAX *010/6500–2871. 400 rooms, 70 suites. 4 restaurants, bar, pool, beauty salon, car rental. AE, DC, MC, V.*

$$$ ⊞ **Jingguang New World Hotel.** Modern China's obsession with blue glass finds its most monstrous expression in this 53-story hotel, the tallest (albeit temporarily) skyscraper in town. Hard to miss on the eastern third ring road not far from the downtown area, this Hong Kong joint-venture is split between residential/office and hotel guests. Numerous facilities include a medical center and a supermarket. The restaurants serve Cantonese, Korean, and Western food. ⊠ *Jingguang Centre, Hujialou, Chaoyang District, 100020,* ☎ *010/6500–8888,* ℻ *010/6501–3333. 426 rooms, 20 suites. 4 restaurants, 2 bars, pool, beauty salon, sauna, exercise room, dance club, car rental. AE, DC, MC, V.*

$$$ ⊞ **Kempinski Hotel.** The hotel forms part of the Lufthansa Centre, together with a luxury shopping center and the Kempinski apartments. It is within walking distance of the Sanlitun embassy area and dozens of bars and restaurants. The hotel deals mainly with business people, providing excellent business service, with a ballroom and six function rooms. There's a gym and swimming pool on the 18th floor and another one in the basement of the apartment block, where a Western tutor gives good aerobics classes. ⊠ *50 Liangmaqiao Lu, Chaoyang District, 100016,* ☎ *010/6465–3388,* ℻ *010/6465–3366. 500 rooms, 100 suites, 14 deluxe suites. 11 restaurants, 2 bars, pool, exercise room, bicycles, car rental. AE, DC, MC, V.*

$$$ ⊞ **Mövenpick Hotel.** Close to the airport, the joint-venture Mövenpick has a fantastic outdoor pool and good food. Horse-rides in nearby woods attract Beijing expats for weekend breaks from city smog. An interesting variety of food includes Swiss, Japanese, barbecues, and Mongolian hotpot served inside a traditional felt yurt. ⊠ *Xiao Tianzhu Village, Capital Airport, Shunyi County, 100621,* ☎ *010/6456–5588,* ℻ *010/6456–5678. 408 rooms, 35 suites. 5 restaurants, bar, indoor and outdoor pools, sauna, exercise room, dance club. AE, DC, MC, V.*

$$$ ⊞ **New Otani Chang Fu Gong Hotel.** Efficient Japanese management is obvious as soon as you walk into this neat and tidy 24-story hotel, conveniently located on Jianwaidajie, near the Friendship Store and the old observatory. Not surprisingly, most guests are Japanese tour groups and business people, and the main restaurant serves expensive and delicious Japanese food. ⊠ *26 Jianguomenwai Dajie, Chaoyang District, 100022,* ☎ *010/6512–5555,* ℻ *010/6513–9810. 500 rooms, 20 suites. 2 restaurants, bar, pool, sauna, health club, bicycles, car rental. AE, DC, MC, V.*

$$$ ⊞ **Peace Hotel.** Well situated in downtown Wangfujing, opposite the Palace Hotel, this joint venture offers guests large and comfortable rooms. ⊠ *3 Jinyu Hutong, Wangfujing Dajie, Dongcheng District,* ☎ *010/6512–8833,* ℻ *010/6512–6863. 420 rooms, 30 suites. 5 restaurants, bar, pool, sauna, exercise room, bicycles, dance club, car rental. AE, DC, MC, V.*

$$$ ⊞ **Radisson SAS Hotel.** This standard, comfortable, and pleasant Radisson chain hotel stands near the large international exhibition center in northeast Beijing. The restaurants—one open-air—offer outstanding food, including a good-value Western Sunday brunch with music. The Scandinavian restaurant is excellent; there's also Chinese food available. ⊠ *6A Beisanhuan Donglu, Chaoyan District, 100028,* ☎ *010/6466–3388,* ℻ *010/6465–3186. 360 rooms. 3 restaurants, bar, pool, sauna, exercise room, bicycles, dance club, car rental. AE, DC, MC, V.*

$$$ ⊞ **Swissotel.** This hotel is a joint venture between Switzerland and the Hong Kong and Macau Affairs Office of the State Council (hence its Chinese name—the Hong Kong Macau Centre). The Hong Kong connection means Hong Kong Jockey Club members can place bets here, while another boast is that it was one of the first hotels in Asia to provide facilities for people with disabilities. In the large lobby you can enjoy excellent jazz every Friday and Saturday evening. The restaurants offer Chinese, Swiss, Japanese, and Italian food; the Italian place is particularly good. ⊠ *Dongsishiqiao Flyover Junction (2nd Ring Road), Chaoyang District, 100027,* ☎ *010/6501–2288,* FAX *010/6501–2501. 424 rooms, 30 suites. 7 restaurants, bar, pool, sauna, exercise room, car rental. AE, DC, MC, V.*

$$$ 🏨 **Traders' Hotel.** Another part of the World Trade Centre complex, Traders is independently managed and located just behind the China World (☞ *above*). A more businesslike atmosphere pervades the comfortable and well-run establishment. Of the two restaurants, one is Chinese and the other is Western. ⊠ *1 Jianguomenwai Dajie, Chaoyang District, 100004,* ☎ *010/6505–2277,* FAX *010/6505–0838. 567 rooms, 20 suites. 2 restaurants, bar, health club, car rental. AE, DC, MC, V.*

$$$ 🏨 **Zhaolong Hotel.** Handy to the Sanlitun embassy area and pub land, the Zhaolong was a gift to the nation from Hong Kong shipping magnate Y.K. Pao, who named it for his father. It has most amenities, plus a theater and banquet facilities. ⊠ *2 Gongren Tiyuchang Beilu, Chaoyang District,* ☎ *010/6500–2299,* FAX *010/6500–3319. 260 rooms, 20 suites. Bar, pool, sauna, exercise room, bicycles, dance club, car rental. AE, DC, MC, V.*

$$ 🏨 **Beijing Asia Hotel.** This centrally located hotel was built in 1990 by Shanghai's Jingjiang Group for the Olympic Asian Games, which were held in Beijing that year. Well run, it supplies rooms with daily fresh flowers and fruit. The San Francisco Brewing Company provides beer brewed on site and video shows. ⊠ *8 Xinzhong Xijie, Gongren Tiyuchang Beilu, Dongcheng District,* ☎ *010/6500–7788,* FAX *010/6500–8091. 300 rooms. Bar, sauna, exercise room, car rental. AE, DC, MC, V.*

$$ 🏨 **Beijing International Hotel.** The building of this white monolith in the mid-'80s inspired the construction boom along Dougchangan Dajie. Administered by the China International Travel Service, it symbolized the take-off of China's tourist industry. It offers most facilities and acceptable service. It stands opposite the old train station, only a few minutes' ride from Tiananmen Square. The restaurants serve Chinese food. ⊠ *9 Jianguomenwai Dajie, Dongcheng District, 100005,* ☎ *010/6512– 6688,* FAX *010/6512–9972. 1,008 rooms, 42 suites. 2 restaurants, bar, pool, bowling, exercise room, shops, car rental. AE, DC, MC, V.*

$$ 🏨 **Continental Grand Hotel.** In the Asian Games village in north Beijing, this massive structure with eastern and western wings came into being for the 1990 Olympic Asian Games. It has modern facilities for conferences and functions, though service could be improved. There is no health club, but the Olympic Sports Centre across the road should suffice. Dining options include both Western and Korean food. ⊠ *8 Beichen Donglu, Andingmenwai, Chaoyang District, 100101,* ☎ *010/ 6491–5588,* FAX *010/6491–0106. 1,000 rooms, 50 suites. 20 restaurants, bar, sauna, dance club, car rental. AE, DC, MC, V.*

$$ 🏨 **CVIK Hotel.** This is part of the CVIK complex, which is comprised of the CVIK tower, plaza, and luxury shopping center. The joint-venture Sino-Hong Kong hotel enjoys a good location on busy Jianguomenwai Dajie opposite the Friendship Store. The interior, facilities, and service are pleasant if not spectacular. There is a small fountain in the lobby, with a tea house on one side. ⊠ *22 Jianguomenwai Dajie, Chaoyang District,* ☎ *010/6512–3388,* FAX *010/6512–3543. 300 rooms, 15 suites. Indoor pool, sauna, exercise room, dance club, car rental. AE, DC, MC, V.*

$$ 🏨 **Fragrant Hills Hotel.** This rather unusual garden-style hotel takes its name from a beautiful park in the western suburbs of Beijing, a retreat favored by emperors through the centuries. Designed by the Chinese-American architect I.M. Pei, the hotel opened in 1983. It has a large lake and a miniature stone forest. The lobby is a traditional courtyard and rooms are spread out along a hillside. Each large room

has a balcony overlooking the park, though, sadly, the management has been remiss in its maintenance. The outdoor swimming pool beloved of Beijing expats has been covered for year-round use, but the hotel remains peaceful, with marvelous walks in the nearby woods. The three restaurants are enormous; one serves Western-style food. ⊠ *Fragrant Hill Park, Haidian District,* ☎ *010/6259–1166,* FAX *010/6259–1762. 200 rooms, 27 suites. 3 restaurants, bar, pool, sauna, dance club, car rental. AE, DC, MC, V.*

$$ 🖭 **Friendship Hotel.** One of the few garden-style hotels in Beijing proper, the Friendship reveals its background with its name; it was built in 1954 to cater to the foreign experts, mostly Soviet, who had come to help build new China. Nowadays, a few surviving Old China hands remain, together with new arrivals working for the Chinese government in areas such as education and publishing. This giant complex comprises many separate compounds of attractive design in Chinese motifs. All manner of facilities are available, such as tennis, an Olympic-size pool, a driving range, and a theater. The restaurants provide both Chinese and Western food. ⊠ *3 Baishiqiao Lu, Haidian District,* ☎ *010/6849–8888,* FAX *010/6831–4661. 800 rooms, 32 suites. 14 restaurants, bar, pool, sauna, dance club, car rental. AE, DC, MC, V.*

$$ 🖭 **Jinglun Hotel.** The former Beijing Toronto Hotel, a Sino-Canadian joint-venture built in 1982, is now the Sino-Hong Kong Jinglun, and the service and comfort remain the same. The Jinglun is known for its good Chinese food on the fourth floor. From spring to autumn, an outdoor café serves drinks and barbecue beside a fountain. ⊠ *3 Jianguomenwai Dajie, Chaoyang District, 100020,* ☎ *010/6500–2266,* FAX *010/6500–2022. 400 rooms, 4 suites. 6 restaurants, bar, pool, sauna, exercise room, bicycles. AE, DC, MC, V.*

$$ 🖭 **Minzu Hotel.** At its birth in 1959, the Minzu (Nationalities) Hotel was proudly labeled one of the Ten Great Buildings in Beijing (it neighbors the Nationalities Cultural Palace). This paean to the unity of China's different peoples welcomed many prominent foreign visitors. Disappointingly, it has been renovated/marbleized into yet another shiny pleasuredome. The hotel lies on western Changan Dajie, 10 minutes' ride west of Tiananmen Square, opposite the San Wei Teahouse. ⊠ *51 Fuxingmennei Dajie, Xicheng District, 100031,* ☎ *010/6601–4466,* FAX *010/6601–4849. 600 rooms, 52 suites. 4 restaurants, bar, sauna, car rental. AE, DC, MC, V.*

$ 🖭 **Beifang Hotel.** Built in 1953, this small hotel distinguished by occasional Chinese architecture is conveniently in the city center near Wangfujing. The restaurant serves northern Chinese (Beifang) food. ⊠ *45 Dongdang Beidajie, Dongcheng District,* ☎ *010/6525–2831,* FAX *010/6525–2928. Restaurant. AE, DC, MC, V.*

$ 🖭 **Jinghua Hotel.** Cheap, adequate, and friendly, it is located way down south on the third ring road. Rooms have showers, telephone, and air-conditioners. In addition to double rooms, the hotel has dorm rooms. ⊠ *Xiluoyuan Nanlu, outside Yongdingmen, Fengtai District, 100077,* ☎ *010/6722–2211,* FAX *010/6721–1455. 168 rooms, dorm rooms with 110 beds. No credit cards.*

$ 🖭 **Qiaoyuan Hotel.** Long a backpacker favorite (charmless but for its shoestring price), the Qiaoyuan has gone predictably upmarket since renovation in 1996. In the far south of the city, it is well connected by bus (Yongdingmen station) to the "old" train station. Numerous inexpensive restaurants outside the hotel offer down-to-earth but tasty Chinese as well as Western food. Plenty of bike rental places are nearby. ⊠ *Dongbinhe Lu Youanmen Wai, Fengtai District,* ☎ *010/6301–2244,* FAX *010/6318–4709. 440 rooms. Restaurant. AE, DC, MC, V.*

Traditional Hotels

$$ ☷ **Zhuyuan Bingguan** (Bamboo Garden Hotel). This charming small hotel was converted from the residence of Sheng Xuanhuai, a high-ranking Qing official, and of Mao's henchman Kang Sheng, who lived here after Liberation. A powerful and sinister character, responsible for "Public Security" during the Cultural Revolution, Kang nevertheless had fine taste in art and antiques. The Bamboo Garden cannot compete on comfort and facilities with the high-rise crowd, but its lovely courtyards and gardens bursting with bamboo make it a genuine Chinese pleasure. You can take an interesting 10-minute hutong stroll from the hotel to the old Drum Tower. ✉ *24 Xiaoshiqiao Hutong, Jiugulou Dajie, Dongcheng District, 100009,* ☎ *010/6403–2229,* FAX *010/6401–2633. 40 rooms, 1 suite. Restaurant, bar, beauty salon, sauna, bicycles. AE, DC, MC, V.*

$ ☷ **Lusongyuan.** In 1980, China Youth Travel Service set up this charm-
★   ing courtyard hotel on the site of an old Qing Mandarin's residence, a few lanes south of the Youhao Guesthouse (☞ *below*). It is guarded by two stone lions sitting in front of the traditional wooden entrance. The hotel comprises five courtyards, decorated with pavilions, rockeries, and plants. Rooms are elegant with large Chinese window panels. Though the place calls itself an International Youth Hostel, there are no self-catering facilities, but it is inexpensive and delightful to boot. The Chinese restaurant is lovely. ✉ *22 Banchang Hutong, Kuanjie, Dongcheng District, 100009,* ☎ *010/6401–1116,* FAX *010/6403–0418. 38 rooms. Restaurant, bar. No credit cards.*

$ ☷ **Youhao Guesthouse.** Behind a high gray wall with a wrought iron gate, deep in hutong land near the Drum Tower, the lovely Youhao (Friendly) Guesthouse forms only a small part of the large traditional compound where Nationalist leader Chiang Kaishek once stayed. From each comfortable room in the two-story guesthouse, you have a view of either the spacious front courtyard or the back garden where there are trees, flowers, and Chinese-style corridors. The main building has sadly been converted for karaoke use, but other pleasures remain, such as a Roman-style folly and rockery gates. The somewhat surly staff would do well to remember the name of their hotel and work unit—the Chinese People's Association for Friendship with Foreign Countries runs the hotel. There are some intriguing hutong houses nearby. Of the pair of restaurants, one is Japanese and one is Chinese. ✉ *7 Houyuanensi, Jiaodaokou, Dongcheng District,* ☎ *010/6403–1114,* FAX *010/6401–4603. 30 rooms. 2 restaurants. No credit cards.*

NIGHTLIFE AND THE ARTS

China's economic boom has also awakened dormant cultural proclivities—noble or otherwise. In eastern Beijing, sleazy new cabarets decorate the Third Ring Road. With names like the Kissy Club and Rainbow Plaza, they offer customers (mostly male) karaoke, imported spirits, and short-term female companionship. The Hot Spot, a discotheque owned by China's military, features caged teenage boys whose carnal gyrations have become the club's trademark—and made the place Beijing's hottest gay hangout. Underground punk clubs and even ecstasy bars make up the radical fringe. Typically, these establishments keep quiet and move often. Beijing's expatriate scene centers around a strip of outdoor cafés in the Sanlitun diplomatic quarter. They serve cappuccinos and croissants by day and double as bars with live music after sundown.

The Arts

By Bill Smith

Peking Opera

Guanghe Juchang (Guanghe Theater; ✉ 46 Qianmenroushi Jie, Qian-men Dajie, Chongwen District, ☎ 010/6701–8216) stages plays and films as well as operas. Performances at **Lao She Chaguan** (Lao She Teahouse; ✉ 3rd Floor, 3 Qianmenxi Dajie, Chongwen District, ☎ 010/6303–6830) vary, but usually include Peking opera and a variety of other folk arts such as acrobatics, magic, or comedy named for one of China's best-known playwrights. In the popular **Liyuan Juchang** (Liyuan Theater; ✉ Qianmen Hotel, 175 Yongan Lu, Chongwen District, ☎ 010/6301–6688, ext. 8860), a Peking opera venue for tourists, performances feature acrobatics as well as singing, with English sur-titles. The authentic wood-built **Zhengyici Juchang** (Zhengyici Theater; ✉ 220 Xiheyuan Dajie, Xuanwu District, ☎ 010/6318–9454) holds nightly performances in a traditional setting.

Theater

At the **Zhongyang Shiyan Huajuyuan Xiao Juchang** (China Experimental Performance Small Theater; ✉ 45 Maoer Hutong, Dianmen, Dougcheng District, ☎ 010/6403–1099) lesser known directors and actors put on avant garde theater and Chinese dramatizations of modern Western plays. **Beijing Zhanlanguan Juchang** (Beijing Exhibition Center The-ater; ✉ Xizhimenwai Dajie, Xicheng District, ☎ 010/6835–1383) in a Soviet-style building inside the Exhibition Center complex stages Chi-nese and Western plays, opera and ballet.

Acrobatics

Chaoyang Juchang (Chaoyang Theater; ✉ 36 Dongsanhuan Beilu, Hu-jialou, Chaoyang District, ☎ 010/6507–2421) has nightly, spectacu-lar individual and team acrobatic displays employing bicycles, seesaws, catapults, swings, and barrels. At the **Tiandi Juchang** (Universal The-ater; ✉ Dongsishi Qiao, Chaoyang District, ☎ 010/6502–3984) the mostly young performers of the China Acrobatics Troupe run through their nightly repertoire of breathtaking, usually flawless stunts.

Music, Variety, Puppets

Beijing Yinyueting (Beijing Concert Hall; ✉ 1 Beixinhua Jie, Dongcheng District, ☎ 010/6605–5812), Beijing's main venue for Chinese and Western classical music concerts, also has folk dancing and singing, and many celebratory events throughout the year. **Tianqiao Le Chaguan** (Tianqiao Happy Teahouse; ✉ 113 Tianqiao Shichang, Xuanwu Dis-trict, ☎ 010/6304–0617) in an old, traditional theater, recreates the Chi-nese variety shows that were so popular before 1949, including opera, acrobatics, crosstalk, jugglers, illusionists and contortionists. At Zhong-guo Mu'ou Juyuan (China Puppet Theater; ✉ 1 Anhuaxili, Chaoyang District, ☎ 010/6424–3698) traditional stories acted out by shadow- and hand-puppets provide lively entertainment for children and adults alike.

Nightlife

Bars/Pubs with Live Music

At **Arcadia** (Tian Yu; ✉ Building 3, Jindu Apartments, Fangchengyuan Block 1, Fangzhuang, Fengtai District, ☎ 010/6764–8271), modern abstract decor, live Chinese rock bands every Friday and Saturday, and a mainly Chinese clientele create a different atmosphere from the more popular expat bars. **CD Cafe** (CD Kafei; ✉ Dongsanhuan Lu, Chaoyang District, ☎ 010/6501–6655, ext. 5127), next to one of Beijing's major roads, has jazz and blues bands performing standard numbers in a large, informal setting that attracts a crowd of mixed age and nationality. At **Goose and Duck** (Eya Jiuba; ⊠ Ritandongyi Jie, Chaoyang District, ☎ 010/6509–3777) you can enjoy an English draft beer while you listen to folk, country, and easy listening music played by Chinese and Western musicians, Tuesday to Saturday. **Hard Rock Café** (Yingshi Canting; ⊠ 8 Dongsanhuan Beilu, Chaoyang District, ☎ 010/6501–6688, ext. 2571) is an expensive Western bar with live bands nightly and frequent special promotions. **Henry J Bean's** (Henli Canting; ⊠ China World Trade Center/Guo Mao, Jianguomenwai Dajie, Chaoyang District, ☎ 010/6505–2266), an upmarket beer and burger bar decorated with gingham, football memorabilia, and other Americana, has a resident band Monday to Saturday. **Minder Cafe** (Mingdaxi Canting; ⊠ Dongdaqiao Xiejie, Chaoyang District, ☎ 010/6599–6066), packed with revelers dancing to the resident band every weekend, is probably Beijing's best-known meeting place for young expats. Above the **Sanwei Bookstore** (Sanwei Shudian; 60 Fuxingmenwai Dajie, Xicheng District, ☎ 010/6601–3204) in a traditional teahouse setting, Friday is jazz night, and Saturday changes to Chinese classical music played on instruments such as the pipa and the guzheng.

Bars/Pubs

The spacious **San Francisco Brewing Company** (Jiujinshan Pijiuwu; ⊠ 8 Xinzhong Xijie, Gongti Beilu, Chaoyang District, ☎ 010/6500–7788, ext. 7156) bar, part of the Asia Hotel complex, has oak-effect tables and chairs, its own micro-brewery, and film nights. **Sentiment Bar** (Sandimen Jiuba; ⊠ Sanlitun Lu, Chaoyang District, ☎ 010/6415–3691), a light, airy, and quiet bar with predominantly white decor and tables outside in summer, is on the main expat shopping and nightlife street. The American-style **Schiller's** (Xile Jiuba; ⊠ Liangmaqiao Lu, Chaoyang District, ☎ 010/6461–9276) bar, named for the German poet, is popular with Beijing's younger expats.

Nightclubs

Hotspot (Ridian; ⊠ Sanhuan Donglu, Chaoyang District, ☎ 010/6531–2277; free entry for foreigners) is frequented by affluent, trendy young Chinese and owned by the People's Liberation Army; the lively venue offers frenetic disco dancing, cage dancers, and karaoke singers in an industrial atmosphere created by a tin entrance tunnel, matte black decor, and steel balustrades. At **Nightman** (Caite Man; ⊠ 2 Xibahenanli, Chaoyang District, ☎ 010/6466–2562) multi-level, black tiered seating and dancing areas house young Chinese and Westerners enjoying non-stop dancing to hip-hop, techno, and everything else served up by the imported DJs.

OUTDOOR ACTIVITIES AND SPORTS

Bicycling

Hotels generally have rental bikes for their guests. ☞ Old Peking by Bicycle *in* Exploring Beijing, *above.*

Golf

Beijing Chaoyang Golf Club. Just beyond the Third Ring Road in downtown Beijing, this short 9-hole course takes less than two hours to play and caters to Japanese expatriates. The course is convenient and—by Beijing standards—inexpensive. Facilities include a driving range and practice green. ⊠ *Shangsi Lu, Chaoyang District,* ☎ *010/6507–3380 or 10/6500–1149.* ☜ *Greens fee: Y600 weekends, Y400 weekdays.* ☉ *Course, daily 9–6; driving range, daily 9–9:30.*

Beijing Country Golf Club. Known as the farmer's course, this Japanese-managed complex offers two 18-hole courses reclaimed from wheat fields. ⊠ *35 km (22 mi) northeast of Beijing in Shunyi County,* ☎ *010/ 6944–1005 or 10/6944–1108.* ▣ *Greens fee: Y900 weekends. Rental clubs, caddies available.* ⊙ *Mar.–Nov. 7–5.*

Beijing International Golf Club. Nestled on a hillside above the Ming Tombs, this spectacular 18-hole course is Beijing's finest. Long (par 72), challenging, and meticulously groomed, it has hosted professional tournaments. Facilities include a restaurant, pro shop, and driving range. ⊠ *46 km (29 mi) north of Beijing near Changping,* ☎ *010/6974– 5678.* ▣ *Greens fees: Y600/weekdays, Y1,200/weekends. Caddy (mandatory): Y120. Rental clubs (full set): Y300.* ⊙ *Mar.–Nov. 7–5.*

Health Clubs

Most high-end hotels in Beijing have extensive fitness centers. Some of these are open to the general public. Typically, facilities include a lap pool; a weight room with step-machines, treadmills, exercise bikes, and modern weight-lifting machines; and even squash, racquetball, and tennis courts.

Great Wall Sheraton Fitness Center offers a modern weight room, an indoor lap pool, a sauna, and tennis courts (Y70/hr., reservations required). ☎ *010/6500–5566, ext. 2251.* ▣ *Y150.* ⊙ *Daily 6–10.*

New Otani Health Club offers a lap pool, a well-equipped exercise room, a tiny indoor track, tennis (Y70/hr., reservations required), sauna baths, and steam rooms. ☎ *010/6512–5555.* ▣ *Y120.* ⊙ *Daily 7–10:30.*

Shangri-La Health Club has an indoor lap pool, a weight room, tennis courts (Y160/hr., reservations required), and ping pong. ☎ *010/6841– 2211.* ▣ *Y150.* ⊙ *Daily 6–10:30.*

SHOPPING

Despite the arrival of numerous modern department stores and groceries, Beijing remains a city of traditional markets. Most people still rely on street stalls for their produce, meat, dry goods, and other household items. The city's trendiest shopping district, Wangfujing (☞ *below*), offers shoppers (and window shoppers) an array of swank boutiques and department stores. For a more traditional flavor—and bargains—try the Sunday market at Panjiayuan (☞ *below*).

Department Stores

The **Beijing Friendship Store** (⊠ 17 Jianguomenwai Dajie, ☎ 010/6512– 4488), a long-time tourist favorite, sells the widest range of traditional Chinese goods and handicrafts under one roof, including hand-drawn table cloths, silk and cashmere yard-goods and clothing, porcelain, watercolor paintings, traditional Chinese medicine, jade and gold jewelry, rugs (both silk and wool), and groceries. The **Lufthansa Centre** (⊠ 52 Liangmaoqiao, Chaoyang District, ☎ 010/6465–1188), among Beijing's top department stores, stocks cosmetics, consumer electronics, wool and cashmere clothing, and new rugs; a Western grocery store occupies the basement.

Specialty Stores

Arts and Antiques

Antiques began pouring out of China more than a decade ago, despite strict rules banning the export of precious "cultural relics." According to Chinese law, nothing that pre-dates the death of Qing Emperor Qianlong (1795) can be legally exported. The same holds for religious items, including Buddha statues and Tibetan tankas, certain imperial porcelains, and any item deemed important to China's Communist revolution. In fact, older objects—from ubiquitous Tang dynasty tomb art to priceless Zhou ritual bronzes—are smuggled across the border daily. In most cases, you needn't worry that your purchases are illicit or will be seized at customs.

MARKETS

Beijing Curio City (⊠ Dongsanhuan Nanlu, Chaoyang District, exit Third Ring Road at Anjiayuan Bridge, ☎ 010/6774–7711) is a four-story complex housing scores of kitsch and curio shops and a few furniture vendors. Prices are high (driven there by tour groups) so don't be afraid to low-ball. **Chaowai Market** (⊠ Shichangjie, Chaoyangmenwai Dajie, Chaoyang District), Beijing's best-known venue for affordable antiques, in a grubby warehouse in the diplomatic quarter, houses scores of independent vendors who sell everything from authentic Qing furniture to traditional baskets, ceramics, carpets, and curios. Be sure to bargain; vendors routinely sell items for less than half their starting price. **Houhai Market** (⊠ at Houhai Gongyuan) is a small lane lined with tiny antiques shops. It can be tough to find on weekends, when a surrounding produce market fills the neighborhood with shoppers. Follow the footpath that hugs the shore on the west bank of Houhai Lake. Look for a sign (in English) advertising ANTIQUES. In **Liangmahe Market** (⊠ 49 Liangmaqiao Lu, just north of Kempinski Hotel, Chaoyang District) stalls offer curios, antiques, collectibles, and fakes—and vendors that beckon shoppers to "lookee, lookee." Prices are higher than at Chaowai, so good bargaining skills are imperative. Toward the north of the market are several shops selling high-quality antiques. One of these, the **Hua Yi Classical Furniture Co.,** has a warehouse/factory complex outside Beijing that is open to the public. Ask a salesperson to accompany you. **Liulichang Market** (⊠ Liulichang, Xuanwu District) occupies a narrow lane that has been carefully restored to its Ming-era grandeur. Its classical architecture is as much an attraction as the art and antiques shops, which sell a variety of curios, Cultural Revolution kitsch, and authentic antiques. Artists come here for the selection of brushes, paper, and ink stones. The Sunday market at **Panjiayuan** (⊠ Huaweiqiaoxinan Jie, Dongsanhuan, Chaoyang District) is Beijing's liveliest. Vendors, many from faraway provinces, fill hundreds of open-air stalls with a dizzying array of collectibles, as well as lots of junk. Old clocks, new porcelain, jade, bronzes, tomb art, wood carvings, Tibetan rugs, "Maomorabilia"—it's all here. The market is grubby so dress down. Arrive at sunrise to beat the crowds. Some stalls also do business on Saturdays.

STORES

There are other small stores that are worth a look. If time permits, comparison shop before making a purchase. Try the **Beijing Jewelry Import & Export Corporation** (⊠ 229 Wangfujing Dajie, ☎ 010/6525–5380) for collectibles. **The Beijing Painting Gallery** (⊠ 289 Wangfujing Dajie) deals in contemporary art. **Han's Gallery** (⊠ Ritan Dongyijie) is a small private venue specializing in contemporary Chinese painters and antique embroidery. The **Huaxia Arts & Crafts Store** (⊠ 293 Wangfujing Dajie) has a selection of crafts work.

Books

Many hotel kiosks sell international newspapers and magazines. The **Beijing Foreign Languages Reference Bookstore** (⊠ 219 Wangfujing Dajie, Dongcheng District, ☎ 010/6525–5140) sells specialized texts and dictionaries. The **Beijing Friendship Store** (☞ *above*) has a small bookstore with titles (most on history or culture) from China's official foreign language presses. It also stocks a limited selection of foreign news magazines, imported fiction, and a few children's books. For more variety try the **Foreign Languages Bookstore** in Wangfujing (☞ Exploring, *above*), which stocks foreign-language novels, textbooks, tapes, maps, and art books.

Clothing

Silk Alley (✉ Ends at junction of Xiushui Nanjie and Xiushui Dongjie) has long been popular with both expatriates and fashion-conscious Chinese. If you start at the south end of Silk Alley near the Beijing Friendship Store, you can follow the alley north to browse open-air clothing stalls specializing in silks, cashmere and made-for-export apparel. Depending on season (and what happens to fall off the truck) you can find everything from Esprit sportswear to designer women's suits to North Face parkas. Beware of hawkers who troll the area with gym bags full of pirate CDs and CD-ROM; these illicit copies are often damaged or virus-tainted. Made-for-export clothing abounds in **Yabao Market** (✉ West side of Ritan Lu), also known as the Russian Market; the quality is (in general) inferior to that found at Silk Alley. Russians and Eastern European traders buy here for export back home. Popular items include cotton apparel, (hideous) fur coats, and bedding. Some vendors only deal in bulk. Another market known for its export-quality clothing runs along **Gongren Tiyuchang Beilu,** west of Gongren Tiyuchang Donglu, and then continues along Sanlitun Lu in the Sanlitun diplomatic quarter. Come here to stock up on cotton and linen. Some children's clothing is also available.

Fabric, Embroidery, and Drawn Work

Most department stores sell silk, satin brocades, and wools. Beijing's best yardage shop, the **Yuanlong Embroidery and Silk Store** (✉ 55 Tiantan Lu, Chongwen District, across from north gate of Temple of Heaven Park, ☎ 010/6701–2859) has sold silks and yard goods for more than a century. It also offers custom tailoring and shipping. For drawn work, try the **Baizihfang Embroidery Factory** (✉ A44 Liren Jie, Xuanwu District, ☎ 010/6303–6577. The **Golden Peacock Art World** (✉ 13 Dongtucheng Lu, Chaoyang District, ☎ 010/6421–4757 has drawn work among many other art products. The **White Peacock Art World** (☞ Rugs, *below*) has a wide range of arts and crafts including drawn work.

Jewelry

Everything from porcelain to toilet paper is sold at the **Hongxiao Market** (✉ Tiantan Lu, between Chongemenwai Lu and Tiyuguan Dajie, ☎ 010/6702–9103), but the main attraction, on the third floor, is freshwater pearls. This market offers a good selection at affordable prices. The **Shard Box Store** (✉ 1 Ritan Beilu, Chaoyang District, ☎ 010/6500–3712) specializes in silver, jade, coral, and turquoise jewelry worn by China's national minorities. Many pieces are one-of-a-kind items from Tibet or Yunnan provinces. The store takes its name from traditional jewelry boxes, which were often made from pottery shards.

Rugs

Antique Chinese, Mongolian, Tibetan, and Central Asian rugs are sold in many of Beijing's antiques shops. Many offer shipping services. At the **Beijing Carpet Import & Export Corporation** ✉ 1st Floor, Hong Kong Macao Center, Dongsishitiao, Chaoyang District, ☎ 010/6501–2568) the walls and floors are covered with a large selection of wool and silk carpets in modern and traditional Chinese and Middle Eastern designs, a few antique, in a variety of sizes and prices. The **Beijing**

Qianmen Carpet Factory (✉ 44 Xingfu Dajie, Chongwen District, in bomb shelter behind theater, ☎ 010/6701–5079; call before visiting) outlet offers a small selection of older rugs. The **Beijing Yihong Carpet Factory** (a.k.a. the Women's Carpet Cooperative, ✉ 35 Juzhang Hutong, Chongwen District, ☎ 010/6712–2195), a back-alley showroom, is managed by women from a state-owned (and nearly bankrupt) carpet factory. Its showroom is stacked with dusty rugs from Mongolia, Xinjiang, and Tibet. Cleaning and repairs are free. While it's primarily an outlet for old rugs, new items are on sale as well, and copies of old designs can be made to order, usually within weeks. The **White Peacock Art World** (✉ Beibinhe Lu, Deshengmenwai Dajie, Haidian District, ☎ 010/6201–3008) carries a large selection of new rugs in silk and wool; it will also make rugs to order. Among department stores with good new rug selections are the Beijing Friendship Store (☞ *above*) and the Lufthansa Centre (☞ *above*).

Stamps and Coins

For new Chinese stamp sets, visit the **Wangfujing Post Office** (✉ 2 Xuanwumendong Dajie at Wangfujing Dajie across from Dunkin' Donuts). For old stamps, try the **Yuetan Shichang** where stamp traders occupy stalls along the west side of Yuetan Gongyuan (Yuetan Park).

Coins are sold at many antiques/curio shops. Old coins and paper currency are traded outside the **Gudai Qianbi Zhanlanguan.** ☞ Exploring Beijing, North and East of the Forbidden City, *above*).

Supermarkets

For Western groceries, the **Welcome Supermarket** (✉ Basement of China World Hotel, ☎ 010/6505–2288) offers Beijing's best selection. The **Lido Supermarket** (Jichang Lu, Jiangtai Lu, Chaoyang District, ☎ 010/6437–6688) at the Holiday Inn Lido is another option. There's a smaller supermarket at the **CVIK Plaza** (22 Jianguomenwai Dajie, Chaoyang District, ☎ 010/6512–4488).

Wangfujing

Wangfujing Dajie, Beijing's premier shopping street, is undergoing a facelift. The tiny one- and two-story shops that used to be its hallmark are disappearing fast as featureless department stores move in. Still, Wangfujing has retained much of its charm and remains worth a browse.

Begin at the corner of Dengshikou and Wangfujing Dajie. On the northwest corner is a newcomer, the Century Plaza department store. To the south, on the west side of Wangfujing Dajie, find the **China Silk Store** (✉ 133 Wangfujing Dajie, ☎ 010/6525–7945), where you can order a *qipao*, a traditional silk dress. A few doors south is the **Beijing Medical Department Store** (✉ 153 Wangfujing Dajie), which stocks an amazing range of Western and Chinese medicines and medical equipment. The **Wangfujing Medical Apparatus Company** (✉ 267 Wangfujing Dajie), a bit farther down the street, has similar merchandise. The **Foreign Language Book Store** (✉ 235 Wangfujing Dajie) contains four floors of books, maps, videotapes, CDs, and school supplies. The **Beijing Sports Department Store** (✉ 201 Wangfujing Dajie) has the city's best selection of sporting gear, including ice skates for winter. Just south is an official condom and birth control outlet; look for the health workers in white lab coats. Wangfujing's grand dame, the **Beijing Department Store** (✉ 255 Wangfujing Dajie, ☎ 010/6512–6677) has Soviet-inspired design features such as marble columns and fancy ceiling moldings. Sandwiched between two construction sites is the state-run

Chengguzhi Antique Store (⊠ 281 Wangfujing Dajie, ☎ 010/6555–2265), which sells more handicrafts than actual antiques.

SIDE TRIPS FROM BEIJING

Changcheng

60–120 km (37–74 mi) north and west of Beijing.

No Beijing visit is complete without a trip to the **Changcheng** (Great Wall). Built by successive dynasties over two millennia, the wall isn't actually one structure but a collection of many defensive installations, erected to repel marauding nomads, that extends some 4,000 km (2,480 mi) from the East China Sea to Central Asia. Built of wood, the earliest walls and signal towers have long since disappeared. The more substantial brick-and-earth ruins that snake across the mountains north of Beijing date from the heyday of wall-building, the Ming dynasty.

China's first wall-builder, Qin Shihuang, began fortifying the northern border after he established the Qin dynasty in 221 BC. His work, which stood far to the north of the present-day wall, extended some 5,000 km (3,100 mi) from Liaoning province in the east to Gansu in the west. By some accounts, Qin mustered nearly a million people, or about a fifth of China's total workforce, a mobilization that claimed countless lives and gave rise to many tragic folk tales. Later dynasties repaired existing walls or built new ones. The Ming, which took power in 1386, committed vast resources to wall-building as a defense against increasingly restive northern tribes. The Ming wall, which is about 26 ft tall and 23 ft wide at its base, could accommodate six horsemen riding abreast. It incorporated small wall-top garrisons linked by beacon towers used for sending smoke signals or setting off fireworks to warn of enemy attack. In the end, however, wall-building failed to prevent the Manchu invasion that toppled the Ming in 1644.

That historical failure hasn't tarnished the Great Wall's image. Whereas China's official "line" once cast it as a model of feudal oppression—focusing on the brutality suffered by work crews and the vast treasures squandered on the useless fortification—the Great Wall is now touted as a national patriotic symbol. "Love China, Restore the Great Wall," declared Deng Xiaoping in a 1984 campaign that kicked off the official revisionism. Since then, large sections of the Great Wall have been repaired and opened to visitors.

Badaling Changcheng

Close to Beijing, 9 km (5½ mi) above the giant Juyongguan garrison and an hour by car from downtown, the **Badaling Fortress** is where visiting dignitaries go for a quickie photo-op. Its large sections of restored wall rise steeply to either side of the fort in rugged landscape. Convenient to the Ming Tombs (☞ *below*), Badaling is popular with group tours and often crowded. People with disabilities find access to the wall at Badaling better than elsewhere in the Beijing area. ⊠ *70 km (43 mi) northwest of Beijing, Yanqing County,* ☎ *010/6912–1308.* ☜ *Y30; cable car, Y80 one-way, Y100 round-trip.* ☉ *Daily 6:30 AM–sunset.*

Mutianyu Changcheng

★ ㊹ A bit farther from downtown Beijing, the **Great Wall at Mutianyu** is more spectacular and (usually) less crowded than Badaling. Here, a long section of restored wall is perched on a high ridge above serene wooded canyons. Views from the top are truly memorable. The lowest point on the wall is a strenuous one-hour climb above the parking lot. Alternately, a Japanese-built cable car offers a breathtaking ride to the highest restored section, from which several hiking trails descend. If you don't plan to hike, phone ahead to make sure the gondola is running. ⊠ *90 km (56 mi) northeast of Beijing, Huairou County,* ☎ *010/6964–2022.* ⌨ *Y30; cable car, Y80 one-way, Y100 round-trip.* ⊙ *Daily 7 AM–sunset.*

Simatai Changcheng

★ ④⑤ Remote and largely unrestored, the **Great Wall at Simatai** is ideal if you're seeking no-handrails adventure. Near the frontier garrison at Gubeikou, this section of wall traverses towering peaks and hangs precariously above cliffs. In some places, the trail along the top of the wall is so steep that the journey is more a crawl than a hike. Stairways are uniformly crumbling and, in places, situated above deadly sheer drops. Several trails lead to the wall from the parking lot. The hike takes about two hours. A cable car serves a drop-off point about 40 minutes on foot from the wall. ⊠ *Near Gubeikou, Miyun County.* ⌨ *Y18; cable car, Y40 one-way, Y60 round-trip.* ⊙ *Daily 8–5.*

Ming Shisanling

★ ④⑥ *48 km (30 mi) north of Beijing.*

A narrow, dead-end valley just north of Changping is the final resting place for 13 of the Ming dynasty's 16 emperors (the others were buried in Nanjing). Ming monarchs would journey here each year to kowtow before their clan forefathers and make offerings to their memory. The area's vast scale and imperial grandeur conveys the importance attached to ancestor worship in ancient China.

The road to the Mingshisan Ling (Ming Tombs) begins beneath an imposing stone portico that stands at the valley entrance. Beyond, a **shen lu** (spirit way; ⌨ Y16; ⊙ 9–5:30) once reserved for imperial travel passes through an outer pavilion and between rows of imperial advisers and charming, huge stone elephants, lions, camels, and horses on its 7-km (4½-mi) journey to the burial sites.

This road leads to **Changling,** the grand tomb built for Emperor Yongle in 1427. Architecturally, it matches the design of Yongle's great masterpiece, the Forbidden City, which he built after moving the Ming's imperial capital north to Beijing.

Changling and a second tomb, **Dingling,** were rebuilt in the 1980s and opened to the public. Unfortunately, both complexes suffer from over-restoration and crowding. Do visit, if only for the tomb relics on display in small museums at each site, but allow ample time for a hike or drive northwest from Changling to the six unrestored tombs located a short distance farther up the valley. Here, crumbling walls conceal vast courtyards shaded by ancient pine trees. At each tomb, a stone altar rests beneath a stela tower and hill-like burial mound. In some cases, the wall that circles the burial chamber is accessible on steep stone stairways that ascend from either side of the altar. At the valley's terminus (about 5 km/3 mi northwest of Changling), the Zhaoling tomb rests beside a traditional walled village. This thriving hamlet is well worth exploring.

Picnics amid the Ming ruins have been a favored weekend activity among Beijing-based diplomats for nearly a century. Ignore signs prohibiting this, but do carry out all trash. ⊠ *Near Changping, Changping County.* ⌨ *Restored tombs, Y30; unrestored tombs, free.* ⊙ *Daily 9–5:30.*

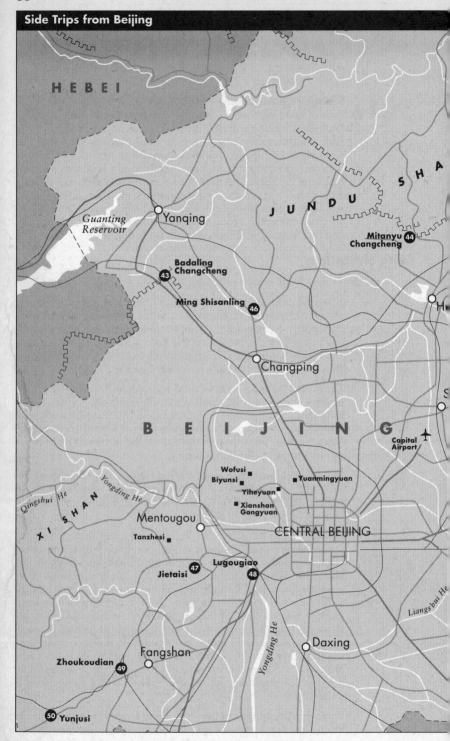

HEBEI

JUNDU SHA

Guanting Reservoir

Yanqing

Mitanyu
Changcheng ④④

Badaling
Changcheng
④③

Ming Shisanling ④⑥

Changping

BEIJING

Capital
Airport

Wofusi ■
Biyunsi ■   ■ Yuanmingyuan
Yiheyuan ■

Qingshui He   *Yongding He*

XISHAN

■ Xianshan
Gongyuan

Mentougou

Tanzhesi ■

CENTRAL BEIJING

Jietaisi ④⑦ Lugouqiao
④⑧

Yongding He   *Liangshui He*

Daxing

Zhoukoudian ④⑨ Fangshan

⑤⓪ Yunjusi

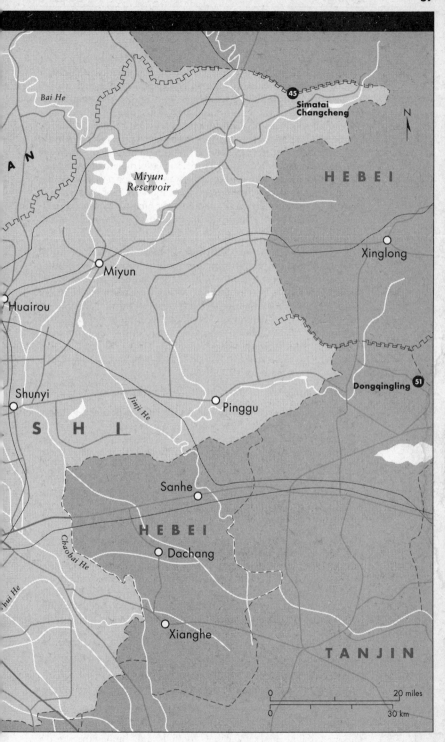

Bai He

Simatai
Changcheng

45

N

HEBEI

Miyun
Reservoir

Xinglong

Miyun

Huairou

Dongqingling 51

Shunyi

Jiuji He

Pinggu

SHI

Sanhe

HEBEI

Chaobai He

Dachang

hui He

Xianghe

TANJIN

0				20 miles

0				30 km

Jietaisi

47 *35 km (22 mi) west of Beijing.*

Standing on a wooded slope beyond Beijing's industrialized western suburb, Jietai Temple is one of China's most famous ancient Buddhist sites. Its four main halls occupy a row of step-like ledges that ascend Ma'an Shan (Saddle Hill). Originally built in AD 581, the temple complex expanded over the centuries and grew to its current scale in a major renovation conducted by Ming-era devotees from 1436 to 1450. The temple buildings, plus three magnificent bronze Buddhas located in the Mahavira Hall, date from this period. To the right of this hall, just above twin pagodas, is the Ordination Terrace, a platform built of white marble and topped with a massive bronze Sakyamuni seated on a lotus flower. Tranquil courtyards, where ornate stelae and well-kept gardens bask beneath the Scholar Tree and other ancient pines, augment the temple's beauty. ⊠ *In hills above Shijingshan District, Mentougou County.* 🎫 *Y10.* ⊙ *Daily 7:30–6.*

En Route Farther along the road past Jietai Temple, **Tanzhe Si** (Tanzhe Temple) is a Buddhist complex nestled in a grove of three-bristle *zhe* (cudrania) trees. Established around AD 400 and once home to more than 500 monks, Tanzhe was heavily damaged during the Cultural Revolution. Restoration continues—slowly—and the complex makes for an ideal side trip from Jietai Temple or Marco Polo Bridge (☞ *below*). ⊠ *10 km (6 mi) past Jietai Temple, 45 km (28 mi) west of Beijing, Mentougou County.* 🎫 *Y13.* ⊙ *Daily 8:30–4.*

Lugouqiao

48 *16 km (10 mi) southwest of Beijing's Guanganmen Gate.*

Also known as Marco Polo Bridge because it was praised by Italian wayfarer Marco Polo, this impressive span is Beijing's oldest. Built in 1192 and reconstructed after severe flooding during the Qing dynasty, its 11 segmented stone arches cross the Yongding River on the ancient imperial highway that linked Beijing with central China. The bridge's marble balustrades support nearly 500 carved stone lions that decorate elaborate handrails. Note the giant stone slabs that comprise the bridge's original roadbed. Carved imperial stelae at either end of the span commemorate the bridge and surrounding scenery.

The Marco Polo Bridge is best remembered in the 20th century as the spot where invading Japanese armies clashed with Chinese soldiers on June 7, 1937. The assault began Japan's brutal eight-year occupation of eastern China that would last until Tokyo's unconditional surrender to allied forces at the end of World War II. The bridge has become a popular field trip destination for Beijing area students. On the Beijing side of the span, a **Kangri Zhanzheng Jinianguan** (Memorial Hall of the War of Resistance Against Japan), underwent renovation and expansion in 1997. Below the bridge on the opposite shore, a local entrepreneur rents horses for Y120 per hour and leads tours of the often-dry riverbed. ⊠ *Near Xidaokou, Fengtai District.* 🎫 *Y5.* ⊙ *Daily 8:30–6.*

Zhoukoudian Peking Man Site

49 *48 km (30 mi) southwest of Beijing.*

This area of lime mines and craggy foothills ranks among the world's great paleontological sites. In 1929, anthropologists drawn to Zhoukoudian by apparently human "dragon bones" found in a Beijing apothecary unearthed a complete skull cap and other fossils dubbed Homo Erectus Pekinensis, or Peking Man. These early remains, believed to be almost 700,000 years old, suggest (as do similar Homo Erectus discoveries in Indonesia) that man's most recent ancestor originated in Asia, not Europe. Funded by the Rockefeller Foundation, a large-scale excavation done in the early 1930s unearthed six skull caps and other hominid remains, stone tools, evidence of fire plus a multitude of animal bones, many at the bottom of a large sink hole believed to be a trap for woolly rhinos and other large game. Sadly, the Peking Man fossils disappeared under mysterious circumstances during World War II, leaving researchers only plaster casts to contemplate. Subsequent digs at Zhoukoudian have yielded nothing equivalent to Peking Man, although archaeologists haven't yet abandoned the search. Trails lead to several hillside excavation sites. A small museum showcases a few (dusty) Peking Man statues, a collection of paleolithic artifacts, and some fine animal fossils, including a bear skeleton and a sabre-toothed tiger skull. ⊠ *Zhoukoudian,* ☎ *010/6930–1272.* ☒ *Y21.* ☉ *Daily 9–4:30.*

Yunjusi

50 *121 km (75 mi) southwest of Beijing.*

Yunju Temple is best known for its collection of 14,278 stone tablets carved with Buddhist scriptures between the 6th and 17th centuries. A small pagoda at the center of the complex commemorates Jing Wan, the Tang-era monk who carved the earliest 146 stone tablets and ordered that the work continue after his death. Many of these tablets were once stored in vault-like caves carved into the cliffs on Shijing Mountain behind the temple complex. Today, these carvings are visible in store rooms built along the temple's southern perimeter.

Four central prayer halls, arranged to ascend the hillside above the main gate, contain impressive Ming-era bronze buddhas. The last in this row, the Dabei Hall, displays a spectacular Thousand Armed Avalokiteshvara. This 13-ft-tall bronze image—which actually has 24 arms and five heads and stands in a giant lotus flower—is believed to embody boundless compassion. A group of pagodas, most notably the 98-ft-tall Northern Pagoda, are all that remain of the original Tang complex. These heavily damaged structures are nonetheless remarkable for their Buddhist reliefs and ornamental patterns. Heavily damaged during the Japanese occupation and again by Maoist radicals in the 1960s, the temple complex is currently under renovation. ⊠ *Off Fangshan Lu, Nanshangle Xiang, Fangshan County.* ☒ *Y16.* ☉ *Daily 8–6.*

Dongqingling

★ **51** *125 km (78 mi) east of Beijing.*

Modeled on the Ming Tombs near Beijing, the Eastern Qing Tombs replicate the Ming-style "spirit ways," walled tomb complexes, and subterranean burial chambers. But they are even more extravagant in their scale and grandeur. The ruins contain the remains of five emperors, 15 empresses, and 136 imperial concubines, all laid to rest in a broad valley chosen by Emperor Shunzhi while on a hunting expedition. By the Qing's collapse in 1911, the tomb complex covered some 18 sq mi of farmland and forested hillside, making it the most expansive burial ground in all China.

The Eastern Qing Tombs are in much better repair than their older Ming counterparts. While several of the tomb complexes have undergone extensive renovation, none is overdone. Peeling paint, grassy courtyards, and numerous stone bridges and pathways preserve the area's imperial grandeur. Often, visitors are so few that you may feel as if you've stumbled upon an ancient ruin unknown beyond the valley's farming villages.

Of the nine tombs open to the public, two are not to be missed. The first, **Yuling,** is the resting place of the Ming's most powerful sovereign, Emperor Qianlong, who ruled China for 59 years during the later 18th century. Beyond the outer courtyards, Qianlong's burial chamber is accessible from inside the Stela Hall, where an entry tunnel descends some 65 ft into the ground and ends at the first of three elaborately carved marble gates. Beyond, exquisite carvings of Buddhist images and sutras rendered in both Sanskrit and Tibetan adorn the tomb's walls and ceiling. Qianlong was laid to rest, along with his empress and two concubines, in the third and final marble vault, amid priceless offerings that were looted by warlords early this century.

The second must-see tomb, **Dingdongling,** was built for the infamous Empress Dowager Cixi (1835–1911). Known for her failure to halt Western imperialist encroachment, Cixi once spent funds allotted to strengthen China's navy on a traditional stone boat for the lake at the Summer Palace. Her burial compound, reputed to have cost 72 tons of silver, is the most elaborate (if not the largest) at the Eastern Qing Tombs. Many of its stone carvings are significant in that the phoenix, which symbolized the female, is level with, or even above, the imperial (and male) dragon. A peripheral hall paneled in gold leaf displays some of the luxuries amassed by Cixi and her entourage, including embroidered gowns, jewelry, a selection of imported cigarettes, and even a coat for one of her dogs. In a bow to tourist kitsch, the compound's main hall contains a wax statue of Cixi sitting Buddha-like on a lotus petal flanked by a chamber maid and a eunuch.

The Eastern Qing Tombs are a four-hour drive from the capital. Poor roads and road construction slow the journey. But the rural scenery is dramatic, and the trip is arguably the best full-day excursion outside Beijing. ⊠ *Near Malanguan, Hebei Province.* ☞ Y32. ☉ *Daily 8:30–5.*

BEIJING A TO Z

Arriving and Departing

By Bus
Beijing is served by four long distance bus stations. They are: Dongzhimen (northeast; ⊠ Dongzhimenwaixie Jie, Chaoyang District, ☎ 010/6348–4995), Haihutun (south; ⊠ Yongwai Chezan Lu, Fengtai District, ☎ 010/6256–6232), Beijiao, also called Deshengmen (north; ⊠ Deshengmenwai Dajie, Xicheng District, ☎ 010/6403–3980), and Majuan (east; ⊠ Guangqumenwai Dajie, Chaoyang District, ☎ 010/6525–7877). Long distance buses are usually quite basic—much like an old-fashioned school bus—although some overnight buses now boast two decks with reclining seating.

By Plane
Beijing Capital Airport (☎ 010/6456–3604) is 25 km (16 mi) northeast of city center. It has outgrown its capacity to handle Beijing's burgeoning passenger loads, both international and domestic, and functions in near chaos during peak periods. A new, larger terminal is under construction south of the main building.

Departing international passengers must pay a Y90 **airport tax** (payable only in RMB) before check-in. Coupons are sold at booths inside the terminal and collected at the entrance to the main departure hall. After checking in, plan on long lines at immigration, especially in the morning.

BETWEEN THE AIRPORT AND CITY CENTER

The easiest way to get from Capital Airport to Beijing is by **hotel shuttle.** Most major hotels have representatives at the airport able to arrange a car or minivan. Departing visitors should pre-book transportation through their hotels.

The **taxi** queue is just outside the terminal beyond a small covered parking area. The line (usually long) moves quickly. Do not accept rides from drivers who try to coax you from the queue. These privateers are often crooks. At the head of the line, a dispatcher will give you your taxi's number, useful in case of complaints or forgotten luggage. Insist that drivers use their meters, and do not agree to negotiate a price. If the driver is unwilling to comply, feel free to change taxis. Most of the taxis that serve the airport are large models. Flag fall is Y12 (good for 3½ km) plus Y2 per additional km. Passengers are expected to pay the Y10 toll for the airport expressway. If you're caught in rush hour traffic, expect standing surcharges. In light traffic, it takes about 30 minutes to reach Beijing's eastern district. During the morning and evening commutes, allow at least 45 minutes. For the city center, expect a one-hour cab ride. After 11 PM, taxis charge a 20% late-night surcharge. There are no extra charges for luggage.

The **shuttle bus** (🚐 Y12) terminal is outside gate 5 of the terminal building. There are two routes (A or B) clearly marked in English and Chinese to indicate areas served. On board, stops are announced in English and Chinese. Route A runs between the airport and the Beijing railway station, stopping at the airport expressway/Third Ring Road intersection, Lufthansa Centre, Kunlun Hotel, Great Wall Sheraton Hotel, Dongzhimen subway station/Second Ring Road, Hong Kong Macau Center (Swissotel), Chaoyangmen subway station, and one block north of the Beijing train station/Beijing International Hotel. Route B runs from the airport to the CAAC ticket office on Changan Dajie. It travels west along the Third Ring Road, following it south to Changan Jie. Stops include the SAS Hotel, Asian Games Village, Friendship Hotel, and Shangri-La Hotel.

By Train

Beijing is served by four stations: the Beijing Main Station and the Beijing West, North, and South stations. Most domestic routes depart from the massive Beijing Xi Zhan (West Station; ✉ Lianhuachi Dong Lu, Haidian District, ☎ 010/6321–4269), Beijing's most modern, but some major city routes still depart the Beijing Zhan (Main Station; ✉ Beijing Zhan Jie, Dongcheng District, ☎ 010/6563–4422), as do international routes to Hong Kong or Siberia. Foreigners must buy tickets at the Main Station's International Passenger Booking Office. Tickets are sold up to five days in advance. Book early to insure a seat. Ticket office hours are 5:30–7:30 AM, 8 AM–5:30 PM, and 7 PM–12:30 AM.

Getting Around

By Bicycle

Beijing is made for pedaling. All of the city's main boulevards and many secondary streets have wide, well-defined bike lanes often separated from other traffic by an island with hedges or trees. If a flat tire or sudden brake failure strikes, seek out the nearest street-side mechanic (they're everywhere), easily identified by their bike parts and pumps.

By Bus

Getting on or off a Beijing city bus is often, quite literally, a fight. Buses are hot and crowded in summer and cold and crowded in winter. If you choose the bus—and you shouldn't—watch your belongings very carefully.

By Car

Drivers in China navigate by following road signs and asking directions. Most roads don't have names or numbers. Taxi drivers who don't know an exact location will find out what town a sight is near, drive to that town, and ask for specific directions.

By Pedicab

Pedicabs were once the vehicle of choice for Beijingers laden with a week's worth of grocery shopping or tourists eager for a street-eye city tour. Today, however, residents are wealthy enough to bundle their purchases into taxis, and the tourist trade has moved on to the tight schedules of air-conditioned buses. But pedicabs still can be hired outside the Friendship Store on Jianguomenwai Dajie and near major tourist sites. Be sure to negotiate the fare in advance, clarifying which currency will be used in payment (Y or US$), whether the fare is considered a one-way or round-trip (some drivers will demand return fares whether or not you come along), and whether it is for one person or two. Fares start at Y10 for short distances.

By Subway

Beijing's two subway lines are packed during rush hour but offer convenient travel on off-hours. There are two lines: one circles Beijing beneath the Second Ring Road and the other bisects the city east-to-west from Xidan to the western suburbs. The lines run close (but do not meet) near Fuxingmen. The subway runs from 5 AM to 10:30 PM daily. Fares are Y2 per ride for any distance.

By Taxi

There are three classes of taxis in Beijing. The cheapest—and most ubiquitous—are the *miandi* (breadloaf vans), tiny minivans usually painted bright yellow. These vehicles cost only Y10 at flag fall and must travel 10 km (6 mi) before the Y1.5 per km meter kicks in. While miandi are certainly a bargain, these people's taxis are often filthy and falling apart. Two other drawbacks: many miandi drivers are newcomers to Beijing and therefore don't know their way around the city; and miandi are banned from certain roads, so cross-city trips in them can take a whole lot longer than in bigger cabs. A second, and better, grade of taxi is the *xiali,* a domestically produced car reminiscent of the first Honda hatchbacks. Tall people find xialis cramped. Flag fall for these taxis is Y10.4 for the first 3½ km (2 mi) and Y1.6 per km thereafter. A 20% nighttime surcharge is added after 11 PM. At the top end are the sedans found waiting at the airport, major hotels, and large tourist sites. They're clean, comfortable, and expensive. Flag fall is Y12 for the first 3½ km (2 mi) and Y2 per km thereafter. A 20% nighttime surcharge kicks in at 11 PM. Be sure to check that the meter has been engaged (the meter is usually found near the gear shift) to avoid fare negotiations at your destination.

On Foot

Beijing is sprawling. City blocks are very large. To avoid arriving exhausted at sites that appeared deceptively close on the map, walk around sites rather than between them. Ration your foot time for Beijing's intriguing back alleys.

Contacts and Resources

Embassies

U.S. (⊠ 2 Xiushui Dongjie, Chaoyang District, ☎ 010/6532–3431 ext. 229 or 010/6532–3831 ext. 264, FAX 010/6532–2483). **Australia** (⊠ 21 Dongzhimenwai Dajie, Chaoyang District, ☎ 010/6532–2331, FAX 010/6532–3101). **Canada** (⊠ 19 Dongzhimenwai Dajie, Chaoyang District, ☎ 010/6532–3536, ℻ 010/6532–4972). **U.K.** (✉ 11 Guanghua Lu, Chaoyang District, ☎ 010/6532–1961, ℻ 010/6532–1937).

Emergencies

Call your embassy first (☞ *above*); embassy staff are available 24 hours a day to help handle emergencies and facilitate communication with local agencies. **Asia Emergency Assistance Center** (AEA; ✉ 2-1-1 Tayuan Diplomatic Office Bldg., 14 Liangmahe Nanlu, Chaoyang District, ☎ 010/6462–9112 during office hours, or 010/6462–9100 after hours) has 24-hour emergency and pharmacy assistance. **International Medical Clinic** (IMC; ✉ Beijing Lufthansa Center, Regis Office Building, Rm. 106, 50 Liagmaoqiao Lu, Chaoyang District, ☎ 010/6465–1561, or 010/1562–1563) has 24-hour emergency and pharmacy services, as well as a dental clinic. **Police** (☎ 110).

English-Language Bookstores

Foreign Languages Bookstore (✉ 235 Wangfujing Dajie, Dongcheng District, ☎ 010/6512–6922). **The Friendship Store** (✉ 17 Jianguomenwai Dajie, Chaoyang District, ☎ 010/6500–3311). Most major hotels now sell international newspapers and magazines.

Guided Tours

Every major hotel will offer guided tours to sites outside Beijing. Tour buses pick passengers up at their hotels. **China International Travel Service** (CITS; ✉ 28 Jianguomenwai Dajie, Chaoyang District, ☎ 010/6515–8570) is the official government agency. New travel agencies are springing up all the time in Beijing; ask at your hotel about alternatives to CITS.

The **Beijing Hutong Tourist Agency** (☎ 010/6524–8482 or through most hotels) offers the only guided pedicab tours of Beijing's back alleys. This half-day trip winds its way through what was once Beijing's most prestigious neighborhood, stops at the Drum and Bell Towers and finishes with tea at Prince Kung's Palace. These tours offer a glimpse of buildings usually closed to the public. Advance reservations are advised. Tours begin on Dianmexi Dajie near the back entrance of Beihai Park.

Visitor Information and Travel Agencies

China International Travel Service (CITS; ✉ 28 Jianguomenwai Dajie, Chaoyang District, ☎ 010/6515–8570), China's official travel agency, maintains offices in many hotels and at some tourist venues.

3 Northeastern China

Northeastern China contains within it just about every aspect of modern China. It has huge urban centers— some booming, some bust, wide-open country spaces, and wilderness, high mountains, and flat plains. The vast area runs from one of the cradles of Chinese civilization in the south almost to the wilds of Siberia in the north. It has witnessed the rise of the Manchu dynasty, Russian adventurism, European colonialism, Japanese invasion, Chinese resistance, and Cold War hostility. Architecture, strangely, provides the most fascinating evidence of this area's turbulent history, from the German houses in Qingdao to the onion domes of Harbin.

PRINCIPAL AMONG THE REGIONS within Northeastern China is Manchuria—what the Chinese call
Dongbei (the Northeast)—made up of the provinces
By David   of Liaoning, Jilin, and Heilongjiang. This land was home to China's
Murphy   last Imperial house, the Qing, who conquered Beijing in 1644 and ruled
China until the 1911 republican revolution brought about their col-
lapse. The Qing were Manchus, who still survive as a distinct ethnic
group in the Northeast, though an outsider would have great difficulty
in distinguishing them from the majority Han.

Until 1911 Han were forbidden to settle in Manchuria, and the area,
though agriculturally rich, was sparsely inhabited. In the 1920s, driven
by war and poverty, people flocked from neighboring Shandong
province across the Bohai Gulf to work as farmers or in the many Japanese factories that had been established in the puppet state of
Manchukuo. After the success of the 1949 Communist revolution,
China's new leader, Mao Zedong, encouraged people to fill the empty
parts of China. This resulted in another massive flood of settlers, again
mostly from Shandong, with the result that today many people from
these three northeasterly provinces claim Shandong as their *laojia* (ancestral home). The other provinces of the region, mountainous Shanxi
and the high-tech municipality of Tianjin, have their own identities.

Most outsiders who come here are on business. Tourism facilities are
not as plentiful as they are in other parts of the country, but often in
China this can be a blessing.

Pleasures and Pastimes

Dining
The variety and value of food to be encountered in this region are as
good as anywhere in China. Cheap, clean restaurants are the best bet.
The high turnover gives you a better chance of avoiding stomach bugs.
The more expensive ones, unless very popular, are rarely worth it. Every
city has its own special local dish. Many outlets specialize in dishes
from other provinces, notably Sichuan. The coastal cities, Qingdao,
Tianjin, and Dalian, enjoy a plentiful range of good seafood. Dalian
in particular has some of the best seafood in China. Farther north, hotpot is a great favorite; you can choose from any number of ingredients and spices to cook food at your own table. Snacks, including yogurt,
are available at street corners and are also quite tasty.

If you want to take a break from Chinese food, you'll find Korean and
Japanese street-front and hotel restaurants in many cities. For Western
food, it is better to stick to the restaurants in leading foreign-managed
or joint-venture hotels. Often these offer excellent value Western-style
buffet lunches.

WHAT TO WEAR
Dress in China is always casual, and reservations are unheard of in this
region, except in a few Japanese or Korean restaurants.

CATEGORY	COST*
$$$$	over $40
$$$	$20–$40
$$	$10–$20
$	under $10

Per person for a three-course meal, excluding tax, tips, and beverage.

Lodging

Nearly all hotels in this region are relatively modern and without any special character. Most state-run hotels are an extremely poor value; rooms are musty, service is poor, and facilities are inadequate—particularly given the price charged. Some even impose extra charges on foreigners. Western-, Hong Kong-, or Singaporean-managed hotels are far better. Occupancy is as low as 30% in some top-class hotels, and special deals are available; fax ahead to request the hotel's best rate. The table below is based on rack rates and significant reductions are readily available.

CATEGORY	COST*
$$$$	over $150
$$$	$110–$150
$$	$90–$110
$	under $90

For a standard double room with bath; no tax is charged.

Nightlife

In good weather the entire Chinese population seems to empty onto the streets or gather in public places at evening time. Young and old carry on a wide range of activities from ballroom dancing to badminton in the public squares and thoroughfares. Taking a stroll around these areas at night is hard to beat if you enjoy people-watching. Conventional nightlife is patchy. The karaoke plague is widespread, unfortunately, but there are signs that it has peaked.

Shopping

There are a number of places that are fun to look around and where curios may take your fancy. Among these is Ancient Culture Street in Tianjin and the Qingdao Antiques Market. Bargaining is advisable at all stalls and is possible in many stores.

Exploring Northeastern China

Of the three provinces of Dongbei, Jilin and Heilongjiang are heavily agricultural, while Liaoning, the more southerly of the three, is very industrial, home to many of China's big state-owned enterprises, which were built up during the 1950s and '60s.

Farther south lies Shandong province, through which the Yellow River flows to meet the sea. Lifeline of China's ancient civilization, the Yellow River has changed its course many times, but in recent years, hit by recurring drought, it has shrunk dramatically in its lower reaches.

To the north lies the municipality of Tianjin, a former treaty port filled with colonial architecture and now at the vanguard of Northern China's economic development, with numerous high-tech global companies.

To the west is Shanxi, which was once the political and cultural center of China. The geography is mountainous, something that was used to good effect by Communist guerrillas during the anti-Japanese war.

Great Itineraries

The itineraries below are based on train journeys, but a combination of rail and flight is possible on any tour of this region.

Numbers in the margin correspond to points of interest on the Northeastern China, Dalian, Qingdao, and Tianjin maps.

IF YOU HAVE 3 DAYS

The coastal cities of **Qingdao,** with its German colonial architecture, and **Dalian,** former colonial center and today one of China's smartest cities, offer an excellent weekend out from Beijing. Comfortable

overnight sleeper trains are available from Beijing, departing at night-
fall to either city. Stay one night in a hotel and take the train back to
Beijing the following night.

IF YOU HAVE 5 DAYS

From **Dalian** take the train to **Changchun** (about 8 hours), spend a couple of days here, and on the way back take a look at **Shenyang,** one of
China's great industrial cities. From Shenyang take a day trip to the steel
town of **Anshan,** a sooty city of industrial dinosaurs that evokes Man-
chester in the heyday of England's industrial revolution. From Dalian
there are departures to Beijing (train, plane) and Shandong (boat, train).
Alternatively you can take a few days to explore Shandong province.
Starting in **Jinan,** go to Confucius's birthplace, **Qufu,** and climb famous
Taishan. Then take the train to **Qingdao** and enjoy the seaside and German colonial architecture.

IF YOU HAVE 8 OR MORE DAYS

Spend a couple of days in **Harbin;** then move south by train (4 or 5
hours between cities) to stay two days each in **Changchun,** then
Shenyang, and finally **Dalian,** on the tip of the Liaodong peninsula.
These four cities combined give a very full flavor of today's China. **Tianjin,** two hours from Beijing, merits a trip of its own. **Datoug** is not close
to the other cities in the region. Visit **Jilin** if you have extra time.

When to Tour Northeastern China

Spring is probably the best time; the emergence of natural colors in
springtime is a heartening relief from the unrelenting grayness. Fall is
next-best, when the countryside takes on rich natural hues and the climate remains comfortable. At the lone winter attraction, Harbin's Ice
Festival, you can view impressive ice carvings, but there is not much
else to do. In many cities, restaurants and other service- or visitor-ori-
ented businesses close early in winter. Summer is hot and humid. Good
hotels have air-conditioning, but many taxis and most offices do not.

HEILONGJIANG

Heilongjiang is China's northeasternmost province. It has a land area
of nearly 470,000 sq km (181,500 sq mi) and more than 35 million
inhabitants. Relatively underpopulated for a Chinese province, it is making a name as an outdoor destination, with an emphasis on fishing and
bird-watching. Heilongjiang (Black Dragon River) was one of the
points where imperial European expansion (in this case Tsarist Russia) met imperial China in the last century. Heilongjiang belonged to
the vast swath of empty territory in east Asia that was colonized this
century by European Russians and Han Chinese. Native tribes that survived in Heilongjiang, for example the Oroqen, are now happy modern citizens of the PRC, at least that's what the offficial press says.

The province is renowned for its rich black soil and is a major producer of grain. The Heilong River, known to the Russians as the Amur,
provides the boundary between the province and Russia, though even
today the border is not fully delineated.

Harbin

❶ *16 hours northeast of Beijing by train and just over 2 hours by plane.*

Harbin, on the banks of the Songhua River, takes its name from the
Manchu word *Alejin,* suggesting fame and reputation. It is the capital
of the province and was once a Russian railway terminus for the line to
Vladivostok. The city bounced between the Russians and the Japanese
until after World War II. Today, Russians are again on the scene; this

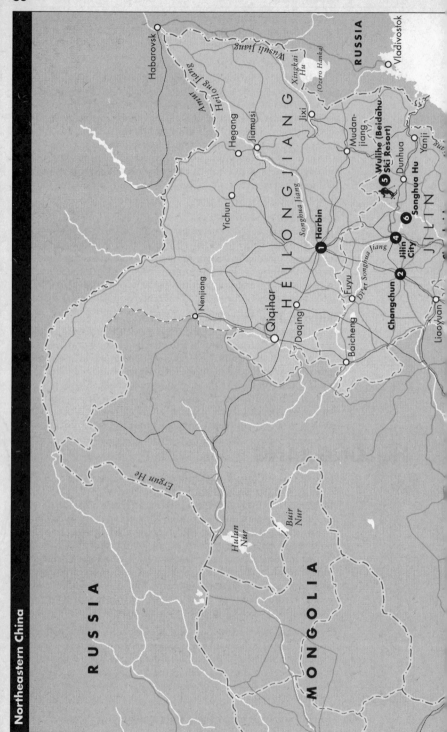

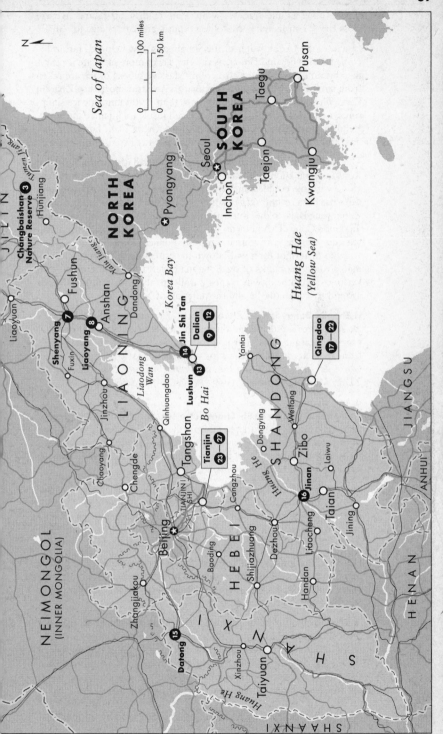

time as tourists and traders. Winters are cold; temperatures average close to −4°F in January, the coldest month, and can plunge to −36°F.

In winter the frozen water of the Songhua is now helping Harbin become famous beyond China, as the city's ever-more intricate ice carvings become a significant attraction. Massive blocks of ice are taken from the river by mechanical excavators and transported to Zhaolin Park. There they are carved into more than 1,000 fantastic ice sculptures, many with colored lanterns placed inside to enhance the effect. Exhibits regularly include versions of the Great Wall, famous pagodas, and the Xian warriors. The festival usually begins on January 5.

The **Daoli** district contains numerous buildings dating from the era of Russian domination in Harbin. Many have been restored in recent years, along with the cobblestone streets. The area centered on **Zhongyang Dajie** has been revitalized as a commercial district. A good stroll is down Zhongyang Dajie to the river embankment and the huge **Fanghong Jinian Ta** (Flood Control Monument) where people practice tai chi in the morning and *yang ge* (a rhythmic traditional dance) in the evenings. Here you can turn right for a walk down the **esplanade** (a favorite kite-flying spot) on the banks of the Songhua or left through the **night market** (mostly clothes), which runs parallel to the river and then winds around to Tongjiang Jie and the junction of Youyi Lu.

Li Zhaolin Gongyuan (Li Zhaolin Park) is where the bulk of Harbin's ice sculptures are displayed during the Ice Festival. At other times of year it a pleasant place to stroll—you can barely hear the honking horns from here. Its weekend outdoor amusement park includes a Ferris wheel. ⊠ *Corner of Youyi Lu and Shangzhi Dajie, Daoli district.* ⌨ *Y1.* ☉ *May–Sept., daily 7 AM–9 PM; Oct.–Apr., daily 8–7.*

About five minutes' walk east of the Flood Control Monument (☞ *above*), **Dao Wai Jie Yu Shi Chang** (Dao Wai Street Fish Market) is not very well stocked in winter, but during the rest of the year a wide range of tropical fish (in jam jars and trays) are on sale here, as well as caged birds, flowers, teapots, raw tobacco, and much more. ⊠ *Dao Wai Jie, east of Flood Control monument.*

☺ **Youle Yuan** (Youle Park) has kiddie rides, an indoor children's playground, and a large roller coaster. On the street leading up to the park entrance is a monastery that has been heavily restored; the pavements around it are lined with stalls selling Buddhist tokens, trinkets, and joss sticks. ⊠ *Dongda Zhi Jie.* ⌨ *Y2.* ☉ *May–Sept., daily 8 AM–9 PM.*

In winter, Harbinites build snow sculptures at **Taiyandao.** The park is home to a small military museum and an amusement park. It is a favorite walking and jogging spot for locals. ⊠ *North of city, across river, to right-hand side of bridge.*

Harbin has quite a quite a few surviving Christian **churches,** many of them architectural as well as cultural novelties in the remote reaches of northern China. The **Russian Orthodox church** (⊠ 268 Dong Dazhi Jie; service, Sat. 2 PM), built of red brick with cupolas, stands in its own grounds, a reminder of the time when Russians dominated Harbin. Across the street is a rather unimpressive **Catholic church** (☉ daily). Farther up the road, also in its own grounds, the busy **Protestant church** (⊠ 252 Dong Dazhi Jie; ☉ Wed., Sat., Sun.) built in 1910 by German missionaries is a thriving center for the Harbin Protestant community. One of the most impressive churches in Harbin is the now bricked-up and burned-out **St. Sofia's Cathedral** (⊠ Tou Long Lu, off Zhaolin Jie), built in 1907, which until the 1960s served the more than 100 Russian residents of Harbin. The cathedral was closed down when the Russians were returned to Russia during the Cultural Revolution. The building's huge green onion dome atop a red brick nave is striking in its incongruity with its surroundings. The cathedral is contained by a tight square of old six-story workers' apartments and a timber yard.

Dining and Lodging

Note: In Harbin particularly—though the practice can be seen elsewhere in the Northeast—red lanterns are hung outside Chinese restaurants to denote cost and quality. The greater the number—the maximum is usually five—the higher the cost and quality. Blue lanterns denote Hui (a Muslim minority) restaurants. The Qianjin district contains a number of fish restaurants, regarded highly by locals.

$$ ✕ **Million Land House Restaurant.** This large open-plan restaurant is one of the best in Harbin. It serves some excellent seafood, including pearl fish cooked in a light batter and dipped in salt; scallops; and North Pole shrimp, which is first cooked and then frozen before being served. Also on the menu is frozen tofu. ✉ *169 Zhongshan Lu, Nangang District,* ☎ *0451/2611–111. No credit cards.*

$$ ✕ **Shun Feng.** This 24-hour restaurant is plainly furnished with wooden tables and chairs. It specializes in beef hotpot. ✉ *107 Wen Chang Jie, Nangang District,* ☎ *0451/2688–888. No credit cards.*

$ ✕ **Huamei Restaurant.** Opposite the Modern Hotel on Zhongyang Dajie, this novel restaurant was built in the 1920s by Russian Jews. Of the three floors, much the best is the second, with its wooden floor and high, ornate ceiling supported by Greek-style columns. The walls are hung with pastoral Russian scenes. Russian food is served. Cold dishes include caviar and sour cucumber and thick slabs of white bread accompanied by plates of jam. The main courses are Russian, Chinese, and French—chicken and fish au gratin, braised mutton chops, and shashlik à la russe are among the main courses. ✉ *112 Zhongyang Dajie, Daoli District,* ☎ *0451/4641–648. No credit cards.*

$ ✕ **Jin Qiao.** Residents recommend the seafood hotpot in this simple restaurant. ✉ *Jing Jie, no phone. No credit cards.*

$ ✕ **Lao Du Yiqu.** Here you'll find excellent *jiaozi* (dumplings). Look for the big "1" sign outside. ✉ *Shisan Lu (13 St.), off Zhaoyang Dajie, no phone. No credit cards.*

$ ✕ **Lao Guangdong.** The fare—Beijing duck and Cantonese food, including dim sum—is sure to please. ✉ *Youyi Jie and Jingwei Jie, no phone. No credit cards.*

$$ 🏨 **Holiday Inn.** This modern hotel is well located in the Daoli district. Standard rooms are a little dark but otherwise comfortable. They are equipped with a minibar and color TV with movie channels. The restaurants serve Chinese or Western food. ✉ *90 Jingwei Jie, Daoli District, 150010,* ☎ *0451/4226–666,* FAX *0451/4221–661. 144 rooms. 2 restaurants, bar, health club, nightclub. AE, DC, MC, V.*

$ 🏨 **Gloria Inn.** Large and modern, this hotel occupies an impressive building constructed in the old style near the Flood Control Monument. Standard rooms are bright and comfortable and are equipped with a minibar, refrigerator, and satellite TV. There is a Cantonese restaurant, and a coffee shop serving Western and Asian food. ✉ *257 Zhongyang Dajie, Daoli District, 150010,* ☎ *0451/4638–855,* FAX *0451/4638–533. 304 rooms. 2 restaurants, nightclub, business services. AE, DC, MC, V.*

$ 🏨 **Hong Kong Palace Hotel.** Overlooking Zhaolin Park, this friendly hotel belongs to the same owner as Beijing's Jiangguo Hotel. Rooms are clean and bright with a minibar and satellite TV. The restaurant serves Chinese food and the café offers Western and Southeast Asian cuisines. ✉ *210 Shangzhi Jie, 150010,* ☎ *0451/4691–388,* FAX *0451/4610–894. 106 rooms. 2 restaurants, business services. AE, DC, MC, V.*

$ ▦ **Modern Hotel.** The rooms in this newly renovated Russian-era hotel are comfortable, with high ceilings and drapes suspended to create a four-poster effect on the beds. Try to get a room overlooking fashionable Zhongyang Dajie, unless you are a light sleeper. There are also simply furnished rooms. The restaurants serve Western or Chinese cuisine. ⊠ *89 Zhongyang Dajie, 150010, ☎ 0451/4615–846,* FAX *0451/4614–997. 160 rooms. 2 restaurants, bar, business services. AE, DC, MC, V.*

Nightlife

Harbin nightlife is fairly quiet. One place that's worth a visit is **Hans International Bar** (⊠ 254 Zhongshan Jie, ☎ 0451/2669–999), which is spacious and tastefully decorated, serves good beer, and doesn't have a karaoke facility. Local musicians playing various styles (e.g. classical, jazz) provide the entertainment.

Shopping

In addition to the area around Zhongyang Dajie and the night market near the Flood Control Monument, there are a couple of other places in Harbin of interest to shoppers. The outdoor **Minmao Shi Chang** (Minmao Market) deals mostly in clothes but also sells souvenirs, antiques, fishing rods, and an inordinate number of binoculars, telescopes, and hand-held periscopes. Soviet-era stamps, watches, ginseng, and dried penises—several varieties—are also available. The market is busiest on the weekends and many Russians come from the border city of Khabarovsk to buy goods for resale at home. The touts and money-changers speak Russian to foreigners.

A massive bomb shelter built at a time of high tension between China and Soviet Russia is now home to a booming shopping center in the **Nangang** district (⊠ Dongda Zhi Jie), where clothes, leather, and household goods are available.

Heilongjiang A to Z

Arriving and Departing

BY PLANE

Regular flights link Harbin with major Chinese cities including Beijing and Shanghai.

BY TRAIN

There are regular rail connections between Harbin and Changchun (4 hours) and points south, including Shenyang, Dalian, and Beijing.

Getting Around

Taxis are the easiest way to get around **Harbin.** Flag fall is Y10, and all cabs have a meter. In Daoli district, going by foot gives you more time to appreciate the area's unique architecture.

Contacts and Resources

CITS (⊠ Modern Hotel, 2nd floor, 129 Zhongyang Dajie, Harbin 150010, ☎ 0451/4687–875.

JILIN

Jilin is the smallest of the three provinces that together make up the Chinese region of Dongbei. It is bordered by North Korea to the southeast, Liaoning to the south, Inner Mongolia to the west, and Heilongjiang to the north. It has a population of about 24 million, the bulk of whom are Han; sizable numbers of ethnic Koreans live in the Korean border area.

Changchun

❷ *1½ hours by plane or 12 hours by train north of Beijing.*

Changchun (Long Spring) is a name based more in hope than reality, given the long, cold winters of China's northeast. Under Japanese rule from 1931 to 1945, Changchun was renamed Xijing (New Capital) when it was made capital of the puppet state of Manchukuo. It is now the provincial capital of Jilin. After the 1949 revolution Changchun was established as China's very own motor city—home to First Auto Works (FAW), which today dominates industry here. Chinese President Jiang Zemin worked here as a factory director in the late 1950s.

The pleasant city of 2.6 million has wide avenues lined with evergreen trees.

In **Weihuanggong** (The Puppet Emperor's Palace), Puyi, China's last emperor before the 1911 revolution, was set up by Japan to be the nominal head of the state of Manchukuo. Appropriately, the palace of the puppet emperor has a puppet feel to it. The buildings are more suited to a wealthy merchant than to the successor to a nearly 300-year-old dynasty and offer no sense that power resided here. Puyi's former house is now a museum documenting his life from childhood through his role as a pawn of the Japanese and then after Liberation to his conversion as a citizen of the new China. Some of the rooms are fitted out in period furniture. Photos are on display in an adjacent courtyard house—one shows Hitler and the Manchukuo economic minister shaking hands during the latter's trip to Europe. Some torture instruments, including a bed of nails, depict the savagery of the Japanese war in China. There are also details on the notorious Camp 731, where crude experiments were carried out on prisoners of war. Upstairs in the same building is Puyi's office and a banquet room. Next door is the Painting Hall of the Imperial Palace, which houses a display of stuffed animals and dinosaur remains. ⊠ *Guangfu Lu,* ☎ *0431/5667–139.* ▨ *Y15.* ⊙ *Daily 9–4:30.*

The **Changchundianying Zhipianchang** (Changchun Film Studio), home to a large slice of China's movie industry, contains screen props of palaces, castles, and scenery. Changchun hosts an international film festival every second year. The next festival is scheduled for August 1998. ⊠ *92 Zhen Yang Lu,* ☎ *0431/7628–804.* ▨ *Y25.* ⊙ *Daily 8:30–5.*

Bai Quen Di Yi Ke Daxue (Bethune First Medical University) is named for Canadian surgeon Norman Bethune, who was with the Republicans in 1930s Spain before coming to China to work with the Communists at their base in Yanan in Shaanxi province. Built between 1933 and 1936, the university was modeled on the parliament building in Tokyo; during the Japanese occupation, it housed the Manchukuo Parliament. The ground floor shop stocks a range of ginseng and medicinal products. The prize of the tour is on the third floor, where a collection of specimens of human body parts, numbering more than 4,000, is stored. Visitors are guided past shelves and row upon row of formaldehyde jars containing some fairly gruesome samples of diseased bodies and body parts. It is interesting, though not for the overly squeamish. ⊠ *Xin Min Jie, next to Wenhua Guangchang and opposite HQ of Military Department of Manchukuo government.* ⊙ *Daily 9–7.*

Banruo Si (Banruo Monastery) was established in 1921, turned into a cardboard box factory in 1966 at the beginning of the Cultural Revolution, and restored to its role as a monastery after 1982. Forty monks now live here. The Grand Hall occupies the center of a courtyard complex that includes the reception, meditation, dining, and head monk's halls. In the Great Hall you can write down a prayer, strike a bell, and hope your prayer is answered. Inside the main gate are two drum towers. The drums are sounded on the arrival of an important visitor. ⊠ *Changchun Lu.* ☉ *Apr.–Oct., daily 8–3; Nov.–Mar., daily 8–2.*

A monument in the center of **Renmin Guangchang** (People's Square)—actually a circular green area—commemorates the Soviet liberation of Changchun from the Japanese in 1945. It is a great place for people-watching in the evenings or early mornings. ⊠ *Bounded by Renmin Lu, Changchun Lu, Minkang Lu, and Xian Lu.*

Around **Xingfa Lu**, on pleasant tree-lined avenues—good for strolling—are a number of buildings dating from the Japanese era, now occupied by the current provincial government.

Dining and Lodging

$$$ ✕ **Rongda Seafood Restaurant.** The restaurant's tropical feel comes from the fact that many of the interior fittings are made of bamboo. A whole wall at the rear of the restaurant is lined with cages and glass fish tanks containing snakes; king crabs; prince crabs; fire, red, and green dragon lobsters; rock fish; shark; and dozens of other varieties of fish. ⊠ *59 Tongzhi Lu,* ☎ *0431/5655–666. No credit cards.*

$$$ ✕ **Tai San Hotel Korean Restaurant.** On the ground floor of the Tai San Hotel this dimly lit open-plan restaurant serves familiar Korean food, including spring onion pancakes and ginseng chicken soup. ⊠ *35 Tongzhi Lu,* ☎ *0431/5634–991. AE, DC, MC, V.*

$ ✕ **De Li Mi Fish Restaurant.** This basement restaurant specializes in carp steamed with vegetables and herbs, cabbage fried with spices, and Sichuan *tanrou* (stewed pork, beef, and chicken). The framed photos of sultry western maids on the walls are probably intended to add a touch of cosmopolitanism. ⊠ *61 Renmin Lu,* ☎ *0431/2725–385. No credit cards.*

$ ✕ **Eastern King of Dumpling Restaurant.** Walk the length of this unpretentious restaurant, which has several sections, to see the chefs rolling the dough and preparing the fillings for the thousands of tasty jiaozi served here daily. You can mix your own dip with mustard, garlic, chili, soy sauce, and vinegar. Try the *qin cai jiaozi* (dumplings filled with vegetables and fresh chopped ginger). ⊠ *59 Gongnong Lu,* ☎ *0431/5688–800. No credit cards.*

$ ✕ **Mao Jia Wan.** This is a red restaurant in every sense. Named for Mao Zedong's home in Shaoshan, Hunan province, it is dedicated to his memory. Communist memorabilia decorates the walls, and the waiters are dressed as Red Guards. Immediately inside the front door is a statue of Mao, in front of which is an altar complete with smoking joss sticks. The wall at the back of the restaurant is bedecked with Red Guard badges in the shape of two red flags and a line wishing Chairman Mao 10,000 years of life. The excellent food includes Mao's favorite dish, *hong shao rou* (a Hunan dish of pork fat served with Chinese cabbage). Also a house specialty is a spicy tofu dish. ⊠ *Qinghua Lu,* ☎ *0431/5622–206. No credit cards.*

$ ✕ **Tongda Restaurant.** Marked by garish plastic greenery draped from ceiling beams, it does, however, serve good northeastern cuisine, including stewed pork, and such southern imports as spare ribs steamed in lotus leaves. ⊠ *60 Tongzhi Lu,* ☎ *0431/5632–681. No credit cards.*

$$$$ ⊞ **Shangri La.** Changchun's best hotel is modern, centrally located, stylish, and charming throughout. The widespread use of wood paneling in the public areas and the friendly staff give it a slightly old-world feel. All rooms have a color TV and in-house movies, minibar, refrig-

erator, 24-hour room service, a full-size executive desk, and fax, phone, and personal computer outlets. There are both Chinese and Western restaurants. ✉ *9 Xian Lu, 130061,* ☎ *0431/8981–818,* FAX *0431/ 8981–919. 458 rooms. 3 restaurants, bar, pool, tennis, health club, business services. AE, MC, V.*

$$$ 🏨 **Changchun Nobel Hotel.** This 25-floor hotel is the only one in northeast China that has a Thai restaurant. The spacious lobby gleams with its polished stone floor and pillars. The elegant rooms have color TVs with in-house movie channels and 24-hour room service. ✉ *135 Renmin Lu, 130021,* ☎ *0431/5622–888,* FAX *0431/5665–522. 300 rooms. 3 restaurants, bar, pool, bowling, health club, business services. AE, MC, V.*

$$ 🏨 **Changchun Overseas Chinese Hotel.** Overlooking South Lake, this was the top hotel in Changchun until newer hotels arrived. Rooms are fitted with color TV and minibar. There are both Western and Chinese restaurants. Service is not outstanding. ✉ *1 Hu Bin Lu, 130022,* ☎ *0431/5388–719,* FAX *0431/5386–099. 3 restaurants. AE, MC, V.*

$$ 🏨 **South Lake Hotel.** This post-revolution hotel renovated in 1991 has high ceilings and the musty smell of Chinese state-run hostelries. The rooms are average, but the hotel is set in huge wooded grounds with guest buildings and villas scattered around. Many of the villas are occupied by VW staff from the FAW factory. Top leaders stay here when they come to Changchun. ✉ *2 Nan Hu Lu, 130032,* ☎ *0431/5683– 571,* FAX *0431/5682–559. 250 rooms. AE, DC, MC, V.*

$$ 🏨 **Swiss Belhotel.** Its revolving Hotpot restaurant is worth a visit for the view it offers of the city, or at least the FAW-owned part of it nearby. Standard rooms are spacious, well furnished, and have color TVs with in-house movies, minibar and refrigerator, and an executive desk. The restaurants serve Chinese or Western food. ✉ *39 Chuang Ye Da Jie, 130011,* ☎ *0431/5988–888,* FAX *0431/5989–999. 230 rooms. 3 restaurants, bar, pool, tennis court, health club, business services. AE, MC, V.*

Nightlife and the Arts

The **Cultural and Entertainment Center** (✉ Near junction of Renmin Lu and Jiefang Lu) frequently puts on plays, all in Chinese.

A number of bars have opened in Changchun recently, some of them with live music. **Again Pub** (✉ 72 Changchun Lu between Renmin Guangchang and Banruo Si monastery, ☎ 0431/8918–684) is busy with live music and a young Chinese crowd. **Fridays Bar** (✉ 3 Xian Lu, ☎ 0431/8923–364), well designed, with large amounts of wood and a small stage area for live music, is popular with young Chinese. **Second Home** (✉ across from Shangri La and down side of International Building) is a favorite for foreigners; on weekends you'll see a crowd of German auto workers ordering Johnny Walker Black by the bottle and singing Bayern Munich football songs.

Outdoor Activities and Sports

Changchun is home to the Jilin Tigers (✉ Renmin Lu), one of the stars of the CNBA (China National Basketball Alliance, ☎ 010/6501– 9474); they compete against the likes of the Beijing Lions, Guangzhou Rams, and Shanghai Nanyang. The season runs from November to March and games are played on Tuesday and Friday evenings.

Shopping

DEPARTMENT STORES

The most modern department store in Changchun, **The Mall** (✉ International Commercial Building), is opposite the railway station. **Changbai Da Sha** (✉ Renmin Lu) is another department store. The **International Trade Center** (✉ Renmin Lu) has a range of depart

store goods. The **Friendship Store** (⊠ Ziyou Lu), not the best department store in town, does sell Chinese paintings and furniture.

MARKETS

The best place for souvenir buying in Changchun is at the four-story
Guwan shichang (antiques market; ⊠ Qing Ming Jie opposite northeast corner of Banruo Si). The ground floor is taken up with stamps
and phone cards; the stairwell to the second floor is lined with metal
and ceramic badges from the Cultural Revolution. The second floor
has more stamps and phone cards plus coins, banknotes, and second-
hand cameras. The third floor houses paintings, calligraphy posters,
carved jade, wood and walnut carvings, wall clocks, phonographs, and
a whole shop dedicated to Mao paraphernalia.

Guilin Lu Market is a large indoor market for one-stop shopping. Meat,
fruit, and vegetables are displayed in open stalls, as well as fish of all
kinds—brought from Dalian—cigarettes and spices, alcohol, tinned
foods, and household hardware.

In the Guangfu Lu vicinity is a large **indoor wholesale market** selling
everything from household furniture to Pepsi, which is made locally.
The streets nearby are lined with stalls. The **French Bakery** (⊠ Longli
Lu, beside Nobel Hotel), bakes reasonable breads.

Side Trips from Changchun

Jingyue Hu (Clear Moon Lake) was built by the Japanese as a reservoir to serve Changchun. It lies in a large pine-wooded area where horse
riding and boating facilities are available. A hotel and villas are concentrated near the entrance to the area; on the far side of the lake is a
practice ski slope. ⊠ *20 min. southeast of city center by car.*

Kalun Hu (Kalun Lake) offers boating facilities. ⊠ *30 min northeast
of Changchun.*

Changbaishan Nature Reserve

★ ❸ *300 km (185 mi) southeast of Changchun or Jilin.*

The main attraction in this huge forest reserve is **Tianchi** (Heavenly Pool),
a lake in the crater of a now extinct volcano, on the Chinese-North
Korean border. Sacred to Korean culture, it draws thousands of South
Korean visitors every year and offers spectacular views, particularly
in autumn and winter. The area is part of the Yanbian Korean Autonomous Prefecture and is home to large numbers of ethnic Koreans.
The lower slopes are densely wooded, but vegetation becomes sparse
higher up. Bathing in hot springs and hiking are just two of the activities possible here. ⊠ *Tours available from Changchun or Jilin through
CITS; 3-day trips early June–early Sept.*

Jilin City

❹ *2½ hours by car or train east of Changchun.*

Jilin City, on the banks of the winding Songhua River, is the second-largest
city in the province but small by Chinese standards, home to only 1.3
million people. Although it is an industrial center, local authorities are
making a determined effort to draw tourists by promoting winter activities. Ski resorts around the city, an ice festival, and the phenomenon
of ice-rimmed trees are all being peddled as worthy attractions.

The twin spires of the Gothic-style **Catholic Church** reach nearly 150
ft. Catholics first arrived in Jilin province in 1898 and began construction
of the church in 1917. Its doors opened in 1926, and it still serves the

local Catholic community, who come in large numbers for the main Christian festivals. ✉ *Song Jiang Lu,* ☎ *0432/2025–142.*

The city is set in picturesque lake and mountain scenery, such as that in **Bei Shan Gongyuan** (North Mountain Park). On the south side of the park's lake are a number of pavilions. The main attraction here is the **Guan Di Si** (Guan Emperor Temple), founded in 1701 and named 50 years later by the emperor Qian Long for one of his predecessors. Among several lesser temples nearby are the **San Wang Miao** (Three Emperor Temple) and the **Yao Wang Miao** (King of Medicine Temple). ✉ *West side of city behind Beishan Railway station,* ☎ *0432/4841–741.*

Jilin has made a virtue out of ugly industrial development in the form of its **rime trees.** A hydroelectric plant, which supplies power to Jilin's industries, takes in cold water from the Songhua River and expels warm water. The vapor, which rises from the river as it flows along in the depths of winter, freezes on the trees overhanging the river bank, resulting in the sort of picturesque scene beloved by Japanese, Korean, and Chinese tourists. ✉ *Take No. 9 bus from roundabout north of Xiguan Hotel on Songjiang Lu to Hydroelectric Plant.*

Dining and Lodging

$ ✕ **Dong Sheng Islamic Restaurant.** This two-story restaurant serves traditional Hui food, such as lamb, beef, and noodle dishes. ✉ *Tianjin Lu (opposite Xin Hua Theater),* ☎ *0432/2439–188. No credit cards.*

$ ✕ **Hao Meng Gourmet City.** The house specialties are "wild chicken" and venison. There is one open-plan dining area on the ground floor and seven private rooms upstairs. ✉ *33 Guangzhou Lu,* ☎ *0432/2456–978. No credit cards.*

$ ✕ **Xin Yuan Jiao Zhi Restaurant.** Jiaozi and northeastern dishes are the specialty in this white two-story restaurant. ✉ *115 He Nan Lu,* ☎ *0432/2024–393. No credit cards.*

$ ✕ **Zhong Hua Restaurant.** This two-story restaurant has a number of private rooms upstairs and an open plan eating area on the ground floor. It serves a range of Chinese dishes. ✉ *Zero Building, Chao Yang Lu,* ☎ *0432/2448–788. No credit cards.*

$$ 🏨 **Jilin Crystal Hotel (aka Rime Hotel).** On the banks of the Songhua River and near the foot of scenic Longtan mountain, this seven-story hotel has a short, sloping roof. Rooms are equipped with TV and a minibar. There are both Western and Chinese restaurants. ✉ *29 Longtan Lu, 132021,* ☎ *0432/3986–200,* FAX *0432/3986–501. 113 rooms. 2 restaurants, bar, pool, bowling, fitness center. AE, DC, MC, V.*

$ 🏨 **Jiangcheng Hotel.** This seven-story hotel has the huge gleaming lobby common in China's newer hotels. It is located beside Qingnian Park on the banks of the Songhua River. Rooms are equipped with TV. ✉ *4 Jiangwan Lu, 132001,* ☎ *0432/2457–721;* FAX *0432/2458–973. Restaurant, pool, health center, business services. AE, MC, V.*

$ 🏨 **Yinhe Hotel.** The lobby in this Hong Kong joint-venture hotel is all bright lights and gleaming surfaces. Rooms are equipped with satellite TV. Standard rooms are small. Both Western and Chinese food is available. ✉ *79 Songjiang Lu, 132011,* ☎ *0432/4841–780,* FAX *0432/4841–621. 174 rooms. 2 restaurants, business services. AE, DC, MC, V.*

Shopping

Jilin Department Store (✉ 179 Jilin Lu, ☎ 0432/2455–488) has four floors of household goods and food. **East Shopping Building** (✉ 131 Henan Lu, ☎ 0432/2024–831) is an all-purpose shopping center with an emphasis on domestic appliances and clothing.

Side Trips from Jilin City

❺ **Beidahu Ski Resort,** 65 km (40 mi) from the city center, has five slopes. Snow stays on the ground here for 160 days of the year. The resort has a small hotel and restaurants that serve Western and Muslim food. ⊠ *Wu Li He Town, Yong Ji County.* ☎ *0432/42–02–168.*

The Songhua River flows from the Changbaishan mountains into long,
❻ narrow **Song Hua Hu** (Song Hua Lake) before continuing on its way about 24 km (15 mi) southeast of the city center. It was built as a reservoir between 1937 and 1943. Boating facilities are available on the lake amid beautiful natural surroundings. ⊠ *For tours: 105 Jilin Jie, Jilin,* ☎ *0432/4654–147.*

Jilin A to Z

Arriving and Departing

BY BUS

Buses from **Jilin** to Changchun depart every 20 minutes during the day from the long-distance bus station, a block west of the train station (☞ By Train, *below*).

BY PLANE

Changchun airport is 30 minutes northwest of the city center. Regular flights link it with Beijing, Shanghai, Guangzhou, Shenzhen, and less frequently, Hong Kong and Irkutsk in Siberia. **Jilin City** airport (☎ 0432/4542–60) is 25 km (15 mi) outside the city and has scheduled flights to Beijing, Shanghai, Guangzhou and Shenyang, Dalian and Harbin.

BY TRAIN

The **Changchun** railway station is about 15 minutes from downtown. Trains link it with Harbin, Shenyang, Dalian, and Beijing regularly. **Jilin City** train station (⊠ off Yanan Lu, ☎ 0432/4545–29) is served by trains from Beijing, Shenyang, Dalian, Harbin, and Changchun.

Getting Around

In both Changchun and Jilin taxis are inexpensive and the most convenient means of transportation. For longer trips outside the cities, check with the hotels or tour operators. On foot, Changchun's wide, tree-lined streets provide some reasonably pleasant walks, notably in the areas around Xingfa Lu and Renmin Guangchang.

Contacts and Resources

EMERGENCIES

Changchun: Hospital (⊠ 148 Ziyou Lu, ☎ 0431/4646–924; open 24 hours; foreigners' ward). State-owned medicine shop (⊠ Tongzhi Lu; open 24 hours; stocks Chinese-style Western medicines). Lobby shop, Shangri La Hotel (some Western medicines).

VISITOR INFORMATION AND GUIDED TOURS

Changchun: Changchun Overseas Tourist Corporation (⊠ 37 Jiefang Lu, ☎ 0431/8692–002, FAX 0431/8692–001); China Jilin Overseas Tourist Corporation (⊠ 14 Xinmin Lu, ☎ 0431/5671–266); China Travel Service (⊠ 8 Nancang Lu, ☎ 0431/8569–519). The better hotels can also provide basic local information. **Jilin City**: CITS (⊠ 2 Jiangwan Lu, ☎ 0432/4567–86, FAX 0432/4567–87.

LIAONING

Liaoning is the most southerly of the three provinces that make up Dongbei, or the Northeast. Home to a large percentage of China's state-owned industry, the province was better off than many during the post-revolution period when steel mills and a wide range of manufacturing industries were set up. Then it was China's powerhouse. Nowadays state-owned industry is in terminal decline, teetering under the strong winds of market reform. Unemployment is rife, and the province has so far failed to attract the levels of investment that have allowed the other great industrial center, Shanghai, to create new jobs to replace old ones. The one success story in Liaoning, Dalian is blessed by natural and administrative advantages—among them a port and preferential tax breaks—but it too is being limited by the poverty of its hinterland.

Shenyang

❼ *280 km (170 mi) southwest of Changchun; 600 km (370 mi) northeast of Beijing.*

The modern provincial capital Shenyang (formerly Mukden) became the capital of Manchuria under the warrior king Nurhachi in the 16th century. In 1644 when the Manchus took Beijing and founded the Qing Dynasty, which ruled China until the 1911 revolution, Manchuria remained a place apart from the rest of China, and Mukden remained its capital. Mao Zedong's new China added to the industry the Japanese had established here and Shenyang was a key city in the industrial drive of the 1950s and '60s. With the switch to market reforms Shenyang has lost its edge to the busy coastal cities. Today it is a place of high unemployment and industrial decay.

Although no beauty spot, Shenyang has something to offer in the way of imperial tombs and the old Manchu Palace, which despite the hype bears hardly any resemblance to Beijing's Forbidden City.

Zhongshan Guangchang (Sun Yatsen Square) makes for a great after-dinner stroll, weather permitting. By 8 PM it is filled with Shenyang citizens of every generation. Old people, mostly women, do *yang ge*— a rhythmic traditional dance done to a drumbeat—the middle-aged practice their ballroom dancing, the young play casual badminton or *tian jizi* (a kind of Hakki sack), and teenagers disco dance to a boom box. Hawkers sell everything from books to yogurt, and kids rent roller skates. All of this is conducted at the foot of a huge fiberglass statue of the late Chairman Mao surrounded by heroic workers, peasants and soldiers. Mao's majestic wave is interpreted by the local youngsters as him trying to flag down a taxi. ⊠ *Nanjing Jie and Zhongshan Lu.*

Wu Ai Shishang (Five Loves Wholesale Market), set up in 1983, is a great place to see the free market in operation. It contains literally acres of stalls, mostly clothes but also shoes and light consumer goods. Most of the goods are made locally. Russians come to buy and bring the goods home for resale. ⊠ *Renao Lu, Shenhe district.* ☉ *3 AM–1 PM.*

The sight of stern, gray Gothic-style **Nanguan Catholic Church of the Sacred Heart of Jesus** set amid the apartment blocks and hutongs of urban China is arresting. Built in 1878 and burned during the Boxer rebellion in 1900, the spires of the church climb 120 ft into Shenyang's gray sky. ⊠ *40 Le Jiao Nan Lu, Xiao Nan Da Jie, Shenhe District.* ☏ *024/4843–986.* ☉ *About 5:30 AM–about 6 PM.*

The courtyard of the Buddhist **Fo Zhao Si** (Fo Zhao Temple) has seen a lot. Founded in the Tang dynasty, it was rebuilt in the Qing and during the Cultural Revolution was turned into a factory. The reforms of the 11th Party Congress in 1977 paved the way for its restoration, though the factory did not finally pull out until 10 years later. There are now 25 monks living here. The alleys around the monastery are lined with stalls selling Buddha statues, trinkets, and incense. ✉ *Ci Anshi Hutong, Da Nan Jie.*

Set in parkland in the north of the city, **Beiling** (North Tomb) is the burial place of Huang Taiji (1592–1643), founder of the Qing dynasty. Inside the entrance a short avenue is lined with stone animals surrounded with pine trees, good feng shui tokens. The burial mound is at the rear of the complex and can be viewed from the top of the wall that encircles the two large central courtyards. The outer buildings house souvenir shops; one contains the 400-year-old bodies of a government official and his wife on open display. ✉ *Chongshan Xi Lu, north side of city.*

Dining and Lodging

$$ ✕ **Dong Lai Shun.** Cook your own beef, squid, shellfish, rice noodles, green vegetables, or a host of other dainties in a copper hotpot of constantly boiling water placed on your table in this clean, reasonably priced restaurant. Hotpot is a winter favorite in the north of China, though it is eaten all year round. You can also choose cold plates and enjoy the sesame sauce, soy, chili, bean curd sauce, and sour mustard dips that come with the hotpot. ✉ *39 Si Ping Lu, Heping district,* ☏ *024/ 386–4979. No credit cards.*

$$ ✕ **Hwa Won Korean Restaurant.** Served in a stylish setting of flagstone and wood floors, light timber paneling, and blue upholstered straight back chairs, the food is traditional. In addition to the public dining area there are seven private dining rooms. Among the favorite dishes here are *haemuljungol* (assorted seafood cooked with vegetables in bouillon), *chapchae* (stir-fried sticky noodles with vegetables and beef), and a delicious seafood soup. The restaurant also serves Japanese food such as modum sashimi and beef, chicken, or seafood cooked on skewers. ✉ *Traders Hotel, 2nd floor, 68 Zhong Hua Lu, Heping district,* ☏ *024/34122–88. AE, DC, MC, V.*

$ ✕ **Lao Bian Dumpling Restaurant.** Claiming to be 150 years in business and now in the hands of the fourth generation of the founding family, this Spartan two-story restaurant is famous in Shenyang for its jiaozi. ✉ *57 Beishi Yi Lu, Heping district,* ☏ *024/2721–819. No credit cards.*

$ ✕ **Xing Long Xuen Jiaozi Guan.** This busy restaurant serves 30 kinds of jiaozi, the steamed light dough encasing vegetable or meat or mixed fillings. Its all-red exterior contrasts with the simple interior. ✉ *25 Zhongshan Jie, Shenghe district.* ☏ *024/2700–207. No credit cards.*

$$$ 🏨 **Traders Shenyang Hotel.** Part of the rapidly growing Shangri La hotel chain, the Traders Shenyang is modern and centrally located. Comfortable, tastefully furnished standard rooms are equipped with minibar, refrigerator, executive desk, and satellite TV. The restaurants serve Chinese, Korean, and Western fare. ✉ *68 Zhong Hua Lu, Heping district, 110001,* ☏ *024/34122–88,* ℻ *024/3413–838. 592 rooms. 3 restaurants, health club, nightclub, business center. AE, DC, MC, V.*

$$ 🏨 **Gloria Plaza.** This modern hotel stands opposite the North Railway station in Shenyang's commercial district, just 10 minutes from the Imperial Palace. Standard rooms are bright and comfortable and all are equipped with satellite TV channels, minibar, and refrigerator. The restaurants serve Chinese food; a café serves Western dishes. ✉ *32 Yingbin Jie, Shenhe District,* ☏ *024/2528–885,* ℻ *024/2528–533. 289 rooms. 2 restaurants, bar, health club, business services. AE, DC, MC, V.*

$ 🏨 **Liaoning Guesthouse.** The lobby and dining room interiors in this hotel are of real character. Built by the Japanese in 1927 to a European design, they have wood paneling and tiled and wooden floors, high ceilings, and a strong hint of the style of 18th-century Europe. Standard guest rooms are a bit shabby for the price. It is still state-run, and though some renovation is going on, there are no plans for a joint venture. Japanese visitors like it for its good feng shui. The hotel restaurants serve Shandong, Liaoning, or Western food. ⊠ *97 Zhongshan Lu, on Zhongshan Square, Heping District, 110001,* ☎ *024/3839–166,* FAX *024/3839–103. 3 restaurants, air-conditioning, tennis court, exercise room, billiards. AE, DC, MC, V.*

Outdoor Activities and Sports

The **Summer Palace** (⊠ 215 Qing Nian Jie, ☎ 024/3844–506) is a three-story complex that houses an ice-rink, a bowling alley, an amusement arcade, and adult and kiddies' swimming pools with water slides and spiraling chutes. Swim wear is for sale.

Shopping

Tai Yuan Jie Market (⊠ next to Traders Hotel) mainly sells clothing, some electronic goods, and CDs. The **Gong Yi Meishu Shangdian** (⊠ Taiyuan Jie) has art and craft items— scroll paintings, tea sets, vases, small and large pieces of jade, and other tourist pieces—on the fourth and fifth floors.

The **Cashmere Building** (⊠ 67 Sanjing Jie, Shenhe district, ☎ 024/2846–759) carries a reasonable collection of cashmere garments.

Side Trips from Shenyang

The road out of Shenyang in the direction of Dalian puts you on the first highway in China, built in the early 1980s. Along it, in the town **❽** of **Liaoyang,** the **Baita** (White Tower) is worth a look. Built in the time of the local Liao kingdom during China's Song dynasty about AD 1000, the White Tower is an impressive octagonal structure with a tier of 13 eaves and Buddhist statues and reliefs carved around it. Repaired several times since it was first built, it was last restored in 1986 but does not bear the kitschy new look of so much restoration in China. ⊠ *Road to Dalian, 30 km (18 mi) south of Shenyang.*

Dalian

❶ *4 hours by train south of Shenyang; 12 hours by train, 1 hour by plane east of Beijing*

Dalian is easily one of the most charming cities in China. Lying at the tip of the Liaodong peninsula between the Yellow Sea and the Bohai Sea, this small city (pop. 1.3 million) is at once a postcard from China's past and a signpost to the country's future. In the 19th century, Russia, seeking an ice-free port, established a trading center here but lost it to Japan in their 1904–5 war. Later other Europeans traded here, and the combination of Russian, Japanese, and West European architecture that survives in public buildings and houses gives Dalian a special atmosphere. In 1955 the Russian presence finally ended when Soviet troops stationed here pulled out. Dalian is a great city for walking. Its wide, colonial-era streets and public squares and parks, including Zhongshan Square, Renmin Square and Laodong Park, are its most striking features. With the sea on three sides, it has something else that is rare in a Chinese city—relatively clean air.

But more important than history are the present economic boom and rising wealth that give Dalian the sort of sophistication for which Shanghai is frequently noted. Many of the large colonial buildings have been renovated, new hotels are springing up, and Japanese and Korean fashions dominate the streets.

The city's special economic status (a package of tax and investment breaks to attract foreign companies) and general economic health are often attributed to the charismatic and politically savvy Mayor Bo Xilai.

Dalian

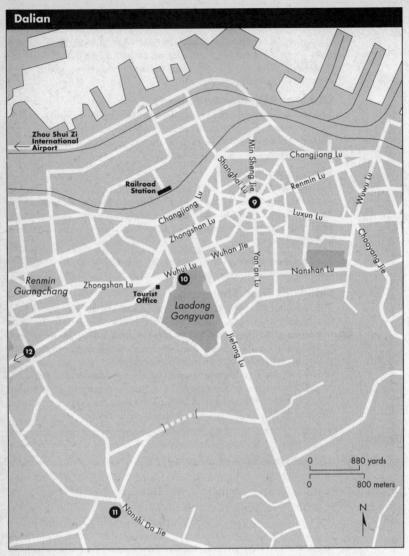

Zhou Shui Zi
International
Airport

Changjiang Lu

Railroad
Station

Min Sheng Jie

Shanghai Lu

Renmin Lu

Wuwu Lu

Changjiang Lu

9

Luxun Lu

Zhongshan Lu

Chaoyang Jie

Wuhan Jie

Wuhui Lu

Yan'an Lu

Nanshan Lu

Renmin
Guangchang

Zhongshan Lu

10

Tourist
Office

Laodong
Gongyuan

Jiefang Lu

12

0   880 yards

0   800 meters

N

11   Nanshi Da Jie

Rong Sheng Guang
Chang Xinsheng, **10**

Dalian Dong Wu
Yuan, **11**

Ocean World
Aquarium, **12**

Zhongshan
Guangchang, **9**

He is the son of the Long March veteran Bo Yibo. The source of the area's economic boom is its good port facilities (Dalian is also China's biggest ship-building center) and the Dalian Economic and Trade Development Zone, 25 minutes from the city, where Japanese, Korean, European, and U.S. companies are based.

❾ **Zhongshan Guangchang** (Sun Yatsen Square) is actually a large circle at the center of Dalian where in good weather locals gather in the evenings to practice genteel ballroom dancing and the lazy version of badminton that is common throughout China. Scenes from the movie *The Last Emperor* were filmed in the square, which is encircled by stately colonial-era buildings, most of which are today occupied by banks.

❿ How do you like your fish? Alive, dead, fresh, or frozen? You will find all kinds at **Rong Sheng Guang Chang Xinsheng** (Rong Sheng Underground Market), everything from flat fish to salmon steaks, plus shrimp, prawn, squid, octopus, sea cucumbers, turtle, tortoise, lobster, crab, eels, abalone, sea urchins, barnacles, and scallops, as well as stalls of fresh fruit and tinned goods. The upper part of the two-level underground complex is dedicated to household furniture. ⊠ *Jiefang Lu, at front of Laodong Park below TV tower and amusement arcade.* ⊙ *Daily 9–6.*

⓫ The **Dalian Dong Wu Yuan** (Dalian Zoo) is where Dalian proudly shows off its Siberian tigers in natural surroundings. The zoo occupies an expansive parkland setting. ⊠ *60 Ying Chun Lu, Nanshi Dao Lu, Xigang District,* ☎ *0411/2480–694.* ☒ *Y30.* ⊙ *Daily 7:30–6.*

⓬ Next to a small beach in Xinghai Park, **Ocean World Aquarium** has a 380-ft plexiglass walk-through tunnel where you can get a full view of the more than 200 varieties of resident fish. ⊠ *Huanghe Jie,* ☎ *0411/ 4685–136.* ☒ *Y35.* ⊙ *Daily 8:30–5.*

Dining and Lodging

$$$$ ✕ **Hyakunin Isshu.** This upscale Japanese restaurant is furnished with plain black Japanese tables and chairs. It serves good Kobe beef grilled or in a hotpot. ⊠ *580 Hwang Hu Lu,* ☎ *0411/4620–088. AE, DC, MC, V. Closed every 2nd and 4th Sun.*

$$ ✕ **Café Igosso.** This offbeat Japanese-owned Italian restaurant is decorated in cream colors and serves pizza, pasta, and cappuccino. There is jazz at night and outdoor seating on a veranda in the summer. The manager plays saxophone and his partner, who runs the kitchen, plays bass. ⊠ *45 Nanshan Lu,* ☎ *0411/2656–453. No credit cards. Closed Mon.*

$$ ✕ **Market Place.** On the first floor of the Holiday Inn, overlooking busy Chang Jiang Lu, this restaurant has a German chef and serves the best Western food in town. It runs special theme menus, such as traditional Italian, New Zealand lamb, or barbecues. ⊠ *18 Shengli Guangchang,* ☎ *0411/2808–888. AE, DC, MC, V.*

$$ ✕ **Sorabol.** Here delicious Korean food is cooked by staff at your table. Among the offerings are the traditional *boolgogi* and *boolgahlbi* (marinated beef served on and off the bone). The restaurant has both private rooms and open booths. Wooden floors and surroundings and friendly service give the place a warm feel. ⊠ *18 Qishi yi Lu,* ☎ *0411/ 2631–460. AE, DC, MC, V.*

$$ ✕ **Tian Tian Yu Gang.** One of the best in a chain of six restaurants around the city serving excellent Dalian seafood, Number 5 offers sea cucumber sautéed and served with asparagus, carrots, and cucumber; abalone—raw or braised—and prawn and crab. The names of the restaurants in the chain vary, but most of them end in Yu Gang, e.g. Tian Tian Yu Gang, Bei Hai Yu Gang, and so on. The restaurant style and layout varies; in Tian Tian Yu Gang the entrance is guarded by fish tanks and basins from which you can choose your meal. There is an open din-

ing area on the ground floor, and upstairs are half a dozen private dining rooms. ⊠ *26 Huachang Jie,* ☎ *0411/2802–708. No credit cards.*

$$ ✕ **Uminosato.** This unsophisticated, open-plan Japanese restaurant specializes in sea urchin, sea cucumber, and Japanese-style rice risotto. You can sit on the floor, Japanese style, or at a regular table. ⊠ *46 Century St.,* ☎ *0411/2656–942. Reservations essential. No credit cards.*

$ ✕ **Metropolis Food Plaza.** For reasonable late-night food, try the restaurants here. Those on the second floor serve a variety of Chinese food with an emphasis on Dalianese. On the fourth floor the food is Cantonese. Both have buffets. ⊠ *52 Youhao Jie,* ☎ *0411/2643–232. No credit cards.*

$$$$ 🏨 **Furama Hotel.** Next door to the Shangri La (☞ *below*), the Furama has executive floor rooms, offices, apartments, and suites. Its massive atrium lobby decked out in marble links its two towers. Standard rooms are spacious and nicely furnished and are equipped with mini-bar and in-house movie channels. The restaurants serve Chinese, Western, or Japanese cuisines. ⊠ *60 Renmin Lu,* ☎ *0411/2630–888,* ℻ *0411/2804–445. 832 rooms. 6 restaurants, 3 bars, pool, tennis court, exercise room, squash, business services. AE, DC, MC, V.*

$$$$ 🏨 **Shangri La Dalian.** Opened in October 1997, this modern high-rise building is part of the rapidly expanding Shangri La chain in China. The rooms are tastefully decorated and comfortable; all come with mini-bar, refrigerator, executive desk, and color TV with movie channels. Several floors are given over to the Horizon Club, which has its own business center and offers complimentary breakfast, cocktails, and express check-in and check-out. The restaurants offer Chinese, Japanese, or Western food. ⊠ *66 Renmin Lu, 116001,* ☎ *0411/2823–131;* ℻ *0411/2823–232. 563 rooms. 3 restaurants, bar, indoor pool, hot tub, tennis court, exercise room, business services. AE, DC, MC, V.*

$$ 🏨 **Holiday Inn.** Just two minutes' walk from the railway station, this hotel is probably the best lodging value in Dalian. Opened in 1988 the red-fronted 23-story building was one of the first high rises in the city. All rooms offer TV and in-house movie channels and a mini-bar. The restaurants serve Cantonese, Sichuan, or Western food. ⊠ *18 Sheng Li Guangchang, 116001,* ☎ *0411/2808–888,* ℻ *0411/2809–704. 405 rooms. 3 restaurants, 2 bars, pool, sauna, exercise room. AE, DC, MC, V.*

$ **Grand Hotel.** This modern hotel houses the Dalian International Exhibition Center, which hosts trade fairs. The plain, red-carpeted rooms come with color TV and minibar. The restaurant serves Chinese and Japanese food. ⊠ *1 Jiefang Jie, 116001,* ☎ *0411/2806–161,* ℻ *0411/2806–969. 248 rooms. Restaurant, 2 bars, exercise room, business services. AE, DC, MC, V.*

Nightlife and the Arts

The **Er Tong Le Yuan** (Children's Palace; ⊠ Renmin Guangchang) hosts occasional photographic and painting exhibitions. The **International Exhibition and Meeting Center** (⊠ Next to Xinghai Park, ☎ 0411/4800–154) hosts industrial exhibitions and trade fairs. The new eight-story **Dalian Wenhua he Meishu Guan** (Dalian Culture and Art Mansion; ⊠ Shidao Nan Jie) houses the city's dance and theater ensembles.

Spring Festival (Chinese New Year: Jan. or Feb.) is the big annual holiday in China. Traditional festivities include a fireworks display. An ice lantern and **ice sculpting** show also takes place at Bingyugou (2½ hrs drive northeast of Dalian) over the Chinese New Year. **Acacia Flower Festival** (last week in May) culminates with a song-and-dance performance in Labor Park in celebration of the blooming lotus.

Nightclubs are relatively new to China. **Casablanca** (✉ 35 Renmin Lu, ☎ 0411/2646–598), a bar with a DJ and small dance floor, is frequented by young Chinese and some foreigners. **The Century Club** (✉ 6 Renmin Lu, 10th floor, ☎ 0411/2825–888), in the Dalian Friendship Club, has singers with a backing band (Western and Chinese rock music) and a dancing show. The strobe-lighted dance floor of **JJ's** (✉ No. 4, 55 St., ☎ 0411/2705–518), with a capacity of about 1,200, is packed on weekends with young Chinese rocking to DJ music.

Outdoor Activities and Sports

The 36-hole **Dalian Golden Pebble Golf Course** (✉ Dalian JinShitan State Tourist and Vacation Zone, ☎ 0411/7350–159; Dalian Office, ☎ 0411/4634–505), on the coast, half an hour northeast of the city center, is open to members only, but arrangements are under way to allow guests in leading hotels to use the facilities.

Shopping

Tianjin Jie market (next to Holiday Inn; ☞ *above*) is a bustling mix of clothing and music stalls good for browsing. **Ti Yu Chang outdoor market** (Xigang district) sells food, clothes, and electronic goods and is busiest on weekends. Five minutes' walk from the Holiday Inn lies the commercial district around **Qingni Jie,** where you'll find department stores, markets, and fast food outlets.

Dalian Friendship Shopping Center (✉ 6–8 Renmin Lu) is a modern department store stocking a wide range of men's and women's clothing, cosmetics, and luxury goods. **Wanlu Liping Shop** (✉ 54 Zhongshan Jie, ☎ 0411/2635–240) sells quality Chinese wood carvings, scrolls, pottery, and interesting lamps and lampshades; you can bargain here.

Side Trips from Dalian

The 32-km-(20-mi-) long **road** that winds **south of Dalian** along the peninsula has some attractive views and a number of good beaches, including Lao Hu and Fujiazhuang. Local couples drive out here following their marriage ceremony to use the coastline and sea as backdrops for wedding photographs.

⓭ **Lushun Prison,** built in the early years of this century by the Russians and later used by the Japanese to hold Chinese prisoners, now houses a museum documenting the Japanese occupation of China. ✉ *139 Xiangyang Jie, Lushun, 42 km (26 mi) north of Dalian,* ☎ *0411/6614–409.*

⓮ **Jin Shi Tan** (Golden Stone Beach), a series of small coves strung along the coast, is near the Dalian Golden Pebble golf course (☞ *above*). ✉ *½ hr northeast of city center.*

Liaoning A to Z

Arriving and Departing

BY BOAT
Frequent passenger service links Dalian with Yantai in Shandong and Shanghai (Dalian Marine Co., ☎ 0411/4623–064.

BY PLANE
Dalian airport (international, ☎ 0411/3645–892; domestic, ☎ 0411/3626–151) is 30 minutes northwest of the city center. There are regular flights to Beijing, Shanghai, Guangzhou, Hong Kong, and Tokyo.

BY TRAIN
From **Dalian** station (✉ Shengli Guangchang, Zhongshan district) the overnight train to and from Beijing has two-berth sleeper cabins and

four-berth hard sleepers, making it more comfortable than most other trains in China. Regular services link Dalian with Shenyang and beyond.

Shenyang has two train stations: Bei Huo Che Zhan (North Railway Station) (☎ 024/2043–522) and Nan Huo Che Zhan (South Railway Station; ☎ 024/2032–222).

Getting Around

The most convenient mode of transport in **Dalian** is taxi. Flag fall is about Y10, though you may have to ask that the meter be used. You can negotiate a price for longer trips outside the city. There are three tram lines (5 mao flat fare).

The easiest way to get around **Shenyang** is by taxi. Flag fall is Y8.

Contacts and Resources

CONSULATE
United States (✉ 52 Shisi Wei Lu, Heping District, Shenyang 110003, ☎ 024/3221–198, FAX 024/3222–374).

EMERGENCIES
Dalian: Hospital, ☎ 120. Ambulance, ☎ 119. Police, ☎ 110.

TRAVEL AGENCIES AND VISITOR INFORMATION
Dalian: China International Travel Service (CITS; ✉ 1 Changtong Jie, Xigangqu 116011, ☎ 0411/3687–956.

SHANXI

Shanxi was at or near the center of Chinese power from about 200 BC until the fall of the Tang Dynasty in the early 10th century. Since then it has remained relatively backward, a frontier area used as a defense against predatory northern neighbors; nevertheless, its very lack of development has allowed a large number of historic sites to survive.

Today lorries and even donkey carts heavily laden with coal dominate the roads of Shanxi, providing a constant reminder that the province produces one third of China's coal. It wasn't until the Japanese occupation that serious exploitation of the coal reserves began, but the mountainous terrain in Shanxi also worked against the Japanese, providing plenty of cover for Chinese guerrillas fighting the anti-Japanese war.

Datong

⑮ *275 km (170 mi) west of Beijing; 724 km (450 mi) by plane northwest of Dalian.*

Datong, in the heart of China's coal mining region, is drab and polluted, but it has some good restaurants and shopping areas, as well as a few historic buildings. The city's chief attractions are the nearby historic sites, where China's ancient history is deeply rooted.

In northern Shanxi near the border with Inner Mongolia, Datong lies close to the old Chinese frontier with the Mongolian and Turkic clans who lived beyond the Great Wall. Datong was a heavily defended city and the countryside around it contained chains of watchtowers where, at the approach of enemy troops, huge bonfires were lit and the warning passed on, giving defenders time to prepare for attacks.

The old city area, within the confines of the still partially surviving city walls, is square and is neatly divided into quarters. The chief areas of interest are within this square.

Originally a screen wall in front of the gate of the palace of the 13th son of the first emperor of the Ming Dynasty, the impressive ceramic tiled **Jiu Long Bi** (Nine Dragon Screen) is about 150 ft long and features colorful depictions of, well yes, nine dragons. ⊠ *East of Da Dong Lu and Da Bei Lu intersection.*

The **Huayan Si** (Huayan Monastery), built in the Liao dynasty, is in the west of the city. Divided into an Upper and Lower Monastery, it has very well-preserved statues, frescoes, built-in bookshelves, and ceilings. The main hall of the Upper Monastery is the largest Buddhist hall extant in China and houses five gilded Buddha statues seated on lotus thrones. The Bhagavat Storage Hall of the Lower Monastery was used for storing Buddhist scriptures and today houses religious statues. ⊠ *Off Da Xi Lu.* ☉ *8–6.*

The **Shanhua Si** (Shanhua Monastery), set in peaceful grounds, dates originally from the Tang dynasty. The four surviving buildings provide important material for the study of Tang and Song dynasty architecture. The main hall contains statues of 24 divine generals. ⊠ *Off Xiao Nan Lu.* ☉ *8–6.*

Trainspotting is possible only through a CITS (☞ Visitor Information, *below*) tour of the **Datong Jiche Cheliang Chang** (Datong Locomotive Works), which made steam engines until the late 1980s, the last factory in China to do so. These black workhorses can still be seen on minor lines or in rail yards away from the boom areas of China. They are reputedly modeled on a 19th Century British steam locomotive. A visit to the works—which now makes diesel engines–includes a ride on one of the old steam engines. ⊠ *Daqing Lu, western suburbs.*

Dining and Lodging

$ ✕ **Hong Sheng Restaurant.** Here, you'll find steamed dumplings and regular Chinese food. ⊠ *3 Yingbin Dong Lu,* ☏ *0352/5037–994. No credit cards.*

$ ✕ **Hong Ya Restaurant.** The two-story family run restaurant has a few specialties, including Beijing-style duck. ⊠ *1 Yingbin Dong Lu,* ☏ *0352/ 5022–467. No credit cards.*

$ ✕ **Yong He Restaurant.** Serving the best food in Datong, it has the same menu on all three floors, but the ground floor—stylish, wood paneled— also serves hotpot, which is what you need to eat if you are in Datong in winter. The regular menu contains a full range of excellent Chinese food, including Beijing duck, and seafood, including turtle, crab and crayfish. ⊠ *Xiao Nan Lu, Shanhua Sikou,* ☏ *0352/2047–999. Reservations essential. No credit cards.*

$ 🏨 **Datong Hotel.** The hotel consists of a main building (renovated Stalinist) and a brand-new smaller facility at the rear. Standard rooms are equipped with satellite TV. The restaurant serves Chinese food. ⊠ *8 Yingbin Xi Lu, 037008,* ☏ *0352/2324–76,* 𝖥𝖠𝖷 *0352/2351–74. 157 renovated rooms, 30 new rooms. Restaurant, bar, pool, health club. No credit cards.*

$ 🏨 **Yungang Hotel.** In the south of the city, this is where most foreigners stay in Datong. Standard rooms are small but adequate and have TVs. Datong CITS main office is in the hotel complex. The restaurant serves Chinese food. ⊠ *Yingbin Dong Lu, 037008,* ☏ *0352/5216–01,* 𝖥𝖠𝖷 *0352/5249–27. 160 rooms. Restaurant, bar, nightclub. No credit cards.*

Shopping

Although far from any of China's booming coastal regions, Datong's main shopping street, Daxi Lu, has its share of fashionable clothing chains and department stores. The most modern department store is the six-story **Hualin Market** (⊠ Xiao Nan Lu), which sells groceries and just about every household item you might want.

Side Trips from Datong

The **Yungang Shiku** (Yungang Grottoes), the oldest Buddhist caves in China, are Datong's most famous site. Built mainly in the latter part of the 5th century, the grotto complex, containing various religious icons, from huge Buddha statues to scores of intricate carvings, stretched over 15 km (9 mi) from east to west. Today only a kilometer of this survives, encompassing 53 major grottoes. Most are now railed off at the front, but visitors can peer in for a better look. ⊠ *16 km/10 mi west of Datong.*

The 1,400-year-old **Xuankong Si** (Hanging Monastery) is attached precariously to the side of a sheer cliff face in the Hengshan mountains, one of China's five sacred mountain ranges. The all-wooden monastery holds China's three historical belief systems within its buildings: Daoism, Buddhism, and Confucianism. In one temple there are statues of Lao zi, Sakyamuni, and Confucius. ⊠ *75 km/46 mi south of Datong via CITS tour only.*

Built around AD1100, the octagonal **Yingxian Muta** (Yingxian Timber Pagoda) is thought to be the oldest wooden building in China. Reflecting the dangers of the bad old days in Shanxi, it began life as a watchtower and waited 400 years before being converted into a temple. In something of an architectural trick, the pagoda's 220 ft appear to contain five floors but in fact holds nine. Whatever its construction, it has been strong enough to survive three powerful earthquakes, although most of the statues and relics inside were destroyed by the upheavals of the Cultural Revolution. A notable survivor is the huge statue of Sakyamuni on the ground floor. ⊠ *70 km/43 mi south of Datong.*

Shanxi A to Z

Arriving and Departing

Daily trains link Datong with Beijing. Datong is also on the route to Inner Mongolia to the north and Lanzhou in the west.

Getting Around

Taxi (flag fall Y5) is the easiest mode of transportation in Datong.

Visitor Information

CITS (⊠ Railway station; ⊠ Yungang Hotel, 21 Yingbin Dong Lu, Datong 037008, ☎ 0352/5101–326, ℻ 0352/5102–046).

SHANDONG

Shandong is one of the most important birthplaces of China. Confucius was born here (in Qufu), and it is home to two of China's holy mountains (Taishan and Laoshan). These sites, along with the city of Qingdao, are among the province's highlights. It is also the *laojia* (old home) of many current inhabitants of the northeastern provinces of Liaoning, Jilin, and Heilongjiang who escaped from poverty and war into Shandong in the decades after 1911 or colonized the area in Mao Zedong's post-revolution China.

The Yellow River, hard hit by drought in recent years, enters the Yellow Sea on the Shandong coastline. To the north lies the Bohai Gulf, and on land Shandong is bordered by Hebei, Henan, Anhui, and Jiangsu provinces. Shandong is one of the most populous provinces in China (pop. 87 million) and, while Qingdao is relatively prosperous, cities such as Heze and much of the countryside are still very poor.

Jinan

🔟 *6 hours by train south of Beijing; 6 hours by train east of Qingdao.*

The old city of Jinan was given a new lease on life by the construction of a railway line linking it to the port city of Qingdao around the turn of the century. German, English, and Japanese concessions operated here and a good number of buildings survive from this era in the downtown area. Jinan is a pleasant city and the locals are friendly—something for which Shandong people in general enjoy a good reputation.

Today's city center, the most interesting part of Jinan, where European influence lingers, is laid out in a grid to the south of the railway station. An exploration of the city should begin here.

Zhongshan Gongyuan (Sun Yat-sen Park) is a quiet retreat from the city traffic. Early in the morning it is full of small groups of elderly people doing tai chi. People hang birdcages on nearby trees while they exercise. ⊠ *Jing San Lu.*

Qianfoshan (Thousand Buddha Mountain), on the southern outskirts of the city, is still the focus of religious festivals though most of the Buddhas have been lost to the ravages of time and the Cultural Revolution. The mountain does offer a good view of Jinan—pollution permitting. ⊠ *Off Qianfoshan Lu beside Qilu Hotel, on south side of city.*

One interesting architectural legacy of the foreign occupation is an imposing red brick **Protestant Church,** with its landmark twin towers. Built in 1927, it is still in use. ⊠ *425 Jing Si Lu.*

Dining and Lodging

$$ ✕ **Jinsanbei Restaurant.** Customers here choose their meals in a novel way: Ingredients—meat, fish, vegetables, and so on—are stocked in open coolers off the lobby, and live fish are in nearby tanks. After you take your pick, the staff carry it to the kitchens while you retire to the large wood-paneled dining room to wait for the meal. ⊠ *5 Qianfoshan Lu,* ☎ *0531/2961–616. No credit cards.*

$ ✕ **California Restaurant.** This place is an odd mixture of Chinese restaurant and micro brewery. It receives mixed reviews from Jinan residents, but in a city where not much goes on it makes some people happy. ⊠ *30 Chaoshan Jie,* ☎ *0531/6925–114. No credit cards.*

$ ✕ **Luneng Shaoezai Restaurant.** Very popular with locals, it presents a buffet of a vast array of fresh seafood, vegetables, and meat for customers to stock up on and cook hotpot style at their tables. Fresh fruit, desserts, and cooked food are also provided. ⊠ *Jing Si Lu, in Linxiang Dasha complex,* ☎ *0531/6011–888. No credit cards.*

$ ✕ **Shandong Danlian Hai Xian.** At this simple open-plan restaurant specializing in seafood, customers can choose their meal from the selection of live (in tanks) and frozen seafood displayed in the lobby. ⊠ *86 Jing Ba Lu,* ☎ *0531/2901–618. No credit cards.*

$$ 🏨 **Qilu Hotel.** Jinan's most lavish hotel is on the fringes of the city near Thousand Buddha Mountain. Standard rooms are decorated in light colors and come with satellite TV and a minibar. The restaurants serve Chinese, Japanese, or Western food. ⊠ *Qian Foshan Lu, 250014,* ☎ *0531/2966–888,* FAX *0531/2967–676. 246 rooms. 4 restaurants, bar, pool, tennis court, bowling, exercise room, nightclub, business services. AE, DC, MC, V.*

$ 🏨 **Guidu Hotel.** This modern hotel is on a side street off Wei San Jie. Rooms are clean and tastefully decorated and are equipped with satellite TV, a business desk, and a minibar. The restaurants serve Chinese or Western food. ⊠ *1 Sheng Ping Lu, 250001,* ☎ *0531/6900–888,* FAX

0531/6900–999. 225 rooms, 15 suites. 2 restaurants, bar, nightclub, business services. AE, DC, MC, V.

$ ▥ **Lakeside Hotel.** This three-story hotel is Chinese style on the outside—green roof tiles and red lanterns hanging on the balconies—and fitted with Western furnishings inside. Clean and comfortable standard rooms are equipped with satellite TV and minibar. ⊠ *271 Minghu Lu, 250011,* ☎ *0531/6021–146,* FAX *0531/6012–113. 50 rooms. AE, DC, MC, V.*

Nightlife

There is little in the way of conventional nightlife in Jinan. What exists is concentrated in a short strip near the Qilu Hotel.

The cool brick and timber **Downtown Café** (⊠ 9 Qianfoshan Jie, opposite Qilu Hotel) plays everything from Irish folk music to the Rolling Stones on its sound system and serves a range of Western beers and spirits, steaks, sandwiches, and noodle dishes. The slightly cavernous **100 C** (⊠ 9 Qianfoshan Lu) bar is furnished in timber, has a dance floor in the middle, a dart board on the wall, and a cooler full of imported beers. **Shandong Elite Teahouse** (⊠ Qianfoshan Lu) serves all kinds of tea at polished dark wooden tables in a traditional Chinese teahouse setting, decorated with lattice wooden paneling, vases, and musical instruments.

Shopping

The best department store in Jinan is the **Yin Zuo** (Silver Plaza; ⊠ Luo Yuan Lu), with a shiny seven floors of everything from domestic appliances to cosmetics, plus a basement supermarket and Chinese fast food outlets.

Side Trips from Jinan

The top of **Taishan** (Mt. Tai) is 5,067 ft above sea level. It is one of China's five holy Taoist mountains. The walk up—on cut stone steps—by open mountainside, steep crags, and pine woods takes about three to four hours. Some people stay overnight to watch the sun rise, but the classic sunrise over cloud-hugged mountainside seen in photos is a rare sight. Confucius is said to have climbed the mountain and commented from its height, "The world is very small." Much later Mao Zedong climbed it and, even more famously, said, "The East is red." At the foot of the mountain is the unremarkable town of Taian. ⊠ *About 50 km (30 mi) south of Jinan.*

Qufu is the birthplace of the great sage himself. About 20% of Qufu's population claim to be descendants of Confucius. The **Confucius Temple, Confucius Family Mansion,** and the **Family Graveyard** are the focus of today's visitors. Confucius has been honored in Qufu almost consistently since his own time 2,500 years ago. Money was regularly sent from Beijing by the Emperors to extend and keep up the extensive buildings devoted to his memory. ⊠ *3 hours by car south of Jinan.*

Qingdao

12 hours by train or 2 hours by plane southeast of Beijing; 6 hours by train east of Jinan.

Qingdao was a sleepy fishing village until the end of the 19th century when German imperialists, using the killing of two German missionaries in the area as a pretext, set up another European colony on the coastal fringe of China. The German presence lasted only until 1914, but the city continued to build in the German style, and large parts of the old town make visitors feel as if they have stumbled into southern Germany. Today it is one of China's most charming cities and home to the country's best-known brewery, Tsingtao (the old-style Roman-

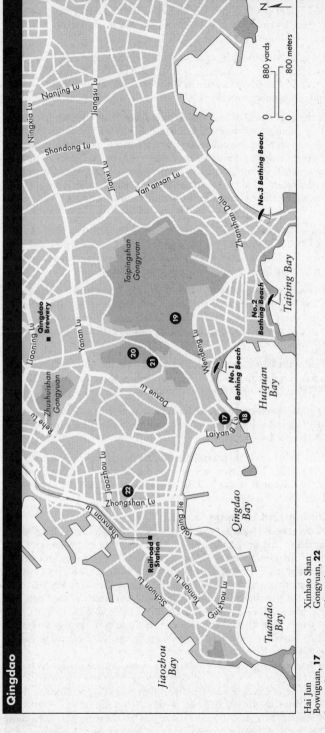

Qingdao

Hai Jun
Bowuguan, **17**
Luxun Gongyuan, **18**
Protestant
Church, **20**
Tianzhu Jiaotang, **21**

Xinhao Shan
Gongyuan, **22**
Zhongshan
Gongyuan, **19**

ization of Qingdao), founded in 1903. Located east of the main harbor, Tsingtao still does a fair impression of a good German lager and produces a sweet black stout as well. The city is also nursery to a growing wine industry.

Qingdao, with its seafront promenades, winding colonial streets, parks, and red tiled roofs, is made for strolling. The main shopping areas are around Zhongshan Lu; nearby is the city's landmark building, a twin-spired Catholic church.

⑰ In the upper yard of the **Hai Jun Bowuguan** (Navy Museum) is an indoor exhibition documenting the history of the Chinese navy and displaying an extensive collection of uniforms and plaques presented by visiting navies. Outdoors in the lower yard stands a range of military equipment, including Russian-made fighter aircraft, fixed turret and anti-aircraft naval guns, rockets, tanks, ground artillery, naval vessels (including three moored in the adjacent harbor), and even an old biplane. ⊠ *8 Lai Yang,* ☎ *0532/2866–784.* ⊡ *Y10.* ☉ *Daily 7:30–7:30.*

⑱ **Luxun Gongyuan** (Luxun Park), built in 1929, faces onto Huiquan Bay. In 1950 it was named for the distinguished Chinese writer and commentator Lu Xun. It combines traditional Chinese garden art with the rocky coastline. ⊠ *West end of No. 1 Bathing Beach.*

⑲ **Zhongshan Gongyuan** (Sun Yat-sen Park), named for Dr. Sun Yat-sen, is the largest park in the city and is best seen in spring. It has an oriental cherry path, an osmanthus garden, and other exotic plant gardens and contains the Qingdao zoo. ⊠ *North of Huiquan Dynasty Hotel, off Wendeng Lu.*

One of the best views of old Qingdao is from the three red mushroom
⑳ towers on the top of Xinhao Shan in **Xinhao Shan Gongyuan** (Xinhao Hill Park). ⊠ *Off Daxue Lu.*

㉑ Qingdao's **Protestant Church** has a bell tower with a clock. It was built in 1910 and is located at the southwest entrance of Xinhao Park. ⊠ *15 Jiangsu Lu.*

㉒ A landmark in Qingdao is the **Tianzhu Jiaotang** (Catholic Church), with its towering 200-ft twin steeples and red tiled roof. Originally named St. Emil Church, it was built by the Germans in 1934. ⊠ *15 Zhejiang Lu.* ☉ *Sun. 7 AM–8 AM, 6 PM–7 PM.*

Dining and Lodging

$$$ ✕ **Good World Seaside Palace.** Occupying part of a large golf ball-shape structure that sits on the edge of the promenade in downtown Qingdao, this Hong Kong-managed restaurant specializes in seafood. Sashimi, shark's fin, and bird's nest soup jostle for space on the menu with more conventional dishes such as Peking duck. The kitchens open onto the spacious restaurant and diners can watch as the chefs prepare the food. ⊠ *2 Xiling Xia Lu,* ☎ *0532/2652–828, DC, MC, V.*

$ ✕ **Gaoli.** One of the better Korean restaurants in the city serves on-table barbecues and relatively cheap dishes. ⊠ *2 Huiquan Lu,* ☎ *0532/3865–301. No credit cards.*

$ ✕ **Shuangsheng Yuan.** Housed in a colonial-era building, this restaurant has a large, bright, airy dining room with big windows overlooking the street. It serves regular Chinese dishes as well as good local seafood. ⊠ *5 Yanerdao Lu,* ☎ *0532/5876–485. No credit cards.*

$ ✕ **Wests.** This coffee shop and restaurant has the atmosphere of a cheap café with its brown covered booths, background pop music, and friendly service, and is a favorite with westerners and other foreigners. Downstairs specializes in breads, sweet cakes and cookies. Upstairs serves iron plate beef, chicken steaks, pork chops, ice cream, and milk shakes. ⊠ *Zhongshan Lu. No credit cards.*

$ ╳ **Xia Wenqian.** This restaurant has a light wood interior with Greek-style columns, a tiled floor, and wooden tables. The friendly staff serves good hotpot and local seafood. ⊠ *11 Tangba Jie,* ☎ *0532/2826–985. No credit cards.*

$$$$ 🏨 **Shangri La.** This top-class hotel opened in late 1997 with standard Shangri La facilities. All rooms have a color TV and in-house movies, mini bar, refrigerator, an executive desk, and fax, phone, and personal computer hookups. ⊠ *9 Zhan Liu Gan Lu, 266071,* ☎ *0532/3883–838,* 𝔽𝔸𝕏 *0532/3886–868. 502 rooms. 3 restaurants, bar, pool, tennis court, fitness center, business services. AE, MC, V.*

$$$ 🏨 **Grand Regency Hotel.** Extravagantly modern, the hotel has a huge foyer and an immense ballroom made with materials imported from Italy, England, and South Africa. Rooms are tastefully decorated and spacious, the only drawback being the relatively poor view due to the hotel's location in the industrial and commercial district. All rooms offer minibar, in-house movie channels, and satellite TV. The restaurants serve Cantonese, French, Japanese, or international fare. ⊠ *1 Taiwan Lu, 266071,* ☎ *0532/5881–818,* 𝔽𝔸𝕏 *0532/5881–888. 448 rooms. 4 restaurants, 2 bars, pool, tennis court, health club, nightclub, business services. AE, DC, MC, V.*

$$$ 🏨 **Haitian Hotel.** Overlooking Qingdao's Number 3 bathing beach, it has clean, modern rooms with minibars, satellite TVs, and good coastal views. The restaurants serve Chinese, Japanese, Korean, or Western fare. ⊠ *39 Zhanshan Dalu, 266071,* ☎ *0532/3871–888;* 𝔽𝔸𝕏 *0532/3871–777. 626 rooms. 4 restaurants, bar, pool, health club, business services. AE, DC, MC, V.*

$$ 🏨 **Dongfang Hotel.** In the university area within walking distance from downtown, the hotel has good views of colonial Qingdao from its comfortable guest rooms. All are equipped with minibar and satellite TV. The restaurants serve Chinese or Western food. ⊠ *4 Daxue Lu, 266003,* ☎ *0532/2865–888;* 𝔽𝔸𝕏 *0532/2862–741. 146 rooms. 2 restaurants, bar, tennis court, health club, nightclub, business services. AE, DC, MC, V.*

$$ 🏨 **Huiquan Dynasty Hotel.** This modern hotel overlooks the Number 1 beach and sea east of the downtown area. In the newest part, a 23-story tower, every guest room has a private balcony overlooking the Yellow Sea. The revolving restaurant—serving Chinese and Western breakfast and evening meals—on the 25th floor affords views of the beautiful old city of Qingdao. Spacious and comfortable standard rooms come with minibar and color TV with in-house movies. The restaurants serve Chinese, Japanese, Korean, or Western cuisine. ⊠ *9 Nanhai Lu, 266003,* ☎ *0532/2873–366;* 𝔽𝔸𝕏 *0532/2871–122. 420 rooms. 4 restaurants, bar, pool, tennis court, health club, nightclub, business services. AE, DC, MC, V.*

$ 🏨 **Qingdao Ying Bingguan.** This small hotel has only a handful of rooms.
★ Despite being state-run, it is one of the most charming hotels in China. Built in 1903 as the official residence of the Governor-General of the then-German colony of Qingdao, it is set on a hill in mature gardens overlooking the old city. The interior is warm with wood paneling and a wide staircase leading from the ground-floor foyer to the guest rooms. Among the famous leaders who stayed here were Mao Zedong, his wife Jiang Qing, Zhou Enlai, Deng Xiaoping, and Cambodia's Prince Sihanouk. Rooms are spacious with good views, and there is a large dining room on the ground floor. Advance booking is essential. ⊠ *26 Longshan Lu, 266003,* ☎ *0532/2866–120;* 𝔽𝔸𝕏 *0532/2861–985. 8 rooms. No credit cards.*

Nightlife and the Arts

Cavalier Bar (✉ 26 Xushan Lu, ☎ 0532/9051–755), near the middle gate of Hai Yang University, is very small and gloomy but has a friendly staff and character. **Century End Café** (✉ 2 Jiangsu Lu, ☎ 0532/2864–530) is a cozy U.S. theme bar made up of three small red and black rooms whose walls are hung with Jack Daniels flags and U.S. Navy crests. **Hanbo Beer Bar** (✉ 2 Rongling Jie, ☎ 0532/2826–301), in a German-era building, is airy with loads of standing room and only a few high stools. **Tsingtao** (✉ 31 Taiping Lu, ☎ 0532/2961–988) is a basement bar with a white grand piano on which the resident pianist churns out a mix of classical, Chinese, and ragtime music with the help of a violinist. The **Yi Du Jiudian** has a tree growing in the middle of the restaurant; it serves jiaozi and regular Chinese dishes until late.

The **International Beer Festival** in August is Qingdao's biggest event of the year, with fireworks and gallons of beer for tasting. There are also several **harvest festivals,** including the **Taidong Radish Festival** and the **Sugar-coated Haws Festival,** both in January; the **Cherry Festival** in April and May; and the **Mount Daze Grape Festival** in early September.

Shopping

Qingdao Antique Store (✉ 40 Zhongshan Lu, ☎ 0532/2864–436) is a serious antique shop that also has a smattering of cheaper gifts as well as items such as calligraphy materials, seals, and art books, but is blessedly devoid of tourist junk; the staff has a professional attitude. The **Art and Craft Shop** (✉ 212 Zhongshan Lu, ☎ 0532/2817–948) deals in scroll paintings, silk, gold, and jade and other stones. **San Yuan Art and Craft Shop** (✉ 10 Feicheng Jie) sells a range of pottery, dolls and figurines, artificial flowers, and vases. **Jinmo Lu Small Wares Market** contains cheap clothes, shoes, and knapsacks; inside is a pearl market.

There are a number of **street markets** in Qingdao. Among the best are **Ping Gu Jie** (you can join an offshoot of this market by the Catholic Church), where, in the right season, a rainbow of color is produced by stocks of fruit such as guava, lychee, cherries, melons, oranges, and apples. All year-round chilies, turmeric, peppers, and curry powders are just some of the spices on sale here along with dried seahorse, squid, octopus, prawns, shellfish, and abalone.

Department stores include **Fada Mansion** (✉ junction of Zhongshan Lu and Hunan Lu), **Number 1 Department Store of Qingdao** (51 Zhongshan Lu), and the **Shandong International Trade Mansion** (✉ Taiping Jie).

Side Trips from Qingdao

Huadong Winery, Shandong's best winery, near Laoshan (☞ *below*), is not yet as famous as the province's brewery but has already won a string of prizes. The winery's equipment comes from France and the United States, and the vines came from France in the mid-1980s. The chardonnay is on a par with any good American wine, perhaps because the wine-growing area of Shandong is on the same latitude as California's Napa Valley.

The holy **Laoshan,** which rivals Shandong's other famous mountain, Taishan, rises to a height of over 3,280 ft above sea level. A repository of Taoism, during its heyday it had 9 palaces, 8 temples, and 72 convents. It is physically beautiful, with sheer cliffs and cascading waterfalls, and is widely recognized in China as a source of the country's best-known mineral water. The mountain area covers 400 sq km (154 sq mi), but paths to Laoshan proper lead from the Song dynasty Taiqing Palace. ✉ *40 km (25 mi) east of Qingdao.*

Shandong A to Z

Arriving and Departing

Regular boats link **Qingdao** with Dalian (every four days) and Shanghai (daily). Ask at CITS or buy tickets at the Passenger Ferry Terminal (⊠ Xinjiang Jie near Friendship Store).

Regular buses link **Qufu** with Jinan, three hours away, and Taian, two hours away by public bus. **Taian** is about an hour from Jinan by bus.

Regular flights link **Jinan** and Hong Kong and other major Chinese cities. The airport is 70 km (43 mi) northeast of Jinan.

Qingdao airport is 30 km (19 mi) from the city center. Direct flights link Qingdao with Osaka, Macau, and Seoul, as well as Hong Kong and other major Chinese cities. Flights can be booked through hotels or at CAAC (⊠ 29 Zhongshan Lu).

Jinan is on the Beijing–Shanghai rail line and the Beijing– Qingdao line, so there is no shortage of trains. The trip to Beijing takes about 5½ hours. Trains link **Qufu** station (6 km/4 mi from town) with Jinan and Beijing. **Taian** is on the main Beijing–Shanghai rail line with onward connections in either direction.

Direct trains link **Qingdao** with Beijing, Dalian, Shanghai, Shenyang, Yantai, Xian, and Lanzhou.

TIANJIN

The Tianjin municipality has a population of over nine million and a thriving seaport with an extensive hinterland that includes Beijing, only two hours away. Numerous multinational businesses, including nearly 1,000 from the United States alone, have set up here. Most are located in the new satellite city, known as Teda (Tianjin Economic Development Area), to the south of old Tianjin.

Tianjin is one of China's four municipalities—meaning it reports directly to China's State Council instead of to a provincial government. The others are Beijing, Shanghai, and Chongqing. The city occupies the banks of the Hai River, 50 km (31 mi) from where it flows into the Gulf of Bohai. A large number of European-style buildings survive here, a legacy of European and Japanese colonialism, and in spring and autumn Tianjin's narrow, leafy streets offer an alternative to the wide avenues of nearby Beijing.

Tianjin signifies "the point where the Son of Heaven forded the river" and refers to the route taken by the Ming dynasty Emperor Yongle to a key battle in the south, where he succeeded in establishing his reign, beginning in 1403. Thereafter Tianjin grew in stature and was viewed as the gateway to the Imperial capital of Beijing.

The second Anglo-Chinese war in 1858 forced Beijing to sign the Treaty of Tianjin, which made the city a treaty port similar to Shanghai. Concessions were established by the British and the French, followed by the Belgians, the Germans, the Italians, the Russians, the Austro-Hungarians, and the Japanese. The city they called Tientsin became a major international port and manufacturing center, producing the Tientsin carpets that are still a major export. In the first part of this century it was a temporary home for the last emperor—whose parties in the Astor Hotel were recreated here in the movie of the same name—engineer Herbert Hoover in his pre-presidential career, Sun Yat-sen, and Zhou Enlai.

In modern times Tianjin was badly damaged in the 1976 Tangshan earthquake but was rebuilt in time to benefit from the Open Door policy. Its port is the biggest in northern China and the new California-like suburb of Teda contains some of China's most successful joint ventures among its 3,000 foreign-funded enterprises.

Exploring Tianjin

An official count reckons there are more than 1,000 buildings in Tianjin surviving from the colonial period. The old quarter is a virtual museum of European architecture.

A Good Walk

Set off from the Hyatt Hotel and head north along the riverside promenade, Taierzhang Lu. A block away is the Astor Hotel, well worth a quick visit as the occasional home of the last emperor. Continue along the promenade, where you'll find groups of pigeon fanciers comparing and selling birds and other people playing Chinese chess. As well as lawns with topiary animals, fountains, and small cafés, the promenade has an inimitable view across the river of surviving colonial mansions that could have been transplanted from 19th-century Europe. Make a detour on Chifeng Lu to Jiefang Lu to see collection of Chinese art in the **Yishu Bowuguan** ㉓, then continue along the waterfront to Beima Lu. Follow it for a block to reach **Gu Wenhua Jie** ㉔. Explore the shops and the Tianhou Gong, then take the main road, Dongma Lu, south until it becomes Heping Lu. Turn right on Rongji Dajie to **Shi Pin Jie** ㉕, where you can stop for lunch. Return to Heping Lu. In British concession times, this was Cambridge Road, lined with fashionable shops and banks, many of which are still here, in the same businesses, albeit with different owners. One classic reminder is the **Quanyechang Baihuoshangchang** ㉖, modeled on Harrod's. Two blocks farther on is Zhongxin Park, with playgrounds and tree-shaded benches and surrounded by some grand old buildings. From here you can take Jiashe Lu back to the Hyatt or head down the modern avenue Yingkou Dao to the Catholic **Xikai Jiaotang** ㉗.

TIMING

This walk should take about 2½ hours, plus an hour if you include lunch.

Sights to See

㉔ **Gu Wenhua Jie** (Culture Street). During foreign concession days the area in the north of the city was a traditional "Chinatown." In the 1980s Tianjin's mayor decided to restore some of the old buildings with their carved wooden facades and ornate balconies hung with silk banner advertisements. Some contain shops selling antiques, reproductions, carpets, swords, paintings, books, coins, and assorted craft items. Others are restaurants serving such local delicacies as *goubuli* (dumplings filled with meat) and soup. At one end of the street is the **Tianhou Gong** (Tianhou Temple), dedicated to the goddess of seafarers, with prayer pavilions set in garden courtyards. ⊠ *Beima Lu.* 🎟 *Free.* ✆ *Daily 9 AM–11 PM.*

㉖ **Quanyechang Baihuoshangchang** (Quanyechang Department Store). Built in the 1920s and modeled on London's Harrod's, this was a landmark of the old British concessional. Today it's an upmarket store with imported brand-name fashions, Chinese luxury items, and a selection of arts and crafts. Its handsome facade has been restored. Other grand colonial buildings in the neighborhood that have been renovated include City of London–style banks now used by Chinese financial institutions, apartment blocks, and trading houses that now contain the offices of multinational firms. Many have candy-striped window awnings. ⊠ *Heping Lu at Binjiang Dao.* ☉ *Daily 10–10.*

㉕ Shi Pin Jie (Food Street). Actually more of a food city, this three-story block contains more than 100 shops selling food and drink from all over China and around the world. The dishes range from *caoji* (donkey meat) and burnt rice to pizzas and hamburgers. The complex has pagoda roofs and city gate-like entrances bearing the characters for "People's lives depend on food." ⊠ *Rongji Dajie.* ☉ *Daily 6 AM–midnight.*

㉗ Xikai Jiaotang (St. Paul's Catholic Church). Built by French Jesuits in 1917, this extraordinary building is a landmark, with its twin domed towers and tan-and-cream brickwork. It amazingly survived the Cultural Revolution with no more than a broken window and in recent years has been beautifully restored. It is regularly full for Sunday services and well attended at daily morning mass. ⊠ *Xining Jie.* ☉ *Daily 10–5.*

㉓ Yishu Bowuguan (Art Museum). The setting of this collection is itself a prime exhibit, being a restored colonial mansion that recalls the architecture of the Belle Epoch. Attractively displayed are some fine examples of traditional Chinese paintings and calligraphy on the first floor; folk art, particularly elaborate giant paper kites, on the second; and temporary exhibitions on the third. ⊠ *77 Jiefang Bei Lu.* 🖾 *Y5.* ☉ *Daily 9–5.*

Dining and Lodging

$$$ ✕ Ganbeiyiding. This streetfront restaurant furnished with wooden tables and lattice chairs serves set Japanese meals. Upstairs are smaller rooms with KTV. ⊠ *12 Zhangde Jie,* ☎ *022/2331–0439. AE, DC, MC, V.*

$$ ✕ Bader Brauhaus. On the third floor of Kiesslings Bakery (founded in 1911), this restaurant is tastefully furnished; the floors are wooden, the walls are hung with scenes from old Tianjin, and behind the bar, which occupies the middle of the floor, are two large copper vats where the Brauhaus special is brewed. The menu lists dishes from 10 countries and includes tortilla and wiener schnitzel. On the floor below is a hotpot restaurant. ⊠ *29 Zhejiang Jie,* ☎ *022/2332–1603. No credit cards.*

$$ ✕ Tianjin Kaoya Dian. Here are five floors serving Peking duck. The ground floor serves cheap roast duck fast-food style. Prices shoot up in the room where Mao Zedong chewed the crisp fat on August 13, 1958. His likeness is on the door to the room, and photographs of the occasion hang on the walls. The restaurant decor varies from the plastic bucket seats on the ground floor to elegant wood-paneled rooms on the upper floors. ⊠ *146 Liaoning Jie,* ☎ *022/2730–3335. No credit cards.*

$ ✕ Goubili Restaurant. Tianjin's most famous restaurant is the proud purveyor of the Tianjin-style *baozi* (steamed dumpling filled with chopped meat and vegetables). The restaurant has three floors. The ground floor has gone for fast food (fast baozi). The second and third floors are a mixture of large dining areas and smaller, more exclusive rooms. Both serve regular Chinese food as well as baozi. ⊠ *77 Shandong Jie,* ☎ *022/7302–540. No credit cards.*

$ Shi Pin Jie (Food Street). The greatest variety of food in Tianjin is here in this huge cross-shape two-story building. The stalls on the ground floor sell everything from cooked donkey penis to preserved fruits. There are between 30 and 40 restaurants on the ground and first floors specializing in a range of Chinese cuisine including hotpot, seafood, Sichuan-style, Chaozhou, Chinese fast food, and roast duck. ⊠ *Rongji Dajie.*

Tianjin

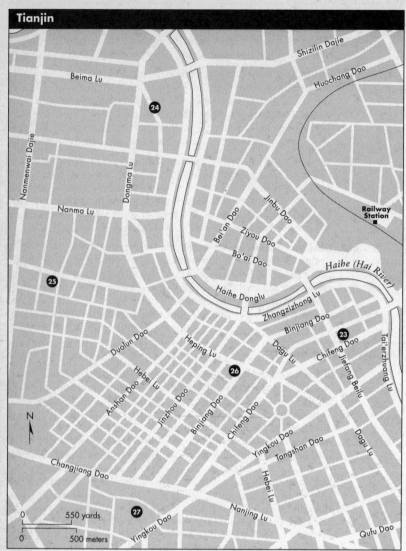

Gu Wenhua Jie, **24**
Quanyechang
Baihuoshangchang,
26
Shi Pin Jie, **25**
Xikai Jiaotang, **27**
Yishu Bowuguan, **23**

$$$$ ⊞ **Sheraton Hotel.** This hotel with an adjacent apartment building stands in its own gardens in a quiet part of town. The comfortable rooms are decorated in light colors and are equipped with a business desk, minibar, and satellite TV. The restaurants have Japanese, Chinese, and Western food. ⊠ *Zi Jinshan Lu, He Xi District, 300074,* ☎ *022/3343–388,* FAX *022/3358–740. 230 rooms. 3 restaurants, bar, pool, tennis court, bowling, health club, business services. AE, DC, MC, V.*

$$$$ ⊞ **Tianjin Hyatt.** The Hyatt backs onto the Hai River and is one of the more established high-class hotels in Tianjin. Old-style green Chinese tiles gird the upper floors of this Hong Kong-managed hotel, making it something of a landmark. Inside is a spacious three-story atrium lobby. Standard rooms are bright, clean, and comfortable and are equipped with a business desk, minibar, and satellite TV. The restaurants serve Chinese, Japanese, and Western cuisines. ⊠ *219 Jiefang Bei Lu, 300042,* ☎ *022/3301–234,* FAX *022/3311–234. 450 rooms. 5 restaurants, bar, driving range, putting green, health club, business services. AE, DC, MC, V.*

$$$ ⊞ **Crystal Palace.** Near the International Exhibition Center, this modern, seven-story hotel sits on a corner of Youyi Lu. At the rear is Yingbing Lake. Plainly furnished standard rooms come with satellite TV. Chinese, Japanese, or Western cuisines are served at the restaurants. ⊠ *28 Youyi Lu, 300061,* ☎ *022/2835–6666,* FAX *022/2835–1970. 346 rooms. 4 restaurants, bar, tennis court, exercise room, business services. AE, DC, MC, V.*

$$$ ⊞ **Holiday Inn.** In this hotel on the banks of the Hai River comfortable standard rooms are equipped with satellite TV. The restaurants serve Chinese, Japanese, or Western food. ⊠ *288 Zhongshan Lu, Hebei District, 300141,* ☎ *022/2628–8888, 300141,* FAX *022/2628–6666. 265 rooms. 3 restaurants, bar, pool, health club. AE, DC, MC, V.*

$$$ ⊞ **New World Astor.** Facing the Hai River, the Astor, the oldest hotel in Tianjin (founded in 1863), was under renovation at the time of writing. It has played host to such luminaries as Sun Yat-sen, Herbert Hoover, and Pu Yi, China's last Emperor. Rooms have satellite TV and minibar. The restaurants offer Chinese, Italian, or international cuisines. ⊠ *33 Taier Zhuang Jie, 300040,* ☎ *022/2331–1112,* FAX *022/2331–6282. 195 rooms, 28 suites. 3 restaurants, health club, nightclub, business services. AE, DC, MC, V.*

$ ⊞ **Geneva Hotel.** This hotel is connected to the Tianjin International Exhibition Center and plays host to trade fair delegates. Standard rooms are bright and equipped with satellite TV, but the beds are a little on the small side. Chinese, Japanese, Korean, or Western cuisines are served at the restaurants. The nightclub has Russian dancers. ⊠ *32 Youyi Lu, Hexi District, 300061,* ☎ *022/8352–2222,* FAX *022/2835–9855. 270 rooms. 4 restaurants, bar, bowling, health club, nightclub. AE, DC, MC, V.*

Shopping

Department Stores
The **International Market** (south end of Binjiang Dao) has a wide variety goods, as well as a supermarket. **Isetan** (Nanjing Lu), a Japanese department store, has five floors of mostly Western or Japanese cosmetics, household wares, consumer durables, and clothes.

Districts
Binjiang Dao is the center of shopping in Tianjin. Department stores and Western upscale boutiques are concentrated at the northern end of the street. To the south these give way to market stalls selling clothes and a few other bargains.

On the long **Gu Wenhua Jie** (Ancient Culture St.) culture and kitsch vie with each other side by side at stalls and shops. On the culture side there are traditional Chinese instruments, scroll paintings, loads of calligraphy paraphernalia and thousands of teapots, wood carvings, jade, vases, and urns. Whatever element of kitsch you might find among the aforementioned is put firmly into the shadows by the offerings of cheap glass baubles, replica clipper ships, and "sexy" posters of blonde white couples in varying states of undress. Whatever your taste in culture, there is something here for you.

Side Trips from Tianjin

Panshan. This range of peaks is at the northern end of the Tianjin municipality. Noted for its pine trees and beautiful scenery, Panshan is one of China's 15 famous mountains. In the past it was home to numerous monasteries and temples. ✉ *75 km (46 mi) east of Beijing; trains and buses run from Tianjin.*

Du Le Si (Du Le Temple). The 1,000-year-old temple lies in Jixian county. It houses a 52-ft statue (among the largest clay statues in China) of Guanyin, Goddess of Mercy, that stretches to the octagonal ceiling three floors up. The walls on the ground floor are covered with Buddhist murals. ✉ *3 hrs north of Tianjin municipality by train.*

Tianjin A to Z

Arriving and Departing

BY PLANE

The airport is half an hour southeast of the city center. There are regular flights to and from Hong Kong and other major Chinese cities as well as South Korea.

BY TRAIN

There are half a dozen departures and arrivals from Beijing every day. Trains run regularly to Jinan, Nanjing, Shanghai, Qingdao, and other cities.

Getting Around

Taxi is the easiest way to get around. Flag fall is Y10.

Travel Agency and Visitor Information

CITS (22 Youyi Lu, opposite Friendship Store, ☎ 022/3318– 550).

4 Shanghai

Shanghai, the most notorious of Chinese cities, once the "Paris of the East," now calls itself the "Pearl of the Orient." No other city can better capture the urgency and excitement of China's opening and reform. Beauty and charm coexist with kitsch and commercialism. From the colonial architecture of the former French Concession to the neon-lit high rises jutting above the city, Shanghai is a city of paradox and change.

By Lily Tung

SHANGHAI, literally the "City on the Sea," has in the 1990s become the center of China's economic resurgence. Shanghai's allure begins with its glamorous past of sepia-lit halls, opium dens, and French villas. A gathering of cultures, it once was a place where rich taipans walked the same streets as gamblers, prostitutes, and beggars, and Europeans fleeing the Holocaust lived alongside Chinese intellectuals and revolutionaries.

Although the Communist party was born here, its strict tenets could not stifle the city's unflagging internationalism, which was determined at its creation. Although the nation has a history thousands of years old, Shanghai itself could be called a new Chinese invention. Lying on the Yangzi River delta, it marks the point where Asia's longest and most important river completes its 5,500-km (3,400-mi) journey to the Pacific. Until 1842, Shanghai's location made it merely a small fishing village. After the first Opium War, the British named Shanghai a treaty port, forcing the city's opening to foreign involvement.

The village was soon turned into a city carved up into autonomous concessions administered by the British, French, and Americans independent of Chinese law. Each colonial presence brought with it its own culture, architecture, and society. Although Shanghai had its own walled Chinese city—what is now known as the "Old City"—many native residents still chose to live in the foreign settlements. Thus began a mixing of cultures that shaped Shanghai's openness to Western influence. Shanghai became an important industrial center and trading port that attracted not only foreign business people (60,000 by the 1930s), but also Chinese migrating from other parts of the country.

Shanghai was the place to be. In its heyday, it was known for the best culture and arts in Asia, the greatest architecture, the strongest business. Dance halls, brothels, glitzy restaurants, international clubs, even a foreign-run race track made it a city with everything for anybody who was rich. Poverty ran alongside opulence, and many of the lower-class Chinese provided the cheap labor that kept the city running.

The Paris of the East became known as a place of vice and indulgence. Amidst this glamour and degradation the Communist Party held its first meeting in 1921, starting a movement that would change all of China. The city weathered the Japanese invasion and then the victory of the Communists in 1949, after which foreigners left the country. Shanghai then fell into a deep sleep, closed from the outside world it had become so comfortable with. Fashion, music, and romance gave way to uniformity and the stark reality of Communism.

Today Shanghai has once again become one of China's most open cities ideologically, socially, and economically. It is striving to return to the internationalism that defined it before the Revolution. Shanghai's path to renewed prominence began in 1990 when China's paramount leader, Deng Xiaoping, chose it as the engine of the country's commercial renaissance, aiming to rival Hong Kong by 2010. Having embraced competition and a market-driven economy within a few years, it now hosts the nation's stock market, accounts for one-sixth of the country's GNP, and houses the most important industrial base in the nation.

Today's metropolis of 13 million is the New York City of China. Nowhere else in the country can you feel the same pulse, dynamism, and fervor. Unlike sprawling Beijing, Shanghai is a true city laid out on a grid. It is one of the world's most crowded urban areas. The Chinese claim that the city's main thoroughfare, Nanjing Lu, contains a higher concentration of people, buses, cars, and bicycles than any other city in the world.

Other parts of the country call the cosmopolitan Shanghainese proud, arrogant, quick to learn, sly, sharp, shrewd, open-minded, glamorous, sophisticated, vulgar, business-minded, and money-driven. The Shanghainese themselves would probably agree, for they are convinced they have the motivation and attitude to achieve their place as China's powerhouse. Across the Huangpu River, which joins the Yangzi at Shanghai, the city's most important project is being built—Pudong New Area, a 21st-century financial, economic, and commercial center. Rising from land dominated just a few years ago by rice paddies is the people's pride and joy, the Oriental Pearl TV Tower—a gaudy, flashing, spaceship-like pillar, the tallest in Asia.

Since 1992 Shanghai has gone through staggering change. Charming old houses are making way for shiny high rises. The population is moving from alley housing in the city center to spanking-new apartments in the suburbs. Foreign shopping centers and malls pop up on every corner. Residents walk down to their favorite store only to find it's been torn down to make room for a new architectural wonder. In 1987 there were about 150 high-rise buildings in the city. Today there are more than 1,500 and the number continues to grow. Shanghai is reputed to be home to one-fifth of all the world's construction cranes.

Shanghai's open policy has also made the city the new hot attraction for foreign investors. As millions of dollars pour in, especially to Pudong, Shanghai has again become home to tens of thousands of expatriates. Foreign influence has made today's Shanghai a Chinese consumer heaven. Domestic stores rub shoulders with the boutiques of Louis Vuitton, Christian Dior, and Ralph Lauren. Shanghainese women are among the most fashionable in China, having abandoned Mao's blue uniforms. Among the youth, mobile phones and pagers are de rigueur, essential accessories for their newfound stylish image.

In Shanghai, it's all about image, and the owner of the highest-priced goods goes home the winner. It's not surprising, then, that the Shanghainese enjoy one of the highest living standards in China. Higher salaries, more goods, and more and more venues for entertainment, nightlife, and culture complement the lives of China's most cosmopolitan and open people.

Pleasures and Pastimes

Architecture
Shanghai's history has been eclectic, and so is its architecture. Although significant portions of the city are making way for skyscrapers, much that has defined its charm still exists. From the neo-classicism of the Bund to the Art Deco of the French Concession to the quaint Chinese alleys of the old city, a walk through town is sure to evoke romantic old Shanghai.

Dining
Although Communism once put a damper on Shanghai's culinary creativity, the city and the outlying region have a history of cooking that survives. Following the push to re-make Shanghai an international city, more tastes from around the world are arriving here than at any time since 1949.

Shanghainese food is one of China's main regional cuisines, along with Cantonese from the south and Sichuan-style from the west. Shanghai's restaurants tend to serve an amalgam of dishes from different regions, and it may be difficult to weed out a restaurant that serves true "Shanghainese" food. Still, when you can find it, the resulting mix of tastes is in itself unique, what the people like to call "home-style" cooking. Typical Shanghai fare includes *jiachang doufu* (homestyle tofu), *pao fan* (a soupy rice concoction), and *su ban dou* (cold vegetables with bean mash). Shanghainese chefs like to use high doses of oil and sugar, and brown-based sauces. River fish is often the highlight of the meal, with Shanghai hairy crab a specialty in winter. Shanghai is also known for its own style of dim sum. You can often find dumplings, wontons, *you tiao* (dough sticks), Shanghainese fried noodles, and baked and fried breads being sold by street vendors throughout the city.

Western food has also become increasingly available, with foreign establishments arriving on the scene monthly. In addition, China's opening has made fast-food joints popular among locals, who frequent KFC and McDonald's. Today it's become more a way of life than just a meal, with families taking their one child for a hamburger treat or couples lovingly sharing a pizza.

Chinese people follow a very strict eating schedule, so if you're dining at a more traditional Chinese restaurant, you can expect larger crowds between 11:30 AM and 12:30 PM and between 5:30 and 6:30 PM. At some restaurants you must arrive early for dinner (at least by 6 PM) or you'll miss all the best food. Many restaurants also have English menus, and you may find it difficult to order at the ones that don't. If you can't find a server who can translate for you, pantomime and drawings usually work fairly well.

You're not obliged to tip, as it's not a custom in China. Actually, almost all restaurants in Shanghai tack on a 10%–15% service charge, which technically takes care of the tip even though your server may not see any of it. If there is no mandatory service charge, tipping is still not required or expected.

CATEGORY	COST*
$$$$	over $45
$$$	$20–$45
$$	$10–$20
$	under $10

Prices are per person for a standard meal, excluding drinks

Lodging

Since the early 1990s the number of foreign hotels has exploded, pushing up the standards and quality of domestic-run hotels as well. Room rates have also skyrocketed. Hotels cater mostly to business travelers, but hotel service and quality in Shanghai still do not excel. Shanghai's hotels can be divided into two categories. The first are modern Western-style hotels that are elegant and nicely appointed, but unmemorable. The second are hotels built in old Shanghai's glory days that became state-run after 1949. These may lack great service, modern fixings, and convenient facilities, but they make up for it in charm, tradition, and history. All hotels have cashier counters where you can change foreign currency into yuan.

CATEGORY	COST*
$$$$	over $200
$$$	$150–$200
$$	$75–$150
$	under $75

Prices are for a standard double room with bath at peak season unless otherwise stated; 15% service charge is not included

Nightlife

Other cities in China may close down after dinner, but Shanghai never sleeps. The neon stays ablaze past the wee hours. Whether playing pool at an American bar or discoing the night away at a chic club, young Shanghainese and expatriates alike have a fairly good selection of nighttime entertainment.

Although most of the city's popular bars are in the city center, they are concentrated at several different points. Old bars close down and new bars pop up out of the blue. Because Shanghai is small, the light traffic in the evenings makes it ideal for quick bar-hopping by cab. Karaoke is ubiquitous; KTV (Karaoke TV) establishments with private rooms complete with serving girls, XO cognac, and fruit platters are even more popular. Just beware of the prices.

Shopping and Markets

Because of Shanghai's commercial status and internationalism as China's most open port city, it has the widest variety of goods to be found in the nation, with the exception of Hong Kong. Foreign name brands can be found in any department store. High-quality domestic goods inundate the consumer. Ritzy chrome shopping malls stand alongside the local state-run food store. Two of Shanghai's main roads—Nanjing Lu and Huaihai Lu—have become the city's shopping meccas.

Traditional treasures, Chinese arts and crafts, and such Chinese special exports as silk and linen are also available in established stores as well as on the street. In the city's nooks and crannies outdoor markets give a good view of Shanghai's bustling street life. Food markets are scattered in every neighborhood. Bird and flower markets offer anything from bonsai plants to prize-winning songbirds. Most interesting, however, are the antiques markets, at which local hawkers sell their pieces of Chinese history—some real, some not.

EXPLORING SHANGHAI

Shanghai as a whole encompasses a huge area. However, the city center is a relatively small district in what is collectively called Puxi (west of the river). On the east side lies Pudong (east of the river). Shanghai's main east–west roads are named for Chinese cities, while its north–south streets are named for Chinese provinces.

The city was once delineated by its foreign concessions, and to some extent, the former borders still define the city. The old Chinese city is now surrounded by the Zhonghua Lu–Renmin Lu circle. North of the Chinese city, the International Settlement, run by the British, Americans, Europeans, and Japanese, was the area between the Huangpu River and Huashan Lu bordered by Suzhou Creek to the north and Yanan Lu to the south. The former French Concession lies south of Yanan Lu, north of Zhaojiabang Lu. The southwest corner of the Concession lies at Xujiahui, from which point it runs all the way east to the Bund, with the exception of the northern half of the old Chinese city.

Although technically most Shanghainese consider the city center to be whatever lies within the Ring Road, the heart of the city is found on its chief east–west streets—Nanjing Lu, Huaihai Lu, and Yanan Lu—cut off in the west by Wulumuqi Lu and in the east by the Bund. The closer you get to the Bund, the stronger the heartbeat becomes. The most crowded and busiest part of town lies between Suzhou Creek and Yanan Lu, bordered by Xizang Lu on the west side and the Bund on the east.

To the east and west of city center lie Shanghai's new development areas. In Hongqiao, the area outside the Ring Road to the west, are new office and commercial buildings for foreign and domestic business and the new residential area of Gubei. Rising from countryside across the Huangpu River to the east is Pudong, the new concrete behemoth that Deng Xiaoping designated as China's future financial, economic, and commercial center.

Parts of Shanghai are easily explored on foot, and taxis are readily available. In compact central Shanghai, cab rides would be short if not for the outrageous traffic. Some spots outside Shanghai offer getaways from the city's urban chaos, but because public transportation can be unreliable and roads are not well maintained, day trips, with the exception of a few places, can be difficult.

Numbers in the text correspond to numbers in the margin and on the Shanghai map.

Great Itineraries

IF YOU HAVE 3 DAYS

Start with a trip to **Yu Garden,** sip some tea, and take a walk around the surrounding old Chinese city. Afterward, work your way over to the **Bund** for a leisurely stroll, take a quick look at the historic **Peace Hotel,** and walk down **Nanjing Lu** to experience Shanghai's busiest street. For dinner, the Peace Hotel Chinese restaurant offers good views of the river and the Bund lit up at night. The next day, take a cab north to the **Jade Buddha Temple,** head back to Nanjing Lu if you didn't finish its sights the day before, and then spend an afternoon at **Renmin Square,** people-watching and taking in China's ancient treasures at the **Shanghai Museum.** If there's still time, you can stop in at the **Great World** for some Chinese entertainment. Day three can be spent walking in the **French Concession,** particularly around Huaihai Lu, for a view of old Shanghai and the city's new chic stores. Here you can also tour **Sun Yatsen's former residence** and the **site of the first Communist Party meeting.** The evenings of day two and three can be spent catching a **show of the Shanghai acrobats,** reputedly the world's best, or relaxing on a **night cruise of the Huangpu River.**

IF YOU HAVE 5 DAYS

Follow the three-day itinerary (☞ *above*) and on the fourth day, make a trip to the southern part of the city to see the **Longhua Temple and Pagoda.** Afterward, you can swing over to view the **Xujiahui Cathedral** and **Madame Soong Ching Ling's** former residence. Go farther west and you'll find yourself at the **Shanghai Zoo,** adjacent to the old **Sassoon Villa.** On day five cross the river and go to the top of the **Oriental Pearl TV Tower** for a bird's-eye view of the city. Head back across the river and then north to view **Lu Xun's memorial.** Alternatively, you can spend a whole day at Shanghai's antiques markets, antique furniture warehouses, and arts and crafts stores.

IF YOU HAVE 7 DAYS

Start with the five-day itinerary (☞ *above*). On the sixth day, to see Shanghai's economic future, go back to **Pudong** for a drive through its financial development zones of Lujiazui, Jinqiao, and Waigaoqiao all the way to the East China Sea. Alternatively, you can get away from it all with a day trip to **Zhouzhuang,** the canal city outside Shanghai. The next day go for a boat ride on **Dianshan Lake** or drive out to Sheshan and Tianmushan in Songjiang County to see the leaning **Huzhou Pagoda.** If you're willing to take a two-hour train ride, **Suzhou** or **Lake Tai** (☞ Jiangsu *in* Chapter 5) also make good one-day trips. Hangzhou (☞ Zhejiang *in* Chapter 5) is even doable, but you'll have to fly if you want to spend a good day there.

The best time to visit Shanghai is early fall. The weather is at its best in September and October, with a good chance of sunny days and mild temperatures. Winters are cold and rainy. In spring the days grow warmer, but the rain continues, sometimes unceasingly for weeks. The summers can be pleasant in June, but come July you can bet that the days will be hot and excruciatingly humid.

The Old City and the Bund

When Shanghai was carved up by foreign powers, one part of the central city remained under Chinese law and administration. These old winding back alleys eventually became notorious as a gangster- and opium-filled slum. Today the narrow meandering lanes, crowded but quaint neighborhoods, tiny pre-1949 houses, and cobblestone streets are still standing (though the vices have disappeared for the most part). A walk through the Old City gives an idea of how most Shanghainese once lived and many still do. The city's most important sightseeing spot, the Bund, on Shanghai's waterfront, showcases the outstanding foreign buildings from pre-1949 times.

A Good Walk

Start at the **Yuyuan** ①. Stroll through the garden, check out the bazaar surrounding it, and stop at the teahouse for a serene rest. You can also wander the small alleys of the Old City, which lies inside the Renmin Lu–Zhonghua Lu circle.

From wherever you come out of the Yuyuan, walk directly east until you reach the water. Shiliupu (Dock No. 16), the main dock for tourist ships to outlying islands, will most likely be south of you (to your right). Turn left along Zhongshan Dong Lu and go north. The **Wai Tan** ② begins along the river on your right. A raised concrete promenade borders the side of the street nearest the river. Continue to the intersection of Zhongshan Dong Lu and Jinling Lu, marked by a triangular commercial building on the water. Near this building is the Huangpu River Cruises dock (☞ Guided Tours *in* Shanghai A to Z, *below*).

As you continue north, historic buildings begin appearing on the west side of the street facing the river. Just north of Yanan Dong Lu is the **Dongfeng Fandian** ③, formerly the Shanghai Club. As you continue walking, you'll pass the **Former Hong Kong and Shanghai Bank** ④ and the present and former **Haiguan Lou** ⑤, which houses the "Big Ching," or clock tower. As you near Shanghai's main thoroughfare, Nanjing Lu, you'll see one of the city's most famous historic monuments: The **Heping Fandian** ⑥ consists of the two buildings on the corner of the Bund and Nanjing Lu. Just north of the Peace is the **Zhongguo Yinhang** ⑦, the main bank in the city. You can spot it by all the black market money changers loitering in front of it.

Across the street on the river lies **Huangpu Gongyuan** ⑧, which has a statue of Chen Yi, Shanghai's first mayor after 1949. North of him is the obelisk-like Memorial of the Heroes of the People. At this point you have come to the junction of the Bund and Beijing Dong Lu. Across the old Waibaidu Bridge on Suzhou Creek in front of you are three more pre-1949 buildings: the Art Deco Shanghai Dasha (Shanghai Mansions) is in front of you to the left, and the **Shanghai Stock Exchange** ⑨ and the blue **Emeng Lingshiguan** ⑩ are to the right.

It can take about three hours to stroll the above route casually without stopping at any sights. Allow another two hours to wander through the Yuyuan Gardens, bazaar, and teahouse. Many of the old buildings

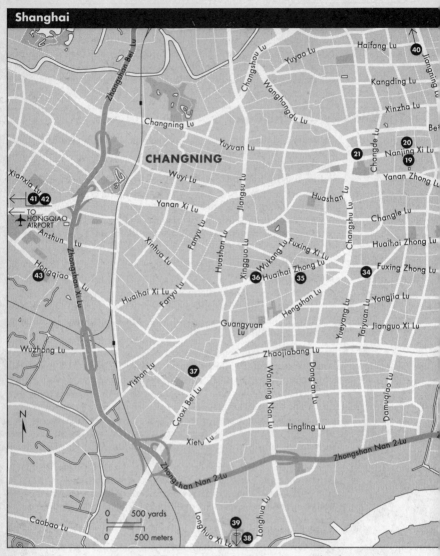

Cathay Cinema, **32**

Da Ju Yuan, **13**

Da Shijie, **14**

Dongfeng Fandian, **3**

Dongfeng
Mingzhu, **22**

Emeng
Lingshiguan, **10**

Former Hong Kong
and Shanghai Bank, **4**

Fuxing Gongyuan, **31**

Guoji Fandian, **16**

Haiguan Lou, **5**

Heping Fandian, **6**

Huangpu
Gongyuan, **8**

Jingan Gu Si, **21**

Jinqiao, **28**

Lao Shanghai
Tushuguan, **17**

Longhua Gu Si, **38**

Lujiazui, **26**

Luxun Gongyuan, **23**

Lyceum Theatre, **33**

Moxi Huitang
and Huoshan, **24**

Nanpu and Yangpu
Bridges, **25**

Renmin
Gongyuan, **15**

Renmin Guang
Chang, **11**

Sassoon Villa, **41**

Shanghai
Bowuguan, **12**

Shanghai
Dongwuyuan, **42**

Shanghai Gongyi
Meishu Yanjiusuo
Jiugong Yipin Xiufu
Bu, **34**

Shanghai Lishi
Bowuguan, **43**

Shanghai Meishu
Guan, **18**

Shanghai
Shangcheng, **20**

Shanghai
Tushuguan, **35**

Shanghai Zhanlan
Zhongxin, **19**

Shanghai Zhenquan
Jiaoyisuo, **9**

Shanghai
Zhiwuyuan, **39**

Song Quingling
Guju, **36**

Sun Zhongshan
Guju, **30**

Xujiahui
Dajiaotang, **37**

Wai Tan
(The Bund), **2**

Waigaoqiao, **27**

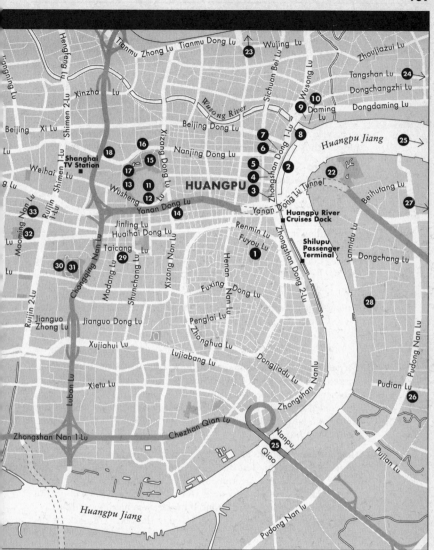

are now government offices and access is not allowed, but to go inside the ones that are open to visitors, allow 15 minutes per building. For a cruise on the Huangpu River, count on one to three hours.

Yuyuan is most crowded on weekends, so if you go on a Sunday, you definitely won't find the walk serene. Shanghai's most popular tourist sights, including the Bund, are most crowded on the weekends, with hordes of domestic tourists and locals enjoying their day off.

On National Day, October 1, and Labor Day, May 1, the Bund is closed to bicycle and automobile traffic, and the roads are choked with people. On those days, a fireworks show is usually put on over the water.

Sights to See

❸ Dongfeng Fandian (Tung Feng Hotel). Built in 1910, the former Shanghai Club limited membership to wealthy British men. The building once contained the longest bar in the world. That first-floor establishment has since been occupied by a fast-food chain restaurant, but much of the building remains in its original glory. The lobby still showcases its marble floor, oak paneling, columns, barrel ceiling, and beautiful old cage elevator. Upstairs is the Seaman's Club, which houses the new "long bar" and is frequented by sailors passing through Shanghai's harbors. ✉ *2 The Bund (Zhongshan Dong Lu).*

❿ Emeng Lingshiguan (Russian Consulate). On the waterfront north and east of the Waibaidu Bridge, the consulate still occupies its pre-1949 building, unlike the other consulates, which have all lost their original quarters. ✉ *20 Huangpu Lu,* ☎ *021/5324–8383.*

❹ Former Hong Kong and Shanghai Bank. After 1949, the building was turned into Communist Party offices and City Hall; now it is used by another foreign bank. One of the Bund's most impressive buildings, the domed structure was built by the British in 1921–23, when it was the second-largest bank building in the world. ✉ *12 The Bund (Zhongshan Dong Lu).*

❺ Haiguan Lou (Customs House). Built in 1927, the Customs House continues as the headquarters of customs authorities, although now in the service of a different government. The old clock tower is now called "Big Ching" by the Shanghainese. During the Cultural Revolution, the bells were taken down and replaced by speakers blaring out Mao Zedong's theme, "The East Is Red." Today the bells are back in the tower, but they can't be heard amid the cacophony of the city. ✉ *13 The Bund (Zhongshan Dong Lu).*

★ ❻ Heping Fandian (The Peace Hotel). This hotel at the corner of the Bund and Nanjing Lu is among Shanghai's most treasured old buildings. If any establishment will give you a sense of Shanghai's past, it is this one. Its high ceilings, ornate woodwork, and Art Deco fixtures are still intact, and the ballroom evokes old Shanghai cabarets and gala parties.

The south building was formerly the Palace Hotel. Built in 1906 by the British, it is the oldest building on the Bund. The north building, formerly the Cathay Hotel, built in 1929, is more famous historically. It was known as the private playroom of its owner, Victor Sassoon, a wealthy landowner who invested in the opium trade. The Cathay was actually part of a complete office and hotel structure collectively called Sassoon House. Victor Sassoon himself lived and entertained his guests in the green penthouse. The hotel was rated along with the likes of Raffles in Singapore and The Peninsula in Hong Kong. It was *the* place to stay in old Shanghai; Noel Coward wrote *Private Lives* here. For a memorable view, take the middle elevators to the top floor of the north building and then climb the last two flights of stairs to the roof. From here you can see Sassoon's former penthouse and the action on the streets and river below (☞ Lodging, *below*). ⊠ *20 Nanjing Dong Lu,* ☎ *021/ 6321–6888.*

❽ Huangpu Gongyuan (Huangpu Park). This uninteresting piece of greenery contains the **Statue of Chen Yi,** Shanghai's first mayor, as well as the **Memorial of the Heroes of the People.** During colonial times, Chinese could not enter the park; a sign stood at the entrance saying, "No Dogs or Chinese Allowed." ⊠ *North end of Bund, next to river.*

❾ Shanghai Zhengquan Jiaoyisuo (Shanghai Stock Exchange). An old building north of the Waibaidu Bridge is the former site of the exchange. The new building is in Pudong (528 Pudong Nan Lu, ☎ 021/6880–8888). Visitors cannot enter the trading floor. ⊠ *15 Huangpu Lu,* ☎ *021/6306–8888.*

★ **❷ Wai Tan** (The Bund). Shanghai's waterfront boulevard best showcases the city's mesh of pre-1949 past and focus on the future. The name of the district is derived from Anglo-Indian and literally means a muddy embankment. In the early 1920s the Bund became the city's foreign street. Americans, British, Japanese, French, Russians, Germans, and other Europeans built banks, trading houses, clubs, consulates, and hotels on this strip of land in styles from neo-classical to Art Deco. As Shanghai grew to be a bustling trading center in the Yangzi Delta, the Bund's warehouses and ports became the heart of the action. With the Communist victory, the foreigners left Shanghai and the Chinese government housed its own banks and offices here.

Today the municipal government has renovated the old buildings of this most foreign face of the city, highlighting them as a tourist attraction, and is in the process of selling them back to the very owners it forced out after 1949.

On the riverfront side of the Bund, Shanghai's street life is in full force. The city recently rebuilt the promenade, making it an ideal gathering place for both tourists and residents. In the mornings just after dawn, the Bund is full of people ballroom dancing, doing aerobics, and practicing kung fu, qigong, and taijiquan. The rest of the day people walk the embankment, snapping photos of the Oriental Pearl TV Tower, the Huangpu River, and each other. In the evenings, lovers come out for romantic walks amid the floodlights accenting the buildings and the Tower. ⊠ *5 blocks of Zhongshan Dong Lu between Jinling Lu and Suzhou Creek.*

★ **❶ Yuyuan** (Yu Garden). This is among Shanghai's main attractions. Since the 18th century the complex, with its traditional red walls and upturned tile roofs, has been a marketplace and social center where local residents gather, shop, and practice qigong in the evenings. Although not as impressive as the ancient palaces in Beijing, Yu Garden is a piece of Shanghai past, one of the few old sights left in the city.

Surrounding the Garden is a touristy bazaar of stores that sell traditional Chinese arts and crafts, medicine, and souvenirs. In the last few years, city renovations have turned the bazaar into a mall, complete with chrome and shiny glass.

To get to the Garden, you must wind your way through the bazaar. The ticket booth is just north of the central man-made lake and the pleasant **Huxingting Teahouse** (☞ *below*). The Suzhou-style rock and tree garden was built from 1559 to 1577 by the Pan family, who were officials in the Ming dynasty. In the mid-1800s the Society of Small Swords used the Garden as a gathering place for meetings. It was here that they planned their uprising with the Taiping rebels against the French colonialists. The French destroyed the Garden during the first Opium War, but the area was later rebuilt and renovated.

Within the winding walkways, bridges, artificial mountains and lakes, carp-filled ponds, dragon-lined walls, and pavilions are a **museum** dedicated to the Society of Small Swords rebellion and the **Chenghuang Miao** (Temple of the City God). The temple was built during the early part of the Ming dynasty but was later destroyed. In 1926 the main hall was rebuilt and sometime after was renovated. The temple went through its most recent renovation in the early 1990s. ⊠ *Bordered by Fuyou Lu, Jiujiaochang Lu, Fangbang Lu, and Anren Lu, Old City.* ☎ *Gardens Y15, Bazaar free.* ☉ *Gardens, daily 8:30AM–4:30PM.*

NEED A
BREAK?

The **Huxingting Teahouse** (Mid-lake Pavilion; ⊠ 257 Yuyuan Lu, ☎ 021/6373–6950), Shanghai's oldest, opened in 1856, stands on a small man-made lake in the middle of the Yuyuan Gardens and Bazaar. Be sure to sit on the top floor by a window overlooking the lake. Every night from 6:30 to 7:30 a traditional tea ceremony is performed.

---

❼ **Zhongguo Yinhang** (Bank of China). The Bank of China showcases old Shanghai's Western architecture (British Art Deco in this case) mixed with Chinese elements. In 1937 it was built to be the highest building in the city and surpassed the neighboring Cathay Hotel (now the Peace Hotel) by a hair, except for the green tower on the Cathay's roof. ⊠ *23 Zhongshan Dong Lu,* ☎ *021/6329–1979.*

Nanjing Lu and Huangpu and Jingan Districts

The city's *zhongxin*, or center, is primarily in Huangpu and Jingan districts. These two areas make up most of what was known in imperial and republican times as the International Settlement. Nanjing Lu, Shanghai's main thoroughfare, crosses east–west through these two districts. You'll be able to spot it at night by its neon extravaganza and in the day by the sheer amount of business going on. Hordes of pedestrians compete with one another and with bicycles, and cars move at a snaillike pace in traffic jams.

A Good Walk

Go west on the shopping street Nanjing Lu from the Heping Fandian (☞ Peace Hotel, *above*), meandering among the crowds and stores. The first blocks of Nanjing Dong Lu are shorter and still showcase some of the architecture of old Shanghai. On the blocks north and south of the street you can still sense the atmosphere of the place in the 1920s. Turn left (south) on Xizang Lu, and in a block you'll arrive at the city's huge social and cultural center, **Renmin Guang Chang** ⑪, overlooked by an enormous TV screen on its southern end. At the square you'll also find the wonderful **Shanghai Bowuguan** ⑫, the new Municipal Offices, and the **Da Ju Yuan** ⑬, which is under construction. The **Da Shijie** ⑭ entertainment center lies southeast of the square, on the corner of Yanan Lu and Xizang Lu.

Just north of the square is **Renmin Gongyuan** ⑮, Shanghai's largest and most important, if not necessarily the nicest. On the other side of the park is the historic **Guoji Fandian** ⑯.

On its western side, the People's Square is bordered by Huangpi Lu. Turn right (north) on Huangpi Lu, past the Bird and Flower Market (☞ Shopping, *below*), and to your right will be the **Lao Shanghai Tushuguan** ⑰ at the corner of Nanjing Lu. Turn left and continue on Nanjing Lu past the rather mundane **Shanghai Meishu Guan** ⑱ on the right side. Once you pass Chengdu Lu, the street of the overhead Ring

Road, the Shanghai Television Station and Tower is on the left with a very large TV screen in front. About 5 blocks down, after the intersection of Xikang Lu, you'll see the huge hall built by the Russians that is now the **Shanghai Zhanlan Zhongxin** ⑲. It sits directly across from the convenient **Shanghai Shangcheng** ⑳. Two blocks farther west on Nanjing Lu, on the corner of Huashan Lu, is the **Jingan Gu Si** ㉑.

TIMING

The above walk is fairly long and doesn't have to be done all at once. When you get tired, it's also easy to jump into a cab between sights. The distance from the Bund to Jingan Temple is about 4 km (2½ mi). The whole walk without stopping will probably take you an hour to an hour and a half. Leave two to three hours for the Shanghai Museum. If you go to the Great World, Jingan Temple, or the Bird and Flower Market, block off an hour for each of these sights. The rest you can walk through or by very quickly.

Nanjing Lu and the People's Square are both most crowded and most exciting on weekends. You may have to fight the hordes, but you'll get a good idea of what life is like in Shanghai. On Saturday evenings from 5 to 10, the east side of Nanjing Lu from Xizang Lu to the Bund is closed to car and bike traffic, and it seems like the city's entire population is walking the street.

Sights to See

⓭ **Da Ju Yuan** (Grand Theatre). Slated for completion in October 1998, this magnificent theater, along with the **Shanghai Museum** (☞ Shanghai Bowuguan, *below*) and **Shanghai Library** (☞ *Shanghai Tushuguan, below*) is part of Shanghai's project to make itself a cultural center. The theater will have three stages and put on the best international and domestic performers. The curved roof sitting atop a square base is meant to invoke the Chinese traditional saying, "The earth is square and the sky is round." Shanghai's goal is to make the theater outshine the Sydney Opera House and New York's Lincoln Center. ⊠ *190 Huangpi Lu,* ☎ *021/6387–5480.*

⓮ **Da Shijie** (The Great World). Old Shanghai's notorious gambling, cabaret, drug, and prostitution den has been recently restored. Today, the entertainment center with its wedding-cake-style tower has an eclectic set of performances—acrobatics, opera, magic, comedy, Chinese period films. Some take place in the outside courtyard. Other attractions include fortune tellers, a Guinness Book of Records hall, fantasy rides, bumper cars, and a hall of mirrors. The center also houses fun-fair booths, bowling, a dance hall, and food stalls. ⊠ *1 Xizang Nan Lu,* ☎ *021/6326–3760.* ▧ *Y20.* ⊙ *Daily 9–9.*

⓰ **Guoji Fandian** (Park Hotel). This Art Deco structure overlooking People's Park was originally the tallest hotel in Shanghai. Completed in 1934, it had luxury rooms, a nightclub, and chic restaurants; today it's more subdued (☞ Lodging, *below*). ⊠ *170 Nanjing Xi Lu,* ☎ *021/ 6327–5225.*

㉑ **Jingan Gu Si** (Jingan Temple). Originally built about AD 300, the Jingan Temple has been rebuilt and renovated numerous times. The temple's most important historical piece is its bell, which was cast in 1183. It is now an active Buddhist center. ⊠ *1700 Nanjing Xi Lu,* ☎ *021/ 6248–6366.* ▧ *Y2.* ⊙ *7:45–3:30.*

⓱ **Lao Shanghai Tushuguan** (Old Shanghai Library). At the northwest corner of People's Park, the former site of the Shanghai Library was once a clubhouse for old Shanghai's sports groups, including the Shanghai

Race Club. The building will soon become the new site of the Shanghai Art Museum. ⊠ *Nanjing Lu at Huangpi Bei Lu.*

⑮ Renmin Gongyuan (People's Park). Shanghai's largest and most central park is one of its least impressive. In colonial days it was the race track. Today the 30 acres of flower beds, lotus ponds, trees, and fairground (which is rarely open) also contain a high percentage of concrete. The park is known for its English corner, where locals gather to practice their language skills. Expect to be approached by people wanting to try their English on you. ⊠ *231 Nanjing Xi Lu,* ☎ *021/6327–1333.* ⊙ *Daily 6–6.*

NEED A BREAK?

At the **Yunnan Lu Night Bazaar** (⊠ left side of Nanjing Lu as you're walking west) every evening after dusk until about 10 PM, hawkers sell, for pennies, such Chinese snack foods as dumplings, spring rolls, and fried noodles. You can walk and eat at the same time or sit down at one of the simple outdoor tables.

⑪ Renmin Guang Chang (People's Square). Shanghai's main square was built for the people and has become a social and cultural center. Before 1949, it made up the south half of the city's race track. The **Shanghai Museum** (☞ Shanghai Bowuguan, *below*), Municipal Offices, Telecommunications Building, and site of the future **Grand Theatre** (☞ Da Ju Yuan, *above*) ring this square. In the daytime, visitors and residents stroll, fly kites, and take their children to feed the pigeons. In the evening, kids roller skate, people watch shows on the huge TV screen, ballroom dancers hold group lessons, and families relax together. Weekends here are especially busy. ⊠ *Bordered by Weihai Lu on south, Xizang Lu on east, Huangpi Lu on west, and Fuzhou Lu on north.*

★ **⑫ Shanghai Bowuguan** (Shanghai Museum). The Shanghai Museum moved in 1995 to its new location in the center of People's Square and opened in 1996. Truly one of Shanghai's treasures, this urn-shape museum is the foremost showcase of relics and artifacts in the country. Its 11 state-of-the-art galleries house China's first international-standard exhibits of paintings, bronzes, sculpture, ceramics, calligraphy, jade, Ming and Qing dynasty furniture, coins, seals, and minority art. The bronze collection is among the best in the world. Three additional halls house rotating exhibitions. Information is well presented in English, but the highly informative acoustic guide is also excellent and shouldn't be missed. You can relax in the museum's pleasant tea room. The excellent museum shops offer antiques, crafts, and quality reproductions of the artworks in the museum. ⊠ *201 Renmin Da Dao,* ☎ *021/6372–3500.* ⊠ *Y20, Y60 with acoustic guide; students Y10, free Sat. 5 PM—8 PM.* ⊙ *Sun.–Fri. 9–5, Sat. 9–8.*

⑱ Shanghai Meishu Guan (Shanghai Art Museum). This state-run museum built in typical Communist-bloc style rarely shows its permanent collection and of late has become an art gallery, leasing space to whatever exhibitor can pay the fee. ⊠ *456 Nanjing Xi Lu,* ☎ *021/6327–0557.* ⊠ *Y5.* ⊙ *Daily 9–11 and 1–4.*

⑳ Shanghai Shangcheng (Shanghai Centre). In the Shanghai Centre are a premier office building that's occupied by multinational companies; the important **Shanghai Centre Theatre**, where international name acts and the Shanghai acrobats perform; two expatriate housing complexes; a major hotel, and a shopping arcade including a supermarket, a drug store, foreign airline offices, and restaurants. ⊠ *1376 Nanjing Xi Lu,* ☎ *021/6279–8600.*

NEED A
BREAK? **Espresso Americano** (✉ Shanghai Centre, 1376 Nanjing Xi Lu, ☎ 021/
6247–9750) is one of the only places in the city to find a real espresso,
latte, or cappuccino. The tiny café has tables outside as well as in.

⑲ Shanghai Zhanlan Zhongxin (Shanghai Exhibition Centre). This mammoth piece of Russian architecture was built as a sign of Sino-Soviet friendship after 1949. Special exhibitions are held here, and the complex has a shopping area, bowling alley, and restaurant. ✉ *1000 Yanan Zhong Lu,* ☎ *021/6279–0279.*

The East and Northeast:
Pudong New Area and Hongkou District

East of the Huangpu River lies a constantly changing urban experiment that before 1990 was farmland and rice paddies. Here you'll find the biggest of everything: the tallest tower in Asia, the largest department store on the continent, and the future tallest building in the world. The modern architectural wonders, the Yangpu and Nanpu Bridges, connect Pudong to Puxi. The new Shanghai international airport, to open in 1999, will be here, and the Shanghai Stock Exchange moves to its new building in Pudong in 1998.

On the west side of the river, you can move back from Pudong's timeline to old Shanghai. North of Suzhou Creek are the northeastern districts of Hongkou and Yangpu. At the turn of the century Shanghai was not only an international port but also an open one, where anyone could enter regardless of nationality. As the century wore on and the world became riddled with war, Jews, first fleeing the Russian Revolution and then escaping Hitler, arrived in Shanghai from Germany, Austria, Poland, and Russia. From 1937 to 1941, Shanghai became a haven for tens of thousands of Jewish refugees. In 1943, Japanese troops who invaded Shanghai forced all the city's Jews into the "Designated Area for Stateless Refugees" in Hongkou District, where they lived until the end of the war. Today you can still see evidence of their lives in the buildings and narrow streets of the area. Hongkou District is also the location of Lu Xun Park and Memorial.

Sights to See

㉒ Dongfang Mingzhu (Oriental Pearl Television Tower). The tallest tower in Asia is the pride and joy of the Shanghainese. It has become a symbol of the city and fully captures the brashness and glitz that are today's Shanghai. This UFO-like spaceship rising over the city is especially kitschy at night, facing off the classic beauty of the Bund. Its several spheres are supposed to represent pearls (as in "Shanghai, Pearl of the Orient"). An elevator takes you to the top sphere for a 360-degree bird's-eye view of the city. ✉ *No. 2, Lane 504, Lujiazui Lu, Pudong,* ☎ *021/5879–1888.* 🎟 *Y50.* ☉ *Daily 8 AM–9:30 PM.*

㉘ Jinqiao. Industry is focused in this part of Shanghai's development zone.

㉖ Liujiazui. This is the central financial area of Shanghai's new development zone.

㉓ Luxun Gongyuan (Lu Xun Park and Memorial). Lu Xun—scholar, novelist and essayist—is considered the founder of modern Chinese literature. He is best known for his work *The True Story of Ah Q.* The park holds the tomb and a statue of the writer, as well as a **museum** of manuscripts, books, and photos related to his life and career. ✉ *146 Jiangwan Dong Lu,* ☎ *021/6596–1181.* 🎟 *Park, Y1; memorial and museum, Y3.* ☉ *Park, daily 5 AM–10 PM; memorial and museum, daily 8:30-4:30.*

㉔ **Moxi Huitang and Huoshan Gongyuan** (Ohel Moshe Synagogue and Huoshan Park). Built in Hongkou by Shanghai's Jewish residents in 1927, the Ohel Moshe Synagogue now has a small museum with photos and information about the Ashkenazi Jewish community of old Shanghai. Nearby Huoshan Park bears a memorial tablet erected in memory of the Jewish refugees who emigrated to the city.

Around the synagogue are lanes and old buildings that were once inhabited by Shanghai's Jewish residents. More than 20,000 Jewish refugees—engineers, lawyers, doctors, musicians, actors, writers, and academics—crowded into the district. They created their own community with newspapers, magazines, cultural performances, and schools. Despite the crowded and unsanitary conditions, most of the Jews survived to see the end of the war, at which point the majority returned to Europe. ⌧ *62 Changyang Lu,* ☏ *021/6512–0229.*

㉕ **Nanpu and Yangpu Bridges.** These two bridges, the third-longest and second-longest in the world, cross the Huangpu River, connecting Pudong to Puxi. The Nanpu Bridge is more accessible, south of the Bund off Zhongshan Nan Lu and the Ring Road. The Yangpu Bridge is farther up the river, on the way to Wusong. Cruises of the Huangpu River (☞ Shanghai A to Z, *below*) pass under both bridges.

㉗ **Waigaoqiao.** In this bonded area of Shanghai's development zone international trade is concentrated.

The Old French Concession

The former French Concession is in the Luwan and Xuhui districts. Once populated primarily by White Russians, the area is today a charming historic district known for its shopping, bars and cafés, and consulates. Most of the action centers on the main east–west thoroughfare, the tree-lined Huaihai Lu, a relaxed, upscale, international shopping street. Many of the old consulates and French buildings still line it; some have become the boutiques of European and American fashion houses.

A Good Walk

You can start your walk at the **Zhonggong Yidahuizhi** ㉙ on Xingye Lu and Huangpi Lu. From here, take a cab or walk 15 or 20 minutes to **Sun Zhongshan Guju** ㉚. If you walk, go south on Huangpi Lu until you reach Fuxing Lu, where you turn right. On the corner of Chongqing Nan Lu and Fuxing Lu is **Fuxing Gongyuan** ㉛. Across the way on the southeast corner of the intersection is a beautiful old arrowhead-shape apartment building that was once American journalist and communist sympathizer Agnes Smedley's residence. If you continue west on Fuxing Lu, turn right at the first corner (Sinan Lu); Sun Yatsen's Former Residence will be just ahead on your right, at Xiangshan Lu.

From here, turn right (north), back onto Sinan Lu. At Huaihai Lu, the main street of the old French Concession, take a left. This middle stretch of the shopping street—Huaihai Zhong Lu—is the heart of the Concession. State-run and foreign shops and department stores dominate the area.

Continue down a couple of blocks on Huaihai and turn right on Maoming Lu at the old **Cathay Cinema** ㉜. At the intersection with Changle Lu stand the historic Jinjiang and Garden hotels (☞ Lodging, *below*). On the northeast corner is the old **Lyceum Theatre** ㉝.

Back on Huaihai Lu, continue west. After another 2 blocks, turn left on Fenyang Lu. The **Shanghai Gongyi Meishu Yanjiusuo Jiugong Yipin Xiufu Bu** ㉞ is in an old French mansion on this street. If you choose to return to Huaihai Lu and continue going west, the shopping will give way to the consulate area. You can end your walk anywhere between Fenyang Lu and Wulumuqi Lu. If you decide to continue walking, eventually you'll pass the **Shanghai Tushuguan** ㉟ on your left (south) side past Wulumuqi Lu. Farther down the street at the corner of Xingguo Lu is **Song Qingling Guju** ㊱.

Besides walking down Huaihai Lu, an excellent way of seeing the French part of town is to hop on the double decker bus that runs up and down the thoroughfare. If you sit on the upper level, you can sneak a good view of the old homes that are otherwise hidden by compound walls at street level.

Farther away in Xuhui District is the **Xujiahui Dajiaotang** ㊲; from Huaihai Lu, go south on Hengshan Lu, which will end in Xujiahui. The church is on the west side of Caoxi Bei Lu. You'll need to take a taxi to **Longhua Gu Si** ㊳.

TIMING
Huaihai Lu, like Shanghai's other main thoroughfares, is most crowded on the weekends when hordes of shoppers enjoy their weekly day out. Allow yourself at least an hour to an hour and a half just to walk the above itinerary without stopping at any shops or taking a look around at the old houses. Allow about half an hour to an hour for each of the sights such as Sun Yat-sen's former residence and the Shanghai Arts and Crafts Research Institute. Some of the historic buildings you can walk through, while others will only require a short look from the outside.

Sights to See

㉛ **Fuxing Gongyuan** (Fuxing Park). This European park was called French Park before 1949. The grounds provide a rare bit of greenery in crowded Shanghai. You'll find people practicing taijiquan and lovers strolling hand in hand. ✉ *2 Gaolan Lu,* ☎ *021/6372–0662,* ⊙ *Daily 6–6.*

㊳ **Longhua Gu Si** (Longhua Temple). The 131-ft-high Longhua Pagoda at Shanghai's largest temple affords views of the city and surrounding countryside. The pagoda dates from the 10th century but has been rebuilt. The temple's numerous halls have hexagonal windows, arched entryways, and roofs of curved eaves. They are surrounded by walls in the shape of a perfect rectangle in accordance with traditional Buddhist symmetry. The grounds contain a small traditional garden and a carp-filled pond. You sometimes come upon Buddhist monks praying in incense-filled courtyards here. Attached is the Longhua Hotel and vegetarian restaurant for Buddhist and secular travelers (☞ Lodging, *below*). ✉ *2853 Longhua Lu,* ☎ *021/6456–6085.* ⊙ *Daily 7– 4.*

㉝ **Lyceum Theatre.** The old stage is still in use as a theater presenting acrobatic shows. In old Shanghai it was the home of the British Amateur Drama Club. ✉ *Corner of Maoming Lu and Changle Lu.*

㉞ **Shanghai Gongyi Meishu Yanjiusuo Jiugong Yipin Xiufu Bu** (Shanghai Arts and Crafts Research Institute). Shanghai's artisans create pieces of traditional Chinese arts and crafts right before your eyes here. Works you can purchase include everything from papercuts to snuff bottles, lanterns, and engraved chops. Formerly, the old French mansion housed an official of the Concession's pre-1949 government. ✉ *79 Fenyang Lu,* ☎ *021/6437–0509,* ⊙ *Daily 8:30–4:30.*

㉟ **Shanghai Tushuguan** (New Shanghai Library). Part of Shanghai's drive to become an international cultural center, the Shanghai Library, one of the 10 largest in the world, opened in 1996. The library employs state-of-the-art information technology in two main buildings that house 20 reading rooms, including a foreign book reading room, and

13 million books and manuscripts, as well as electronic and audiovisual publications and books in braille. Specialized reading rooms hold 1.7 million rare books that are up to 1,400 years old. An especially interesting room contains ancient genealogical manuscripts. ⊠ *1555 Huaihai Zhong Lu,* ☎ *021/6445–5555.* ⊘ *Daily 8:30–8:30.*

③⑥ Song Qingling Guju (Soong Chingling's Former Residence). The residence from 1949 until 1963 of the wife of Dr. Sun Yat-sen has been partially preserved to represent the home as it was when she lived here. Madame Soong was sympathetic with the Communists, while her sister, Meiling, was married to Chiang Kaishek. ⊠ *1843 Huaihai Zhong Lu,* ☎ *021/6431–4965.* ⊘ *Daily 9–11, 1–4:30.*

③⓪ Sun Zhongshan Guju (Sun Yat-sen's Former Residence). Dr. Sun Yat-sen, the father of the Chinese republic, lived in this two-story house for six years, from 1919 to 1924. His wife, Soong Ching Ling, continued to live here after his death until 1937. Today, it's been turned into a museum, and you can tour the grounds. ⊠ *7 Xiangshan Lu,* ☎ ☎ *021/6437–2954.* ⊘ *Daily 9–11:30, 12:30–4:15.*

③⑦ Xujiahui Dajiaotang (Xujiahui Cathedral). Built by the Jesuits in 1848, this Gothic-style cathedral still holds regular masses in Chinese. ⊠ *158 Puxi Lu,* ☎ *021/6469–0930.*

②⑨ Zhongguo Gongchangdang Di Yi Ci Quanguo Daibiao Dahui Huizhi Jinian Guan (Zhonggong Yidahuizhi; Site of the First National Congress of the Communist Party of China). The secret meeting in July 1921 that marked the first National Congress was held at the Bo Wen Girls School, where 13 delegates from Marxist, Communist, and socialist groups gathered from around the country. Today you can enter the house, which was renovated in 1951, and view its relics, documents, and photos. Deep in the back is the very room where the first delegates worked. It remains in its original form, complete with a table set for 13 people at tea. ⊠ *76 Xingye Lu,* ☎ *021/6328–1177.* ⊒ *RMB3.* ⊘ *Daily 8:30–11, 1–4.*

The West: Changning and Putuo Districts

West of Hongkou District is Putuo, in the northern part of the city, site of one of Shanghai's most important landmarks, the Jade Buddha Temple. Just south of Putuo, west of Jingan District, is Changning District, with the Shanghai Hongqiao Airport at its western end, the commercial development area of Hongqiao, and the booming residential construction of Gubei New Area. In old Shanghai, Hongqiao Lu was an elite road lined with glamorous country villas of rich foreigners escaping the center of the city. Most of the gardens are gone, but some of the homes are still standing.

A Good Tour

Start at the **Yufo Si** ⑩, one of Shanghai's most important Buddhist temples. Take a cab west to Changning District and check out the **Shanghai Lishi Bowuguan** ㊷ for an hour or two. Farther west on the same street, Hongqiao Lu, is the **Shanghai Dongwuyuan** ㊷. You'll have to take a cab there as well.

Sights to See

④① Sassoon Villa. The owner of the former Cathay Hotel, Victor Sassoon, was the socialite of old Shanghai. His country villa was designed in the style of an English manor and surrounded by acres of greenery, trees, and a lake. It is now privately owned and not open to the public. The **Shanghai Zoo** (☞ Shanghai Dongwuyuan, *below*) occupies part of the grounds, and the Cypress Hotel now stands here as well. ⊠ *Hotel: 2419 Hongqiao Lu,* ☎ *021/6268–8868.*

㊷ **Shanghai Dongwuyuan** (Shanghai Zoo). The pandas here are the highlight, but the zoo doesn't quite meet international standards. More space needs to be allocated to the animals, and the general up-keep improved, but efforts are currently under way to rectify the situation. The city recently started a program in which sponsors adopt an animal and contribute to its care. Before 1949, the grounds of the zoo held a private golf club. ⊠ *2381 Hongqiao Lu,* ☎ *021/6268–7775.* ⊠ *Y15.* ☉ *Daily 6–6.*

㊸ **Shanghai Lishi Bowuguan** (Shanghai History Museum). This small museum recalls Shanghai's pre-1949 heyday with the bronze lions that once ornamented the front of the former Hong Kong and Shanghai Bank Building, among other curiosities. ⊠ *1286 Hongqiao Lu,* ☎ *021/ 6275–5595.* ⊠ *Y10.* ☉ *Daily 9–3:30.*

㊴ **Shanghai Zhiwuyuan** (Shanghai Botanical Gardens). This spacious and pleasant park, a welcome spot of green in the busy cityscape, has a lake and walks lined with a wide variety of shrubs, flowers, plants, and trees. ⊠ *1100 Longwu Lu,* ☎ *021/6436–5523.* ⊠ *Y6.* ☉ *Daily 8–5.*

★ ㊵ **Yufo Si** (Jade Buddha Temple). Completed in 1918, this temple is fairly new by Chinese standards. During the Cultural Revolution, in order to save the temple when the Red Guards came to destroy it, the monks pasted portraits of Mao Zedong on the outside walls so that the Guards couldn't tear them down without destroying Mao's face as well. The temple is built in the style of the Song dynasty with symmetrical halls and courtyards, upturned eaves, and bright yellow walls. The temple's great treasure is its 6½-ft-high, 455-lb seated Buddha made of white jade with a robe of precious gems, originally brought to Shanghai from Burma. Other Buddhas, statues, and frightening guardian gods of the temple populate the halls, as well as a collection of Buddhist scriptures and paintings. The 70 monks who live and work here can sometimes be seen worshiping. On Chinese New Year, tens of thousands of Chinese Buddhists descend upon the temple to worship. ⊠ *170 Anyuan Lu,* ☎ *021/6266–3668.* ⊠ *Y15.* ☉ *Daily 8–11, 1–5.*

DINING

American

$$ ✕ **Hard Rock Café.** Although not a premier Hard Rock, as in Beijing or London, the Hard Rock Shanghai attracts tourists and big crowds of up-and-coming young Shanghainese. Shanghai's Hard Rock serves the typical Hard Rock dishes—burgers, steaks, salads, sandwiches, and pastas—as well as some Asian specialties. It's one of the only places in the city to get a decent salad. (☞ *Nightlife, below.*) ⊠ *Shanghai Centre, 1376 Nanjing Xi Lu,* ☎ *021/6279–8133. AE, DC, MC, V.*

$$ ✕ **Malone's.** This sports bar and grill serves American favorites such as Philly cheese steaks, buffalo wings, burgers, and pizza, as well as Asian specialties. The food isn't superb but is satisfying for a casual meal in a cheerful bar setting. You can watch sports on TV and play pool between bites. Malone's also serves a pleasant weekend brunch of such items as eggs Benedict, omelettes, pancakes, and French toast. ⊠ *257 Tongren Lu,* ☎ *021/6247–2400. AE, DC, MC, V.*

$$ ✕ **Tony Roma's a Place for Ribs.** This U.S. chain arrived in Shanghai in 1995 to serve their standard American ribs. If you're missing an American meal, Tony Roma's should do the trick. It's best known for its ribs, of course, but like the Hard Rock, it serves some of the best sal-

ads in town. ⊠ *Shanghai Centre, 1376 Nanjing Xi Lu,* ☎ *021/6279–7129. AE, DC, MC, V.*

$ ✕ **Johnny Moo.** This cute, tiny malt shop dotted with cow spots is a little-known bastion of burger-making. The cheeseburger here is a sure contender for the "Best in Shanghai" award. Besides great burgers, Johnny Moo offers excellent twister fries and outstanding shakes. ⊠ *Vanke Plaza, 37 Shuicheng Lu, Gubei,* ☎ *021/6270–8686. No credit cards.*

Cantonese

$$$ ✕ **The Dynasty.** Once known as the best Cantonese restaurant in Shanghai, the establishment keeps its reputation for great Cantonese cuisine despite the arrival of more competition. It has the typical hotel restaurant carpet, big tables, and white tablecloths. Although the food is mostly Cantonese, some other cuisines have entered the picture, such as the first-rate Peking duck and the Sichuan-influenced hot-and-sour soup. The Cantonese seafood dishes, especially the prawns and lobster, are particularly good. At lunch time, great dim sum is served. ⊠ *Yangtze New World Hotel, 2099 Yanan Xi Lu,* ☎ *021/6275–0000. Reservations essential. AE, DC, MC, V.*

$$$ ✕ **Forum Palace.** This eatery is designed in Hong Kong style: large, carpeted open spaces with big circular tables and lots of children running around. Still, there's something classy about the pastel tones. The tasty Cantonese offerings here give one the feeling of being in Hong Kong. The dim sum is some of the best in the city, but it's served to order rather than from carts. The congee and the shrimp dumplings are especially good. ⊠ *188 Huaihai Zhong Lu,* ☎ *021/6386–2608. Reservations essential. AE, DC, MC, V.*

$$$ ✕ **Huai Sian Lou.** This pastel-hued Cantonese restaurant serves up sophisticated cuisine with a Hong Kong-like brashness. Visual and gastronomic delights include immense pincer-less Australian lobsters served sashimi-style or cooked in a hot pot, with the remaining tail and legs stuffed and baked. The babao tea is served in the traditional Sichuan manner, poured theatrically two feet from the table top from a teapot with a foot-long spout. The seafood is all well-executed, as are the shark's fin soups, pan-fried noodles, and barbecued suckling pig. ⊠ *Isetan Department Store, 527 Huaihai Zhong Lu,* ☎ *021/5306–1616. Reservations essential. AE, DC, MC, V.*

Chaozhou

$$$ ✕ **Chaozhou Garden.** This restaurant has an elegant Chinese setting and excellent service. The Chaozhou dishes here are superb: The core seafood offerings are prepared with exuberance and creativity; the poultry dishes are hearty, yet virtually greaseless (a welcome respite from Shanghai's relatively oily fare); and the vegetable and noodle selections are a sheer delight. The soya goose with *doufu* (tofu) appetizer is a classic Chaozhou dish. Try the crab claw with bamboo shoots and bird's nest and the braised shrimp and turnip in casserole. Chaozhou dim sum is served during lunch, along with the regular menu. ⊠ *Yangtze New World Hotel, 2099 Yanan Xi Lu,* ☎ *021/6275–0000. Reservations essential. AE, DC, MC, V.*

Chinese

$$$ ✕ **Dragon and Phoenix Room.** The food is good, but the chief draw
★   is the atmosphere. On the 8th floor of the Peace Hotel, the restaurant offers spectacular views of the Oriental Pearl TV Tower, the Huangpu River, and the Bund. (Be sure to reserve a table by the window.) A light-

green motif tints the room's original art deco design. In the corner a group of traditional Chinese musicians plays quietly. The menu represents a good variety of Chinese dishes, and the fried noodles are some of the best in town. ⊠ *Peace Hotel, 20 Nanjing Dong Lu,* ☎ *021/6321–6888. Reservations essential. AE, DC, MC, V.*

$$$ ✕ **Revolving 28.** On the east side of the river 28 stories up, this revolving restaurant offers dizzying views of the Bund and the surrounding area. Cantonese and Sichuanese food is served, but the restaurant's most famous dish is the Sichuan smoked duck. Other good dishes include sautéed prawn balls in spicy sauce and the Chaozhou-style double-boiled snow frog with bamboo pith. Although the cooking here is not the best in Shanghai, the view compensates. ⊠ *Ocean Hotel, 1171 Dong Da Ming Lu,* ☎ *021/6545–8888. Reservations essential. AE, DC, MC, V.*

$$–$$$ ✕ **Park Hotel.** In one of old Shanghai's premier hotels, the atmosphere of the main restaurant evokes that of a large and loud Chinese eatery. It's even difficult hearing the live traditional Chinese music above the din of the clientele. People come here to eat Peking duck, which is reputedly better than any to be found in Beijing. The duck, served with pancakes, scallions, cucumbers, and duck sauce, can be ordered whole or by the half. Be sure to arrive early for dinner (around 5 or 6 PM), as by 7 or 8 PM the best food is gone, including the Beijing ducks. ⊠ *170 Nanjing Xi Lu,* ☎ *021/6327–5225. Reservations essential. AE, DC, MC, V.*

$$ ✕ **Meilongzhen.** Probably Shanghai's most famous restaurant, the
★ Meilongzhen is one of the oldest establishments in town, dating from 1938. You dine in traditional Chinese rooms with mahogany and marble furniture and intricate woodwork. Most of the dishes are Sichuanese, but the flavors are combined with Shanghai cooking styles, which use more grease. The Sichuan duck is one of its more famous dishes. It's best to eat here early, as all the good food is gone by 7 or 8 PM. ⊠ *1081 Nanjing Xi Lu,* ☎ *021/6256–6688, 021/6256–2718. Reservations essential. AE, DC, MC, V.*

$$ ✕ **Shenji Liang Tang.** Shen Ji, as it's called by regulars, is a massive establishment that does a thriving business 24 hours a day. The specialties of the house are soup and dim sum. The waitresses and suited-up managers use walkie-talkies to communicate with each other. The dim sum tables roll from 9 to 11 AM, 2 to 4:30 PM, and after 9 PM. For a real Shanghai atmosphere, come here at four or five in the morning, when the place is filled with smoke and completely packed with slightly disheveled but well-dressed and red-eyed Chinese people, and you have to wait for 45 minutes for a table. ⊠ *860 Beijing Xi Lu,* ☎ *021/ 6258–7929, 021/6256–6699. No credit cards.*

$$ ✕ **Soho.** This chic restaurant has much to offer: Western-style atmosphere, an attentive, professionally trained wait staff, and a menu that is Chinese but with a Western twist. In sophisticated surroundings amid modern art, you can eat great Chinese food. The menu, in side-by-side Chinese and English, features Yangzhou-style cuisine. One house specialty—*su bao cui san* (scissor-shredded black tree mushrooms)—is not to be missed; it looks and tastes like barbecued eel. *Songren yu mi* (fish with corn and pine nuts), the assorted vegetables, and the *songsu guiyu* (crisp sweet and sour Mandarin fish) are also recommended. ⊠ *2077 Yanan Xi Lu,* ☎ *021/6219–2948. Reservations essential. AE, DC, MC, V.*

$ ✕ **Chang An Dumpling Restaurant.** The city's most famous—and best—dumpling house offers more than 100 types of dumplings, many served in the shapes of birds and small animals. The dumplings are sweet or not-so-sweet; steamed, boiled, or fried; stuffed with meats, vegetables, seafood, fruits, or intriguing combinations. And it all

Shanghai Dining and Lodging

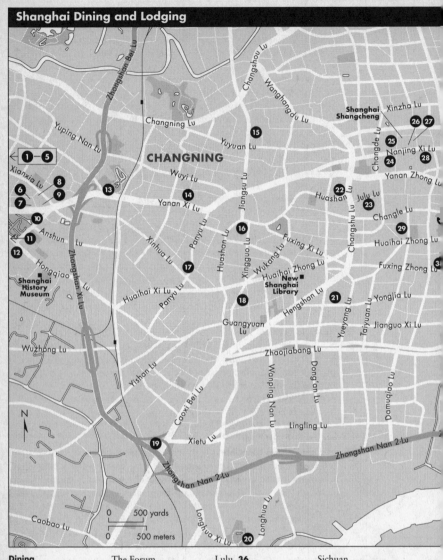

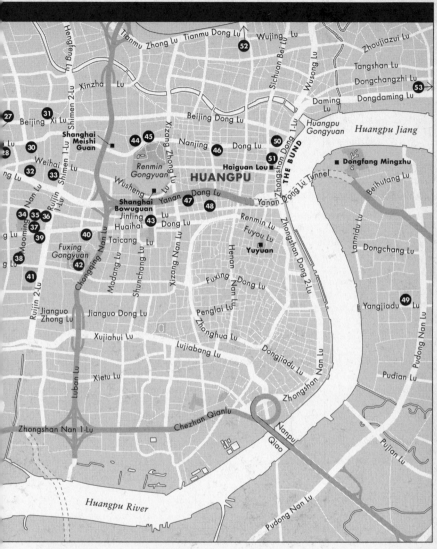

Lodging

Cypress Hotel, **1**

Garden Hotel, **34**

Holiday Inn Crowne Plaza, **17**

Hotel Sofitel Hyland, **49**

Huating Hotel and Towers, **8**

Jinjiang Hotel, **35**

Jinjiang Tower, **40**

Longhua Hotel, **24**

Park Hotel, **45**

Peace Hotel, **50**

Portman Ritz-Carlton at the Shanghai Centre, **27**

Radisson SAS Lansheng, **52**

Ruijin Guesthouse, **41**

Shanghai Hilton, **20**

Shanghai JC Mandarin, **28**

Shanghai New Asia Tomson Hotel, **54**

Westin Tai Ping Yang, **6**

Xijiao Guesthouse, **2**

Xingguo Guesthouse, **16**

Yangtze New World Hotel, **7**

comes at a bargain 24 hours a day. ✉ *2 Yunnan Lu,* ☎ *021/6328–5156, 021/6328–0695;* ✉ *1588 Pudong Lu, Pudong,* ☎ *021/5885–8416. No credit cards.*

$ ✕ **The Grape.** During the mid-1980s the Grape, a hole in the wall with eight tiny booths and dim lighting, became a haven for the small expatriate community. Over the years, the small Grape was torn down, and two bigger outlets were built just across the street from one another. Today the two new Grapes bustle with foreign and Chinese clientele, friendly service, great food, and even better prices. The atmosphere is still simple, with wooden tables and checkered tablecloths. Dishes that won't disappoint are the garlic shrimp, *jiachang doufu* (home-style bean curd), and fried chicken wings. ✉ *55 Xinle Lu,* ☎ *021/6472–0486;* ✉ *142 Xinle Lu,* ☎ *021/6472–0499. No credit cards.*

Chinese Vegetarian

$–$$ ✕ **Gongdelin.** Serving vegetarian specialties for over 50 years, the restaurant combines cuisines from all over the country in its creations. An outstanding dish is the mock duck made of tofu. If you've never tried this vegetarian delicacy, it's absolutely delicious. Be sure to get there early. If you arrive after 6 PM, you may not be able to eat. ✉ *Huanghe Lu at Nanjing Lu,* ☎ *021/6327–1532. No credit cards.*

$–$$ ✕ **Jue Lin Shu Shi Chu.** Jue Lin is one of a handful of vegetarian restaurants in the city that draw on both the incredibly varied produce in Shanghai markets and the myriad ways Shanghainese have concocted to create dishes out of tofu. Mock ham is a good appetizer. Even better is the mock eel and mock sweet-and-sour pork made of mushrooms. The mock Beijing duck is the specialty of the house. The restaurant has a somewhat spartan but elegant Buddhist-inspired interior design. Simple Chinese calligraphy prints adorn the walls. As at most Buddhist establishments, meals are eaten early (6 AM–1:30 PM, 5 PM–7:30 PM). ✉ *250 Jinling Lu,* ☎ *021/6326–0115. No credit cards.*

Continental

$$$$ ✕ **Continental Room.** Perched at the top of the Garden Hotel, this very elegant restaurant offers fine French food and views of the surrounding former French Concession. It's all very chic in a traditional way here. The atmosphere is extremely quiet and subdued, a perfect setting if you want to impress business clients. ✉ *Garden Hotel, 58 Maoming Lu,* ☎ *021/6415–1111. Reservations essential. AE, DC, MC, V.*

$$$$ ✕ **Park 97.** A sure sign of Shanghai's return to glamour and decadence,
★   Park 97 opened in 1997 on the grounds of Fuxing Park. The très chic establishment, where attitude is everything, encompasses a massive space divided into café, restaurant, ultra-late lounge, and art gallery. The nouvelle design and decor is perfected to the last detail, from the single lilies on the tables to the scented candles glowing with subdued light. Park's elegant furnishings in wood and fabric, and its warm coloring in hues of orange and green, recall the feel of Art Deco, while soft jazz plays in the background. Eating in the café can be casual, but the small, elite restaurant serves some of Shanghai's most elegant gourmet fare. Among the most raved-about dishes are tartar of salmon and sea scallops, pickled pear with goat cheese and black bean caviar, seared tuna, and Turkish delight dessert. At night, Park 97 is a popular place to drink and hang out. The waitstaff is also part of the image—too cool to be friendly—and a packed restaurant and bar sometimes translates into slow service. ✉ *Fuxing Gongyuan, 2 Gaolan Lu,* ☎ *021/6318–0785. Reservations essential. AE, DC, MC, V.*

$$$$ ✕ **Shanghai Jax.** The grill restaurant, named for an early-1900s Shanghai expatriate, Horatio S. Jax, known for his exquisite taste in food,

lives up to its namesake. It is best known for its grilled prime cuts and pastas and serves some of the tastiest steaks in town. In summer, it opens an outdoor terrace for al fresco barbecues. Periodically, the restaurant brings in guest chefs for weekly stints. Its bar has live music in the evenings. ⊠ *Portman Ritz-Carlton Hotel, 1376 Nanjing Xi Lu,* ☎ *021/ 6279–8888. Reservations essential. AE, DC, MC, V.*

$$$ ✕ **AD.** When the former head chef of the Westin's Giovanni's, Antonio Donnaloia, decided to open his own place, he sacrificed nothing in bringing elegant Italian dining to Shanghai. From the marble to the antique furniture to the staff's Gianni Versace uniforms, it is overly apparent that the chef spared no cost in erecting his masterpiece. Everything is done at AD with an operatic flourish. Its dramatic décor—vaulted ceilings, pastel hues, a fireplace placed inside what looks like a plaster-of-Paris head of Zeus, and Italian fabric on the walls and furniture—makes AD almost overwhelming. With the exception of a few appetizers, the food is superb: the deep-fried calamari and prawns, the mixed seafood Amalfi soup, the hearty but delicious risotto, some of the best veal in Shanghai, and grilled portions of fresh, imported seafood. Don't miss the to-die-for desserts. Especially life-stopping are the poached pear with cinnamon mousse and the tartufo bianco. ⊠ *3896 Hongmei Lu,* ☎ *021/6262–5620. Reservations essential. AE, DC, MC, V.*

$$$ ✕ **50 Hankou Lu.** This nicely appointed restaurant is in a beautiful old British building right off the Bund (with original ornamentation intact). The fare is a mix of East and West, but the decor is Southeast Asian. Primitive Indonesian and New Guinean full-figure wooden sculptures stand everywhere. If it's available, don't miss the aubergine and feta cheese appetizer; it's divine. A crescent-shaped bar serves good drinks and a selection of wines. ⊠ *50 Hankou Lu,* ☎ *021/6329–8999, 021/ 6323–8383. AE, DC, MC, V.*

Indian

$$$ ✕ **The Tandoor.** Beautifully appointed and serving excellent food, this
★ restaurant is among the best in Shanghai. The entire management and staff have been flown in from India and offer impeccable service. Don't miss the unbelievable *murgh malai kebab* (tandoori chicken marinated in cheese); try some vegetable curries—*palak aloo* (spinach with peas) or *dal makhani* (lentil); and complement everything with a selection of rice and bread. Traditional Indian dancers and musicians perform nightly. Decorated with mirrors, Indian artwork, and Chinese characters dangling from the ceiling, the restaurant is ingeniously designed to show the route of Buddhism from India to China. ⊠ *Jinjiang Hotel, 59 Maoming Nan Lu,* ☎ *021/6258–2582, ext. 9301. Reservations essential. AE, DC, MC, V.*

Italian

$$$$ ✕ **DaVinci's.** This trés chic eating establishment offers top-notch nouvelle Italian food. For starters, a colorful selection from the antipasto table can include carpaccio, eggplant salad, calamari, and Italian cold cuts. In addition to the excellent pastas and risotto, the meat dishes are outstanding, especially the lamb dusted with rosemary. ⊠ *Shanghai Hilton, 250 Huashan Lu,* ☎ *021/6248–0000, ext. 8263. Reservations essential. AE, DC, MC, V. Closed lunch.*

$$$ ✕ **Giovanni's.** At this upscale Italian bistro the food and service are
★ excellent. The interior has a European feel, and from it you catch a good view of the Hongqiao area. The *zuppa di pesce alla Veneziana* (Venetian fish soup) is spectacular, as are the calamari, and the pastas are served perfectly al dente. Be sure to try the flat bread with aromatic olive oil—a treat in Shanghai. The crème brûlée with blueberry sauce

is extraordinary. ⊠ *Westin Tai Ping Yang, 5 Zunyi Nan Lu,* ☎ *021/ 6275–8888. Reservations essential. AE, DC, MC, V.*

\$\$ ✕ **Pasta Fresca da Salvatore.** This casual trattoria has two outlets in Shanghai. The food isn't outstanding, but it's the only place to go for good casual Italian food at a reasonable price. The pizza here is better than the pasta, but the selection is wide. ⊠ *Friendship Shopping Centre, 6 Zunyi Nan Lu,* ☎ *021/6270–4693, 021/6270–0000, ext. 1211;* ⊠ *115 Changshu Lu,* ☎ *021/6248–1705. AE, DC, MC, V.*

\$\$ ✕ **Savini's.** A Hong Kong and Japanese joint-venture, Savini's brings diners authentic Italian food in a sophisticated, elegant setting. Savini's imports all its fixings—beautiful silverware and dishes, Italian cheeses and spices, wine, and grappa. The Italian chef prepares appetizers such as buffalo mozzarella and tomatoes, beef carpaccio, and bruschetta. The risotto is excellent, the pastas are pleasing, and there are also meat and fish dishes, as well as a gourmet imported food store and deli. ⊠ *823 Huangjin Jie,* ☎ *021/6278–9876. AE, DC, MC, V.*

Japanese

\$\$\$\$ ✕ **Sakura.** Although the prices are outrageous (up toward \$100 U.S. ★ per person), the best sushi (try salmon and yellowtail) in town can be found here. In addition, the simply but elegantly appointed restaurant offers sashimi (especially sea bream and deep-purple tuna) and an impressive array of Japanese hot and cold dishes: everything wonderfully fresh, superbly presented, and absolutely delectable. The sweet shrimp is some of the best to be had anywhere in the world—surprising in Shanghai, where sweet shrimp is usually unavailable. ⊠ *Garden Hotel, 58 Maoming Nan Lu,* ☎ *021/6415–1111. Reservations essential. AE, DC, MC, V.*

\$\$\$ ✕ **Hanazen.** On a narrow, charming street in the former French Concession stands one of the most authentic and picturesque Japanese restaurants in town. With close to 80% Japanese clientele, Ms. Wang, the manager, oversees a multilingual wait staff beautifully dressed in traditional Japanese garb who are polite and eager to help with the ordering. Besides the raw fish, try the beef *takaki* (grilled) and the *agedashi tofu* (cold tofu in special broth). ⊠ *574 Yongjia Lu,* ☎ *021/ 6474–6427. Reservations essential. AE, DC, MC, V.*

\$\$\$ ✕ **Itoya.** In a dark back alley behind Watson's on Huaihai Lu, an unexpected light box marks this little-known paradise for sushi hedonists. The small, unassuming restaurant, the main branch of a chain of four, serves imposing portions of some of the freshest and tastiest fish in town. The non-English menu is filled with a variety of traditional Japanese dishes, but the place to head for is the sushi bar. Try the tuna, salmon, and eel. ⊠ *24 Ruijin Er Lu,* ☎ *021/6473–0758;* ⊠ *Longhua Xidao, Lane 19, No. 6,* ☎ *021/6473–0758;* ⊠ *400 Changle Lu, 2/F,* ☎ *021/ 6466–2929;* ⊠ *111 Ruijin Yi Lu,* ☎ *021/6318–4722. Reservations essential. AE, DC, MC, V.*

\$\$ ✕ **Sushi and Bowl.** The sushi at SAB, as it's called, isn't the freshest; nor is the selection that great. Nevertheless, it is the only place in Shanghai where you can get decent sushi for below \$20 U.S. per person. Seating surrounds a central sushi bar, while a circular conveyor belt transports dishes around the dining area. It's better to order directly from the chef rather than picking from the belt; you never know how long the food's been sitting up there. ⊠ *136 Maoming Nan Lu,* ☎ *021/ 6466–1763. No credit cards.*

Korean

\$\$ ✕ **Alilang.** One of Shanghai's stalwarts in Korean food, Alilang serves *kimchi* (pickled cabbage), unlimited cold appetizers, tender and delicious meat and seafood barbecued right before your eyes, rice, and noodles. The meat dishes are the best choice here. Another specialty that is always delicious is the *congyoubing* (onion cake). The Spartan restaurant is made homey by the excellent service. ✉ *28 Jiangsu Bei Lu,* ☎ *021/6252–7146. AE, DC, MC, V.*

$$ ✗ **Kum Gang San.** Servers bombard you here with free cold appetizers and kimchi. For meat eaters, *kalbi* (short ribs of beef) and *bulgogi* (beef strips) are great, grilled at your table to a tender finish, and wonderful with rice. *Chap chae* (vermicelli noodles) is another must try, as well as the *kimchi chi gae* (pickled cabbage stew). The seafood grill selection is among the best buys in town. Although the menu is all in Chinese, the servers understand the names of the dishes in Korean. ✉ *756 Yanan Zhong Lu,* ☎ *021/6255–2710. AE, DC, MC, V.*

Mexican

$$ ✗ **Viva El Popo.** A stone staircase, Spanish paintings, an open-grill kitchen, wood floors, and terra-cotta tile countertops set the tone in the two-story restaurant. The chef was trained in Mexico and southern California, and creates his own Shanghai-meets-Mexico dishes—burritos, chimichangas, enchiladas, tacos, and fajitas. All these generously sized entrées are served on terra-cotta plates complete with rice and refried beans. ✉ *Golden Lion Garden, Longhua Xidao, Lane 19, No. 12,* ☎ *021/6219–9279. No credit cards.*

$ ✗ **Badlands.** Serving simple Mexican dishes, this tiny restaurant draws foreign residents for quick and cheap Mexican food and the cheerful, friendly environment. The favorites here are the burrito and taco plates and the "buffalo balls" (fried cheese balls), plus the all-you-can-eat bottomless chili bowl. ✉ *897 Julu Lu,* ☎ *021/6466–7788. No credit cards.*

Shanghainese

$$ ✗ **Big Fan.** The restaurant's exclusive feel is deserved, as the Big Fan is unique in flavor and location. Customers are mostly Chinese and foreign officials and delegations. The restaurant is down an alley in a 1930s-vintage apartment village, and the decor adds to the pre-1949 feel. The walls are wood-paneled and decorated with nicely framed colonial advertisements and bank notes, along with photos of street scenes, garden parties, and men's clubs from the 1930s. As you're seated, a waiter will pour you Sichuanese tea in the traditional style from a pot with a foot-long spout. Be sure to try some seafood dishes. ✉ *1440 Hongqiao Lu,* ☎ *021/6275–9131, ext. 268. No credit cards.*

$$ ✗ **Gap Salon.** Sure, the Gap Salon serves good Shanghainese food, but it's the whole experience that will grab you. This 20,500-sq-ft establishment offers its mostly Chinese clientele just about everything—food, music, dancing, karaoke—with European decor (or at least what the Hong Kong-Chinese owners perceive as European). A genuine antique Red Flag—the car exclusively used by Shanghai officials of yesteryear—overhangs the entrance, hinting at the grandiosity to come. A huge central area mocks an outdoor courtyard. Filipino bands and Chinese dance girls take over the stage during your meal. ✉ *127 Maoming Nan Lu,* ☎ *021/6433–9028. AE, DC, MC, V.*

$$ ✗ **The Village.** Run by a Hong Kongese mother-daughter team, the restaurant serves only Shanghainese food. The atmosphere is traditional and cozy, but contemporary paintings by local Shanghainese artists decorate the walls. Most dishes are done homestyle without MSG (an oddity in Shanghai). The *chuipi doufu* (crisp tofu) is excellent. The homemade chicken soup is just that—simmered for over six hours with tender chunks of chicken. ✉ *137 Tianping Lu,* ☎ *021/6282–8018. Reservations essential. No credit cards.*

$-$$ ✕ **Lulu.** Small, crowded, and smoke-filled, this excellent restaurant has
★   become the hip, late-night place to go for Shanghai's young fashionable crowd. Lulu is known for its fresh seafood; you'll be able to see
what you're getting in the tanks lined up inside the entrance. The
shredded pork and scallion wrapped in pancakes is perfectly executed.
Other great dishes are the cold braised tofu, *sucai mianjing* (sticky,
browned vegetable dumpling) and the *cai fan* (vegetable rice). Sometimes it's difficult to get a table, even at three in the morning, so be
prepared to wait, especially on weekends. ⊠ *69 Shimen Yi Lu,* ☎ *021/
6258–5645. Reservations essential. No credit cards.*

$-$$ ✕ **1221.** This stylish and chic, but casual, eatery is run by the same
★   owners as The Village. Since opening in 1997, 1221 has become a favorite of its expatriate regulars. Like The Village, 1221 prides itself on
home-cooked Shanghainese food. The dishes are imaginative, the service attentive, the atmosphere pleasing, and the prices reasonable.
From the extensive 11-page menu (in English, pinyin and Chinese) you
can order dishes like sliced *you tiao* (fried bread sticks) with shredded
beef, a whole chicken in a green onion soy sauce, shredded pork with
sweet bean sauce served with small pancakes, and Shanghainese stuffed
duck. ⊠ *1221 Yanan Xi Lu,* ☎ *021/6213–6585 or 021/6213–2441.
Reservations essential. No credit cards.*

Sichuanese

$$$ ✕ **Sichuan Court.** The sleek, sky-high eatery at the top of the Hilton
serves Sichuanese dinners with views overlooking the city. The atmo-
sphere is chic and upscale. The Sichuan treasure box is a good array
of delicacies to start off with. The tea-smoked duck (smoked on order
in Chengdu) and the *dan dan* (noodles) are typical of the Sichuanese
dishes served. ⊠ *250 Huashan Lu,* ☎ *021/6248–0000. Reservations
essential. AE, DC, MC, V.*

$$ ✕ **Sichuan Restaurant.** The restaurant is on the outskirts of Tianshan
Park, and tables on the second floor offer views of the surrounding
greenery. The most popular dish, which you'll see on almost all the tables, is the stewed beef. If you want something really spicy, typical of
Sichuan food, try the crisp chicken. The restaurant also serves 14 varieties of Sichuan dim sum that come at a bargain (Y1.30 a piece). More
daring choices such as fish maw, turtle, snake, pigeon, and frog are served
up with unexpected flavors like almond bean curd, chili and peanuts,
preserved eggs, and dried fried squid shreds with chili. ⊠ *1733 Yanan
Xi Lu,* ☎ *021/6259–4583. Reservations essential. AE, DC, MC, V.*

Southeast Asian

$$ ✕ **Brasserie Tatler.** Despite its hotel coffee shop atmosphere, the Tatler
serves excellent Singaporean dishes made by a Singapore Malay chef.
The *hainan ji fan* (chicken rice) is outstanding. The *laksa* (Malaysian
noodle dish) and the *nasi goreng* (fried rice) are also good choices. If
you want something a bit more exotic, try the *rou ga cha,* (pork and
herbal stew served with terrific noodles). ⊠ *Shanghai JC Mandarin, 1225
Nanjing Xi Lu,* ☎ *021/6279– 1888, ext. 5108. AE, DC, MC, V.*

$-$$ ✕ **Frankie's.** Bare decor and a-bit-too-bright lighting don't discourage
★   lovers of Singaporean specialties. Especially good are the fried *kway
teow* (an absolutely delicious version of the Singaporean noodle dish),
the chicken curry, and the stir-fried broccoli with garlic. The stellar choice
is the pepper crab. Don't miss the refreshing dessert made with coconut
milk. ⊠ *Nanjing Xi Lu at Changde Lu. No credit cards.*

Taiwanese

$–$$ ✗ **Xiao Muwu Beer Garden.** This restaurant made of bamboo is a great place to go in summer and early fall. When the weather's warm and it's not raining, they take the glass off the windows, making it an open-air eatery reminiscent of Thailand. The specialty of the house is barbecued meat and seafood marinated in Taiwanese hot spices. You order by the piece, and the chef cooks it on the spot. The best items are the barbecued squid, chicken, and tofu. ✉ *61 Yili Lu,* ☎ *021/6275–6072. Reservations essential. No credit cards.*

LODGING

Nanjing Lu and the Bund

$$$$ ⊞ **Portman Ritz-Carlton at the Shanghai Centre.** Outstanding facilities,
★ elegant furnishings, and great location are the draws here. The hotel's 50 stories make it the tallest in the city. The rooms, including the Horizon Club executive rooms, are furnished in a modern East-meets-West style with wooden Ming-influenced furniture and equipped with electronic amenities. It's elegant, if a bit impersonal. The health club is the most comprehensive in the city. The hotel has four good food outlets, and the Portman Deli in the supermarket is a great place to grab a bite to eat. ✉ *1376 Nanjing Xi Lu, 200040,* ☎ *021/6279–8888,* FAX *021/6279–8887. 600 rooms and suites. 4 restaurants, 2 bars, indoor and outdoor pools, beauty salon, sauna, tennis court, exercise room, racquetball, squash, dance club, shops, business services, meeting rooms. AE, DC, MC, V.*

$$$$ ⊞ **Shanghai JC Mandarin.** In the city center, the 30-story hotel is Singapore-managed. Its towers of blue glass stand east of the Shanghai Exhibition Center. In the lobby is a five-story-high hand-painted mural depicting the voyage of the Ming dynasty admiral, Cheng Ho. Rooms are bright with earthy tones and natural wood and are equipped with useful electronic amenities. The coffee shop serves good Southeast Asian food. ✉ *1225 Nanjing Xi Lu, 200040,* ☎ *021/6279–1888,* FAX *021/6279–1822. 576 rooms, 24 suites. 4 restaurants, bar, deli, pool, sauna, tennis court, exercise room, squash, dance club, shops, business center, meeting rooms. AE, DC, MC, V.*

$$$ ⊞ **Hotel Sofitel Hyland.** Smack in the middle of downtown, the French-owned hotel is managed by Accor. Transportation isn't particularly convenient, as the area is subject to traffic jams. It is well located, though, for walking through the city center, shopping, and trips to the Bund. The 34-story hotel has eight floors of Sofitel Club rooms designed for business travelers. The top-floor Sky Lounge offers good views of downtown and a pleasant Sunday brunch. ✉ *505 Nanjing Dong Lu, 200001,* ☎ *021/6351–5888,* FAX *021/6351–4088. 400 rooms and suites. 4 restaurants, bar, deli, beauty salon, exercise room, shops, business services, meeting rooms. AE, DC, MC, V.*

$$ ⊞ **Peace Hotel.** This hotel has been called the most romantic in Asia
★ and is among Shanghai's most treasured historic buildings. If any establishment will give you a sense of Shanghai's past, this one will. Its high ceilings, ornate woodwork, and Art Deco fixtures are intact, and the ballroom evokes old Shanghai cabarets and gala parties. The south building was formerly the Palace Hotel. Built in 1906 by the British, it is the oldest building on the Bund. The more popular north building, formerly the Cathay Hotel, built in 1929, is more famous historically. It was known as the private playground of its owner Victor Sassoon. The rooms are not glamorous anymore, but they are homey and still retain a charming old-Shanghai ambience. The eighth-floor

Dragon and Phoenix Room (☞ Dining, *above*) is a good choice for dinner. ⊠ *20 Nanjing Dong Lu, 200002,* ☎ *021/6321–6888,* ℻ *021/6329–0300. 420 rooms and suites. 2 restaurants, bar, beauty salon, exercise room, shops, billiards, business services, meeting rooms. AE, DC, MC, V.*

$ 🏨 **Park Hotel.** This historic 1934 Art Deco structure overlooking People's Park was once among Shanghai's more luxurious and fashionable hotels. Today it has been renovated to recapture its pre-1949 glory. ⊠ *170 Nanjing Xi Lu, 200003,* ☎ *021/6327– 5225,* ℻ *021/6327–6958. 208 rooms. 3 restaurants, beauty salon, shop, dance club, business services. AE, DC, MC, V.*

Old French Concession

$$$$ 🏨 **Garden Hotel.** Managed by the Japanese Okura Group, this 33-story
★   hotel is beautifully appointed but presents luxury with a sort of Japanese chill. The first three floors, which were once old Shanghai's French Club, have been renovated with many of the former Art Deco fixtures and frescoes still intact. The huge, perfectly kept garden is good to look at, with a carpet of green grass. The third-floor terrace, overlooking the garden, is a great place for a romantic drink in summer. The hotel is also known for its excellent, and high-priced, Japanese food. The rooms are spacious and tastefully decorated, and have electronic amenities. The indoor swimming pool is gorgeous. ⊠ *58 Maoming Lu, 200020,* ☎ *021/6415–1111,* ℻ *021/6415–8866. 478 rooms and 22 suites. 4 restaurants, 3 bars, pool, beauty salon, sauna, tennis, exercise room, shops, business services, meeting rooms. AE, DC, MC, V.*

$$$$ 🏨 **Holiday Inn Crowne Plaza.** This hotel in the western side of the French Concession is known for its service. The staff here is the friendliest in town and makes guests feel right at home. Although a bit outside the city center, the hotel is still close to the Huaihai Lu shopping district and Hongqiao area. The comfortable, bright guest rooms and suites have a wide range of electronic amenities. There are six floors of executive rooms. The Sichuan restaurant Fu Rong Zhen is solid, while Cheers offers good, innovative Western food. Charlie's Fun Pub always houses the best hotel bands. ⊠ *400 Panyu Lu, 200052,* ☎ *021/6280–8888,* ℻ *021/6280–3353. 466 rooms and 30 suites. 4 restaurants, bar, deli, pool, beauty salon, sauna, tennis court, exercise room, business services, meeting rooms. AE, DC, MC, V.*

$$$$ 🏨 **Huating Hotel and Towers.** The first Western hotel to open in Shanghai was managed by Sheraton until the contract reverted to Chinese management in 1996. The Huating is just southwest of the old French Concession, in the Xujiahui area. Some of the interior is a bit kitschy. The exterior looks like an S-shape tiered wedding cake. Rooms and suites are modern and comfortable. The Towers make up the hotel's executive floors. Because it's just across from the Shanghai Gymnasium and the new Sports Stadium, many visiting athletes stay here. ⊠ *1200 Caoxi Bei Lu, 200030,* ☎ *021/6439–1000,* ℻ *021/6255–0830. 1,008 rooms and 56 suites. 4 restaurants, bar, pool, tennis court, bowling, exercise room, squash, shops, billiards, dance club, business services, meeting rooms. AE, DC, MC, V.*

$$$$ 🏨 **Shanghai Hilton.** The 43-story triangular building has some of the
★   best dining in town and top-rate accommodations. Rooms have modern fixtures and are rather luxurious for Shanghai. All include marble bathrooms and electronic amenities. There are four executive floors, as well as two Japanese floors. The lobby is elegantly designed; the hotel coffee shop has a lovely sun-lit atrium. Everything is well-appointed here, from the health club to the upscale shopping area. The view from the top-floor Penthouse Bar and Sichuan Court is spectacular, a great

place for watching fireworks on Chinese New Year. ✉ *250 Huashan Lu, 200040,* ☎ *021/6248–0000,* ℻ *021/6248–3848. 775 rooms and suites. 6 restaurants, 2 bars, deli, pool, beauty salon, sauna, tennis court, exercise room, squash, billiards, shops, business services, meeting rooms. AE, DC, MC, V.*

$$$ 🏨 **Jinjiang Hotel.** Built before 1935, the former Cathay Mansions, Grosvenor Gardens, and Grosvenor House were some of the old French Concession's most popular addresses, housing everyone from diplomats to taipans. Now known collectively as the Jinjiang Hotel, they are among the few Art Deco buildings left standing in the city. The Cathay was built in 1928 as an apartment building. Three years later the outrageously glamorous Grosvenor House was built. This southern wing of the Jinjiang has some of the most decadent suites in town at the most decadent prices. All rooms have been left in their original design, with the beautiful Art Deco ornamentation still intact. Standard rooms in the North Building also have an old-Shanghai feeling. They're comfortable, traditionally furnished, and homey but not luxurious. Halls are a bit dark, in keeping with the old feeling of the building. Since its opening in 1951, the Jinjiang Hotel has received 300 heads of state from 120 countries—among them, Margaret Thatcher, Helmut Kohl, and Presidents Nixon, Ford, and Reagan. The Indian restaurant is one of the best dining experiences in town. ✉ *59 Maoming Lu, 200020,* ☎ *021/6258–2582,* ℻ *021/6472–5588. 487 rooms and 28 suites. 4 restaurants, bar, beauty salon, sauna, shops, dance club, business services, meeting rooms. AE, MC, V.*

$$$ 🏨 **Jinjiang Tower.** Called "Xin Jinjiang," or New Jinjiang, by the Chinese, it is not to be confused with the "Lao Jinjiang," or Old Jinjiang, Hotel (☞ *above*). The Tower is the first Chinese-managed luxury hotel in Shanghai, and the first to be listed on international and domestic stock markets. Although it's Chinese-run, it retains a foreign orientation. In the middle of the old French Concession, it stands next to the Old Jinjiang and a block from the shopping district of Huaihai Lu. The round, 43-story building is covered in reflective glass. At the top, a revolving restaurant affords great views of the city. The interior isn't as elegant as the other luxury hotels in town, but it's still fairly upscale. Rooms are small but well-appointed and equipped with electronic amenities. ✉ *161 Changle Lu, 200020,* ☎ *021/6415–1188,* ℻ *021/ 6415–0048. 728 rooms and suites. 4 restaurants, pool, exercise room, shops, dance club, business services, meeting rooms. AE, DC, MC, V.*

$ 🏨 **Longhua Hotel.** Just outside the old French Concession by the southern Ring Road, this hotel caters to followers of China's ancient culture and religion. The monks at Longhua Temple in 1991 opened the hotel within the walls of the temple. Directed by the Master Abbot of Longhua Temple, Ming Yang, the hotel is the first in China with a distinct Buddhist character. Simply decorated in a Chinese style tinged with modern Western influences and post-1949 Communist starkness, the Longhua is much like any other mid-range Chinese hotel. Rooms are simply furnished. The hotel's labyrinth design and circuitous halls are fashioned according to traditional Chinese architecture and beliefs. Along with Chinese and Western cuisine, the hotel also serves vegetarian dishes. ✉ *2787 Longhua Lu, 200232,* ☎ *021/6457–0570,* ℻ *021/6457– 7621. 140 rooms and suites. 3 restaurants, beauty salon, billiards. AE, DC, MC, V.*

$ 🏨 **Ruijin Guesthouse.** The Morriss Estate, now Ruijin Guesthouse, was built by a Western newspaper magnate. Today, the estate's houses still stand amid huge green lawns and trees. Five old villas have rooms traditionally renovated in an old-fashioned style. You can have a drink or a cup of tea on the lawn or in the bar on the south side of the main mansion. Stroll around the estate to view the ornate details, including a stained glass window in the rear house. ⊠ *118 Ruijin Er Lu, 200020,* ☎ *021/6472–5222,* ℻ *021/6473–2277. 47 rooms. 3 restaurants, bar, beauty salon, business services. AE, DC, MC, V.*

$ 🏨 **Xingguo Guesthouse.** This collection of old Shanghai villas, like the Ruijin, sits around a huge green lawn. The villas are old and traditionally furnished. The service and food are not as top-rate as at the Western hotels, but the quaint atmosphere definitely has more charm. Both restaurants serve Chinese cuisine. ⊠ *72 Xingguo, 200052,* ☎ *021/6212–9998,* ℻ *021/6251–2145. 2 restaurants, business services. AE, DC, MC, V.*

Hongqiao Development Zone

$$$$ 🏨 **Westin Tai Ping Yang.** This luxurious Japanese-managed high-rise hotel is extremely formal, and everything is done with a flourish, down to the "welcome" gauntlet that meets you at the front entrance and follows you all the way to the elevator. The hotel is within easy access of the Shanghai International Exhibition Centre and Shanghai Mart. Getting to the airport requires only a short ride. Rooms are fresh and equipped with electronic amenities. Giovanni's is one of the best Italian restaurants in town, and the deli on the second floor offers a great selection of pastas, cold cuts, and breads. ⊠ *5 Zunyi Nan Lu, 200335,* ☎ *021/6275–8888,* ℻ *021/6275–5420. 541 rooms and 39 suites. 5 restaurants, deli, outdoor pool, beauty salon, sauna, tennis court, exercise room, shops, billiards, business services, meeting rooms. AE, DC, MC, V.*

$$$ 🏨 **Yangtze New World Hotel.** Adjacent to the International Trade and Exhibition Center and Shanghai Mart, the hotel has several executive floors. It is especially noted for its excellent Chinese restaurants. The modern, comfortably furnished rooms have a good range of electronic amenities. ⊠ *2099 Yanan Xi Lu, 200335,* ☎ *021/6275–0000,* ℻ *021/ 6275–0750. 553 rooms and suites. 5 restaurants, deli, outdoor pool, beauty salon, sauna, exercise room, shops, dance club, business services, meeting rooms. AE, DC, MC, V.*

$$ 🏨 **Cypress Hotel.** The grounds here are filled with trees, ponds, streams, bridges, and lawns. In the huge sports center are an indoor swimming pool and bowling. Close to the airport, Cypress lies in the west of Hongqiao. The rooms are simple but comfortable. ⊠ *2419 Hongqiao Lu, 200335,* ☎ *021/6268–8868,* ℻ *021/6242–3739. 157 rooms. 5 restaurants, bar, pool, sauna, tennis court, bowling, exercise room, squash, billiards, business services, meeting rooms. AE, DC, MC, V.*

$$ 🏨 **Xijiao Guesthouse.** In the western part of Hongqiao, the Xijiao has pleasant villas set in a large, well-laid-out garden. The tennis courts are among Shanghai's best. ⊠ *1921 Hongqiao Lu, 200335,* ☎ *021/ 6219–8800,* ℻ *021/6433–6641. 110 rooms. 2 restaurants, bar, pool, beauty salon, tennis court, bowling, squash, dance club, business services, meeting rooms. AE, DC, MC, V.*

Pudong and Northeastern Shanghai

$$$ 🏨 **Radisson SAS Lansheng.** The only Western-managed hotel in northeastern Shanghai is easily accessible from the Ring Road, as well as from Pudong New Area. The modern rooms are spacious and elegantly appointed with bathrooms that have separate bath and shower. ⊠ *1000 Quyang Lu, 200437,* ☎ *021/6542–8000,* ℻ *021/6544–8447. 380 rooms and 37 suites. 4 restaurants, bar, beauty salon, sauna, bowling, exercise room, business services, meeting rooms. AE, DC, MC, V.*

$$$ 🏨 **Shanghai New Asia Tomson Hotel.** The first luxury hotel in Pudong is in the heart of Lujiazui financial district. The pièce de résistance of the 24-story hotel is a nearly 200-ft-high Italian Renaissance-inspired atrium with an interior garden that brings in natural light to 18 floors of guest rooms. The spacious, elegant rooms are equipped with elec-

tronic amenities. There are three executive floors. ⊠ 777 Zhangyang Lu, Pudong 200120, ☎ 021/5877–2237, 021/5878–8584, ʄʌX 021/5887–9111. 344 rooms and 78 suites. 7 restaurants, indoor pool, outdoor pool, beauty salon, sauna, exercise room, shops, billiards, nightclub, business services, meeting rooms. AE, DC, MC, V.

NIGHTLIFE AND THE ARTS

For up-to-date information about what's going on in the city, check out *Shanghai Talk,* the monthly expatriate magazine available at Western bars, restaurants, and hotels throughout town, and the *Shanghai Star,* the English newspaper published by the *China Daily,* available at most hotels and bookstores.

The Arts

Acrobatics
Shanghai is home to China's, and possibly the world's, best acrobatic troupe. The **Shanghai Acrobatic Troupe** performs remarkable human feats and stunts at the Shanghai Centre Theatre (⊠ 1376 Nanjing Xi Lu, ☎ 021/6279–8663) daily at 7:15 PM.

Chinese Opera
Not only Beijing opera, but also China's other regional operas, such as Huju, Kunju, and Shaoxing, are performed regularly at the **Yifu Theatre** (⊠ 701 Fuzhou Lu, ☎ 021/6322–6478). Call the box office for schedule and ticket information. On Sundays at 1:30 PM, students from the **Shanghai School of Music and Opera** perform a selection of acts from different operas at the Yifu Theatre. Ticket prices range from YB5 to YB20.

Dance and Music
The modern **Shanghai Centre Theatre** (⊠ 1376 Nanjing Xi Lu, ☎ 021/6279–8663) is the place in town to see quality musical events. Until construction of the Grand Theatre (☞ *below*) is completed in late 1998, this remains the only international-standard venue in the city. Domestic theater and dance acts also perform here from time to time. Asian and Western acts sporadically appear at the **Shanghai Gymnasium** (⊠ 1111 Caoxi Bei Lu, ☎ 021/6473–0940). The **Majestic Theatre** (⊠ 66 Jiangning Lu, ☎ 021/6217–4409, 6267–6366) also hosts both Asian and Western performances.

In October 1998, the magnificent **Grand Theatre** (⊠ 90 Huangpi Lu, ☎ 021/6387–5480) opens, presenting domestic and international entertainment in each of its three theaters.

The **Jingan Hotel** (⊠ 370 Huashan Lu, ☎ 021/6248–1888) has Chamber Music Series performances every Friday at 8 PM.

Theater
Modern theater in China is primarily dominated by state-run companies. The **Shanghai People's Art Theatre** (⊠ 284 Anfu Lu, ☎ 021/6431–3523) presents regular performances of Chinese plays, as well as foreign plays in Chinese translation. The **Shanghai Theatre Academy** (⊠ 630 Huashan Lu, ☎ 021/6248–2920, ext. 3040) has three venues that periodically present student and professional works.

Nightlife

Bars
Small and intimate, **Blues and Jazz** (⊠ 44 Sinan Lu, ☎ 021/6327–2475) has one of the best collections of jazz CDs in the city and, on

Fridays and Saturdays, live blues and jazz performed by expatriate and Chinese musicians. **The Cotton Club** (⌗ 1428 Huaihai Zhong Lu, ☎ 021/6437–7110), a comfortable, unassuming, and relaxed jazz lounge, presents the best live blues and jazz acts in Shanghai.

Shanghai's **Hard Rock Café** (⌗ 1376 Nanjing Xi Lu, ☎ 021/6279–8133), not as impressive as the one in Beijing, does have the latest loud DJ'd and live pop and rock music, a spirited atmosphere, a merchandise shop, a high cover charge (Y80 including one free drink on weekdays, Y100 on weekends), and crowds of Chinese yuppies. The casual **Judy's Too** (⌗ 176 Maoming Nan Lu, ☎ 021/6473–1417) is a beautiful two-level café with a strong old Shanghai colonial theme. Live rock and jazz acts appear some weeknights; the disco floor fills up with a mix of Chinese and foreign dancers on weekends. **Jurassic Pub** (⌗ 8 Maoming Nan Lu, ☎ 021/6253–4627, 021/6258–3758) lives up to its Spielberg-inspired name with dinosaur skeletons wrapped around a central bar beneath a willow tree; *teppanyaki* (Japanese grilled meat) is cooked and served right at your table.

In the Shanghai Centre, the narrow, horse-shoe shape **Long Bar** (⌗ 1376 Nanjing Xi Lu, ☎ 021/6279–8268), reputed to be the longest in town, has a loyal expatriate businessman clientele, and an eclectic jukebox most nights.

Malone's American Café (⌗ 257 Tongren Lu, ☎ 021/6247–2400), the first China edition of a sports bar chain from Vancouver, Canada, has TVs broadcasting sports events, pool tables, darts, sports legend decor, and live jazz or Chinese bands covering rock-and-roll. One of the favorite expatriate pubs in town, **O'Malley's** (⌗ 42 Taojiang Lu, ☎ 021/6437–0667) serves the city's only Guinness beer on tap; Irish staff and Irish music give it a true Irish flavor. The outdoor garden is a great place to relax. A soaring three stories, plus atrium, **Paulaner Brauhaus** (⌗ 150 Fengyang Lu, ☎ 021/6474–5700) combines beer house, pub, and restaurant under one roof—all German, complete with imported oak furnishings and stained glass. The historic and romantic **Peace Hotel** (⌗ 20 Nanjing Xi Lu, ☎ 021/6321–6888) has a German-style pub that has gained fame due to the nightly performances (☞ Y45) of the Peace Hotel Old Jazz Band—men in their 60s and 70s who played jazz in dance halls in pre-1949 Shanghai. **Shanghai Sally's** (⌗ 4 Xiangshan Lu, ☎ 021/6358–1859, 021/6375–2248) has a ground-level bar with a pool table and a basement horseshoe bar where you can eat hamburgers and French fries, and listen to a live reggae band or jazz or rock.

Clubs

The most infamous late-night spot in Shanghai, **D.D.'s Club** (⌗ 298 Xingfu Lu, ☎ 021/6280–8670) only gets really hopping after 1:30 AM on weekends, when people continue their evenings here after the other bars close, merging drunk foreigners with chic, hip, and fashionable Shanghainese (☞ non-members, Y50–100); the small, smoky underground club has intimate scarlet velvet booths and curtains, huge mirrors, antique lamps, coed bathrooms, and DJs spinning techno and disco tunes. **Groove** (⌗ 308 Hengshan Lu, ☎ 021/6471–8154) attracts foreigners, fashionable Shanghainese, and those of alternative lifestyles to enjoy one another and listen or dance to DJ'd acid jazz or jungle music; the club consists of an upstairs bar, a downstairs psychedelic dance floor, and a huge back garden.

The brilliant marquee, seemingly from the 1920s, makes the building look romantically like an old movie theater, but inside, **New York, New York** (⌗ 146 Huqiu Lu, ☎ 021/6321–6097) is one of Shanghai's biggest discos (☞ Y50, includes drink), with a Manhattan setting, techno and disco music, a sunken dance floor, two bars, a pool table, a KTV area, and a lounge. For spectacle, **Time Disco** (✉ 550 Huaihai Zhong Lu, ☎ 021/6327–0302; 💳 Y50–75, includes one drink) offers Shanghai extremism at its best: two crowded floors of lights and mirrors, popular Shanghainese singers draping themselves over moving balconies, the entire roof rolling open to the sky at midnight, and 20 KTV rooms. The small, mellow **Ying Yang** (✉ Nanchang Lu, ☎ 021/6431–2668) club lined with black velvet and illuminated with blue light is a place with character, where an eclectic group of people hangs out, from foreign yuppies to Shanghai's alternative types.

Karaoke

The "only" way to do karaoke these days is to book a KTV room for the evening. This favorite Chinese pastime involves sitting in a private room with three to 20 friends, in front of a TV, songbook, microphone, and drinks. A KTV culture has even begun in China, complete with KTV girls who sing along with (male) guests, and serve cognac and expensive snacks. Be aware that at some establishments, KTV girls practice the world's oldest profession. One of Shanghai's most popular KTV establishments is the giant **Cash Box** (✉ 457 Wulumuqi Lu, ☎ 021/6374–1111). The **Golden Age** (✉ 918 Huaihai Zhong Lu, ☎ 021/6415–8818) is a huge, mind-boggling operation with a wealthy clientele.

Hotel Bars

The Holiday Inn Crowne Plaza's **Charlie's Fun Pub** (✉ 400 Panyu Lu, ☎ 021/6280–8888) hosts the best hotel bands in the city. The Portman Ritz-Carlton's **Shanghai Jax** (✉ 1376 Nanjing Xi Lu, ☎ 021/6279–8888) hosts a two-person band that plays pop favorites. The Hilton's **Penthouse Bar** (✉ 250 Huashan Lu, ☎ 021/6248–0000) offers a quiet, elegant drink overlooking a great view of the city.

OUTDOOR ACTIVITIES AND SPORTS

Basketball

Professional league basketball is growing increasingly popular in Shanghai, with foreign-sponsored teams that include American professional players. The Hilton Basketball League, for instance, plays an annual season from November to April at the **Luwan Gymnasium** (✉ 128 Jiaozhabang Lu). Call IMG Sports Management (☎ 021/6427–8673) for ticket information. Games are also occasionally played at the **Shanghai Gymnasium** (✉ 1111 Caoxi Bei Lu, ☎ 021/6473–0940).

Golf

Golf has only recently hit China, but dozens of courses have sprung up in the last few years. All clubs and driving ranges run on a membership basis, but most allow non-members to play when accompanied by a member. Some even welcome the public. Most clubs are outside the city, in the suburbs and outlying counties of Shanghai.

Grand Shanghai International Golf and Country Club (✉ Box 18, Zhengyi, Kunshan, ☎ ++??++/6210–3350) is an 18-hole par-72 championship course and driving range. **Shanghai Dianshan Lake Golf Club** (✉ Rm. 7010, Rainbow Hotel, 2000 Yanan Xi Lu, ☎ 021/6275–3388), a 27-hole course on Dianshan Lake designed by Bobby J. Martin, includes a driving range. **Shanghai East Asia Golf Club** (✉ 135 Jianguo Xi Lu, ☎ 021/6433–1351) has a driving range. **Shanghai Golf Club** (✉ 12, Tang Hang Zhen Shuang Tang Cun, Jiading County, ☎ 021/5954–0111) is an 18-hole par-72 course. **Shanghai Grand City Golf Club** (✉ 5188 Huaxing Lu, Qibao, ☎ 021/6270–4861) has a 9-hole course and a driving range. **Shanghai International Golf and Country Club** (✉ Zhu Jia Jiao, Qingpu County, ☎ 021/5972–8111), an 18-hole par-72 course, has a driving range and a 3-hole practice course. **Shanghai Links Golf and Country Club** (✉ Tianxu Township, San Jia Bay, Pudong, ☎ 021/5882–2700), a Jack Nicklaus Signature–designed 18-hole championship course, should be completed in 1998–99. **Shanghai Riviera Golf Resort** (✉ Xiang Er, Nanxiang, Jiading County, ☎ 021/5912–8836) is an 18-hole course and driving range. **Sun Island International Club** (✉ Sun Island, Shenxiang, Qingpu County, ☎ 021/5983–0888), an 18-hole course designed by Nelson Wright Haworth, also has a driving range. **Tomson Pudong Golf Club** (✉ 1 Longdong Lu, Pudong, ☎ 021/5855–4001) is an 18-hole course designed by Shunsuke Kato with a driving range.

Health Clubs, Swimming Pools, and Tennis Courts

The best health clubs, gyms, and pools are at the western hotels. The largest and most comprehensive, at the **Portman Shangri-La** (✉ 1376 Nanjing Xi Lu, ☎ 021/6279–8888), has an aerobics room, weight room, swimming pool, and tennis, squash, and racquetball courts; if you're not a hotel guest or a member, you can enter only with a member at a fee of Y100. The **Shanghai Hilton** (✉ 250 Huashan Lu, ☎ 021/6248–0000) has a good health club. The **Garden Hotel** (✉ 58 Maoming Nan Lu, ☎ 021/6415–1111) is especially noted for its Olympic-size indoor pool. If you're looking for an outdoor pool, you can find a beautiful one at the **Shanghai International Convention Hotel** (✉ 2106 Hongqiao Lu, ☎ 021/6270–3388).

Other hotel gyms with **tennis and squash courts** are the **Shanghai JC Mandarin** (✉ 1225 Nanjing Xi Lu, ☎ 021/6279–1888) and **Holiday Inn Crowne Plaza** (✉ 400 Panyu Lu, ☎ 021/6280–8888). Some of the city's best tennis courts can be found at the **Xijiao Guesthouse** (✉ 1921 Hongqiao Lu, ☎ 021/6433–6643). You can also try the new **Shanghai International Tennis Centre** (✉ 516 Hengshan Lu, ☎ 021/6415–5588).

Yachting

Shanghai isn't known for its boating, but if you go out to Dianshan Lake, you can enjoy water sports in style at the **Regency International Yacht Club** (✉ 1860 Hongqiao Lu, ☎ 021/6242–3632), an elite, members-only club (that admits non-members for a fee) with a clubhouse, a pool, and food and beverage outlets. It provides boats, sailboats, jet skis, kayaks, surfboards, water skis, parasailing, and overnight accommodations in cabins right on the lake.

SHOPPING

China's shopping capital, Shanghai has more commercial goods available than any other place in the country except Hong Kong. Shopping is an important part of the city's lifestyle, so most shops and department stores on the main shopping streets of Nanjing Lu and Huaihai Lu and in the Xujiahui area stay open from 10 AM until 10 PM.

Antiques and Furniture

Antiques markets, shops, and furniture warehouses abound in Shanghai, as increasing numbers of foreigners, allured by news of great deals, flock to the city. Great deals, however, are gradually becoming only good deals. No matter what or where you buy, bargaining is an inescapable part of the sales ritual. Note that fake antiques are often hidden among real treasures. Also be aware of age: The majority of pieces date from the late Qing (1644–1911) dynasty; technically, only items dated after 1797 can be legally exported. When buying antique furniture, it helps to know age, of course, and also what kind of wood is used. Although the most commonly used is elm, a whole variety of wood can be found in Chinese antiques.

Antiques buying was once charming at the **Fuyou Lu** Sunday Market in the Old City. Now the market is open daily, and since it moved off the streets into a nondescript warehouse (⌗ 457 Fangbang Zhonglu), most of the fun is gone, but hawkers still sell a wide selection of antiques. The daily **Dongtai Lu Market** (⌗ off Xizang Lu) offers goods similar to those at the Fuyou Lu but stalls are set up outside lining the street. The **Haobao Building** (⌗ Yuyuan Garden, 265 Fangbang Lu, ☎ 021/6355–9999) houses a basement floor with 250 booths selling antiques. The government-owned **Shanghai Antique and Curio Store** (⌗ 218-226 Guangdong Lu, ☎ 021/6321–4697) has some good pieces; there's no bargaining, but you're sure not to get a fake and the receipts are official.

Some **warehouses** to try are at ⌗ 307 Shunchang Lu, ☎ 021/6320–3812 and ⌗ 1430 Hongqiao Lu, 1970 Hongqiao Lu, ☎ 021/6242–8734 and the **Li Brothers** (⌗ 1220 Hongmei Lu, ☎ 021/6436–1500, ext. 195). All shops will renovate any pieces you buy.

Arts and Crafts

Shanghai's artisans create pieces of traditional Chinese arts and crafts right before your eyes at the **Arts and Crafts Research Institute** (⌗ 79 Fenyang Lu, ☎ 021/6437–0509), where you can purchase everything from papercuts to snuff bottles, lanterns to engraved chops. The state-owned **Friendship Store** (⌗ 40 Beijing Dong Lu, ☎ 021/6329–4600), one of a chain of stores started in major Chinese cities as a sign of friendship between the Chinese and foreigners when China first opened to the outside world, was originally open only to foreigners; the quality products it carried were unavailable in regular stores. Now it has evolved into a six-story department store selling foreign and domestic goods that welcomes everyone. It is an especially good source of Chinese arts and crafts and silk: snuff bottles, jewelry, calligraphy, cloisonné, porcelain, batik, traditional furniture, fans, vases, carpets, jade, linen, lanterns, and silk jackets, robes, lingerie, and other clothing. **ShanghART** (⌗ Portman Shangri-La, 2nd floor, 1376 Nanjing Xi Lu, ☎ 021/6279–7135), the only contemporary Chinese art gallery in Shanghai, can give you a good idea of where Chinese avant garde art is heading in the new millennium. The state-owned **Shanghai Jingdezhen Porcelain Store** (⌗ 1175 Nanjing Xi Lu, ☎ 021/6253–3178) has a large selection of porcelain ware and other arts and crafts.

Carpets

Beijing has always been a better place to buy Chinese rugs, but Shanghai has a few shops that may give you a good deal: The **Carpet Factory** (⌗ 783 Honggu Lu, ☎ 021/1391603148), the **Friendship Store** (☞ Arts and Crafts, *above*), the **Shanghai Arts and Crafts Trading Co.** (⌗ Shanghai Exhibition Centre, 1000 Yanan Xi Lu, ☎ 021/6279–0279, ext. 62222), the **Shanghai Pine and Crane Carpet Store** (⌗ 410 Wukang Lu, ☎ 021/6431–7717), and **Zhaohu Carpet Factory** (⌗ 98 Gubei Nan Lu, ☎ 021/1391711047).

Chinese Medicine

Many pharmacies sell Chinese medicine and herbs. You can try: **Caitongde Drugstore** (✉ 320 Nanjing Dong Lu, ☎ 021/6350–4740), **Jinsong Ginseng and Drug Store** (✉ 823 Huaihai Zhong Lu, ☎ 021/6437–6700), and **Shanghai No. 1 Dispensary** (✉ 616 Nanjing Dong Lu, ☎ 021/6473–9149).

Daily Necessities

Shanghai's modern supermarkets should be able to supply you with most personal use and food products. **Watson's Drug Stores** (✉ Shanghai Centre, 1376 Nanjing Xi Lu, ☎ 021/6279–8381; ✉ 789 Huaihai Zhong Lu, ☎ 021/6474–4775) is the most reliable pharmacy. **Wellcome Supermarket** (✉ Shanghai Centre, 1376 Nanjing Xi Lu) can be counted on for products you can't find anywhere else in the city.

Department Stores and Malls

The large, state-run **Hongqiao Friendship Shopping Centre** (✉ 6 Zunyi Lu, ☎ 021/6270–0000) has everything, including Western finesse—household items, gifts, cosmetics, clothing, furniture and audio/video equipment, and a grocery store and deli. The Japanese-run **Isetan** (✉ 527 Huaihai Zhong Lu, ☎ 021/6375–1111; ✉ 1038 Nanjing Xi Lu, ☎ 021/6218–7878) department store, one of the most fashionable in Shanghai, carries such brands as Lancôme, Clinique, Benetton, Esprit, and Episode. **Printemps** (✉ 939-947 Huaihai Zhong Lu, ☎ 021/6431–0118), the leader in French department stores, opened a beautiful branch designed in the same style as the 130-year-old Printemps in Paris in the center of Shanghai's old French Concession; most goods sold are at a price far too high for the common Chinese. The famous **Shanghai No. 1 Department Store** (✉ 830 Nanjing Dong Lu, ☎ 021/6322–3344) is Shanghai's largest state-owned store and attracts masses of Chinese shoppers, especially on weekends; its seven floors have an amazing plethora of domestic items. The **Orient Shopping Centre** (✉ 8 Caoxi Bei Lu, ☎ 021/6407–1947), in Gotham City-like Xujiahui, is the biggest and most comprehensive of three major department stores in the area. **Yaohan Department Store** (✉ 501 Zhangyang Lu, Pudong, ☎ 021/5830–1111), otherwise known as Ba Bai Ban, claims to be the biggest mall in Asia; the 10-story Japanese-owned mega-mall sells everything—clothes, household goods, shoes, accessories, cosmetics, sporting goods, arts and crafts, exercise equipment, stationery, audio/visual equipment, office equipment, even cars.

Fabrics and Tailors

The **Golden Dragon Silk and Wool Company** (✉ 816 Huaihai Zhong Lu, ☎ 021/6473–6691) has the best fabric selection in town. The **Jinling Silk Company** (✉ 363 Jinling Dong Lu, ☎ 021/6320–1449) has a wide choice. The **Shanghai Silk Commercial Company** (✉ 139 Tianping Lu, ☎ 021/6282– 5021) offers good quality. For silk clothing, the **Friendship Store** (☞ *above*) has a good selection.

Shanghai is home to many tailors who make clothing at reasonable prices. The most inexpensive are to be found at **Tailor Lane,** a small alley leading to Hunan Lodge on Wuyuan Lu (numbers 52 and 72) near Maison Mode; bring in a garment to copy. For better, more complicated work, try **Ascot Chang** (✉ Dickson Center, 400 Chang Le Lu, Room 211, ☎ 021/6472–6888). **Hansheng** (✉ Shanghai Centre, 1376 Nanjing Xi Lu, ☎ 021/6279–8600); **Sakurai Yofuku** (✉ Friendship Shopping Center, 6 Zunyi Lu, ☎ 021/6270– 0000); and **Taylor Lee** (✉ 2018 Huaihai Lu) also produce good clothing.

A few tailors specialize in making Chinese *qipaos* (cheongsams). The one at ✉ 258 Shimen Yi Lu does good work. **Long Feng** (✉ 942 Nanjing Xi Lu) turns out good cheongsams.

Outdoor Markets

Most of Shanghai's outdoor markets sell food and produce. The **Bird and Flower Market** (✉ Huangpi Lu between Nanjing Lu and Weihai Lu) gives a good slice of Shanghai life: You'll find hawkers selling pets such as fish, birds, turtles, cats, and frogs, and a whole range of plants, bonsai trees, orchids, and clay pots. You can find good, cheap Western clothing—seconds, irregulars and knock-offs—at **Huating Market** (✉ Huating Lu between Changle Lu and Huaihai Zhong Lu). The biggest market in Shanghai is the **Zhonghua Xin Lu Market** (✉ 100 Hengfeng Lu), which attracts private hawkers that sell everything under the sun.

Tea

Shanghai Huangshan Tea Company (✉ 853 Huaihai Zhong Lu, ☎ 021/6545–4919) sells a huge selection of China's best teas by weight; the higher the price, the better the tea is. Beautiful Yixing pots are also for sale.

SHANGHAI A TO Z

Arriving and Departing

By Boat

Boats running between Shanghai and Hong Kong (2½ days) and Shanghai and Japan dock at **Waihongqiao Harbor** (✉ 1 Taiping Lu). Tickets can be booked through CITS (☞ Travel Agencies, *below*).

Most domestic boats leave from the **Shiliupu Dock** (✉ Zhongshan Dong Lu just south of the Bund) for such destinations on the Yangzi (Changjiang) River as Wuhan, Chongqing, Nanjing, Wuhu, and Jiujiang, as well as for such coastal cities as Guangzhou, Qingdao, Dalian, Ningbo, and Fuzhou. Overnight boats for the outlying island of Putuoshan leave every other day; a faster boat leaves daily, but the overnight boat is more practical. All domestic tickets can be purchased at the foreigner ticket booth on the 2nd floor of the Boat Ticket Booking Office (✉ 1 Jinling Dong Lu), as well as at CITS (☞ Travel Agencies, *below*). River passenger transport information can be obtained by calling ☎ 021/6326–1261.

There's a wide range of boats, although most domestic boats are not luxurious. They do, however, offer different levels of berths, the most comfortable being first class.

By Bus

Getting to and from Shanghai by bus is usually less convenient than by train. A deluxe coach bus (✉ 58 Laochongqing Nan Lu, ☎ 021/6358–8089) does run between Shanghai and Nanjing (3½ hours). Regular buses, most of which lack comfort, run from the long-distance bus station (✉ Qiujiang Lu west of Henan Bei Lu). These are acceptable for shorter distances such as to Hangzhou and Suzhou. The ticket office for Suzhou tickets is at the eastern end of People's Square. Check out train tickets before taking the bus.

By Car

Although most travelers arrive in Shanghai by train or plane, the city is connected by some new highways to Suzhou and Nanjing in the west and Hangzhou in the south. Travel by car is generally difficult in China, as there are few roads and road facilities. It is virtually impossible for people not residents of China to drive.

By Plane

The new Shanghai International Airport opens in Pudong in 1999; until then all air traffic comes through the **Hongqiao International Airport** in western Shanghai, about 15 km (9 mi) from the city center. Porters and trolleys are available for a nominal fee. You can call for 24-hour airport information (☎ 021/6268–8918).

Many offices of international carriers are located in the Shanghai Centre and the Shanghai Hilton. Major foreign airlines that serve Shanghai are: Dragon Airlines (✉ Shanghai Centre, 1376 Nanjing Xi Lu, ☎ 021/6279–8099), Japan Airlines (✉ Ruijin Dasha, 205 Maoming Nan Lu, ☎ 021/6472–3000), Lufthansa (✉ Shanghai Hilton, 250 Huashan Lu, ☎ 021/6248–1100), Northwest Airlines (✉ Shanghai Centre, ☎ 021/6279–8088), Qantas (✉ Shanghai Centre, ☎ 021/6279–8660), SAS (✉ Jin Jiang Hotel, 59 Maoming Nan Lu, ☎ 021/6472–3131), Singapore Airlines (✉ Shanghai Centre, ☎ 021/6279–8000), Swiss Air (✉ Shanghai Centre, ☎ 021/6279–7381), United Airlines (✉ Shanghai Centre, ☎ 021/6279–8009).

Domestic carriers that connect international destinations to Shanghai include Air China (✉ 600 Huashan Lu, ☎ 021/6327–7888) and China Eastern (✉ 200 Yanan Xi Lu, ☎ 021/6247–5953, domestic; ☎ 021/6247–2255, international).

A number of regional carriers serve Shanghai, but China Eastern Airlines (✉ 200 Yanan Xi Lu, ☎ 021/6247–5953, domestic; ☎ 021/6247–2255, international) is the main carrier connecting it with other cities in China.

BETWEEN THE AIRPORT AND CITY CENTER

Depending on the traffic, the trip can take anywhere from 30 minutes to an hour. Plenty of taxis are available at the queues right outside both the international and domestic terminals. Don't take a ride with drivers who tout their services at the terminal entrances; their cars don't have meters, and they'll try to charge you exorbitant rates. To get into the city, most drivers use the recently opened expressway that connects to the Ring Road. Expect to reimburse the driver for the toll.

By Train

Shanghai is connected to many destinations in China by direct train. The **Shanghai Railway Station** (✉ 303 Moling Lu) is in the northern part of the city. Several trains a day run to Suzhou, Hangzhou, Nanjing, and other nearby destinations. The best train to catch to Beijing is the overnight express that leaves around 7 PM and arrives in Beijing the next morning. An express train also runs to Hong Kong.

You can buy train tickets at CITS (☞ Travel Agencies, *below*), but they charge you a service fee. Same-day, next-day, and sometimes third-day tickets can also be purchased at the ticket office in the Longmen Hotel (✉ 777 Hengfeng Lu, ☎ 021/6317–0000) on the western side of the train station. For 24-hour train information, call ☎ 021/6317–9090.

Getting Around

By Bus

With few exceptions, Shanghai buses are very old and uncomfortable, primarily standing-room-only, and extremely inconvenient. Often you'll have to change buses several times to get where you're going. During busy traffic hours, they're unbelievably crowded. On most buses, the fare is Y0.50 for any stop on the line.

One exception to the above is the double-decker bus running down Huaihai Lu through the old French Concession. It's a pleasant ride, as there are many seats on these vehicles imported from Hong Kong. If you sit on the top deck, you have a great view over the many compound walls at the beautiful old Shanghai buildings that line the thoroughfare. Fares on this bus line will run you a few yuan.

By Car

Traffic is chaotic and exasperating due to the sheer number of bicycles, mopeds, motorcycles, pedestrians, cars, buses, and trucks simultaneously vying for the right-of-way.

By Subway

The Shanghai Metro is now under construction. The one line in service runs in both directions from the Jinjiang Amusement Park in southern Shanghai north to Xujiahui, turns northeast on Hengshan Lu, continues eastward through the old French Concession with stops at Changshu Lu, Shaanxi Lu, and Huangpi Lu, then shifts northeast and runs through the center of the city with a stop at People's Square and continues north to the last stop at the Shanghai Railway Station.

The subway is not too crowded except at rush hour, and trains run regularly. However, the line closes at 10 PM. Trains start operating in the morning at 8 AM. Tickets cost Y2 for one ride to any stop on the line.

By Taxi

By far the most convenient way to get around Shanghai, taxis are plentiful and easy to spot. Most are red Volkswagen Santanas, although they also come in white, yellow, and blue. They are all metered. You can spot the available ones by the red "for hire" sign on the dashboard on the passenger side. The Santanas start at Y14.40, with each km (½ mi) thereafter costing Y1.60. After 10 km (6 mi), the price per km goes up to Y2.70. You also pay for waiting time in traffic. There are other cabs such as Citroens and smaller Volkswagens that start at Y13.50. The really small cabs, the Daihatsu TJ7100, are less comfortable and usually don't have air-conditioning, but the ride is cheaper at a starting rate of Y10.80 and Y1.20 each km thereafter.

Cabs can be hailed on the street or called for by phone. Some major taxi companies are: **Dazhong Taxi Company** (☎ 021/6258–1688), **Shanghai Taxi Company** (☎ 021/6258–0000), and **Friendship Taxi Company** (☎ 021/6258–3484).

Most cab drivers don't speak English, so it's best to give them a piece of paper with your destination written in Chinese. Hotel doormen can also help you tell the driver where you're going. It's a good idea to study a map and have some idea where you are, as many drivers will take you for a ride, literally, if they think they can get away with it. You'll usually get where you want to go, but it may take you more time and more money!

On Foot

When crossing streets the best tactic is to thread your way carefully and steadily among the vehicles. Try to cross with a group of other pedestrians. Don't try to dart ahead of a car or bike.

Contacts and Resources

Community Organizations

American Chamber of Commerce (☎ 021/6279–7119). **Australia Chamber of Commerce** (☎ 021/6352–3155). **British Chamber of Commerce** (☎ 021/6278–5975). **Canadian Business Forum** (☎ 021/6279–8400). **Hong Kong Chamber of Commerce** (☎ 021/6386–6688, ext. 420).

Consulates

United States ✉ 1469 Huaihai Zhong Lu, ☎ 021/6433–6880; emergencies, ☎ 021/6433–3936). **Australia** (✉ 17 Fuxing Xi Lu, ☎ 021/6433–4604). **Canada** (✉ Shanghai Centre, No. 604, 1376 Nanjing Xi Lu, ☎ 021/6279–8400). **Great Britain** (✉ Shanghai Centre, No. 301, 1376 Nanjing Xi Lu, ☎ 021/6279–7650). **New Zealand** (✉ Qihua Dasha, 15th floor, 1375 Huaihai Zhong Lu, ☎ 021/6433–2230).

Emergencies

Police ☎ 110. **Fire** ☎ 119.

In a medical emergency, never call for an ambulance. The Shanghai Ambulance Service (☎ 120) is merely a transport system. If possible take a taxi; you'll get there faster.

New Pioneer Medical Centre (✉ 910 Hengshan Lu, 2nd floor, ☎ 6469–3898). **World Link Medical Center** at the Shanghai Centre (✉ 1376 Nanjing Xi Lu, ☎ 021/6279–7688). **Huadong Hospital** (✉ 221 Yanan Xi Lu, 2nd floor Foreigner's Clinic, ☎ 021/6248–3180, ext. 6208/6201). **Huashan Hospital** (✉ 12 Wulumuqi Lu, 19th floor Foreigner's Clinic, ☎ 021/6248–3986).

Shanghai Dental Medical Centre Cooperative (✉ Ninth People's Hospital, 639 Zhizaoju Lu, 7th floor, ☎ 021/6376–3174). **Shen Da Dental Clinic** (✉ 83/1 Taiyuan Lu, ☎ 021/6437–7987).

English-Language Bookstores

Foreign Language Bookstore (✉ 390 Fuzhou Lu; branches in hotels and Friendship stores) carries maps, photography books, and non-fiction, literature and poetry about China, as well as foreign periodicals and a small selection of contemporary English-language novels.

Guided Tours

CITY TOURS

Guided bus tours of the city can be booked through CITS (☞ Travel Agencies, *below*) and are led in several languages.

CRUISES

Huangpu River Cruises (✉ 239 Zhongshan Dong Er Lu, ☎ 021/6374–4461), 3½-hour trips (Y45–Y100) up and down the Huangpu River between Wusong and the Bund, include buffet and depart from the Bund at Jinling Lu at 2 PM and 3:30 PM. You'll see barges, bridges and factories, but not much scenery; night-time cruises are better, as you get great views of the Bund beautifully floodlit. One-hour cruises (Y30) from the Bund between the Nanpu and Yangpu Bridges leave at 10:45 AM and 4:15 PM. You can purchase all tickets at the dock.

Regal China Huangpu River Cruises (✉ 108 Huangpu Lu, ☎ 021/6306–9801, FAX 021/6306–9902), China's only foreign-owned and managed cruise line, runs high-class dinner cruises (Y250) that blend views of the Bund and the Nanpu and Yangpu Bridges with a comfortable sit-down buffet or Chinese à la carte dinner aboard a German-made 426-ft-long river liner. Boats leave at 7:30 PM and dock at 10:30 PM. The line also runs cruises (US$70–$150) to Wusong—the point where the Huangpu meets the Yangzi River—docking overnight before returning to Shanghai the next morning; dinner and breakfast are served.

For **Yangzi River cruises** to the Three Gorges from Shanghai, CITS (☞ Travel Agencies, *below*) handles bookings.

Telephones
Local directory assistance, ☎ 114 (Shanghai). Domestic directory assistance, ☎ 116 (other Chinese cities). Time ☎ 117. Weather, ☎ 121.

Travel Agencies
China International Travel Service (CITS; ✉ Guangming Building, 2 Jinling Lu, ☎ 021/6321–7200). **American Express** (✉ Shanghai Centre, 1376 Nanjing Xi Lu, ☎ 021/6279–8600). **Evrokantakt** (✉ 9T Tseng Chow Commercial Mansion, 1590 Yanan Xi Lu, ☎ 021/6280–9579). **Harvest Travel Services** (✉ 16-A6 Harvest Building, 585 Longhua Xi Lu, ☎ 021/6469–1860). **IRS International Travel Agency** (☎ 021/6486–0681, 021/6486–0682). **Jebsen and Co. Ltd.** (✉ 16 Henan Lu, ☎ 021/6355–4001).

Visa Service
To extend your visa or ask for information about your status as an alien in China, stop by the **Public Security Bureau division for aliens** (✉ 333 Wusong Lu, ☎ 021/6357–6666; ⊙ Weekdays 9–11 and 2–5). The office is extremely bureaucratic, and the visa officers can be difficult at times. Most of them can speak English. It's usually no problem to get a month extension on a tourist visa. You'll need to bring in your passport and your registration of temporary residency from the hotel at which you're staying. If you are trying to extend a business visa, you'll need the above items, as well as a letter from the business that originally invited you to China saying that it would like to extend your stay for work purposes. Rules are always changing, so you will probably need to go to the office at least twice to get all your papers in order.

Visitor Information
Shanghai Tourist Information Services (✉ Hongqiao Airport, ☎ 021/6268–7788, ext. 6750; ✉ People's Square Metro Station, ☎ 021/6438–1693; ✉ Yuyuan Commercial Building, ☎ 021/6355–4909; Spring Travel Service, ☎ 021/6252–0000, ext. 0; Tourist Hotline, ☎ 021/6439–0630.

5 East Central China

"*Above, there is heaven. Below, there are Hangzhou and Suzhou.*" *Even the most space-age travel agencies may have trouble arranging tours of heaven, but this traditional comparison marks East Central China as home to some of the country's oldest and best-known landmarks. In the western part of the region lie major sites and artifacts of Chinese history, both ancient and modern.*

ONE OF THE FIRST areas where Chinese civilization developed, the six provinces of Jiangsu, Zhejiang, Hubei, Shaanxi, Henan, and Anhui are home to some of archaeology's most stupendous finds, ranging from Neolithic remains to pre-dynastic artworks to an enormous army of sculptures built to outlast death. Five of China's six major dynastic capitals are found here: Hangzhou, Kaifeng, Xian, Luoyang, and Nanjing, leaving only Beijing in the north. In the 20th century the region witnessed its own share of tumult during the struggle between Nationalist and Communist forces, which was based largely in this densely populated stretch of China.

By Anya
Bernstein
with Saul
Thomas

Han Chinese civilization originated along the banks of the Yellow River near where the cities of Luoyang and Zhengzhou now stand, in the small but populous province of Henan. The name of the province, which literally translates as "south of the river," is a constant reminder of the river's importance. Traces of what was, 36 centuries ago, the capital of the Shang dynasty can still be faintly seen in modern-day Zhengzhou, Henan's capital. Archaeological finds suggest that another capital in the same area predated even this early city. The river itself still holds a certain fascination, largely for its potential destructive power.

West of Zhengzhou, Henan harbors the starting point of another aspect of Chinese civilization. Buddhism, brought to China in the 1st century AD, found its first home in White Horse Temple on the outskirts of present-day Luoyang. The religion, once translated and adjusted a bit to Chinese sensibilities, gained enormous popularity, inspiring Henan's extraordinary Dragon Gate Caves. In the 6th and 7th centuries AD, artisans carved thousands of Buddhist figures into a stretch of mountain faces near Luoyang. Time has not been kind to these astounding art works, but despite foreign looting and the ravages of wind and rain, they remain one of the region's most important, and most impressive, sights.

The region also includes some of the most important cities of 20th-century China. Wuhan, in eastern Hubei province, was home to major Communist uprisings in the 1920s and also base for a time of the left-leaning faction of the Nationalist Guomindang party. To the east, Jiangsu province's Nanjing housed the main conservative opposition to the Wuhan group and the Communists. It served as national capital under Chiang Kai-shek from 1927 to 1937, a time referred to as the "Nanjing decade."

To the west, in the province of Shaanxi, another marvel of ancient craftsmanship stands poised for attack in Xian. Discovered accidentally in 1974 by farmers digging a well, the army of terra-cotta warriors, created in the 3rd century BC, has still not been fully excavated. Ranks of soldiers stand at attention while hundreds of square feet of land wait to reveal further treasures.

Another tribute to ancient creativity, the Grand Canal runs from Beijing to Zhejiang's Hangzhou to form the longest artificial waterway in the world. It can be viewed to flattering effect on a boat trip between Hangzhou and Suzhou in Jiangsu, both of which are themselves marvels of artistic creation. Hangzhou's focal point for visitors is Xihu, or West Lake, which was purposely cut off from the river centuries ago. Tang dynasty poets, painters, and other artists came here to relax, recite, and re-create the culture around them. Hangzhou has remained a major draw for visitors ever since, even after a Taiping rebellion army laid siege to the city and burned much of it to the ground in the 1860s.

Suzhou's numerous gardens, scattered about the city, fall somewhere between sculpted artwork and playground maze, exhibition hall and romantic refuge. Many districts in both of these cities retain a flavor of the past despite efforts at modernization that have caused whole blocks to be rebuilt. They provide some of the best opportunities in China for strolling and discovering unexpected vistas of beauty.

East Central China also has its share of natural beauty. Two of China's traditional "five famous mountains"——one for each direction and one in the center——are found here. The twisted, slanted pines of Huangshan are the original, non-miniature bonsai trees. These mountains in eastern Anhui province rise in sheer cliffs out of mist. After a visit here, you suddenly see old-style Chinese landscape paintings as realism and not the fanciful invention that they appear to most Western eyes. The mountain range of Huashan, between Xian and Luoyang, has its own particular flavor. The Three Gorges region of the Yangzi River is in Western Hubei province.

Pleasures and Pastimes

Cruises

Ferries travel the Yangzi River and the Grand Canal, affording views of many of the region's landmarks. A boat between Wuhan and Chongqing takes you through the Three Gorges. You can travel on the Grand Canal between the old-style cities of Hangzhou and Suzhou. Hotel travel desks and CITS, as well as other private travel agencies, can arrange tickets.

Dining

East Central China covers a lot of ground, both physically and culinarily. While the same basic dishes—cooked with greater or lesser success—can be found at cheap sit-down eateries pretty much everywhere in China, both the more serious specialty restaurants and the ubiquitous street foods vary here. The emphasis here is on fish; the region is rich in water, with two major rivers and an ocean coast, as well as numerous lakes. Another tendency, especially in the more eastern cities, is an unfortunate liberality with oil. Concentrations of the Hui Islamic minority in the western cities lend much of the food a Muslim flavor. Sweets tasting slightly like halvah and sticky rice with dates and sweet sauces bear the marks of a Middle Eastern influence, while lamb or beef dumplings, steamed or fried, differ from regular Han Chinese versions only in the absence of pork.

In some cities, restaurants commonly frequented by the locals provide great enough variety and high enough quality to render them a desirable choice—you can see how the populace eats without compromising your own expectations of taste and cleanliness. Other cities have a less developed dining culture; the local restaurants tend toward a Chinese version of fast food and provide fair-to-middling quality in a setting not quite up to many visitors' standards. Your best alternatives here usually lie with the city's high-class restaurants and the often excellent food served in the local hotels. Even the fancier venues are often affordable by Western standards. Most sizable hotels serving foreigners have a western as well as a Chinese kitchen. The Chinese restaurant may serve specialties of other regions, such as Sichuan and Canton, which are more famous for their cuisine than is East Central China.

Dress is usually casual by western standards in even the more upscale places, but tends to be more formal in the hotel restaurants, especially the western sections. Reservations are almost never necessary; in fact, many restaurants are loath to give out their phone numbers at all.

CATEGORY	COST*
$$$$	over $20
$$$	$12–$20
$$	$5–$12
$	under $5

per person, excluding drinks and service (usually 15%)

Hiking

Spread across the region are a variety of famous mountain ranges—some sacred to Buddhists, some to Daoists, and some just part of Chinese lore and the widespread classifications that rank visitor sights. This system has been known to fail with regard to man-made sights, but it is rarely wrong when it comes to nature. Hiking on the well-worn paths has its own particular flavor. This is not trekking through the wilderness—stone steps built through the centuries on many of these mountains make for more civilized travel. On all of them, you will periodically come upon temples built for the gods or pavilions honoring famous people or beliefs; several are likely to be packed with Chinese tourists, for whom these trips can be an almost patriotic outing to see the beauty and history of their country. Lodging and dining in these areas tend toward the simple and basic; the views, the fresh air, and the relative quiet make up for that.

Lodging

The chief cities of the region have built up an impressive array of joint venture or upscale domestic hotels over the last few years of foreign tourism. Many offer comfortable, well-appointed and well-managed establishments with facilities and staff training based on western hotels of the same caliber. Other hotels are simpler, sometimes lagging in the customer service department. What's often really missing in city hotels, though, is charm. Don't expect the decoration or the architecture to be enchanting in the metropolis. Reservations are strongly advised at major tourist spots like Huangshan at any time of year; Luoyang in April is particularly crowded. Hangzhou and Suzhou are also popular tourist destinations and may require reservations, especially during the spring and autumn.

CATEGORY	COST*
$$$$	over $100
$$$	$60–$100
$$	$25–$60
$	under $25

All prices are for a standard double room with bath, excluding service charge (usually 15%).

Nightlife

Some cities in the region have begun a nightlife industry over the last few years. Bars, pubs, and dance clubs have started popping up about town—often only to close down in a couple of months. Outdoor markets provide a more traditional form of nighttime entertainment as clusters of people wander through them in the evenings, eating and chatting. In a culture where many people still have few opportunities, outside of relatively structured and quite expensive banquets, these markets provide a kind of excuse to gather for no other reason than to be social. The markets in Nanjing, Suzhou, and Hangzhou are well known for their variety of products, ranging from silk scarves and clothing to ceramic teapots to Cultural Revolution memorabilia. Street food, also a main part of these markets, is a cuisine unto itself. Snacking reaches its apex in Kaifeng, a short ride east of Zhengzhou, where the considerable local Muslim population sets up a nightly porkless market stretching for blocks around the center of town. A blend of goods and foods can be found in Xian's Muslim quarter, centered around the mosque.

Shopping

In the east, silk rules. Suzhou and Nanjing, as well as Hangzhou, all have plentiful and well-priced silk products, from scarves and skirts to Mao-style jackets and bolts of cloth that you can take to any number of tailors. Many of these wares are easily available at small shops around town and in the nightly markets. Western local products often focus around archaeological finds and historical traditions: imitation Tang dynasty ceramics in Luoyang, reproduction terra-cotta warriors in Xian. Friendship stores sell local arts products as well as some antiques, and major tourist sites are surrounded by peddlers selling souvenirs. Small tradespeople occupying endless stands sell handmade trinkets that are sometimes quite precious; pushcart owners in Zhengzhou quickly and expertly convert long, flat pieces of grass into various cute-looking insects. Souvenirs like this are usually quite reasonably priced; for larger items, bargaining is the rule in the outdoor markets, while prices are taken somewhat more seriously inside stores.

Exploring East Central China

Great Itineraries

The far-flung area we call East Central China encompasses a variety of dialects both linguistic and cultural. Nevertheless, you can get a glimpse of a good many things if you plan your trip carefully. Even taken in small bits, this is a big chunk of land to cover, and transportation, although constantly improving, is not always up to western expectations of speed, cleanliness, or convenient access. If you treat the journey as part of the tour, you will have a much better time than if you stay too focused on reaching your final destinations with all possible haste.

Numbers in the text correspond to numbers in the margin and on the East Central China, Nanjing, Suzhou, and Xian maps.

IF YOU HAVE 3 DAYS

If you're flying into Shanghai or **Nanjing,** trains leave every couple of hours to take you into **Suzhou** for a day of wandering, exploring gardens, and shopping for silk, Suzhou's specialty. An overnight ferry down the Grand Canal gets into **Hangzhou** in the morning, and you can spend a day here exploring. You might take a sleeper train back up to Nanjing if you want a day on the town there, or stay another day in Hangzhou to walk in the outlying area before training back up to Shanghai.

Alternatively, if Chinese culture and history are your interests, fly to **Xian** to see the army of Qin dynasty terra-cotta warriors and the Great Mosque in the center of the city, among many other historic attractions. Take the 10 AM "tourist train" to **Luoyang** for a walk through the Dragon Gate Caves and, if it's spring, a glimpse of budding peonies, before heading back east.

IF YOU HAVE 5 DAYS

For a look at the scenery that has inspired Chinese art, follow first the three-day itinerary (☞ *above*) to **Hangzhou,** but catch a bus to **Huangshan** instead of returning eastward. The day-long trip passes through enthralling countryside as you wind around mountain curves past villages and farms. After a day of mountain climbing, you can take a train back from Tunxi to Shanghai, catch another bus, or fly. Another nature-oriented trip would take you by plane to **Wuhan,** where you can start the four-day trip up the Yangzi River, past the Three Gorges into Chongqing.

A more historically oriented five days could be spent expanding the second three-day itinerary (☞ *above*). Give yourself a little more time to explore the plentiful sights around **Xian**: the hot springs and Neolithic village, as well as the ancient dynastic tombs unearthed a few decades ago. Then, in **Luoyang,** be sure to see the Bai Ma Temple, China's first Buddhist temple, as well as the martial arts Shao Lin Temple between Luoyang and Zhengzhou. End up by going past Zhengzhou into **Kaifeng,** an ancient capital that has managed to hold on to its small neighborhoods and vibrant culture.

IF YOU HAVE 8 OR MORE DAYS

Flying into **Nanjing,** spend a day exploring the city—Zijinshan in sunny weather is particularly pleasant, and Fuzimiao is a good evening hangout spot. Catch the 10 AM train into **Zhenjiang** the next day. The trip takes only an hour, so you will have plenty of time to stroll around this small city before heading off that evening or the next morning to **Wuxi.** Then go to **Suzhou** and the gardens, taking the overnight Grand Canal ferry down to **Hangzhou** before continuing on to **Huangshan** for a couple of days of climbing (☞ *above*). For a more unusual experience, fly to **Wuhan** and explore some of the western region of Hubei—up to **Wudangshan,** then back down to the Yangzi for a final view of the Three Gorges.

A good way to combine the historic with the aesthetic is to take the second 5-day itinerary (☞ *above*) through **Xian** to **Kaifeng,** then catch an overnight train (11 hours) from **Kaifeng** to **Nanjing.** Spend a day exploring Nanjing before taking the train in to **Suzhou** for a final fragrant, relaxing day among flowers and ponds.

When to Tour East Central China

Nanjing and Wuhan share the distinction of being two of China's three summer "furnaces," but summer heat does not do much to moderate winter cold: The region tends toward seasonal extremes. The best time to visit is early to mid-fall, when Huangshan is cool but not cold, and Suzhou gardens still have flowering trees but fewer visitors than during the summer months. March and April are good months in Luoyang, famed for its peonies, and Nanjing, with its plum blossoms.

The Spring Festival, the Chinese lunar new year, which usually falls in early February, is a great time to see popular culture in action, especially in east coast cities such as Nanjing, Suzhou, and Hangzhou. However, try to keep actual travel around this period to a minimum as trains, stations, and hotels tend to become even more crowded and disorganized.

JIANGSU

One of China's richest provinces and home to some of its best land, Jiangsu has long been an economic and political center. It was raised to province status under the Ming dynasty (1368–1644), which brought the capital to Nanjing for a time before moving it back north to Beijing. Nanjing and Jiangsu retained their nationwide importance owing partly to the Grand Canal, which cuts southward through the province. After the mid-19th-century Opium War, which saw British armies in the Yangzi Delta, the stretch between Nanjing and the sea was built up into the major metropolitan area of Shanghai and the smaller Wuxi. Japanese occupation from 1937 to 1945 caused serious damage in the province, but restoration has taken place.

Jiangsu has a wealthy cultural heritage. The Sun Yat-sen Memorial in Nanjing is a national pilgrimage goal, while the gardens of Suzhou are a showcase of Chinese artistry and tradition. Autumn tends to be

INNER
MONGOLIA

HE

Yulin

Huang He

Huang He

Anyang

Yan'an

SHANXI

NINGXIA

GANSU

Zhengzhou

Luoyang 41

40 Kaifeng

Baoji

Weinan

Xuchar

Wei He

Xian
31 — 39

HENAN

Zhumadian

Hanzhong

Shiyan

Nanyang

SHAANXI

Ankang

Wudang
Shan 30

Tongbai Shan

Xi

Shennongjia
29

Xiangfan

Han Shui

HUBE

SICHUAN

Jingmen

Tianmen

Yichang 28

27 Jingzhou

Xiantao

Chongqing

Chang Jiang

*Dongting
Hu*

S

Yuan Jiang

HUNAN

Changsha

GUIZHOU

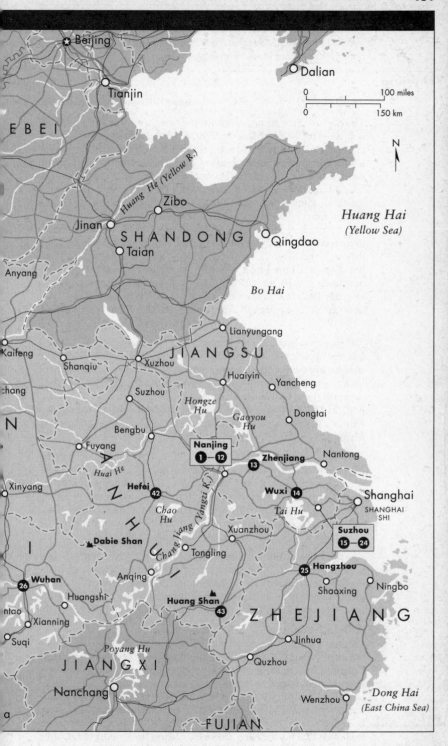

warm and dry here, with ideal walking temperatures; spring can be rainy and windy, but it also brings the blooms to Nanjing's Plum Blossom Hill and Zhenjiang's Nanshan Park. Summers are oppressively hot and humid; winters are bearable though cold and misty.

Nanjing

2½ hours west of Shanghai by "tourist train;" 4½ hours by normal trains.

The city's present name, which means "southern capital," was originally used by the first Ming emperor, who relocated the imperial court here in 1356. Although his son returned the capital to Beijing, Nanjing has retained a special place in Chinese history, and in the Chinese heart. The Taiping Rebellion started here in 1851 and went on to conquer a large portion of southern China with its promises of egalitarianism, morality, and wealth—not to mention its significant armies. The Ming tombs on Zijinshan Hill are a reminder of the city's glorious dynastic past, as the Sun Yat-sen Mausoleum, nearby, is a reminder of more recent honors. Sun Yat-sen harked back to the indigenous Ming dynasty in his determination that Nanjing should be the capital of the new Republic, opposing it to Beijing, which had housed the non-Chinese Qing dynasty until 1912. The city served as the republican capital from 1927 to 1937, a time known as the "Nanjing decade," and again as the Guomindang (GMD) capital during the civil war from 1945 to 1949.

Nanjing was also the scene of some of the first unequal treaties, which forcibly opened Chinese ports to the west after the Opium Wars. The treaties and the European encroachment on Chinese sovereignty have been a sore point for more than a hundred years. In the 1930s Japan occupied the area. The atrocities committed during the "rape of Nanjing" in 1937—when hundreds of thousands of civilians were killed within a few days—are commemorated at the Nanjing Massacre Memorial.

Sections and some gates of the 33-km (20-mi) Ming wall built around Nanjing in the 14th century still stand. The city is composed of a series of small neighborhoods with winding streets, separated by major thoroughfares. You may want to explore one or two by simply taking a turn down an alleyway. However, be careful: there's very little physical danger for foreigners walking around in the daytime, but it's quite easy to get lost on these small, twisting, unmarked lanes.

The rural areas under Nanjing's administrative control supply the city with most of its food. Vegetables, fresh meat, and fish fill huge, lively markets held daily in every neighborhood. Nanjing University, a quiet, green, tastefully constructed campus, now ranks as China's number two educational institution, second only to Beijing University.

A Good Walk

The best place for a long stroll in Nanjing, ironically, lies just outside the city proper, in **Zijinshan** (Purple Mountain). People come to this delightful area to escape the noise and traffic of the city, particularly in spring and autumn. A wealth of historic sites are located on the mountain. Take a taxi to Mingling Lu, or take bus number 20 to its penultimate stop, ending up by **Meihuashan** ① and the **Zhongshan Zhiwuyuan,** both just east of the road. After a stroll on the hill and in the gardens, head west again to the **Ming Xiaoling** ②, where the founder of the Ming dynasty is buried. Continue on uphill. In warm weather, shuttle buses run to **Zhongshan Ling** ③, Sun Yat-sen's mausoleum. If the weather is warm enough, you can take a cable car up to the top of the mountain as well. Otherwise, keep on going west to **Linggu Si** ④ and **Linggu Ta.**

Catch the shuttle back and walk or ride south along Lingyuan Lu to stop by the **Meiling Gong** ⑤, Chiang Kai-shek's weekend house. A bit farther south you reach the city wall at the **Zhonghua Men** ⑥. Northward along Zhongshen Nanlu, to the right just off Jiankang Lu, is **Fuzimiao** ⑦, a Confucian temple sitting in the midst of a shopping and entertainment district. Just to the west is **Mochou Hu Gongyuan** ⑧, a restful park. Northward just west of Zhongshan Lu is the **Gulou** ⑨ drum tower. Farther north, east of Zhongshan Lu, you can take in the lakes of **Xuanwu Hu Gongyuan** ⑩. Take a bus or cab across the Qinhuai River southwest of the city to visit the **Datusha Jinianguan** ⑪, commemorating those killed during the Japanese occupation of the city. Another taxi ride will take you across the **Yangzi River Bridge** ⑫, to the northwest of the city.

Sights to See

⑪ **Datusha Jinianguan** (Nanjing Massacre Memorial). This monument commemorates the victims of the Japanese occupation of Nanjing. Commonly known as the "rape of Nanjing," the Japanese invasion saw hundreds of thousands of deaths in the space of a few days. On the anniversary of the invasion, city-wide sirens remind the populace of the horrors suffered by their compatriots. The memorial also displays artifacts from the Sino-Japanese reconciliation after World War II, ending on a less strident, more hopeful note. ⊠ *Just outside Jiangdong Men (River East Gate) of city wall, on western side of city; No. 7 bus or taxi.* ⊙ *Daily 8:30–5.*

❼ **Fuzimiao** (Confucian Temple). The traditional-style temple on the banks of the Qin Huai, a tributary of the Yangzi, sits in the midst of the city's busiest shopping and entertainment district. The original statue of Confucius, now replaced by a modern replica, has been moved to the side of the temple. Here, the master presides over children in bumper cars and their older siblings playing video games in an arcade in one of the temple's pavilions. The streets around are busy with shops and outdoor stalls that sell silks, antiques, and souvenirs as well as stuffed animals, snacks, and trinkets. The area is at its best in the early evening, when the lights shine off the water and the crowds pour in. ⊠ *Zhongshan Lu and Jiankang Lu.*

❾ **Gulou** (Drum Tower). The traditional center of ancient Chinese cities, the tower housed the drums used to signal events to the populace, from the changing of the guard to an enemy attack or a fire. Nanjing's tower, constructed in 1382, still has a certain centrality although it now holds only one drum. Its first floor is used as an exhibition hall for local art. ⊠ *Dafang Kiang 1,* ☎ *025/442–1495.* 🎫 *Y2.* ⊙ *Daily 8AM–11PM.*

★ ❹ **Linggu Si and Linggu Ta** (Spirit Valley Temple and Pagoda). The 14th-century Wuliang Dian (Beamless Hall)—made entirely of brick—leads you into the Linggu Temple, which has a hall with relics and altars dedicated to Xuan Zang, the monk who brought Buddhist scriptures back from India. The 200-ft-high Linggu Pagoda is much more recent; it was built in 1929 as a memorial to revolutionaries. ⊠ *Ta Lu, eastern suburbs.* 🎫 *Y5.* ⊙ *Daily 8:30–5.*

❶ **Meihuashan and Zhongshan Zhiwuyuan** (Plum Blossom Hill and Middle Mountain [Sun Yat-sen] Botanical Gardens). Plum Blossom Hill is a favorite early spring outing for Nanjing residents, who delight in the myriad blossoms on the rolling hill. Pavilions stand here and there along the paths. The hill leads into the Botanical Gardens, which have over 300 species of plants lining small walkways, as well as small ponds with covered bridges. ⊠ *Taiping Men Lu, eastern suburbs.* 🎫 *Y5 (Y10 in spring).* ⊙ *Daily 8:30–5.*

Nanjing

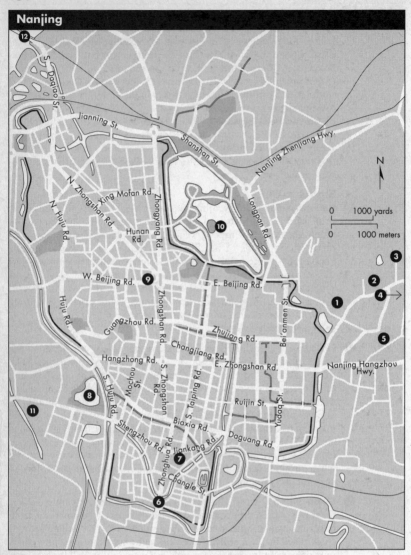

❺ Meiling Gong (Meiling Palace). Chiang Kai-shek built this house as a vacation and weekend retreat for himself and his wife, Song Meiling, who was a sister of Sun Yat-sen's wife, Song Ching-ling. The sisters were heavily involved in the politics of their day, Song Ching-ling joining with the Communist forces after her husband's death. The house, with its photographs, portraits, and historical blurbs, is mostly interesting as an artifact of modern Chinese views of this period's history. Although it is supposedly furnished with original furniture, it's well known that the place was looted several times over. ⊠ *Lingyuan Lu, eastern suburbs.* 🚃 *Y6.* ☉ *Daily 8:30–5.*

❷ Ming Xiaoling (Ming Tomb). The tomb of Zhu Yuanzhang—the Emperor Hong Wu, founder of the Ming dynasty, who died in 1398 at age 71—was completed in 1383. The vault of the tomb has been left unexcavated. The long, curving path leading up to it is lined on both sides by pairs of large stone animals—camels, horses, lions—meant as guards. As it bends northward, statues of military and civil officials replace the animals. The path then leads over some bridges and through a gateway, taking you to two consecutive courtyards. The second of these has an altar tower that you can climb for a view of the burial mound and its surrounding wall. ⊠ *Mingling Lu, eastern suburbs.* 🚃 *Y5.* ☉ *Daily 8:30–5.*

❽ Mochou Hu Gongyuan (No Sadness Lake Park). In the southwest of the city, it's a lovely escape from the pace of life in Nanjing. ⊠ *North of Shuixi Menwai Dajie.*

❿ Xuanwu Hu Gongyuan (Xuanwu Lake Park). A favorite getaway, this area offers more lake than park. The grounds are covered by three enormous bodies of water whose banks are set with benches along peaceful paths. The outer rim goes along the old city wall on the south and west sides. Jimin Park, with its small temple, and Jiuhuashan Park, with its pavilion, lie almost directly south of the main park. ⊠ *Off Hunan Lu eastbound or north of Beijing Donglu.*

⓬ Yangzi River Bridge. The second bridge ever to span the Yangzi, it was the first built without foreign aid. Completed in 1968 at the height of the Cultural Revolution, it's the longest rail and road bridge in the world. At either end, a statue of Red Guards places the bridge historically; some inscribed slogans popular at the time were removed after the Cultural Revolution, but you can still see their impressions on the side of the bridge. ⊠ *Northwest side of city.*

❻ Zhonghua Men (South Gate of City Wall). This gate was the planners' pride. The caves built into the structure could hold 3,000 soldiers. The gate was held to be absolutely impenetrable, and in fact it has never been taken or even attacked. Aggressive armies wisely avoided it in favor of the less heavily fortified areas to the north. ⊠ *South side of city wall.*

❸ Zhongshan Ling (Sun Yat-sen Memorial). Both the Communists and the GMD recognize Sun Yat-sen as the father of the Chinese revolution; he is widely admired and honored on the mainland today. Sun always insisted that the capital of China should lie in Nanjing, and after his death in 1925, this mausoleum was erected in his honor. Completed in 1929, it covers a total area of about 95,600 sq yds. The enormous stairway echoes the ascent to ancient emperors' tombs. Several bronzes stand in the middle and at the top of the stairway—some of these bear bullet marks incurred during the war with Japan. The ceiling of the first room of the mausoleum itself bears Sun's design for the flag; although it was used as the GMD flag, the Communist government has not covered it out of respect for the dead leader. The second room has a circular walkway from which visitors view a likeness of Sun lying in a coffin. Millions of Chinese come here every year to pay their respects. ⊠ *Lingyuan Lu, eastern suburbs.* 🎫 *Y10.* ⊙ *Daily 8:30–5.*

Dining and Lodging

$$$$ ⨯ **Dingshan Meishi Cheng.** In the Fuzimiao area, this is one of Nan-
★ jing's finest upscale restaurants. Built in traditional Chinese style, it has wooden latticework on the windows. The cuisine is the local Huainan—not as spicy as Sichuan (farther up the Yangzi River), not as sweet as Shanghai (farther down the Yangzi). ⊠ *Changhan Lu 2,* ☎ *025/880–5931. No credit cards.*

$$$ ⨯ **Sichuan Restaurant.** A Nanjing classic, this four-story restaurant increases in formality as you climb the stairs. Excellent Sichuan specialties mingle with more general Chinese cuisine. It's also a great place to host banquets or formal dinners. ⊠ *Taiping Lu 171,* ☎ *025/440–2038. MC, V.*

$$$ ⨯ **Swede and Kraut.** If you want some western food, this small side-street restaurant is your best bet—homemade bread, homemade cheese, homemade just about everything. The Italian food here is a lot more authentic than you're likely to get in other restaurants in China. Opened in spring 1997 by—predictably—a Swede and a German, it instantly became a haven for those who have spent a while on the road. They also stock an excellent bar. ⊠ *Ninghai Lu 137,* ☎ *025/663-8020. AE, MC, V.*

$$ ⨯ **Dechangxing Jiaozi Restaurant.** *Jiaozi* (boiled or steamed meat or vegetable dumplings) are a regional specialty throughout the east of China. The Dechangxing makes a special delight of this common fare, preparing dumplings in various shapes and sizes, and offering *pupu* (variety) platters for willing experimenters. They don't have an English menu, but the pupu platters on the second page are hard to miss. Share a Y100 two-person variety and choose what you like. ⊠ *Hunan Lu 38,* ☎ *025/361–9879. No credit cards.*

$$ ⨯ **Jimingsi Restaurant.** This establishment offers excellent Chinese fare with absolutely no meat, a rare occurrence in mainland China. The food is not the only draw, however—the restaurant stands in the quiet and charming Jiming Park and provides a lovely view of the grounds as well as access to the Ming dynasty wall, which runs directly to the north of the park. The wall in this area has been restored, and from here you can climb up to get a closer look at the structure as well as the parks surrounding it. ⊠ *Jiming Park, north side,* ☎ *025/771– 3690. No credit cards. No dinner.*

$$ ⨯ **Piano Café.** With good western cooking, this restaurant has a cozy atmosphere and reasonable prices. There is also a small selection of tasty Chinese dishes. The café serves a Chinese version of American cuisine and attracts adventurous and fashionable Chinese as well as many expats and travelers. ⊠ *Shigu Lu 121,* ☎ *025/420–4252. AE, MC, V.*

$$ ⨯ **Tiandi Restaurant.** This charming restaurant standing on old tem-
★ ple grounds is surrounded by a small wooded area on a little hill off the road. Seating is in pavilions. Outdoor seating near a man-made rock wall with a stream and pond provide a quiet setting from which to view the pavilions. The staff speak a little English and will be happy to guide you through their Jiangsu specialties and Chinese cuisine. ⊠ *Huju Lu 175,* ☎ *025/371–0463. No credit cards.*

$$$$ 🏨 **Central Hotel.** Just off the Xinjiekou traffic circle, the effective business and shopping center of town, the hotel caters to foreign guests. It arranges day tours of Nanjing and has 24-hour travel services. Fanciful touches, like double rooms in the styles of various countries—Arabian, Japanese, French—accompany practical amenities, like brand-new computers in the reception area. ⊠ *Zhongshan Lu 75,* ☎ *025/440–0888,*

FAX *025/441–4194. 354 rooms and suites. 2 restaurants, bar, coffee shop, pool, sauna, health club, shops, dance club, business services, meeting rooms. AE, MC, V.*

$$$$ ⊡ **Grand Hotel.** Not as central as the other upscale hotels in town, nev-
★ ertheless the Grand has much to offer. The 24th-floor western restaurant gives you a good circular view of Nanjing, while downstairs you'll find some of the best Japanese food around. The health center offers traditional Chinese medical services and massages, as well as acupuncture treatments. There's a nice roof garden on top of the lower building. ⊠ *Guangzhou Lu 208, 210024,* ☎ *025/331–1999,* FAX *025/331–9498. 311 rooms and suites. Restaurant, bar, café, pool, beauty salon, sauna, tennis court, health club, bookstore, meeting rooms, travel services. AE, MC, V.*

$$$$ ⊡ **International Conference Hotel of Nanjing.** This sprawling resort is fully equipped to handle major conferences, with simultaneous interpretation facilities and a host of meeting rooms. Each all-suite villa near the main building has its own meeting rooms and restaurant. The hotel is in the best part of town, on Purple Mountain, near the city's major historical sights, the botanical garden, and Plum Blossom Hill. ⊠ *Sifangcheng 2, Zhongshan Ling, 210014,* ☎ *025/443–0888,* FAX *025/443–9255. 681 rooms and suites. 10 restaurants, beauty salon, sauna, exercise room, squash, nightclub, business services, meeting rooms. AE, MC, V.*

$$$$ ⊡ **Jinling Hotel.** Nanjing's best-known hotel, the Jinling stands on the corner of Xinjiekou, in the city's busy central area. It's a huge, modern building with an excellent staff geared toward catering to foreign business and leisure travelers. The hotel is connected to a shopping center, and the travel agency on its first floor provides friendly and efficient service. The top floor of the hotel has a revolving lounge with live music. ⊠ *Xinjiekou, northwest corner, 210005,* ☎ *025/445–5888, 025/445–4888,* FAX *025/470–3396. 818 rooms and suites. 6 restaurants, bar, beauty salon, exercise room, billiards, dance club, business services, meeting rooms. AE, MC, V.*

$$$$ ⊡ **Mandarin Garden Hotel.** Contrary to the impersonal bent of most hotels of its caliber, this well-appointed establishment is warm and friendly, geared toward a quiet intimacy. Its setting on the north side of Fuzimiao lets you view the city center while keeping the noise out of your room. The excellent rooftop bar/lounge on the eighth floor affords a good view of the Fuzimiao area. The Huicui Ting (Galaxy Restaurant) on the second floor serves Cantonese food. ⊠ *Zhuang Yuan Jing 9, Fuzimiao, 210001,* ☎ *025/220–2555, 025/220–2988,* FAX *025/220–1876. 500 rooms and suites. 12 restaurants, bar, no-smoking floors, indoor pool, beauty salon, sauna, miniature golf, health club, squash, business services, meeting rooms. AE, MC, V.*

$$$ ⊡ **Hongqiao Hotel.** Northwest of the popular Shaanxi outdoor market and shopping area, the hotel has friendly and efficient service. ⊠ *Zhongshan Beilu 202,* ☎ *025/340–0888,* FAX *025/663–5756. 194 rooms and suites. 12 restaurants, bar, beauty salon, health club, dance club, business services, meeting rooms. AE, MC, V.*

$$$ ⊡ **Nanjing Hotel.** Originally built in 1936, the hotel is set back from the road, surrounded by lawns and trees that seem pleasantly out of place in such a busy area of town. The well-trained, friendly staff is used to receiving tour groups and official visitors as well as individual travelers. A separate section has rooms at half the standard rate. ⊠ *Zhongshan Beilu 259,* ☎ *025/341–1888,* FAX *025/342–2261. 310 rooms, 21 suites. 14 restaurants, beauty salon, massage, sauna, exercise room, business services, meeting rooms. AE, MC, V.*

$$$ ⊡ **Xuanwu Hotel.** Just across the street from Xuanwu Park, the hotel has a 20th-floor restaurant that affords an excellent view of Nanjing and the park. The health club has an unusual feature: it offers lessons in basic Qigong—a traditional Chinese healing movement practice related to Tai Chi—and examination by a trained specialist in traditional Chinese medicine. ✉ *Zhongyang Lu 193, 210009,* ☎ *025/335–8888,* ℻ *025/336–6777. 408 rooms and suites. 14 restaurants, bar, massage, sauna, health club, business services, meeting rooms. AE, MC, V.*

$$ 🏨 **Huaqiao Grand Hotel.** The overseas Chinese hotel is near the northern shopping district around Shaanxi Lu. The service is a little slow but friendly, and the prices are quite reasonable. This is an easy area from which to reach other city sights. ✉ *Zhongshan Beilu 277,* ☎ *025/ 334–4888,* ℻ *025/334–3132. 190 rooms and suites. 10 restaurants, beauty salon, massage, business services. AE, MC, V.*

Nightlife

BARS

Banpo Village (✉ Qingdao Lu 32, ☎ 025/332–4627) provides a relaxing atmosphere for drinks and snacks. The **City Hunter** (✉ Beijing Xilu 1–1, ☎ 025/663–2584), a stylish pub popular with Nanjing's expat population, has good beers and snacks, a pool table, and a quiet and intimate atmosphere. A music bar that enjoys its jazz, blues, and rock & roll, **The Good Men** (✉ Hanjia Xiang 10/2, ☎ 025/452–3681) offers Friday-night foreigner specials to lure in the expat crowd. A current favorite with the Chinese population, **Scarlet** (✉ Gulou Chezhan Dongxiang 29, off Zhongshan Beilu, ☎ 025/335–1916)—as in O'Hara— has red wood furnishings and two-story seating that reproduce an authentic western pub; the food could use a little work.

DANCE CLUBS

The **Casablanca** (✉ Xuanwu Hotel, ☎ 025/335–8888), the city's most upscale dance club, draws a mostly over-30 crowd for dancing, drinking, and mingling. The **Manhattan** (✉ Yanling Xiang 5, ☎ 025/550–8888) draws young business people for dancing and relaxation on weekend nights. **Orgies** (✉ Zhongshan Lu 202, ☎ 025/341–9991), an instant success in 1997, is actually quite prim by American big-city standards; the good bar and small dance floor attract a mix of locals and ex-pats ranging in age from mid-twenties to late forties. **Zhongshan Paradise** (✉ Zhongshan Lu and Zhujian Lu, ☎ 025/336–1888, ext. 0057) is the most basic of the city's dance clubs, draws foreign students as well as for Chinese of varying ages.

Shopping

The main shopping districts center around the Zhongshan Beilu and Shaanxi Lu traffic circle in the northern section of town, the Xinjiekou traffic circle in mid-town, and Fuzimiao in the south.

The **Jiangsu Antiques Store** (✉ Zhongshan Donglu 321, ☎ 025/664–4701) has regional specialties in antiques and replicas. The **Nanjing Antique Co.** (✉ Taiping Nanlu 72, 5/F, ☎ 025/664–2027) runs several antiques stores in the area. The **Nanjing Arts & Crafts General Company** (✉ Beijing Donglu 31, ☎ 025/771–1574) has a great variety of items, from jade and lacquerware to silk qipaos and tapestries; they also will carve seals and draw calligraphy to order. The **Xinhua Bookstore** (✉ Baiziting 34, ☎ 025/771–1793) has a good selection of calligraphy scrolls, along with brushes and other paraphernalia, as well as phrase books and dictionaries. Your best bet for silks—both off the roll and ready-made—are the market areas; Fuzimiao has an excellent selection of shops and stalls; the **Shaanxi Lu Nightmarket** has a wide array of goods; the market to the south of Xinjiekou is also worth a look. The **Friendship Store** (✉ Hanzhong Lu 16) here does not do so well in clothing, but it has a small selection of antique-style arts on the fourth floor. For the latest in fashion, try the **Golden Eagle Department Store** (✉ Hanzhong Lu and Tieguan Xiang).

Side Trip to Zhenjiang

⑬ *1-hr train ride from Nanjing on Shanghai–Nanjing rail line.*

Zhenjiang was once a city of great administrative and economic importance, a vital grain shipping point as well as a tax collection center at the junction of the Grand Canal and the Yangzi River. By the 20th century, the entrance to the canal had become heavily silted and virtually unusable. The city was damaged in the Opium Wars as well as during the Taiping Rebellion, when rebels used their base here to help defend Nanjing. Several old temples and pavilions are still standing. These and the parks make Zhenjiang a delightful day trip from Nanjing.

The **Dinghui Si,** the functioning Buddhist temple in **Jinshan Gongyuan** (Jinshan Park) attracts tourists and pilgrims from the surrounding regions. The temple stands on a hill that also contains four interesting caves: the Fahai Dong (Buddhist Sea), the Bailong Dong (White Dragon), the Zhaoyang Dong (Morning Sun), and the Luohan (Arhat). ✉ *Xinhe Lu and Jinshan Lu.* 🎫 *Y15.* ⏰ *8–5:30.*

South along the Yangzi shoreline from Su Bie Lu, in **Boxian Gongyuan** (Boxian Park), the **Zhenjiang Museum** occupies the former British consulate building. The park and surroundings are good exploration grounds on a nice day, and the museum has a small selection of pottery, bronzes, and Tang dynasty paintings, as well as a section devoted to the war with Japan. ✉ *Jingji Lu.* ⏰ *Museum, daily 8:30–12:30, 2:30–5:30.*

Also on the banks of the Yangzi, **Beigushan Gongyuan** (Beigushan Park) houses the **Ganlu Temple** and its Song dynasty pagoda. Views of the pagoda are more interesting than views from it. ✉ *Off Zhenjiao Lu.*

In the middle of town, the restored **Mengxi Yuan** (Dream Spring Garden) provides pleasant walkways and rock formations in the Jiangsu garden style. ✉ *Huancheng Lu between Zhongshan Lu and Zhengdong Lu.*

To the south of the city, the **Nanshan Gongyuan** (South Mountain Scenic Park) provides some good hiking and scenery. Partway up the mountain stands the **Zhulin Si** (Bamboo Forest Temple), worth a walk not only for itself but for the peaceful area around it. Buses stop near the mountain, but the park is accessible only by taxi or minivan.

On a small Yangzi island east of the city, **Jiaoshan Gongyuan** (Jiaoshan Park) contains the **Dinghui Si** monastery, whose monks display artworks and miniature trees. The area has numerous pavilions as well as an 11th-century iron pagoda. From the top of the hill, you get an excellent view of the river traffic. ✉ *Ferry near terminal of No. 4 bus (also accessible by taxi) takes you to island.*

DINING AND LODGING

As Zhenjiang is best visited on a day trip from Nanjing or Suzhou, the few hotels here are most useful for their dining rooms.

$$$ 🏨 **Zhenjiang Hotel.** Located near the train station, this hotel is a convenient stop if you plan to stay the night. You can order western food, but you might as well stick with the Chinese selections, which include regional specialties and river catches. ✉ *Zhongshan Xilu 92, 212004,* ☎ *0511/523–3888,* FAX *0511/523–1055. 186 rooms and suites. Restaurant, bar, beauty salon, health club, business services. AE, MC, V.*

$$ ☎ **Southern Magnolia Hotel.** This fancifully named hotel is really the
only choice in Zhenjiang besides the Zhenjiang Hotel (☞ above) for
the foreign visitor. Their dining halls deserve a try if you are in the area.
⊠ *Zhongshan Donglu 256, 212001,* ☎ *0511/501–2053,* FAX *0511/502–
2700. 80 rooms and suites. 2 restaurants, bar, health club, business ser-
vices. AE, MC, V.*

SHOPPING

Like the cities around it, Zhenjiang has a number of small roadside
shops selling silks, and markets spring up around tourist sights and tem-
ples. An **Arts and Crafts Store** (⊠ Jiefang Lu 191) sells wares such as
porcelain, jade, and chops.

Wuxi

⓮ *2¾ hr by train southeast of Nanjing; 1¾ hr southeast of Zhenjiang; 40
min northwest of Suzhou.*

To see it now, you'd never know Wuxi was once one of China's major
grain markets, combining the harvests of its own fertile surroundings
with those being transported on the Grand Canal. The Canal, which
passes by the northeast edge of Wuxi's Taihu (Lake Tai), once linked
the city with other major economic and cultural centers. Shanghai in-
dustrialists, many of whom came from the Wuxi area, built up the city's
textile works in the early part of the 20th century, making it China's
largest silk-reeling center. Taihu covers more than 2,200 sq km (850
sq mi) and is dotted with 48 islands; its fish provide much of the local
cuisine. Wuxi is best seen as a day-trip from Suzhou or Shanghai.

Jutting into the southern part of the lake, **Yuantouzhu** (Turtle Head
Isle) is actually a small peninsula that affords a great view of the lake.
It also houses a few interesting old structures. **Guangfu Si** (Broad Hap-
piness Temple), originally built in the 6th century AD, stands on the
site of a nunnery, and **Chenglan** (Clear Ripples Hall), a well-preserved
prayer hall, now holds a tea house. The park by the lake is laid out in
four sections, each with its own pavilions and artistic remnants. ⊠ *End
of Hubin Lu, southeast of city.*

A 20-minute ferry ride from Turtle Head Isle, **Sanshan Dao** (Three Hills
Isles) offer more scenic spots, as well as a tea house where you can sit
and enjoy the view.

★ Just outside the city, **Xihui Gongyuan** (Xihui Park) is home to the two
hills that are Wuxi's symbols. Xishan (Tin Hill) is supposed to resem-
ble a pearl. At its top, **Longguang Ta** (Dragon's Light Pagoda) gives
you a good view of the surrounding city and lake. Pavilions dot the
paths, and there is a small zoo at the bottom of the hill. The coiling
paths of Huishan (Generosity or Wisdom Hill), which rises to 1,077
ft above sea level, were laid out to suggest a dragon's tail. The hill also
has scattered pavilions as well as the **Tianxia Dier Quan** (Second
Under Heaven Spring), once thought to bear the second-best tea-brew-
ing water in China. At the eastern foot of Huishan, the Ming-style **Jichang
Yuan** (Attachment to Freedom Garden) was the model for Beijing's Sum-
mer Palace Garden of Harmonious Interest. The garden's own land-
scape has been created to blend with the surrounding scenery. ⊠
Renmin Xi Lu and Hehui Lu, west side of city.

The **Mei Yuan** (Plum Garden) is famed for its thousands of spring plum
trees, which come in over 30 varieties. Several pavilions provide views
of the garden and the surrounding scenery. Early March, when the trees
bloom, is the time to visit. ⊠ *7 km (4 mi) west of city, near bus No. 2
terminal.* ☎ *Y10.* ⊙ *Daily 8:30–5:30.*

Dining and Lodging

$$ ✕ **Wuxi Restaurant.** Here you'll find typical Wuxi appetizers and "small eats," like Wuxi-style pork ribs in soy sauce. ✉ *Gongnongbing Lu 26,* ☎ *0510/580–6789. No credit cards.*

$$ ✕ **Zuiyue Lou Restaurant.** The "Drunken Moon" has a selection of Wuxi specialties, snacks, and cold dishes. The seating is nothing special, but it's one of Wuxi's better-known venues. ✉ *Tongyun Lu 73,* ☎ *0510/ 272–0423. No credit cards.*

$$$ 🏨 **Shuixiu Hotel and Hubin Hotel.** Next door and connected to one another, these hotels share management and service facilities; the Hubin is a bit more upscale than the Shuixiu. They lie close to the lake in a quiet area next to the Plum Garden. ✉ *Off Hubin Lu,* ☎ *0510/510– 1888,* 🖷 *0510/510–2637. Hubin, 202 rooms; Shuixiu, 161. 2 restaurants, pool, barber, theater. AE, MC, V.*

$$$ 🏨 **Taihu Hotel.** Between Lake Tai and Mei Garden, this was the city's first hotel to receive overseas guests. At villas attached to the hotel you can get a massage, acupuncture, and lessons in Tai Chi. The restaurant serves fresh-caught Lake Taihu fish. ✉ *Off Meiji Lu,* ☎ *0510/ 551–7888,* 🖷 *0510/510–6135. 156 rooms. Restaurant. AE, MC, V.*

Nightlife and the Arts

Wuxi has several song-and-dance ensembles, as well as its own style of Chinese opera. You can see these periodically at the **Renmin Theater** (✉ Gongyuan Lu 134), the **Dazhong Theater** (✉ Renmin Lu 90), or the **Jiefang Theater** (People's Bazaar No. 13, Beitang District).

Shopping

Wuxi is mostly famed for silk, selling products made along traditional Chinese lines as well as more western-style clothing and scarves. The city has a tradition of Huishan clay figurines, which, however, are not as attractive as the pottery brought in from Yixing County. In addition, you can find embroidery, carved seals, and jade carvings at small shops in the city center. Try the **Friendship Store** (✉ Zhongshan Lu 8, ☎ 0510/286–8414). The **Wuxi Arts and Crafts Store** (✉ Renmin Lu 192, ☎ 0510/272–8783) is another major emporium.

Suzhou

On Nanjing–Shanghai rail line; approximately 3½ hr by train southeast of Nanjing, or 1¼ hr west of Shanghai.

If the renowned gardens of Suzhou form a thriving monument to the city's past, the passages leading up to them speak of a time of transition. Entire blocks of old-style houses still line some of the city's canals. Decorated gates and doorways from centuries ago catch the eye, but they now lead into shops selling silk and cashmere in Chinese and western styles; the ramshackle houses from past eras border on tall office buildings and shiny new hotels; and the sloping, tiled roofs often sit atop structures built in the last few years. This mixture of old styles with new makes Suzhou's central districts a pleasure to explore.

Suzhou's many canals once formed the basis of its economy. Now falling into disuse, the waterways still line many a lamplit street. These canals, however, are really only the younger cousins of the Da Yunhe (Grand Canal), which passes through the outskirts of town. Probably begun as early as the 4th century BC, and rebuilt in AD 607, it was gradually expanded and became the world's longest artificial waterway, stretching from Beijing to Hangzhou. Just 5 km (3 mi) south of the city is the Baodai Qiao (Precious Belt Bridge), one of the most famous and grandiose on the canal. The canal used to be a main transportation route for eastern China but has been gradually replaced with newer, faster modes. The section south of Suzhou is still navigable and navigated; you can take an overnight boat (✉ CITS, Shiquan Lu 115, ☎ 0512/522–3175) to Hangzhou if you want to explore the canal more thoroughly.

Suzhou's main claim to fame is its fabulous array of gardens, which set a style and standard for Chinese gardens in general. They were originally created by retired officials or unaffiliated literati as places in which to read and write poetry and philosophy, to stroll and drink with their friends, and to meditate and spend quiet hours. In these gardens neither the rock formations nor the thoughtfully planted trees and flowers are the main attraction. Rather, each garden is meant to be enjoyed for its overall atmosphere, as well as for its unique style and layout. Each is an artistic creation in which impressions of space were carefully considered. Sit in a teahouse near the pond and enjoy the peaceful breeze blowing over the water, or stroll along the various pathways leading to an artfully planted tree winding its way up the garden wall, a glimpse of lake you catch from a small man-made cave, a pavilion displaying Qing dynasty tree-root furniture, or one of the region's famed unusual rock formations. The gardens are generally open from 7:30 AM to 5:30 PM. Although spring is considered prime viewing time, each season works its own magic.

A Good Walk

Starting where Renmin Lu meets Xibei Jie in the northern section of town, check out the **Beisi Ta** ⑮, a tall pagoda that offers views of the city. Walk east along the restored street with its traditional style fronts and shops until you come to the **Zhuo Zheng Yuan** ⑯, Suzhou's largest garden. Then turn south along Yuan Lin Lu, checking out the silk shops that line the street. **Shizi Lin** ⑰, a garden filled with caves, will be on your right about halfway down the short street. At the end of the street turn right and then left onto Lindun Lu; follow that south to Guanqian Lu and turn right to reach the **Xuanmiao Guan** ⑱, an ancient temple in a market square. To the south along Lindun Lu, off Ganjiang Lu, is **Suzhou University** ⑲. Follow Fenghuang Jie south to Shiquan Jie and turn left for the small, exquisite **Wangshi Yuan** ⑳. From this garden, go left on Shiquan Jie to Renmin Lu, turn left again and follow it to **Canglang Ting** ㉑, a large garden off the street to the left. Back up Renmin Lu, just north of Ganjiang Lu, stop to visit a more recent garden, **Yi Yuan** ㉒. Take a bus or taxi north and west across the city moat and a branch of the Grand Canal to **Liu Yuan** ㉓ a large, well-designed garden. Just to the west, at the end of Liuyuan Lu, is the Buddhist **Xi Yuan Si** ㉔.

Sights to See

⑮ **Beisi Ta** (North Temple Pagoda). You can climb up the nine-story pagoda for a view of the surrounding city. The pagoda has large windows on every floor, balconies, and wider staircases than most. The grounds here form a garden of their own; behind the pagoda are a couple of art galleries selling local paintings and woodcuts, name chops, and other souvenirs. They also display traditional musical instruments and miniature trees. There is a rather nondescript teahouse here as well. ✉ *Xibei Jie and Renmin Lu.* 🎫 *Y10.*

㉑ **Canglang Ting** (Blue Wave Pavilion). In one of Suzhou's larger gardens you can thread your way through a maze of oddly shaped doorways, around an artificial pond, and into a large, man-made cave with a small stone picnic table. The garden was originally built in the 11th century and, although lovely in its own way, is not as delicately wrought as

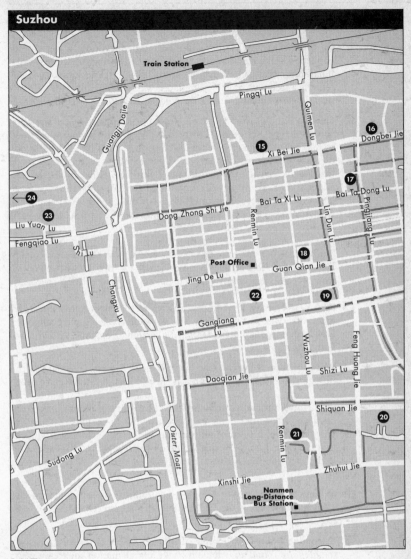

Suzhou

Beisi Ta, **15**
Canglang Ting, **21**
Liu Yuan, **23**
Shizi Lin, **17**
Suzhou University, **19**
Wangshi Yuan, **20**
Xi Yuan Si, **24**
Xuanmiao Guan, **18**
Yi Yuan, **22**
Zhuo Zheng
Yuan, **16**

some of the smaller gardens.✉ *Off Renmin Lu between Shiquan Jie and Xinshi Lu.* 🎫 *Y10.*

㉓ Liu Yuan (Lingering Garden). In the western part of the city is another of Suzhou's larger gardens, originally installed during the Ming dynasty. It has impressive rock formations and calligraphy expositions, and masters the garden art of carefully placed windows that provide an artistically determined view. ✉ *Liuyuan Lu.* 🎫 *Y20.*

⑰ Shizi Lin (Lion's Grove Garden). Here, a maze of man-made caves surrounds a small scenic lake. Its wall is divided and pavilions are sited to make the garden seem more spacious than it really is. The illusions of space are expertly created here, and the bridges on the lake provide many a couple with a romantic photo spot. The paths around the lake allow you to take in a wider expanse of garden, while the cave maze lets you concentrate on minutely detailed landscaping decisions. At the garden's exit is a small marketplace with antique replicas and silks of all sorts. ✉ *Yuan Lin Lu,* 🎫 *Y10.*

....

NEED A BREAK?   Lion's Grove Garden has one of the more charming **teahouses** around. Situated on the second floor of a pavilion on the lake, it gives you a view of the garden with its romping children and meandering couples.

....

⑲ Suzhou University. Here European architecture emerges unexpectedly in this otherwise so-Chinese city. The assemblies building and gymnasium look like reproductions of Harvard's version of England. ✉ *Off Ganjiang Lu.* a

★ **⑳ Wangshi Yuan** (Master of the Nets Garden). Experts consider this the best garden in Suzhou, though it is the smallest. It is a haven of peace and beauty, with its carefully planted flora and artful rocks, whose original arrangement dates from the 12th century. It was redone in the 18th century. The former living quarters now house exhibits of Qing dynasty tree-root furniture and other artworks. One placard announces that the **Dianchun Yi** (Spring Cottage) was reproduced for exhibition in the Metropolitan Museum of Art in New York in 1981. ✉ *Shiquan Jie.* 🎫 *Y10.*

㉔ Xi Yuan Si (West Garden Temple). A Buddhist temple dating from the Ming, it was rebuilt in the 19th century after a destructive fire. ✉ *Xiyuan Lu.* 🎫 *Y10.*

⑱ Xuanmiao Guan (The Temple of Mystery). One of the best old-style temples you'll find anywhere, it backs a large market square on what used to be temple grounds. Founded in the 3rd century, the temple has undergone fewer restorations than most its age, still retaining parts from the 12th century. It suffered very little damage in the Cultural Revolution. ✉ *Guanqian Jie,* 🎫 *Y10.*

㉒ Yi Yuan (The Joyous Garden). A more recent example of Suzhou styles, this one also has a pleasant blending of pavilion and rockery, courtyard and pond. ✉ *Off Renmin Lu at Changchun Xiang.*

⑯ Zhuo Zheng Yuan (The Humble Administrator's Garden). Suzhou's largest, this 10-acre garden is renowned for its "high and low" architecture and expansive lake area. It was built as the private retreat of a Tang poet and official. Here he wrote poetry and entertained his friends. Through the centuries, the garden has had a number of owners, at one time even serving as a local temple. The street leading east to the garden has been restored in a traditional style. ✉ *Dong Bei Jie.* 🎫 *Y20.*

Dining and Lodging

$$$ ✕ **Deyuelou Restaurant.** Specializing in Old Suzhou styles, this restaurant has a wide array of fish dishes, as well as local-style dim sum. It also specializes in a particularly attractive type of food presentation, the ancient art of "garden foods"—an assortment of dim sum specialties arranged to resemble various sorts of gardens, with flowers, trees, and so on. ✉ *Taijian Nong 27,* ☎ *0512/523–8940. No credit cards.*

$$$ ✕ **Songhelou Restaurant.** With more than 250 years of history, this is one of Suzhou's most famous restaurants. It serves Suzhou specialties and catches from the river that, in the old days, were actually eaten on river boats during banquet cruises— hence their popular designation, "boat food." The restaurant has nine separate dining halls decorated with Suzhou regional arts and calligraphy. ✉ *Taijian Nong 18,* ☎ *0512/523–7969. No credit cards.*

$$ ✕ **Huangtianyuan Restaurant.** Here the specialty is the local favorite of *mifen* (rice gluten), made by pounding rice to a fine paste. In business for over 170 years, it has different seasonal menus, serving the foods traditionally considered most appropriate for specific times of year. Other house specialties include *babao fan* (a bowl of syrupy rice with various sweets, nuts, and fruit bits), and *tang tuan* (a kind of dim sum whose skin is made of the thick dough of mifen). These come in a variety of sizes and with both meaty and sweet fillings. ✉ *Guanqian Jie 86,* ☎ *0512/727–7033. No credit cards.*

$$$$ 🏨 **Bamboo Grove Hotel.** A modern facility, the Bamboo Grove caters to international business travelers and tourists. It is one of the city's choice establishments in terms of service quality and facilities, but its location is somewhat out of the way. ✉ *Zhuhui Lu 108, 215006,* ☎ *0512/520–5601,* FAX *0512/520–8778. 360 rooms and suites. 2 restaurants, bar, beauty salon, health club, business services, meeting rooms. AE, MC, V.*

$$$$ 🏨 **Nanlin Hotel.** This hotel has a quiet setting somewhat back from the road. Master of the Nets Garden and Blue Wave Pavilion are both within walking distance. ✉ *Gunsiufang 20, Shiquan Jie, 215006,* ☎ *0512/519–4641,* FAX *0512/519–1028. 253 rooms and suites. 2 restaurants, bar, beauty salon, health club, business services, meeting rooms. AE, MC, V.*

$$$ 🏨 **Suzhou Hotel.** This is an ideally located establishment with excellent service and facilities. It's a short walk down a popular street lined with silk and cashmere stores that leads to the Master of the Nets Garden. ✉ *Shiquan Jie 115, 215006,* ☎ *0512/520– 4646,* FAX *0512/520–5191. 308 rooms and suites. 2 restaurants, bar, beauty salon, health club, business services, meeting rooms. AE, MC, V.*

$$–$$$ 🏨 **Nanyuan Hotel.** Priced just above the more budget accommodation, the Nanyuan relies on its excellent location to draw guests. Near the most fashionable hotels in town, it's an easy walk from several gardens. ✉ *Shiquan Jie 249, 215006,* ☎ *0512/519–7661,* FAX *0512/519–8806. 100 rooms and suites. 2 restaurants, bar, beauty salon, health club, business services, meeting rooms. AE, MC, V.*

$$ 🏨 **Friendship Hotel.** The original hotel for foreign guests, it seems less and less deluxe as joint venture hotels proliferate. However, it's quiet and clean with prompt service and decent facilities. In a peaceful courtyard built in Suzhou garden style you can enjoy your breakfast or a cup of coffee. ✉ *Zhuhui Lu, 215007,* ☎ *0512/529–1601,* FAX *0512/520–6221. 116 rooms and suites. 2 restaurants, bar, beauty salon, health club, business services, meeting rooms. AE, MC, V.*

$$ 🏨 **Lexiang Hotel.** Catering mainly to Chinese guests, this budget option is more basic in its approach than the hotels on the fashionable Shiquan Jie. It does have a fine location, just down the street from the

Joyous Garden and a block from the beautiful Temple of Mystery. ✉ *Dajingxiang 18*, ☎ *0512/522–2890*, FAX *0512/524–4165. 39 rooms. 2 restaurants, bar, beauty salon, health club, business services, meeting rooms. AE, MC, V.*

Nightlife and the Arts

On warm nights, you can see Suzhou regional **traditional opera performances** at the Master of the Nets garden (☞ *Wangshi Yuan, above*). Chinese operas are often performed by scene rather than by play (an entire opera can last hours or days), so you are likely to see several bits from several different stories. Check at the entrance gate of the garden or with CITS about times and tickets.

Across the street from the North Temple Pagoda, **Pro Golf and Coffee Club** (✉ Renmin Lu 656, ☎ 0512/752–2012) is the first mini-golf-cum-bar to open in Suzhou; it has a classy lounge with imported coffees and imported and domestic teas, as well as alcoholic drinks and light snacks.

Shopping

Districts around the gardens and temples teem with silk shops and outdoor markets. The **Friendship Store** (✉ Renmin Lu 504, ☎ 0512/727–2070) has a selection of local products in silk, wood, and jade. Since 1956, the **Suzhou Antiques Store** (✉ Renmin Lu 328, near Leqiao bridge, ☎ 0512/523–3851) has been selling antiques, calligraphy, jades, and other "cultural products." You can get jewelry and carvings at the **Suzhou Precious Stones Store** (✉ Baita Xilu 33, ☎ 0512/727–1224). The **Suzhou Silk and Printing Store** (✉ Baijia Xiang 7, ☎ 0512/729–9600) sells silks and designs to print on them. The **Suzhou Silk Clothing Store** (✉ Lujia Xiang 46, ☎ 0512/727–1453) is a silk outlet. The **Suzhou Silk Museum Shop** (✉ Renmin Lu 661, from North Temple Pagoda, ☎ 0512/727–6507) is really the reason to come to the Silk Museum in the first place. For local artworks and calligraphy, visit the **Suzhou Wumen Artstore** (✉ Liuyuan Lu 105, ☎ 0512/533–4808).

Jiangsu A to Z

Arriving and Departing

BY BOAT

You can get to a great many places by boat from Nanjing, but for faraway destinations the prospect is risky: sanitary conditions are rarely good, and schedules are not convenient. A trip down the Yangzi to Shanghai is scenic enough, and boats leave every morning and three afternoons a week from the dock in the northwest side of town. You can get to Nanjing via boat by starting an eastbound Yangzi river cruise in Wuhan (☞ Hubei, *below*).

The overnight ride from Suzhou to Hangzhou along the Grand Canal takes you through some great countryside scenery between two of China's prettiest cities. For information and tickets, talk with a travel agent or your hotel travel desk or call ☎ 025/440–8583 in Nanjing.

BY BUS

Frequent bus service runs between Nanjing, Zhenjiang, Wuxi, and Suzhou, with connections or direct lines to Shanghai as well. Some runs offer modern tourist buses with air conditioning. **Nanjing's** bus station (Jianing Lu and Zhongyang Lu) lies west of the railway station. A new direct air-conditioned coach to Shanghai takes about 3½ hours. In **Zhenjiang,** the station (Jiefang Lu) is in the southeast corner of the city center. Direct buses run frequently to Nanjing, Suzhou, and Wuxi. In **Wuxi,** the station (Tonghui Donglu) is right across from the railway station. The **Suzhou** bus station (southern tip of Renmin Lu) offers trips to other Jiangsu destinations. For all of these, it's best to have the name of your destination written in Chinese to avoid misunderstanding. Buses are the most convenient choice for short trips like Nanjing–Zhenjiang and Wuxi–Suzhou. Otherwise, trains are more comfortable.

BY PLANE

International flights go through Shanghai or Beijing before continuing on to Nanjing. From **Nanjing,** several flights leave daily for Shanghai, Beijing, Guangzhou, Xiamen, Wuhan, and Hong Kong; flights leave daily for Xian and Chengdu; and several flights leave weekly for Zhengzhou and Hangzhou. Buy tickets at the CAAC office (⊠ Ruijin Lu 52, ☎ 025/664–9275), at major hotels like the Jinling (⊠ Xinjiekou, northwest corner, ☎ 025/445–5888), or at CITS (⊠ Zhongshan Beilu 202/1, ☎ 025/334–6446, ext. 8102). Dragonair also has a desk in the Grand Hotel (⊠ Guangzhou Lu 208, Room 810, ☎ 025/331–1999, ext. 810) that offers daily flights to Hong Kong.

In Wuxi and **Suzhou,** CITS can arrange plane tickets through the Shanghai or Nanjing airports for you, or you can get in touch with China Eastern Airlines in Suzhou (⊠ Renmin Lu 192, ☎ 0512/522–2788).

BY TRAIN

Nanjing, Zhenjiang, Wuxi, and Suzhou are all on the same rail line, which continues on to Shanghai. Two air-conditioned "tourist trains" run daily between Nanjing, Wuxi, Suzhou, and Shanghai, leaving Nanjing at 9 AM and 5 PM, reaching Wuxi in about an hour, Suzhou in about 2 hours, and Shanghai in about 2 hours and 45 minutes. Other trains between all these destinations leave quite frequently. Several daily trains from Nanjing will take you on a day-trip to Zhenjiang in about an hour, and several from Suzhou will take you on a day-trip to Wuxi in about 40 minutes.

Getting Around

Taxis are plentiful and quite inexpensive in all of these cities and are a better bet than the crowded and confusing bus systems. Motor tricycles are inexpensive and convenient if you have only a couple of people. Taxis from **Nanjing** airport to the center of town should take about 20 minutes and cost around Y30 to Y40. Make sure the meter is on as the car is starting.

Zhenjiang's buses are relatively easy to handle. The No. 4 goes east to the Yangzi, where you can catch a ferry to Jiaoshan. Buses 6 and 21 go south, almost to Nanshan Scenic Park; bus No. 2 takes you out to Jinshan Park.

Contacts and Resources

EMERGENCIES

Nanjing: First Aid Station (⊠ Zhongshan Lu 231, ☎ 025/330–4392; 025/663–3858, 025/663–6872 for emergencies). **Suzhou:** People's Hospital No. 2 (⊠ Daoqian Jie 26, ☎ 0512/522–3691). **Wuxi:** People's Hospital No. 1 (⊠ Renmin Zhong Lu 111, ☎ 0510/270–0778), Wuxi People's Hospital No. 3 (⊠ Tonghui Donglu 320, ☎ 0510/270–7391).

GUIDED TOURS

Major hotels will often arrange a tour guide for a group, as will CITS. Individuals may offer you day-tours; just make sure the price is set and their English is good enough to make it worthwhile. Because the major sights in Jiangsu lie inside the cities, they are generally quite accessible to individual travelers.

VISITOR INFORMATION

Hotels are the chief source of tourist information in Zhenjiang and Wuxi. It's best to do any planning you need in Nanjing or Suzhou, where both hotels and special agencies tend to be much better informed.

Nanjing: CITS (⊠ Zhongshan Beilu 202/1, ☎ 025/334–6444); Jiangsu Jinling Business International Travel Service (⊠ basement of Jinling Hotel, ☎ 025/470–4149). **Suzhou:** CITS (⊠ Shiquan Lu 115, ☎ 0512/ 522–3175); Suzhou Taihu International Travel Service (⊠ South Renmin Lu 105, ☎ 0512/527–9694); Suzhou Women's International Travel Service (⊠ Miaotang Hutong 31, ☎ 0512/524–8517).

ZHEJIANG

Zhejiang is a worthy province to house one of China's two "heavens on earth," the city of Hangzhou. Its scenery is known for lush beauty, and despite being one of China's smallest provinces, it is also one of the wealthiest. The river basin area to the north is countered by mountains in the south, and cultivated greenery is everywhere. The province was dynastically important starting in the 12th century, when Hangzhou was the capital of the Southern Song dynasty. It continued in importance even when the capital was moved away, largely because of its grain production and its scenic and cultural attractions. Zhejiang's farms are among the most prosperous in the country, producing tea, rice, wheat, barley, corn, and sweet potatoes. This province also provides fully one-third of China's silk. It's famous for its crafts and wares, including fine porcelain, silk products, embroideries, lace, wood and stone carvings, and sculptures. Zhejiang is also home to Putuoshan, one of the sacred Buddhist mountains.

Hangzhou

㉕ *4 hours southwest of Shanghai by train.*

The terminus of the Grand Canal, Hangzhou was destined for greatness as an economic center from the canal's completion in AD 609. In 1126, the Song dynasty fled south from Kaifeng to Hangzhou to escape the Jurchen invaders. The era that ensued, later known as the Southern Song, witnessed the rise of Hangzhou's cultural and administrative importance. Its proximity not only to the canal but to river and ocean, as well as its position in an area of unusual fertility, made Hangzhou a hub of southern Chinese culture. By the 13th century, the city had a population of between 1 and 1.5 million people. In 1861 it was captured by the Taipings, and in the ensuing battles with the imperial forces—which didn't win the city back for over two years—the city, along with its cultural artifacts and monuments, was largely destroyed.

As the center of so much traditional and imperial history, Hangzhou also made a natural target during the Cultural Revolution, when Red Guards smashed to bits much of what had survived the previous century's turmoil. However, many of the city's monuments have been repaired or reconstructed, and even the Red Guards couldn't destroy West Lake, which lends Hangzhou much of its romantic beauty. A little way outside the city, you can visit the plantations that produce the area's famous Long Jing tea, or stroll in forested hills to take in the views of the surrounding area. The lake, in the southwestern section of town, provides a setting of serenity rarely seen in a Chinese city.

To explore Hangzhou's sights, you can start at the lake, which is the effective, if not geographic, center of town. From the lake you can go on to visit the city proper and then move out to the less populous region to the southwest.

Hangzhou culture revolves around **Xihu** (West Lake). The lake, originally a lagoon cut off from the nearby river by a man-made dike, is traversed by two causeways, the Baidi and the Sudi. They were built from the earth left over from the dredging of the lake. Both dikes are named for important Tang dynasty officials and poets who held posts in Hangzhou. Both are bordered by a tree-lined, grassy lawn and interrupted by several bridges.

Officially run multi-seat boats leave every half hour or so from near the Hangzhou Overseas Chinese Hotel (⊠ Hubin Lu 15, ☞ Lodging, *below*) to take you to the lake's islands, and a slew of smaller private boats are moored around the lake. If you want your own boat with no rower, you can rent a paddle boat—some of them look like science fiction inventions, which is fun for the kids.

The lake's largest island is actually accessible on foot: **Gushan** (Solitary Hill) island houses the **Zhongshan Gongyuan** (Sun Yat-sen Park ⊠ Gushan; ☎ Y5). It's more flowered and greener in spring than most.

Another point of interest on Gushan is the **Seal Engravers' Society**. (⊠ Gushan. ☎ Y3 or Y4) Once a professional organization, it has turned into a hobby for most of the artisans who gather here. The grounds are lovely, with a small stream, a statue of Confucius, and an ancient tablet of dedication.

The park is connected to the **Fanghe Ting** (Crane Releasing Pavilion ⊠ Gushan. ☎ Y5. ☉ Daily 8:30–dusk), marred a bit by its recent acquisition of a semi-abstract concrete crane. The pavilion grounds have a pleasant lakeside garden with early-blooming plum trees that make up for the statue.

Gushan is also home to the important **Zhejiang Bowuguan** (Zhejiang Provincial Museum ⊠ Gushan. ☎ Y20. ☉ Daily 8:30–noon and 2–5:30). On display are recently unearthed 2,000- to 3,000-year-old jade implements wrought with extraordinary technological skill, as well as some fine bronzes. There are natural history and ceramics and a section for contemporary local works, focusing more on fine arts than on crafts exhibits.

You can reach the island of **Santan Yinyue** (Three Pools Reflecting the Moon) by taking a boat across West Lake's placid waters. The large manmade pools on the island are famed for their reflections of the August moon, but they make a lovely sight during other months and at other times of day as well. There are several Buddhist pavilions on the island.

The east side of the lake borders the happening section of town, where most of the city's entertainment takes place. About halfway down the east side is **Ertong Gongyuan** (Children's Park), with a playground and rides. ⊠ *Nanshan Lu and Kaiyuan Lu.* ☎ Y10. ☉ *Daily 8:30–6.*

Farther down, at the southeastern end of the lake, is a less touristy park where local chess lovers and *erhu* (traditional northern violin with a long neck and small, hollow body, played propped on the knee) musicians often converge for informal bouts and performances.

The neighborhood directly north of the lake is a combination of two scenic spots that make a good walk. The **Huanglong Dong** (Yellow Dragon Cave) has not only a cave but a variety of sights, including a stream that rushes off the mountainside through the mouth of—of course—a yellow dragon head of relatively recent vintage. The magic of the stream, it is said, is that even in times of drought it never runs dry. On a stage in this park local Yue opera is performed daily in good weather, starting around 2 PM. You can sit and have some tea here and listen to this traditional art form, now performed mostly in villages or specialty theaters. There is also a bamboo grove with rare "square bamboo." You can't tell the difference just by looking, but if you touch a few stalks, especially of the younger trees, you'll notice the angles. ✉ *Tiyuchang Lu.* 🎫 *Y10.* 🕐 *Daily 8:30–dusk.*

Bao Chu Ta (Protect Chu Pagoda) stands atop Baoshi Liuxia (Precious Stone Hill). The tower was built around 970 in hopes of ensuring the safe return of Hangzhou's reigning official from an audience with the emperor. Its most recent reconstruction was in 1933. The tower is surrounded by small stone cliffs that afford a view of the lake and cityscape. Paths lead out from it down to the lake and Baidi by way of pavilions and small temples. ✉ *Baoshi Liuxia.*

Near Gushan stands the **Yue Fei Mu** (Yue Fei Mausoleum), a temple built to honor the 12th-century Song general Yue Fei, a commander against the Jurchen invaders. A jealous courtier convinced the emperor that Yue Fei was a traitor, and the emperor ordered him executed. Before submitting himself to the emperor's will, Yue Fei had the words "Loyal to the last" tattooed on his back. Twenty years later he was rehabilitated and deified, and is now one of China's national heroes, a symbol of patriotic duty. The temple wall replicates the tattooed inscription, while a statue of the traitorous official kneels in shame nearby. Traditionally, you're supposed to spit on statues of traitors, but a recent sign near the statue asks visitors to refrain. ✉ *Beishan Lu, west of Gushan.* 🎫 *Y7.* 🕐 *Daily 8:30–5:30.*

A short ride southwest of the lake takes you to the **Longjing Wencha** (Dragon Well Tea Park), where you can buy the local Long Jing green tea from people who are serious about quality. This park, set in the middle of some tea plantations, is the site of the well from which water for the best tea comes. In fact, though, you will see people at several of Hangzhou's parks scooping up well or stream water with which to make tea. Tea sellers may invite prospective buyers to taste the tea, often at the seller's house. The prices seem ridiculous until you take a sip: there really is a difference. Polite bargaining is acceptable but haggling is looked down upon. Long Jing tea, famous throughout China, makes an excellent gift. ✉ *Southwest off Huanhu Xi Lu.*

Across the lake, on the northwestern side, is the **Hangzhou Zhiwuyuan** (Hangzhou Botanical Garden), a beautiful place in autumn or spring. ✉ *Lingyin Lu and Yuquan Lu.* 🎫 *Y10.* 🕐 *Daily 8:30–6.*

Almost directly south of the lake, about 15 minutes by bus, the **Hupao Meng Quan** (Running Tiger Dream Spring) has a temple built on a dream. According to legend, a traveling monk decided this setting would be perfect for a temple, but as there was no stream or other water in the place, he couldn't build one. Sleeping on the ground, he dreamed that two tigers came and ripped up the earth around him. When he awoke, he was lying next to the stream that they had dug for him. He duly built the temple. The grounds have a bamboo grove, a nondescript teahouse, a modern statue of the dreamer with his tigers, and an intriguing "dripping wall." This cut-out part of the mountainside is so porous and moist that it exudes water from its surface. ✉ *Hupao Lu, just south of lake.* 🎫 *Y10.* 🕐 *Daily 8:30–6.*

The **Hangzhou Dongwuyuan** (Hangzhou Zoo) lies south of the lake. Better than most Chinese zoos, which tend to be in a depressing condition, this one houses some rarities and makes a good visit. ✉ *Hupao Lu.* 🎫 *Y10.* 🕐 *Daily 8:30–6.*

★ The **Lingyin Si** (Temple of Inspired Seclusion) was founded in the 4th century facing a rocky formation in the hills. A Buddhist monk from India thought the rocks looked so much like a mountain he knew in India that he was convinced it had migrated and called the formation

Fei Lai Feng (Peak that Flew Here). The length of the cliff is covered with Buddhist carvings done from the 10th to the 14th centuries, many demolished during the Cultural Revolution but many more left intact or at least discernible. A fat laughing Buddha is the cliff's hallmark, but there are also some excellent caves closer to the entrance, where Buddhist believers burn candles and incense before the dim statues.

The temple becomes so crowded on holidays that you can hardly get in. It has been rebuilt or restored numerous times. The current main building dates from the Qing, but many parts were restored in 1956 and again after the Cultural Revolution. Luckily, the Red Guards just missed the temple, due to intervention from higher up in the government. Many of the statues are quite recent, but several pillars and stupas are thought to be at least 1,000 years old.

The small **Fei Lai Feng Zaoxiang** (Peak that Flew Here Artificial Statues) park, near the entrance, has gigantic fiberglass statues that are poor reproductions of all the most famous Buddhist statues from all over China. Temple, peak, and funhouse park all come under one ticket. ⊠ *Lingyin Lu, west of lake; take No. 7 or No. 507 bus.* ☎ *Y15.* ☉ *Daily 8:30–6.*

A bit outside of town, the **Jiuxi Yanshu** (Nine Streams) area provides one of the most restful scenic spots around. The hill, traversed by streams and brooks, has bright foliage in autumn and spring. At the top of the hill is a teahouse for resting and enjoying the view. Minibuses from your hotel can take you here, as public buses do not run this far out. ⊠ *Jiuxi Lu, a few km southwest of lake.*

Dining and Lodging

Hangzhou is one of China's most heavily visited cities; reservations for hotels are recommended any time of year, but are absolutely essential during spring and autumn weekends, when crowds from outlying regions descend on the city.

$$$$ ✕ **Louwailou Restaurant.** On the banks of Xihu, this is Hangzhou's ★ most famous restaurant. It serves festive afternoon teas as well as excellent meals. The fish dishes are made with fish grown in a small sectioned-off area of West Lake in front of the restaurant; for the real specialty dishes, you can go outside and point out the fish you want. The Hangzhou specialties include a shrimp dish made with Long Jing tea leaves, and a cooked fish that comes to the table still smacking its lips. ⊠ *Waixihu 30,* ☎ *0571/796–9023. No credit cards.*

$$$ ✕ **Tianxianglou Restaurant.** This major restaurant caters banquets as well as to smaller groups, serving up tasty regional specialties of fish and seafood in light sauces as well as choice dishes. ⊠ *Jiefang Lu 166,* ☎ *0571/706–3104. No credit cards.*

$$$$ 🏨 **Shangri-La Hotel Hangzhou.** On the lakeside, the Shangri-La is the best-placed hotel in Hangzhou. The hotel's own gardens merge into the walkways around Xihu, and boat rides and parks are a few minutes' walk away. Suites face out onto the lake. ⊠ *Beishan Lu 78,* ☎ *0571/797–7951, from U.S. 800/942–5050,* ℻ *0571/707–3545. 387 rooms and suites. 2 restaurants, meeting rooms. AE, MC, V.*

$$$ 🏨 **Dragon New World Hotel Hangzhou.** In the hilly area around Yellow Dragon Cave and Dragon Well, it stands in relatively peaceful and attractive surroundings and makes a good starting point for walking tours of the city. You can reach the Bao Chu pagoda and the lake on foot. ⊠ *Shuguang Lu, 310007,* ☎ *0571/799–8833,* ℻ *0571/799–8090. 536 rooms and suites. 3 restaurants, outdoor pool, beauty salon, mas-*

sage, sauna, tennis courts, health club, bicycles, baby-sitting, business services, meeting room, travel services. AE, MC, V.

$$$ 🏨 **Hangzhou Overseas Chinese Hotel.** Now open to visitors of any origin, the hotel is across a large intersection from the lake. Rooms on upper floors offer good views of Xihu. The restaurant serves local specialties and traditional foods of the Hang, Ye, and Chuan cuisines. You can also rent a car here to tour the area. ⊠ *Hubin Lu 15, 310006,* ☎ *0571/707-4401,* FAX *0571/707-4978. 300 rooms and suites. 2 restaurants, bar, beauty salon, business services, meeting rooms. AE, MC, V.*

$$$ 🏨 **Wanghu Hotel.** A couple of minutes' walk from the lake, the Wanghu is oriented toward business travelers. It offers a special "business club" service with a 24-hour business center and meeting rooms as well translation services and PC's. The hotel also serves complimentary breakfasts and teas to give business travelers a chance to meet. ⊠ *Huancheng Xilu 2, 310006,* ☎ *0571/707-1024,* FAX *0571/707-1350. 364 rooms and suites. 2 restaurants, bar, pool, beauty salon, sauna, health club, business services, meeting rooms. AE, MC, V.*

$ 🏨 **West Lake Hotel.** This is one of Hangzhou's few budget options. Facilities are sparse, but the hotel is clean and comfortable, the service friendly, and the location—a couple of blocks from the lake—ideal. ⊠ *Renhe Lu 80,* ☎ *0571/706-6933, for reservations 0571/706-2630,* FAX *0571/706-6151. 87 rooms. Restaurant. AE, MC, V.*

Nightlife and the Arts

Shaoxing Opera performances take place daily at the **Huanglong Dong Yuanyuan Mingshu Yuan** (⊠ 16 Shuguang Lu, ☎ 0571/798-5860) theater.

The nightlife craze is still in its early stages, and places come and go with relative frequency. The **Casablanca Country Pub** (⊠ set back from Hubin Lu, northwest of Joe Eagle complex next to lake) has a decor true to its name with long wooden benches and tables and serves imported beers to a diverse (but mostly local) crowd. The understated, somewhat sophisticated **Golden Saxophone** (⊠ Banqiao Lu 1, ☎ 0571/703-5542) offers drinks, live jazz, and both Chinese and western snacks and small meals. The Mexican-style bar and snack shop **Have a Bite** (⊠ Beishan Lu next to Shangri-La Hotel) is a nightspot with a lovely view onto the lake and the causeways; the clientele is largely foreign. To see how far the Western influence extends, check out the **L.A. Club** (⊠ Jinsi Hua, Hubing Lu 18, 4th floor, ☎ 0571/707-7838), a one-floor dance club with an extensive CD and LP collection. **Paradise Rock** (⊠ Hubin Lu next to Overseas Chinese Hotel) caters to Western tastes with beer, drinks and music.

Shopping

The best things to buy in Hangzhou are tea and silk, but all sorts of wooden crafts, silk fans and umbrellas, and antiques are available, too. The local **Friendship Store** (⊠ Hubin Lu and Qinchun Lu) sells crafts and silks, but a great variety of smaller shops are also sprinkled around. For the best Long Jing tea, you can go out to the tea plantations themselves (☞ Longjing Wencha, *above*). You can check out a range of tea stores on Yanan Lu. One to look out for is the **Long Jing Tea Shop** (⊠ Yanan Lu 89, ☎ 0571/702-9605).

Where Hubin Lu goes along the lake, an informal shopping district stretches out to the east, culminating in the **night market** (⊠ Wushan Lu between Pinghai Lu and Youdian Lu, nightly). One of the best in China, this is a market where you can find all the choice products of the area: silks, from dresses to boxers to straight off the reel, and artifacts from the Qing to the Cultural Revolution. Try the north end of the market for the clay teapots of Yixing County.

Zhejiang A to Z

Arriving and Departing

BY BOAT

You can travel overnight between Hangzhou and Suzhou by ferry up and down the Grand Canal. Tickets are available through CITS, or at the dock (✉ Huancheng Lu and Hushu Nanlu, Hangzhou).

BY BUS

The bus hub of the province is Hangzhou. The **West Bus Station** (Tianmushan Lu) has buses to Huangshan (☞ Anhui, *below*). Buses to major northbound destinations like Shanghai leave from the **Main Station** (Hushu Nanlu).

BY PLANE

You can travel between Hong Kong and Hangzhou daily on CAAC (✉ Tiyuchang Lu 160, ☎ 0571/515–4259) or Dragonair (☎ 0571/799–8833 ext. 6061). Silk Air flies to and from Singapore (☎ 0571/799–8833 ext. 6070). Both Dragonair and Singapore airlines have offices in the Dragon New World Hotel Hangzhou (✉ Shuguang Lu, ☎ 0571/799–8833). There are regular flights to all other major Chinese cities, often daily, depending on the season.

Between the Airport and Hangzhou. Major hotels offer limo service to the airport. Taxis to the airport cost between Y50 and Y75. A bus leaves from CAAC (✉ Tiyuchang Lu 160) every 40 minutes during the day for about Y15.

BY TRAIN

Travel between Shanghai and **Hangzhou** is quick and convenient: normal trains take about three hours; the new "tourist train" takes only two. The train station (✉ Jiang Cheng Lu, in western part of city) is crowded and difficult to manage, but hotel travel desks can often book tickets for you for a small fee. CITS seems uncertain about its own ability to book rail tickets, so stick with the private offers.

Getting Around

BY BICYCLE

Traffic makes biking a dodgy endeavor in Hangzhou. The lakeside and the Bai Causeway are the least congested. Major hotels have bike rentals, as does the Liulangwenying Park (✉ Nanshan Lu, on east side of lake), south of the Children's Park. The rental rate is usually a couple of yuan per hour.

BY BOAT

You can take a two- or four-seat paddle boat by yourself in Hangzhou's Xilu, but these can't be docked at the islands. Official boats run to Santanyinyue Island whenever they have enough passengers—usually about every 40 minutes. Walking around the lake, you will be approached by vendors selling rides on private four-seaters. These are more expensive but quieter and will go wherever you want.

BY BUS

Nearly every street in Hangzhou except the causeways has bus stops; the buses come frequently and cost Y1. Unfortunately, you're lucky to find an uncrowded bus anytime before 9 PM. If you are willing to brave the crowds, though, ask at your hotel desk or the Xinhua Bookstore about English-language bus maps. Nos. 7, 505, and 507 go out to the Temple of Inspired Seclusion; No. 514 goes to Tiger Dream Spring; Nos. 16 and 28 take you to Yellow Dragon Cave. Nos. 7, 27, and 507 all run along the north side of the lake.

BY TAXI

Red four-door cabs are in great supply in Hangzhou. Some larger taxis cost more. Beware of drivers who take the scenic route instead of the straight one, and make sure the meter is on when the car starts.

Contacts and Resources

EMERGENCIES

Hangzhou Red Cross Hospital (⊠ Huancheng Donglu 38, ☎ 0571/518–6042, 0571/518–3137). **Zhejiang Medical University Affiliated Hospital No. 1** (⊠ Qingchun Lu 261, ☎ 0571/707– 2524).

GUIDED TOURS

Hotels can set up tours for interested groups, and **CITS** (☞ *below*) is willing to oblige for a fee. Hawkers or taxi drivers at the Hangzhou train station or in front of your hotel may offer tours; although these can be as good as the official ones, their English is often minimal.

TRAVEL AGENCIES

Most hotels have their own agencies, as well as visitor information. **CITS** (⊠ Shihan Lu 1, ☎ 0571/515–2888). **Zhejiang China International Travel Service** (⊠ Shihan Lu 1, ☎ 0571/515–2888). **Zhejiang Women International Travel Service** (⊠ Huancheng Xilu 1, ☎ 0571/703–5094). **Zhejiang Comfort Travel** (⊠ In Shangri-La Hotel, Beishan Lu 78, ☎ 0571/796–5005).

Visitor Information

Hangzhou Travel and Tourism Bureau (⊠ Yanan Lu 484, ☎ 0571/515–2645).

HUBEI

The Yangzi River cuts lengthwise from west to east through Hubei, giving the province an age-old edge on transportation and a whole stretch of densely foliated land. Centrally located, Hubei, with over 50 million people and a host of waterways, has long been one of China's most important provinces. From 1850 to 1860, it suffered battles between the Taiping rebels and imperial troops. Shortly afterward, several of its cities were opened to European trade, which spread some Western influence through parts of the province. The 1911 revolution started here, toppling the already unsteady Qing dynasty. Over the next 38 years, the province hosted some of the country's leading politicians and military leaders as they vied for control of China's future. Known for both its scenery and its history, the province offers water travel, hiking, mysterious wildlife—and Mao Zedong, who lived in the city of Wuhan for a time before and during the Cultural Revolution.

Wuhan is the port for river cruises through the Three Gorges, which range from western Hubei to eastern Sichuan province. The Three Gorges dam is scheduled for completion in the first decade of the next century; building it will mean flooding much of the Three Gorges area.

The Wudangshan mountain range in the west holds several important Daoist temples, while the Shennongjia region in the northwest is China's cross between the Bermuda Triangle and the abode of the abominable snowman. Travelers are warned of ghostly beasts of unknown origin and purpose, and rumor has it that if you go, you should be prepared not to return. Nevertheless, the number of people around to testify to the existence of the unidentifiable animals seems surprisingly high. As long as you aren't too overwhelmed by the beauty of the place, you'll probably make it back, too.

Wuhan

㉖ *13 hours by train south of Beijing; 6 hours by train south of Zhengzhou; 30 hours by train southwest of Nanjing.*

Whether you're coming into town on a train or in a shuttle from the airport, you can't miss the water. The area around Wuhan seems permanently half-submerged, a swampy marshland traversed by tributaries of the Yangzi River. This impression does not stop when you get to the city. Various lakes, large and small, appear all around town, among which Donghu (East Lake) is often named as a sort of little sister counterpart to Hangzhou's famous Xihu—West Lake. (The fact that East Lake actually lies far to the west of West Lake does not faze anybody. Dozens of East and West Lakes are scattered all over the country, but these two are certainly the most famous.)

The city was a hotbed of revolutionary activity of one sort or another for over a century. It was a center of anti-Qing unrest during the Taiping Rebellion of 1850–1864 and the cradle of the 1911 Republican revolution. During the uneasy 1920s, it was the site of one of the decade's most prominent, and most brutally put down, railway strikes. In 1926 it hosted an unlikely and short-lived coalition government of Guomindang and Communist forces; an even shorter-lived left-wing Guomindang faction ran the city against the wishes of Chiang Kai-shek, whose headquarters were in Nanjing. Mao Zedong ran a Peasant Movement Institute here until the city was taken by the right-wing Guomindang in 1928. During the civil war in the late '40s, the uprisings and strikes led by students and workers in the city speeded the Communist victory in the area in 1949. Nowadays it is home to major iron and steel complexes, as well as such other industries as textiles, heavy machinery, glass, railroad cars, and trucks.

Wuhan is actually a conglomerate of what used to be, until the middle of this century, Wuchan, Hankou, and Hanyang—three distinct towns. Wuhan is the only city in China to lie on both sides of the Yangzi River, which separates Hankou and Hanyang in the west from Wuchang in the east. The smaller Hanshui River separates Hankou from its southern partner, Hanyang. All of these waterways make Wuhan a little cumbersome to traverse. Taxi rides are long, bus rides almost always require at least two buses, and ferry rides across the river, although fun, take a bit of planning. A two-day layover here can be broadly divided along the river: one day for the east and one for the west. Because of Wuhan's natural beauty, it's good to get here during the pleasant seasons of early spring and autumn. Wuhan also is one of China's summer "furnaces."

Wuhan has post-revolution status as one of the Great Helmsman's favorite getaways. **Mao Zedong Bieshu** (Mao Zedong's Villa) near East Lake, now open for viewing, takes on some cult aspects that come with his presence. The villa offers guided tours and lots of photos. ⊠ *Zhongnan Lu.* 🎫 *Y20.* ☯ *Daily 8:30–noon and 2– 5.*

★ The **Hubei Sheng Bowuguan** (Hubei Provincial Museum), west of East Lake, has Mao memorabilia—from photos of Mao lounging by the river to odder relics like a playing card he chose when asked by schoolchildren to pick a card. The rest of the museum holds a magnificent collection of artifacts: the entire contents of a 5th-century BC tomb are housed here, including thousands of ceremonial objects, decorations, and, most impressively, a set of 65 bronze bells that are still taken out and played on special occasions. Most, though not all, of the exhibits are labeled in English. ⊠ *Just south of Donghu Lu and Huangli Lu.* 🎫 *Y10.* ☯ *Tues.–Sun. 8:30–noon and 2–5.*

Dong Hu Gongyuan (East Lake Park) covers 87 sq km (34 sq mi) divided into six "districts" that surround the lake on three sides. Various pavilions—the **Huguang Ge** and the **Xingyin Ge** are the most famous—are scattered about. Some have been recast as teashops overlooking good views. You can cross the lake eastward along a narrow land bridge or hire a boat to end up at Moshan, a lakeside hill, and visit its **Tangshan Zhiwuyuan** (botanical garden). ⊠ *Off Donghu Lu, Wuchang, east side of city.*

On the way back from Wuchang to Hankou, **Hongshan,** a hill lying southeast of the lake, is a pretty place to wander around. At the top stands a small pagoda. ⊠ *Off Wulou Lu.*

The **Changchun Daoist Temple** hosts a small market on the surrounding grounds where you can get sweets and small souvenirs. ⊠ *West of junction of Wulou Lu and Zhongshan Lu.*

Sheshan (Snake Mountain) holds the **Baiyun Ge** (White Cloud Pavilion). The park leads almost to the Yangzi River bridge. It also leads up to the **Huanghe Lou** (Yellow Crane Tower). This gorgeous pagoda, first built in AD 223, has been restored numerous times since then, but it retains the aged elegance that so few restorations can manage. The combination of the tower and the pavilion behind it embodies architecturally Wuhan's more literary name: Yellow Crane White Cloud. ⊠ *Wulou Lu and Jiefang Lu.*

Other than the faint traces of Mao, 20th-century pride seems focused around the southernmost **Wuhan Changjiang Daqiao** (Yangzi River Bridge). Begun with Soviet aid in 1955 and completed in 1957, it was the first bridge ever built across the river, linking Wuchang and Hanyang. The railings display an early example of socialist realism with Chinese characteristics. The two-tiered bridge runs 1670.4 m (5,480 ft) across the river.

South of the Hanyang end of the bridge lies the **Guiyuan Chansi** (Temple of Return to First Principle), one of Hubei's four largest and oldest. First built in 1658, the temple has more than 200 rooms and pavilions. The hall of arhats contains some 500 statues carved in the 19th century. These serve to display Buddhism's current fashionable status more than its historical importance in China. ⊠ *Cuiweiheng Lu at Cuiwei Lu, Hanyang.* 🎫 *Y10.* 🕐 *Daily 8:30–5.*

Near the bridge up to Hankou you can stop in at the **Guqin Tai** (Platform of the Ancient Lute), built in honor of Yu Boya, an ancient lute player, and his friend and avid listener, Zhong Ziqi. Constructed during the Northern Song dynasty (AD 960–1126), the building has retained that dynasty's style through subsequent restorations. ⊠ *Eastern end of Qinhe Lu.* 🎫 *Y5.* 🕐 *Daily 8:30–5.*

Guishan (Tortoise Mountain) lies across the road from the Yangzi and holds another object of Wuhan pride: the **Dianhsi Ta** (Hubei TV Tower), completed in 1986—the first in China to be built without foreign aid. It stands in the park as a symbol of China's modernizing drive.

Wuhan's main hotels and restaurants are in Hankou, but that section of the city also holds the fewest places of interest. The stretch of Hankou that runs along the river between the two bridges—Yangjiang Dadao as well as the street directly west of it, Shengli Jie—retains some pretty buildings from the late 19th century. The city was open then to European concessions, and Chinese architects eagerly accepted but used their own interpretation of the foreign influence. There are also several parks that are nice to stumble upon during a walk. **Zhongshan Gongyuan** (Sun Yat-sen Park) has some rather intricate waterways and paths. ⊠ *Jiefang Dadao, 2 blocks east of Qingnian Lu.* 🚳 *Y5.* 🕔 *7 AM–10 PM.*

Jiefang Gongyuan (Jiefang Park) has a small lake with a historical preservation center on its island. ⊠ *Jiefang Dadao at Jiefang Gongyuan Lu.* 🚳 *Y5.* 🕔 *7 AM–10 PM.*

Dining and Lodging

$$$ ✕ **Little Nanjing.** This is Wuhan's current eating hot spot, favored especially by fashionable young professionals eager to forge a dining culture in their circles. Little Nanjing serves East Central fare in a relatively subdued and tasteful setting. ⊠ *Hankou, Nanjing Lu 104,* ☎ *027/284–2906. No credit cards.*

$$ ✕ **Da Zhonghua.** Once the favorite of Chairman Mao, this restaurant serves Hubei "small eats" like roast squab as well as regional seafood specialties. Visitors go for the history, but locals go for the food. ⊠ *Wuchan, Peng Liu Zhou Lu 198,* ☎ *027/887–3775. No credit cards.*

$ ✕ **Sili Meitang Dumpling Restaurant.** The "Four Li" restaurant, named for the brothers who founded it, has a rather basic setting and decor. But its dumplings—a specialty throughout East Central China—are well known in Wuhan for their juicy fillings. ⊠ *Hankou, Zhongshan Dadao 898,* ☎ *027/283–2842. No credit cards.*

$$$$ 🏨 **Asia Hotel.** The Asia vies with the recently constructed Tianan Holiday Inn (☞ *below*) for pride of place as Wuhan's most favored business-tourist enclave. With similar facilities and equally convenient location, they are now sharing the custom that used to be the Asia's alone. ⊠ *Jiefang Lu 616, Hankou,* ☎ *027/380–7777,* FAX *027/380–8080. 350 rooms and suites. 2 restaurants, bar, beauty salon, exercise room, business services, meeting rooms, travel services. AE, MC, V.*

$$$$ 🏨 **Ramada Inn/Huamei Hotel.** On a small, quiet street a short walk
★ from two city parks, the Inn is known for its excellent service. The accommodations are comfortable without being imposing, and the western restaurant and coffee shop are serious about quality. It also stands directly across the street from one of the best CITS offices in the country. ⊠ *Taibei One Rd. 9, Hankou,* ☎ *027/578–7968,* FAX *027/580–3581. 200 rooms and suites. 2 restaurants, bar, beauty salon, sauna, exercise room, business services, meeting rooms. AE, MC, V.*

$$$$ 🏨 **Tianan Holiday Inn.** This is Wuhan's most upscale hotel, carefully decorated and amply staffed. Near the Hankou city center, it offers a variety of eating options, satellite TV and IDD telephones in every room, and sound travel advice. ⊠ *Danzhou Xiao Lu 4, Hankou,* ☎ *027/568–6054. 400 rooms and suites. 2 restaurants, bar, beauty salon, exercise room, business services, meeting rooms, travel services. AE, MC, V.*

$$ 🏨 **Victory Hotel.** Housing one of Wuhan's very best Chinese restaurants, the Victory stands on a quiet street in the Hankou's pretty riverside district, where colonial-style houses are scattered along with more modern Chinese structures. The hotel provides excellent, friendly service. ⊠ *Siwei Lu 11,* ☎ *027/281–2780. 130 rooms and suites. 2 restaurants, beauty salon, business center. AE, MC, V.*

Nightlife
In Wuhan as in many large Chinese cities, favorite local hangouts include the bars, discos and, especially, the karaoke rooms of the major joint-venture hotels.

Shopping
Impromptu markets surround every temple and pagoda, and the **train station area** also hosts stands catering to tourists. The **Gongyi Dalou** (⊠ Zhongshan Dadao and Minsheng Lu) carries antiques and local artifacts. The **Wuhan Antiques Store** (⊠ Zhongshan Dadao 169, ☎

027/585–6538) sells local antiques and replicas. **Wuhan Friendship Co.** (✉ Zhongshan Dadao 263, ☎ 027/586–4814) offers typical Friendship Store artifacts and prints. The **Xinhua Bookstore** (✉ Hankou, Jianghan Lu 87, ☎ 027/382–4040) carries a limited selection of English language books, as well as useful maps. **Yuehan Matou** (✉ Yanjiang Dadao at Huanliao Shichang shopping center) has a wide selection of goods ranging from everyday to artistic and antique.

Side Trips from Wuhan

The real reason to come to Hubei is not for the capital but for the scenery in the west and northwest of the province. Wuhan is the stopover on the way to wilder locations. The city is a major Yangzi ferry port, and many river tours start or end here. You can buy tickets at your hotel travel desk or book them through CITS (☞ Visitor Information, *below*), which will also be able to arrange unusual, tailor-made, or brand-new packages.

EASTWARD

If you are traveling west to east and have been through Hubei already, or if you want to skip the western section of the province altogether, you can travel downriver to Shanghai (☞ *below*). The two-day trip down the scenic river ends at what is arguably China's most cosmopolitan city.

The trip downriver also provides side trip possibilities of its own. The boat stops at Jiujiang in Jiangxi (☞ Chapter 7) province. From here, Jiangxi's Lu Shan mountains are easily accessible. Guichi and Wuhu in Anhui (☞ *below*) province are both excellent places to start a trip to one of China's most famous, and most beautiful, mountain ranges: Huangshan. Because the mountains are not well served by railroad lines, this combined river-land approach is not any more inconvenient than others, but is certainly more unusual. The boat also passes the major metropolis of Nanjing (☞ *above*) and the small but attractive city of Zhenjiang (☞ *above*) in Jiangsu province, both worth exploring if you have the time.

WESTWARD

The trip upriver is slower because of the current, but it also offers a view of some of China's most fabulous scenery. A four-day trip southwest to Chongqing in Sichuan (☞ Chapter 9) province will take you

㉗ through a variety of sights. You first pass **Jingzhou** in the southern part of Hubei province. This city, which still retains part of its ancient wall, was a major center during the Spring and Autumn and Warring States periods (770 BC–221 BC) and has been the site of several productive archaeological digs. A 2000-year-old male body in the museum is China's oldest preserved corpse. The boat also passes Shennong River, which flows into the Yangzi from **Shennong mountain. Nanjin Pass** in

㉘ **Yichang,** western Hubei, marks the easternmost entrance point of the

㉙ Three Gorges: Qutang, Wu, and Xiling. **Shennongjia** is the wildest part of Hubei, and one of the strangest in the country. The area, thought to hold over 1,000 types of trees, is named for the legendary peasant Shennong, who discovered and collected medicinal herbs here. Possessed of amazing natural beauty, Shennongjia also carries an aura of magic and mystery. With enough time and the help of a travel agent or CITS, you may find this one of the most interesting trip possibilities in China.

㉚ The **Wudang Shan** range in northwest Hubei holds a number of ancient Daoist temples—some atop mountain peaks, and some built right into the mountainside, as though the monks had grown tired of walking and decided to settle right where they were. Building started in the Tang but really took off in the Ming dynasty, with Daoist myths and fengshui requirements in mind. Among the 72 peaks, of which Tianzhu is the highest, you can hear Daoist music and liturgy and see religious ceremonies as well as displays of Taijiquan (or tai chi), transformed over the centuries from its original martial uses to a sort of meditative dance. Trains and buses from Yichang can take you to the Wudangshan village.

Hubei A to Z

Arriving and Departing

BY BOAT

Boats run in either direction from Wuhan along the Yangzi River, going to Chongqing in the west and Shanghai in the east. A few private ferries offer a first class; these are definitely advisable for sanitation and service, but cost more. Tickets can be purchased at your hotel travel desk; check also with CITS (☞ Travel Agencies, *below*).

BY BUS

Buses run daily to Xiamen and Nanchang, northern Hubei, northern Anhui, and Yichang. Planes are preferable if you are going between Wuhan and Hangzhou, Nanjing, or Xian.

BY PLANE

Wuhan offers daily flights to Beijing, Kunming, Shanghai, Guangzhou and Shenzhen; four times a week to Fuzhou, Xian, and Nanjing. Purchase tickets at major hotels or at CAAC (✉ Yanjiang Dadao 102, Hankou, ☎ 027/284–4841). You can also try the Hubei International Airline Service Ltd. (✉ Jianghan Beilu 4, Wuhan, ☎ 027/586–3177). Taxis out to the airport take just under an hour and cost around Y110.

Getting Around

BY BOAT

Ferries cross the Yangzi between Hankou and Wuchang frequently. This is a faster and more enjoyable way of getting around than riding buses.

BY BUS AND TAXI

Buses traverse **Wuhan,** but its size and their number renders the whole system a little unwieldy. You can expect to switch buses one or two times if you're crossing the river between city-sections. Taxis and the ferry are more convenient. Taxis are easy to flag down on any major street.

Contacts and Resources

EMERGENCIES

Hubei Medical University Affiliated Hospital No. 1 (✉ Jiefang Lu, Wuchang, ☎ 027/884–4437). **Wuhan Hospital No. 1** (✉ Zhongshan Dadao, Hankou, ☎ 027/585–5900).

GUIDED TOURS

CITS (☞ *below*) has the latest information on tours of northern Hubei and of the Three Gorges area. Look into tours especially if you are planning to go into the northwest—the region can be difficult going without a working knowledge of Chinese.

TRAVEL AGENCIES

CITS (✉ Taibei Yi Lu, Xiaonanhu Building 7/F, Wuhan, ☎ 027/578–4107). **Wuhan Overseas Tourist Corp.** (✉ Jiefang Dadao, Hankou, ☎ 027/585–6473).

VISITOR INFORMATION

CITS (☞ Travel Agencies, *above*). **Wuhan Tourism Administration** (✉ 17 Hezuo Lu, Hankou, ☎ 027/283–2389).

SHAANXI

One of the oldest habitations of Chinese people, with evidence of pre-historic occupation, Shaanxi was also home of the first unifier of China, Qin Shihuang—first (and penultimate) emperor of the Qin dynasty. Because of the prestige of its capital city, then called Changan, the province grew in importance until the Tang, when it reached new heights of prosperity and artistic productivity. A locus of Asian trading routes, it prospered from its association with the Silk Road. At the same time, the Muslim, Buddhist, and to a lesser extent Christian, influences coming from the west added to the vibrant, diverse culture encouraged during the Tang.

As China's focus turned inward and the outside seemed to grow more and more distant, the capital was moved east. With a slackening of trade and a clamp-down on religious and cultural diversity, Shaanxi's assets became its losses. Minority Muslim unrest caused major rebellions in the 14th and 17th centuries, and harsh repressions of uprisings caused thousands of deaths during the late Qing. The complex web of irrigation canals that sustained the populace fell into disrepair and the province was ravaged by famine. These cultural conflicts and natural disasters ensured that it would never again reach the heights it had known in the 10th century.

The late 19th and early 20th centuries saw poverty and famine sweep this once-prosperous area; millions died as the country was wracked by military unrest and, finally, civil war. In the late 1920s, the young Communist Party started a countrywide effort to win over Chinese peasants; the state of disaffection and despair in this province gained them enthusiastic recruits. When the embattled Communists embarked on their Long March in 1934, it was from Shaanxi that they chose to emerge. They set up a camp in Yanan that would last them for more than 10 years of intermittent Japanese and Guomindang conflict. It was here that much Party theory was first wrestled out, and here that Mao Zedong consolidated his power over the Party. In 1947 the Communists were finally routed by the GMD and fled the province, to return two years later.

Xian

7 hours by train southwest of Luoyang; approximately 2 hours by plane northwest of Nanjing.

Xian lures visitors with men in uniforms: the huge tomb of Qin Shihuang, emperor of the Qin dynasty, holds thousands of terra-cotta warrior figures in battle gear. The emperor Qin, acceding to the throne in 221 BC at the age of 38, ruled China with an iron hand until his death just 11 years later. He not only ruled it, he created it. At the time of his accession, the lands we now call China were splintered into numerous small kingdoms. Qin took it upon himself to "unite"—that is, to conquer—a huge territory during his lifetime. He imposed military unity and instigated a series of bureaucratic reforms to centralize the country's governmental systems as well. He standardized money and measurements, divided the country into administrative units under central control, started construction on the Great Wall, and burned any books he could find that challenged state decrees—including many of the ancient classics. His son inherited his father's throne, but the dynasty crumbled four years after Qin's death. Nevertheless, his conquered lands and his administrative ideas formed the basis of what China was and would become.

The area met with changing fates for the next millennium. The Han dynasty, which overthrew the Qin, established its capital just north-west of modern-day Xian, but when in AD 23 the Later Han moved its capital to Luoyang, the region's prestige declined. In the 6th century, the Sui dynasty returned to Changan, as the city was then called—a name meaning "eternal peace." Over the next centuries, under the Tang dynasty, Changan grew to become one of the largest and most cultured cities in the world. A complex web of communication systems united the capital with the rest of the country. It also became an important center for what is considered China's most cultured and artistic dynasty. Xian (western peace) was a name given during the Ming, per-haps a less idealistic time. The city is studied by historians as a model of ancient capital city planning. It was carefully arranged from ancient times and expanded during the Tang. Much of it lies on a grid that fo-cuses on what used to be the exact center of the city, where the bell tower stands.

More recently, in 1936, Xian hosted Chiang Kai-shek when his own general, Zhang Xueliang, had him arrested. Zhang used the arrest to convince Chiang to join the Communist party in opposing the Japa-nese invasion of China, which Chiang had been more or less ignoring in his attempt to exterminate the Communist menace. Chiang agreed—although Zhang later paid heavily for the betrayal. Xian contains a wealth of cultural artifacts and architecture, chiefly concentrated in the south-eastern and the western quarters.

A Good Walk

Start at the **Da Qingzhen Si** ③. The Muslim neighborhood around the mosque is also a great place to wander and shop. Head east and south to pass under the **Gulou** ②. Next, follow Xi Da Jie east to the **Zhong-lou** ③, which stands at the intersection with Dong Da Jie. From here you can go south and east to the **Shaanxi Sheng Bowuguan** ④, which holds the Forest of Stone Stelae. Exiting, turn west (right) onto Sanxue Jie, which will quickly lead you to **Shu Yuan Men** ⑤, a small street with old-fashioned architecture. At the crossing with Nanda Jie, notice the **Nanmen** ⑥ on your left. This is one of the city wall's access points. Just south of the South Gate is the pleasant **Xiao Yan Ta** ⑦. A bit far-ther south and east, the **Shaanxi Lishi Bowuguan** ⑧ contains terra-cotta warriors from the Qin tomb farther outside town, among other im-portant dynastic relics. Southeast of the museum, you can visit the **Da Yan Ta** ⑨, one of the best-known pagodas in the country.

The chief places of interest in the Xian vicinity—**Banpo Bowuguan** (Ne-olithic village), **Huaqing Chi** (hot spring), the **Imperial Tombs,** several **Si** (temples), and especially, the **Qin Shihuang Ling** (Tomb of Qin Shi-huang) and the **Qin Shihuang Bing Ma Yong Bowuguan** (Museum of Qin Terra-cotta Warriors)—lie outside the city and can be visited on tours or by minibus.

Sights to See

★ **Banpo Bowuguan** (Banpo Neolithic Village). Unearthed in 1953, this settlement east of the city holds the remains of the earliest Yangshao culture yet discovered. The village was populated from around 4500 BC to 3750 BC, and though villagers survived mainly by fishing, hunt-ing, and gathering, there is evidence of animal domestication (pigs and dogs, and perhaps cattle or sheep) as well as farming in the surrounding areas.

This was also one of China's earliest pottery sites, with kilns reaching temperatures of 1,000°C (1,800°F) to produce cooking ware as well as ceremonial containers, many of which are decorated with animal

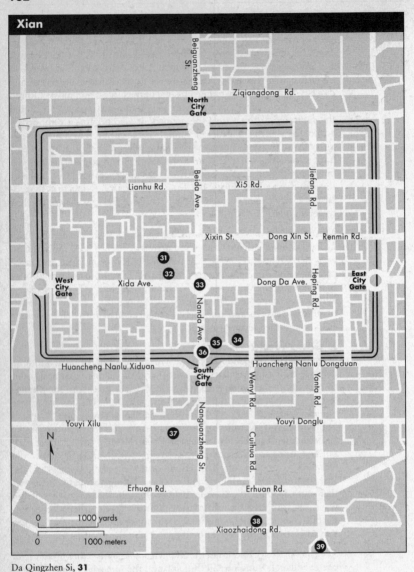

Xian

designs. Banpo is part village, part museum: an attempt has been made to re-create the conditions of the ancient village to give a sense of the past. The museum displays actual archaeological finds and sells explanatory guidebooks of the artifacts. ⊠ *Off Changdong Donglu, east of city; take bus No. 11 from train station.* 🚇 *Y10.* 🕑 *Daily 9–6.*

31 **Da Qingzhen Si** (Great Mosque). The mosque may have been established as early as AD742, during the Tang, but the remaining buildings date mostly from the 18th century. Amazingly, it was left standing during the Cultural Revolution and has been significantly restored since then. Stone tablets mark the various pavilions, often bearing inscriptions in both Chinese and Arabic. Be sure to look above the doors and gates: there are some remarkable designs here, including 3-D stone Arabic script that makes the stone look as malleable as wedding cake frosting. The northern lecture hall holds a handwritten Koran from the Ming. Non-Muslims are not allowed in the prayer hall. The **Muslim Quarter,** in the small side streets surrounding the mosque, is the center of the city's Muslim community, with shops and a market. ⊠ *East of Beiguangji Jie.* 🚇 *Y15.* 🕑 *Daily 8:30–noon and 2–6.*

39 **Da Yan Ta** (Great Goose Pagoda). Southeast of the city wall's south gate, the pagoda was originally built in the 7th century AD but was rebuilt during the Qing, in a Ming style. Parts have been restored since 1949. This Buddhist pagoda is one of the best known in the country. It was directly connected to the imperial palace during the Tang and in fact houses the tumulus of the emperor Qin Shihuang. Inside the pagoda, statues of Buddhist figures in Chinese history line the various chambers. The building also houses the **Tang Dynasty Arts Museum,** which collects originals and reproductions from that era of high artistic production. ⊠ *Yanta Lu.* 🚇 *Y20.* 🕑 *Daily 8:30–6.*

32 **Gulou** (Drum Tower). This ancient building, which used to hold the alarm drums for the imperial city, marks the southern end of the Muslim Quarter. Both the street on which the tower is located and the side street running left directly after the tower are restored market streets on which endless peddlers offer you anything from Chinese Muslim-style clothing to Mao Zedong memorabilia to seals engraved on the spot, in Chinese or English, by old men bent over their metal picks. ⊠ *Bei Yuan Jie.*

Huaqing Chi (Huaqing Hot Spring). The spring, which stands amid gardens east of the city, provides natural hot water for 60 pools, as well as private baths. There are several pavilions and ponds around to remind you of the Tang emperors who once enjoyed this place as a romantic retreat; but it has gone downhill over the last millennia. There is a museum on the grounds. ⊠ *30 km (19 mi) east of Xian.* 🚇 *Y30.* 🕑 *Daily 8–5.*

Imperial Tombs. This series of tombs north and west of the city can be seen most conveniently on a day tour organized by a travel agency or hotel. The **Qian Ling** (Qian Tomb; 85 km/53 mi northwest of Xian) is the burial place of the Tang Emperor Gao Zong and his wife, the Empress Wu, whose 21-year reign after his death was marked by an effective acquisition of power through such age-old means as political intrigue and murder. The surrounding area holds many statues depicting animals, imperial guards, and the tribute-payers and minority representatives who dealt with the emperor. **Zhang Huai Mu** and **Yong Tai Gongzhu Mu** (Prince Zhang Huai and Princess Yong Tai's Tombs; ⊠ near Qian Tomb) hold murals and engravings, although the princess's have stood the test of time better than the prince's. Both of these royals—he, the second son of Empress Wu; she, Emperor Gao Zong's granddaughter—

fell out of favor with the Empress. The Princess was killed, and the Prince exiled; both were posthumously rehabilitated and their remains returned to Xian.

Many of the most important artifacts in the **Zhao Ling** (Zhao Tomb; ✉ 70 km/43 mi northwest of Xian) have been transported to other sites, notably the Philadelphia and Xian museums, but the tomb itself, built for the second Tang emperor, is still a sight to see. Tai Zong died in AD 649 and was buried surrounded by his retainers and relatives. A small museum holds murals and examples of tri-color Tang pottery.

The largest Han dynasty tomb around, the **Mao Ling** (Mao Tomb; 40 km/25 mi west of Xian), was built for the Han's strongest leader, Emperor Wu. It's about 47 m (154 ft) high. The emperor was interred with retainers and horses, clad in a burial garment of jade and gold.

Lishan. This small mountain east of the city has several pavilions along its paths, as well as the local Taoist temple. It's an inviting stroll if your tour stops at Huaqing and you want to get away from the crowds. ✉ *30 km (19 mi) east of Xian.*

❸❻ **Nanmen** (South Gate). The south gate of the city wall hosts a small market during the day, where peasants from nearby villages come to sell their produce. This is also one of the points at which the city wall can be climbed; if you have the time, take a stroll along this ancient structure. The walls mark the site of Tang dynasty walls; the present ones were built at the beginning of the Ming. Although many city walls in China were torn down during the 20th century, these were left standing and used as storage and protection areas when small caves were hollowed out during the Japanese invasion. They rise to a height of 39 ft. ✉ *South end of Nan Da Jie.* 🚊 *Y10.* ☉ *8:30–6.*

★ **Qin Shihuang Ling** (Tomb of Qin Shihuang). The first Qin emperor started construction on his enormous tomb to the east of the city almost as soon as he took the throne. The **Bing Ma Yong,** an army of thousands of hand-shaped, life-size terra-cotta warriors was buried nearby. Complete with weapons and horses, they were to be his garrison in the afterlife. After the fall of the Qin to the Han—during which it was damaged—the tomb was forgotten, only to be found again in 1974, when some farmers digging a well unexpectedly came up with a piece of sculpture instead of the formless soil they were expecting. Only a part of the entire area has been excavated, and the process of unearthing more warriors continues. In fact, no one is sure just how many warriors there are or how far their "tomb" extends beyond the 700-ft-by-200-ft section being excavated. You can see what they've dug up so far in three vaults about a mile from the unexcavated tomb.

The first part of the **Qin Shihuang Bing Ma Yong Bowuguan** (Museum of Qin Terra-cotta Warriors) holds about 6,000 warriors, well shaped and fully outfitted except for their weapons, whose wooden handles had decayed over the centuries, although the bronze blades were still sharp upon excavation. Be sure to walk around the entire vault: in the back, a less fully excavated section dramatically displays half-formed figures emerging from the rock of the ground. Vault No. 2 holds 1,000 statues, while Vault No. 3 has 68 warriors and a chariot. The warriors in the second two vaults are much like those in the first. Nearby, in a room to the side, stand two miniature **bronze chariots** unearthed in the western section of the tomb. Found in 1980, these chariots are of exemplary quality, containing intricate detail on their finely crafted surfaces.

Please note that absolutely no photographs or videos are allowed in the vaults. Your film will be confiscated if a guard notices your camera. Postcards and other souvenirs are available in the shops outside the vaults and the movie, or from hawkers outside the main gates who sell them for under half the museum's price. CITS and practically every hotel arranges tour buses out, or you can go solo on public buses No. 306 or 307, which leave from the train station. ⊠ *30 km (19 mi) east of Xian.* 🎫 *Site, Y50; museum, Y80 (foreigners), Y35 (Chinese).* 🕐 *Daily 9–5.*

★ ㊳ **Shaanxi Lishi Bowuguan** (Shaanxi Historical Museum). The museum is rated at the top of its class. Much of the collection used to be housed in the Shaanxi Provincial Museum (☞ Shaanxi Sheng Bowuguan, *below*), but some of it is newly available for public viewing. First opened in 1992, the two-story museum is arranged chronologically to show artifacts from the Paleolithic and New Stone Ages, later Zhou dynasty bronzes and burial objects, and several terra-cotta warriors taken from the tombs outside town. This is the closest you can get to these statues, which are housed here behind glass. In the actual tomb area, they are unapproachable in their original pits and can only be seen from the scaffolding erected around the vaults. The exhibit also shows Han, Wei, and northern Zhou dynasty relics, ending with more recent technological displays from the Sui, Tang, Ming, and Qing, as well as impressive bronze and jade artworks and religious statues. The exhibits have English labels. Foreigners enter through a door to the left of the main gate. ⊠ *Xiao Yan Xi Lu and Cuihua Lu.* 🎫 *Y40.* 🕐 *Daily 8:30–6.*

㉞ **Shaanxi Sheng Bowuguan** (Shaanxi Provincial Museum). The first thing you see as you walk in is the impressive Forest of Stone Stelae. As the name suggests, there is no shortage here of historical stone tablets. More than 1,000 stelae bear inscriptions ranging from descriptions of administrative projects 1,000 years ago to artistic renditions of landscape, portraiture, and even calligraphy. One of the world's first dictionaries, the oldest map of China, and Tang dynasty inscribed classics are housed here. One, known as the Popular Stela, dates from AD 781. It records the interaction between the emperor and a traveling Nestorian priest, Raban. After presenting the empire with translated Nestorian Christian texts, Raban was allowed to open a church in Xian. The rest of the museum holds Silk Road artifacts. ⊠ *San Xue Jie west of Duanlu Men.* 🎫 *Y20.* 🕐 *Daily 8:30–6.*

㉟ **Shu Yuan Men** (Calligraphy Yard). The houses on this lively, bustling street are built in a traditional style. Lining the sides of the road are peddlers and shops selling various wares such as calligraphy brushes, souvenirs, and artworks, including calligraphy scrolls and watercolors.

Si (Temples). A number of temples near Xian are worth a visit. To the south, **Daxingshan, Caotang, Huayan, Xiangji,** and **Xingjiao** were all built to house Buddhist scriptures or to commemorate famous monks. Several schools of Buddhism begun in this area grew to renown and popularity throughout Asia. To the northwest, **Famen Si** (Famen Temple), originally built in the 3rd century AD, was renovated in 1981. It turned out to hold a crypt that housed thousands of coins and various sacrificial objects of jade, gold, and silver. These can be viewed at the museum on the temple grounds. All of these temples are best seen on an organized tour.

㊲ **Xiao Yan Ta** (Small Goose Pagoda). Once part of a 7th- century AD temple and monastery, it is directly south of the city's south gate. The remaining buildings were actually constructed during the Ming, later damaged in an earthquake, and rebuilt more recently. The grounds are pleasant and the pavilions are a good place to relax and stroll. Near the entrance, a pavilion houses a small art shop that sells local imitations of ancient styles as well as more modern paintings that still bear the marks of their Chinese origin. There are some excellent reproductions here at reasonable prices. ⊠ *Youyi Xilu, west of Nanguan Zhengjie.* 🎫 *Y10.* ⊙ *Daily 8:30–6.*

㉝ **Zhonglou** (Bell Tower). The Bell Tower was built in the late 14th century to mark the center of the city. Subsequent changes in city organization have displaced it from this prominent position, but the city still revolves around it. Despite its lack of centrality, it marks the point where West Main Street becomes East Main Street and North Main Street becomes South. You can cross to the tower, which stands in the middle of a traffic circle, through an underground passage and climb up to see its centuries-old pillars and roofs, as well as an art exhibit on its upper floor. ⊠ *Traffic circle at intersection of Dong Da Jie, Xi Da Jie, Bei Da Jie and Nan Da Jie.* 🎫 *Y10.* ⊙ *Daily 8:30–6.*

NEED A   Try one of Xian's indigenous Muslim specialties, paomo: Join the crowd
BREAK?   at the **Laosunjia Restaurant** (⊠ southeast corner of Dong Da Jie and Du-
          anlumen intersection, ☎ 029/721–6828) and pick up two rounds of
          hard bread and a bowl. Tear the bread into pieces as small as possi-
          ble—you can tell the experienced eaters by the speed of their hands
          and the circumference of their crumbs. When you are done, a waitress
          takes your bread-filled bowl, returning it in a few minutes filled with hot
          mutton soup with thin, clear noodles.

Dining and Lodging

$$$$ ✕ **De Fa Chang Restaurant.** If you think dumplings are just occasional snack food, think again. This is one of Xian's fanciest and most famous restaurants; it caters exclusively to groups. Its claim to fame is its dumpling banquet. ⊠ *Dong Da Jie,* ☎ *029/723–1127. No credit cards.*

$$$ ✕ **Tangle Gong.** Using recipes preserved from ancient times, the Tang-
★   le Gong specializes in Tang dynasty imperial cuisine—a taste you are not likely to find at your local Chinese restaurant. Book in advance for an unusual evening of entertainment, a full-length imperial banquet, complete with Tang dynasty singing and dancing. ⊠ *Changan Lu,* ☎ *029/526–1620. Reservations essential. No credit cards.*

$$ ✕ **Dongya Restaurant.** An old establishment predating the current government, the Dongya, or East Asian, is centrally located. Head upstairs for some of the best Chinese food in Xian. ⊠ *Luoma Shi 46,* ☎ *029/721–8410. No credit cards.*

$$ ✕ **Xian Fanzhuang.** The oldest and largest restaurant in the city, the Xian specializes in local foods with a Muslim flavor as well as local "small eats"—street food spruced up for the visitor. The private rooms upstairs serve banquets. ⊠ *Dong Da Jie,* ☎ *029/727–3185. No credit cards.*

$ ✕ **Jiefang Lu Jiaozi Guan.** *Jiaozi* is Chinese for dumplings, specifically boiled ones with meat fillings. The glorification of meat-filled pastry seems to be a Xian theme. This restaurant has become so popular for its handmade delights that visitors are now advised to call ahead. ⊠ *Jiefang Lu,* ☎ *029/727–3185. Reservations essential. No credit cards.*

$ ✕ **Laosun Jia.** Otherwise known as the Xian Muslim Restaurant, this
★   traditionally family-run affair serves some of the local Islamic specialties in lamb and beef. The first floor has a snack bar style, while the second floor has a more formal atmosphere and friendly service. ⊠ *Southeast corner of Dong Da Jie and Duanlumen intersection,* ☎ *029/721–6828. No credit cards.*

$$$$ 🏨 **Grand New World.** This luxurious hotel benefits from its proximity to an access point in the city wall as well as from its association with the Xian Cultural Center, which holds performances of plays and

local style operas in the hotel's theater. The courtyard containing some statues of historic figures lets you get away from the busy street outside. Several bus routes run on Lianhu Lu to take you to more central areas of town. ⊠ *Lianhu Lu 48*, ☎ *029/721–6868*, FAX *029/721–9754. 519 rooms. 2 restaurants, food court, pool, tennis court, health club, business services, travel services. AE, MC, V.*

$$$$ 🏨 **Hyatt Regency Hotel.** This deluxe establishment provides excellent service and high-quality Chinese food. It's located a short ride away from the best Xian sights, as well as being within walking distance of the East Gate of the city wall. ⊠ *Dong Da Jie 158*, ☎ *029/723–1234*, FAX *029/723–1234. 404 rooms and suites. restaurant, bar, café, nightclub, business services, meeting rooms. AE, MC, V.*

$$$$ 🏨 **Shangri-La Golden Flower Xian.** Its glassy veneer shields a well-lit property with excellent service and facilities. One of the most imposing and up-scale hotels in the city, the Shangri-La maintains the chain's usual strict quality. The hotel offers bicycle rentals and tours of the area. Every room comes with mini-bar, satellite TV, and IDD telephone. In-room movies are also available. ⊠ *Changle Xi Lu 8*, ☎ *029/323–2981, or from U.S. 800/942–5050*, FAX *029/323–5185. 453 rooms and suites. 2 restaurants, 2 bars, indoor pool, health club, nightclub, business services, meeting rooms. AE, MC, V.*

$$$ 🏨 **Bell Tower Hotel, Holiday Inn.** Right in the middle of the city, with views of the Bell Tower and a nearby park across the street, it is home to some of Xian's best western food and has excellent service. Upstairs, the Golden Gate Travel Agency and a less useful branch of CITS have offices. You can rent bicycles here or set up tours of the area. ⊠ *Nan Da Jie, 710001*, ☎ *029/727–9200*, FAX *029/721–8767. 300 rooms and suites. 2 restaurants, business services, travel services. AE, MC, V.*

$$$ 🏨 **Sheraton Hotel.** This is a joint venture with international quality standards. Unfortunately, it's some distance from town; staying here adds roughly half an hour to 40 minutes to a terra-cotta warriors excursion. ⊠ *Fenghao Lu 12, 710077*, ☎ *029/426–1888*, FAX *029/426–2188. 476 rooms, 15 suites. 2 restaurants, bar, pool, health club, business services. AE, MC, V.*

$$ 🏨 **Jiefang Hotel.** Right across from the railway station, the Jiefang is a standard hotel that caters mostly to Chinese guests. Its service is nothing special, but it's very convenient if you are coming in late at night or want to be at the hub of Xian excursion possibilities. CITS has a ticketing office upstairs. ⊠ *Jiefang Lu*, ☎ *029/721–2368. 150 rooms and suites. Restaurant, business services, travel services. AE, MC, V.*

$$ 🏨 **People's Hotel.** This interesting structure, where two pagodas frame the long torso of the building, combines 1950s socialist realism with traditional Chinese touches. It stands near a small park and, although less impressive than some of the other hotels in town, is a fine choice for an overnight stay. ⊠ *Dongxin Lu 39, 710004*, ☎ *029/721–5111*, FAX *029/721–8152. 600 rooms and suites. 2 restaurants, tennis court, exercise room, business center, meeting room. AE, MC, V.*

Nightlife and the Arts

The **Shaanxi Provincial Dance and Song Assembly** (⊠ Wenyi Bei Lu, ☎ 029/727–1180) and the **Shaanxi Provincial Drama Assembly** (⊠ Wenyi Bei Lu, ☎ 029/721–4498) have periodic performances of regional-style traditional opera and plays.

The busiest part of town in the evening is definitely the **Muslim Quarter,** where crowds converge to shop, stroll, and eat virtually any night of the week. Bars and clubs are located in the hotels.

Shopping

Predictably, Xian swarms with terra-cotta references in various flavors and styles: aside from postcards and picture-books, you can get imitation terra-cotta warriors at virtually every tourist site in town. Made with detail that quite resembles the original, these range in size from ones that fit in the palm of your hand to others that look eye-to-eye with a standing adult.

But there is more to buy here than Qin reminders. The **Art Carving Factory** (⊠ Nanxin Jie, ☎ 029/721–6308) carries local art wares. All kinds of crafts and souvenirs can be bought at the **Friendship Store** (⊠ Nanxin Jie, ☎ 029/721–0551). The **Jade Carving Factory** (⊠ Nanxin Jie, ☎ 029/721–8232) sells the works of local artists. The **Overseas Chinese Department Store** (⊠ Nanxin Jie, ☎ 029/723–2269) has local artists' wares. A bit outside of town but well worth the trip if you are interested in art, the **Xian Chinese Painting Institute Shopping Center** (⊠ Naner Huan Lu at Lingyuan Lu, ☎ 029/526–4775–228) displays and sells local artworks.

Xian also has a number of market streets where peddlers sell foods, replica antiques, and whatever else comes to mind. You can sometimes find lovely souvenirs and antiques here, if you are prepared to look around and to bargain. The **Dajue Xiang** market is near the mosque. There is a market on **Fangu Jie**. The area around the **North Gate** has antiques sellers. **Sanxue Jie** market is near the South Gate.

Side Trip from Xian

A few hours east by train from Xian lies one of China's five "famous mountains," **Huashan**. The 7,218-ft mountain has some lovely scenery, including tall, sloping pines whose distinctive tufts of green are reminiscent of a Dr. Seuss creation, and granite walls that rise shockingly out of the surrounding flatter lands. This is not a trip for the faint-hearted: hiking the main trail takes a good seven to nine hours, some of it along narrow passes on sheer cliffs. You can take a train to Huashan Village, at the base of the mountain. It's best to check with CITS about arrangements; some new hotels may be opening up to foreigners.

Shaanxi A to Z

Arriving and Departing

BY BUS

The long-distance bus station, across the street from the train station (☞ *below*), has buses to Huashan and other Shaanxi destinations, as well as Henan stops. These last are better covered by train.

BY PLANE

About an hour out of town by bus, Xian's airport has daily or almost daily service to major Chinese cities. It is also well connected internationally, with daily flights to Japan. If you're coming to Xian by plane, you can book tickets at CAAC's office in Xiguan Airport (☎ 029/420–1001); otherwise, it's most convenient to use CITS or your hotel travel desk. For Hong Kong flights, you can take the domestic carrier or Dragonair (⊠ Fenghao Lu 12, ☎ 029/426–2988).

BY TRAIN

The train station, Xian Zhan (⊠ Huancheng Bei Lu Dong Duan and Jiefang Lu), lies on the same rail line as Luoyang and Zhengzhou (8 hours) to the east. You can also get direct rides farther east to Nanjing, Shanghai, and Beijing, or southeast to Wuhan. Chengdu is a major western destination. The foreigners' ticket window is upstairs above the main ticket office. First order your destination at one of the windows on the far left, then take the receipt and line up on the other side of the room. CITS will book tickets for a fee. The main Huashan stop is about an hour out of Xian on the train.

Getting Around

BY BICYCLE

Many Xian hotels rent bicycles for a song. In good weather, this is a great way to see the city—all the sights within the city walls are close enough to bike to, and you might want to ride around to the park that surrounds the moat.

BY BUS AND TAXI

Xian's bus center stands directly south of the Bell Tower; just about every bus in the city passes through here. From here you can also catch convenient, and less crowded, buses to out-of-town sights. Buses run frequently and traverse the city, but they are very crowded and the driving tends to be a little fast and loose. It's best to stick to the cabs, which are plentiful and easily hailed.

BY CAR

Because so many of the sights lie outside the city proper, hiring a car is convenient and allows you the freedom to leave when you like instead of waiting for the rest of the tour. Major hotels have car services.

Contacts and Resources

EMERGENCIES

Xian Medical University Affiliated Hospital No. 1 (⊠ Jiankang Lu, ☏ 029/526–2981).

GUIDED TOURS

Every hotel offers its own guided tours of the area, usually dividing them into eastern area, western area, and city tours. More upscale hotels have special English-language tour guides, but their availability often depends on the number of people in your group. You do not have to be staying at the hotel to participate in a tour. The **Golden Bridge Travel Agency** (☞ *below*) arranges tours similar to these.

TRAVEL AGENCIES

CITS (⊠ North Changan Lu 32, ☏ 029/524–1864, FAX 029/526–1454). **Golden Bridge Travel Agency** (Bell Tower Hotel, 2nd floor, ⊠ Nan Da Jie, ☏ 029/727–9200). **Xijing Travel Agency** (⊠ 77 Qingnian Lu, North Building, 3/F, ☏ 029/721–7951).

VISITOR INFORMATION

CITS (☞ Travel Agencies, *above*).

En Route The population explosion has led to a housing crisis in China's big cities, but in the Shaanxi–Henan countryside, people have been making creative homes for years. If you're taking the train anywhere between Xian and Zhengzhou, keep your eyes peeled for the cave dwellings that periodically line the railroad tracks. When the Communists were based in Shaanxi before the civil war, they lived in cave houses, but what has become a virtual symbol of their simple life and inventiveness had actually been around long before they came here. Thousands of Chinese live in houses completely or partially built into the rising ground; compared to normal standing houses, these are easy to heat in winter and keep cool in summer, making them an efficient choice.

HENAN

Henan is both a source of pride and a sore point for the nation. The Huang He (Yellow River) area supports the popular conception of China's "5,000-year history," a ubiquitous phrase in any discussion of Chinese culture; but the economy of the current province is in sad shape. The Shang dynasty, established in the 17th century BC, set their capital in Henan, moving it to several different cities throughout their 600-year reign. The northern Song dynasty also returned the capital to this region, occupying Kaifeng. This city, just west of Zhengzhou, remains one of Henan's most enchanting. Threatened by invaders in the 12th century AD, the Song fled south, leaving Kaifeng and the surrounding region to its own devices.

Henan's fertile land supported a growing population, which in the end may have been its downfall. Apart from the periodic flooding of the Yellow River, which wreaks havoc on crops and lives, the steady increase in population has made Henan the home of some of the nation's most impoverished people. Refugees of a sort, fleeing the poverty of their home regions, the majority of China's millions of migrant workers come from Henan and Sichuan.

The area's most famous sight, the Dragon Gate Caves, is close to Luoyang; you might start in Luoyang (☞ *below*), visit Shaolin Temple on the way from Luoyang to Zhengzhou, spend the night in Zhengzhou, and go on to Kaifeng (☞ *below*) the next afternoon.

Zhengzhou

40 *3 hours by train east of Luoyang; 11 hours by train northwest of Nanjing.*

Archaeological finds indicate that the region around this city has been populated since the Neolithic period. It was the Shang dynasty capital for a time and became an important transportation and economic center under the Sui and Tang dynasties, when canals connecting the Yellow River to the northwest terminated in Zhengzhou's great grain market. When the Song moved their capital east to Kaifeng, the city's importance waned. In the 20th century, Zhengzhou once again became an important transportation center. It was the site of one of the chief railway strikes of the 1920s and, later, of a major wartime disaster. When Chiang Kai-shek's retreating Nationalist army blew up the dams on the Yellow River in a vain attempt to stop Japanese military progress into the country, millions suffered from the ensuing floods. The Nationalists also moved Zhengzhou's industry to avoid its falling into Japanese hands. After 1949, the Communist government rebuilt industry in what was at that point only an administrative and commercial center. The city is spread out below the Yellow River in fits and starts of industrial development. The heavy industrialization of recent years has given an otherwise nondescript provincial capital a level of pollution, traffic, and noise befitting a major urban center. Cultural attractions, unfortunately, have not kept pace.

Zhengzhou, along with Luoyang, provides a suitable base for exploring some of China's oldest and best-known sights. The area around Zhengzhou is one of the most important in Chinese ancient history.

Sights are organized below in order of their proximity to the central restaurant and hotel district along Jinshui Lu.

If you're lucky, you can catch a glimpse of some city ruins in the far eastern section of **Zijingshan Gongyuan** (Zijingshan Park). The park also has a playground for children, a minimally functional miniature golf course, and several pretty wooden pagodas. It's a nice place to get away from the noise of the city, especially if you are traveling with children. A classic of socialist realism, a sculpture dating from the Cultural Revolution, guards the entrance. ☒ *Jinshui Lu between Renmin*

Lu and Chengdong Lu, entrance at intersection of Jinshui Lu and Ren-min Lu. 🖼 *Y1.* ⊙ *Daily 8–dusk.*

Renmin Gongyuan (People's Park) provides a relaxing alternative to the city's dusty streets. It contains a small lake with a large island and provides a favorite dawn and dusk Tai Chi venue for the local popu-lace. ⊠ *Jinshui Lu between Wenhua Lu and Nanyang Lu, entrance on Nanyang Lu just south of Jinshui Lu.* 🖼 *Y1.* ⊙ *Daily 8–dusk.*

Zhengzhou's **Henan Sheng Bowuguan** (Henan Provincial Museum) has an excellent collection of archaeological finds from this area as well as others. You can see some of the Neolithic remains found on the Yel-low River, Shang bronzes found in and around the city itself, and other ancient artifacts such as earthenware pots and ceramics from var-ious dynasties. ⊠ *Nongye Lu.* 🖼 *Y10.* ⊙ *Daily 8:30–noon and 2–5:30.*

Zhengzhou was the site of one of several important and bloody rail-way strikes that took place in the early 1920s. On February 7, 1923, striking railway workers halted the busy rail line to Wuhan, angering the regional strongman Wu Peifu as well as the British business com-munity in Wuhan. Wu ended the strike by ordering his troops to fire on a crowd of demonstrators and then publicly executing the strike leaders. Fifty-two people were killed, over 300 wounded, and over 1,000 workers were fired. The event shook the confidence of the two-year-old Chinese Communist Party and put a damper on the burgeoning Chinese labor movement for the next two years. This early Commu-nist martyrdom is commemorated in the **Er Qi Ta** (February 7th Pagoda), whose fresh colors and distinctive shape ornament a major traffic cir-cle a short way from the train station. Inside, documents and pictures concerning the strike and Communist history in Zhengzhou are on dis-play. ⊠ *Junction of Wenhua Lu, Renmin Lu, and Zhengguang Jie.* 🖼 *Y5.* ⊙ *Daily 8:30– noon and 2–5:30.*

A short ride from the city, the **Huang He Youlan Qu** (Yellow River Park) offers an impressive view of the river itself as well as a clean and re-laxing environment. Exhibits document the importance of the river as both the origin of ancient civilization and a major destructive force in recent times. Its flooding has claimed millions of lives over the years. Several dams now harness the river's power for hydroelectric use. To get to the park, catch a minibus from outside the train station or ask at your hotel travel or information desk about rides. ⊠ *30 km (19 mi) northwest of city.* 🖼 *Y10.* ⊙ *Daily 8:30–dusk.*

One of the lesser known attractions in this area, **Zhongyue Si** (Tem-ple of the Central Peak), stands amid beautiful mountains. Officially, it is the local Taoist temple, but China has a long tradition of inter-mingling religions. Like most temples of its kind, Zhongyue in fact bears as many Buddhist implications as Taoist ones: locals come to pray, and who they pray to is completely up to them. You can stop in on the way to or from Shaolin Monastery (☞ Shaolin Si, *below*). ⊠ *60 km (37 mi) southwest of town; accessible by minibus or hired car.* 🖼 *Y10.* ⊙ *Daily 8:30–dusk.*

If you like martial arts, you'll want to see where it started in China at ⟳ **Shaolin Si** (Shaolin Monastery). Chinese combat martial art is thought to have been invented here by Buddhist monks who needed some di-version from their meditation. Amid gorgeous hills checkered with large patches of farmed land, the site actually extends up and down a fairly long street, including far more than just the temple. The large temple has a bamboo grove surrounded by stone stelae and a pavilion illus-trated with scenes from the Confucian Classic of Filial Piety. Across the street, something resembling a wax museum portrays famous martial artists in various fighting positions and battle arrays. Children tend to enjoy this bit. The martial arts school at the temple often has performances and competitions, so you may get to see actual monks, and other students, showing off their skill. Farther up the hill, famous monks of the past are commemorated in the "Forest of Pagodas." ⊠ *70 km (43 mi) southwest of town; accessible by minibus or hired car.* ⊠ *Y40; one ticket buys entry to all sights.* ⊙ *Daily 8:30–5:30.*

Dining and Lodging

$$$$ ✕ **Huayuan.** Probably the best-dressed building in Zhengzhou—in terms of both architecture and clientele—this is the current hotspot for fashionable dining. The newly invented class of young, urban professionals flocks to see and be seen at the tastefully decorated restaurant and bar. Geared slightly toward Western customs, it has fewer banquet rooms and more opportunities for private dining and drinking than most upscale Chinese restaurants. ⊠ *Jinshui Lu, south side, between Chengdong Lu and Renmin Lu,* ☎ *0371/595–2541. Reservations essential. No credit cards.*

$$$$ ✕ **Yuexiu, or YX.** Zhengzhou's most famous restaurant, near several major international hotels, the YX is aware of its foreign clientele. It offers western classical music from a string quartet near the bar and lounge section, and from a small shop in back sells not only Chinese books but framed calligraphy scrolls that non-Chinese speakers can also enjoy. Unlike many restaurants of its status, which expect to serve banquets or at least groups of four or more, it reserves a section for people eating in pairs and even offers to accommodate solo diners, a rarity in China. Decorated in red—the color of luck and happiness—it serves up a tasty selection of some favorite Cantonese foods, including more daring specialties like snake gall. ⊠ *Jinshui Dong Lu, north side, between Jin 3 Lu and Jin 4 Lu,* ☎ *0371/594–8568,* FAX *0371/596–3526. No credit cards.*

$$$ ✕ **Tianlun.** Near Zijinshan Park, this large restaurant focuses on Chinese banquet-style dining. Its decor is not exciting; like most restaurants of its type it tends to be a little on the loud side, without much patience for after-dinner lingering (don't expect coffee and dessert). Nonetheless, it remains one of the best places around for seafood and Henan specialties made from the fresh water catches of the Yellow River. ⊠ *Jinshui Lu 111, south side, between Chengdong Lu and Renmin Lu,* ☎ *0371/597–6880. No credit cards.*

$$$ ✕ **Yangguang.** This restaurant specializes in delicious Fujien dishes from the south of China. ⊠ *Huayuan Lu 17,* ☎ *0371/594–2579. No credit cards.*

$$$$ ▥ **Holiday Inn Crowne Plaza.** At the edge of Zhengzhou's restaurant row, set back from the street behind a tall fountain, this appealing hotel provides everything you would need during a stay in Zhengzhou. The Shang Palace restaurant on the first floor tends toward formality and serves a variety of excellent Chinese dishes in a tasteful and quiet environment. Mama Mia's Pizzeria claims actual American-style oven-baked pizzas, and the downstairs Patisserie serves fine coffee and a variety of cakes and cookies. Geared toward foreign business travelers, the hotel has a friendly staff whose English tends to be quite good. ⊠ *Jinshui Lu 115, 450003,* ☎ *0371/595–0055,* FAX *0371/599–0770. 150 rooms and suites. Restaurant, bar, pool, health club, nightclub, business services, meeting rooms, travel services. AE, MC, V.*

$$$ ▥ **Asia Hotel.** Walk out the door and see the February 7th Pagoda. This hotel has an excellent location if you plan to do much sightseeing outside Zhengzhou: it's close to the train and long-distance bus stations.

The facilities in the hotel are excellent and the staff is very helpful. Each room comes with satellite TV, IDD telephone, and a minibar. ⊠ *Jiefang Xi Lu 165,* ☎ *0371/696–8866,* FAX *0371/696–9877. 145 rooms, 15 suites. 3 restaurants, bar, food court, beauty salon, sauna, health club, billiards, dance club, business services, meeting room. AE, MC, V.*

$$$ 🏨 **Hai Tian Hotel.** Occupying most of a high-rise off Jinshui Lu, this hotel has great service and an enjoyable indoor environment even though the street outside is not the most attractive. The rooms are very light. A major travel service has its offices on two floors of the building. ⊠ *Chengdong Bei Lu, Section 288,* ☎ *0371/595–9988,* FAX *0371/ 596–1603. 40 rooms, 8 suites. Restaurant, bar, beauty salon, business services, meeting room. AE, MC, V.*

$$$ 🏨 **International Hotel Zhengzhou.** A bit bland on the outside, the International Hotel is part of the Novotel group. Its restaurants, one Chinese and one western, are quite nice, if lacking in character. Each room comes with IDD telephone, satellite TV, and a minibar. A new wing, opened in 1997, houses 215 rooms and 32 suites, two restaurants, a nightclub, a bar, a swimming pool, and a health club. ⊠ *Jinshui Lu 114, 450003,* ☎ *0371/595–6600,* FAX *0371/595–1526. 241 rooms, 9 suites. 2 restaurants, bar, business services, travel services. AE, MC, V.*

$$ 🏨 **Friendship Hotel.** The best buy for budget travelers, the Friendship offers few outstanding facilities but has good service at a good price. It's a few blocks north of the February 7th Pagoda. ⊠ *Jinshui Lu 97,* ☎ *0371/622–8807. 120 rooms and suites. 2 restaurants, bar, beauty salon, sauna, shops, business services. AE, DC, MC, V.*

$$ 🏨 **Golden Sunshine Hotel.** This hotel has business class tourists in mind. Directly north of the railway station, it makes up for its distance from most restaurants by offering a western kitchen as well as an excellent Chinese restaurant that prepares specialties from various regions. Each room comes with IDD telephone and television. ⊠ *Erma Lu 6,* ☎ *0371/ 696–9999,* FAX *0371/871–2921. 400 rooms and suites. 2 restaurants, bar, beauty salon, billiards, business services. AE, MC, V.*

$$ 🏨 **Greenland Hotel.** This long-established hotel stands next door to the railway station. A joint venture that places particular emphasis on customer service, it is well furnished and offers a variety of rooms and suites. The revolving restaurant on the 32nd floor has probably the best view you can get of Zhengzhou. ⊠ *Datong Lu 93,* ☎ *0371/696–8888. 510 rooms and suites. 2 restaurants, beauty salon, business services, meeting room. AE, V.*

$$ 🏨 **Henan Province Henan Hotel.** Tending toward monumental Soviet style, this is a clean building with minimal facilities. It is a better buy if you are traveling with several people; the cost of singles here is on a par with the rates of other moderately priced hotels. There is no western restaurant. ⊠ *Jinshui Lu 26,* ☎ *0371/394–3117,* FAX *0371/394– 4619. 500 rooms. 2 restaurants. No credit cards.*

Nightlife

In Zhengzhou the few bars that spring up now and then tend to have a short and uncertain lifespan. By far the most promising venue is the easy-going **Richmond Brewery** (⊠ Jinshui Lu 111); its Western-style bar has 24 varieties of imported beer on tap in a clean, spacious setting.

Shopping

Zhengzhou has several night markets where the local Muslims set up food stands and local merchants peddle wares. You can find anything from baby clothes to the most recent publications here, but the main attraction is usually the people. The **Erqi Area Nightmarket** (⊠ along the small side streets off Minzhu Lu, 1 block west of Erqi Lu) starts doing business around 7 PM and keeps going until the crowd gets tired—usually around 10 PM.

The best shopping for regional crafts and reproductions of famous archaeological finds can be found at the sights outside Zhengzhou. The local **Friendship Store** (⊠ Erqi Bei Lu 96 ☎ 0371/622–6110) sells prints and antiques. The **Henan Museum Shop** (⊠ Nongye Lu, in the Henan Provincial Museum, no phone) sells local art, reproductions of its own exhibits, carved jewelry, and the like. **Shaolin Monastery** (☞ Shaolin Si, *above*) is surrounded by stands selling everything from art reproductions to little martial arts figurines. The **Zhengzhou Friendship Department Store** (⊠ Main Building, Zhenxing Shopping Center, Yi Malu, ☎ 0371/696–3360) has prints and antiques.

Side Trip from Zhengzhou

Once the capital of the Song dynasty, **Kaifeng,** east of Zhengzhou, was abandoned by the court in the 12th century when northern invaders forced the Song south to Hangzhou. Amazingly, it has managed to retain many of its attractions, as well as large chunks of its city wall, without having been turned into a heavy industrial center or a tourist trap. It's a relatively quiet, friendly city that has preserved its neighborhood feel. The Muslim population has a strong influence in the city, and two brand-new mosques in white and green tile, complete with Middle Eastern onion domes, have been built in the last few years. Older, Chinese-style mosques, as well as Buddhist temples, dot the side streets. The Muslims also run one of the busiest food and wares markets.

The city's most famous sight stands near Tieta Hu (Tieta Lake). The **Tie Ta** (Iron Pagoda) is not made of iron but of brick covered with tiles that look like iron. You can climb to the top on a narrow, pitch-black staircase that leads to several small windows. You can also see the lake and wander around the pretty surroundings. ⊠ *Northeast corner of town, near No. 3 bus terminus.* 🎫 *Pagoda, Y5.* ☼ *Daylight hours.*

☙ **Longting Gongyuan** (Dragon Pavilion Park), Kaifeng's major park, includes three lakes and a pavilion. It is a favorite family outing spot. ⊠ *North end of Zhongshan Lu.* 🎫 *Y10.*

The **Xiangguo Si** (Xiangguo Temple), originally built in the 6th century, was most recently rebuilt in the 18th century. It houses some old artifacts. A food and souvenirs market has sprung up around it. ⊠ *Ziyou Lu.* 🎫 *Y5.* ☼ *Daily 8–5.*

Near the middle of town, the **Yangqing Guan** (Yangqing Taoist Temple) is a two-story structure with a strikingly ornate exterior around an unusually bare interior. A shop displays some calligraphy scrolls. ⊠ *Off Yingbin Lu.* 🎫 *Y10.* ☼ *Daily 8:30- -5:30.*

Luoyang

❹ *3½ hours by train west of Zhengzhou, 7 hours by train northeast of Xian.*

First established by the Zhou in the 12th century BC, Luoyang became the dynastic capital in 771 BC. Although well known as one of the "ancient capitals," Luoyang became more important for its religious and artistic history. Not only did it serve as capital to ten successive dynasties, it also welcomed and built a temple for the first monk to bring Buddhism to the Middle Kingdom. Under instructions from the emperor of the Northern Wei dynasty, cave temples were constructed slightly south of the city. These temples are now regarded as some of the most important monuments to Buddhist art. Buddhism's incorporation into indigenous beliefs and everyday lives was so complete that even restrictions and periodic purges by various dynasties as well as by modern governments have not kept people from praying to the arhats. In fact, with increased government openness—fueled perhaps partly by a desire to attract tourists, particularly those from Taiwan, Hong Kong, and Singapore—Buddhism seems to be on the rise again today.

The art that Buddhism fostered once adorned Luoyang's many temples and monasteries, but the city reached its cultural apex centuries ago, and for hundreds of years its symbolic importance as a name associated with religious and dynastic powers carried more weight than the fact of its existence. Nowadays it is a growing industrial center; the city itself holds few important sights. You'll need about a day to see the chief places of interest around Luoyang. If you can get here in April, you should give yourself an afternoon to see the blooming peonies that are Luoyang's pride, second only to the Buddhist grottoes. All sights but Wangcheng Park lie outside the city proper.

Spring means peonies in Luoyang. Stroll through the peony show in **Wangcheng Gongyuan** (Park of the Royal Town) during the third week of April every year, when Luoyang is crowded with visitors from the region. Families come out to enjoy the sight and college students skip class and take the seven-hour train ride from Xian to participate. At other times of year, the park is a restful, if unremarkable, recreation area. It has a small zoo in the back, and a playground for kids; in winter, a small indoor rink has exhibits of ice lanterns. ⊠ *Just northwest of Yanan Lu and Wangcheng Lu, no phone.* 🚋 *Y1.* ☉ *Daily 8:30–dusk.*

The **Gumu Bowuguan** (Ancient Tombs Museum) stands north of the city atop Mangshan mountain, which was viewed as an auspicious site. The museum displays 22 of the thousands of ancient tombs found in the area. The underground tombs come from dynasties from the Han to the Song. ⊠ *4 km (2½ mi) north of city; tour or minibus.* 🚋 *Y15.* ☉ *Daily 8:30–5.*

East of town is the site of the original Buddhist temple. **Baima Si** (White Horse Temple)—named for the white horses believed to have carried the first scriptures from India to China—became a focal point for China's powerful fascination with this imported religion. The temple has been destroyed several times over, and the buildings we see now date from the Ming and Qing dynasties. Statues of white horses stand to either side behind the central hall as emblems of its origins. ⊠ *13 km (8 mi) east of city; accessible by minibus or hired car.* 🚋 *Y15.* ☉ *Daily 8:30–5.*

South of the city lies **Guanlin** (Grove of Guan), a large enclosure with tree-lined paths between its many prayer halls. Not far from the Dragon Gate Grottoes, it provides a peaceful setting for an afternoon walk as well as a glimpse of contemporary Buddhist practice. ⊠ *7.5 km (4½ mi) south of town; accessible by minibus or chartered car, no phone.* 🚋 *Y10.* ☉ *Daily 8:30–5.*

★ To the southeast, the **Longmen Shiku** (Dragon Gate Grottoes) are a tribute to Buddhism's immense force in the Chinese past. Carved during two successive dynasties over several centuries, these thousands of Buddhist figures are ranged along the mountainside overlooking the Luo river. Although some of the grottoes are labeled in English, you rarely get more than a dynasty name and an uninformative blurb. The Chinese blurbs are not much better. The atmosphere of the ruins is part artwork, part ruins—exposure to the elements has done its bit to wear away the intricacy of the work. The real damage was done by the English and other western enthusiasts who, in the 19th century, decided to take some of the artwork home with them. Many figures now stand headless, their faces decorating European museums or private collectors' shelves. At the end of the grottoes stands another tribute of sorts, a recently constructed **funhouse,** with a dragon mouth for a door and fiberglass caves, moving installations, and the obligatory roller-coaster track inside. You can visit the caves on your own or take one of numerous guided tours offered by CITS and the local hotels. ⊠ *16 km (10 mi) southeast of town; accessible by chartered car and buses Nos. 53, 60, and 81 and private minibuses with the same numbers.* 🎫 *Y25.* ⊙ *Daily 8:30–5.*

Dining and Lodging

$$ ✕ **Yaxiang Lou.** "Elegant Scent Restaurant" is one of the two dining options in Luoyang outside of the big hotels. It serves a variety of Chinese dishes. ⊠ *Xiyuan Lu,* ☎ *0379/492–3030. No credit cards.*

$$ ✕ **Zhen Butong.** The name means "Truly Different"; not surprisingly, it is the only restaurant around that specializes in real "Luoyang flavor." The house specialty is a "water banquet," named for the rapidity of each successive course, but perhaps also referring to the soupy sauces that each dish swims in. These include both spicy entrées and a soothing dessert that tastes something like a Middle Eastern version of rice pudding. You don't have to order a whole banquet to enjoy some of its component parts. ⊠ *Zhongzhou Dong Lu,* ☎ *0379/395–2338. No credit cards.*

$$$ 🏨 **Peony Hotel.** This joint-venture hotel lies a short walk from Wangcheng Park, where Luoyang's peony festival takes place. Its rooms are fresh, and its small restaurant serves fairly good western food as well as some excellent Chinese dishes. More than half of its guests are foreign tourists and business people. The staff is friendly, and the atmosphere is tasteful and quiet. ⊠ *Zhongzhou Xi Lu,* ☎ *0379/491– 3699. 194 rooms and suites. Restaurant, bar, recreation room, travel services. AE, MC, V.*

$$$ 🏨 **Peony Plaza.** This towering edifice opened with much pomp in the center of town. While it's obviously built to cater to business travelers and upscale tourists, it also offers some great weekend deals and tour prices. The building is light, clean, and well furnished, with a professional and energetic staff. ⊠ *Nanchang Lu 2, 471003,* ☎ *0379/493– 1111,* 📠 *0379/493–0303. 163 rooms and suites. 2 restaurants, 2 bars, food court, pool, health club, nightclub, recreation room, business services, convention center, meeting room, travel services. AE, MC, V.*

$$ 🏨 **Friendship Guesthouse.** A joint venture, it has tasteful amenities and a lovely courtyard out back whose artificial lake, curved bridge, and rock arrangement are inspired by the gardens of Suzhou. ⊠ *Xiyan Lu 6,* ☎ *0379/491–2780,* 📠 *0379/491–3808. 125 rooms and suites. 2 restaurants, food court, pool, beauty salon, sauna, business services, travel services. AE, MC, V.*

$$ 🏨 **New Friendship Hotel.** Don't be confused by the addresses— the New Friendship is in fact neighbor to the Guesthouse (☞ *above*). Not surprisingly, they quite resemble each other. This one's main attraction is the Suzhou-style garden out back, whose arched bridges, small pavilions, and peony blossoms outdo those at the Guesthouse. ⊠ *Xiyuan Lu 6,* ☎ *0379/491–9201,* 📠 *0379/491–9702. 168 rooms and suites. 2 restaurants, health club, nightclub, recreation room, travel services. AE, MC, V.*

Nightlife

Locals head to the outdoor market that springs up between Jinguyuan Lu and Kaixuan Lu and bustle around the shopping district on Zhongzhou Dong Lu in the old city. For dancing, drinking, and entertainment, you're best off staying in your hotel.

Shopping

The tricolor pottery associated with the Tang dynasty developed here. The lot in back of the Longmen Grottoes has many Tang-style figurines. The Ru ceramics of the Song dynasty are also local; the greenish glaze has a distinctive thick, opaque quality. Reproductions of these creations are sold at hotel shops and specialty stores. The **Friendship Store** (✉ Zhongzhou Zhong Lu, ☎ 0379/492–1795) carries local wares. The **Meitao Cheng** (✉ Wangcheng Lu, ☎ 0379/393–5941) carries regional products. **Wenwu Shandian** (✉ Zhongzhou Dong Lu) specializes in antiques, including calligraphy, pottery, and jewelry.

Henan A to Z

Arriving and Departing

BY BUS

Kaifeng: From the long-distance bus station (just south of Baogong Lake on Yingbin Lu; take No. 4, 6, 10, 12, or 13 bus) buses run to Zhengzhou every hour on the half-hour until 6:30 PM. Less frequent service is available to Luoyang. This is the most convenient way to get in and out of Kaifeng, as the train station is not computerized and cannot guarantee seats.

Luoyang: The bus station is right across from the train station and provides several daily buses to Zhengzhou, 3 hours away, and to Shaolin temple, about 1½ hours away.

Zhengzhou: The long-distance bus station is directly across from the train station (☞ By Train, *below*) and offers buses to just about everywhere in China. The best places to get to by bus are Luoyang and Kaifeng (departures every hour).

BY PLANE

Luoyang is not as convenient to reach by plane as Zhengzhou. There are flights to Xian on weekdays and to major cities several times a week. Book through the travel offices in the Peony Hotel or in the Friendship hotels, or through CAAC at the Luoyang Airport (✉ Daobei Lu, ☎ 0379/393–1120).

Zhengzhou airport is about 40 minutes' ride from town and offers daily flights to major Chinese cities. Tickets can be purchased at the central CAAC office (✉ Yima Lu 51, ☎ 0371/696–4789) or at CAAC outlets in the Greenland Hotel, Holiday Inn, the International Hotel, and the Henan Hotel.

BY TRAIN

Kaifeng is easily accessible by rail: any train going west out of Zhengzhou will pass through here. Getting out is harder: the train station can't guarantee seats, and the place is often crowded and unruly. Leaving Kaifeng, it's best to take a bus.

Luoyang is on the rail line between Xian (6–7 hours) and Zhengzhou (about 3 hours). Trains run often to and from these destinations. The double-decker "tourist trains" are the most comfortable option.

Zhengzhou is one of the best-connected cities in China, lying on the intersection of both north–south and east–west lines. You can buy tickets to most major Chinese cities. Foreigners are encouraged to go to ticket windows numbers 1 or 2; you can also go to the advance booking office (✉ Erqi Lu 193) to avoid the crowds. Some hotels will book tickets for you.

Getting Around

BY BUS

Kaifeng's bus system covers all points of interest in the city. The No. 4 bus goes from the effective center of town at Gulou to the long-distance bus station.

A number of buses run the route down **Luoyang**'s main drags, Zhongzhou Xi Lu and Zhongzhou Dong Lu; these are crowded at rush-hour but are otherwise not bad. Public buses go out to the Buddhist grottoes and to White Horse Temple, but private minibuses are usually more comfortable.

Zhengzhou is a rather sprawling metropolis, and buses are a convenient way of getting around it. Public buses do not run to the out-of-town sights, but you can catch minibuses at the train station, or ask at your hotel information desk—many hotels run their own services.

BY CAR

It may be convenient to hire a car for a tour of the sights surrounding Zhengzhou and Luoyang. Check with a major hotel for hiring information. Kaifeng is smaller and best handled by bus or on foot.

BY TAXI

Kaifeng's friendly drivers have red taxis and pedicabs. **Luoyang** has vans and four-doors that congregate mostly on Zhongzhou Lu, east and west. These are easy to flag down and aren't expensive. Unless you know how much a ride should cost, it is usually to your advantage to make sure the driver follows the meter, rather than agreeing on a price beforehand. Canary yellow minivans and dark red four-doors roam the streets of **Zhengzhou,** particularly around the hotel and restaurant strip of Jinshui Lu.

Contacts and Resources

EMERGENCIES

Luoyang: Police (have hotel contact precinct). Second People's Hospital of Luoyang (⊠ Zhongzhou Zhong Lu 288, ☎ 0379/393–8401). **Zhengzhou:** Police (have hotel contact precinct). Henan People's Hospital (⊠ Weiwu Lu, ☎ 0379/595–1553).

GUIDED TOURS

Kaifeng: Here, the sights are within the city proper and don't require minibus hauls out of town. You're best off just getting a map and exploring the sights on your own.

Luoyang: Hotels offer minibus service out to the Longmen Grottoes and White Horse Temple. Other guided tours of the area can be arranged with CITS and include Mangshan and the ancient tombs.

Zhengzhou: Most hotels offer their own buses to Shaolin Temple and the Yellow River, and some will create custom tours if you want to see more of what lies between Zhengzhou and Luoyang. There are no guided city tours.

TRAVEL AGENCIES

Kaifeng: CITS (⊠ Yingbin Lu 14, ☎ 0378/595–5131). **Luoyang: CITS** (⊠ Zhongzhou Xi Lu 26, ☎ 0379/492–3467 or 491–3091). **The Peony Hotel** (⊠ Zhongzhou Xi Lu, ☎ 0379/491–3699). **Zhengzhou:** It's best to stick with the hotel travel agencies— every major hotel has one. **The Haitian Hotel** (⊠ 288 Chengdong Lu Bei Duan, 8th floor, ☎ 0379/595–9988). **CITS** (⊠ 15 Jinshui Lu, ☎ 0379/595–1134, 0379/595–4305).

VISITOR INFORMATION

CITS (☞ Travel Agencies, *above*). Hotels are the best source of visitor information in all three cities.

ANHUI

The last two centuries have not been kind to Anhui, but with increasing control over the Yellow River and growing industrial production, the province seems to be pulling itself up. In 1850, the Yellow River flooded and changed course, causing major famine and destruction, and widespread disenchantment led to peasant revolts. The revolts, put down by imperial forces, led to further famine and destruction. In 1938, the province suffered another flood, this one caused by its own military forces. Despite their efforts to cut off the Japanese advance, Anhui was occupied by the invading troops during World War II, before the Guomindang re-occupied it in 1946. Until the Communists took it in 1949, Anhui was considered the most backward province in Eastern China.

The Yangzi River runs from Nanjing west through the southern half of Anhui, and the province's best sights are defined by this natural boundary. Between the river and Anhui's southern border lies one of China's most famous mountain ranges. In the popular consciousness, Huangshan is one of the five great mountains of China. These mountains undeniably present some of the most spectacular scenery in the country, and perhaps in the world. Anhui is not well known for cultural, historic, or scenic spots; but the mountains have drawn a steady influx of visitors for hundreds of years, from Tang dynasty emperors to modern families on vacation.

Hefei

㊷ *450 km (280 mi) southeast of Zhengzhou; 5½ hours by train (3½ hours by car) west of Nanjing.*

For a provincial capital, Hefei is surprisingly clean and calm. On warm spring days, families picnic at the city fountains and kids take a bumper car ride and go for an ice cream cone at a nearby park. The park that forms a ring around the center of the city has no gates and no closing hours, and couples stroll on its darkened paths long into the night. There is something less anxious and less polluted about Hefei than about many other cities its size. It's a fine place to break up a longer journey or to end up in for business reasons. What historical importance Hefei has held has been mainly administrative; it was the site of a small ancient state and the capital of a Tang prefecture, but never a great cultural center. Before World War II, it was a trade center, and since the 1930s it has steadily increased its industrial output. From the mid-1930s to the mid-1950s, the city's population increased 10 times. It became the capital of Anhui in 1949.

Both the most frustrating and the most pleasing aspect of Hefei is its total lack of tourist culture—most people come for business and few are foreign. Few hotels are allowed to accept foreigners, and there is no central tourist agency. No particularly intriguing restaurants exist outside of the major hotels. On the other hand, it is precisely this unprepared quality that gives Hefei its small-city charm.

The best thing to do in Hefei, especially in early spring or in autumn, is to take relaxing walks around the **ring of parks** at the city's center. The grass is unusually lush and the plum blossoms start blooming in March. The long park is broken up by roads passing through town; each section has its own pond with various fairly new and attractive architectural structures like small pagodas, pavilions set out on the pond, and an old-fashioned steeply arched bridge.

🐦 The eastern end of **Yuhua** (Yuhua Pond) has a playground with bumper car rides, an ice cream vendor, and chairs for relaxing adults. It's a nice place to pass the afternoon if you have children with you. ✉ *Jinzhai Lu.*

Baohebin Gongyuan (Baohebin Park ✉ Y5. ☉ Daily 8:30–5), in the southeast part of the ring, holds a pretty temple and several small tombs. **Xiaoyaojin Gongyuan** (Xiaoyaojin Park), **Heichi** (Heichi Pond), and **Xinghua Gongyuan** (Xinghua Park) make up the rest of the ring, but aside from the roads and bridges separating them, there are no distinguishing marks.

Dining and Lodging

$$ ✕ **Jiu Jiu Long Restaurant.** Not exactly the fanciest or best-decorated place you could imagine, this all-you-can-eat hot pot restaurant provides a more active eating style than most. Each table is outfitted with a gas burner and a pot with boiling water, and for a very reasonable price each customer is provided with a plate on which to load a variety of seafood, shellfish, meats, vegetables, noodles, and so on. For more saucy foods, there is also a small buffet. ✉ *Jinzhai Lu 327,* ☎ *0551/ 281–5868. No credit cards.*

$$$ 🏨 **Anhui Hotel.** Hefei's best-appointed hotel caters to business travelers and government officials as well as to tourists. The high-rise opens out onto the park and has excellent service and fully modern facilities. ✉ *Meishan Lu 18, 230022,* ☎ *0551/281–1818,* FAX *0551/282–2581. 320 rooms and suites. 2 restaurants, beauty salon, health club, dance club, recreation room, business services, meeting rooms. AE, MC, V.*

$$$ 🏨 **Anhui Overseas Chinese Hotel.** This three-building complex near the center of town contains a range of room types and prices. Half of the hotel is expensive, while the other half is moderate. Suites come with musical entertainment facilities and television. The various kitchens cook specialties of Anhui province as well as Huaiyang, Sichuan, Guangdong, Beijing, and western foods. ✉ *Changjiang Lu 98,* ☎ *0551/265–2221,* FAX *0551/264–2861. 268 rooms and suites. 14 restaurants, bar, beauty salon, health club, business services, travel services. AE, MC, V.*

$$ 🏨 **Meishan Guest House.** "Guest house" is an odd term for this hotel whose numerous buildings cover more than 7 acres of land. On a little side street across a waterway from one of the city parks, and set back from the road as it is, it promises a quiet stay. Restaurants inside the complex serve foods in a variety of Chinese styles, including several ethnic minority specialties. ✉ *Yi Huan Lu, off Meishan Lu,* ☎ *0551/281–3355,* FAX *0551/281–6584. 149 rooms, 2 suites, 4 villas. 3 restaurants, health club, business services. AE, MC, V.*

Shopping

The **Anhui Antiques Shop** (✉ Renmin Lu 57, East Building, ☎ 0551/ 265–5989) has a limited selection. The local **Department Store** (✉ Changjiang Lu 124, ☎ 0551/265–3261) offers a small choice of goods. You can restock on English books at the **Foreign Languages Bookstore** (✉ Yimin Jie 29, ☎ 0551/265–8392).

Side Trips from Hefei

★ By far the most important attraction in Anhui is **Huangshan** (Huang Mountain). A favorite retreat of emperors and poets of old, its peaks have inspired some of China's most outstanding artworks and literary endeavors. They were so beguiling, in fact, that years of labor went into their paths, which are actual stone steps rising up—sometimes gradually into the forest, sometimes sharply through a stone tunnel and into the mist above. The mountain is known particularly for three common sights. The "grotesque pines" are cliffside trees growing into the wind to end up twisted and knotted. The "unusual rock formations" come in animal shapes: thus a rock might be named rooster or rabbit. And the "sea of mist" that sweeps in and out of the upper reaches of the peaks lends the mountain its almost cinematically meaningful aura. What you really should see, though, is the sunrise from the top of the mountain. Hundreds of people gather to observe the stunning sight before walking sleepily back down for some breakfast.

Getting to Huangshan takes a bit of planning. The town at the base of the mountain, Tangkou, is not on a rail line; the best you can do is either take a bus directly here or catch a train to Tunxi, from which you can get a local bus into town. Although Huangshan is in Anhui, it actually lies farther from Hefei than from Hangzhou in neighboring Zhejiang province. A bus route from Hangzhou to Tangkou follows mountain passes to reveal a patchwork of small, sloping, graded fields traversed by thin irrigation canals. You'll get a glimpse of peasant life in the hills as you pass small-time farmers dipping long-handled wooden ladles into the canals to water their crops, or working with sickles and other hand tools to set their lands in order. Alternatively, you could get to Huangshan by bus from Wuhu or Guichi, towns on the Yangzi River at which the Wuhan-Shanghai ferry stops. (☞ Side Trips *in* Hubei, *above.*)

The stone steps of the pathways can be wearying on the legs. The whole way usually leads you from the Eastern Gate up the Eastern Steps, around the top of the range and down the Western Steps. The other way around, although equally and differently beautiful, is recommended only for the most stalwart and aerobically fit: the Western Steps are considerably longer and steeper than the Eastern. If you want the beauty without the pain, just past the Eastern Gate a cable car takes you almost all the way to the top of the mountain. Halfway down the Western Steps, another cable car station opened recently to take you down to the Western Gate. From either of these gates you can catch a minivan or bus down to the Main Gate in Tangkou. If you are planning to do the entire mountain in one day, it's best to take at least one cable car to make sure you have time. However, if you are staying at a hotel near the mountain top, you might have time to walk both.

DINING AND LODGING

Reservations are essential for any hotel in the Huangshan area, as this is one of China's major tourist spots. Food in the area tends to be less than amazing; after a day of hard climbing and breathtaking scenery, you probably won't care.

$$$$ ☷ **Xihai Hotel.** This joint venture is ideally located at the top of the mountain, providing a convenient location for sunrise watching as well as for comfortable living. It is not a luxury hotel, but it is one of the two best lodgings around. ☎ *0559/256–2132. Restaurant, bar. AE, MC, V.*

$$$ ☷ **Beihai Hotel.** This is the other mountain-top hotel that accepts foreigners. Less well-appointed than the Xihai, and less expensive, it still provides the amenities you'd need for a one- or two-day stay. ☎ *0559/ 556–2558. Restaurant, bar. AE, MC, V.*

$$ ☷ **Peach Blossom Hotel.** A winding road takes you over a bridge, past a waterfall to this enchanted-looking resort between the Main Gate of the mountain park and the beginning of the Western Steps. The Peach Blossom has the best food (both Chinese and western) of the three mountain hotels. You'll have to hustle to catch the sunrise if you stay here, but the hot springs next door are great to come back to after a day of hiking. ☎ *0559/556–2666. Restaurant, bar. AE, MC, V.*

Anhui A to Z

Arriving and Departing

BY BUS

Buses are the fastest way to get to **Hefei** from Nanjing. Coaches go between the cities about four times a day and take only three and a half hours; however, not all of these are air-conditioned travel vehicles, and they can be crowded and bumpy.

As the mountain town of **Huangshan** itself has no railway station, you'll have to take a bus, either from Tunxi or from some point farther off. Although buses from Hangzhou (9 hours) and Hefei (11 hours) go through some gorgeous scenery, they often do not provide the most comfortable ride. You can try going to or from Hangzhou by bus and traveling the other direction by train or plane—the views really are worth the ride.

BY PLANE

The **Hefei** airport has daily flights to major cities; it also has daily flights to Tunxi, from which you can catch a minibus to Huangshan. There are twice-weekly flights to Xian and Hong Kong. You can book flights at most major hotels, or at China Eastern Airlines (✉ Jinzhai Lu 246, ☎ 0559/282–2357).

Huangshan's airport at Tunxi has daily flights to Hefei, as well as flights to Beijing and Guangzhou several times a week, Shanghai almost daily, Xian once a week, and Hong Kong twice a week. It's best to buy tickets at your hotel, or in advance at your starting point.

BY TRAIN

The train tracks between Nanjing and **Hefei** sweep through upper Anhui before descending south to Hefei, adding a good 2 hours onto what, by highway, is a 3½-hour ride. There is only one train a day from Nanjing to Hefei. Hefei is also connected to Beijing, Chengdu, and Xiamen; the direct connection to Zhengzhou passes through Kaifeng. Sleeper tickets can be purchased in the ticket office east of the train station at window number 2.

Trains to **Huangshan** stop in Tunxi from where you can catch a minivan or cab to the Huangshan gates. The ride takes about an hour. It's best to arrive early in the day as many drivers are not eager to traverse the winding road in the dark, although they will for about Y100.

Getting Around

BY BUS AND TAXI

In **Hefei,** the most useful buses are the No. 1, which passes through the center of town, and the No. 10, which travels just south of the southern parks and passes most of the foreign hotels. Both of these terminate at the train station (☞ By Train, *above*). Otherwise, taxis are readily available and easily flagged down on the streets or at the numerous taxi stops designated on each major road.

Minibuses and taxis from Tunxi to Tangkou congregate around the train station and will take you to the **Huangshan** main gates at the bottom of the mountain or up to the actual entrance to the climbing section.

Contacts and Resources

EMERGENCIES

Anhui Medical University Affiliated Hospital No. 1 (✉ Jixi Lu 218, Hefei, ☎ 0559/363–6474).

GUIDED TOURS

As you approach the main gates of Huangshan, street-side peddlers will offer you guided tours of the area, including transportation to various gates. These are usually reasonably priced; however, the guides' English tends to be minimal. You are usually better off just buying a map and hiring a taxi or taking a minibus up to the East Gate. At the Tunxi train station, you will also be offered day-tours, sometimes complete with meals—usually not very tasty—and hotel accommodations. Unless your Chinese is good enough to set the terms, it's not worth it.

TRAVEL AGENCIES
Aside from hotel information desks, there are no travel agencies in Hefei or in Huangshan. It's best to plan from an agency in Nanjing or other major city.

VISITOR INFORMATION
Hotels are the primary source of information in this region.

6 Guangzhou

During the 19th century the only place westerners were allowed to visit in China was Canton, where they traded for silk, tea, porcelain, lacquer screens, lace shawls, ivory fans, and other chinoiserie. Since the late 1970s, this port city, now known as Guangzhou, has again become a gateway for the West, to do business, recall a shared experience, sample Cantonese food in its homeland, and shop for those familiar treasures.

RIGHT PLACE, RIGHT TIME would be a far more apt slogan for Guangzhou than its rather tame promotional name, City of the Rams, because for the better part of the last 2,000 years it has prospered—and at times survived—thanks to what we now call an ideal location.

By Shann
Davies

It all began with the Silk Road, when some merchants chose to take their caravans south and transport their silk and other luxuries by sea through the sheltered port of Guangzhou. From southeast Asia, more merchants came to do business, selling pepper, nutmeg and other spices, bird's nests for soup, and aromatic sandalwood for incense. Gradually they were joined by traders from farther afield. It is recorded that merchants from Ancient Rome arrived to buy silk—at semi-annual fairs that foreshadowed today's Canton Fair—during the Han dynasty (206 BC–AD 220), but it was the Arabs who came to dominate trade between East and West. In the 7th century they introduced Islam to Guangzhou, where they built China's first mosque.

The Cantonese talent and enthusiasm for business was as keen then as now, so the city's inhabitants welcomed the Portuguese explorer-merchants who arrived in the 16th century looking for a trading post. At the time, the Ming court in Beijing banned all foreign trade, but, as the saying went, the emperor was far away. On their own initiative, the local mandarins allowed the Portuguese to settle in Macau, to act as entrepreneurs for their trade with Japan and the West.

Dominated by Japanese silver; Chinese silk, porcelain, and tea; Indian muslin; Persian damascene; African ivory; and European manufactures, this trade flourished for a century, until Japan closed its doors to the outside world. The Portuguese lost their sealanes and cargoes to the newly mercantile nations of Europe, led by Britain, which used Macau as a base for doing business in Guangzhou. The British called Guangzhou Canton, an anglicized version of the Portuguese Cantão.

From the late 18th century western merchants set up trading houses in Guangzhou where they negotiated the purchase of tea. The beverage became so important to Britain that the British East India Company had to find an import to match it in value. The problem was that China didn't want more European manufactures or woolen cloth, but there was a market for opium. The British colonial government took control of the Bengal opium market, and private British companies were soon making fortunes from the opium trade.

The Chinese authorities tried to stop it and in 1839 engaged in the brief Opium War, with naval battles in the Zhujiang (Pearl River) estuary. Defeated, they were forced to cede the island of Hong Kong to Britain and open treaty ports like Shanghai to foreign trade and influence.

Guangzhou lost its pivotal importance as an international trading hub and went into decline. Times were tough for many Cantonese, but now they knew about the outside world, and in the 19th century tens of thousands of them left in search of a better life, often in coolie ships. Among the scholars who found an education overseas was Dr. Sun Yat-sen, who was born a few miles north of the Macau border. He led the movement to overthrow the Manchus that culminated in the 1911 Revolution.

Guangzhou next became a hotbed of revolutionary zeal and a battle-ground between Nationalists and Communists. Chiang Kai-shek founded the Whampoa Academy and Mao Zedong taught at the Peasant Movement Institute, as did Zhou Enlai.

Following the 1949 Revolution, Guangzhou re-instituted the bi-annual trade fairs (April and September) and welcomed foreign business, but it wasn't until the Open Door policy of Deng Xiaoping in 1979 that the port city was able to resume its role as a commercial gateway to China. Since then the city has become an economic dynamo; in 1995 it had an urban population of 6.5 million. The city is currently growing up, down, and sideways, with some of Asia's tallest skyscrapers, a new metro, a second railway terminal, a modern sea terminal, and new suburbs that extend along new expressways in all directions.

Pleasures and Pastimes

Cantonese Opera

There was a form of Chinese opera as early as the mid-16th century, as can be seen from the superb Wanfutai (Ten Thousand Blessings) stage in Foshan's Taoist temple. Built in 1658, it is the oldest surviving wooden stage in China. In the early 18th century, one of the great men of Chinese theater, Master Zhang, moved to Foshan from the capital and set about establishing a distinctive Cantonese operatic tradition, which eventually led to the replacement of Mandarin by the local dialect.

In the north Peking opera was very much an aristocratic entertainment, but in the south opera became popular with everyone. The merchant class, which had grown rich from international trade, provided valuable patronage of the art. Operatic performances became an integral part of all major festivals, such as the Feast of the Hungry Ghosts, feasts honoring the seafarer's goddess, Tin Hau, and the Lunar New Year.

For these special occasions temporary stages were set up, with bamboo boards and roofs of rattan matting, in temple courtyards and village squares. Everybody came to watch and listen to stories based on well-known myths and legends. The troupes consisted of about 40 players, including six principals, acrobats, and martial arts experts. There were no scripts, only numbers to indicate the kind of action and music needed, and very little rehearsal for performances that typically consisted of 40 or 50 acts.

The performers belonged to acting families, learning from example and tradition the complex rules that governed everything that happened on stage. Each movement was prescribed: trembling arms indicated fear, an outstretched palm in front of the face meant tears. The music, often adapted from folk melodies, was sung according to the role—many tunes were used, with different words, for a wide variety of operas—with actors frequently using shrill falsetto to make themselves heard from stages in busy market squares.

Everyone in the audience knew the plots, which could be episodes from classics such as *Journey to the West, The Romance of Three Kingdoms, Dream of the Red Chamber,* or any of the action-packed epics of the Qing era. It wasn't *what* was being sung but *how* that mattered, so actors and actresses had to put all their energy and inspiration into a performance without breaking any traditional rules. This helped make Cantonese opera more exuberant and vital than the northern variety, a major reason why, unlike Peking opera, it continues to flourish in the modern age. It was also more flexible. In the latter part of the 19th century, for instance, writers would adapt plots to include subtle criticism of the Manchu government, while in this century there have been experiments using western instruments to augment the traditional gongs, drums, clappers, fiddles, and various kinds of lute.

Cantonese audiences remain dedicated, as can be seen at regular evening opera performances in Guangzhou's Culture Park. For the uninitiated, however, the art form needs some preparation. The music sounds cacophonous to western ears, and the stylized movements are strange until you accept them as in a ballet. The costumes are brilliant, with silk robes embroidered, sequined, or covered with glittering beads, while headdresses have jeweled crowns, pompoms, or long feathers. Makeup is equally exotic, with colors to emphasize the character of the role. White means sinister, green is cruel, and black obedient; yellow stands for nobility and purple for royalty.

Sets are very basic and stage props simple: an actor striding behind two banners shows he's in a carriage, a player with a lantern indicates that it's night. Large fans are used to tell the audience that a character is commanding an army, inviting a lover, or hiding from an enemy. It's very much up to the players to hold the stage, especially as a Cantonese audience doesn't like to sit in rapt attention, preferring to stroll around, chat with friends, and take a snack. Visitors are welcome to do the same.

Dining

Few foreigners really appreciate the incredible diversity and ingenuity of Cantonese cuisine, which has developed from both abundance and scarcity. Guangdong Province has some of the most fertile land in China, thanks to silt brought down by the Pearl River into its extensive delta. Here you have two crops of rice a year, vegetables of every kind—including European varieties introduced by the Portuguese from Macau—orchards of litchi, oranges, and other fruit; chicken farms; duck ponds; and tropical waters rich in dozens of kinds of fish and seafood.

Cantonese chefs over the years learned to prepare these ingredients in the most satisfactory ways. Fresh fish needs steaming; meats are barbecued and roasted; vegetables are stir-fried; seafood is steamed or cooked in casseroles; suckling pigs are roasted on a spit with a glaze of honey, plum, and soy. Then to bring out the individual flavors, various sauces were devised, from black beans, garlic, oysters, and lobsters to lemon, plum, and soy. Meanwhile, another tradition grew up, in poverty-stricken regions where poor soil and rapacious landlords forced the people to eat whatever was edible. This included fungi and mushrooms, bamboo shoots and tree bark, seaweed and sea cucumbers, as well as any creature found in the forest.

With the most varied cuisine in the world, in Guangzhou eating is everyone's favorite activity and restaurants are prime hubs of society. It is possible to have a Cantonese meal for 2 or 4 people, but ideally you need 12 or at least 8, so that everyone can share the traditional 8 to 10 courses. The table is never empty, from the beginning courses of pickles, peanuts, and cold cuts to the fresh fruit that signals the end of the meal. In between you'll have mounds of steamed green vegetables (known rather vaguely as Chinese cabbage, spinach, and kale), braised or minced pigeon, bean curd steamed or fried, luscious shrimp, mushrooms in countless forms, bird's nest or egg drop soup, fragrant pork or beef, and a large fish steamed in herbs, all accompanied by steamed rice, beer, soft drinks, and tea.

Although Cantonese restaurants predominate in Guangzhou, the city also offers excellent opportunities to enjoy the other great dining tradition from Guangdong Province, **Chiu Chow cuisine**, better known as Chaozhou in China. It originated in the area around Shantou (formerly Swatow) on the coast east of Guangzhou and has been introduced to Chinatowns around the world by Chiu Chow people, who make up the largest number of overseas Chinese.

Like the Cantonese, Chiu Chow cooks can take advantage of bountiful supplies of fish and seafood but have far fewer resources on land that is mostly arid. As a result farms are devoted to vegetables—which are served salted and pickled—and livestock, particularly chickens and lion-head geese, which average 26 pounds and stand 4 ft or more tall. These birds have been bred and treasured in the region for centuries, producing feathers, down, and a most delectable meat that is fried in goose blood and served cold with a sauce of vinegar and chopped garlic.

Many Chiu Chow dishes are fried, including such favorites as chicken wings stuffed with glutinous rice, shrimps, chopped mushrooms and chestnuts, served with tangerine oil; *xinxing* beef balls, combining beef, shrimp, and fish; and milk mixed with corn flour and fruit. The Chiu Chow also like to combine sweet and salty tastes, for instance wrapping the yolk of a salted duck egg with sweetened rice in thin sheets of bean curd; or cooking goose with pepper, aniseed, tangerine peel, licorice root, sugar, ginger, and mango, and serving it with garlic and vinegar.

As tangerine bushes grow well here, the fruit is a staple for flavoring. The name was given to the little oranges after they were discovered by the Portuguese in Macau and transplanted to Tangiers.

No account of Chiu Chow cuisine would be complete without a mention of Iron Buddha tea, also known as *kungfu* tea because of its strength. The Oolong is brewed three times in an elaborate ceremony and served in tiny white bowls. It is tossed back in one gulp for the full mule-kick effect.

Least known of the cuisines found in Guangdong is Hakka, which was brought from the north in the 13th century by migrating Hakka people. They are of frugal peasant stock and their cooking utilizes preserved vegetables and every part of an animal. Their most popular dish is salt-baked chicken. The bird, including all its insides, is wrapped in rice paper and cooked in rock salt, to produce golden brown, tender meat, crunchy intestines and moist liver. It is served with ginger and scallion or sesame sauce.

Other favorite dishes are stewed pork with preserved cabbage—a kind of Chinese sauerkraut—steamed beancurd with minced pork; deep-fried intestine stuffed with shrimp paste; pig's brain with wine sauce; and pig's tripe and bone marrow soup. To end the meal, Hakka fried noodles are served, dipped into a bowl of sugar before eating.

CATEGORY	COST*
$$$	over $37
$$	$18–$37
$	under $18

per person for a three–course Western or six–course Chinese meal, excluding drinks and 15% service

Golf
The development of first-class golf courses has given the Pearl River Delta a new appeal as rapid industrialization has erased the area's more traditional attractions. The first clubs were built by and for golfers, but their success has given developers visions of big profits from corporate memberships. How many will achieve this remains to be seen, but for now there is a wide choice of clubs that welcome guests and members of affiliated clubs.

Lodging
Superlatives are well deserved when describing the hotels of Guangzhou. Here you'll find China's tallest hotel (GITIC Plaza), the hotel that consistently tops the list of the most profitable business ventures in the country. The words "opulent," "sumptuous," and "no expense spared" apply

equally to the White Swan and Garden hotels, while the Victory on Shamian Island recalls a bygone colonial era. All hotels have business services and excellent telecommunications, and many have health clubs and evening entertainment. Unfortunately, the standard of English is not very high among hotel staff, although some are now employing native English speakers at their front desks.

Guangzhou is overbuilt with hotels, so there are very substantial discounts on published rates, perhaps 30%–40%, especially on weekends, *except* during trade fairs when prices are double or more the regular rates. Even so the elevated rates can be maintained only for the first few days of a two-week fair, and some gentle bargaining usually gets results.

CATEGORY	COST*
$$$	over $80
$$	$40–$80
$	under $40

per standard double room, excluding tax

EXPLORING GUANGZHOU

Because of its rapid modernization during the 1980s and '90s, many parts of Guangzhou no longer evoke the once easygoing port city with its waterfront row of colonial mansions, streets lined with China coast shophouses, verdant parks, and skyline dominated by a 7th-century minaret, a 10th-century pagoda, and a Ming dynasty tower. Today highrise blocks and new highways dominate the old town, while new suburbs advance toward every horizon, bristling with skyscrapers and shopping malls. Fortunately the city has preserved some of its heritage in the splendid parks and busy temples, in some excellent museums, and, most of all, on Shamian Island.

Great Itineraries

It would take three days to visit Guangzhou's most important sights, and three more to take in the rest. The city can be divided into neighborhoods but, thanks to heavy traffic and construction works, walking itineraries are only practical on Shamian Island, in the parks, and in the oldest part of town. With the city's wealth of good restaurants, it's tempting to stop for leisurely lunches, but not advisable, as museums and temples close at 5. Save the big meal for dinnertime.

The best itineraries combine historic sites, temples that are works of art, landscaped parks, good museums, and opportunities for shopping and picture-taking. Depending on the season you might also be able to include a Chinese festival, which in Guangzhou usually means floral spectacles—sculptures made of chrysanthemums in November, flower fairs before the Lunar New Year.

Numbers in the text correspond to numbers in the margin and on the Guangzhou and Side Trips from Guangzhou maps.

IF YOU HAVE 3 DAYS
Start by walking around **Shamian** (Shamian Island), with its restored colonial mansions. Cross the bridge to the **Qingping Shishang** (Qingping Market) and the Antiques Market. Stop for lunch at a restaurant with views of the Pearl River (Cantonese at the Datong or east/west at Lucy's; ☞ Dining and Lodging, *below*). In the afternoon take a taxi to the **Huaisheng Si Guang Ta** (Huaisheng Mosque) and stroll from there to the **Liu Rong Si Hua Ta** (Six Banyan Temple) and **Guangxiao Si** (Bright Filial Piety Temple). Take a taxi to the **Chen Jia Ci** (Chen Family Temple) and spend the evening in **Liuhua Gongyuan** (Liuhua Park), with dinner at a garden restaurant. The next day, begin at **Yuexiu Gongyuan**

(Yuexiu Park) and the **Guangzhou Bowuguan** (Guangzhou Museum). Have lunch in the park, then cross the street to the **Nan Yue Wang Mu** (Museum and Tomb of the Southern Yue Kings). Stroll to the **Lanpu** (Orchid Garden) and take traditional tea in one of the pavilions. On the third day, begin at the **Sun Zhongshan Jinian Tang** (Sun Yat-sen Memorial Hall) and continue on to the **Nongmin Yundong Jiangxi Suo** (Peasant Movement Institute). After lunch proceed to the **Lieshi Lingyuan** (Memorial Garden for the Martyrs) and Revolutionary Museum. End the day at the **Huanghua Gang Qishi'er Lieshi Mu** (Mausoleum of the 72 Martyrs and Memorial of Yellow Flowers).

IF YOU HAVE 6 DAYS

Follow the itinerary of the first three days (☞ *above*); on Day 4 take a taxi to the **Eastern Suburbs,** with its post-modern architecture and fine sports stadium. After lunch go by taxi to **Studio 2000,** Guangzhou's answer to Hollywood's Universal Studios. On Day 5 take a bus or train to Foshan, where you can spend a day exploring the **Zu Miao** (Ancestral Temple) and shopping for papercuts and Shekwan pottery. On Day 6 take a bus to the town of Cuiheng in Zhongshan County and see the **Sun Yatsen Guju** (Sun Yatsen's Birthplace). Have lunch at the Chung Shan Hot Springs Resort.

IF YOU HAVE 10 DAYS

Follow the six-day itinerary (☞ *above*); on Day 7 take a bus or ferry to Shenzhen Bay for a day at the **Jin Xiu Zhong Hua and Zhong Hua Minzu Wen Hua Cun** (Splendid China and China Folk Culture Villages) theme parks. From either Guangzhou or Shenzhen airport take a flight to **Shantou** and spend two days exploring the Chiu Chow homeland, sampling the cuisine and shopping for ceramics, embroidery, lace, and wood carvings.

Colonial Canton

To recapture the days of Canton as it looked to the foreign merchants in the latter half of the 19th century and first part of the 20th, stroll around Shamian Island and have lunch within sight and sound of the Pearl River traffic, which once included tea clippers and opium ships. Cross the small bridge to visit the antiques shops of Qingping.

A Good Walk

Start from the White Swan Hotel, leaving by the rear entrance. Follow the three streets that run parallel along the length of **Shamian** ①. Here you can see restored buildings and watch the locals at leisure in the small central park. Then cross the north bridge to visit **Qingping Shishang** ②.

TIMING

This walk can be done in three hours, but lunch and shopping can add another two to three hours.

Sights to See

② **Qingping Shishang** (Qingping Market). Across the short bridge from the north shore of Shamian is the bustling, noisy complex of alleys packed with shops and market stalls. The Qingping Market caters to a wide variety of shoppers. The central alley contains herbalists, spice sellers, and fruit and vegetable stalls. To the left is the infamous meat market, with dogs, cats, and various endangered species on sale. Turn right on Dishipu Lu and on the left is a collection of jade shops, along with stores selling reproduction antiques, old watches and jewelry, Mao memorabilia, and other collectibles. Farther north, on Daihe Lu, is the private **Antiques Market,** where you'll find plenty of old furniture, porcelain, jade, and bank notes. ⊠ *Dishipu Lu and Daihe Lu.*

In case you want to be welcomed there.

We're here to see that you're always welcomed at establishments everywhere. That's why millions of people carry the American Express® Card – for peace of mind, confidence, and security, around the world or just around the corner.

do more ®

Cards

In case you're running low.

We're here to help with more than 118,000 Express Cash locations around the world. In order to enroll, just call American Express before you start your vacation.

do more

Express Cash

And just in case.

We're here with American Express® Travelers Cheques and Cheques *for Two*.® They're the safest way to carry money on your vacation and the surest way to get a refund, practically anywhere, anytime.

Another way we help you...

do more ®

Travelers Cheques

❶ **Shamian** (Sandbank Island). More than a century ago, the mandarins of Guangzhou designated a 44-acre sandbank outside the city walls in the Pearl River as an enclave for foreign merchants. They had previously lived and done business in a row of houses known as the Thirteen Factories, near the present Shamian, but local resentment after the Opium War—sometimes leading to murderous attacks—made it prudent to confine them to a protected area, which was linked to the city by two bridges that were closed at 10 every night.

The island rapidly became a bustling township, as trading companies from Britain, the U.S., France, Holland, Italy, Germany, Portugal, and Japan built stone mansions along the waterfront. With spacious gardens and private wharves, these served as homes, offices, and warehouses. There were churches for Catholics and Protestants, banks, a yacht club, football grounds, a cricket pitch, and the Victory Hotel (☞ Dining and Lodging, *below*).

Shamian was attacked in the 1920s but survived until the 1949 Revolution, when its mansions became government offices or apartment houses and the churches were turned into factories. In recent years, however, the island has resumed much of its old character. Many of the colonial buildings have been restored, and both churches have been beautifully renovated and reopened to worshippers. **Our Lady of Lourdes Catholic Church** (✉ Shamian Dajie at Yijie), with its cream-and-white neo-Gothic tower is particularly attractive. A park with shady walks and benches has been created in the center of the island, where local residents come to chat with friends, walk their caged birds, or practice tai chi, shadow-boxing.

The island has also resumed its role as a foreign enclave, with business people at the deluxe White Swan hotel (☞ Dining and Lodging, *below*) and budget travelers at the re-established and renovated Victory Hotel. Continental-style sidewalk cafés have opened, and the delightful Lucy's (☞ Dining and Lodging, *below*) became the only restaurant on the river's edge. In addition, Shamian has developed into a shopping district, with brand-name, but bargain-priced, boutiques in the White Swan and dozens of small shops selling Chinese paintings, pottery, minority handcrafts, and assorted souvenirs.

The biggest attractions, however, are the finely restored colonial buildings, now put to new uses. The old British Consulate is now the Foreign Affairs Office of Guangdong Province; the former U.S. Consulate is now a restaurant, as is the stately, colonnaded Hongkong and Shanghai Bank; the Banque de l'Indochine and offices of Butterfield & Swire house modern businesses; and the stuffy old Shamian Club is now the International Club Karaoke Lounge. ✉ *Shamian Island.*

Ancestral Guangzhou

To explore what used to be the walled city of Guangzhou takes a full day. The major attractions are scattered, and the narrow streets are invariably congested with human and vehicular traffic. Nevertheless it's interesting to cover some of the itinerary on foot, to experience the dynamism of Cantonese city life.

A Good Walk

It's best to start with a taxi ride to the **Huaisheng Si Guang Ta** ③, except on Fridays when it is closed to non-Moslems. You can walk from here to the **Liu Rong Si Hua Ta** ④ and on to the nearby **Guangxiao Si** ⑤. After lunch take a taxi to the **Chen Jia Ci** ⑥ and end the day with a stroll in **Liuhua Gongyuan** ⑦.

Guangzhou

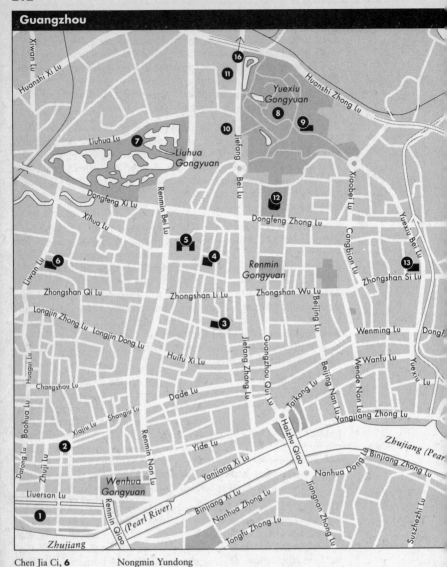

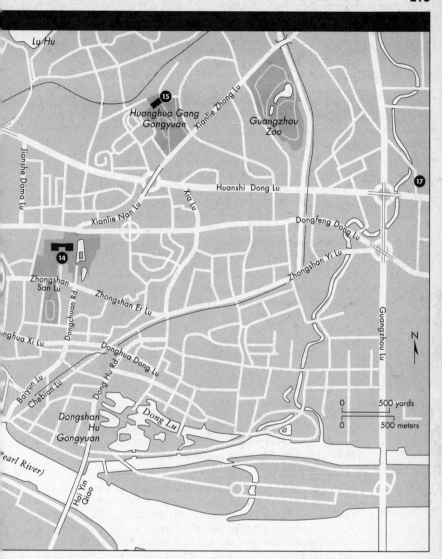

Lu Hu

15 Huanghua Gang Gongyuan

Xianlie Zhong Lu

Guangzhou Zoo

17

Jianshe Dama Lu

Huanshi Dong Lu

Xianlie Nan Lu

Xia Lu

Dongfeng Dong Lu

14

Zhongshan Yi Lu

Zhongshan San Lu

Dongchuan Rd

Zhongshan Er Lu

Guangzhou Lu

nghua Xi Lu

Donghua Dong Lu

N

Baiyun Lu

Dong Hu Rd

Chebian Lu

Dongshan Hu Gongyuan

Dong Lu

| 0 | | 500 yards |

| 0 | | 500 meters |

Pearl River)

Hai Yin Qiao

TIMING

This itinerary should take six to seven hours, depending on how much walking you do and how long you take for lunch.

Sights to See

❻ **Chen Jia Ci** (Chen Family Temple). There are many brilliantly orna-mented ridgepoles to be found in Guangdong and neighboring Fujian. Crafted by masters from local clay into birds, flowers, mythical beasts, sacred images, and historical tableaux, they usually crown a temple pavilion or study hall, representing one of the great folk art traditions of all China.

Of such works of art one of the most marvelous is to be found on the Chen Family Temple, where it stretches 90 ft along the main roof, de-picting scenes from the epic *Romance of Three Kingdoms* with thou-sands of figures against a backdrop of ornate houses, monumental gates, and lush scenery. This is the showpiece of the temple but only one of its treasures. Elsewhere in the huge compound of pavilions and court-yards are friezes of delicately carved stone and wood, as well as fine iron castings and a dazzling altar covered with gold leaf.

The Chen family is one of Guangdong's oldest and most numerous clans. In the late 19th century local members, who had prospered as merchants, decided to build a memorial temple. They invited contri-butions from the Chens—and kindred Chans—who had emigrated over-seas. The money flowed in from 72 countries, and no expense was spared to make this a tribute to a successful family. The temple also houses a folk arts museum and shop. ✉ *7 Zhongshan Xilu.* 🎫 *Y10.* 🕐 *Daily 8–5.*

❺ **Guangxiao Si** (Bright Filial Piety Temple). A short walk from the Six
★ Banyan Temple, this Buddhist temple is the oldest in Guangzhou. It was originally the residence of the Nan Yue kings but became a tem-ple in AD 401. During the Tang dynasty, Huineng, the monk who founded the southern sect of Buddhism, studied here. In 1629 it was rebuilt after a fire, with new prayer pavilions added.

It is among the most charming of Guangzhou's temples, with a warm, welcoming atmosphere. A gilded wooden Laughing Buddha sits at the entrance, and a huge bronze incense-burner, usually wreathed in joss-stick smoke, stands in the main courtyard. Beyond the main hall, noted for its ceiling of red-lacquered timbers, is another courtyard that contains several treasures, among them a small brick pagoda, said to contain the tonsure of Huineng, and a couple of iron pagodas that are the oldest of their kind in China. Above them spread the leafy branches of a myrobalan plum tree and a banyan called Buddha's Tree because it is said Huineng was given tonsure in its shade. ✉ *Guangxiao Lu.* 🎫 *Y5.* 🕐 *Daily 8–5.*

❸ **Huaisheng Si Guang Ta** (Huaisheng Mosque). In the cosmopolitan era of the Tang dynasty (618–907) a Muslim missionary named Abu Wan-gus, said to be an uncle of the Prophet Muhammad, came to South-ern China. He converted many Chinese to Islam and built this mosque in Guangzhou as their house of worship. Ever since he died here, his tomb in the northern part of the city has been a place of pilgrimage for visiting Muslims. The mosque, however, is his best-known memo-rial. The first mosque in China, it originally stood on the banks of the river and for 1,300 years provided a beacon for merchant ships from Southeast Asia, India, Arabia, and Europe. Following progressive land reclamations, it is now almost downtown and surrounded by modern skyscrapers, yet manages to retain an old-world dignity and an atmo-sphere of peaceful devotion.

A high wall encloses the mosque, which is dominated by the smooth, white minaret that rises 108 ft. It can be climbed by an interior spiral staircase, and the views from the top—where a muezzin calls the faithful to prayer—are still spectacular. Below is a gate-tower that was rebuilt in Tang style during the late 17th century, and the main prayer hall, which was refurbished in Ming dynasty style in 1936. Around the mosque are courtyards and gardens where local Muslims and visitors can rest and meditate. ⊠ *Guangta Lu.* ⊡ *Free.* ☉ *Sat.–Thurs. 8–5, except special holy days.*

★ ❹ **Liu Rong Si Hua Ta** (Six Banyan Temple). Look at any ancient scroll painting or lithograph by early Western travelers and you will see two landmarks rising above old Guangzhou. One is the minaret of the mosque, the other is the 184-ft pagoda of the Six Banyan Temple. Still providing an excellent lookout, the pagoda appears to have nine stories, each with doorways and encircling balconies. Inside, however, there are 17 levels. Thanks to its arrangement of colored, carved roofs, it is popularly known as the Flowery Pagoda.

The temple was founded in the 5th century, but following a series of fires, most of the existing buildings date from the 11th century. It was built by the Zen Master Tanyu and is still a very active place of worship, with a community of monks and regular attendance by Zen Buddhists. It was originally called Purificatory Wisdom Temple, but changed its name after a visit by the Song dynasty poet Su Dongpo, who was so delighted by six banyan trees growing in the courtyard that he left an inscription with the characters for six banyans.

The trees are no longer to be found, but the stone bearing his calligraphy can be seen in the temple, along with tablets telling the history of the place and a 1,000-year-old bronze statue of Zen Master Huineng. In one prayer hall there are also three statues of Buddha—each weighing five tons—and one of the Goddess of Mercy, all made of brass and cast in 1663. ⊠ *Haizhu Beilu.* ⊡ *Y15.* ☉ *Daily 8–5.*

❼ **Liuhua Gongyuan** (Liuhua Park). Next to the China and Dong Fang hotels, as well as the trade fair hall, this park is ideal for relaxation, people-watching, and dining. It has a serpentine lake, groves of trees, flower beds, and plenty of benches. You can sit and watch men gather to compare the talents of their pet songbirds, finches that are kept in exquisite bamboo cages fitted with porcelain feeding bowls and decorated with pieces of jade. In late afternoon the scene changes as young lovers come in search of secluded benches. As for dining, the glittering white palace in the lake is the Sun Kwong restaurant (☞ *Dining, below*). ⊠ *Dongfeng Xilu and Renmin Beilu.* ⊡ *Y3.* ☉ *Daily 6 AM–10 PM.*

Station District

The area around the main railroad station and exhibition hall offers an agreeable combination of ancient history and natural history. Dominated by the Zhenhai Tower, Yuexiu Park is Guangzhou's answer to New York's Central Park, while the Nan Yue Tomb Museum uncovers an extraordinary era in the city's past, and the Orchid Garden proves you can find peace and quiet in the busiest part of town.

A Good Walk

Begin at **Yuexiu Gongyuan** ⑧, strolling to pay respects to the Five Celestial Rams before visiting the **Guangzhou Bowuguan** ⑨ housed in the 14th-century Zhenhai Tower. Have lunch in the park, then cross Jiefang Beilu to the **Nan Yue Wang Mu** ⑩. End the day with a stroll through the **Lanpu** ⑪, where you can stop for tea in a classic tea pavilion.

TIMING
This walk, including lunch, should take about five and a half hours.

Sights to See

9 **Guangzhou Bowuguan** (Guangzhou Museum). Dominating Yuexiu Park is the five-story, 92-ft **Zhenhai Lou** (Tower Controlling the Sea), which was first built in 1380. Three centuries later it was converted into a watchtower overlooking the old port. Today its entrance is still guarded by a dozen old cannons and three Krupp guns, but now it houses the municipal museum, whose displays outline the history of the city from prehistoric times to the present. On the first floor is a huge anchor from the Ming era, which was found in the river mud, and a bas relief model of Guangzhou as it is projected to look in the 21st century.

On the next floor are the remains of pottery from a Han dynasty (206–220 BC) tomb; Han bronzes; and examples of early trade goods such as rhinoceros horns, hawksbill turtle shells, and precious stones. The third floor is devoted to Guangzhou's experience of the western world. Here is the original clock face from the Roman Catholic cathedral, bibles, exportware porcelain, models of the first railway car and first plane, pictures of the foreign factories on Shamian, and a bas relief of the city in the 19th century.

Guangzhou after the Opium War is the subject of exhibits on the fourth floor. There are pictures of the first brewery, the first sugar refinery, and early sewing machines, along with displays of an old fire engine, telephone, radio, household implements, and a sedan chair. On the top floor are shops selling antiques, tea, jade, *cheongsams* (high-neck, split-skirt Chinese dresses), and such local specialties as snake wine. Tea, beer, soft drinks, and snacks are served at tables on the balcony, which affords marvelous views of the park. ⊠ *Yuexiu Gongyuan, Jiefang Beilu,* ☎ *20/8333–0627.* ☞ *Y5.* ☉ *Daily 8:30–5.*

11 **Lanpu** (Orchid Garden). Across the square from the main railroad and bus terminals, and opposite Yuexiu Park, this garden offers a wonderfully convenient retreat from the noise and crowds of the city. It's spread over 20 acres, with paths that wind through groves of bamboo and tropical trees, beside carp-filled ponds, to a series of classic teahouses. Here you can sit and enjoy a wide variety of Chinese teas, brewed the traditional way. There are tables inside and on terraces that overlook the ponds. As for the orchids there are 10,000 pots with over 2,000 species of the flower, which present a magical sight when they bloom. ⊠ *Jiefang Beilu.* ☞ *Y5.* ☉ *Daily 8:30AM– 11PM.*

★ **10** **Nan Yue Wang Mu** (Museum and Tomb of the Southern Yue Kings). Until quite recently only specialist historians realized that Guangzhou had once been a royal capital. In 1983 bulldozers clearing ground to build the China Hotel uncovered the intact tomb of Emperor Wen Di, who ruled Nan Yue (Southern China) from 137 to 122 BC. The tomb was faithfully restored and its treasures placed in the adjoining Nanyue Museum.

The tomb contained the skeletons of the king and 15 courtiers— guards, cooks, concubines, and a musician—who were buried alive to attend him in death. Also buried were several thousand funerary objects, clearly designed to show off the extraordinary accomplishments of the southern empire. Now attractively displayed in the museum, with intelligent labeling in Chinese and English, they include jade armor, gem-encrusted swords and crossbows, gold jewelry, lacquer boxes, pearl pillows, 139 pottery pi-discs, 1,000 bronze and iron cooking pots, and an orchestra of bronze and stone chimes that are still in tune.

The tomb itself—built entirely of stone slabs—is behind the museum and is remarkable for its compact size. Divided into two parts, it is 66 ft deep, 40 ft wide, and 35 ft long. The emperor was buried in the central chamber, while six smaller adjoining rooms were packed from floor to ceiling with the funeral objects and the courtiers.

On the second floor, an incomparable collection of 200 ceramic pillows—from the Tang, Song, Jin, and Yuan dynasties—was donated by Hong Kong industrialist Yeung Wing Tak and his wife. ⊠ *Jiefang Beilu.* 🚇 *Y20.* ⊙ *Daily 9:30–5:30, no entry after 4:45.*

8 **Yuexiu Gongyuan** (Yuexiu Park). To take a break from business or get away from the bustle, residents and visitors alike adjourn to Yuexiu Park in the heart of town, truly a "central park" with a wide range of attractions and facilities. It covers 247 acres and includes Yuexiu Hill and six hillocks, landscaped gardens, man-made lakes, theme parks, restaurants, and recreational areas.

The best known sight in Yuexiu Park is the **Wuyang Suxiang** (Five Rams statue), which celebrates the legend of the five celestials who came to Guangzhou riding on goats to bring cereals to the people. Today Guangzhou families take each other's photo in front of the statue before setting off to enjoy the park. They hire boats on the three man-made lakes, which contain islands accessible by hump-backed bridges, or stroll along paths lined with flowering bushes, bamboo groves, and small forests of pine, cypress, and kapok.

For a different kind of enjoyment, the park has a stadium for soccer matches and other sports, a "Journey to the West" theme park—with a giant wooden cockerel that crows at the entrance—and a children's playground with fairground rides. ⊠ *Jiefang Beilu.* 🚇 *Y3.* ⊙ *Daily 8 AM–10 PM.*

Revolutionary Guangzhou

In the center of the city are memorials to people who changed Chinese history in this century, using Guangzhou as a base of operations. The most famous were local boy Dr. Sun Yat-sen, who led the overthrow of the Qing dynasty, and Communist Party founders Mao Zedong and Zhou Enlai. There were many others, among them thousands who died in the struggles. All are recalled in different ways that are revealed in this itinerary.

A Good Walk

Start with a taxi ride to the **Sun Zhongshan Jinian Tang** ⑫, visit the hall and its grounds, then walk, or take a taxi, to the **Nongmin Yundong Jiangxi Suo** ⑬ to recapture the days when youthful revolutionaries Mao and Zhou taught their followers how to organize a peasant revolt. Walk on to the **Lieshi Lingyuan** ⑭ and Revolutionary Museum, and finish with a cab ride to the **Huanghua Gang Qishi'er Lieshi Mu** ⑮.

TIMING

This itinerary should take three to four hours.

Sights to See

⑮ **Huanghua Gang Qishi'er Lieshi Mu** (Mausoleum of the 72 Martyrs). In a prelude to the successful revolution of 1911 a group of 88 revolutionaries staged the Guangzhou Armed Uprising, only to be defeated and executed by the authorities. Of them, 72 were buried here. Their memorial incorporates a mixture of international symbols of freedom and democracy, including replicas of the Statue of Liberty. ⊠ *Xianlie Zhonglu.* 🚇 *Y5.* ⊙ *Daily 5 AM–7:30 PM.*

⑭ **Lieshi Lingyuan** (Memorial Garden for the Martyrs). Built in 1957, this garden has been planted around a tumulus that contains the remains of 5,000 revolutionaries killed in the 1927 destruction of the Guangzhou Commune by the Nationalists. This was the execution site of many victims. In the grounds is the **Revolutionary Museum,** which displays pictures and memorabilia of Guangdong's 20th-century rebellions. ⊠ *Zhongshan Sanlu.* 🚇 *Y5.* ⊘ *Daily* 6 AM–9 PM.

⑬ **Nongmin Yundong Jiangxi Suo** (Peasant Movement Institute). Today the atmosphere of the Institute—with its quiet courtyards and empty cells—recalls its origin as a 14th-century Confucian Temple, but it doesn't take long to detect the ghostly presence of the young idealists who came here in the early 1920s to learn how to create a new China based on equality and justice.

The institute was established in 1924 by some of the founders of the Chinese Communist party, who had set up a Guangzhou Commune modeled on the 19th-century Parisian example. Young people came from all over the country to listen to party leaders. In 1926 Mao Zedong became director of the school, and Zhou Enlai was a staff member. They and their colleagues lectured on "the problem of the Chinese peasantry," "rural education," and geography to students who were then sent to the countryside to educate the peasants.

The venture proved short-lived, as it soon became obvious that the Nationalists under Chiang Kai-shek were planning to drive the Communists from the city. The institute was closed in late 1927, just before the Commune was crushed and 5,000 revolutionaries killed. In 1953 the Beijing government restored the buildings and made it into a museum. The result is very evocative. The main lecture hall, with desks ranged in front of a blackboard, looks as if the students might return any minute. Instead they can be seen in photographs displayed along the corridors: keen young men and women, bright-eyed with expectation, but in most cases doomed. As the captions reveal, a majority were captured and killed by the Nationalists. As for their leader, Mao is recalled in a re-creation of his room. It is a simple cell, with a metal frame bed, desk, and bookcase. ⊠ *42 Zhongshan Silu.* 🚇 *Y5.* ⊘ *Daily* 9–5.

⑫ **Sun Zhongshan Jinian Tang** (Sun Yat-sen Memorial Hall). By the end of the 19th century the Qing dynasty was in its last throes. The moribund court and its corrupt mandarins were powerless to control the westerners who had taken over much of China's trade, or the warlords who kept the peasantry in feudal misery. Dissent was widespread, but it was Guangzhou that became a center for rebellion. The leader was Sun Yat-sen, a young doctor from a village in the Pearl Delta, who had studied in Honolulu and graduated from Hong Kong's medical college. Inspired by democratic ideals, he set up the Revive China Society in Guangzhou in 1892 and petitioned the emperor, demanding equality and justice. In return a price was put on his head and he was forced to spend the next years as an exile in Japan, the United States, and Europe.

Everywhere that he went he gathered supporters and funds for a revolution, which finally took place in 1911, when he returned to Guangzhou to be proclaimed "Father of the Revolution" and provisional president. However, Dr. Sun was no politician and soon lost Nationalist leadership to Chiang Kai-shek. He spent his last years in Shanghai and died in Beijing in 1925, but he remains a favorite son of Guangzhou.

This can be seen from his Memorial Hall, a handsome pavilion that stands in an attractively landscaped garden behind a bronze statue of

Dr. Sun. Built in 1929–31 with funds mostly from overseas Chinese, the building is a classic octagon with sweeping roofs of blue tiles over carved wooden eaves and verandahs of red lacquered columns. Inside is an auditorium with seating for 5,000 and a stage for plays, concerts, and ceremonial occasions. ⊠ *Dongfeng Zhonglu.* ⊙ *Daily 8—5.*

Airport Area

One of the newest entertainments of Guangzhou is a reproduction film studio where you can get a close-up view of the action taken from kungfu and Shanghai gangster films. The studio is in the northern suburbs, next to Baiyun Airport. You can reach it by taxi in 10 minutes from the China Hotel.

🐾 ⑯ **Oriental Studio 2000.** Modeled on Hollywood's Universal Studios, this new entertainment complex has two movie sets. Probably the two best-known genres of Chinese movie-making are the kungfu epic and the good old bad days of Shanghai, so they were chosen for Oriental Studio 2000. On the "Shanghai in the roaring '30s" set, a chorus line of scantily clad girls entertains slick-haired gangsters in the Paramount Ballroom. Suddenly a rival gang bursts onto the scene riding motorcycles and firing machine guns. Others burst from the upper balcony of the ballroom and apparently fly through the air to do battle. The "traditional Chinese courtyard" set has stables and workshops. A figure in bright silk appears on the roof and sails down to the ground, flashing a tasseled sword. It is the Lion King, who summons his army to fight the enemy lions. The enemies leap high into the air with battle banners and perform breathtaking acrobatics until they are subdued and made to pay homage.

The Studio opened in 1996 in the Dong Fang Amusement Park. The two shows utilize all the equipment to be found in local film studios, so there are overhead wires for "flying," facades that "collapse," mats that become springboards, and blowers to provide a snowfall or smoke. The introductions are in Chinese and there's no program, but this isn't important because it's totally visual. The shows last 15 minutes with three performances a day, at 3, 7, and 8:45 PM for the *Shanghai Tan;* 4, 6, and 8 PM for the *Lion King.*

Along with the sets, the park has restaurants, some modeled on old films, serving Chinese and Western food; shopping arcades with souvenirs; staged folk dancing; acrobatics; and street performances by conjurors, magicians, and *qigong* (traditional Chinese exercise said to release the inner power or *qi* of the spirit) experts. In the main part of the vast amusement park there's a huge Ferris wheel, a rollercoaster, and other fairground rides, plus a lake with pleasure boats. ⊠ *Jiefang Beilu, Baiyun, next to airport,* ☎ *020/8669–6882.* 🎟 *Y120.* ⊙ *Daily 8:30 AM–11 PM.*

Eastern Suburbs

Since 1980 Guangzhou has grown out of all recognition, and the result is a city bursting at the seams. In response the local government decided to create a new downtown, to the east of the city, where there was space. The first move to lure residents from their traditional venues was the construction of a world-class sports stadium. The second was to invite China's biggest foreign investor, Hong Kong's New World Company, to build a brand-new suburb of apartments and offices. The third was the most drastic. The direct rail link between Guangzhou and Hong Kong is a vital artery, so the terminal for Hong Kong trains was moved to Tianhe, the new downtown.

A Good Walk

Take a taxi to Guangzhou East train station, look inside, and from here stroll around **Tianhe** ⑰. See the handsome sports stadium and some attractive modern statuary, then take a look at the eclectic architecture of the city's newest skyscrapers, which combine Doric-columned courtyards, neo-Gothic archways, colored glass-clad facades, and traditional Chinese roofs. Drop by the multi-storied book shop and the newest shopping arcades of Teem Plaza.

TIMING

An hour and a half is enough to see the highlights of Tianhe, unless there is something happening in the stadium that is worth watching.

Sights to See

⑰ **Tianhe.** There might be other contenders for the title of Asia's tallest building, but Guangzhou has a very prominent claimant, the **GITIC Plaza,** which soars 1,300 ft with 80 stories of office space. It is already a city landmark, especially when viewed together with the neighboring **Metro Plaza**'s two gold-walled romanesque towers. All three are located next to the **Guangzhou East Station** (⊠ Linhe Lu), the new terminus for trains from Hong Kong. The station is light, airy, and very spacious, with a vast entrance hall and long distances to walk between trains and the immigration hall.

Tianhe is designed to be a hub of sports activity. The two outdoor and indoor stadiums of the **Tianhe Stadium Complex** (⊠ Huanshi Donglu, East Guangzhou) appeal to the eye and are equipped for international soccer matches, track and field, and athletics competition, as well as pop concerts and large-scale ceremonies. Around the stadiums is a pleasant landscaped park, with outdoor cafés and tree-shaded benches. The park surrounding the complex also contains a bowling center with 38 lanes and a floor of TV games.

Around this core of Tianhe, construction is underway for the Guangzhou Pearl River New City, a development of offices, apartments, hotels, shops, and recreational facilities. Already the area is drawing the shoppers. The **Guangzhou Book Center** (⊠ Huangshi Donglu, East Guangzhou) has seven floors with space for books on every subject (including some bargain-priced art books in English), computer programs, and exercise equipment. Across the street is **Teem Plaza,** a vast complex of shops and supermarkets.

DINING AND LODGING

The problem of dining in Guangzhou is choosing from the extraordinary range of restaurants. (There are an estimated 157,000.) The following selection includes tried-and-true favorites for Chinese and western meals. Unless specified, all restaurants are open daily for lunch and dinner, with most Chinese establishments also serving traditional breakfast of rice porridge and dim sum snacks. Reservations are usually not necessary except in western restaurants during the fair periods. Chinese banquets are part of all business deals here; you can organize a meal for local colleagues by contacting the restaurant at least a day in advance and either choosing the menu (if you're very familiar with banquet dishes) or specifying the number of guests—to fill each table with 12—and price range, and leaving it in the restaurant's experienced hands.

The purpose of your visit to Guangzhou is likely to determine your choice of hotel, not least because heavy traffic on every road, exacerbated by encroaching construction sites, can make cross-town travel very time-consuming. Traditionally the hotels close to the main train station and trade fair headquarters were the choice of business people, but since the terminal for Hong Kong train service has been moved to the eastern suburbs at Tianhe, where the local government is encouraging businesses to relocate, there has been a shift to hotels both in the east and on Huanshi Donglu, the major thoroughfare between the two business areas.

$$$ ✕ **All Seasons.** Four cuisines in one restaurant is the very successful
★ concept here, with menus from Shanghai, Beijing, Sichuan, and Taiwan. The frequently displayed FULL-HOUSE signs testify to the standard of the food, and the setting is coolly elegant. As in other outlets in the GITIC Plaza, no msg is used in the cooking. ✉ *GITIC Plaza Hotel, 339 Huanshi Donglu,* ☎ *020/8331–1888. AE, DC, MC, V.*

$$$ ✕ **Connoisseur.** You could almost be in Regency France in the Garden's premier restaurant. The arched columns with gilded capitals, the gold-framed mirrors, lustrous drapes, and the immaculate table settings are just right. And the food doesn't disappoint. A French chef is in charge, and the finest Continental fare is on the menu. ✉ *Garden Hotel, 368 Huanshi Donglu,* ☎ *020/8333–8989. AE, DC, MC, V.*

$$$ ✕ **Guangzhou.** Established in 1936, with branches in Hong Kong and Los Angeles, as well as two more in Guangzhou, this is probably the busiest Cantonese restaurant in town, serving a total of 10,000 diners a day. The setting is classic, with courtyards of flowery bushes surrounded by dining rooms of various sizes ranged along arcaded corridors. The house specialties are abalone sprinkled with 24-carat gold flakes; Mao-tai chicken; plus Eight Treasures—game, chicken, ham, and mushrooms—in winter melons carved to make a bowl; duck feet stuffed with shrimp; roast sliced goose; and Wenchang chicken. ✉ *2 Wenchang Nanlu,* ☎ *020/8188–7840. AE, DC, MC, V.*

$$$ ✕ **The Roof.** China Hotel's fine dining restaurant is tops in both ways. It sits in understated splendor on the 18th floor, with panoramic views of night-time Guangzhou (it's open only for dinner and closed Sundays). The menu changes with seasonal food specialties, but there are such staples as saddle of lamb marinated in mint and yogurt, fettuccini, scallops in saffron sauce, and prime cuts of U.S. beef. ✉ *China Hotel, Liuhua Lu,* ☎ *020/8666–6888. AE, DC, MC, V.*

$$$ ✕ **Silk Road Grill Room.** As you'd expect from the superlative White Swan, the grill room is the ultimate in sophistication. It's furnished with brass fittings and big silver food covers, gleaming candlesticks, and crisp white linen. The service is impeccable and the menu a fine selection of Continental dishes. It is open for dinner only. ✉ *White Swan, Shamian Yi, Shamian,* ☎ *020/8188–6968. AE, DC, MC, V.*

$$$ ✕ **South Sea Fishing Village.** There's nothing rustic about this "village" except the traditional pavilion gate at the entrance, where limousines pull in with Guangzhou's new rich. To greet them are waitresses in slinky cheongsams, with sides split up to the thigh, and fur capes over their shoulders. On the menu you find lobsters fresh from Hainan and the choicest of Chiu Chow cuisine. The restaurant has an equally upmarket branch opposite the Dong Fang Hotel. ✉ *350 Huanshi Donglu,* ☎ *020/8346–1111. AE, DC, MC, V.*

$$$ ✕ **Sun Kwong.** It looks like a European folly, a four-story belle epoch palace in a lake surrounded by a park, which you approach either by small canopied gondola or by land through a courtyard dominated by a statue of a mounted medieval knight. The restaurant, a Sino-Hong Kong joint venture, was opened in 1993. In the main restaurant, with marvelous views from picture windows, the menu offers Beijing duck, shark's fin, pigeon, and a wide range of seafood. There are 28 private banquet rooms upstairs. ✉ *Liuhua Park,* ☎ *020/8668–8928. AE, DC, MC, V.*

Guangzhou Dining and Lodging

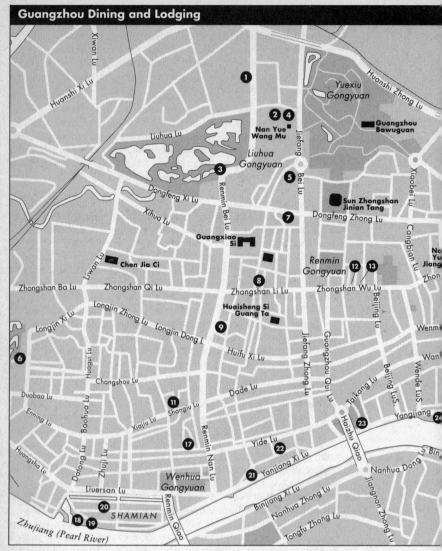

Restaurants

All Seasons, **10**
Banxi, **6**
Beiyuan, **7**
Caigenxiang
Vegetarian
Restaurant, **8**
Chiu Chou City, **23**
Connoisseur, **14**
Datong, **21**
Dongjiang , **12**
Food Street, **4**
Guangzhou, **11**
Lai Wan Market, **14**

Lucy's, **19**
Oscar's, **16**
The Roof, **4**
Silk Road Grill
Room, **18**
Snake Restaurant, **17**
South Sea Fishing
Village, **15**
Sun Kwong, **3**
Tang Banquet Hall, **2**
Tong Kong, **13**
Xin Jia Lu, **9**

Hotels

China Hotel, **4**
Dong Fang Hotel, **2**
Equatorial
Guangzhou, **1**
Furama Guangzhou
Hotel, **22**
Garden Hotel, **14**
GITIC Plaza, **10**
GITIC Riverside, **24**
Holiday Inn City
Centre, **16**
Landmark
Canton, **23**
Parkview Square, **5**

Ramada Pearl, **25**
Victory, **20**
White Swan, **18**

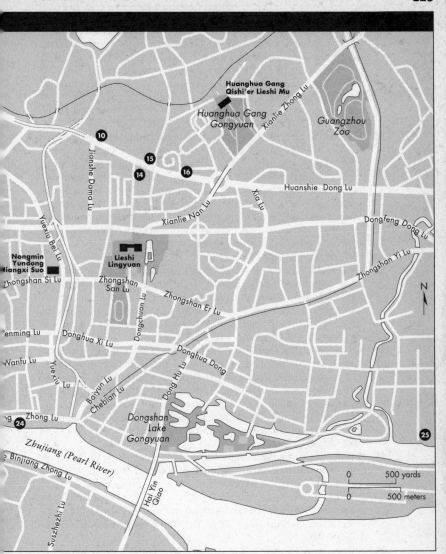

Huanghua Gang
Qishi'er Lieshi Mu

Huanghua Gang
Gongyuan

Xianlie Zhong Lu

Guangzhou
Zoo

Jianshe Dama Lu

Yuexiu Bei Lu

Huanshie Dong Lu

Xia Lu

Xianlie Nan Lu

Dongfeng Dong Lu

Nongmin
Yundong
Jiangxi Suo

Lieshi
Lingyuan

Zhongshan Si Lu

Zhongshan
San Lu

Zhongshan Er Lu

Zhongshan Yi Lu

Dongchuan Lu

enming Lu

Donghua Xi Lu

Wanfu Lu

Yuexiu
Lu

Baiyun Lu
Chebian Lu

Donghua Dong

Dong Hu Lu

Dongshan
Lake
Gongyuan

g Zhong Lu

Zhujiang (Pearl River)

e Binjiang Zhong Lu

Suszhezhi Lu

Hai Yin
Qiao

N

0   500 yards
0   500 meters

10
15
14
16
24
25

$$$ ✕ **Tang Banquet Hall.** The Dong Fang Hotel has 45 restaurants serving a dozen different cuisines, but the most outstanding, for setting and superb Cantonese food, is the Tang room with its ivory-inlaid screens, carved furniture, gilded archways, and red carpets. This is the place for a special banquet, with roast suckling pig a house specialty (cooked on a spit and glazed with honey, plum, and soy), plus shark's fin, salt-baked chicken cooked in clay, and floating flower soup, which contains poached quail eggs made to look like flowers. ✉ *Dong Fang Hotel, Liuhua Lu,* ☎ *020/8666–9900. AE, DC, MC, V.*

$$ ✕ **Banxi.** You feel like you're entering a Taoist temple or private estate, beautifully located on the shore of Liwan Lake, but it's actually one of the city's most attractive traditional restaurants. It consists of rooms of various sizes in rambling teahouses, one of them built on a floating houseboat. Between are landscaped gardens networked by zigzag paths over bridges across ornamental lakes and through bamboo groves. The food is just as good on the eye as the tongue, with vegetables sculptured into birds for cold cuts, scallop and crab soup, and quail eggs cooked with shrimp roe on a bed of green vegetables among the huge selection. ✉ *151 Longjin Xilu,* ☎ *020/8181–5955. AE, DC, MC, V.*

$$ ✕ **Beiyuan.** Like its meaning, "north garden," this traditional teahouse restaurant is surrounded by ornamental pools connected by paths and lined with tropical plants. There are rooms for parties of all sizes and a huge menu, with specialties like shark's fin soup with shredded chicken, chopped crab balls, and chicken cooked in Shaoxing wine. ✉ *320 Dongfeng Xilu,* ☎ *020/8333–0087. MC, V.*

$$ ✕ **Chiu Chou City.** One of the best places for authentic food from the Shantou area is this restaurant in the Landmark Canton hotel on Haizhou Square. It has an extensive main room and several private rooms, which are invariably packed for lunch and dinner. The house special is the famous Chiu Chow goose, served as cold cuts or cooked in its own blood and dipped into a sauce of white vinegar and chopped garlic. ✉ *Hotel Landmark Canton, Qiao Guang Lu,* ☎ *020/8335–5988. AE, DC, MC, V.*

$$ ✕ **Datong.** Occupying all eight stories of an old building on the riverfront, with an open terrace on the top floor, this is one of the city's veteran dining places. It is famous for its morning dim sum, and a 1,000-dish menu that includes peacock chicken—braised and cut in the shape of a peacock with its tail fanned—served with vegetables and ham; crisp-skin chicken; and Xishi duck. ✉ *63 Yanjiang Xilu,* ☎ *020/8188–8441. AE, DC, MC, V.*

$$ ✕ **Dongjiang.** This city-center stalwart has a simple setting, but a brilliant menu. Among the favorites are braised duck stuffed with eight delicacies and glutinous rice, stuffed giant prawns, crab in black bean sauce, salt-roast chicken, stuffed beancurd, and steamed pork with salted dried mustard cabbage. ✉ *337 Zhongshan Wulu,* ☎ *020/8333–5568. MC, V.*

$$ ✕ **Lai Wan Market.** This is a wonderful re-creation of the old Canton waterfront, with booths shaped like the "flower boats" that used to offer food, drink, opium, and girls; and small wooden stools at low counters. This "market" is known for its dim sum and two kinds of rice gruel, one made with pork, beef, fish, and seafood, the other with fish, beef, and pork liver. ✉ *Garden Hotel, 368 Huanshi Donglu,* ☎ *020/8333–8989. AE, DC, MC, V.*

$$ ✕ **Oscar's.** Holiday Inns in China have built up an enviable reputation for first-class Continental cooking, thanks to their European chefs. Oscar's is no exception. Its prices and decor might suggest a coffee shop, but this is dining at its best. In addition to set meals and à la carte, there are also frequent food festivals, with ingredients specially flown in from around the world. ✉ *Holiday Inn City Centre, 28 Guangming Lu,* ☎ *020/8776–6999. AE, DC, MC. V.*

$ ✕ **Caigenxiang Vegetarian Restaurant.** Established by Buddhists, this
★ is a joy for visiting vegetarians. Its menu lists 200 dishes and 100 snacks.
It features vegetables with herbs to give the taste of duck, sausage, and
meatballs. Fungi are used to create such delicacies as Snow Mountain
consommé made from woodear fungus. The restaurant has tables,
chairs, and walls made of bamboo. ⊠ *167 Zhongshan Lilu,* ☎ *020/
8334–4363. No credit cards.*

$ ✕ **Food Street.** The concept of a "food street," with half a dozen open
kitchens preparing food from different regions of China, was created
here. Since then it has become a staple of all New World hotels, and
plenty of other places. It is especially attractive for foreigners, who can
see what's cooking before choosing from the menu. It's also ideal for
casual meals at any time, and service is efficient and helpful. ⊠ *China
Hotel, Liuhua Lu,* ☎ *020/8666–6888. AE, DC, MC, V.*

$ ✕ **Lucy's.** Amazingly, this is the only place in Guangzhou where you can
eat alfresco at umbrella-shaded tables in a garden beside the river. It's
on Shamian, next to the White Swan, and it has air-conditioned inside
rooms as well. The choice of fare is astonishingly eclectic, and the prices
extremely reasonable. On the main menu are Asian curries, mixed grills,
TexMex dishes, fish and chips, noodles, burgers, sandwiches, and much
more. Then there are menus for snacks, tea-time, desserts, and happy
hour, which extends from 2:30 to 9 PM. Drinks are also very inexpensive. ⊠ *5–7 Shamian Yi, Shamian.* ☎ *020/8191–0203. No credit cards.*

$ ✕ **Snake Restaurant (Shecanguan).** This 80-year-old establishment
specializes in snake meats. The living creatures fill tanks in the windows and are taken out as ordered. If you like, you can watch the waiters extract their bile for "healthy soup" or skin them. Otherwise it's
done in the kitchen, which prepares dishes such as snake in maotai,
chicken soup with three kinds of snake, and a clear broth with boa
constrictor. ⊠ *41 Jianglan Lu,* ☎ *20/8188–2317. No credit cards.*

$ ✕ **Tong Kong.** This is one of the best Hakka restaurants in the region
and is famous for its salt-baked chicken and preserved vegetables. ⊠
337 Zhongshan Wulu, ☎ *020/8333–5568. No credit cards.*

$ ✕ **Xin Jia Lu.** This is the infamous restaurant that serves what it eu-
phemistically calls super deer. In fact, it's rat meat and not for the faint-
hearted. ⊠ *383 Renmin Zhonglu,* ☎ *020/8188–7992. No credit cards.*

$$$ 🏨 **China Hotel.** This city within a city contains a hotel, office and apart-
ment blocks, and shopping malls that include a supermarket, exhibi-
tion and banquet halls, and restaurants to suit all tastes. It stands
opposite the Trade Fair Exhibition Hall—with bridge links over the
road—and is a great favorite of fair regulars and year-round business
visitors. It has a 66-room Executive Floor with spacious private lounges
just below The Roof, possibly the best European restaurant in
Guangzhou. In the basement is the Hard Rock Café and Catwalk, an
entertainment center with bar, disco, and karaoke areas. ⊠ *Liuhua Lu,
510015,* ☎ *020/8666–6888,* FAX *020/8667–7014; in Hong Kong,* ☎
852/2724–4622, FAX *852/2721–0741. 1,017 rooms. 6 restaurants, pool,
tennis court, bowling, health club, shops, nightclub, business services,
meeting rooms. AE, DC, MC, V.*

$$$ 🏨 **Dong Fang Hotel.** This vast luxury complex is across from Liuhua
Park and the trade fair headquarters. It is built around a 22½-acre gar-
den with pavilions, carp-filled pools, rockeries, trees, and assorted
statuary. There are miles of arcaded corridors, 45 restaurants, plus shops
and service outlets. The shopping concourse holds an interesting selection of Chinese antiques and carpets. It also has a large fitness club
for members and regular guests, plus a complete spa. The four-story
Times Square, a block of shops and restaurants, includes a McDonald's and branches of just about every name Hong Kong store. ⊠ *120*

Liuhua Lu 510016, ☎ 020/8666–9900, FAX *020/8666–2775; in Hong Kong, ☎ 852/2575–5866,* FAX *852/2591–0335. 1,300 rooms. 45 restaurants, beauty salon, shops, recreation room, business services, meeting rooms. AE, DC, MC, V.*

$$$ 🏨 **Garden Hotel.** In the northern business suburbs, this hotel, which is part of a huge complex that includes apartments and offices, lives up to its name with a spectacular garden that includes an artificial hill with a waterfall and pavilions. Inside is an extensive lobby decorated with enormous murals and featuring a bar lounge set in an ornamental pool. There are some great restaurants, a cheerful pub, meeting rooms, and a convention center with a capacity of 1,800 for receptions, 1,000 for banquets. Furnishings include genuine antiques, fine reproductions, and modern art. ⊠ *368 Huanshi Donglu 510064, ☎ 020/8333–8989,* FAX *020/8335–0467. 1,112 rooms. 8 restaurants, pub, pool, health club, squash, shops, business services, convention center. AE, DC, MC, V.*

$$$ 🏨 **GITIC Plaza.** The tallest hotel in China, this new landmark is part of a spectacular complex, built as a flagship property by GITIC, China's second-largest financial institution. The hotel occupies the top floors of the 63-story tower, next to a complex with 14 restaurants and lounges, banquet halls, and a large shopping mall with fashion boutiques. There are also extensive recreation facilities in an indoor-outdoor health spa. ⊠ *339 Huanshi Donglu 510098, ☎ 020/8331–1888,* FAX *020/8331–1666. 402 rooms, 300 suites. 14 restaurants, pool, 2 tennis courts, bowling, health club, shops, business services. AE, DC, MC, V.*

$$$ 🏨 **White Swan.** The first international hotel in town, the White Swan occupies a marvelous site on historic Shamian Island beside the Pearl River. It is a huge luxury complex on the river bank, with landscaped gardens, two outdoor pools, a jogging track, and a separate health spa. Its restaurants are among the best in town and the elegant lobby bar and coffee shop have picture windows to frame the panorama of river traffic. Many rooms have replicas of Chinese antique furniture and porcelain. Even if you don't stay here, visit the lobby and take a look at the spectacular indoor waterfall. ⊠ *Shamian Yi, Shamian 510133, ☎ 020/8188–6968,* FAX *020/8186–1188; in Hong Kong, ☎ 852/2524–0192,* FAX *852/2877–0811. 843 rooms. 12 restaurants, bar, pool, health club, shops, business services, meeting rooms, travel services. AE, DC, MC, V.*

$$ 🏨 **Furama Guangzhou Hotel.** This modest hotel is well located beside the river downtown. Rooms are small but adequate, and the Gourmet Court restaurant serves excellent, reasonably priced Cantonese meals. ⊠ *316 Changdi Damalu, 510120, ☎ 020/8186–3288,* FAX *020/8186–3388. 360 rooms. 3 restaurants, bar, dance club, business services. AE, DC, MC, V.*

$$ 🏨 **GITIC Riverside.** Next to the river, this hotel really uses its location to its advantage, with restaurants extending onto open terraces overlooking the river. It tends to be bustling with Hong Kong and mainland groups, and with children playing around its vast lobby and fountain. ⊠ *298 Yanjiang Zhonglu, 510100, ☎ 020/8383–9888,* FAX *020/8381–4448. 338 rooms. 5 restaurants, bar, pool, health club, shops, dance club, business services, meeting rooms. AE, DC, MC, V.*

$$ 🏨 **Holiday Inn City Centre.** Conveniently located for both train stations in the northern suburbs, it is next door to the Guangzhou World Trade Center. The hotel is a good, reliable place to stay with typically expert Holiday Inn management and superb restaurants for European and Cantonese food. An adjoining 800-seat cinema is sometimes used for film festivals. ⊠ *Huanshi Donglu, Overseas Chinese Village 28, Guangming Lu 510060, ☎ 020/8776–6999,* FAX *020/8775–3126. 431 rooms. 3 restaurants, pool, health club, shops. AE, DC, MC, V.*

$$ ⊞ **Landmark Canton.** Towering above Haizhu Square and the main bridge across the river, this hotel is very much in the heart of central Guangzhou. It is managed by China Travel Service (Hong Kong) and gets much of its business from Hong Kong. Most of the guest rooms have great views of the river or city. The Chiu Chow restaurant is famous, as is the 39th-floor Continental restaurant and karaoke lounge. For a different kind of karaoke, go to the square in the morning, where locals practice their vocal skills with competing sound systems! ⊠ *8 Qiao Guang Lu, 510115,* ☎ *020/8335–5988,* FAX *020/8333– 6197. 900 rooms. 5 restaurants, pool, health club, shops, dance club, business services, meeting rooms. AE, DC, MC, V.*

$$ ⊞ **Parkview Square.** On the edge of Yuexiu Park and close to the trade fair hall, this friendly little hotel is one of the most pleasant in town. It has rooms and service apartments that are spacious and newly decorated; half have wonderful park views. The dining rooms serve Chinese and Western food. ⊠ *960 Jiefang Beilu, 510030,* ☎ *020/8666–5666,* FAX *020/8667– 1741. 207 rooms. 4 restaurants, business services. AE, DC, MC, V.*

$$ ⊞ **Ramada Pearl.** In the eastern part of the city, this full-service hotel on the Pearl River has interesting views of the river traffic. One of its great assets is a two-story health club and a large garden with two swimming pools, tennis courts, and a children's playground. Its Canton 38 entertainment center has a pub, a disco, and a karaoke lounge. The Ramada now benefits from being 10 minutes from the East Railway Station, new terminus for Hong Kong trains. ⊠ *9 Ming Yue Yilu, 510600,* ☎ *020/8777–2988,* FAX *020/8776– 7481. 394 rooms. 5 restaurants, pub, meeting rooms. AE, DC, MC, V.*

$ ⊞ **Equatorial Guangzhou.** Within easy walking distance of the fair hall and main railroad station, this hotel is managed with friendly efficiency by a Singaporean company. It has Chinese and western restaurants and a busy little bar. ⊠ *931 Renmin Beilu, 510010,* ☎ *020/8667–2888,* FAX *020/8667–2583. 300 rooms. 7 restaurants, bar, dance club, business services, meeting rooms. AE, DC, MC, V.*

$ ⊞ **Victory.** This hotel on Shamian Island has two wings, both origi-
★ nally colonial guesthouses that have been superbly renovated. The main building has a pink-and-white facade, an imposing portico, and twin domes on the roof, where the pool is located. Nevertheless, it is basically for budget travelers, with small rooms and inexpensive dining rooms. The setting among restored old mansions is priceless. ⊠ *53 Shamian Dajie, 510130,* ☎ *020/8186–2622,* FAX *020/8186–1062. 400 rooms. 4 restaurants, pool, health club, dance club, business services, meeting rooms. AE, DC, MC, V.*

NIGHTLIFE AND THE ARTS

The Arts

Except for the survival of Cantonese opera, performed in temporary bamboo theaters in People's Park and at annual festivals, Guangzhou has little to offer in the way of performing arts.

Nightlife

Until recently Guangzhou's nightlife scene was the sole preserve of Chinese businessmen in search of relaxation and recreation at karaoke lounges staffed by hostess "singing companions." Recently the situation has improved with the opening of some agreeable pubs.

Bars

All of the leading hotels have bars, where it's pleasant to relax after a hard day's work or sightseeing. The popular **Corner Bar** (⊠ Lobby, China

Hotel, ☎ 020/8666–6888) has big, comfortable bar stools, quiet tables for two, and a rack of the latest foreign newspapers. The big attraction of the **Hare & Moon** (✉ White Swan hotel, ☎ 020/8188–6968) is the panorama of the Pearl River as it flows past the picture windows.

Dance Clubs

A Go-Go (✉ Swan Club, 68 Binjiang Lu, ☎ 020/8430–8888) has some very sophisticated lighting and a huge dance floor. For energetic dancing to the latest pop music, without the hassle of karaoke, a good place is **Catwalk** (✉ Basement, China Hotel, ☎ 020/8666–6888). **JJ's** (✉ 18 Jiao Chang Xi Lu, ☎ 020/8381–3668) has a piano lounge and catwalk with Shanghai models. **Rock & Roll** (✉ 101 Yanjiang Xilu, ☎ 020/8189–2995) features that music.

Pubs

Café Elles (✉ 119 Shiu Yin Erlu, ☎ 020/8764–2939), opened in late 1996, caters to French expatriots and francophiles with French music and food and a small dance floor. The **Hard Rock Café** (✉ Basement, China Hotel, Liuhua Lu, ☎ 020/8666–6888, ext. 2059) has Elton John's trousers, Tina Turner's black dress, and stained glass pictures of rock icons such as John Lennon and Michael Jackson; there's live and taped rock music and a choice of hamburgers and Chinese dishes. Opened in 1996 by a Canadian-Chinese, **Kathleen's** (✉ 60 Tao Jin Lu, ☎ 020/8359–8045) has become a popular meeting and drop-in place for many local expats and regular visitors from Hong Kong and overseas; it's where you find out what's going on in Guangzhou. **L'Africain** (✉ 707 Dong Feng Zhonglu, ☎ 020/8778–2433) is the place for late night dancing, to African, reggae, Spanish and American pop music. **360 Degrees** (✉ 62 Tao Jin Lu, ☎ 020/8357–9688) offers jazz by African residents (who came to China originally as students) and by local musicians; there's a dance floor and long bar in front of a huge mural picturing jazz greats.

SHOPPING

The city has long offered goods at prices well below those in Hong Kong, but only recently has the range grown to compare with that available in the former colony, with the addition of international name-brand boutiques and branches of Hong Kong department stores, such as Sincere and Jusco. Shops are usually open from 9 or 10 AM to late into the evening.

Antiques and Traditional Arts and Crafts

Guangdong Arts Centre (✉ 698 Renmin Beilu) has a fine selection of painted scrolls. **Guangzhou Arts & Crafts Corporation** (✉ 11 Guangjiu Da Ma Lu) sells a wide variety of Foshan pottery. **Guangzhou Fine Arts** (✉ 46 Shuiyin Hengsi Ma Lu) specializes in scrolls and painted screens. **Guangzhou Ji Ya Zhai** (✉ 7 Xinwen Lu, Zhongshan Wulu) is a specialist in Chinese calligraphy and painting. **Guangzhou South Jade Carving Factory** (✉ 15 Xia Jiu Lu) offers visitors a perfect opportunity to watch jade being carved and buy the finished products at wholesale prices.

Bookstores

Guangzhou Book Center (✉ main square, Tianhe) has seven floors of books on every subject, including some bargain-priced art books in English, as well as computer programs and exercise equipment. **Xinhua Bookshop** (✉ 276 Beijing Lu) sells an extensive catalog of books on a wide range of subjects at very affordable prices.

Department Stores

Friendship Store (✉ 369 Huanshi Dong Lu) occupies a five-story building with departments selling a huge array of goods. There are fashions with such brand names as Pierre Cardin and Levi, cosmetics by Nina Ricci, Max Factor and Revlon, shoes by Puma, and a wide range of children's wear, luggage, and household appliances. **Guangzhou Merchandising Building** (✉ 295 Beijing Lu) has 11 departments on its six floors, selling watches, ladies' and men's garments, shoes and leather goods, children's wear, cosmetics, household appliances, and daily necessities.

Malls

GITIC Plaza Shopping Arcade (✉ Huanshi Donglu) has stores in the mid- to up-market range. Some are contained in the Monte Carlo Shopping Center, where ladies' and men's fashions, accessories, cosmetics, stationery, and such are sold. Then there are clothing boutiques, jade shops, and Chinese arts and crafts. The spacious arcade is particularly busy from 8 to 9 in the evening. **Nanfang International Shopping Arcade** (✉ Huanshi Donglu) is aimed at the top of the market, with Hong Kong-style boutiques selling name-brand products from Chanel, Christian Dior, and Pierre Cardin, plus Mickey Mouse licensed goods, Swatch watches, and Ulferts furniture. **White Swan Arcade** (✉ Shamian Island) has some of the city's finest up-market specialty shops. They sell genuine Chinese antiques, traditional craft items, works of modern and classical art, Japanese kimonos and swords, jewelry, cameras, and books published in and about China. There are also fashion boutiques that include China's first Benetton outlet and an Elizabeth Arden salon.

OUTDOOR ACTIVITIES AND SPORTS

Golf

Opened in 1995, the **Guangzhou Luhu Golf & Country Club** (☎ 020/8350–4957 or 020/8359–5576, ext. 3282) has 18 holes spread over 180 acres of Luhu Park, 20 minutes from Guangzhou train station and 30 minutes from Baiyun Airport. The 6,820-yard, 72-par course was designed by Dave Thomas. The club also offers a 75-bay driving range and a clubhouse with restaurants, a pro shop, and a health spa. Members' guests and those from affiliated clubs pay HK$500 greens fees for 18 holes on weekdays, HK$800 on weekends. Caddies can be hired for HK$180 per 18 holes and clubs rented for HK$150. The club is a member of the International Associate Club network.

Horse Racing

The Chinese passion for horse racing has found a home in Guangzhou, at the handsome **Guangzhou Jockey Club** track in the new downtown of Tianhe. It has a five-tier grandstand, electronic display boards, closed-circuit television, floodlights, and computerized betting. There are races from 1:30 PM every Sunday. ✉ *Tianhe Beilu, East Guangzhou,* ☎ *20/8753–9899.* 🎟 *RMB10.*

SIDE TRIPS FROM GUANGZHOU

Pearl River Delta

The booming economy of the Pearl River Delta region seems to have transformed even the smallest village into an industrial estate surrounded by acres of ersatz Mediterranean villas, assuming, that is, that the rural retreat hasn't been concreted over for a super expressway. The sturdy Cantonese heritage does survive in small pockets, overshadowed but undaunted by the modern highrise, high-tech world.

Foshan

⑱ *20 km (12½ mi) southwest of Guangzhou.*

Foshan (Buddha Mountain) is on the main circuit of the delta region. The city's history goes back 1,200 years. At one time it was an important religious center with a population of a million. Today, after centuries of obscurity, it is again a prosperous town with numerous joint enterprises involving overseas cousins.

Happily, this prosperity has encouraged residents to maintain the legacy of their past, dramatically in the city's **Zu Miao** (Ancestral Temple). It dates from the building of a Taoist temple on this spot during the Song dynasty (960–1279). Rebuilt during the Ming, without using nails, the main prayer hall is a masterpiece of art and architecture. Its wooden roof, with its interlocking beams, has a ridgepole crowded with porcelain figurines depicting the epic story of the *Romance of Three Kingdoms.* This is possibly the greatest example of porcelain tableaux art, which was developed by the potters of the nearby town of **Shiwan**, also known as Shekwan, where the art continues to flourish. You can visit workshops to see the artisans at work and buy their wares.

Inside the temple is a gilded altar table carved with scenes of Chinese defeating long-nosed foreign invaders. On the altar is a bronze statue of the Northern Emperor, cast in the Ming era and weighing 5,500 lb. On either side are examples of old spears, swords, and other weapons, plus gongs and an Iron Cloud Board, which were carried by a mandarin's entourage.

In the courtyard outside is the **Wanfutai** (Wantu Stage), built in 1658 and the oldest surviving wooden stage in China. It consists of a large platform with a great sweeping roof. The wall panels are inset with gilt carvings and colored glass. You can go behind the stage, where there is a display of old theater masks. ⊠ *Zumiao Lu.*

The vibrant artistic heritage of Foshan is not confined to historic buildings, however. At the **Renshou Si** (Folk Art Center), built into the former Renshou Temple, craftsmen make intricate paper cutouts, huge paper lanterns, butterfly kites, and heads for lion dances. There are also shops displaying calligraphy, scroll paintings, and carvings of jade, wood, and bone. In addition, there are many examples of Shiwan pottery, including a set depicting Bruce Lee in different kungfu postures. All are for sale, at very reasonable prices. ⊠ *Renmin Lu at Aumiao Lu.* ☉ *Daily 8–6.*

Zhongshan

⑲ *35 km (22 mi) southeast of Guangzhou.*

Zhongshan is the county, south of Foshan, that abuts Macau. In the 16th century, mandarins and merchants from here agreed to let the Portuguese settle on the tiny peninsula, and over the years this proximity has made it the source of vast numbers of emigrants. Formerly Heungshan (fragrant mountain) the area was renamed Zhongshan (central mountain) in honor of local hero Sun Yat-sen, who used the name as his nom-de-guerre. The county covers 690 sq mi of the fertile Pearl River Delta.

With substantial help from overseas Chinese investors, many new industries have been developed here in recent years, mostly footwear, tex-

Side Trips from Guangzhou

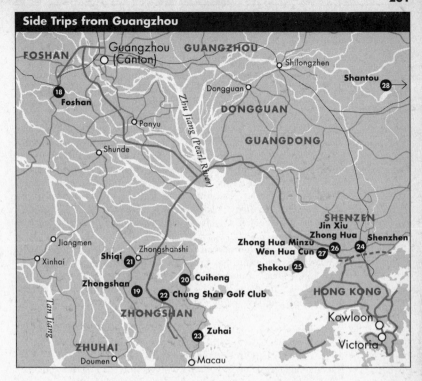

tiles, medicines, processed food, and electronic components. There are still farms to be seen, but increasingly, ancestral villages are being converted into suburbs of apartment houses and so-called villas. Some are inhabited by the newly rich farmers, but most were built speculatively as second homes for big-spending Hong Kong folk.

⑳ Cuiheng (106 km [65 mi] southeast of Guangzhou, 33 km [20 mi] north of Macau), is famous as the village where Sun Yat-sen was born in 1866. Located in a park is the **Sun Yat-sen Bowuguan** (Sun Yat-sen Museum; ☎ Y10; ⊙ daily 9–5), that has rooms ranged around a patio, each showing the life and times of Sun as man and revolutionary. Next to the museum is the **Sun Yat-sen Guju,** the house that Sun built for his parents during a visit in 1892. It is a fine example of China coast architecture, with European-style verandas facing west. Bad geomancy for traditional Chinese, it underscored Sun's reputation for rebellion. The interior, however, is traditional, with high-ceilinged rooms, ancestral plaques, gilded carvings, and heavy blackwood furniture that includes a roofed Chinese marriage bed. Nearby is the **Sun Yat-sen Memorial High School,** with splendid blue tile roofs and a traditional Chinese gateway. It was built in 1934 and has about 700 students. ⊠ *Cuiheng.* ☎ *Free.* ⊙ *9–5.*

㉑ Shiqi (formerly spelled Shekkei; also known as Zhongshanshi) is the capital of Zhongshan county, and for 800 years it has been an important market center and inland port. It's about 78 km (48 mi) south of Guangzhou and 61 km (38 mi) northwest of Macau. Until a few years ago it was a picturesque port, where a cantilever bridge over the Qi River was raised twice a day to allow small freighters to pass, but the old town has been all but obliterated by modern high rises, and farms that used to surround it are now covered with factories. Nevertheless you can still join the throngs who stroll along the riverbanks in the evening. The **Sun Zhongshan Jinian Tang** (Sun Yat-sen Memorial Hall; ⊠ Sunwen Zhonglu) and **Xishan Temple** (⊠ Xishan Park), restored in 1994, are also worth a visit.

DINING AND LODGING

$$ ✕🏨 **Chung Shan Hot Springs Resort.** This vast recreational complex consists of a charming compound of villas with pagoda roofs and Chinese antiques in some rooms, built around a traditional Chinese garden landscaped with classical pavilions beside willow-screened ponds filled with carp and lotus. The English-speaking staff is helpful, and there is a large Chinese restaurant (popular with tour groups) and a smaller western restaurant. Outside, extensive grounds contain a swimming pool, a shooting range, a horseback-riding ring, and a shopping center. There are also four baths fed by hot-spring water piped from a neighboring valley. The hotel is 24 km (15 mi) from Macau. ⊠ *Macau–Shiqi Highway, near Sanxiang, Zhongshan,* ☎ *0760/668–3888,* FAX *0760/668–3333. 350 rooms. 2 restaurants, pool, 36-hole golf course, 4 tennis courts, shops. AE, MC, V.*

$$ ✕🏨 **Zhongshan International Hotel.** This 20-story tower, topped with a revolving restaurant, has become a landmark of downtown Shiqi. Its Chinese restaurants are excellent. ⊠ *2 Zhongshan Rd., Shiqi 528400,* ☎ *0760/863–3388,* FAX *0760/887–3368. 369 rooms. 4 restaurants, pool, sauna, bowling, billiards. AE, MC, V.*

$ 🏨 **Cuiheng Hotel.** Opposite the Sun Yat-sen Memorial Park, this hotel consists of low-rise wings and bungalows of contemporary, elegant design. It has gardens around the pool and a riding school next door. ⊠ *Cuiheng Village, Zhongshan 519015,* ☎ *0760/552–2668,* FAX *0760/552–3333. 242 rooms. 2 restaurants, pool, dance club. AE, V.*

OUTDOOR ACTIVITIES AND SPORTS

㉒ The **Chung Shan Golf Club** was the first and is still considered one of the best in China. It was designed by Arnold Palmer's company and opened in 1984, with Palmer among the first to try it out. It's a par-72, 6,552-yd course of rolling hills, streams, and tricky sand traps. Professionals who have competed in China's first international golf tournaments here declare it first-class, and local youngsters who have been trained here now make up what amounts to China's national team. A second 18-hole course, designed by Jack Nicklaus, was added in the early 1990s, making this an ideal championship venue. The clubhouse, with gleaming mahogany paneling and elegant rattan furniture, has a bar, a restaurant, a sauna, and a granite-walled pool, plus a pro shop with everything you'd expect to find in an American or Japanese club. Greens fees for visitors are HK$500 for 18 holes during the week, HK$1,200 on weekends. Caddies cost HK$160 a round, and club rentals cost HK$110. ⊠ *Macau–Shiqi Highway, ½ hr north of Macau, Zhongshan,* ☎ *0760/668–3888.*

Zhuhai

㉓ *103 km (80 mi) southeast of Guangzhou; across border from Macau.*

Zhuhai was one of the first Special Economic Zones set up in 1980 with liberal laws to encourage foreign investment. The zone has been extended from an original 13 sq km (8 sq mi) to 121 sq km (74 sq mi), complete with a long coastline and many small off-shore islands.

Zhuhai has the highest standard of living anywhere in China. It is also one of the most congenial and clean areas, thanks to its high-tech industrial base, which includes factories producing electronics—Canon has its manufacturing headquarters here—textiles, glassware, TV parts, and computer discs. It is the place where pilots from all over Asia take Boeing simulator courses. Tourism is also important. Everyday hundreds of Western visitors cross from Macau and observe hundreds of Chinese tourists, often from remote provinces, who are observing them in return. Domestic tourists come to Zhongshan to pay their respects to Sun Yat-sen, and then they explore the shops and restaurants of Zhuhai, from which you can gaze across at Macau.

DINING AND LODGING

$$$ 🏨 **Grand Bay View Hotel.** This handsome new hotel stands on the bay between the Macau border and the Zhuhai ferry terminal. It is sumptuously furnished and contains some of the zone's best nightlife and dining, as well as imaginative function areas that include a balcony overlooking the water and Macau. ⊠ *Shui Wanlu, Gongbei 519020,* ☎ *0756/887–7998,*🖷 *0756/887–8998. 238 rooms. 4 restaurants, pool, 2 tennis courts, exercise room, billiards, nightclub. AE, DC, MC, V.*

$$$ ✕🏨 **Paradise Hill.** Looking like a belle epoch palace on the French Riviera, this new hotel replaced the modest little Shichingshan Resort. It has a stunning white-and-cream stone facade with balconies overlooking a garden terraced around fountains. To one side are swimming pools beside a man-made lake, and at the back, tennis courts and six villas with guest rooms. The interior boasts a marble-clad atrium lobby and a marble grand staircase. The restaurants, serving Chinese, Continental, Portuguese, and Japanese meals, are equally opulent, and the health center is state-of-the-art. ⊠ *Shichingshan, Zhuhai, 519015,* ☎ *0756/333–7388,* 🖷 *0756/333–3508, in Macau 853/552–739, ext. 406. 180 rooms, 6 villas. 8 restaurants, 2 pools, beauty salon, 2 tennis courts. AE, DC, MC, V.*

$$ ✕🏨 **Zhuhai Resort.** This is a delightful reproduction of a Qing dynasty courtyard mansion. The **Jade City** restaurant serves excellent Cantonese food, which is also served in private dining rooms. ⊠ *Shichingshan, Zhuhai, 519015,* ☎ *0756/333–3718,* 🖷 *0756/332–2339. 340 rooms. 4 restaurants, bar, 2 pools, 2 tennis courts, health club, meeting rooms. AE, DC, V.*

OUTDOOR ACTIVITIES AND SPORTS

In Zhuhai, next to a Formula-1 racing circuit, the **Lakewood Golf Club** is about a half hour by car from Macau, 20 minutes from the Zhuhai Ferry Terminal. It opened its Mountain Course and clubhouse at the end of 1995 and the Lake Course in 1997. The club is a joint venture of Zhuhai and Malaysian companies. Greens fees for visitors are HK$600 weekdays and HK$1,200 weekends, while caddies are HK$120 and golf carts HK$240. ⊠ *Jinding, Zhuhai,* ☎ *0756/335–2502,* 🖷 *0756/335–2504.*

Shenzhen/Shekou

153 km (95 mi) southeast of Guangzhou; across border from Hong Kong.

㉔ **Shenzhen** (Shumchun in Cantonese) was just a farming village across the border from Hong Kong until, in the late 1970s, it was designated a Special Economic Zone and became the first "instant China" excursion for foreign tourists. Since then it has been transformed into a bustling industrial center, complete with one of the highest GDPs in China and the attendant pollution, crowding, and sleaze. Today most visitors to Shenzhen are Chinese from Hong Kong, engaged in business or on family holidays, golfing, and relaxing in lavish but moderately priced resorts. Foreign tourists are drawn to Shenzhen's series of theme parks (☞ *below*).

㉕ **Shekou** came into being in 1978 as the company town of China Merchants, a mainland shipping and trading conglomerate with headquarters in Hong Kong. The company recognized the potential of

Shekou's location, at the entrance to the Pearl River estuary and next door to Hong Kong, not only as a new port but as a base for oil exploration firms. Since then all of the big oil companies have made their regional headquarters here, and it shows. There are spacious California-style suburbs, with balconied villas, swimming pools, and garages (a rarity in China). Nearby are supermarkets, high-rise office blocks, and a row of trendy bars and western restaurants. The streets are clean and the beach immaculate. There's virtually no crime and certainly no unemployment as everyone has to be cleared by China Merchants to live here.

Most foreign visitors come to Shekou by sleek, Norwegian-made catamaran ferries, which commute in 50 minutes from Hong Kong, but the opening of new expressways has made the port-city readily accessible from Shenzhen City, a half hour's drive away, and Guangzhou, less than two hours away. There is also good ferry service between Shekou and Macau and Guangzhou. This is important for the planned development of Shekou into a convention venue.

㉖ Jin Xiu Zhong Hua (Splendid China) draws crowds of Chinese visitors— Deng Xiaoping joined them on his famous journey south—because of the way it presents their historical and geographic heritage. This also appeals to Western visitors, who are equally impressed by the park as a masterpiece of folk art, where 74 of China's best-known attractions are shown in brilliant replicas on a scale of 15 to 1.

Each exhibit in the 74-acre site illustrates the ingenious craftsmanship of the Chinese. There is the incredible, waist-high Great Wall winding over the park's central hillock, and the Forbidden City looking like a celestial emperor's doll house. Nearby is Tibet's Potala Palace and the Buddhist sculptures of the Magao Grottoes, while around the corner is a water village from Jiangsu and the Ming Tombs.

Cleverly arranged between paths for pedestrians and electric hire cars, the exhibits are well labeled in English and Chinese. By some magic they offer individual worlds in spite of their often illogical proximity. For instance, the mausoleum of Genghis Khan, surrounded by a Mongol horde that seems to shimmer in the desert heat, is just a short stroll from the Ice Lantern show of Harbin— with tinted glass for ice. Best of all is the population of this mini-world. Thousands of tiny porcelain people, each one different, come to life in a triumph of folk art. ✉ *Shenzhen Bay, Shenzhen.* 🎫 *HK$/Y110.* ⊗ *Daily 9–6.*

㉗ Zhong Hua Minzu Wen Hua Cun (China Folk Culture Villages), the theme park CTS built next to Splendid China, is a collection of faithfully reproduced buildings from different ethnic areas of China, along with some typical scenery. What was a small spit of flat land on the bayside now has soaring concrete peaks of the Stone Forest with life-size houses of some of Yunnan's many minority peoples nearby: a stone Bouyei house, a bamboo and thatch Yao residence, and a Miao compound. Nearby is the monumental Wind and Rain Bridge and Drum Tower from Guizhou, together with traditional houses. Elsewhere there's a Tibetan house and lamasary, a Moslem mosque beside a Uygur house, and a Beijing quadrangle.

Among the many attractions of the park are the craft workshops set up in some of the houses, where native experts produce local specialties, such as embroidery, weaving, carving, painting, and jewelry, while you watch. The finished articles are for sale. Another popular activity is a dine-around-China tour, on which you can sample regional dishes made by locals using ingredients from back home.

Performances of songs, dances, and acrobatics from diverse parts of the country take place throughout the day. They are held in the relevant villages, on small stages in front of benches for the audience. The show begins at 11 AM when the gates open with a welcoming dance. There follow performances by artists from minorities such as the Miao, Dong, Dai, Kazak, Mongol, Tibetan, Uygur, Hani and Korean. Each lasts 15 minutes, and plenty of time is allowed for the audience to move to the next show. There is also a one-hour performance in the park's Central Theatre at 5 PM. In the evening, the entertainment continues with other programs. At 7 the artists stage a Folk Arts Parade through the park to reach the Central Theatre for a grand performance at 8, with a laser show projected on the park's Water Screen; finally a 75-ft statue of the thousand-eyed Guanyin, Goddess of Mercy, is paraded through the park. ⊠ *Shenzhen Bay, Shenzhen.* 🎫 *HK$130.* ⊙ *Daily 11–9:30.*

DINING AND LODGING

$$ ✕🏨 **Landmark Shenzhen.** This handsome hotel in downtown Shenzhen looks and feels European. Its lobby is like a foyer, with informal check-in counters, and the central Piazza Café is really like an Italian square, with a skylight roof, overhanging balconies, striped canopies, and tables set out as in a sidewalk café. The Landmark is also popular for its Chinese abalone restaurant and 27th-floor Hollywood entertainment center. ⊠ *2 Nanhu Lu, Shenzhen, 518001,* ☎ *0755/217–2288,* FAX *0755/229–0473. 351 rooms. 3 restaurants, pool, health club, shops, dance club, business services, meeting rooms. AE, DC, MC, V.*

$$ 🏨 **Marina Ming Wah Convention Center.** Opened in 1997, this multipurpose, high-tech commercial complex adjoins the original Marina Ming Wah Hotel, which has large, irregularly shaped rooms, many with private terraces. There are Cantonese and western restaurants, and the popular Marina Tavern. The city's first scenic elevators take guests to the 25th- (top-) floor Crow's Nest tea lounge, complete with a dance floor. The floor below is devoted to the Asian buffet Spice Market. ⊠ *Gui Shan Lu, Shekou, 518067,* ☎ *0755/668–9968,* FAX *0755/668–6668. 85 rooms and suites, 28 service apartments. 8 restaurants, bar, pool, bowling, health club, dance club, business services, convention center. AE, DC, MC, V.*

$$ 🏨 **Nan Hai.** This was the first luxury hotel in Shenzhen, designed for international oil company demands. The rooms are large and expensively furnished, and all have terraces. The hotel has its own beach and extensive resort facilities, including a large pool, tennis courts, a golf putting green, and a gym. There are various restaurants, a bar, and karaoke lounge. ⊠ *Next to ferry terminal, Shekou, 518069,* ☎ *0755/669–2888,* FAX *0755/669–2440. 396 rooms. 5 restaurants, bar, pool, beauty salon, miniature golf, tennis court, jogging, shops, billiards, dance club, meeting rooms. AE, DC, MC, V.*

$$ 🏨 **Shangri-La Shenzhen.** Opposite the stations for trains from Guangzhou and Hong Kong and alongside the bus station, this hotel nevertheless has the characteristic Shangri-La class. The top-floor revolving restaurant is furnished like a country house lounge, and the health club has an outdoor pool terrace and marbled spa facilities. The hotel contains a new grand ballroom that can accommodate 1,500 people. It is also home to Henry J. Bean's American grill. ⊠ *Jianshe Lu, Shenzhen, 518001,* ☎ *0755/233–0888,* FAX *0755/233–9878. 553 rooms. 4 restaurants, pool, beauty salon, health club, shops, business services, meeting rooms. AE, DC, MC, V.*

$$ 🏨 **Sunshine.** Although it looks like an average Shenzhen multipurpose building from the outside, this is one of the most attractive hotels in the region. The grand lobby flows from the entrance through the lounge and bar, past the white marble staircase to the executive wing.

Here you find the Sunshine City Health Club, with a vast indoor pool, a golf putting "green" and simulator, a fully equipped gym, and a TV-aerobics room. ☒ *1 Jiabin Lu, Shenzhen, 518005,* ☎ *0755/223–3888,* FAX *0755/222–6719. 372 rooms. 7 restaurants, pool, beauty salon, putting green, 2 tennis courts, health club, squash, shops, dance club, business services, meeting rooms. AE, DC, MC, V.*

OUTDOOR ACTIVITIES AND SPORTS

Mission Hills Golf Club (☒ Dai Hau Yau Lok, Cheng Guanlan, Shenzhen, ☎ 0755/802–2931) scored a signal success, against many expectations, when it hosted the World Cup of Golf in 1995. It has four 18-hole championship courses. Other facilities include a spectacular clubhouse and an adjoining 228-room resort, courts for basketball tournaments, tennis and squash courts, a variety of restaurants, and an indoor/outdoor pool around a stage for concerts or fashion shows. The courses are not open to nonmembers except for resort guests, for whom greens fees are HK$700 weekdays and HK$1,200 weekends; caddies are HK$100 and caddy carts HK$200.

Just inside the border of Hong Kong and Shenzhen, the **Sand River Golf Club** (☒ Shen Nan Lu, Shenzhen Bay, Shenzhen, ☎ 0755/690–0111) offers two courses—one is nine holes and floodlit—designed by Gary Player. There is also a large driving range, a fishing lake, and various resort facilities. Greens fees for visitors are HK$600 weekdays and HK$1,000 weekends. Caddies are HK$150.

Pearl River Delta A to Z

ARRIVING AND DEPARTING

By Boat. Fast, modern catamaran ferries make eight round-trips daily to the pier at **Jiuzhou** (on the coast of Zhuhai, just north of Macau), with five departures from CHKC (☒ Canton Rd., Kowloon) and three from the Macau Ferry Terminal (☒ Shun Tak Centre, Connaught Rd., Central). The trip takes 90 minutes. ☒ *HK$236 first class, HK$211 second, HK$196 third.*

Catamarans make six round-trips daily between Hong Kong and Zhongshan Harbor, close to **Shiqi,** with five departures from the CHKC Terminal and one from Shun Tak Centre on Hong Kong Island. The trip takes approximately 80 minutes. ☒ *HK$251 first class, HK$231 second class, HK$221 third class.*

Comfortable, double-deck catamaran ferries make a pleasant 50-minute trip between Macau and **Shekou** (passing under the new Tsing Ma Bridge), with five departures daily, from the Macau Ferry Terminal. ☒ *HK$145 first class, HK$110 economy class.*

By Bus. Citybus (☎ 852/2873–0818) buses make eight round-trips daily between Hong Kong and Shenzhen, with six continuing on to Shenzhen Bay theme parks. Buses depart Admiralty Station and CHKC Terminal. Fares depend on the destination and day. ☒ *HK$65 one-way to Shenzhen City weekdays, HK$85 weekends. HK$75 one-way to Shenzhen Bay weekdays, HK$95 weekends.*

By Plane. Shenzhen Airport is very busy, with flights to 50 cities. There is commuter service by catamaran ferries and buses between the airport and Hong Kong. Zhuhai International Airport is the largest in size in China but, despite its name, it operates only domestically, to 24 cities.

By Train. There is a rail route from Beijing to Hong Kong via Shenzhen.

GUIDED TOURS

By far the most popular tour is to **Zhongshan** via Macau, which provides a full and interestingly diverse, if rather tiring, daylong outing. All one-day Zhongshan tours begin with an early departure from

Hong Kong to Macau and a bus transfer to the border at Gongbei, in the Zhuhai Special Economic Zone. From here tour itineraries vary, but all spend time in Cuiheng Village, to visit the house built by Sun Yat-sen and an excellent museum devoted to his life and times. A six-course lunch, with free beer and soft drinks, is taken in Shiqi, an 800-year-old inland port that has become an industrial city, at the Chung Shan resort, or in one of the "neo-Qing dynasty" hotels of Zhuhai. Completing the itinerary is a visit to a "typical" farming village, which is kept traditional for tourists. Tours return to Hong Kong in the late afternoon via Zhongshan Harbor. ☎ *Zhongshan tour: HK$880.*

The other established one-day China trip takes in the **Shenzhen Special Economic Zone,** immediately across the border from Hong Kong. This begins with a coach trip to Shenzhen to visit either **Splendid China,** (✉ HK$680) or the adjoining theme park, **China Folk Culture Villages** (✉ HK$650). The tour also includes visits to a Hakka village, a kindergarten, and a market.

Shantou/Chaozhou

㉘ *380 km (236 mi) east of Guangzhou.*

The ancestral homeland of the Chaozhou people—better known outside China by the Cantonese pronunciation Chiu Chow—is the region on the east coast of Guangdong Province, between the port of Shantou (formerly written Swatow) and the historic capital of Chaozhou.

Although there was a settlement here from the 2nd century BC, the original Chiu Chow arrived in the 4th century, fleeing war torn Central China. They developed a distinctive dialect, cuisine, and operatic style, as well as a talent for business, which was conducted through Chaozhou. Silting of the Han River forced business downstream to Shantou, locally known as Swatow, which in 1858 became one of the ports opened up to foreigners by the Treaty of Tianjin.

Companies like Jardine Matheson and British American Tobacco set up shop, but Swatow remained a minor-league treaty port compared with Shanghai. Nevertheless, the local lace and porcelain became world famous. Meanwhile, droughts and warlords spurred the Chiu Chow people to emigrate on a mass scale to Southeast Asia and beyond.

Today there are an estimated 6 million overseas Chiu Chow, half of them in Thailand, 1.2 million in Hong Kong, and large numbers in Taiwan, Malaysia, and North America. An amazing number have made their fortunes in their new homes, but they don't forget their roots, which was why Shantou was, in 1980, chosen as a Special Economic Zone for investment from abroad.

The results have exceeded every expectation, with vast sums flowing in to build a new port and new highways, hospitals, and schools, as well as office buildings and homes. Today the picturesque port of old Swatow lies on 30 international and domestic shipping routes; modern vessels far outnumber the traditional fishing boats. Gleaming high rises have replaced all but a handful of the Victorian houses and offices, with their neo-classical facades and colonnaded verandas. The best of the survivors is the former British Consulate in Jiaoshi Scenic Park, which now houses government offices.

The waterfront **Xidi Gongyuan** (Xidi Park), with its parade of beautifully sculpted stone animals and people alongside tree-shaded benches and open-sided pavilions, is where locals play Chinese chess and read newspapers. From here you have intimate views of the busy harbor with its fleets of fishing boats, ferries, and freighters, which somehow steer clear of oyster farms that produce the key ingredient for delicious oyster pancakes.

The best reason for visiting Shantou is to make the 50-minute drive inland to **Chaozhou.** During the Tang and Song dynasties, it thrived as an inland port with its own sophisticated cultural style. The port succumbed to river silt, but Chaozhou preserved much of its heritage. Thanks to the fine local clay and traditional craftsmen, it continues to produce all kinds of Chinese porcelain in workshops that welcome visitors. One company still makes Chaozhou wood carvings and there are factories producing lace, but the distinctive "sculpted" embroidery is no longer made, for lack of skilled needleworkers.

The **Kaiyuan Si** (Kaiyuan Temple), built in AD 738 as one of the 10 major temples in China, is a Chaozhou treasury that contains three huge gilt statues of Buddha, a 3,300-lb Song dynasty bronze bell, and a stone incense burner said to have been carved from a meteorite. Its prayer pavilions have ridgepole decorations of multi-colored porcelain birds and flowers in exuberant swirling patterns.

Not much is left of the old **Ming dynasty wall,** except for two carved wooden gates that have been attractively restored. There were also plans to restore the original bridge built over the Han in the 12th century. It once rested on 18 wooden boats in a traditional "floating gate," which swung with the tide, a device to overcome the problem of building foundations in the then-swiftly flowing river; they are now replaced by concrete blocks.

DINING AND LODGING

Although Chiu Chow food ranks as one of China's great cuisines, it is not easy to sample it in its homeland unless you have local contacts. There are, of course, plenty of restaurants around Shantou and Chaozhou, but virtually none has an English menu or English-speaking staff, and in most cases even the name is in Chinese only. Happily, however, the major hotels have restaurants that serve Chiu Chow meals. They have English menus and at least one person who speaks English.

$$$ ✕🏨 **Golden Gulf Hotel.** Sophisticated elegance aptly describes this, the only luxury hotel in the region. Guest rooms occupy a white, semi-circular tower. The pool terrace and tennis courts are laid out on an open podium, and the lobby is a circular courtyard with a globe-shape fountain as a centerpiece and a glass domed ceiling. Restaurants and shops are arranged around the colonnaded gallery. The decor is stylish throughout, the Magnificent Palace Chiu Chow restaurant being suitably lavish and the City Bar a cozy retreat with Tiffany lamps, marble-topped tables and a newspaper rack. The food served is as good as the setting, with fresh, beautifully prepared Chiu Chow and Cantonese dishes, plus Japanese and Chinese hot pots and good western food. ✉ *Jinsha Dong Lu, Shantou, 515041,* ☎ *0754/826–3263,* FAX *0754/826–5162. 400 rooms. 5 restaurants, pool, 1 tennis court, health club, dance club, business services, meeting rooms. AE, DC, MC, V.*

$$$ ✕🏨 **Shantou International.** Opened in 1988, this was the first international-class hotel in East Guangdong, and it remains a major landmark with its zig-zag facade and revolving restaurant. It is a few blocks from the Special Economic Zone and close to the shops. The 26th-floor Palace Revolve is where guests and locals come for a comprehensive western and Chinese buffet breakfast. For the rest of the day, it turns into a western restaurant and bar. The Han Jiang Chun, a banquet hall, serves some of the best Chiu Chow food in the region. You can also find the local cuisine, along with dim sum, noodles, Cantonese, Sichuan, and Beijing dishes, in the casual Fragrant Court food street. In the elaborately traditional Tea House, you prepare your own kungfu tea around a carved wooden cabinet that opens up to reveal a small sink, where the first infusions of tea are poured before the powerful brew is ready to drink. The hotel's guest rooms are large and comfortably furnished. ⊠ *Jinsha Lu, Shantou, 515041,* ☎ *0754/825–1212,* 𝔽𝔸𝕏 *0754/825–2250. 350 rooms. 4 restaurants, health club, dance club, business services, meeting rooms. AE, DC, MC, V.*

$$ ╳🖽 **Shantou Harbour View.** Overlooking the harborside park, a block or so from the International Ferry Terminal, this smartly modern hotel has marvelous views of the busy port. It has a nautical theme, with a blue-and-white color scheme and a tower of rooms that suggests a giant sail. The rooms have attractive decor; garden suites have their own private terraces. The Harbor View Restaurant is a superior coffee shop, serving western and Chinese food against a backdrop panorama of the port. For fine dining Chiu Chow and Cantonese style there's the Palace Restaurant. The Paradise Disco and an extensive sauna provide recreation and relaxation. ⊠ *Haibin Dong Lu, Shantou, 515031,* ☎ *0754/ 854–3838,* 𝔽𝔸𝕏 *0754/855–0280. 250 rooms. 2 restaurants, health club, dance club, business services, meeting rooms. AE, DC, MC, V.*

SHOPPING

All kinds of locally made porcelain is available in Shantou shops and roadside stores in **Fungxi,** a village on the outskirts of Chaozhou, where family factories produce customized dinnerware and commemorative mugs, openwork Chinese stools, and waist-high jars encrusted with brightly colored and gilded figures. Most are for export around the world but sold here for the best prices. Most shops pack and ship overseas. Lace is very cheap and abundant in shops in Shantou and Chaozhou. If you're lucky you also might find some of the local three-dimensional wood carvings.

Shantou Essentials

From Guangzhou there are daily flights (45 minutes) and air-conditioned, express bus service (five hours). From Hong Kong there are two flights a day, express buses (six hours) and an overnight ferry.

GUANGZHOU A TO Z

Arriving and Departing

By Boat

There is daily service by **Turbo Cat** (catamaran ferries) between China Hong Kong City (CHKC) ferry terminal (⊠ Canton Rd., Kowloon) in Hong Kong and Guangzhou, departing 7:15 AM and 1:30 PM, returning 10:00 AM and 4:00 PM. The journey takes about 2 hours. 🚢 *HK$370 first class, HK$250 economy from Hong Kong, HK$345 and HK$225 from Guangzhou.*

A **ferry** makes the journey every day, departing CHKC Terminal at 9 PM; it arrives at dawn, and passengers disembark at 7 AM. There are cabins of different classes and restaurants. 🚢 *From HK$202 for a 4-berth cabin.*

By Bus

Citybus (☎ 852/2873–0818; 🚢 HK$180 from Hong Kong, Y170 from Guangzhou) has five round-trips a day between Hong Kong and Guangzhou using new vehicles that have toilets, drinks, snacks, reclining seats, and individual air-conditioning and lighting controls. The trip takes 3½ hours, and buses leave from CHKC and Shatin City One in Hong Kong and the Garden Hotel in Guangzhou. Among other bus services, **China Travel Service** (CTS; 🚢 HK$170) has 11 round-trips a day, with pick-up and drop-off at major Guangzhou hotels. Following CTS's purchase of a stake in Citybus in 1997 there is likely to be a broader, coordinated service by 1998.

By Plane

Guangzhou is an international gateway, served by direct flights from Los Angeles, Singapore, Bangkok, Sydney and Pnom Penh, and from Amsterdam via Beijing. There are four flights daily from Hong Kong, a hop of 20 minutes. It is one of the busiest domestic airports, with at least seven flights a day from both Beijing and Shanghai, as well as services from virtually every other major city in China. The local China Southern Airlines is one of the big three Chinese carriers.

By Train

Five express trains depart daily from **Kowloon Station** (✉ Hong Chong Rd., Tsim Sha Tsui East) at 8:35 AM, 9:25 AM, 11:45 AM, 1:20 PM and 2:45 PM. The trip takes about 105 minutes. The last train back to Hong Kong leaves at 6 PM. 🎫 *HK$280 first class, HK$250 second class.*

Guangzhou is the terminus for daily express trains from Beijing.

Getting Around

By Subway

Guangzhou is not an easy place to get around because of the vast amount of demolition and building going on. The first line of the new Metro, opened in late 1997, connects Huangsha, close to the White Swan hotel, with the southern suburbs. Future lines are planned to link up both the old and new railway stations and downtown areas.

By Taxi

Taxis provide the only viable means of city transport. There are plenty of them, at hotels, outside tourist sights, and on the roads. Some are obviously retired from Hong Kong service, with sagging suspension, broken handles, and inoperative air-conditioning. The large grille around the driver leaves little room in the back. Few drivers speak English, so you need your destination written in Chinese. The flag-fall is RMB9, with increments of 60 *fen* per 250 m, and drivers will always give receipts.

Contacts and Resources

Obtaining information of any kind is extremely difficult in Guangzhou, even for the Chinese. The most valuable sources are the staff in hotel business centers, but even the best have limited knowledge of their city. Getting information over the phone is particularly frustrating. Don't try calling the railway station (☎ 20/8668–2043) unless you have hours and patience to spare. Consulates are a good source of information.

Consulates

U.S. (✉ White Swan hotel Annex, Shamian Nan Jie, Shamian, ☎ 20/8186–2441). **Australia** (✉ 1503 GITIC Plaza Offices, 339 Huanshi Dong Lu, ☎ 20/8331–1888 ext. 1503). **U.K.** (✉ GITIC Plaza Offices, ☎ 20/8331–1888, ext. 5304).

Currency Exchange

You can easily change foreign currency at hotels and banks in Guangdong; the Hong Kong dollar is a very acceptable second currency here.

Emergencies

Tourist Hotline (☎ 20/8667–74220). Foreign Affairs Branch of **Public Security Bureau** (☎ 20/8331–1326). **Guangzhou Red Cross** (☎ 20/8444–6411). **Guangzhou Emergency Treatment Centre** (☎ 120).

Guided Tours

Four-day circular tours of the region (departing Hong Kong Tues., Thurs., and Sat.) begin with a fast ferry to Macau. This is followed by a visit to Cuiheng, an overnight stay in Shiqi, a day in Foshan, a night in Zhaoqing, and a night and day in Guangzhou before a return by train to Hong Kong. ✉ *HK$2,520.*

Travel Agencies

If you're coming from Hong Kong, **China Travel Service** (CTS; ☎ 852/2853–3533) is the most convenient place to book tickets to Guangzhou and the Pearl Delta area, although they add a service charge.

Travel agencies in Guangzhou can arrange tours of Foshan, Zhaoqing, and other nearby places of interest. The biggest are **Guangdong International Travel** (✉ 2/F Dong Fang Hotel, ☎ 020/8666–1646, FAX 020/8668–8921), **Guangdong CITS** (✉ 179 Huanshi Lu, ☎ 020/8666–6271, FAX 020/8667–8048), and **Guangdong CTS** (✉ 10 Qiaoguang Lu, ☎ 020/8333–6888, FAX 020/8333–2247).

Visas

☞ Chapter 1

Visitor Information

There are no local English-language newspapers or magazines. *City life Guangdong,* published in Hong Kong every two months, is quite useful. **Hong Kong Trade Development Council** (✉ 23/F GITIC Plaza Building, 339 Huanshi Donglu, ☎ 020/8331–2889; business advice). **Trade Fair information** (☎ 020/8667–7000).

7 Southeastern China

China's southeast attracts connoisseurs with the wondrous scenery of Guilin and with the modernizing changes taking place in bustling cities such as Xiamen, one of China's first Special Economic Zones. If you want to find out what has happened to the revolution, then you can visit Shaoshan, the birthplace of Chairman Mao and once a shrine as important to the Chinese as Jerusalem is to the Christian, Muslim, or Jew.

Pick up
the phone.

Pick up
the miles.

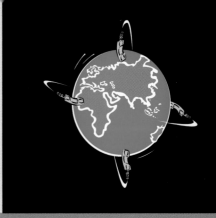

MCI ✦   Calling Card

415 555 1234 2244
J.D. SMITH

WorldPhone

Use your MCI Card® to make an international call from virtually anywhere in the world and earn frequent flyer miles on one of seven major airlines.

Enroll in an MCI Airline Partner Program today. In the U.S., call **1-800-FLY-FREE**. Overseas, call MCI collect at **1-916-567-5151**.

1. To use your MCI Card, just dial the WorldPhone access number of the country you're calling from.
   (For a complete listing of codes, visit www.mci.com.)
2. Dial or give the operator your MCI Card number.
3. Dial or give the number you're calling.

# Bahrain	800-002
# Brunei	800-011
# China ❖	108-12
For a Mandarin-speaking operator	108-17
# Cyprus ♦	080-90000
# Egypt ♦	355-5770
(Outside of Cairo, dial 02 first)	
# Federated States of Micronesia	624
# Fiji	004-890-1002
# Guam (CC)	950-1022
# Hong Kong (CC)	800-1121
# India (CC) ❖	000-127
# Indonesia (CC) ♦	001-801-11
Iran ÷	(Special Phones Only)
# Israel (CC)	177-150-2727
# Japan (CC) ♦	
To call using KDD ■	0039-121▶
To call using IDC ■	0066-55-121
To call using ITJ ■	0044-11-121
# Jordan	18-800-001
# Korea (CC)	
To call using KT ■	009-14
To call using DACOM ■	00309-12
Phone Booths ÷	Red Button 03, then press ★
Military Bases	550-2255

# Kuwait	800-MCI (800-624)
Lebanon ÷	600-MCI (600-624)
# Macao	0800-131
# Malaysia (CC) ♦	800-0012
# Philippines (CC) ♦	
To call using PLDT ■	105-14
To call using PHILCOM ■	1026-14
Philippines IIIC via PLDT in Tagalog ■	105-15
Philippines IIIC via PHILCOM in Tagalog ■	1026-12
# Qatar ★	0800-012-77
# Saipan (CC) ÷	950-1022
# Saudi Arabia (CC)	1-800-11
# Singapore	8000-112-112
# Sri Lanka	440-100
(Outside of Colombo, dial 01 first)	
# Syria	0800
# Taiwan (CC) ♦	0080-13-4567
# Thailand ★	001-999-1-2001
# United Arab Emirates ♦	800-111
Vietnam ●	1201-1022
Yemen	008-00-102

Is this a great time, or what? :-)

Urban planning.

CITYPACKS

The ultimate guide to the city—a complete pocket guide plus a full-size color map.

www.fodors.com

THE SOUTHEAST OF CHINA—the provinces of Fujian, Guangxi, Jiangxi, Hunan, and Guizhou—is a region as varied as it is large, from the temperate coastline of Fujian to the tropical coastline of Guangxi, from the arid hills of Jiangxi and Hunan to the lushness of Guizhou.

By Christopher Knowles

Fujian is popular with overseas Chinese, many of whose ancestors were part of the great 19th-century waves of immigration around the world. Xiamen has excellent seafood, while the offshore island of Gulangyu, empty of traffic, is a fascinating mix of Chinese and Western colonial architecture. In the southwest of the province are the traditional earth dwellings of the Hakka people, and close to Quanzhou is the walled town of Chongwu. This great tea-growing area is also the site of the Tea Art Halls of Fuzhou. Among Jiangxi's treasures are the old imperial porcelain center at Jingdezhen and the hill resort of Lushan. In Hunan, Changsha has an excellent museum, and the small town of Shaoshan is the birthplace of Mao Zedong. Guizhou is the site of China's mightiest waterfall and home to a large number of colorful non-Han peoples.

In Guangxi you'll find the sublime scenery of Guilin. Guilin probably ranks, along with the Taj Mahal and others, as one of the great destinations of the world. Of course it has been commercialized to exploit the world's interest, and there is a lamentable but unavoidable atmosphere of gold-fever about this small town that can be disconcerting; fortunately the scenery remains as it always has been.

Pleasures and Pastimes

Beaches
There are a couple of tolerable beaches on Gulangyu at Xiamen and on Meizhou Island. Perhaps the best beach in this largely inland region is at Beihai, on the tropical south coast of Guangxi.

Dining
The vastness of the area allows for a wide variety of cooking, most of it delicious. The cuisine of **Fujian** is considered by some to have its own characteristics and by others to form part of the Eastern tradition, one of the four major styles of Chinese cooking. It also shares some characteristics of its famous culinary neighbor to the south, Guangdong, but tends to fry more than steam. Spare ribs are a specialty, as are soups, and stews using a soy and rice wine stock. The coastal cities of Fujian offer a wonderful range of seafood, including shark's fin soup, a great delicacy usually served at the beginning of the meal rather than at the end, which otherwise is the usual custom with soups. Other dishes to look for are river eel with leeks, fried jumbo prawns, drunken chicken (chicken soused in Shaoxing wine), and steamed crab.

The cooking of **Hunan** tends to be spicy, not unlike Sichuanese food. Although it lacks Sichuan's variety, it produces some fine dishes, such as hot bean curd, spicy noodles, chicken with peanut sauce, and dishes cooked in a sauce heavily spiced with ginger, garlic, and chili.

As **Guangxi** and **Guizhou** are closer to the tropics, their cooking tends to be more exotic, with strong influences from both Guangdong and the spicy cooking of Hunan and Sichuan. There is a wide range of vegetables and fruit and a love of what are to westerners at best exotic and at worst repellent dishes—snake, dog, and, illegally, rare animals such as the pangolin. Both snake and dog are said to have warming effects and are therefore winter specialties. Guizhou in particular has a wide variety of traditional dishes, as the province is home to so many ethnic groups; bean curd is again a specialty, most famously "fall in love bean curd" (bean curd with chili sauce mixed with wild garlic shoots, vinegar, and soy sauce). An unexpected specialty of Guizhou is beef kebab, introduced by Uigur immigrants from Xinjiang and adapted to local produce. Look also for hotpot and for ginkgo fruit served in beaten egg white. **Jiangxi,** never noted for its cooking, has tended to absorb the traditions of the provinces that surround it. However, there are a few specialties to try—five-flower pork (slices of pork cooked in spice), sautéed frog, and soy-braised chicken.

CATEGORY	COST*
$$$$	OVER $27
$$$	$21–$27
$$	$12–$21
$	under $12

Prices are per person for a five-course meal, excluding drinks, taxes, and tip.

Lodging

The following chart gives an approximate idea of the cost of lodging in the region. It should be kept in mind that as there is no satisfactory method of grading hotels in China, price may have but a superficial bearing on quality.

The $$$$ category generally refers to the new generation of Chinese hotel, often built with foreign money, and with facilities associated with international standards. The $$$ category refers to hotels with good facilities but where service and comfort have been compromised in some way. The $$ category refers to generally older hotels that have been modernized. In the final, $, category, facilities may be simple or even offer dormitory accommodation.

CATEGORY	COST*
$$$$	OVER $102
$$$	$79–$102
$$	$54–$79
$	under $54

Prices are for a standard double room at peak season, including taxes.

Scenery

Perhaps the single greatest highlight of a visit to this part of China is the breathtaking scenery. Most famous, of course, is the fairy-tale scenery of **Guilin,** in Guangxi province, with its hundreds of karst-formation mountains rising sheer out of a vast plain of streams and paddy-fields; the Tang dynasty poet Han Yu likened them to "kingfisher jade hairpins." But Guilin is far from being the only possibility for lovers of natural beauty. In northwest Fujian is **Wuyi Shan,** a land of 36 tree-clad mountains, skirted by the stream known as Nine Bend Creek. In the northeast of Fujian is **Taimu Shan** (Taimu Mountain), an area of exotically shaped rocks and peaks. Guizhou is home to China's highest waterfall at **Huangguoshu.** In Hunan, **Wulingyuan Fengjinqu** (Wulingyuan Scenic Reserve), among the Wuling Mountains, is home to several minority peoples and the largest cave in Asia.[/r]

Exploring Southeastern China

To travel in an area as vast as this, the size of several European countries, and in a country like China, which is still developing its service industries, you need to be well organized. Unless you have limitless patience and time on your hands, set your priorities in advance. In the coastal province of Fujian, particularly in the cities of Fuzhou and Xiamen, the new China of the trader and entrepreneur is very much in evidence. The inland provinces of Hunan and Jiangxi, bordering each other to the west of Fujian, are rugged and deeply rural, perhaps the best places in this region to get a sense of both imperial China—the porcelain kilns at Jingdezhen, the museum at Changsha—and revolutionary China—Mao's birthplace at Shaoshan and the scene of the Communist uprising of 1927 at Nanchang. Guilin is in the heart of the tropical province of Guangxi, which borders Vietnam to the west and the South China Sea to the south. Finally, to the north of Guangxi, is the inland province of Guizhou, a territory of high valleys and low mountains, home to at least nine non-Han ethnic groups, of which 82% are farmers.

Great Itineraries

To get the most out of this large area, a minimum stay of two weeks is recommended, three to explore it properly. However, with good planning, it would be possible to extract some of its flavor within a week or ten days. For shorter stays, you will be limited to one or two destinations in the region.

Numbers in the margin correspond to points of interest on the Southeast China, Fuzhou, Changsha, Guilin, and Nanning maps.

IF YOU HAVE 2 DAYS

Fly directly to **Guilin** and book a place on the cruise along the Li River to Yangshuo. This effectively takes up a whole day but is one of the highlights of any visit to China. On the second day either explore the town on foot or, better still, rent a bicycle and spend the day cycling around the countryside through the mountains and tropical fruit farms, perhaps including a visit to the gaudy attractions of the Reed Flute Cave (remembering to take a flashlight). At night there may be an acrobatic display, or you might join a party following a cormorant fisherman on the river.

IF YOU HAVE 7 DAYS

Start with Guilin, as above; then fly north to **Guiyang** and find your way to Huangguoshu Falls; see also the ways of life of the non-Han peoples who live there. If you have time, go to **Xiamen** on the southeast coast and explore the islet of Gulangyu, a short ferry ride from Xiamen island, which has a fascinating array of colonial architecture.

IF YOU HAVE AT LEAST 10 DAYS

Start by spending a couple of nights in **Xiamen,** followed by a short visit to **Fuzhou** in order to go to Wuyi Shan. Continue on to Guiyang for three nights to visit the Huangguoshu Falls. Next go to **Guilin** for three nights. Finish off on the south coast, relaxing on the beaches at **Beihai.** If you don't want to sunbathe, go instead to **Changsha** to see the excellent museum.

IF YOU HAVE AT LEAST 14 DAYS

After visiting **Guilin, Huangguoshu Falls,** and **Xiamen,** make sure you visit Mao's birthplace at **Shaoshan** and the revolutionary sites at **Nanchang.**

When to Tour Southeastern China

The best time of year is in the spring, in April or early May. The winter months can be surprisingly cold (except on the south coast of Guangxi), and the heat in the summer months is stifling. Mid-September can also be a comfortable time to travel here. The falls at Huangguoshu are at their best in the rainy season between May and October. Inhabitants of coastal areas celebrate the birthday of Mazu or Tianhou, goddess of the sea, on the 23rd day of the third lunar month

(May/June). The minority peoples of Guizhou hold frequent festivals, particularly during the first, fourth, and sixth lunar months. For example, the lusheng festivals, among the Miao people, take place in January or February, when mothers, trying to find a partner for their daughters, present them to local boys who play their lusheng pipes.

FUJIAN

Fujian has a long and distinctive recorded history, dating back at least as far as the Warring States period (475–221 BC). At that time the state of Yue, which covered today's provinces of Jiangsu and Zhejiang, defeated by the neighboring state of Chu, moved southward to an area that included Fujian. Under the Qin dynasty, the first to rule over a united China, what is now Fujian became a prefecture known as Min, a name that even now is sometimes used as an abbreviation for Fujian.

Evidence of early civilizations that predate the Warring States period has been found in abundance. The strange so-called boat coffins from Wuyi almost certainly date from the mysterious Xia dynasty that, it is thought, flourished between 2100 and 1600 BC. Carved pictographs have also been discovered here from the earliest dynasty known to have existed, the Shang (about 1600–1100 BC).

Although very clearly part of mainstream, or Han, China, Fujian is home to a surprising number of non-Han ethnic groups. The Ding and the Guo in the southern part of the province are the descendants of Arabs and Persians who traded here in the Tang and Song dynasties, and the Dan people are thought to be the remnants of the Mongols who settled here during the Yuan dynasty. Best known are the Hakka, with their distinctive fringed hats, who migrated to Fujian from Henan many centuries ago.

Hilly, rural Fujian is particularly associated with the massive waves of emigration that took place from China during the 19th century, when war and decadent government caused widespread poverty here. Its most famous agricultural product is tea, some of which is considered among the very best in China. Wuyi Rock Tea, for example, is said to be an essential traditional drink for the British royal family.

Fujian's main attractions are the principal cities of Fuzhou and Xiamen, which have become bustling paragons of the new entrepreneurial China, and the scenic area of Wuyi Shan in the northeast. Food is distinctive and good in the coastal cities, and for the shopper Fujian is a famed provider of soapstone, much of which is used in the production of chops (traditional seals). Other crafts typical of the region include lacquerware, puppet heads from Quanzhou, and porcelain from Dehua.

Fuzhou

200 km (125 mi) northeast of Xiamen; 1,500 km (930 mi) southeast of Beijing; 700 km (435 mi) northeast of Hong Kong.

The capital of Fujian, lying about 40 km (25 mi) upstream from the Min River estuary, dates from the 3rd century AD, when it was well known as a center of ore smelting. Subsequently it became capital of the independent and rather mysterious kingdom of Minyue, when it was known as Minzhou. In the 8th century, when it was absorbed into the Chinese empire during the Tang dynasty, Fuzhou acquired its present name, which means "happy city." The name may derive from its splendid location close to the Fu mountains on a green, subtropical plain. It became an important commercial port specializing in the export of tea, growing extremely wealthy in the process.

As an important port city, it was the base for the voyages of the Ming eunuch admiral Zheng He. For the same reason, it attracted Western powers in the mid-19th century, becoming one of the first ports opened to foreign traders and residents following the signing of the Treaty of Nanking in 1842.

Marco Polo is supposed to have passed through in the 13th century, referring to Fuzhou as a "veritable marvel." It could not be described as such any longer; on the whole, despite its proliferation of banyan trees planted in the Song dynasty, it is a rather gray town in the modern Chinese idiom. It is, nevertheless, an important city—the home of Fujian University and several industrial plants, including tea production and handicrafts in stone—with some sites of historical significance. It is also a good base for visits to other places of interest in the province. Getting around this sprawling city on foot is difficult—pedicabs or taxis are more efficient.

① The **Foreign Concessions,** where foreign residents lived after 1842, are across the stone bridge spanning the Min River, on the south bank in an area previously used for burials. Around here were the banks, consulates, and houses serving the French, American, Japanese, and British traders and civil servants sent here in the service of their countries or of the great trading houses of the day. Chances are that in the rush to replace old with new, most of what is left will soon disappear. ⊠ *Guanjing Lu and nearby streets, Nantai Island.*

★ **②** In an attempt to preserve something of the city's ancient architecture, a small area of traditional housing, **San Jie Qi Xiang** (Three Lanes and Seven Alleys), has been set aside so that visitors can glean some idea of how the city looked until the early 1980s. Here the high, whitewashed walls and peaceful courtyards of the Ming and Qing dynasties have retained a timeless quality increasingly hard to find. ⊠ *Guanglu, Wenru Lu, and Yijin Lu; Jibi Xiang, Gong Xiang, Ta Xiang, Anmin Xiang, Huang Xiang, Langguan Xiang, and Yangqiao Xiang; behind waterfront.*

③ The artificial **Xi Hu** (West Lake) was dug in AD 282 in order to irrigate the surrounding countryside. It has been used as a park ever since the Min Kingdom (from the 8th century). On his return to Fuzhou toward the middle of the 19th century, after his time as an Imperial official, Lin Zexu (☞ *below*), a native of Fuzhou, had the lake cleared and some of the Tang pavilions restored. Once again they fell into disrepair until 1985, when they were repaired to commemorate the 200th anniversary of Lin's birth. ⊠ *Xihu Yuan, east end of Hualin Lu, in northwest part of town.*

④ Divided into two parts (pre-revolutionary and revolutionary), the **Fujiansheng Bowuguan** (Fujian Provincial Museum) has some items of particular interest. In 1978 a boat-coffin was discovered on Mount Wuyi. It is thought to date from some 3,500 years ago and consists of a raised prow and stern in cedarwood. There is also a collection of locally discovered Tang pottery (many pieces of which appear to have been chamber-pots), as well as Song bronzes and ceramics that include Fujian black ware. There are also items from boat excavations and a collection of Nestorian crosses from Quanzhou. ⊠ *Xihu Yuan, off Hubin Lu.* 🖼 *Y5.* ☽ *Daily 9–5.*

⑤ Perhaps the best-known place associated with the city of Fuzhou, **Gu Shan** (Drum Mountain), east of the city center, rises to some 3,200 ft.

248

Southeastern China

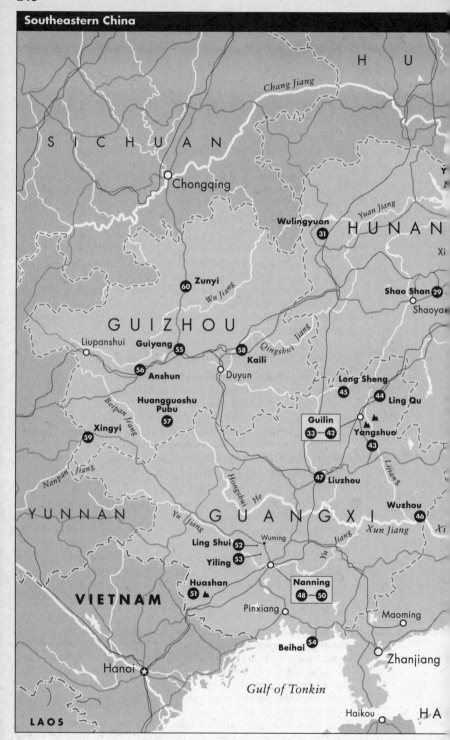

Fuzhou

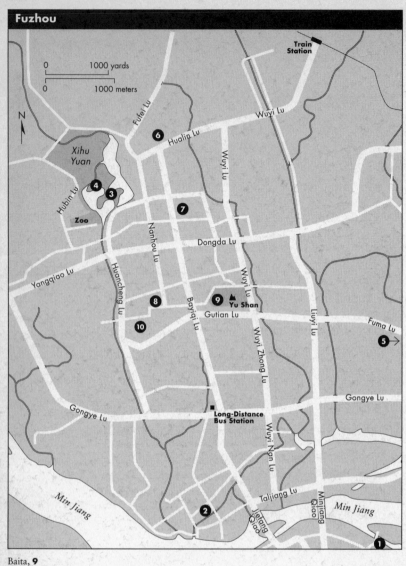

Baita, **9**
Foreign
Concessions, **1**
Fujiansheng
Bowuguan, **4**
Gu Shan, **5**
Hualin Si, **6**
Kaiyuan Si, **7**
Linzexu
Jinianguan, **8**
San Jie Qi Xiang, **2**
Wushan, **10**
Xi Hu, **3**

The stone on its slopes carries a number of Buddhist inscriptions dating from the Song dynasty, particularly in the vicinity of **Yongquan Si**, one of the most important temples in the province.

The much-altered temple, which lies about halfway up the mountain amid pine forest, was founded in 908 by the Duke of Fujian to accommodate the monk Shen Yan. In front of the first of three major halls stand two ceramic pagodas dating from 1082. During the Northern Song dynasty they originally stood in the Longrui Temple on Nantai Island. The temple is home to an outstanding library of more than 10,000 Buddhist sutras, some of which are said to have been written in the blood of disciples. There is also a white jade statue of a reclining Buddha. If you follow a path from here, you can gain the summit of the mountain, which affords fine views. ⊠ *Gutian Lu, 9 km (5 mi) east of city center.*

⑥ North of the city on the slopes of Pingshan, **Hualin Si** (Hualin Temple) dates from the Tang dynasty, although the only building from that period is the **Daixong Baodian** (Sumptuous Hall of the Great Hero). Recent restoration work may have replaced more of the original than was strictly necessary. ⊠ *1 km (½ mi) northeast of Xihu Park, on southern slopes of Pingshan.*

⑦ Originally built in the 6th century during the Liang dynasty, **Kaiyuan Si** (Kaiyuan Temple) is chiefly notable for its iron Buddha, weighing some 40 tons, thought to have been cast in the Tang dynasty. However, during the Qing dynasty restorations of the mid-16th century, a silver pagoda was discovered under the Buddha that was dated to the Northern Song, in the 11th century. ⊠ *East of Guping Lu, in north of city.* ▦ *Free.* ☾ *Daily.*

⑧ In the northern suburbs of the city is the **Linzexu Jinianguan** (Tomb of Lin Zexu). An enlightened Imperial Commissioner, Lin (1785–1850) confiscated 20,000 cases of opium from the British. This act led to the outbreak of the First Opium War in 1840. The tomb is lavish, with six chambers on four levels and a pair of guardian lions in front. ⊠ *Aomen Lu, on Jinshishan.* ▦ *Y5.* ☾ *Daily 8–5.*

⑨ Standing on the slopes of Yushan in the center of the city, the **Baita** (White Pagoda) is decorated with inscriptions that date from the Song dynasty to the present day. Many were placed here in celebration of the Autumn Festival, when it is said that ascent of a "mountain" must be made to ward off evil spirits. There are several temples, too, including the **Guanyin Ge** (Hall of the Great Master), built during the Song dynasty and rebuilt in 1713, where the local officials congregated to pray for good fortune; it served as a headquarters during the 1911 revolution. Now the city museum, it houses a Song tomb discovered in 1986.

Close to the main pagoda is the **Qi Gong Ji Nian Tang** (General Qi Memorial Hall), dedicated to a Ming military strategist who was alleged to have slept here in a drunken stupor after celebrations in honor of his defeats of the Japanese.

The White Pagoda was originally built in 904. The current building, 135 ft high and made of brick and wood, was built in 1548; the pavilions close by, with columns carved in the local stone, date from the Qing dynasty. ⊠ *Center of city close to Gutian Lu.*

⑩ Also in the center of the city, the slopes of **Wushan** (Black Hill) are covered in stone inscriptions, among them an example of the work of the famous Tang calligrapher Li Yangbing and records of the duties of Ming eunuchs, who were put to work in the shipyards. The black granite **Wu Ta** (Black Pagoda), 115 ft high, was originally built in 799 and is covered with fine carving work. ⊠ *1 km (½ mi) west of Yushan near Wushan Lu.*

Dining and Lodging

For cheap food, the area around the train station abounds in street restaurants selling noodles and dumplings.

Fuzhou does not offer much in the way of cheap accommodation but does have a good number of comfortable and modern hotels. These, however, are aimed at business travelers with substantial expense accounts.

$$$ ⊁ **Fuzhou Restaurant.** At this comfortable restaurant you'll find local dishes, especially fish and fried oysters. ⊠ *36 Dongda Lu,* ☎ *0591/753–3057. AE, V.*

$$$ ⊁ **Guolu Restaurant.** The tasty offerings here originate in cuisines from all over China. ⊠ *Liuyi Beilu,* ☎ *0591/755–6283. No credit cards.*

$$$ ⊁ **Juchunyuan.** Founded in 1877, this famous restaurant in an overly modernized old building specializes in Fotianqiang stew, made from various kinds of fish, pigeon eggs, and shark's fin. ⊠ *130 Bayiqi Beilu,* ☎ *0591/753–3230. AE, V.*

$$$ ⊁ **Lakeside Hotel Restaurant.** Both the food and the pretty surroundings are worth the visit. ⊠ *1 Hubin Lu,* ☎ *0591/753–9888. V.*

$$$ ⊁ **Nantai Lezhuang.** The cuisine is local here, and although the atmosphere is unsophisticated, the dishes—which include fresh fish, when available, and subtly flavored soups such as shark's fin—are usually reliable. ⊠ *Guohuo Nanlu,* ☎ *0591/753–2034. No credit cards.*

$$$ ⊁ **Rongcheng.** The menu at this unpretentious place in the center of the city offers choices from a wide variety of Chinese cuisines. ⊠ *Bell Tower, Dongjiekou,* ☎ *0591/755–5816. No credit cards.*

$$–$$$ ⊁ **Beijing Restaurant.** For northern Chinese cuisine—Peking duck, beef kebabs—this restarurant is the best in town. ⊠ *12 Dong Lu,* ☎ *0591/752–2334. V.*

$$–$$$ ⊁ **Guangdong Restaurant.** Not surprisingly, considering the name, the specialty here is Cantonese food, with the emphasis on vegetables and fish. ⊠ *241 Bayiqi Beilu,* ☎ *0591/755–0896. V.*

$$$–$$$$ ⊡ **Taiwan Hotel.** Opened in 1987, this highrise hotel in the north of the city has air-conditioned rooms with TVs and minibars. ⊠ *28 Hualin Lu, Fujian 350003,* ☎ *0591/784–0570,* ℻ *0591/841–409. 2 restaurants, air-conditioning, beauty salon, business services. AE, V.*

$$$ ⊡ **Foreign Trade Centre Hotel.** This hotel in the commercial district has a hot-spring swimming pool. The rooms rooms have standard amenities. ⊠ *Wusi Lu, Fujian 350001,* ☎ *0591/755–0154,* ℻ *0591/550358. 195 rooms. 2 restaurants, air-conditioning, pool, sauna, tennis court, exercise room, business services. AE, V.*

$$$ ⊡ **Tangcheng Mansion.** Opened in 1989, this standard highrise hotel is close to the central part of the city. The rooms are a bit shabby. ⊠ *215 Wuyi Beilu, Fujian 350009,* ☎ *0591/326–9999,* ℻ *0591/268215. 111 rooms. 2 restaurants, air-conditioning, shops, 2 meeting rooms. V.*

$$–$$$ ⊡ **Donghu Hotel.** Convenient to the railway station and reasonably central, this moderately priced hotel built in 1984 has Chinese and Western restaurants and hot springs. The rooms are well-kept and offer good value, though the minibars are meagerly stocked. ⊠ *73 Dongda Lu, Fujian 350001,* ☎ *0591/755–7755,* ℻ *0591/555519. 329 rooms. 2 restaurants, air-conditioning, pool, exercise room. AE, V.*

$$–$$$ ⊡ **Fuzhou Lakeside Hotel.** With simply but comfortably furnished standard rooms, this hotel is close to the West Lake. ⊠ *158 Hubin Lu, Fujian 350003,* ☎ *0591/783–9888,* ℻ *0591/839752. 427 rooms. 2 restaurants, air-conditioning, pool, business center. AE, V.*

$$–$$$ ⊞ **Hot Spring Hotel.** Opened in 1986, this hotel, one of the best in
★   Fuzhou, is in the northern part of the city. ⊠ *Wusi Lu, Fujian 350003,*
☎ *0591/785–1818,* FAX *0591/835150. 311 rooms. 2 restaurants, air-
conditioning, pool, beauty salon, sauna, bowling. AE, V.*

Nightlife and the Arts

There are no specific venues for the performing arts, but there are often
concerts both of traditional music and of the local version of Chinese
opera, which, for the uninitiated, is entirely different from its Western counterpart. Opera is often performed during the day in parks by
local enthusiasts. Check with CITS (⊠ 73 Dong Dalu ☎ 0591/755–
2052) for locations and times.

Bars in the Western sense do not exist outside the hotels. Those who
can raise the money set up small establishments that serve snacks and
beer, but they are usually singularly lacking in atmosphere. New places
come and go, so wander around the main thoroughfares to see what's
available. The best discos are in the expensive hotels. **Karaoke** parlors
are all over the city—look for neon signs with the letters KO included
in them.

Outdoor Activities and Sports

Through CITS (⊠ 73 Dong Dalu, ☎ 0591/755–2052) you can arrange
★   **boat trips** along the **Min River,** 40 km (25 mi) downstream to the sea.
The scenery is attractive—you pass Drum Mountain as you go—and
the various craft on the river make it an absorbing ride.

You can rent a **bicycle** through CITS. For **jogging,** the best place is Xihu
Yuan. The best **swimming pools** are in hotels, where nonresidents
must pay a fee. There are also **beaches** at Meizhou (☞ Beyond Fuzhou,
below). For **walking or hiking,** try the scenic area of Wuyishan (☞
below).

Shopping

Among the local specialties are Shoushan stone carving, using a form
of alabaster; porcelain from Dehua; lacquerware; and lacquer painting. Tea is also a good buy in this part of China. For arts and crafts
try the **Fujian Tourist Souvenirs Corporation** (close to Minjiang Hotel).

Among street markets, the most interesting is the **Flower and Bird Market** (⊠ Liuyi Zhong Lu), where there are also ornamental fish, miniature trees, rockeries, and exotic pets such as monkeys.

Meizhou

⓫ *100 km (62 mi) south of Fuzhou.*

An offshore island, Meizhou is well known for its scenery and temples. According to Taoists it is the birthplace of Mazu, goddess of the
sea. The **Meizhou Mazu Si** (Meizhou Mazu Temple) complex, devoted
to her, is in fact a whole array of temples on a rocky coastline below
a huge statue. Mazu's original name was Lin Mo. She was born in AD
930 in Zhongmen to a prominent Fujian family. According to legend,
as a child she never cried and was clearly exceptionally intelligent. At
the age of 13 she was adopted by a Taoist priest. She then devoted her
life to spiritual matters and became well-known for her acts of charity, her proficiency in medicine, and her astronomical observations and
weather predictions. In 987, deciding that she had had enough of temporal life, Lin Mo climbed Mount Meifeng and sailed away on the clouds.
Thereafter she was often sighted at sea at times of danger and acquired
the name Mazu (ancestral mother).

The main place of worship at the temple is the **Tianhou Dian** (Heavenly Goddess Hall). The busiest day is Mazu's birthday on the 23rd day of the third lunar month, when Puxian opera is performed and all the halls are brightly illuminated. You can reach the island by taking a bus from Fuzhou to Putian County, and then a ferry.

Wuyi Shan Fengjingqu

⑫ *270 km (167 mi) north of Fuzhou.*

★ In the north of Fujian Province, **Wuyi Shan Fengjingqu** (Wuyi Mountain Natural Reserve) is known for its spectacular scenery. Magnificent peaks covered in waterfalls (most notably the Shuilian), bamboo groves, and tea bushes rise from the banks of the Jiuqu Xi (Nine Meanders or Nine Bends Creek). You can enjoy the scenery on boats that wend their way up and down stream. You can climb the mountains simply for the views or to visit the pavilions and temples that stand on the slopes of some—for example, Tianyou Feng.

The cliffs along the river were once used for "boat burials," in which wooden boat-shaped coffins were placed in niches some 160 ft above the river. Some have been dated to 3,000 years ago, but little is known about how and why these burials took place.

You can reach this area by train to Nanping and then bus, or by air. It should be noted that in the early 1990s "pirates" attacked one of these boats and murdered several of the Taiwanese tourists on board. The culprits were apparently caught, but repetitions cannot be ruled out.

Xiamen

⑬ *200 km (125 mi) southwest of Fuzhou; 1,700 km (1,050 mi) south of Beijing; 500 km (310 mi) northeast of Hong Kong.*

Known as Amoy to the foreign traders who made the town on these two islands their home from the middle of the 19th century on, Xiamen, with a total population of about 1 million, is an appealing place, with some interesting corners to explore. By Chinese standards Xiamen is a new town, founded only in 1394 during the Ming dynasty as a defense against pirate attacks. It has remained important ever since, with its well-located natural harbor, as a center of coastal trade.

At the end of the Ming era it became the stronghold of the Ming loyalist Zheng Chenggong, better known as Koxinga, who held out with some success against the Manchus. Born in Japan to a Chinese father and a Japanese mother, he went to China and became a favorite of the court during the final years of the Ming dynasty. When China was overrun by the Qing, he built up a fleet of more than 7,000 junks and a force of some three quarters of a million men, including pirates. In 1661 he succeeded in driving the Dutch from Taiwan and went on to try to extend his power to the Philippines. He murdered both his cousin and his uncle for their ineptitude and killed himself in 1662 on Taiwan.

After 1842 Xiamen became one of the first treaty ports to be opened up to foreign trade, and by the 1950s it had become an important industrial center. Since Deng Xiaoping's open policy, it has been turned into one of the four Special Economic Zones (SEZs), where trade is practiced according to the laws of the free market. Only a few miles farther out to sea are other small islands that still belong to Taiwan.

The city consists of two islands: Xiamen, linked to the mainland by a causeway built in the 1950s, and Gulangyu. The main street, leading down to the port, is Zhongshan Lu.

★ The most interesting part of the city—and also the most attractive to the eye—is **Gulangyu** (Island of Blown Waves), which was where the foreign communities were established after 1842. It can be reached in about 10 minutes on the ferry from the quay on Xiamen Island. Gulangyu's Sino-Colonial buildings, mostly dating from the late 19th and early 20th centuries, are surprisingly large, considering the fact that in 1912 there were only 250 foreign residents.

An exploration of the island takes an hour or two. From the ferry, turn left and follow the path around the island, cutting across the middle at **Baiguangyan** (Sunlight Rock). In so doing you will pass the statue in memory of Koxinga and a variety of handsome villas in peeling pastels, with arched windows, terraces, and doorways in the styles of China, England, Germany, Japan, and Spain. The **Koxinga Bowuguan** (Koxinga Museum; ⊠ Gulangyu; ⊙ daily 8–11 and 2–5) contains displays on the life of Koxinga. The **Protestant Church** is from the quasi-colonialist era. The **Xiamen Bowuguan** (Xiamen City Museum; ⊙ daily), housed in an imposing building with a domed roof, has more than 1,000 exhibits, including some fine porcelain and jade. You can take a cruise around the island and to other places of interest in summer; boats depart from Xiagu Ferry Pier.

Nanputuo Si (Nanputuo Temple), on Xiamen Island in the southern suburbs of the city, dates from the Tang dynasty. It has been restored many times, most recently in the 1980s, and although it has lost its patina of antiquity, it's still interesting in a gaudy sort of way. The roofs of the halls are painted with a colorful array of flowers and traditional ornamentation; pavilions on either side of the main hall contain tablets commemorating suppression of secret societies by the Qing emperors. As it is the most important temple remaining in Xiamen, it is nearly always busy with the comings and goings of worshipers. Behind the temple a rocky path threads its way past a series of stone inscriptions. At the height of summer the lakes in front of the temple are covered with lotus flowers. ⊠ *Siming Nan Lu, Xiamen; take bus 1 or 2 from the port.* ☜ *Y10.* ⊙ *Daily.*

Housed in neo-imperial–style buildings close to the Nanputuo Temple, **Xiamen Daxue** (Xiamen University) was founded in the 1920s with the help of overseas Chinese donations. There are two small museums here—**Lu Xun Bowuguan** (Lu Xun Museum) in the Jimei Building commemorating the stay of China's most prominent writer of the 20th century, Lu Xun, who taught here from 1926 to 1927; and **Zi Ran Bowuguan** (Museum of Anthropology), with a cannon in front, dedicated to anthropology, which has a very good collection of fossils, ceramics, paintings, and ornaments. ⊠ *Xiamen Daxue, Siming Nan Lu.* ☜ *Y5.* ⊙ *Variable; check with CITS.*

Lying southeast of the university is the **Huli Cannon,** made in Germany by the Krupp Company and placed here in 1891, at a cost of 50,000 silver taels, along with 100 other cannons that were already in place. Weighing 60 tons and measuring 45 ft in length, it sits along with other smaller armaments on the bare bones of an old fortress, overlooking the sea, a strange relic from the end of the declining Qing dynasty. It is the only well-preserved coastal cannon left in China. ⊠ *Off Daxue Lu in southeast of city, about 45-min walk from university.* ☜ *Y5.* ⊙ *Daily.*

In the southern part of the city, the **Huaqiao Bowuguan** (Overseas Chinese Museum) is an institution founded by the wealthy industrialist Tan Kah-kee (☞ Jimei Xuexiaocun, *below*). Three halls illustrate, by means of pictures and documents, personal items and relics associated with the great waves of emigration from southeast China during the 19th century. ✉ *Foot of Fengzhao Shan, off Siming Nanlu.* 🎫 *Y5.* ⊘ *Daily 9–4:30.*

The undulating **Wanshi Zhiwuguan** (Wanshi Botanical Garden) has a fine collection of tropical and sub-tropical flora; a pretty artificial lake; strangely shaped rocks and caves; and several pavilions, of which the most interesting are those forming the **Tianje Si** (Temple of the Kingdom of Heaven). Close to the lake is a large gray stone marking the spot where Koxinga killed his cousin before taking over the troops he commanded in order to continue the fight against the Qing. The garden specializes in the flora of southern China and of southeast Asia, including the varieties of eucalyptus that originated in Australia but have been widely planted throughout the south of China. ✉ *Huyuan Lu, in the eastern part of city off Wenyuan Lu.* ⊘ *Daily 8–6.*

A conglomeration of educational establishments on the mainland to the north of the city, **Jimei Xuexiaocun** (Jimei School Village) was set up early in the 20th century by the expatriate Tan Kah-kee, a native of Xiamen who emigrated to Singapore, where he became an industrialist. The school, offering primary and secondary education (as well as kindergarten, a science center, a library, and specialist schools), has a student body of many thousand. It is built in an attractive mixture of traditional Chinese and Western architectural styles, using red brick, glazed tiles, and white stone, and is set in landscaped parkland. Tan's elaborate mausoleum, richly decorated with carved friezes, is to be found here in the Aoyuan (Turtle Garden). ✉ *Northern end of Gaoqi-Jimei Sea Dike.*

Dining and Lodging

There is no shortage of little restaurants on Gulangyu offering all sorts of seafood. You don't have to worry about the menu—just point to what you want.

$$$ ✗ **Taibai Restaurant.** At this somewhat overpriced restaurant the food is good and the service reasonable. ✉ *542–544 Xiahe Lu, Xiamen,* ☎ *0592/202–2575. AE, V.*

$$–$$$ ✗ **Fuhao Seafood Restaurant.** You can eat plenty of excellent seafood here at good prices if you choose with care; make sure you know the price of what is on offer. ✉ *14 Huyuan Lu, Xiamen,* ☎ *0592/202–4127. AE, V.*

$$–$$$ ✗ **Shanghai Restaurant.** Here the specialty is Shanghai-style cooking, with the slightly sweeter sauces that characterize it. ✉ *5–7 Dongmen Lu, Xiamen. No credit cards.*

$$–$$$ ✗ **Yanyun Restaurant.** The food is generally good, but the service is sometimes sloppy. The fish and soups are especially worthwhile. ✉ *103–105 Kunming Beilu, Xiamen,* ☎ *0592/202–6635. V.*

$$ ✗ **Ludao Restaurant.** Well located, it serves good if unexceptional food at reasonable prices. ✉ *232–234 Zhongshan Lu, Xiamen,* ☎ *0592/202–2264. No credit cards.*

$$ ✗ **Tianxin Restaurant.** For a good all-around Chinese meal, try the Tianxin. ✉ *59 Xinhua Lu, Xiamen. No credit cards.*

$$ ✗ **Xinnanxuan Restaurant.** This good-value restaurant offers a wide variety of dishes, both local and from across China. ✉ *17–19 Siming Nanlu, Xiamen,* ☎ *0592/202–3979. AE, V.*

$–$$ ✗ **Puzhaolou Vegetarian Restaurant.** Good food in pleasant surroundings at exceptionally good prices is the threefold draw here. ✉ *Nanputuo Temple, Xiamen,* ☎ *0592/202–2908. No credit cards.*

$$$–$$$$ 🏨 **Holiday Inn Crowne Plaza Harbourview.** This modern hotel has an excellent location overlooking the harbor with comfortable rooms in

the usual reliable Holiday Inn style. There is a medical clinic on the premises. ⊠ 12 Zhenhai Lu, Fujian 361001, ☎ 0592/202–3333, ‾FAX‾ 0592/236666. 367 rooms. 3 restaurants, air-conditioning, pool, business services. AE, V.

$$$ 🏨 **Lujiang Hotel.** This older mid-range hotel has a good location opposite the ferry pier. Rooms are simply furnished. ⊠ 54 Lujiang Lu, Fujian 361001, ☎ 0592/202–2922, ‾FAX‾ 0592/224644. 130 rooms. 2 restaurants, air-conditioning, nightclub. AE, V.

$$$ 🏨 **Xiamen Hotel.** Fairly close to the center, this comfortable hotel has a good range of facilities. The rooms are comfortable and well appointed. ⊠ 16 Huyuan Lu, Fujian 361003, ☎ 0592/202–2265, ‾FAX‾ 0592/221765. 260 rooms. Air-conditioning, pool, exercise room, business services. AE, V.

$$$ 🏨 **Xiamen Plaza.** Close to the railway station, this modern hotel is about 3 km (2 mi) outside the city center. ⊠ 908 Xiahe Lu, Fujian 361004, ☎ 0592/505–8888, ‾FAX‾ 0592/505–7788. 287 rooms. 2 restaurants, pool, clinic, nightclub, business services. AE, V.

$$–$$$ 🏨 **Xinqiao Hotel.** An old but well-located mid-range hotel, it has good facilities, including a Western restaurant. The rooms have been modernized to an acceptable standard. ⊠ 444 Zhongshan Lu, Fujian 361004, ☎ 0592/238883, ‾FAX‾ 0592/238765. 97 rooms. Restaurant, sauna, business services. AE, V.

Nightlife and the Arts

There are often performances of **traditional music, local opera, and acrobatics** by visiting troupes. CITS (☞ below) is likely to be the best source of information. Chongwu (☞ below) is noted for a special form of local opera that had its origins in Taiwan.

Xiamen is more lively than many other cities in China. Nonetheless, the best **bars** are still to be found in hotels like the Holiday Inn and the Lujiang. Otherwise, you will need to trawl the streets around Zhongshan Lu, near the port area. The port area of the city is also sprinkled with **discos. Karaoke** parlors (usually distinguished by the letters KO) of varying standard, some of which also offer "hostesses," dot the area. The best and most reliable places are to be found in hotels like the Lujiang and the Holiday Inn (☞ above).

Outdoor Activities and Sports

Swimming is possible on the beaches of Gulangyu; otherwise, make use of hotel swimming pools, for which a fee will be charged for nonresidents. The best place for **jogging** would also be on Gulangyu Island, where there is no traffic. On Xiamen Island the area around the university is reasonably quiet.

Shopping

Shops along Zhongshan Lu have squeezed out residential buildings. You can buy almost anything you want nowadays; but the local specialties are tea, Hui'an stone carving (stone tablets, stone products for ornamental and daily use), puppet heads, silk figurines, wood carving, and lacquerware. The **Friendship Store** (⊠ Si Ming Beilu) has a reasonably wide selection of wares for sale. Antiques and art shops line Gulangyu. There are also a number of night markets.

Quanzhou

🔟 80 km (50 mi) north of Xiamen.

Quanzhou is an ancient port on the Jin River. During the Song and Yuan dynasties it was the foremost port in China, sometimes described as the starting point of the Maritime Silk Road. As a result, it had a considerable Muslim population, who have bequeathed to the city what is probably the most interesting mosque in China. To Arabs, Quanzhou was Zaiton, from which the English word "satin" is derived.

The mosque, the **Qingzheng Si,** was built in 1009, enlarged in 1309, and restored in 1350 and 1609. Unlike other ancient mosques in China, which were heavily influenced by Chinese styles, this one is mainly in the purely Islamic architectural idiom. Partially ruined, it still retains some impressive features, particularly the entrance, which is 66 ft high. ⊠ *Tumen Jie, in southeast of city.*

★ The **Kaiyuan Si,** a temple founded in the 7th century, is flanked by two pagodas that have some fine bas-relief carving on the niches of each story. The style is a Sino-Indian mix; following the death of the Chinese monk who had initiated the carving, an Indian monk was placed in charge of the work. In the temple's Mahavira Hall, among the roof timbers, are some marvelous carvings of *apsaras,* Buddhist angels. ⊠ *Xi Jie.*

The **Hai Yun Bowuguan** (Museum of Maritime Communications) has on display the hull of a Song dynasty boat retrieved from the bottom of Quanzhou Bay after 700 years. It had 13 cabins and a capacity of 200 tons (which would have required 700 camels to transport across the terrestrial Silk Road). Also in the museum are stone carvings that show evidence of the early presence of Nestorian Christianity. ⊠ *Xi Jie.* ▥ *Y10.* ◔ *Daily 9–5.*

Although there is not a lot left of the **old town,** some of the streets retain their ancient atmosphere—Baguagou Lu (Baguagou Road) and Jingting Jie (Jingting Lane) are two examples.

Close to Quanzhou, the scenic **Qingyuanshan** area has a huge 700-year-old statue of Laotze, the founder of Taoism. Also close to the town are two stone bridges built in the Song dynasty to help with the endless flow of goods into the port—the **Luoyang Qiao** (Luoyang Bridge) and the **Anping Qiao** (Anping Bridge), which is 2½ km (1½ mi) long.

Chongwu

⑮ *40 km (25 mi) northeast of Quanzhou.*

Chongwu is a rarity in China: a town with a city wall and street after street of traditional housing. Built in 1387 as a fortress against Japanese and local pirates, the 2½ km (1½ mi) granite wall has an average height of 22 ft. The local people are known as the Hui'an. Their traditional way of dressing with butterfly scarf and exposed navel ("feudal head, democratic belly") proves that they were never fully assimilated into Han life. The town also has a much-used temple and a Catholic church.

Yongding

⑯ *150 km (93 mi) northwest of Xiamen.*

This town in the rural, hilly southwest of Fujian is the site of the traditional fortress-like, circular or square earthen houses of the Hakka (guest peoples). These buildings are large, at least three stories high, and capacious enough to hold an entire clan. The **Zhencheng** Building, for example, consists of two concentric circles. The **Chengqi** Building, known as the "King of Round Buildings," consists of four circles, with 400 rooms and 57 households. The buildings stand amid rural greenery in countryside where old covered bridges made of wood still span rivers and where (at Liancheng) rice paper is still made in the ancient way.

Fujian A to Z

Arriving and Departing

BY BUS

There are two long-distance bus stations in **Fuzhou,** one in the north of the city near the train station, serving destinations to the north, another (✉ Wuyi Lu) in the south of the city, serving destinations to the south. From Fuzhou it is possible to travel to most of the major coastal cities of the region, including Xiamen and Quanzhou, and as far as Shanghai and Guangzhou. There are also air-conditioned overnight buses to some more distant destinations.

Xiamen has service to Quanzhou and all the main cities along the coast as far as Guangzhou and Shanghai from the long-distance bus station (✉ Hubin Nanlu). Private companies also run air-conditioned long-distance buses from offices around the town.

Buses go to **Yongding** by way of Longyan.

BY PLANE

Fuzhou airport is 12 km (7 mi) from the city center. It has flights to all the other major cities in China, including Hong Kong, as well as to Wuyi Shan. There are buses between the main CAAC office (Wuyi Lu, ☎ 0591/755–4593) and the airport.

Xiamen airport, one of the largest and busiest in China, lies about 12 km (7 mi) northeast of the city. The local branch of CAAC is Xiamen Airlines (☎ 0592/602–2961). There are domestic flights all over China and international flights to Jakarta, Manila, Penang, and Singapore. Other airlines include: **Dragonair** (✉ Seaside Building, Jiang Daolu, ☎ 0592/202–5433). **Philippine Airlines** (✉ Holiday Inn, ☎ 0592/202–3333, ext. 6742).

BY TRAIN

The **Fuzhou** train station (✉ Liuyi Beilu) is on the northern edge of the city, about 6 km (4 mi) from the river. From Fuzhou there are direct trains to Guangzhou, Shanghai, and Beijing. Part of the journey to Wuyishan can also be undertaken by train, as far as Nanping.

Rail travel to and from **Xiamen** is not very convenient. Many journeys will involve a change. There are, however, direct links to Shanghai and also to Fuzhou (a long journey better undertaken by bus). The railway station (✉ Xiahe Lu) is about 3 km (2 mi) northeast of the port; bus service between the two is frequent.

Getting Around

BY BUS

Like most cities in China, **Fuzhou** has a comprehensive and cheap public bus system. Buses can also be slow and very crowded. Route maps are available from hotels, from CITS, or from the railway station.

Maps for the comprehensive bus service around **Xiamen** are available from the railway station, CITS, and hotels. Much of interest in Xiamen (e.g., the port area) can be explored on foot; the island of Gulangyu must be explored on foot as no vehicles are permitted.

BY TAXI

In a city like **Fuzhou,** your best bets for getting around are taxis or pedicabs, which are comfortable and reasonably cheap (though it never harms to try and establish what the fare should be in advance). They are easily hailed in the street or from outside hotels. In taxis, insist that the meter be used.

In **Xiamen,** taxis can be found around hotels or flagged on the streets and will be useful for visiting the sights on the edge of town.

Contacts and Resources

CAR RENTAL

There is no self-drive car rental in **Fuzhou** and surroundings. Cars with drivers can be hired on a daily basis through CITS or through hotels. Self-drive cars are not available in **Xiamen,** but cars with drivers can be hired through CITS.

CONSULATES

There are no consulates in Fuzhou or Xiamen. If you need help, your nearest consulate is likely to be in Guangzhou (☞ Chapter 6) or Shanghai (☞ Chapter 4).

CURRENCY EXCHANGE

Most major hotels in **Fuzhou** have foreign exchange counters that are open during the day (possibly closing for lunch).

Money exchange facilities are in hotels in **Xiamen.** Bank of China (✉ 10 Zhongshan Lu). American Express (Holiday Inn, ☎ 0592/212–0268).

EMERGENCIES

Fuzhou: PSB (Gonganju; Public Security Bureau; ✉ Xian Ta Lu). **Xiamen:** PSB (Gonganju; Public Security Bureau; ✉ off Zhongshan Lu, near Xinqiao Hotel).

VISITOR INFORMATION AND GUIDED TOURS

Fuzhou: CITS (73 Dong Dalu, ☎ 0591/755–2052). **Xiamen:** CITS (Zhongshan Lu near harbor, ☎ 0592/505–1822).

JIANGXI

This inland province (the name means "west river") to the northwest of Fujian has been part of mainstream China since the Qin dynasty. It remained thinly populated until the 3rd century, when Han Chinese arrived, fleeing the steppe peoples beyond the Great Wall, who were threatening to invade. From the 7th century onward the construction of the Grand Canal channeled trade to the southeastern regions and brought more immigrants from the northern regions into what was still a sparsely populated area. Most of those who came to begin with were poor peasants, but as silver mining and tea cultivation took hold, a wealthy merchant class developed, and by the Ming dynasty the province had acquired its present boundaries. After 19th-century coastal shipping ate into the canal trade, Jiangxi became one of the poorest Chinese provinces, which may explain why it was an important guerrilla stronghold for the communists during the civil war.

Jiangxi has an area of 166,000 square km (64,000 square mi) and a population of 39,000,000. Running south to north through the center of most of the province is a river known as the Ganjiang. One of the largest freshwater lakes in China, Poyang Hu, is located here. Much of Jiangxi is flat, but to the east, west, and south it is fringed by mountains that reach 6,500 ft.

Nanchang

 400 km (250 mi) northwest of Fuzhou; 750 km (465 mi) northeast of Hong Kong; 1,200 km (745 mi) south of Beijing.

The capital of Jiangxi province is a useful stepping-off point for more interesting places in the region. It has existed under a variety of names since the Han dynasty, becoming well known as a city of merchants and alchemists. Its current name means "to flourish from the south." It was often used as a transit point for the ceramics made in the imperial kilns at Jingdezhen; indeed, the son of the founder of the Ming dynasty was made ruler of the area. Its fame attracted the attentions of Matteo Ricci, the Jesuit missionary, who came here in the last years of the 16th century. He, in 1601, became the first European to gain access to the Chinese court, through friendship with a eunuch and by disguising himself variously as a Buddhist monk and a Confucian scholar. Bearing gifts, which the Chinese interpreted as tribute, he was allowed to reside in Beijing, where he stayed, demonstrating to the court the latest innovations in European astronomy, until his death in 1613.

Nanchang is best known for events in the early part of the 20th century, which proved to be a turning point in the Chinese revolutionary struggle. On August 1, 1927, there was an uprising in the city, in protest of Chiang Kai-shek's attack on the Shanghai Commune in April of the same year. Several eminent Communists, officers in the Nationalist army—among them Zhou Enlai and Zhu De—were serving in the area of Nanchang. They decided to take the city, and with a force of 30,000 succeeded in holding out for three days before the Nationalists retook it. The defeated soldiers fled to the mountains and later regrouped to form what was to become the Red Army. It was from this moment that Mao began to diverge from Soviet orthodoxy by concentrating on the rural peasantry. The uprising is still celebrated nationally on August 1, known as Army Day.

The **Bayi Jinianguan** (Former Headquarters of the Nanchang Uprising and Revolutionary Museum; ⊠ Zhongshan Lu; 🚅 Y3; ☉ daily 8–5:30) building was a hotel until it was taken over as the headquarters of the leaders of the Communist uprising of August 1, 1927. The somewhat esoteric exhibits consist of furniture of the period and photographs of the protagonists. The marble and granite **Bayi Jinianta** (Memorial to the Nanchang Uprising; ⊠ Renmin Guangchang) was erected in 1977. The **Geming Ying Xiong Jinian Tang** (Memorial Hall to the Martyrs of the Revolution; ⊠ Bayi Dadao) is another revolutionary site. The **Zhou En Lai, Zhu De Guju** (Residence of Zhou Enlai and Zhu De; ⊠ Minde Lu) lets you see how the leaders lived.

The **Shengjin Ta** (Gold Restraining Pagoda) was first built in the 10th century and rebuilt, after it collapsed, between 1708 and 1788 over the remains of a temple. Made of brick in imitation of wood, it is 194 ft high. Built in the belief that it would prevent the outbreak of destructive fires, it has a golden tripod standing at its top to appease the gods. ⊠ *Close to Zhishi jie.* 🚅 *Y3.* ☉ *Daily.*

The country house **Qingyun Pu** (Blue Cloud Garden) belonged to one of the greatest of Chinese painters, Zhu Da (sometimes known as Badashanren—Man of the Eight Great Mountains), who lived from 1626 to 1705. In the suburbs about 10 km (6 mi) south of the center, this retreat has a long history; it had already found favor with Taoists in the 4th century. The rooms have been preserved authentically with reproductions of Master Zhu's works on the walls (the originals are mostly in the Shanghai Museum) and a number of items dating from the Ming dynasty. Zhu was a kinsman of the Ming imperial household, but his art is considered innovative for its time; it is rather simple and direct in style, specializing in the depiction of animals and rocks. ⊠ *Near Dingshan Qiao (Dingshan Bridge); best reached by taxi or bus from Bayi Da Dao near Renmin Guangchang.*

The former site of the provincial imperial examination halls, **Bayi Gongyuan** (August 1 Uprising Park) is a pleasant spot with a lake, islands, and a small traditional garden known as **Suweng Pu** (Old Su's Vegetable Plot). The lake was used for naval exercises during the Southern Song period (1127–1279), while the garden, which is on Baihua Zhou (Hundred Flowers Island), was laid out by a scholar, Su Yunqin, around AD 1000. ⊠ *Zhongshan Lu.*

Daan Si (Daan Temple) was built on the site of a military headquarters in the late 4th century. The iron incense burner here is said to have been cast during the Three Dynasties (220–280) period. ⊠ *Yuzhang hou jie.* ☉ *Daily.*

The **Sheng Bowuguan** (Provincial Museum) contains a number of interesting items relating to the region, most notably a collection of ceramics made between the 4th century AD and the end of the Qing dynasty and a number of funerary items from both the Ming period and the Spring and Autumn Period. ⊠ *Bayi Gongchang.* ☉ *Wed., Fri., Sun. 8–11 and 2–5.*

The huge **Tengwang Ge** (Tengwang Pavilion) on the banks of the Fu River was reconstructed in 1989 on the site of a building that has known some 28 incarnations, the first during the Tang dynasty in AD 653. Made of granite, nine stories high, with exhibit rooms and a tea house, it reflects the architectural styles of the Tang and Song dynasties. ⊠ *Yanjiang Lu.* 🎫 *Y15.* ☉ *Daily 8–6.*

Youmin Si (Youmin Temple), founded in the 6th century, is notable for its Tang dynasty bell cast in 967 by order of a Tang general. There is also a large bronze Buddha in the rear hall and a bronze bell cast during the Ming period. ⊠ *Huanhu Lu.* ☉ *Daily.*

Dining and Lodging
Other than those in the hotels, there are no restaurants of particular note in Nanchang. However, there is no shortage of choice along the main streets and around the railway station, where small, cheap restaurants sell dumplings and other sweetmeats.

$$$ 🏨 **Jiangxi Binguan.** Most foreigners stay at this reasonably comfortable hotel, with its grim 1950s facade and modernized rooms. ⊠ *Bayidadao, 330006,* ☏ *0791/622–1131. 120 rooms. 2 restaurants, bar, air-conditioning, shops. AE, V.*

$ 🏨 **Nanchang Hotel.** This hotel not far from the railway station is short on luxuries but very reasonably priced. ⊠ *Bayidadao, 330006,* ☏ *0791/ 621–9698. 90 rooms. Restaurant. No credit cards.*

Nightlife and the Arts
Although there is the occasional opera or acrobatic performance, the odd bar or karaoke parlor, the main interest is ordinary Chinese life—**night markets** where they exist, or perhaps a visit to the cinema. Ask at the CITS or your hotel about **performances.**

Hotel bars are the focus of nightlife for visitors in Nanchang.

Outdoor Activities and Sports
Ask at your hotel for **bike** rentals. Renmin Park and Bayi Park are good for **jogging.** The best place for **hiking** in this area is at the hill resort of Lushan (☞ *below*).

Shopping
The chief item is **porcelain.** Jingdezhen (☞ *below*) is the best place, but it is widely available in Nanchang and elsewhere. New shops, privately owned, are appearing all the time, and some are selling very good quality wares, especially reproductions of classical porcelain. Otherwise, try the **Nanchang Porcelainware Store** (⊠ Minde Lu).

Jingdezhen

★ ⑱ *136 km (85 mi) northeast of Nanchang.*

The ancient town of Jingdezhen on the banks of the Chang River once created some of the finest imperial porcelain in China. It is still a major manufacturer of ceramics, although the wares are mostly mass produced now.

There were kilns in operation here from as early as the Eastern Han dynasty. From the 4th century AD, the local rulers in Nanking commissioned pottery wares for use in their palaces. At that time Jingdezhen produced mostly white ware, with a transparent or pale blue glaze. As manufacturing methods were perfected, a finer porcelain, using kaolin, was created by firing at higher temperatures. From the Song dynasty, the imperial court, compelled to move southward to Hangzhou, began to place orders on a serious scale partly to satisfy the widespread demand for vessels from which to drink tea and also because metal was in shorter supply. In fact it is from this era that the town, formerly known as Xinping, acquired its current name. One period (1004–1007) of the Song was known as the Jingde, at which time all pieces of porcelain made for the court had to be marked accordingly. Both the custom, and the name, stuck. In later centuries, during the Yuan and Ming dynasties, Jingdezhen became famous for its blue underglaze porcelain (the classic Ming blue and white) which was widely exported to the rest of Asia and to Europe. Much of the export material was fussy and overdecorated—classic porcelain was much simpler.

Although mass production is the norm now, it is not an entirely modern phenomenon. Most of the finest artistic ware was made by special order, such as when the paintings of an artist favored at court were copied onto porcelain; but most production was on a considerable scale, certainly, at least, in the 18th century, when European travelers describe the methods used. It is clear that much depended on organization, certain workers being responsible for certain roles in the creative process, just as in a 20th-century factory.

The kilns here were known as "dragon kilns." They have several chambers and are fired with wood. Many among the population of the town are involved in porcelain production, manufacturing some 400 million pieces each year. Although parts of Jingdezhen resemble a Victorian manufacturing town that Charles Dickens would have relished describing, it is a fascinating place to visit.

Off the main streets, Zhushan Lu and Zhongshan Lu, older, narrower streets close to the river have considerable character. While it is often easy simply to walk into one of the innumerable pottery factories, if you want a more comprehensive tour of the porcelain works, which would include the **Yishu Taochang** (Art Porcelain Factory) and the **Meidiao Taochang** (Porcelain Sculpture Factory), you'll probably need to arrange it through **CITS** (✉ 8 Lianhuating Lu).

The **Gu Taoci Bolanqu** (Museum of Ceramic History; ✉ Cidu Dadao) shows items found among the ancient kiln sites and has workshops demonstrating porcelain techniques of the Ming and Qing dynasties.

In the vicinity of Jingdezhen are a number of **ancient kilns,** for example the **Liujia Wan,** 20 km (12 mi) outside the town, or the **Baihu Wan,** 9 km (6 mi) out on the Jingwu road.

Dining and Lodging

$$$ 🏨 **Jingdezhen Guesthouse.** Built with Hong Kong money, this comfortable hotel stands in a park to the north of the city center. ✉ *Lian-*

shi Bei Lu, 333000, ☎ *0798/225010,* FAX *0798/226416. 2 restaurants, bar, air-conditioning, shops. AE, V.*

Jiujiang

⑲ *120 km (75 mi) north of Nanchang.*

A stopping-off point for a visit to Lushan, Jiujiang, Jiangxi's second city, was once an important entrepôt for the tea and porcelain trade. Before that it was associated with Buddhism. The **Nengren Si** (Nengren Temple; ✉ Yulian Lu) is a reminder. **Jiujiang Bowuguan** (Jiujiang Museum) on an island on scenic Gantang Hu (Gantang Lake) has examples of clothing, porcelain, and antique weapons.

Dining and Lodging

$$$ 🏨 **Bailu.** The best hostelry in town was built as a luxury hotel but has not lasted well. ✉ *33 Xunyang Lu, 332000,* ☎ *0792/822–4404. 250 rooms. Restaurant, bar, shops. V.*

Lushan

⑳ *35 km (22 mi) south of Jiujiang; 85 km (53 mi) north of Nanchang.*

This old hill resort is a relaxing place to pass a couple of days if you can escape the Chinese tourists who flock here in summer. The whole area is a massif of 90 peaks, which reach a height of 4,836 ft, liberally sprinkled with rocks, waterfalls, temples (mostly destroyed), and springs that have charmed visitors for more than 2,000 years.

The focal point of the Lushan region is the town of **Guling,** well known for the fact that eminent politicians, including Chiang Kai-shek, have had villas here, and because it is home, in the Hanbokou Valley, to the Lushan Botanical Garden (☞ *below*). Many of the villas here are European in style, having originally been built for westerners working on the plains below. Like those in Shanghai, they are a fascinating mix of various styles of architecture from the early 20th century. The scenery is a well-known subject for painters and poets. Lushan, since 1949, has often been used for significant party conferences, notably the one in 1959 after the catastrophe of the Great Leap Forward that attempted to sideline Mao and indirectly led to the Cultural Revolution. In 1970 it was the scene of a bitter argument between Mao and his defense minister, Lin Biao, who the following year died in a plane shot down over Mongolia.

Guling is 3,838 ft above sea level; once you are here, most things of interest can be reached on foot. The **Renmin Juyuan** (People's Hall), site of the 1959 conference, is now a museum of party history. ✉ *Hexi Lu.* 🎫 *Y3.* ⊘ *Daily 8–5.*

About 4 km (2½ mi) south of the village is Lulin Hu (Lulin Lake), beside which is the **Lushan Bowuguan** (Lushan Museum). Here you can see an exhibition on local geology and natural history, as well as photographs commemorating important events in Lushan and items relating to the observations made about the area by various poets and scholars. ✉ *By Lulin Lu.* 🎫 *Y3.* ⊘ *Daily 8–5.*

The **Zhiwuyuan** (Botanical Garden) lies about 2 km (1 mi) east of the lake and has a collection of alpine and tropical plants, as well as a cactus display. ✉ *Southeast of Lulin Hu.* 🎫 *Y5.* ⊘ *Daily 9–5.*

About 2½ km (1½ mi) west of Guling is **Ruqin Hu** (Ruqin Lake). You can take a walk beyond it to **Xianren Dong** (Xianren Cave) and **Longshouya** (Dragon Head Cliff).

The only temple of note is the **Donglin Si** (Donglin Temple) on the lower northwest slope of Lushan. Founded in AD 381, it was the home of Hui Yuan, founder of the Pure Land Sect of Buddhism, which taught that there was a life after death for believers. ⊙ *Daily.*

Dining and Lodging

$$ 🏠 **Lushan Hotel.** This old hotel of some character is well managed. It offers comfortable, modernized rooms and an excellent restaurant. ⊠ *446 Hexi Lu, Guling,* ☎ *0792/828–2843. 60 rooms. Restaurant, bar, shops. No credit cards.*

Jinggangshan

㉑ *180 km (112 mi) southwest of Nanchang.*

In the south of Jiangxi on the border with Hunan, this remote and mountainous area, with its picturesque villages, was the scene of Mao's first revolutionary activity in the 1920s. It became the base for the Red Army, which was founded as a result of the abortive uprising in Nanchang. The Long March started from here in 1934. There are some good opportunities for walking in the surrounding hills.

At the **Jinggangshan Geming Bowuguan** (Jinggang Mountain Revolutionary Museum) in the village of Ciping Zhen (on Jinggang Mountain, an 8-hour bus journey from Nanchang), you can visit the **Geming Jiujuqun** (Red Army Dormitory), which includes the old field hospital, and **Mao Zedong Guju** (Mao's House). ⊠ *Ciping Zhen.* ☞ *Y3.* ⊙ *Daily.*

About 10 km (6 mi) northeast of Ciping Zhen is the **Shiyan Dong** (Grotto of the Stone Swallow), a 3,280-ft series of caves with stalagmites and stalactites.

Jiangxi A to Z

Arriving and Departing

BY BOAT

Between Nanchang and Jingdezhen, you can take a ferry from Bayi Bridge across Lake Boyang to Boyang and then continue by bus.

BY BUS

From the **Nanchang** long-distance bus station (⊠ Bayi Dadao) buses leave several times daily for Changsha, Jiujiang (2 hours), and Jingdezhen (6 hours). There is also regular service to Lushan and Jinggangshan (8 hours) in summer.

BY PLANE

The airport lies 40 km (25 mi) south of **Nanchang.** There are flights to most of the main cities in China.

BY TRAIN

Direct trains to Guangzhou, Fuzhou, Shanghai, Jiujiang, and Jingdezhen leave from the **Nanchang** train station (⊠ end of Zhanqian Lu, in southeast part of city).

Getting Around

Nanchang has both buses and trolley-buses. Maps for the system are sold at the train and bus stations. Pedicabs and taxis can be hailed on the streets or outside hotels and at the railway and bus stations.

In Lushan, Jingdezhen, and Jiujiang many, if not most, sights can be visited on foot.

Contacts and Resources

CAR RENTAL
Self-drive is not possible, but cars with drivers can be arranged through CITS (☞ *below*).

CURRENCY EXCHANGE
Jiangxi Binguan Hotel exchange counter (☞ Nanchang Dining and Lodging, *above*); **Bank of China** (✉ Zhanqian Xilu).

EMERGENCIES
PSB (✉ Shengli Lu, Nanchang).

VISITOR INFORMATION AND GUIDED TOURS
Jingdezhen: CITS (✉ 8 Lianhuating Lu). **Jinggangshan:** CITS (Jinggangshan Binguan Hotel). **Jiujiang:** CITS (✉ Nanhu Guesthouse). **Nanchang:** CITS (✉ Jiangxi Binguan Hotel).

HUNAN

This large inland province of rural communities and thinly populated mountainous regions is particularly associated with Mao Zedong, who was born and educated here. It was his upbringing and experiences in rural Hunan that provided the impetus for his revolutionary activities.

Hunan was part of the Kingdom of Chu during the era before the unification of China, known as the Warring States (475–221 BC). There were several waves of migration starting in the 3rd century AD as the northern Han people moved to avoid the constant threat of invasion from the steppe lands of Manchuria and Mongolia. But like its neighbor Jiangxi, Hunan began to develop only from the 8th century AD as a result of ever greater migrations from the north of China. Its population increased many times over up to the 11th century, the rich agricultural land proving a great attraction for settlers. During the Yuan and Ming dynasties, Hunan and its neighbor to the north, Hubei, were united to form the province of Huguang, becoming the principal source of grain and rice for the Chinese empire. In 1664 Hunan became an independent province.

In the 19th century the population outgrew resources, a problem that was aggravated by constant war and corrupt government, so that the Communists found a ready supply of converts here as they became a force to be reckoned with in the early 20th century. Mao was not the only influential revolutionary from Hunan—Liu Shaoqi was born here, and so was Hu Yaobang. Hunan is essentially Han China but is also home to a few non-Han minority peoples, the Miao and Yao (the original natives of the area), the Dong, and the Tujia.

Hunan ("south of the lake") occupies an area of 210,000 square km (81,000 square mi) and has a population of 62 million. The flat northern part of the province falls within the catchment area of the Dongting Hu (Dongting Lake); the remaining regions are hilly or mountainous. The climate is sharply continental with short, cold and wet winters and long, very hot summers. It is still an important agricultural area; half of the cultivated land is devoted to the production of rice.

The capital, Changsha, is a good place to visit not only for its excellent museum but also for its revolutionary sites. Mao's birthplace in rural Hunan at Shaoshan is a worthwhile destination, as is the scenic area of Wulingyuan.

Changsha

300 km (185 mi) west of Nanchang; 675 km (420 mi) northwest of Hong Kong; 1,300 km (805 mi) southwest of Beijing.

The capital of Hunan Province, with a total population of just over 1 million, stands on the banks of the Xiangjiang, a tributary of the Yangzi. Built on a fertile plain, it has been an important settlement for well over 2,000 years. Before acquiring its current name, it was known as Qinyang and was famous for its textiles and handicrafts during the times of turmoil known as the Spring and Autumn Period and the Warring Kingdoms (771–221 BC). During the Warring Kingdoms period it was in fact the capital of the Chu, a people regarded as considerably different from the rest of the Chinese. Their state, while it lasted, was certainly innovative for its time, introducing measures to prevent corruption among officials and paring down the number of hereditary offices. The Chu were ultimately subjugated by the Qin (221–206 BC), who made Changsha one of the most important cities of the newly united China. It was at this time that it acquired its present name.

Nonetheless, the area previously known as Chu, for centuries remained on the fringes of the empire, long a place of exile for dissidents from the north. During later dynasties, it was well known as an educational center and became the provincial capital in 1664.

At the beginning of the 20th century it was opened up to foreign trade, attracting a small number of American and European residents; but it is best known for the fact that it was the home of Mao Zedong between 1911 and 1923. He studied here and then taught at the College of Education. Since 1949 much of the town has been rebuilt, and it has become a port and commercial center of some importance.

★ ㉒ In some ways the highlight of a visit to Changsha, the **Hunan Bowuguan** (Hunan Provincial Museum) on the banks of Lake Nianjia contains some especially interesting exhibits, most notably those referring to the royal graves discovered at Mawangdui. These were the family graves of the Marquis of Dai, who died in 186 BC. The bodies were in extremely good condition, especially that of the Marquis's wife. Her remarkable state of preservation is due to the fact that she was wrapped in 20 layers of silk, and her coffin was sealed in charcoal and white peat, which excludes moisture and air. She appears to have died when she was 50, from some sort of fit after eating melons, although she was already suffering from TB and arthritis. The beautiful coffins are on display, as are many of the funerary objects, including illustrated books and documents and a silk banner depicting Han after-life beliefs. Also exhibited here are Shang bronzes and illustrated items from the Warring States period. ⊠ *Dongfeng Lu.* 🚌 *Y5.* ☉ *Daily 9–12 and 2:30–5:30.*

㉓ Due west of the Provincial Museum, the **Kaifu Si** (Temple of Blissful Happiness) was founded in the 10th century AD, during the Five Kingdoms Period, when the Kingdom of Chu made a brief reappearance. Much added-to and altered over the succeeding centuries, it received its last extension in 1923. Very much in the southern style in its rich decoration, it consists of a *pailou* (decorative, ceremonial gate) and several temple halls. ⊠ *Xiangchun Lu.* ☉ *Daily.*

㉔ Three important places linked to Chinese revolutions are close together in the southern part of the city. **Tianxin Gongyuan** (Heart of Heaven Park), at what was the southeast corner of the old city wall, was occupied by a rebel leader during the 19th-century Taiping rebellion. There is a pavilion here, the **Tian Xin Dian** (Pavilion of the Heart of Heaven), restored in 1759. ⊠ *Jiangxiang Lu.* ☉ *Daily 9–5.*

Changsha

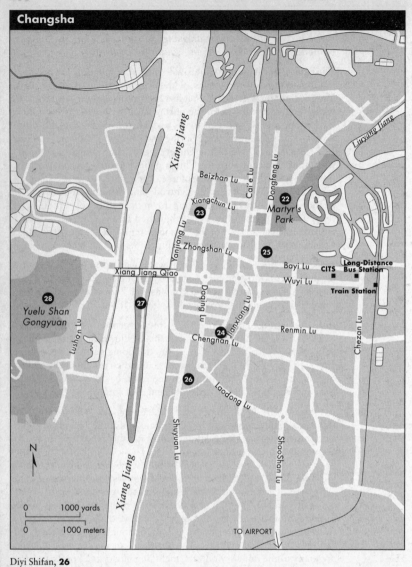

㉕ Nearby you will find the **Zhonggong Xiangqu Weiyuanhui Jiuzhi** (Headquarters of the Local Communist Party), sometimes known as the Qing Shui (Clearwater Pool). It was here that the first meeting of the local Communist party was held, under the auspices of Mao Ze-dong, in July 1921 and where Mao and his first wife, Yang Kaihui, the daughter of one of his teachers at Changsha who was later shot by the Nationalists, lived between 1921 and 1923. It was also home to Yang's mother. On display are a conference room and the room where Mao and his wife lived, with furniture in the traditional Hunan style. ✉ *Qing-shui Tang.* 🎟 *Y5.* 🕐 *8:30–5.*

㉖ The third place of interest is the **Diyi Shifan** (Hunan No. 1 Teacher Training College). Mao studied here between 1913 and 1918, becoming student of the year in 1917 (though presumably not for his various political activities, which were already in full swing by this time). The original school was destroyed in 1938 during the war against the Japanese, but the buildings associated with Mao were later meticulously reconstructed and some parts of them have been turned into a sort of museum. On view here are photographs and documents, including schoolbooks, associated with his time here, as well as newspaper cuttings of the period connected with events, particularly of a revolutionary flavor, around the world. ✉ *Shuyuan Lu.* 🎟 *Y5.* 🕐 *Daily.*

㉗ The narrow 5-km (3-mi) **Juzi Zhou** (Island of Oranges) in the Xiangjiang (Xiang River) is known for its orange orchards. A park at its southern tip affords some fine views. On a tablet here is inscribed a poem written in praise of the town by Mao.

㉘ A well-known beauty spot 975 ft in height, **Yuelushan** (Yuelu Hill) is now the site of Hunan University. There were other educational establishments here before that, most notably the 10th-century Yuelu Academy, one of the most celebrated of the Song dynasty. Several notable figures, including the philosopher Zhu Xi, whose texts became the basis for the Imperial examinations, studied there. Nothing is left of the academy, except a single stela, but there are still some buildings from the Qing dynasty, including the **Aiwan Ting,** with its severe eaves, built in 1792, and at the summit, the **Yunlu Gong,** a pavilion built in 1863. The **Lushan Si,** on the lower slopes, was originally built in AD 268 and is one of the oldest temples in the province. The doorway and a pavilion remain. ✉ *Lushan Lu, west bank of river; bus No. 12.* 🕐 *Daily.*

Just outside Changsha lie Mawangdui village and the **Han graves,** discovered in 1972. The contents of these three graves, over 2,000 years old, have provided much of the interest of the Provincial Museum. They belonged to the Marquis of Dai, Li Cang (Tomb 2), who was prime minister to the King of Changsha between 193 and 186 BC; his wife To Hou (Tomb 1); and their son (Tomb 3), who died in 168. The mummified remains of To Hou are in the Provincial Museum (☞ *above*). The tomb itself was in a pounded earth mound 65 ft high and up to 200 ft in diameter, lying about 50 ft from the top. To Hou lay in the innermost of several coffins, the outer ones highly decorated and covered in bamboo mats. It seems that Tomb 1, the last to be built, completely escaped the depredations of tomb robbers (the other two were less fortunate); bamboo slips listing everything that was placed in the tomb to help To Hou on her way to the underworld showed that nothing had been removed for 2,100 years. ✉ *Mawangdui, 4 km (2½ mi) northeast of Changsha.* 🎟 *Y3.* 🕐 *Daily.*

Dining and Lodging

$$–$$$ ✗ **Changdao.** Centrally located, this restaurant serves a wide variety of standard Chinese dishes. ✉ *Wuyi Xilu, no phone. No credit cards.*

$$–$$$ ✗ **Changsha Restaurant.** One of the original restaurants in Changsha before private restaurants were permitted, it serves good Hunanese food such as *gualieng fen* (cold rice noodles in a hot and spicy sauce). ✉ *116 Wuyi Donglu, no phone. No credit cards.*

$$–$$$ ✗ **Youyicun.** At this conveniently located restaurant you can choose from a wide variety of dishes from all over China. ✉ *225 Zhongshan Lu, no phone. No credit cards.*

$–$$ ✗ **Kaiyunlou Restaurant.** At this simple but usually reliable restaurant you can feast on a large number of snack foods such as dumplings and soups. ✉ *Wuyi Donglu, no phone. No credit cards.*

$$$ ✗🏨 **Hunan Lotus Hotel.** A rambling, mid-range hotel built in the 1980s near the railway station, it has comfortable rooms that are beginning to become a little shabby. In the restaurant, you'll find good Hunanese food—*chou dofu* (fermented beancurd) or *dongan* chicken (poached chicken in a vinegar and soy sauce)—in modern, air-conditioned surroundings. ✉ *8 Wuyi Donglu, 410001,* ☎ *0731/440–1888,* 𝖥𝖠𝖷 *0731/444–5175. 150 rooms. Restaurant, air-conditioning, shops. AE, MC, V.*

$$$$ 🏨 **Hua Tian.** This new luxury hotel has a central location. It is well maintained, provides good service, and is much frequented by the business community. ✉ *16 Jiefang Donglu, 410001,* ☎ *0731/444–2888,* 𝖥𝖠𝖷 *0731/444–3088. 205 rooms. 2 restaurants, bar, air-conditioning, shops, business services. AE, V.*

$$$ 🏨 **Cygnet Hotel.** In the heart of the city, this hotel, of a reasonably high standard, has both a new and an old part. The rooms are simply equipped with basics, including a TV and a minibar. ✉ *26 Wuyi Zhong Lu, 410001,* ☎ *0731/441–0400,* 𝖥𝖠𝖷 *0731/442–3698. 200 rooms. 3 restaurants, air-conditioning, pool, exercise room, nightclub. AE, MC, V.*

Nightlife and the Arts

Besides local opera and acrobatics, Hunan's specialty is **shadow puppets,** and the province has its own troupe. For information ask CITS or at your hotel.

Karaoke is popular here but, as usual, the best bars are in the hotels. The newly opened **Ocean Shore Music Bar** (✉ Wuyi Zhonglu, in center of town) is privately run and has some atmosphere, but these bars tend to come and go, so don't be surprised if it has been replaced with something else.

Outdoor Activities

For **bicycle** rental, ask CITS (☞ *below*). For **jogging,** the best place is Martyr's Park. The best places for **walking and hiking** are in Wulingyuan (☞ *below*); maps with trails are for sale in the area.

Shopping

Tea is a good buy in Hunan, and Changsha embroidery is one of the best known in China. The main shopping area of Changsha is Zhongshan Lu; there is an antiques shop in the Provincial Museum.

Shaoshan

★ ㉙ *130 km (80 mi) southwest of Changsha.*

The small town of Shaoshan, within fairly easy driving distance of Changsha, is in many ways indistinguishable from thousands of similar towns all over China, but was for many years a shrine every bit as potent as

Lourdes. Thousands of pilgrims came here every day, pouring out of the trains that arrived regularly on the railway line especially built for the purpose, eager to see a town that, to them, was just as holy as Bethlehem is to Christians. For Shaoshan is the birthplace of Mao Zedong, the greatest, or at least the most powerful, figure of modern Chinese history. At the height of his cult, in the mid-'60s, particularly during the Cultural Revolution, some 3 million visitors came here every year, 8,000 every day. The numbers declined, of course, as the terrible consequences of the period became clear, but as time has passed those consequences have come to be placed in the context of Mao's overall achievement, and a train still departs every day from Changsha at 7 AM for Shaoshan.

Shaoshan is not without some charm. It is a typical Chinese rural settlement, with its newer uninspiring buildings forming a town around the railway station, while the original town lies about 4 km (2½ mi) away. A farming community just like many others, it stands among glistening paddy fields and is cradled by hills covered in tea plantations, orange orchards, and bamboo groves. Apart from the attractions of the Mao industry, it offers an opportunity to enjoy what is in many ways China's most attractive attribute, its countryside.

Mao arrived at the **Mao Zedong Guju** (House Where Mao Was Born) in 1893. He was the son of a farmer who was perhaps a little better off than the poor peasant of Communist mythology. Mao lived here until 1910 before moving to Changsha to enter college. The house, built in typical Hunan style, became a museum in 1964. It is surprisingly large, with a thatched roof and mud walls, and, of course, in a better state of repair than most of its neighbors. Nonetheless, the spirit of simplicity has been retained, and it has an air of formal homeyness. From the courtyard you enter a room originally devoted to the ancestral altar. Then there is a kitchen, a dining room, three family bedrooms, and a guest room. Personal items belonging to Mao and his family are on display here, as well as photos of his parents and of him from his revolutionary days. ✉ *Northeastern outskirts of village.* 🚃 *Y3.* ☉ *Daily 8:30–5.*

The **Maozedong Tongzhi Jinianguan** (Museum of Comrade Mao), opened during the Cultural Revolution, is devoted to Mao's life in its revolutionary context. It is filled with with photographs and items pertaining to Mao's revolutionary career. ✉ *Village Square.* 🚃 *Y5.* ☉ *Daily 8:30–5.*

When you have had enough of Mao's early life, you may wish to simply explore the countryside around the town. There is a path that will take you up Shaofeng, the hill that dominates the town, meandering among trees and bamboo groves past inscribed tablets up to the Taoist pavilion at the top. **Dishuidong** (Dripping Water Cave) is about 3 km (2 mi) from the village, close to the Mao family tombs where Mao apparently retired for 11 days of contemplation in 1966 just as the Cultural Revolution was getting under way.

Dining and Lodging
Simple dining is available everywhere.

$$ ✕🏠 **Shaoshan Guesthouse.** At this newly built hotel in the old village you can find something a little more sophisticated in the way of dining options. ✉ *Village Square, behind statue of Mao,* ☎ *0731/682127. 50 rooms. Restaurant, shop. No credit cards.*

Nightlife and the Arts

Occasional performances of traditional **opera** or of one of the more modern versions permissible during the Cultural Revolution, which are revived from time to time, take place here.

Outdoor Activities and Sports

If you can find a **bicycle** for hire, then it is always worthwhile to explore the local area as much as possible. **Walking** on the hills around Shaoshan is enjoyable—there are no trails, but there are paths that can be followed across and alongside fields.

Shopping

Apart from a great deal of Mao paraphernalia, there is nothing of note to buy, although you will probably find handicrafts for sale similar to those in Changsha.

Hengyang

🟤 *140 km (87 mi) south of Changsha.*

The second-largest city in Hunan has a few points of interest— **Shigusgan** (Stone Drum Mountain) and the **Huiyanfeng** (Mountain of the Wild Geese) with its temple remains—but the main reason for visiting
★ Hengyang is to go on to the beautiful 4,234-ft **Hengshang Shan** (also known as Nanyue; ⊠ 1 hr by road northeast of Hengyang), one of China's Five Holy Mountains. At the foot of the massif is the large **Nanyue Damiao** (Grand Damiao Temple), originally built in AD 725. Covering a considerable area, it consists of an array of halls and pavilions dedicated to various aspects of Buddhism and, about 4 km (2½ mi) from the main monastery, the tomb of the monk Xi Qian, who founded the Japanese sect of Buddhism in the 8th century.

Wulingyuan

🟤 *350 km (220 mi) northwest of Changsha.*

This nature reserve in northwest Hunan comprises three areas—
★ **Suoxiyu, Tianzishan,** and **Zhangjiajie,** among which the latter is the best known. A spectacular area of peaks eroded into dramatic shapes, waterfalls, and caves, including the largest cavern in Asia, Zhangjiajie is a splendid place for relaxing and for walking along trails (maps are available). The natural scenery speaks for itself, but many of the rocks, pools, and caves have been given names in accordance with their perceived resemblance to buildings, animals, and so on.

Dining and Lodging

$$–$$$ ▦ **Zhangjiajie Hotel.** This, the best option, has a new wing with quite well-appointed and clean rooms and an older part where the rooms are damp and rather shabby. ⊠ *Off main st.,* ☎ *07483/712718. Restaurant, shop. No credit cards.*

Yueyang

🟤 *150 km (95 mi) north of Changsha.*

This small town on the Yangzi has a lively port atmosphere. The **Yueyang Lou** (Yueyang Pavilion), one of the best known south of the Yangzi, is a temple that dates back to the Tang dynasty, famous as a meeting place for such great classical poets as Du Fu and Li Bai. The main tower is surrounded by pavilions, including the **Sancui Ting** (Pavilion of the Three Drinking Sprees), named in honor of the Taoist Lu Dongbin, who became drunk here on three occasions. The brick **Cishi Ta** (Cishi Pagoda) dates from 1242. Both are on the shoreline of

Dongting Hu, the second-largest fresh-water lake in China, with an area of 3,900 sq km (1,500 sq mi). On one of the islands of the lake, Junshan Dao, "silver needle tea," one of the most famous and expensive teas in China, is grown. The island can be easily reached on one of the boats that regularly depart from the town.

It is also possible to board a steamer here for the journey up or down the Yangzi.

Dining and Lodging

$$ ✕ **Yueyang Hotel.** The best hotel in town (given that the other possibilities are not very appealing) has comfortable rooms. ✉ *Dongting Beilu,* ☎ *0730/822–3011. Restaurant, air-conditioning, shop. No credit cards.*

Hunan A to Z

Arriving and Departing

BY BUS

Changsha's long-distance bus station is in the eastern part of the city, close to the train station. There is daily service to major cities across the country, such as Guangzhou (18 hours), Nanchang, and Nanking (30 hours), as well as frequent departures to Hengyang, Shaoshan, Yueyang, and Zhangjiajie (10 hours).

Shaoshan's bus station is in the new town close to the railway station.

BY PLANE

The **Changsha** airport is 15 km (9 mi) east of the city. Buses leave from the CAAC office (✉ 5 Wuyi Donglu). There are flights to all the major cities in China, including a handful of flights every week to Hong Kong.

You can fly to **Zhangjiajie** from Changsha, Beijing, Guangzhou, Shanghai, and Chongqing.

BY TRAIN

The **Changsha** railway station (✉ Wuyi Dong Lu) is in the east of the city. Changsha is linked by direct services to Guangzhou, Guilin, Beijing, Kunming, Lanzhou, Shanghai, and Xian, as well as to Hengyang, Yueyang, Zhangjiajie (15 hours), and the Mao shrine at Shaoshan.

Getting Around

Changsha has comprehensive bus service (maps are available from the railway station and from bookshops). Taxis and pedicabs can be hailed or found at hotels and at the railway station.

Everything in **Shaoshan** village can be reached on foot. Pedicabs and taxis are available around the railway and bus stations to take you to the village.

Contacts and Resources

CAR RENTAL

Self-drive cars are out of the question, but cars with drivers can be rented through CITS (☞ *below*).

EMERGENCIES

PSB (✉ Huangxing Lu, western part of Changsha).

CURRENCY EXCHANGE

Hua Tian, the Lotus, or the Xiangjiang **hotel exchange counters** in Changsha. **Bank of China** (✉ Wuyi Donglu, Changsha).

VISITOR INFORMATION AND GUIDED TOURS

CITS (✉ Wuyi Donglu, close to Lotus Hotel, Changsha).

GUANGXI

The Autonomous Region of Guangxi is famous above all for the town of Guilin, or more particularly the scenery that surrounds it, an oasis of fairy-tale hills that has been celebrated by painters and poets for centuries.

Guangxi has a population of a mere 43 million, occupying an area of 236,000 sq km (91,000 sq mi). Historically it has often been the object of tussles for possession between its indigenous peoples and the Han, who established suzerainty only in the 19th century. At the same time, it drew the attentions of the French and British, who were competing for trade advantages in the region. Several towns and cities were compelled eventually to open themselves up to trade with the Western powers of the era. During the Second World War, Guangxi was occupied at various times by the Japanese. In 1958, as a sop to the indigenous peoples of the region—the Dong, Gelao, Hui, Jing, Maonan, Miao, Shui, Yao, Yi, and, in particular, the Zhuang people—the government in Beijing turned Guangxi into one of five autonomous regions, which in theory have an element of self-government.

Guangxi is an essentially mountainous region, 85% of which is composed of the distinctive karst rock formations that have made Guilin so famous. They rise from the coastal plain in the south, by the Gulf of Tonkin, and reach a height of 7,030 ft. The climate is subtropical, affected by seasonal monsoons, with long, hot and humid, and frequently wet summers, and mild winters.

Besides Guilin, the region's attractions include the city of Nanning, the rural areas beyond Yangshuo, and the subtropical sea resort of Beihai.

Guilin

500 km (310 mi) northwest of Hong Kong; 1,675 km (1,040 mi) southwest of Beijing; 400 km (250 mi) southwest of Changsha.

By Chinese standards Guilin is a small town and architecturally not very distinguished at that, mostly because of the amount of bombing it suffered during the Sino-Japanese War. Yet it is plumb in the middle of some of the most beautiful scenery in the world. This landscape of limestone karst hills and mountains, rising almost sheer from the earth and clustered closely together over hundreds of square kilometers of orchard, paddy field, and shallow streams, has a dreamy quality that is hypnotic.

The town itself does in fact have a surprisingly long history. Its current name dates only from the Ming dynasty; before that it was Shian. The first emperor of a united China, Qin Shihuang, established a garrison here when he made a military expedition to the south in 214 BC. He later built the Lingqu Canal to link the Lijiang (Li River), which flows through Guilin, with the Xiangjiang (Xiang River) to create what was for centuries the most important traffic route between central and south China and between the Zhu (Pearl) and Chang (Yangzi) rivers. During the early years of the Ming dynasty it was the capital of a small kingdom ruled by Zhu Shouqian, a nephew of the dynasty's founder. The last of the Ming royal house took refuge here in the mid-17th century as the Manchurians seized power in the country to begin the last imperial dynasty, the Qing. The town's population grew quickly during the Sino-Japanese War, when refugees fled here from the north. Nowadays the population is swollen, indeed saturated, by a constant flow of visitors, a challenge to which local entrepreneurs, both legal and illegal, have risen with alacrity.

Guilin

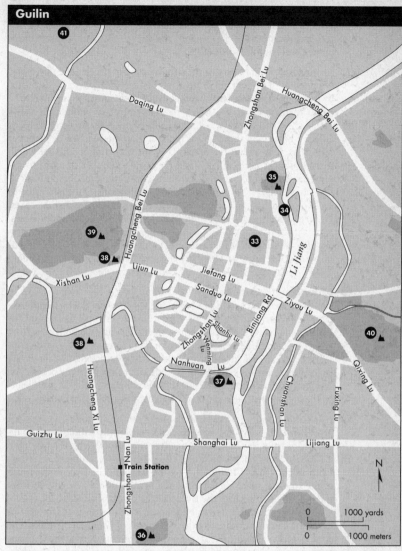

Diecaishan, **35**
Duxiu Feng, **33**
Fuboshan, **34**
Ludi Yan, **41**
Nanxishan, **36**
Qixing Gongyuan, **40**
Xi Shan, **39**
Xiangbi Shan, **37**
Yin Shan, **38**
Zhu Shouqioan
Ling, **42**

Formation of the hills dates back about 200 million years, to when the area was under the sea. As the land beneath began to push up, the sea receded, the effects of the ensuing erosion over thousands of years producing this sublime scenery.

Although the real beauty of the countryside lies outside the town, and is best enjoyed by boat, there are several hills in the town itself. By means of the stairways that have been cut into their flanks it is possible to climb them without too much trouble and enjoy wonderful views **㉝** across the town to the sea of misty hills beyond. **Duxiu Feng** (Peak of Solitary Beauty) is about 492 ft high, the summit reached by just over 300 steps. It is within the precincts of the old Ming palace (of which there is almost nothing left), and there are a number of caves to explore as you climb, decorated with inscriptions, some dating back to the Tang dynasty. A number of these inscriptions, indecipherable to most of us, are in fact important historical records or, in some cases, **㉞** literary masterpieces. **Fuboshan** (Whirlpool Hill) offers similar views, and at its base you will find a huge bell and the **Qian Ren Gang** (Vessel of a Thousand Men) from the Qing dynasty. Here, too, at Fuboshan is the **Huanzhu Dong** (Cave of the Returned Pearl), containing a 10-ft stalactite.

㉟ **Diecaishan** (the Mountain of Piled Brocades), which reaches 732 ft, stands on the banks of the Li River and was for centuries a famous retreat for literary and philosophical figures, who built pavilions and halls here. None survive, but in the past their fame attracted visitors from all over China, long before the idea of modern tourism was even considered. In several grottoes there remain inscriptions and Buddhist statues from the Tang and Song periods, not to mention the poem "Ascending to gaze upon the magical birds amongst the clustered peaks by the light of the Brilliant Moon" by Yuan Mei, the Qing dynasty poet.

㊱ **Nanxishan** (South Creek Hill), to the south of the town, has two almost identical peaks and again is rich in geological formations and inscriptions from the Tang and Song dynasties. Another well-known hill **㊲** is **Xiangbi Shan** (Elephant Trunk Hill), which at one time appeared on Chinese currency bills. Situated on the banks of the river in the south of the town, it takes its name from a branch of rock extending from the hill and arching into the river like the trunk of an elephant. There is also a legend attached to this phenomenon. It seems that an elephant descended from paradise to help the citizens of Guilin in their toil. The King of Heaven, disgusted at this display of charity, turned the elephant to stone as he drank at the river's edge. As with many Chinese legends, one feels that something crucial has been omitted from the story, but nobody seems to know what it is. Behind the trunk is a grotto covered in poetic inscriptions inspired by the beauty of the place, some by the greatest poets of the Song dynasty.

㊳ On the western fringes of the town are other hills of interest. **Yin Shan** has some fine carvings from the Tang dynasty and by a Five Dynasties **㊴** monk. At **Xi Shan** the Buddhist carvings are considered among the finest Tang dynasty works in China.

㊵ The arrangement of the hills in **Qixing Gongyuan** (Seven Star Park) is said to resemble the Great Bear Constellation. The park is an extremely pleasant place in which to get a feeling for the hills, albeit in a sort of captive state. It is dominated by **Putuoshan,** where there are some famous examples of Tang calligraphy, protected by a pavilion. There is also calligraphy on the hillside by the Taoist philosopher of the Ming dynasty, Pan Changjing, while below is an array of interestingly shaped rocks.

Just by Putuoshan is the **Qixing Dong** (Seven Star Cliff) with several large caves. The largest contains rock formations that are thought to resemble a lion with a ball, an elephant, and so on. An inscription in the cave dates from AD 590.

South of Putuoshan is **Yueya Shan** (Crescent Moon Hill). At its foot is **Longyin Dong** (Dragon Lair Cave), rich in carved inscriptions, some of which are said to date back 1,600 years. With imagination, you can see the imprint of a recently departed dragon in the roof of the cave. ⊠ *Jiefang Donglu, east of Li River; take taxi or pedicab from station.* ☉ *Daily.*

④ In the countryside on the northwest fringes of Guilin, **Ludi Yan** (Reed Flute Cave) is an underground extravaganza—curious rock formations gaudily illuminated to emphasize their coincidental similarity with birds, plants, and animals—that you either love or hate. A path, a third of a mile along, threads through what is in many ways quite an entertaining and sometimes dramatic underground palace. Some of the formations are remarkable, but perhaps the most impressive item is the Crystal Palace of the Dragon King, where there is an area of pools and small mounds that resemble a miniature Guilin. Although the cave is illuminated, a flashlight is useful. The hawkers outside the cave can be particularly aggressive and dishonest. ⊠ *Northwest edge of town; take bicycle, taxi, or pedicab from station.* ☎ *Y50.* ☉ *Daily 8:30–11 and 12:30–3:30.*

④ A few miles east of the town is the **Zhu Shouqian Ling** (Ming Tomb), the tomb of Zhu Shouqian, the nephew of the first Ming emperor, who founded a principality here. The tomb is complete with a sacred way and makes a pleasant excursion by bicycle. ⊠ *Cross river on Ziyou Lu, take second left and follow road about 9 km (5 mi).* ☎ *Free.* ☉ *Daily.*

Unless you are willing and able to spend a long time in the Guilin area and to get out into the countryside to explore on foot, then the best **★** way of absorbing the beauties of the landscape is to take the **Li River Cruise,** which operates most days between Guilin and Yangshuo. The shallow and limpid Li River takes you through breathtaking scenery, threading its way between the mountains, overhung by bamboo fronds, disturbed only by the splashing of children and water buffalo cooling themselves in the shallows. Narrow, flat rafts made of bamboo spoon by, perhaps with cormorants, which are used for fishing, tethered to the prow. So, although you are likely to be on one of a fleet of boats, you will hardly know it. Where the route begins will depend on the level of the water. Sometimes it is not possible to start from Guilin, in which case a transfer by bus is made about 40 minutes downstream. The cruise lasts about 4 hours (lunch is served on board and delights like turtle or shrimps, caught en route, are often offered as extras), terminating in the small market town of Yangshuo (☞ *below*), from where it is a 2-hour bus journey back. The peaks that you pass en route all have acquired fantastic names—Dou Ji Shan (Cock-fighting Hill), Siu Hua Shan (Embroidery Hill)—conjuring something familiar out of nature. ⊠ *Boat leaves from docks on Binjiang Lu.* ☎ *Approximately Y450, includes lunch and return by bus.*

Dining and Lodging

The main streets of Guilin are lined at night with tables serving simple, flavorsome and cheap dishes (always check on the price in advance). Other restaurants serve exotic dishes like snake soup—these are easily spotted because of the snakes coiled up in cages outside.

$$ ✕ **Tailian Hotel.** Here you'll find a tasty array of Cantonese dim sum. ⊠ *Zhongshan Lu, no phone. V.*

$$ ✕ **Yueyalou.** This pleasant restaurant in pretty surroundings of a park
★ dominated by its karst rocks and hills serves local and regional dishes. ⊠ *Seven Star Park, no phone. AE, V.*

$–$$ ✕ **Yiyuan Restaurant.** At this friendly restaurant, with its all-wood exterior, the specialty is Sichuanese cooking. ⊠ *Nanhuan Lu, no phone. No credit cards.*

$$$$ ▥ **Sheraton Guilin.** This modern, well-managed, comfortable hotel
★ overlooking the river has good facilities with rooms that are smart, clean, and spacious. The formal restaurant serves excellent Chinese cuisine. A small café attracts homesick Westerners and stylish locals with a '50s rock & roll motif and eclectic snacks such as pizza, steak sandwiches, and pumpkin soup. ⊠ *Binjiang Nanlu, 541001,* ☎ *0773/282–5588,* ℻ *0773/282–5598. 407 rooms, 23 suites. 3 restaurants, bar, air-conditioning, shops, nightclub. AE, MC, V.*

$$$–$$$$ ▥ **Holiday Inn.** Here you'll find the chain's standard comfort and
★ value at a nice location in the older part of town. ⊠ *Ronghu Lu, 541002,* ☎ *0773/282–3950,* ℻ *0773/222101. 259 rooms. 2 restaurants, health club, shops. AE, MC, V.*

$$$ ▥ **Lijiang Hotel.** For many years the main tourist hotel, it still has one of the best locations in town. It is fairly well appointed, though there are now some better hotels in town. ⊠ *Shanhu Beilu, 541001,* ☎ *0773/ 282–2881,* ℻ *0773/282–2891. 120 rooms. 2 restaurants, shops, disco. AE, MC, V.*

$$$ ▥ **Osmanthus Hotel.** This mid-range hotel in a pleasant location has good facilities; the rooms, although modern and basically comfortable, could do with a facelift. ⊠ *Zhongshan Lu, 541002,* ☎ *0773/383–4300,* ℻ *0773/383–5316. 100 rooms. 2 restaurants, air-conditioning, pool, shops, rec room. AE, MC, V.*

Nightlife and the Arts
Performances of **opera** or acrobatics frequently take place; to find out what's on, ask CITS or at your hotel.

Karaoke is popular here as it is everywhere else in China. The best **bars** are in the hotels.

Outdoor Activities and Sports
An interesting diversion might be to take a night excursion on the river to follow a cormorant fisherman at work.

Guilin is an excellent place for **bicycling.** The areas between the hills are almost dead flat, and the countryside can best be appreciated from bicycles, which can readily be hired from around the town. You can go **jogging** in several places, for example around Banyan Lake.

Shopping
A few items of local interest—jewelry, bamboo products, minority people's woven clothes, and handwoven linen and tablecloths and crochet work—are available. Be aware that tourists in Guilin are frequently seen as victims: a favorite technique at stalls is for the seller to bend down to place the chosen item in the bag and switch it for something cheaper.

Yangshuo

❹❸ *60 mi south of Guilin.*

★ The boat cruise from Guilin finishes at the small market town of **Yangshuo.** Most days the whole town seems to have become a giant market. Don't be disappointed at not finding any bargains and watch out for pickpockets, and you will enjoy the experience. A pleasant place to relax, it is also a good base from which to explore the surrounding countryside. If you want more river trips, you can go by boat to the village of Fuli farther down river. In the immediate vicinity of the town are a number of peaks—**Bilian feng** (Green Lotus Peak), **Long Tou Shan** (Dragon Head Hill). Within easy cycling distance are **Heifo Dong** (Moon Hill), a number of caves, and an underground river.

Dining and Lodging

Outside the hotels there are any number of small, informal restaurants where cheap and usually good food can be obtained at rock-bottom prices.

In Yangshuo, there are several simple and cheap hotels, as well as a resort hotel and a joint venture hotel built in 1997.

Nightlife

A number of small **bars** have sprung up here to cater to young individual travelers.

Outdoor Activities and Sports

You can camp in the countryside or rent canoes to explore the river and its creeks.

Shopping

There is plenty to buy in the market—Mao paraphernalia, batiks, T-shirts, and antiques.

Ling Qu

44 *70 km (43 mi) north of Guilin.*

At the market town of Xingan, it is possible to see sections of the 34-km-long (21-mi-long) Ling Qu (Ling Canal), built by the first emperor, Qin Shi Huang Di, in 214 BC to link the Yangzi and Pearl rivers.

Longsheng

45 *120 km (75 mi) northwest of Guilin.*

A small town on the border with Guizhou, in the northwest of Guangxi, Longsheng is in the middle of a mountain area populated by several minority peoples, notably the Dong, Miao, Yao, and Zhuang. The countryside around the town, made up of steeply terraced hills and bamboo forests, is particularly beautiful. North of Longsheng, the town of **Sanjiang** is close to several Dong villages. It is reached on a very bad gravel road. The Dong villages, crowded with beautifully built brown wooden houses, are extraordinary. One impressive spot, about 20 km (12 mi) west of Longsheng, is the **Longji Fitian** (Dragon's Backbone Rice Terraces), which have been cut into the hills up to a height of 2,625 ft and are reachable by bus.

Wuzhou

46 *225 km (140 mi) southwest of Guilin.*

Lying close to the border with Guangdong province, on the Xijiang (Xi River), Wuzhou became an important trading center with the Western powers at the end of the 19th century. Although it was particularly badly affected by the Cultural Revolution, there are a few items of interest remaining: the **Xilan Yuan** (Western Bamboo Temple), the **Zhongshan Gongyuan** (Sun Yat-sen Park and Memorial Hall), and, intriguingly, the largest **shecang** (snake entrêpot) in southwest China, where locally caught snakes are held before being exported to Chinese kitchens around the world.

Liuzhou

47 *130 km (80 mi) southwest of Guilin; 250 km (155 mi) northeast of Nanning.*

This town with a population of three-quarters of a million is a major railway junction on the Liujiang (Liu River). It first attained importance at the time of the unification of China under the first emperor, Qin Shi Huang Di. Historically it is associated with the Tang dynasty scholar and Minister of Rites, Liu Zongyuan (AD 773–819), who was exiled here in 815 after trying unsuccessfully to have government reforms enacted. Notwithstanding his banishment, in Liuzhou he rose to an eminent position and was widely respected for his good works.

Since 1949 Liuzhou has become an industrial town of considerable importance. There is little left of the handsome town described by Liu Zongyuan. The surrounding scenery is a somewhat paler version of that at Guilin, but you are unlikely to find many other foreigners in the neighborhood.

Named for the Tang dynasty man of letters (dubbed a prince during the Song dynasty), **Liuzhou Gongyuan** (Prince Liu Park) in the city center contains his tomb and his ancestral temple, originally built in 821 and rebuilt in 1729. Inside is a stela with Liu's portrait inscribed upon it, as well as a number of others from various dynasties. ✉ *East of Liuzhou Square.* ⊘ *Daily.*

Yufengshan (Fishpeak Hill) is in a park of the same name. It gets its name from the fact that its summit can be seen reflected in the **Xiaolong Tang** (Little Dragon Pool) at its foot, suggesting to some onlookers a fish jumping out of the water. It is also tied up with a legend, according to which a girl named Liu Sanjie used to sing songs on the mountain complaining of the oppressive rule of the local despots. Finally she threw herself into the pool, whereupon a fish sprang out and bore her up to heaven. To commemorate this, a song festival is held every year on the 15th day of the 8th lunar month. ✉ *Longcheng Lu, in Yufeng Gonguan, south of river.* ⊘ *Daily.*

In the south of the city, **Maanshan** (Horsesaddle Mountain) reaches almost 500 ft. So named because of its shape, it has inscriptions in its praise and a cave with interesting geological features. ✉ *Next to Yufengshan.*

Dining and Lodging

$$$ ✕⌂ **Liuzhou Hotel.** The best hotel in town is not wonderful, but it does have air-conditioned rooms and is reasonably well located near Liuzhou Park. In a city not known for its cooking, the Liuzhou's restaurant is an oasis; it serves good and varied regional food. ✉ *Youyi Lu, 545001,* ☎ *0772/357–4388,* ℻ *0772/282–1443. 120 rooms. Restaurant, bar, shops. AE, V.*

Nightlife and the Arts

Check with CITS for performances. Apart from karaoke parlors, there are a couple of entertaining bars on **Liuzhou Square.**

Outdoor Activities and Sports

The chief option is to get out into the countryside and **walk.** Try Liuzhou Park for **jogging.**

Nanning

600 km (375 mi) west of Hong Kong; 350 km (220 mi) southwest of Guilin; 440 km (275 mi) southeast of Guiyang.

In the south of the autonomous region of Guangxi, Nanning, with a population of about 2 million, is built on the banks of the Yongjiang (Yong River), about 200 km (125 mi) north of the border with Vietnam. Now an important industrial city, 1,600 years ago it was the political and military center of southwest China, outside the rule of the Chinese emperors. It was subjugated only during the Mongolian Yuan dynasty (1271–1368), when it received its present name. It became capital of Guangxi Province in 1912 and then, when changes were made in the 1950s, capital of the Zhuang National Autonomous Region of Guangxi. Like Chengdu and Kunming, although it lacks their charm, Nanning has become a busy exponent of economic policies that bear more resemblance to those of the Western democracies than to those normally associated with communism. It is not a beautiful town but has some interesting sites and lies amid attractive countryside. It has also become a transit point for travelers continuing to Vietnam. Visas can be obtained here, and although it may be necessary to change trains at the border, you should be able to reach Hanoi by rail. The link that was built after the Second World War was severed in 1979, but in recent years, as relations between China and Vietnam have thawed, the journey has become much easier.

㊽ Renminyuan/Bailong Gongyuan (People's, or White Dragon, Park) is a pleasant, comparatively tranquil area of flowers and greenery, with some 200 species of rare trees and flowers. The **Bailong Hu** (White Dragon Lake) and some pagodas can be found here, as well as the remains of fortifications built by a warlord in the early part of the 20th century. Within the **old fort,** which offers attractive views of the area, is a cannon built by the German Krupp Company, placed here in 1908 as part of a defensive line against a possible French invasion from Vietnam. The lake is traversed by an attractive zig-zag bridge, a traditional design intended to throw evil spirits, who evidently thrive only on a straight line, off the scent. ⊠ *Renmin Dong Lu.*

㊾ The **Guangxi Bowuguan** (Museum of the Autonomous Region of Guangxi) concentrates on the history of the province with an emphasis on the numerous minority peoples who live here. You can see examples of traditional costumes, as well as reconstructions of their architecture built in the courtyard at the back. There is also a collection of more than 300 bronze drums made by local peoples. ⊠ *Minzu Dadao.* ⊠ *RMB3.* ☺ *Daily 8:30–11:30 and 2:30–5.*

㊿ In the southeast part of the city, **Nanhu** (South Lake) covers 230 acres. You can find a good fish restaurant here, as well as a bonsai exhibition and an orchid garden in the surrounding park. Close by is a botanical garden specializing in the growing of herbs. ⊠ *Gucheng Lu.* ⊠ *Y2.* ☺ *Daily.*

Dining and Lodging

$$ ✕ **Nanhu Fish Restaurant.** In an ugly concrete building prettily located by the lake, it serves some excellent fish dishes, as well as other Chinese food. ⊠ *Nanhuyuan, no phone. No credit cards.*

$–$$ ✕ **American Fried Chicken Restaurant.** Close to the railway station, it serves Western and Chinese snacks. ⊠ *Chaoyang Lu, no phone. No credit cards.*

$$$$ ☒ **Majestic Hotel.** This older hotel has been refurbished reasonably well
★ and is efficiently run by its overseas Chinese management. ⊠ *38 Xin-*

Guangxi
Bowuguan, **49**
Nanhu, **50**
Renminyuan/
Bailong
Gongyuan, **48**

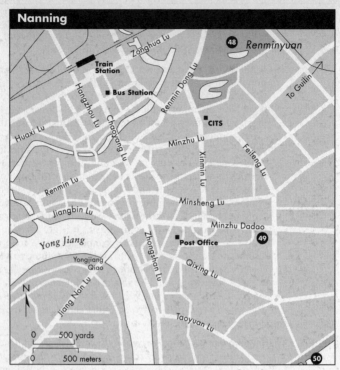

min Lu, 530023, ☎ 0771/283–0808, FAX 0771/283–0811. *150 rooms.
3 restaurants, bar, air-conditioning, shops. MC, V.*

$$$ 🏨 **Yongjiang Hotel.** Fairly centrally located, this is a comfortable hotel
on the riverside, with well-decorated, rooms and an older part where
the rooms are considerably cheaper and also rather worn. ✉ *41 Jiang-
bin Dong Lu, 530012,* ☎ *0771/280–8123,* FAX *0771/280–0535. 6
restaurants, bar, air-conditioning, shops, dance club. AE, MC, V.*

Nightlife and the Arts

The colorful **Duanwujie** (Dragon Longship Festival) takes place on the
5th day of the 5th lunar month, usually sometime in June. Oarsmen
row long, narrow boats, sitting low in the water, on the river, urged
on by a coxswain at the back who screams encouragement as he beats
out a rhythm on a drum. Other festivals include the **Zhuang Zou Ge
Hui** (Zhuang People's Song Festival), on the 3rd day of the 3rd lunar
month.

Theaters (consult CITS for information) often give performances of local
opera, some of which is based on the lore of the Zhuang people.

In Nanning, nightlife is concentrated in karaoke parlors and bars in
the hotels.

Shopping

Nanning is a good place to look for crafts by the local minority peo-
ples, including bamboo ware and traditional clothes. Try the **Arts and
Crafts Store** (✉ Xinhua Lu). There is a reasonable antiques store at-
tached to the **Museum of the Autonomous Region of Guanxi** (☞ *above*).

Huashan and the Zuo River

⑤ *200 km (125 mi) southeast of Nanning.*

★ In the **Huashan** (Hua Mountain) vicinity is spectacular scenery, much like the karst formations more famously found around Guilin. Nearby are several examples of **Zhuang rock paintings,** depicting hunters, animals, and local scenes, sometimes on a gigantic scale. There are several dozen sites all told, in varying states of repair, located within a rough triangle formed by the towns of **Chongzuo, Longzhou,** and **Ningming.** They have yet to be precisely dated, though they are, it is believed, at least 2,000 years old. CITS (☞ Guangxi A to Z, *below*) runs excursions to the area.

Ling Shui

⑤ *42 km (26 mi) north of Nanning.*

Ling Shui (Waters of the Soul) is a 1-km-long (½-mi-long) lake close to Wuming, with clear spring-fed waters that have a constant temperature of 18–22°C all year round. There are bathing pools and pavilions on its shores.

Yiling

⑤ *30 km (18 mi) northwest of Nanning.*

Among the Nanning Hills, the **Yiling Dong** (Yiling Cave) is noted for its exotic and colorful arrangement of illuminated stalactites and stalagmites, through which a path threads for about 1 km (⅔ mi). It is said to have been the refuge of a Taoist hermit who lived here 1,500 years ago and a retreat for people in difficult times.

Beihai

⑤ *175 km (110 mi) southeast of Nanning.*

In a country that has surprisingly few beach resorts with any appeal, the town is a pleasant place and the beaches are good by Chinese standards. **Yintan** (Silver Beach) in particular is worth a visit.

Guangxi A to Z

Arriving and Departing

BY BOAT

There is boat service between Hong Kong and **Wuzhou.** Nightly river service operates from **Liuzhou** to Guangzhou (12 hours), but you must be prepared for dormitory accommodation.

BY BUS

From **Guilin**'s long-distance bus station (✉ Zhongshan Lu, near railway station) you can get regular buses to Liuzhou and Nanning. There are also various types of bus (sleepers, with or without air-conditioning) to Guangzhou (16 hours) and Wuzhou. There are buses to **Beihai** daily from Nanning, Guilin, and Liuzhou. From **Liuzhou** there is frequent direct service each day to Guilin (6 hours) and a departure each day for Yangshuo. There is also direct service to Beihai, Guangzhou, Nanning, and Wuzhou. **Longsheng** is about 4 hours by bus from Guilin. From **Nanning**'s long-distance bus station (✉ corner Chaoyang Lu and Huaxi Lu, close to railway station) there is direct service to Beihai (5 hours), Guangzhou (19 hours), Liuzhou (5 hours), and Wuzhou (9 hours), as well as minibus service to Yiling Caves. **Wuzhou** can be reached by bus from Guilin, Liuzhou, and Nanning. Buses and mini-buses leave regularly from the Guilin railway station for **Yangshuo.**

BY PLANE

There are flights to **Beihai** from Guangzhou, Changsha, Guiyang, and Hong Kong. The **Guilin** airport, amid splendid scenery, is about a half-hour ride outside the town; buses to it leave from outside the CAAC office (✉ Shanghai Lu). There are flights to all the main destinations in China. **Liuzhou** has several flights a week to Guangzhou, Guiyang, Beijing, and Shanghai. **Nanning** (CAAC office, ✉ Chaoyang Lu), has direct flights daily to Guangzhou and Beijing, regular flights to Kunming and Shanghai, and a weekly flight to Guilin, as well as flights to Hanoi and Hong Kong. **Wuzhou**'s newly opened airport has a few flights to and from major cities in China.

BY TRAIN

Guilin's railway station (✉ just off Zhongshan Nanlu) is in the center of the city. There is direct service to most major Chinese cities, but journey times are long, e.g., to Beijing and Kunming, 30 hours; Shanghai and Xian, 35 hours. Guangzhou is a bit better at 15 hours. **Liuzhou** has direct service to Guangzhou, Changsha, Guilin (4 hours), Guiyang, Nanning, Kunming, Beijing, Shanghai, and Xian. **Nanning**'s station (✉ off Zonghua Lu) is at the northwest edge of town; there are direct trains to Beihai, Guilin, Chongqing, Liuzhou, Beijing, Shanghai, Wuhan, and Xian.

Getting Around

In **Guilin** the best way to get around, even in the heat, is by bicycle, which can be hired from several places around town. **Nanning** has motorbike taxis, which means riding pillion or in a sidecar. Bicycles can be hired in **Yangshuo.**

All cities have comprehensive public bus service, with maps available from CITS and the railway station. Otherwise, pedicabs and taxis can be found at hotels and at the railway and bus stations.

Contacts and Resources

CAR RENTAL

A car with driver can be arranged through CITS in any of the cities.

CONSULATES

The nearest consulates are in Guangzhou or Hong Kong. In Nanning, visas for Vietnam can be arranged through CITS.

CURRENCY EXCHANGE

Guilin: Bank of China (✉ Shanhu Beilu, just east of Zhongshan Lu). **Liuzhou:** Bank of China (✉ Feie Lu, south of Liu River). **Yangshuo:** Bank of China (✉ Binjiang Lu, close to river).

Money can also be changed in the major hotels.

EMERGENCIES

PSB (✉ Sanduo Lu, near Banyan Lake, Guilin).

VISITOR INFORMATION AND GUIDED TOURS

Guilin: CITS (Ronghu Beilu, close to Banyan Lake). **Nanning:** CITS (✉ 40 Xinmin Lu). **Liuzhou:** CITS (Youyi Lu). **Yangshuo:** CITS (Yangshuo Resort Hotel).

GUIZHOU

Guizhou is one of the most interesting provinces in China, although, or perhaps because, it is one of the least developed. It remains poor partly because of the unpredictable weather and also because of the difficult terrain with its thin limestone soil.

With an area of 170,000 sq km (65,600 sq mi) and a population of 33,200,000, Guizhou is an inland province of hills and agriculture, and of the so-called minority peoples, including the Dong, Hui, Yao, Zhuang, and Miao, among whom the latter are in the majority. About 85% of the province is high plateau intersected by mountains, which reach a height of 9,520 ft. It has warm, reasonably comfortable summers and fairly mild winters, the main disadvantage of which is the high volume of rain brought by monsoons.

The history of Guizhou has been marked by the constant struggle of the native population, now dominated by the Miao, for independence from Chinese subjugation, a struggle that has come to an end with Guizhou increasingly influenced by Beijing. The Chinese began to exert influence in the region from at least the Han dynasty (206 BC–AD 220), but forces sent to conquer it were only partly successful, real power remaining in the hands of various tribal chiefs. During the Tang dynasty Guizhou was considered part of the Chinese empire, although local chiefs retained at least some power by means of the payment of tribute. The situation remained more or less unchanged until the Ming dynasty, when central power was more in evidence as many more Han people began to settle here. This did not prevent uprisings; one Miao uprising in the 16th century, near Zunyi, lasted more than two years. Various rebellions, in which Han settlers allied themselves with the native tribes-people, continued throughout the Qing dynasty, persisting into the 20th century.

Guizhou's capital, Guiyang, has a few sites of interest, but the main natural attraction in the province is the Huangguoshu Falls. Guizhou provides an opportunity to see the daily lives of a traditional China that is rapidly disappearing.

Guiyang

55 *350 km (218 mi) northwest of Guilin; 425 km (265 mi) northwest of Nanning; 850 km (530 mi) northwest of Hong Kong; 1,650 km (1,025 mi) southwest of Beijing.*

The provincial capital of Guizhou, with a population of about a million, is noted for its mild climate and its convenience as a starting point for a visit to the Huangguoshu Falls. In the center of the province on a high plateau surrounded by mountains, it stands on the banks of the Nanminghe (Nanming River). Its historical name is Zhu, but not a lot is known about its history. There was a settlement here during the Han dynasty (206 BC–AD 220), and it became a military base during the Yuan (Mongol) dynasty in the 13th century. It was only during the following dynasty, the Ming, that the town rose to prominence. Then it acquired its city walls (parts of which still stand). It became known as Xingui, and only acquired its current name in 1913. Although like most cities in China it is fast losing its older quarters, enough still remains to render a short stay here worthwhile.

The main streets of the sprawling town are Zhonghua Lu and Yanan Lu.

The Qing dynasty **Jiaxiu Lou** (Pavilion of the Erudite Man), in the center of the city, was built in 1689. It has a handsome triple roof 65 ft in height. Two 18th-century iron pillars stand in the forecourt. ⊠ *East of Fushui Lu and south of river.*

Qianlingshan Gongyuan (Qianlingshan Park) lies just outside the city. Covering an area of about 740 acres, it has something of everything— thousands of different species of plants and trees, medicinal herbs, a lake and hills, and a collection of birds and monkeys.

At its center the park is dominated by the bulk of Qianlingshan (Mt. Qianling), which reaches a height of 4,265 ft and offers fine views across the town from its western peak. The **Hongfu Si** (Temple of Great Fortune), on the higher slopes of the mountain, was built in 1672. The **obelisk** on the wooded slopes behind the mountain, erected in 1949, is dedicated to those who fell in the Civil War and in the Sino-Japanese War.

The **Qiling Dong** (Cave of the Unicorn), discovered in 1531, was used as a prison for the two Nationalist generals, Yang Hucheng and Chang Hsueliang, who were accused by the Guomindang of collaborating with the Communists when Chiang Kai-shek was captured at Xian in 1937. ⊠ *Zhaoshan Lu, 1.5 km (1 mi) northwest of city.* 🕿 *RMB1.* 🕗 *Daily.*

Huaxi Gongyuan (Huaxi Park) is a scenic park about 18 km (11 mi) south of Guiyang on the banks of the Huaxi, the River of Flowers. The Huaxi Waterfall is nearby; the park itself is filled with tea houses, pavilions, and ornamental scenery. 🕗 *Daily.*

Dixia Gongyuan (Underground Gardens) is the poetic name for a cave about 25 km (15 mi) south of the city, discovered in 1965. In the cave, at a depth of 1,925 ft, a path threads its way through the various rock formations, which are illuminated in such a way as to emphasize their similarity with animals, fruit, and other living things. 🕿 *Y10.* 🕗 *Daily, 8:30–11:30 and 2:30–5.*

Dining and Lodging

$$ ✕ **Jinqiao Fandian.** At this good restaurant the menu offers regional food from Beijing and Canton. ⊠ *34 Ruijin Zhong Lu,* 🕿 *0851/582– 5310. MC, V.*

$$ ✕ **Jue Yuan Vegetarian Restaurant.** Excellent vegetarian food is the draw here. ⊠ *51 Fu Shui Beilu,* 🕿 *0851/529609. No credit cards.*

$–$$ ✕ **Hongfu Temple Vegetarian Restaurant.** You'll find good vegetarian
★   food at very reasonable prices in appealing surroundings. ⊠ *Qianling Park,* 🕿 *0851/625606. No credit cards. No dinner.*

$$$–$$$$ 🏨 **Guizhou Park Hotel.** The most luxurious hotel in town is a highrise
★   standing in the north close to Qianling Park. It has a bank. ⊠ *66 Beijing Lu, 550004,* 🕿 *0851/682–2888,* 🖷 *0851/682–4397. 220 rooms. 2 restaurants, shops, business services. MC, V.*

$$$ 🏨 **Jinzhu.** Here you'll find the Chinese version of Western luxury in a convenient location. It even has a bank. Rooms are a bit shabby. ⊠ *Yanan Donglu,* 🕿/🖷 *0851/682–5888. 3 restaurants, shops, business services. MC, V.*

Nightlife and the Arts

Ask CITS (☞ Visitor Information, *below*) or at your hotel about the occasional performance of **opera** or local song and dance, particularly in the village of Caiguan, near Anshun (☞ *below*).

Nightlife is restricted on the whole to karaoke or to the hotel bars.

Outdoor Activities and Sports

For **jogging,** try the Qianling Park or Hebin Park in Guiyang. You can walk in the countryside around Huangguoshu Falls (☞ *below*).

Shopping

Crafts to buy in Guiyang and surroundings include batik, Miao and Bouyei embroidery and jewelry, Yuping flutes, lacquerware, opera masks, tea, and Jinzhu glazed pottery.

Anshun

56 *80 km (50 mi) southwest of Guiyang.*

This, the most important town in western Guizhou, with some nice old streets, lies in an attractive area of karst rock formations. Its principal attraction is the Ming dynasty **Wen Si** (Wen Temple), in the north of the town, just off Hongshan Donglu. It is also a good base for visiting the Huangguoshu Falls (☞ *below*), which are only 45 km (28 mi) to the southwest, and the **Longgong Dong** (Dragon Palace Caves), only 32 km (20 mi) to the south. The caves, parts of which are adorned with some spectacular rock formations, meander for some 30 km (19 mi) through a chain of mountains; part of them can be seen from tin boats that can be hired here (✉ Y35).

Huangguoshu Pubu

★ **57** *150 km (94 mi) southwest of Guiyang.*

Here the Baishuio River streams over nine sets of rocks, creating nine waterfalls over a course of 2 km (1 mi). At its highest, it drops 230 ft and is 263 ft wide. The **Huangguoshu Pubu** (Yellow Fruit Trees Falls), the largest in China, though not as spectacular as the other great waterfalls around the world, are set in lush countryside that is home to a number of minority peoples. You can enjoy the falls from afar or by wading across the **Xi Niu Jian** (Rhinoceros Pool) to the **Shui Lian Dong** (Water Curtain Cave) behind the main fall. Seven kilometers (4½ mi) downstream are the **Xing Qiao Pu** (Star Bridge Falls). The falls are at their best between May and October.

The people most in evidence at Huangguoshu are the Bouyei, a Thai people, who have a festival in Huangguoshu village at the lunar new year and whose specialty is the production of batik cloth.

Kaili

★ **58** *About 200 km (125 mi) east of Guiyang*

Kaili is in the middle of some of the most interesting countryside in Guizhou, occupied by a number of minority peoples. In the town itself are a few sites: the **Drum Tower** in Jinquanhu Park, the **Zhou Minzu Bowuguan** (Minorities Museum; ✉ RMB5; ☉ Mon.–Sat.), and the **pagoda** in Dage Park. Outside town the local villages are of great interest. At **Shibing,** north of Kaili, it is possible to take boat rides (contact CTS) through spectacular limestone gorges on the Wuyang River.

Xingyi

59 *160 km (100 mi) southwest of Guiyang.*

This small town in the southwest of Guizhou has a minorities museum but is mainly notable for the **Maling Hexiagu** (Maling Gorge), which cuts deeply and impressively into the mountains for 15 km (9 mi), with a path running alongside it. The gorge lies close to the town and is best reached by taxi.

Zunyi

60 *160 km (100 mi) north of Guiyang.*

Zunyi has some interesting old streets and the **Xianshan Si** (Xianshan Temple). The town is of interest mainly because of its associations with the Communists' Long March in 1934. Having set out from Jiangxi in October, the party members reached Zunyi in December. In January they held a conference here to analyze their position, a conference at which Mao distinguished himself, establishing a reputation that was ultimately to lead him to power. The main thing to see is the **Zunyi Huiyi Zhi** (Zunyi Conference Center; ✆ daily), across the river in the west of the town. A 1920s Western-style house built for a wealthy landowner, it is furnished as it would have been in the 1930s. There is also the **Changzheng Bowuguan** (Long March Museum) in the old house and church built by the French in the 19th century. A huge Soviet-inspired monument to the Red Army Martyrs stands in **Fenghuang Shan Gongyuan** (Phoenix Hill Park).

Northwest of Zunyi is the town of **Maotai,** home to the distilleries that produce the liquor of the same name that is considered the best in China. ✉ *100 km (62 mi) northwest of Zunyi.*

Guizhou A to Z

Arriving and Departing

BY BUS

From Guiyang's station (✉ Yanan Xilu) there is regular bus service to Anshun (2 hours), Kaili (5 hours), Xingyi (12 hours approximately over very bad roads) and Zunyi (5 hours). There are also special tour buses to Huangguoshu Falls from the Guiyang railway station. From Anshun the journey to Xingyi is 8 hours.

BY PLANE

The Guiyang airport lies to the southwest of the city. There are direct flights between Guiyang and most of the main cities in China, including Beijing, Chengdu, Guangzhou, Guilin, Hong Kong, Shanghai, Xiamen, and Xian. CAAC office (✉ Zunyi Lu, ☎ 0851/683–0677).

BY TRAIN

Direct trains link Guiyang with Chongqing, Guilin, Kunming, Liuzhou, Nanning, and Shanghai. The railway station (✉ Zunyi Lu) is at the southern edge of the city. There is train service from Guiyang to Kaili (3 hours) and Zunyi (about 3 hours).

Getting Around

Maps for the comprehensive public and minibus network around Guiyang can be obtained from bookshops, stations, or CITS (☞ *below*).

Contacts and Resources

CAR RENTAL

There is no self-drive car rental available, but cars with drivers can be hired through CITS in Guiyang (☞ *below*).

CONSULATES

There are no consulates in Guizhou.

CURRENCY EXCHANGE
Change money at your hotel or at the Bank of China (✉ Ruijin Lu).

EMERGENCIES
PSB (✉ Zhongshan Xilu, Guiyang).

VISITOR INFORMATION AND GUIDED TOURS
CITS (✉ 20 Yanan Zhonglu, Guiyang, ☎ 0851/582–5873).

8   Hong Kong

Hong Kong became a Special Administrative Region (SAR) of China amid much pomp and ceremony on June 30, 1997. After 156 years as a British colony, Hong Kong is still a world apart from the rest of China. It has designer fashions, fast food, places where English is spoken—and yet, Hong Kong is a distinctly Chinese city. Because it never suffered through revolution, Hong Kong has retained more traditional Chinese ways than the mainland has. Temples and miniature Buddhist altars are scattered throughout the city and the outlying islands; in the back streets incense curls into the air and housewives shop twice a day at tiny market stalls.

By Jan
Alexander

THE ISLAND WAS OFFICIALLY CEDED to Great Britain in 1841, at the end of the First Opium War with China. At that time it was hardly considered a valuable prize. It was a sparse little island, 78 sq km (30 sq mi) in size, with only one natural water source—a waterfall above what is now Aberdeen—and a mountainous center. The British foreign minister called Hong Kong "that barren rock."

In the beginning, it was the natural harbor that allowed the territory to grow into a trading center. After Mao's revolution in China in 1949, the population more than doubled as families, mostly from the hated merchant class, escaped persecution by fleeing to Hong Kong—sometimes by swimming across the South China Sea. Many set up manufacturing companies, making goods for export, which fueled double-digit economic growth through the 1960s, '70s and '80s. China's "Open Door" policy since 1978 has brought even more of an economic boom to Hong Kong, as multinational investment banks set up their operations in the glamorous buildings of Central Hong Kong in order to put together multi-million-dollar investment deals in China. Today, the "barren rock" contains some of the world's most expensive real estate and a skyline to rival that of any of the world's major cities.

Hong Kong vibrates with life, energy, and the frantic quest for personal achievement and gain. The intensely developed areas at the center belie the fact that about 75% of Hong Kong's territory is actually rural land. A bird's-eye view reveals the 236 islands that make up the lesser-known part of Hong Kong. Most of these undeveloped islands are nothing but jagged peaks and tropical scrub, just as Hong Kong Island itself once was. Even Hong Kong Island has vast stretches of green, with walking trails that take two days or more to cover. This other side of Hong Kong is easily accessible by boats and buses. You can hike in the woods, stroll through traditional Chinese villages, or spend the afternoon sailing and then, via the city's mega-efficient highways and public transportation, arrive back to civilization in plenty of time for an evening of fine dining and glittering nightlife.

By late 1997 the British bureaucracy had departed and their jobs had been filled by Hong Kong Chinese bureaucrats, most trained under the old system. Street names are still given in English everywhere. Cantonese (as opposed to Mandarin, the official language of the mainland) and English are likely to be the languages of Hong Kong for the foreseeable future.

Pleasures and Pastimes

Chinese Culture

Hong Kong's indigenous culture is tuned in to the modern world through mobile phones and computers but still retains its unique traditions. These you can see at ancient Buddhist temples, at the hands of a fortune teller, or in parks watching the morning tai chi ritual. Visit a karaoke to see a contemporary ritual.

Dining

Anywhere you go in Hong Kong, in any direction you'd care to look, you're bound to see a restaurant sign. Nowhere in the world is cooking more varied than in this city, where Cantonese cuisine (long regarded by Chinese gourmands as the most intricate and sophisticated in Asia) is joined by delights from not only other parts of China, but also virtually every other culinary region on earth.

Five styles of Chinese cooking are prominent in Hong Kong. As 94% of the population comes from Guangdong (Canton) Province, **Cantonese** is considered the indigenous style. The Cantonese ideal is to bring out the natural taste of ingredients by cooking them quickly at very high temperatures. This creates *wok chi,* a fleeting energy that requires food to be served immediately and eaten on the spot.

Hong Kong is also a great place to sample the gutsy, hearty cuisine of **Chiu Chow,** near Canton. It begins with "Iron Buddha" tea and moves on to thick shark's fin soup, soya goose, whelk (tiny snails), bird's nest, and irresistible steamed lobsters served with tangerine jam.

There are also many restaurants in Hong Kong serving **Shanghai, Peking,** and **Szechuan** food.

Tips (15%) are expected at most restaurants, even if there is already a service charge on the bill. In more traditional Chinese restaurants, tips are not expected. However, it is customary to leave small change.

Reservations are always a good idea; we note only when they're essential or when they are not accepted. Unless otherwise noted, the restaurants listed are open daily for lunch and dinner. We mention dress only when men are required to wear a jacket or a jacket and tie.

CATEGORY	COST*
$$$$	over HK$500 (US$64)
$$$	HK$300–HK$500 (US$38–US$64)
$$	HK$100–HK$300 (US$13–US$38)
$	under HK$100 (US$13)

per person, not including 10% service charge

Horseracing

If you're here for the season (September through May) don't miss the excitement of the races—a favorite spectator sport among locals and expatriates alike. Some 65 races are held at the two race courses: Happy Valley on Hong Kong Island and Shatin in the New Territories.

Lodging

Accommodations are very expensive in Hong Kong. Most hotels provide top-of-the-line amenities like magnificent views and hi-tech facilities—and strive to please business clientele with expense accounts at their disposal. To find a guest house for less than U.S. $120 is difficult; expect to pay at least U.S. $150 a night for a room of normal international standards. For that price, you won't have a prime location, but you will have basic and reliable facilities—color TV, radio, telephone, same-day valet laundry service, room service, secretarial service, safe deposit box, refrigerator and minibar, and air-conditioning. Most hotels also have at least one restaurant and bar, a travel and tour-booking desk, and limousine or car rental.

Categories for hotel rates are based on the average price for a standard double room for two people. Prices will be higher for a larger room, or a room with a view. All rates are subject to a 10% service charge and a 5% government tax, which is used to fund the activities of the Hong Kong Tourist Association. Accommodations are listed by three geographical areas—Hong Kong Island, Kowloon, and New Territories and the Outer Islands—alphabetized within each price category.

CATEGORY	COST*
$$$$	over HK$2,500 (US$325)
$$$	HK$1,800–HK$2,500 (US$230–US$325)
$$	HK$1,200–HK$1,800 (US$150–US$230)
$	under HK$1,200 (US$150)

*All prices are for a double room, not including 10% service charge and 5% tax.

Shopping

In this shopaholic capital of the world, the most rewarding spoils are the Chinese clothes, fabrics, antiques, jewelry, tea, and collectibles that you can find on Hollywood Road, in outdoor markets, and even tucked away in high-tech shopping malls.

Water Cruising

The madness of the city disappears when you're viewing Hong Kong from the water. Board a cruise vessel around the harbor, go to Aberdeen and take a sampan ride, or charter a junk for a day.

EXPLORING HONG KONG

The first view you're likely to have of Hong Kong Island is Central, at the center of the north side of the island, where the ferries arrive and embark, and where the most prestigious commercial buildings stand. The Western District, to the west of Central, has small Chinese shops that give way to large residential high rises stretching out to Pok Fu Lam, home of Hong Kong University. East of Central is Wanchai, once known mostly for its topless bars and massage parlors; it, too, has developed into a district of office buildings, popular night spots, and hotels. Farther east along the northern shore are, in order, Causeway Bay, North Point, Quarry Bay, Tai Koo, Shaukeiwan, and Chai Wan. These districts, formerly industrial, have in recent years been the beneficiaries of office development moving out from high-priced Central. Beyond the buildings and factories on the northeastern shore are middle-class and working-class residential buildings. South of Wanchai is the middle-class area of Happy Valley, home of one of Hong Kong's two race tracks.

Much of the center of the island is rolling green space, with residential areas scattered throughout. On the southern side are the residential beach communities of Aberdeen and adjacent Ap Lei Chau island, Stanley, Repulse Bay, and Shek O, and the millionaires' paradise, Deepwater Bay.

The Kowloon Peninsula, which juts down from the mainland, is easily reachable from Central by the Star Ferry. The ferry docks at Tsim Sha Tsui, one of the most densely packed sections of Hong Kong, an area teeming with stores, hotels, restaurants, and offices. North of Tsim Sha Tsui, and reachable by subway, are the equally jam-packed commercial areas of Yau Ma Tei, Mong Kok, and Kowloon Tong. Just north of Kowloon Tong, the New Territories begins. This once-rural section has been developed into a series of so-called satellite towns. Some of the biggest of these towns are Fanling; Shatin, home of the Sha Tin Race Track and Chinese University of Hong Kong; and Tai Po. The beautiful Sai Kung peninsula, which has seaside villages, beaches, and walking trails, lies along a bay in the eastern New Territories.

Great Itineraries

Numbers in the text correspond to numbers in the margin and on the Hong Kong map.

Start day one at Star Ferry Pier in Central, and see Hong Kong's bustling **harbor.** Go to Hollywood Road via the **Mid-Levels Escalator** and browse or buy antiques. Take the **Peak Tram** up to Victoria Peak for a splendid view of the territory. Spend the afternoon at **Ocean Park,** an exciting family theme park, or shopping for inexpensive casual clothes and Chinese souvenirs in **Stanley Village,** which has a pleasant sea view. Take one day to visit **Lantau Island.** See the village of **Mui Wo,** the **Po-Lin Monastery** and **Giant Buddha,** famous sights in Hong Kong and nestled amidst scenic mountains. If you start out early enough, go to **Tai O** to see a traditional Chinese fishing village. Take the Star Ferry to **Tsim Sha Tsui,** where you can shop till you drop, or take a tour through Hong Kong's history at the **Hong Kong Museum of History.** Work your way up to Temple Street and the Kansu Street **Jade Market,** if you want to do more shopping (or wait and go to Temple Street at night), and to **Wong Tai Sin Temple,** to see an excellent example of a large Buddhist temple. Take a break to experience one of the few remaining throwbacks left to colonialism—high tea at the Peninsula Hotel.

Starting at Star Ferry Pier, go to **Hollywood Road** and on to the Western district and **Bonham Strands East and West.** From here go to **Victoria Peak.** Visit the **Happy Valley Race Track** to see the site for racing madness. Go on to **Aw Boon Haw** (Tiger Balm Gardens), for an experience in family entertainment, and the **Law Uk Folk Museum** to see what Hong Kong used to look like. Take a day to visit southern Hong Kong Island. Visit **Ocean Park,** and shop at **Stanley Bay.** If it's a warm day, go to a beach. Take one day to visit **Lantau Island.** Spend a day on Kowloon, in **Tsim Sha Tsui,** the **Hong Kong Museum of History,** shopping on **Temple Street** and at the **Jade Market,** visiting **Wong Tai Sin Temple,** and stopping for tea at the Peninsula. Book a day or half-day tour of the **New Territories.** For a final view of Hong Kong from the water, book a day-time water tour.

Add to the above itinerary a day-long side trip to **Macau** to see a place where Hong Kong residents go for recreation and the popular pastime of gambling. Take a day to visit either **Lamma** or **Cheung Chau Island,** to see a slower-paced side of Hong Kong life and try fresh-caught seafood, Cantonese style.

Hong Kong Island

Walking is often the transportation of choice in Hong Kong's compact commercial areas, where taxis and buses can get stalled in traffic at any time of the day. The best strolling weather is in the dry season from late September to mid-December; the rest of the year you should carry a folding umbrella.

A Good Tour

Start exploring from Central at the **Star Ferry** ① terminal. Walk up the staircase beside the Post Office **Exchange Square** ②, following the signs along the elevated walkway. From Exchange Square, return to the elevated walkway and cross Connaught Road. The walkway ends at Pedder Street. Follow Pedder Street to Queen's Road Central, one of the main shopping arteries. A few blocks down you'll see the **Mid-Levels Escalator** ③. Board the escalator and exit at **Hollywood Road** ④. Stop at **Man Mo Temple** ⑤, on Hollywood Road amid antiques and curio shops. To reach **Upper Lascar Row** ⑥, also known as **Cat Street,** walk down the steps of Ladder Street, just across from Man Mo Temple.

From Cat Street, head toward the Western District. Walk down Ladder Street back to Queen's Road Central. Walking west, you'll begin to find some of the best local color within the urban jungle. Turn right on Cleverly Street, then left. **Bonham Strands East and West** ⑦ have many little shops selling preserved foods such as dried and salted fish, black mushrooms, Chinese medicines, chops, and live birds.

You can take a taxi from here to the **Peak Tram** ⑧ terminal, just behind the St. Johns Building (a modern office building) on Garden Road. Ride the tram to **Victoria Peak** ⑨. When you come down from the Peak, take a taxi toward Happy Valley, to the **Happy Valley Race Track** ⑩ and **Aw Boon Haw** ⑪.

Take a taxi or the MTR blue line, which starts at Sheung Wan west of Central and runs east across the northern side to Chai Wan with intermittent stops, to the **Law Uk Folk Museum** ⑫, at the end of the line. To see the south side, take a taxi from Central downhill to **Ocean Park, Water World, and Middle Kingdom** ⑬, which are mostly of interest to children. You can spend the afternoon here, or skip the theme parks and continue on by taxi from Aberdeen along the scenic waterside road to **Stanley Bay** ⑭, where the main attraction is shopping at **Stanley Market**.

TIMING
You'll need three to four hours for the walk if you stop to shop and browse, and four to five hours for the trip to the peak and the rest of the island.

Sights to See

⑪ **Aw Boon Haw** (Tiger Balm Gardens). Built in 1935 with profits from sales of a popular menthol balm, the gardens were the pet project of two Chinese brothers, who also built a mansion here. Eight acres of hillside are pocked and covered with grottoes and pavilions filled with garishly painted statues and models of Chinese gods, mythical animals, and scenes depicting fables and parables. It's great fun to explore, especially for children. Be forewarned: Some of the scenes of Taoist and Buddhist mythology are decidedly gruesome. There is also an ornate seven-story pagoda containing Buddhist relics and the ashes of monks and nuns. ⊠ *Tai Hang Do, Happy Valley.* ▨ *Free.* ◎ *Daily 9:30–4.*

⑦ **Bonham Strands East and West.** Left relatively untouched by the modern world, the streets here are lined with traditional shops, many open-fronted. Among the most interesting are those selling live snakes, for both food and medicinal uses. The snakes, from pythons to cobras, are imported from the mainland and kept in cages outside the shops. Go ahead and sample a bowl of snake soup or an invigorating snake-gallbladder wine. The main season for the snake trade is October through February.

② **Exchange Square.** Exchange Square consists of three gold- and silver-striped glass towers and contains some of the most expensive rental space on the island—or in the world. The escalator up to the lobby of Exchange Square 1 takes you to the rotunda, which has exhibitions of a fairly trendy collection of contemporary art. The complex is also home to the **Hong Kong Stock Exchange.** You can arrange to tour the exchange during trading hours; call for information. ⊠ *1 Exchange Sq., Central,* ☎ *852/2522–1122.* ◎ *Weekdays 10–12:30 and 2:30–3:30.*

⑩ **Happy Valley Race Track.** Every Wednesday night and one afternoon each weekend from September to mid-June, you can bet on horses here. Completed in 1841, it has been updated with a huge outdoor video screen for close-ups, slow motion, and instant replays. The track is for members only, but you can obtain a special visitor's admission if you

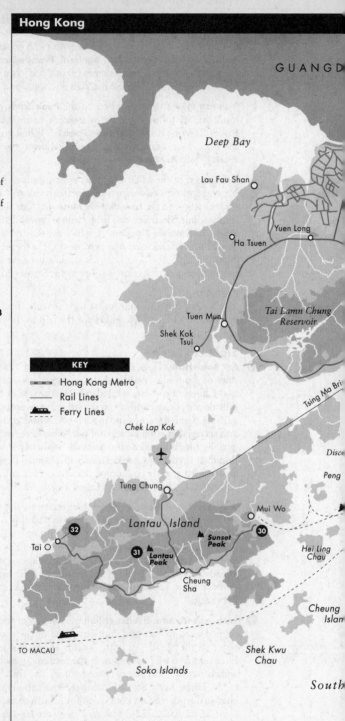

GDONG

Lo Wu

Lok Ma Chau

Sheung
Shut

San Tin

Mai Po

27 Fanling

Wu Kau
Lang

*Plover Cove
Reservoir*

Tolo Channel

28 Taipo

Kam Shan

Pan
Chung

Tolo Harbour

Chek
Keng

29

N E W   T E R R I T O R I E S

26

Shatin

Sai Kung

Tsuen Wan

25

Ho chung

*Kau Sai
Chau*

Bridge

*Tsing
Yi*

Sung Dynasty Village

Port Shelter

Kowloon

15 — 23

24

Discovery Bay

Victoria Harbour

*Kowloon
Bay*

Yau Tong

Junk Bay

*Tai Wan
Tau*

eng Chau

Victoria

Central Hong Kong

1 — 8

9

10   11

12

HONG KONG

*Tei Tong
Tsui*

g

13

*Tung Lung
Chau*

14

Stanley

ng Chau
sland

*Lamma
Island*

*Repulse
Bay*

*Stanley
Peninsula*

*Po Toi
Islands*

N

uth China Sea

0   2 miles

0   3 km

have been in Hong Kong for less than three weeks and are over 18. Your passport with the tourist visa stamp is required as proof. ✉ *Hong Kong Jockey Club, 2 Sports Rd., Happy Valley,* ☎ *852/2966–8111 or 852/2966–8364.* 🖅 *HK$50, entrance badge.*

❹ **Hollywood Road.** Here are many antiques, curio, and junk shops, as well as shops selling every type of Asian art and handicraft. Some items are genuinely old, but most are not. Porcelain, embroidered robes, paintings, screens, snuff bottles, and wood and ivory carvings are among the many items that can be found here in profusion. Bargain hard if you want a good price.

The junction of Hollywood Road and Possession Street was where Captain Charles Elliott of the British Royal Navy stepped ashore in 1841 and claimed Hong Kong for the British Empire. As a result of a century of aggressive land reclamation, today's harbor is far from this earlier shoreline.

⓬ **Law Uk Folk Museum.** It's worth a trip to Chai Wan, the end of the MTR line on the northeastern side of the island, to see this museum, a 200-year-old house that belonged to a family of Hakkas, the farming people who originally inhabited Hong Kong Island and the peninsula all the way into what is now southern Guangdong province. Decorated as a period house, the museum displays rural furniture and farm implements. A photo exhibition shows you what bustling industrial Chai Wan looked like in the 1930s, when it was a peaceful bay inhabited only by fishermen and squatters. ✉ *14 Kut Shing St., 1 block from Chai Wan MTR station (turn left from station, then follow Kut Shing St. as it curves to right),* ☎ *852/2896–7006.* 🖅 *Free.* ☉ *Tues.–Sat. 10–1 and 2–6; Sun. and public holidays 1–6.*

❺ **Man Mo Temple.** Built in 1847 and dedicated to the gods of literature and of war—Man and Mo, respectively—this is Hong Kong Island's oldest temple. The statue of Man is dressed in green and holds a writing brush, while Mo is dressed in red and holds a sword. To their left is a shrine to Pao Kung, god of justice, whose face is painted black. To the right, Shing Wong is god of the city. Coils of incense hang from roof beams, filling the air with a heavy fragrance. The temple bell, cast in Guangzhou in 1847, and the drum next to it are sounded to attract the attention of the gods when a prayer is being offered. To check your fortune, stand in front of the altar, take one of the small bamboo cylinders available there, and shake it until one of the sticks falls out. The number on the stick corresponds to a written fortune. Here's the catch—the English translation of your fortune is in a book on sale in the temple. ✉ *Hollywood Rd.* ☉ *Daily 9–6.*

❸ **Mid-Levels Escalator.** Completed in 1993, this is a half-mile of escalators and walkways that go through the steep incline between Central and Mid-Levels. The painless uphill ride provides an interesting view of small Chinese shops and gleaming residential high rises, as well as the all-green **Jamia Mosque** (built in 1915) at Shelley Street. **Staunton Street,** one level above Hollywood Road, is now known as Hong Kong's "SoHo" (i.e., "South of Hollywood"), with a string of cafés and bars, including the most intriguing Sherpa Himalayan Coffee Shop (you won't find one of these in New York or London!) at 11 Staunton Street.

Ride the escalators up between 10:20 AM and 11:30 PM. After 11:30, the escalators shut down, and in the mornings, from 6 to 10, they reverse direction and move downhill, so that commuters living in Mid-Levels can get to work in Central. You can get off at any point and explore the side streets, with shops selling porcelain, clothes, and antiques (not necessarily authenticated). Notice that almost every building has a tiny makeshift altar to the ancestors, usually made of red paper with gold Chinese characters, and offerings of fruit and incense. ✉ *Begins at Queens Rd. Central across from Central Market.* ⛽ *Free.* ⊙ *Daily 6 AM–11:30 PM.*

✋ ⑬ **Ocean Park, Water World, and Middle Kingdom.** These three attractions, east of Aberdeen, were built by the Royal Hong Kong Jockey Club. **Ocean Park,** on 170 acres of land overlooking the sea, is one of the world's largest oceanariums. On the "lowland" side are gardens, parks, and a children's zoo. A cable car, providing spectacular views of the entire south coast, can take you to the "headland" side and to the 4,000-seat Ocean Theatre, the world's largest marine mammal theater, where dolphins and a killer whale perform. There are also various rides, including a mammoth roller coaster. The adjacent, 65-acre **Water World** is an aquatic fun park with slides, rapids, pools, and a wave cove. **Middle Kingdom** is a theme park depicting architecture, arts, crafts, and industry through 3,000 years of Chinese history. The complex has cultural shows, souvenir shops, and restaurants. ✉ *Wong Chuk Hang Rd.,* ☎ *852/12873–8888 (Ocean Park),* ☎ *852/2870–0268 (Middle Kingdom),* ☎ *852/2555–6055 (Water World).* ⛽ *Ocean Park and Middle Kingdom, HK$140 adult, HK$70 children under 12; Water World, HK$65 adults, HK$30 children.* ⊙ *Ocean Park and Middle Kingdom, daily 10–6; Water World, June–Sept. daily 10–6.*

❽ **Peak Tram.** Starting from the Lower Peak Tram Terminus is the world's steepest funicular railway. It passes five intermediate stations en route to the upper terminal 1,800 ft above sea level. The railway was opened in 1880 to transport people to the top of ☞ **Victoria Peak,** the highest hill overlooking Hong Kong Harbour. Before the tram, the only way to get to the top was to walk or take a bumpy ride up the steep steps in a sedan chair. The tram has two 72-seat cars that are hauled up the hill by cables attached to electric motors. A free shuttle bus to and from the Peak Tram leaves from next to City Hall, at Edinburgh Place. ✉ *Between Garden Rd. and Cotton Tree Dr.* ⛽ *HK$15 one-way, HK$27 round-trip.* ⊙ *Daily 7 AM– midnight; trams run every 10–15 min.*

⑭ **Stanley Bay.** It became notorious as the home of the largest Hong Kong prisoner-of-war camps run by the Japanese during World War II. Today, Stanley is known for its picturesque beaches and its market, where casual clothing is sold at wholesale prices. Hong Kong has dozens of shops offering similar bargains, but it's more fun to shop for them in the countrified atmosphere around Stanley. You can also find ceramics, paintings, and souvenirs. Past the market, on Stanley Main Street, a strip of restaurants and pubs faces the bay. On the other side of the bay is a temple to Tin Hau, goddess of the sea, just beyond land that is being cleared for development. Part of this development is to be a public housing estate that will give low-income residents a chance to live on prime waterfront property.

❶ **Star Ferry.** Since 1898, the ferry terminal has been the gateway to the island for visitors and commuters crossing the harbor from Kowloon. Taking the Star Ferry and riding around Hong Kong Island on a two-decker tram are almost essential for first-time visitors. In front of the terminal you will usually see a few red rickshaws. Once numbering in the thousands, these two-wheel, man-powered "taxis" are all but gone. ✉ *Enter terminal area through tunnel next to Mandarin Hotel on Connaught St.* ⛽ *First-class ticket, HK$2.20; second-class, HK$1.90.* ⊙ *Daily 6 AM–midnight.*

❻ **Upper Lascar Row.** Cat Street, as Upper Lascar Row is often called, is a vast flea market. You won't find Ming vases here—or anything else of significant monetary value—but you may come across an old Mao badge or an antique pot or teakettle. More worthwhile for the art or antiques collector are the shops and stalls known as **Cat Street Galleries** (⌧ 38 Lok Ku Rd.), adjacent to the flea market. This is a growing new complex, with galleries selling every kind of crafted work, old and, most often, new. You can rest your feet and have coffee in the convenient little European café, Somethin' Brewin'. ⌧ *1 block north of Hollywood Rd., between Ladder and Tung Sts.*

★ **Victoria Peak.** The Chinese name for Victoria Peak is Tai Ping Shan (Mountain of Great Peace). It may become known by this name post-handover, but name change or not, this is one site that will last. The top of the peak is 1,800 ft above sea level, and on a clear day the panorama is breathtaking, offering a view of Hong Kong's islands stretching all the way up to the mainland shores. Besides being the most prestigious address to have in Hong Kong, the Peak offers highly hospitable parkland to visitors. It is a popular picnic spot, filled with beautiful walking paths that circle the peak. A lookout pavilion just below the summit was once part of a former Governor's residence. The original gardens and country walks remain and are open to the public.

The **Peak Galleria** shopping mall and the **Peak Tower** next door have numerous restaurants and boutiques selling souvenirs, clothes, and gifts. The Peak Tower has several attractions for children: The Peak Explorer is a virtual reality ride through outer space, while the Rise of the Dragon takes you on a rail car through a series of animated scenes from Hong Kong's history, including a frighteningly accurate rendition of the 1907 typhoon that devastated the territory. There is also a Ripley's Believe It or Not Museum. ⌧ *Enter via Peak Tram from Garden Rd. (there is no road on the tramline).*

NEED A BREAK?   On the Peak, the nicest place to have a drink or a meal and enjoy the view is the **Peak Café** (⌧ 121 Peak Rd., ☎ 852/2819–7868). If the weather is good, ask for a table in the garden.

Kowloon

Kowloon Peninsula juts down from mainland China, directly across Victoria Harbour from Central. Legend has it that Kowloon was named by a Chinese emperor who fled here during the Sung dynasty (960–1279). He counted eight hills on the peninsula and called them the Eight Dragons—so the account goes—but a servant reminded him that an emperor is also considered a dragon, and so the emperor called the region *Gau-lung* (nine dragons), which becomes Kowloon in English.

Kowloon is the site of most of Hong Kong's hotels. In the Old Tsim Sha Tsui district is the Victorian-era clock tower of the old Kowloon–Canton Railway station, the new Hong Kong Cultural Centre, the Peninsula Hotel, and the bustling Nathan Road area. The Tsim Sha Tsui East district, lying on land reclaimed from the harbor, contains many luxury hotels and shopping centers, the Space Museum, and a waterfront esplanade, as well as the new railroad station.

A Good Walk

The **Star Ferry Pier** ⑮ on the Kowloon side is a 10-minute ferry ride from the pier on the Hong Kong side; the ferry ride is the most romantic way to see the harbor, day or night. East of the pier is the long promenade along Salisbury Road. You can visit the **Hong Kong Cultural Centre** ⑯, **Hong Kong Space Museum** ⑰, and the **Hong Kong Museum of**

Art ⑱. The luxurious **Peninsula Hotel** ⑲ is across the street, on the corner of Salisbury and Nathan Road. Walk north on Nathan Road, then on to Haiphong Road to get to **Kowloon Park** ⑳, site of the **Hong Kong Museum of History** ㉑. Continue north on Nathan Road 3 blocks to Jordan Road; make a left and then a right onto **Temple Street** ㉒. Follow Temple Street north to the **Kansu Street Jade Market** ㉓, to the west. From here, take a taxi to **Wong Tai Sin Temple** ㉔.

Sights to See

⑯ **Hong Kong Cultural Centre.** This stark, architecturally controversial building has tiled walls inside and out, sloped roofs, and no windows—an irony, as the view is superb. It houses a concert hall and two theaters. ✉ *10 Salisbury Rd.,* ☎ *852/2734– 2010.*

⑱ **Hong Kong Museum of Art.** The exterior is unexciting, but inside are five floors of well-designed galleries. One is devoted to historic photographs, prints, and artifacts of Hong Kong, Macau, and other parts of the Pearl River delta. Other galleries display Chinese antiquities and fine art and visiting exhibitions. ✉ *10 Salisbury Rd.,* ☎ *852/2734– 2167.* 🎫 *HK$10.* ☉ *Tues.–Sat. 10–6; Sun. and holidays 1–6.*

㉑ **Hong Kong Museum of History.** The museum covers a broad span of the past with life-size dioramas depicting prehistoric scenes, the original fishing village, a 19th-century street, the Japanese occupation, and modern Hong Kong—all complete with sounds and smells. There is also a multiscreen slide show. ✉ *Haiphong Rd.,* ☎ *852/2367–1124.* 🎫 *HK$10.* ☉ *Mon.–Thurs. and Sat. 10–6, Sun. and holidays 1–6.*

☝ ⑰ **Hong Kong Space Museum.** Across from the Peninsula Hotel, the dome-shaped museum houses one of the most advanced planetariums in Asia. It also contains the **Hall of Solar Science,** whose solar telescope permits visitors a close look at the sun; the **Exhibition Hall,** which houses several exhibits at a time on topics such as outer space and astronomy; and a **Space Theatre,** with Omnimax movies on space travel, sports, and natural wonders. Children under 6 are not admitted. ✉ *10 Salisbury Rd.,* ☎ *852/2734–9009.* 🎫 *HK$10.* ☉ *Mon. and Wed.–Fri. 1– 9, weekends and holidays 10–9; Space Theatre, 7 shows daily, first at 2:30, last at 8:30.*

㉓ **Kansu Street Jade Market.** The daily jade market carries everything from fake jade pendants to precious carvings. If you don't know much about jade, take along someone who does, or you may pay a lot more than you should. The best time to visit is from 10 AM to noon. ✉ *Kansu St., off Nathan Rd.* ☉ *10–6.*

⑳ **Kowloon Park.** The former site of the Whitfield Military Barracks is today a restful, green oasis. Signs point the way to gardens with a variety of landscaping themes. Try the Chinese Garden, which has a lotus pond, streams, a lake, and a nearby aviary with a colorful collection of rare birds. The **Jamia Masjid and Islamic Centre** is on the south end of the park, near the Haiphong Road entrance. This is Hong Kong's principal mosque. Built in 1984, it has four minarets, decorative arches, and a marble dome. ✉ *Haiphong Rd. off Nathan Rd.*

⑲ **Peninsula Hotel.** The exterior of this sumptuous hotel draws attention with a fleet of Rolls-Royce taxis and doormen in white uniforms, while the huge colonnaded lobby has charm, grandeur, string quartets, and a plethora of celebrities (though with the opening of the Regent Hotel, no longer a monopoly on them). ✉ *Salisbury Rd.,* ☎ *852/2366– 6251.*

Tsim Sha Tsui is short on quiet cafés, but the **Peninsula Hotel** offers high tea—frankly, the perfect way to rest your shopping feet in style. You even have options: Dine on a majestic array of scones and pastries in the lobby (daily 2–7; HK$145 per person), or settle down for tea in the Verandah Restaurant (daily 3–5; HK$155 per person).

22 Temple Street. The heart of a busy shopping area, Temple Street is ideal for wandering and people-watching. By day you'll find market stalls with plenty of kitsch and a few worthwhile clothing bargains, but the best time to visit is after 8 PM, when the streets become an open-air market filled with street doctors offering cures for almost any complaint, fortune-tellers, and, on most nights, Cantonese opera.

Such nearby lanes as **Shanghai Street** and **Canton Road** are also worth a visit for their colorful shops and stalls selling everything from herbal remedies to jade and ivory. **Ning Po Street** is known for its shops selling paper kites and the colorful paper and bamboo models of worldly possessions that are burned at Chinese funerals.

24 Wong Tai Sin Temple. Have your fortune told at this large, colorful compound with a Buddhist shrine dedicated to a shepherd boy who was said to have had magic healing powers. In addition to the main altar, the pavilions, and the arcade—where you'll find soothsayers and palm readers happy to interpret Wong Tai Sin's predictions for a small fee— there are two lovely Chinese gardens and a Confucian Hall. ⊠ *Wong Tai Sin Rd. and Nga Chuk St.,* ☎ *852/2807–6177.* ☒ *Small donation expected.* ⊙ *Daily 7–5:30.*

New Territories

Only about 25 km (15 mi) of land lie between Kowloon's waterfront and the pre-handover border with China—hence the New Territories' appellation as "the land between." It is called the New Territories because it was the last area of land claimed by the British in extending their Hong Kong colony. Although most of the original farmland has given way to urban development, the village flavor remains in many areas, with small "wet-markets" (the ground beneath them is always wet) selling fresh produce and live chickens and fish in small fishing towns along the water.

Here you can enjoy panoramas of forested mountainsides and visit some of the ancient temples and clan houses of the area. The easiest way to see the region is by taking a tour organized by the **Hong Kong Tourist Association** (☎ 852/2807–6543 Mon.–Sat., ☎ 852/2807–6177 Sun. and holidays). Book through your hotel tour desk or an HKTA Information Center (⊠ lower level of Jardine House—building with round windows directly across from main Post Office next to Star Ferry Terminal, Central; or at Star Ferry Terminal, Tsim Sha Tsui).

A Good Drive
The six-hour "Land Between" tour takes you to the **Chuk Lam Shim Yuen** 25; **Tai Mo Shan** 26, Hong Kong's tallest mountain; **Fanling** 27, a typical wet market; a country park, **Tai Po** 28; and **Chinese University of Hong Kong** 29.

Sights to See
29 Chinese University of Hong Kong. The **Art Gallery**, in the university's Institute of Chinese Studies building, is well worth a visit. It has large exhibits of paintings and calligraphy from periods ranging from the Ming to modern times. There are also important collections of bronze seals, carved jade flowers, and ceramics from South China. Take the KCR to University Station and then take a campus bus or taxi. ⊠ *12*

Miles Tai Po Rd., Shatin, ☎ *852/2609–7416.* ☒ *Free.* ⊘ *Mon.–Sat.
10–4:30, Sun. and holidays 12:30–4:30. Closed between exhibitions
and on major holidays.*

㉕ Chuk Lam Shim Yuen (Bamboo Forest Monastery). One of Hong
Kong's most impressive monasteries, it has three large statues of Buddha. Crowds of worshipers on festival days demonstrate its continuing importance to the Chinese. ☒ *Castle Peak Rd., Tsuen Wan.*

㉗ Fanling. This town combines the serene atmosphere of the Hong Kong
Golf Club with the chaos of rapid growth. The nearby **Luen Wo Market** is a traditional Chinese market, well worth visiting. You might find
snakes for sale here in the winter months, and you're sure to see whole
dried chickens prominently displayed. ☒ *North central part of New
Territories, 2 towns below Chinese border on KCR line.*

㉖ Tai Mo Shan. In the southern central portion of the New Territories is
Hong Kong's highest peak, rising 3,230 ft above sea level. A trail
through the bush allows you to climb to the top if you're fit enough
(☞ Hiking *in* Outdoor Activities and Sports, *below*). From halfway
up, you'll have a nice view of the surrounding country park area. Unfortunately the summit is fenced off, serving as a government com-
munications post.

㉘ Tai Po (Shopping Place). In the heart of the region's breadbasket, Tai
Po has long been a trading and meeting place for local farmers and
fishermen. It is now being developed as an industrial center, with new
housing and highways everywhere you look. It has a fine traditional
market (☒ Tat Wan Rd.; ⊘ 9–6) stretching several blocks alongside
the Tai Po Market KCR station, with most of the action taking place
outdoors. Adjacent to the market is the 100-year-old **Man Mo Temple.**

OFF THE
BEATEN PATH
You can wander the forest and seaside trails of the **Sai Kung Peninsula**
on the eastern shore of the New Territories. Take the MTR to Choi Hung
and then Bus 92, 96R, or Minibus 1 to Sai Kung Town. **Sai Kung Country Park** has one of Hong Kong's most spectacular hiking trails, through
majestic hills overlooking the water. You can also take a taxi along
Clearwater Bay Road, through forested areas and land that is only partially developed, with Spanish-style villas overlooking the sea. Stroll
along the waterfront and you'll see some of the most unusual marine life
ever—in tanks, outside restaurants. (If you choose to eat in one of the
seafood restaurants, note that physicians caution against eating raw
shellfish here because of hepatitis outbreaks.) Rent a *kaido* (pronounced
guy-doe; one of the small boats run by private operators; about
HK$130) for a cruise around the harbor, stopping at tiny **Yim Tin Tsai
Island,** which has a rustic Catholic mission church built in 1890. This excursion will take one day. You should go only in sunny weather.

The Outer Islands

In addition to Hong Kong Island and the mainland sections of Kowloon
and the New Territories, 235 islands make up the special region of Hong
Kong. The four that are most accessible by ferry—Lantau, Lamma, Cheung Chau, and Peng Chau—have become popular residential areas and
welcome visitors. The largest, Lantau, is bigger than Hong Kong Island; the smallest is just a few square feet of rock. Most of them are
uninhabited. Some are gradually being developed, but at nowhere
near the pace of the main urban areas.

You can reach the islands by scheduled ferry services operated by the **Hong Kong and Yaumati Ferry Company** (☎ 852/2542–3081; enquiries hotline, ☎ 852/2525–1108). The ferries are easy to recognize by the large HKF letters painted on their funnels. Leave from the Outlying Districts Services Pier, Central, on the land reclamation area behind ☞ **Exchange Square.** Ferry schedules are available at the information office on the pier. The ferry ride to any of the major islands takes about one hour. Round-trip fares vary from HK$15 to HK$50.

The island of **Lantau** lies due west of Hong Kong. At 143 sq km (55 sq mi), it is almost twice the size of Hong Kong Island. For now—that is until development increases with the opening of the new airport on nearby Chek Lap Kok Island—Lantau's population is only 20,000, compared with Hong Kong Island's 1.5 million.

A Good Tour

The ferry will take you to the town of Mui Wo on **Silvermine Bay** ㉚, which is being developed as a commuter suburb of Hong Kong Island. The island is very mountainous, so for a tour of the outlying villages, plan to hike or take a bus. From the main ferry town, Mui Wo, the island's private bus services head out to **Po Lin Tzi** ㉛, home of a giant Buddha; and **Tai O** ㉜, an ancient fishing village.

TIMING

Take an entire day to tour the island.

Sights to See

㉛ **Po Lin Tzi** (Precious Lotus Monastery). In the mountainous interior of the island you will find the world's tallest outdoor bronze statue of Buddha, the **Tin Tan Buddha.** It is more than 100 ft high and weighs 275½ tons. The adjacent monastery, gaudy and exuberantly commercial, is also famous for the vegetarian meals served in the temple refectory. ⊠ *Look for signs at bus stands or ask dispatcher at Silvermine Bay bus depot.* ☉ *Daylight hours.*

㉚ **Silvermine Bay.** This busy fishing bay is the point of entry from the Lantau Ferry, with some pleasant little seaside cafés. The village of Mui Wo, which lies along the bay, has a few hotels where you can stay overnight or rent bicycles to ride through the side streets and along the rice fields.

㉜ **Tai O.** Divided into two parts connected by a rope-drawn ferry, the village still has many stilt houses and fishing shanties along the water. Visit the local temple, dedicated to Kuanti, the god of war, and taste local catches at the seafood restaurants. ⊠ *Take bus marked Tai O at Silvermine Bay.*

DINING

Hong Kong Island

Central

ASIAN

$$$$ ✕ **Man Wah.** Here you'll find a Zen-like haven in the midst of busy Central. A highlight of the menu is the sautéed fillet of sole with chilies in black bean sauce, which is delicately cooked to bring out the fish's fresh flavor as Cantonese cuisine should. For dessert try poached pear in tangerine tea, an unusual specialty to be savored slowly while watching the ships pass in Victoria Harbour. ⊠ *Mandarin Oriental Hotel, 5 Connaught Rd.,* ☎ *852/2522–0111, ext 4025. AE, DC, MC, V.*

$$$ ✕ **Indochine 1929.** The name directly evokes the period when the
★   French were in possession of what is modern-day Vietnam. The mood of the 1930s is gloriously but subtly summoned by the decor—potted

palms, old pictures, soothing lighting—and dedicated service of the sarong-dressed staff. Must-tries are the soft shell crab and the Hanoi fried fish. ⊠ *California Tower, 2nd floor, Lan Kwai Fong,* ☎ *852/2869–7399. AE, DC, MC, V.*

$ ✕ **Luk Yu Tea House.** Food takes a backseat to atmosphere in this unofficial historical monument, which lets you catch a rare glimpse of old colonial Hong Kong, but from the Chinese perspective. The morning dim sum is popular with Chinese businesspeople, though the fare is no more than standard Cantonese. Reservations can be difficult to get at peak meal hours unless you're a regular. ⊠ *24–26 Stanley St.,* ☎ *852/2523–5464. No credit cards.*

EUROPEAN

$$$$ ✕ **M at the Fringe.** This spot above the Fringe Club has a seasonal menu
★ that mixes Continental with Middle Eastern cuisine. Whether it's pumpkin and almond tortellini, crisp risotto, or grilled scallops wrapped in bacon, the combinations are truly as delicious as they are creative. ⊠ *South Block, 2 Lower Albert Rd., 1st floor,* ☎ *852/2877–4000. Reservations essential. AE, MC, V.*

Mid-Levels
ASIAN

$$ ✕ **Nepal.** If you're feeling adventurous, but not quite up to an assault
★ on Everest, you can stimulate your imagination with a Yaktail or Yeti Foot cocktail in this tiny Nepali restaurant. Take a look at the Nepalese woodcarving, *manne* (praying tools), and musical instruments as you enjoy the background Indian/Nepalese music. The menu has simple explanations of the Royal Nepalese cuisine. For a main course, the royal chicken, a light Nepali curry, is highly recommended. End the meal with the Nepalese ice cream. ⊠ *14 Staunton St.,* ☎ *852/2521–9108. Reservations essential. AE, DC, MC, V.*

EUROPEAN

$$–$$$ ✕ **Casa Lisboa.** Fado music playing in the background and bottles with
★ eruptions of melted candle wax add to the atmosphere. The codfish soup is a divine broth with chunks of the flaked fish and slivers of garlic and coriander. Also ask for the mashed potato *ze do pipa*, a fabulous mash with cheese, fish, and olives. All wines on the list are Portuguese (except for the champagne). ⊠ *21 Elgin St.,* ☎ *852/2869–9361. Reservations essential. AE, DC, MC, V.*

Wanchai
ASIAN

$$$–$$$$ ✕ **Dynasty.** Palm trees and live traditional Chinese music provide a total contrast to the modernity on display outside the windows. If you really want to push the boat out, try the braised imperial bird's nest with bamboo mushrooms and pigeon at HK$1,300. Definitely try the roast suckling pig—thin skins on top of tiny buns, although the melon balls served with this dish may present you with a real chopstick challenge. ⊠ *New World Harbour View, 1 Harbour Rd.,* ☎ *852/2802–8888. Reservations essential. AE, DC, MC, V.*

$ ✕ **Thai Delicacy.** This is a perennial favorite with lovers of inexpensive Thai food. Little chili symbols indicate how fiery each dish will be (they'll mellow the flavor if you ask). The *tom yung kung* (spicy prawn and coconut soup) is wonderful, as is the papaya salad. ⊠ *44 Hennessy Rd.,* ☎ *852/2527–2598. DC, MC, V.*

Causeway Bay
ASIAN

$$ ✕ **Chiu Chow Garden.** Try Iron Buddha tea (served in thimble-size cups and packed with caffeine), cold roast goose on a bed of fried blood

Hong Kong Dining and Lodging

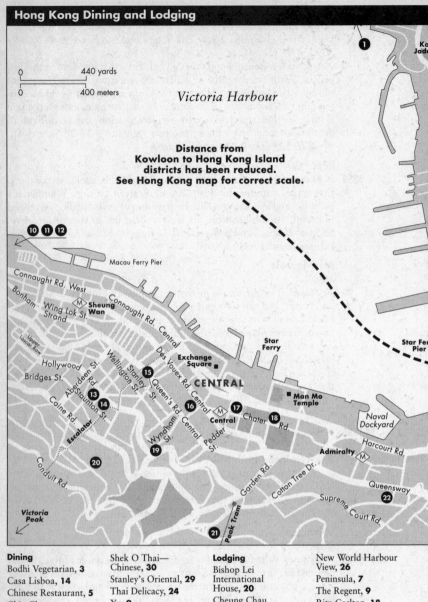

Victoria Harbour

Distance from
Kowloon to Hong Kong Island
districts has been reduced.
See Hong Kong map for correct scale.

0 — 440 yards
0 — 400 meters

Macau Ferry Pier

Connaught Rd. West
Bonham Strand
Wing Lok St.
Strand
Connaught Rd. Central

Sheung Wan

Des Voeux Rd. Central

Exchange Square

Star Ferry

Hollywood
Bridges St.
Aberdeen St.
Staunton St.
Wellington St.
Stanley St.
Queen's St.
Queen's Rd. Central

CENTRAL

Man Mo Temple

Caine Rd.
Escalator

Wyndham St.
Pedder St.
Chater Rd.

Central

Naval Dockyard

Conduit Rd.

Harcourt Rd.

Admiralty

Garden Rd.
Cotton Tree Dr.

Supreme Court Rd.

Queensway

Victoria Peak

Peak Tram

Kan
Jade M

Star Ferry Pier

Dining

Bodhi Vegetarian, **3**
Casa Lisboa, **14**
Chinese Restaurant, **5**
Chiu Chow
Garden, **27**
Dynasty, **26**
Gaddi's, **7**
Indochine 1929, **16**
Lancombe, **10**
Luk Yu Tea
House, **15**
M at the Fringe, **19**
Man Wah, **17**
Nepal, **13**

Shek O Thai—
Chinese, **30**
Stanley's Oriental, **29**
Thai Delicacy, **24**
Yu, **9**
Yunyan Szechuan
Restaurant, **2**

Lodging

Bishop Lei
International
House, **20**
Cheung Chau
Warwick, **11**
The Excelsior, **28**
Garden View
International
House, **21**
Gold Coast, **1**
Grand Hyatt, **25**
Island Shangri-La, **22**
Kowloon, **6**
Mandarin
Oriental, **17**

New World Harbour
View, **26**
Peninsula, **7**
The Regent, **9**
Ritz-Carlton, **18**
Royal Garden, **4**
Salisbury YMCA, **8**
Silvermine Beach
Hotel, **12**
The Wesley, **23**

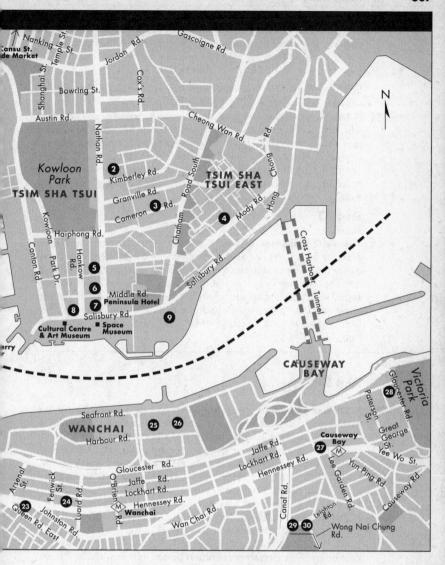

Nanking St.
Kansu St.
de Market
Temple St.
Shanghai St.
Bowring St.
Jordan Rd.
Gascoigne Rd.
Cox's Rd.
Austin Rd.
Nathan Rd.
Cheong Wan Rd.

Kowloon
Park

TSIM SHA TSUI

Kimberley Rd.
2

Granville Rd.

Cameron Rd.
3

TSIM SHA
TSUI EAST

Chatham Road South

Road

Hong
Chong

Mody Rd.
4

Haiphong Rd.

Kowloon
Park Dr.

Hankow
Rd.

Canton Rd.

5

6

Middle Rd.
Peninsula Hotel

7
Salisbury Rd.

8

Cultural Centre
& Art Museum

Space
Museum

Salisbury Rd.

9

rry

Cross Harbour Tunnel

CAUSEWAY
BAY

Victoria
Park

Gloucester Rd.

Paterson
St.

28

Seafront Rd.

WANCHAI

Harbour Rd.

25 **26**

Jaffe Rd.

Lockhart Rd.

Hennessy Rd.

**Causeway
Bay**
27 Ⓜ

Great
George
St.

Yee Wo St.

Lee Garden Rd.

Yun Ping Rd.

Causeway Rd.

Arsenal
St.

Fenwick
St.

Luard Rd.

O'Brien Rd.

Gloucester   Rd.

Jaffe   Rd.

Lockhart Rd.

Hennessey Rd.

Wanchai Ⓜ

Wan Chai Rd.

Canal Rd.

Leighton
Rd.

29 **30**

Wong Nai Chung
Rd.

23

24

Johnston Rd.

Queen Rd. East

N

(far better than it sounds), Fukien abalone in light ginger sauce, and delicious sautéed shrimp and crabmeat balls served over crisp prawn crackers. There are branches of Chiu Chow Garden in Jardine House and at Vicwood Plaza, on Hong Kong Island. ⊠ *Hennessy Centre, 500 Hennessy Rd.,* ☎ *852/2577–3391. AE, DC, MC, V.*

Stanley Bay

ASIAN

$$–$$$ ✕ **Stanley's Oriental.** Designed like an eastern version of an Old Quarter house in New Orleans, complete with ornate balconies and ceiling fans, Stanley's Oriental has a menu that marries Eastern and Western cuisines, matching Cajun and Creole with Thai, Indian, and Japanese. Try Thai curry or Cajun blackfish. For a little romance, reserve a table on an upper level overlooking the water. ⊠ *90B Stanley Main St.,* ☎ *852/2813–9988. AE, DC, MC, V.*

Shek O

ASIAN

$ ✕ **Shek O Thai–Chinese.** There's nothing particularly outstanding in decor or food here, but Shek O Thai–Chinese is a legend in its own dinner time—the casual, noisy, and lively outdoor restaurant is just such fun. The *tom yung kung* (spicy prawn and coconut soup) is always guaranteed to bring color to your cheeks, the green curry is a safe chicken choice, and the honey-fried squid is a must. ⊠ *Main corner of Shek O next to bus stop,* ☎ *852/2908– 4426. Reservations essential on weekends. No credit cards.*

Kowloon

Tsim Sha Tsui

ASIAN

$$$$ ✕ **Chinese Restaurant.** The postmodern interior is a new take on the traditional 1920s teahouse, and the talented kitchen staff's innovative Cantonese cooking is what makes the place stand out. The menu changes seasonally, though papaya soup, crisp chicken skin, and stewed goose in brown ginger gravy are always available and worth tasting. Peking duck here is out of this world, as is braised abalone on a bed of artichoke hearts. ⊠ *Hyatt Regency Hotel, 67 Nathan Rd.,* ☎ *852/ 2311–1234. Reservations essential. Jacket and tie. AE, DC, MC, V.*

$$$$ ✕ **Yu.** Walk in past a huge, curving built-in aquarium where gorgeous fish swim. There are a dozen or so varieties of fresh catch of the day, which is cooked to suit either Asian or Western tastes, as well as such East-meets-West specialties as sautéed Boston lobster with black beans and fine noodles. ⊠ *Regent Hotel, 18 Salisbury Rd.,* ☎ *852/2721–1211. Reservations essential. AE, DC, MC, V.*

$$ ✕ **Bodhi Vegetarian.** This small chain of restaurants offers some of the best Chinese vegetarian food in Hong Kong. A wide array of vegetables, dozens of varieties of mushrooms, bird's nests, and noodles are often combined with tofu, prepared to suggest meat or fish. Try deep-fried *taro* (a potato-like vegetable) or stir-fried Chinese vegetables. Buddhist scrolls decorating the walls emphasize the philosophical roots of the menu. No alcohol is served. ⊠ *56 Cameron Rd., TST,* ☎ *852/2739– 2222. AE, DC, MC, V.*

$$ ✕ **Yunyan Szechuan Restaurant.** If your taste buds are hearty, go for the dishes with three or even four chili signs on the menu, like poached sliced beef served in a pungent sauce, and bean curd with minced meat and chili. For milder palates, deep-fried fish with sweet-and-sour sauce is stimulating. For noodle lovers, tell the waiters how spicy you want your noodles to be: mild, hot, or very hot. ⊠ *Miramar Shopping Centre, 1 Kimberley Rd., 4th floor,* ☎ *852/2375–0800. AE, DC, MC, V.*

EUROPEAN

$$$$ ✕ **Gaddi's.** With huge chandeliers made in Paris, silver candelabras, and ankle-deep Tai Ping carpets, the decor is opulent and sumptuous. So is the food. Pan-fried goose liver, warm lobster salad, lobster with cider sauce, and the roast bresse pigeon are highlights. Don't decline the house soufflé, served in a portion big enough for two. ⊠ *Peninsula Hotel, Salisbury Rd.* ☎ *852/2366–6251, ext. 3989. Reservations essential. Jacket and tie. AE, DC, MC, V.*

Outer Islands

Lamma Island

ASIAN

$ ✕ **Lancombe.** This Cantonese seafood restaurant is Lamma's best source for no-nonsense food at no-nonsense prices. The huge English/Cantonese menu features seafood, seafood, and more seafood. Try deep-fried squid, *garoupa* (local fish) in sweet corn sauce, broccoli in garlic, and beef with black beans. Dishes come in three sizes; the small is sufficient for most. Go through the front of the restaurant via the kitchen (don't loiter, they're busy in there) to the terrace out back, where you'll have a view of the sea and distant Peng Chau Island. ⊠ *47 Main St., Yung Shue Wan,* ☎ *852/2982–0881. No credit cards.*

LODGING

Hong Kong Island

Central

$$$$ 🏨 **Island Shangri-La.** In the Pacific Place complex, the hotel sparkles
★ with more than 780 dazzling Austrian crystal chandeliers—in the lobby, the restaurants, and every single room. This deluxe hotel has the world's largest Chinese landscape painting, "The Great Motherland of China" (16 stories high), which took six months for the 40 artists from Beijing to create. Rooms are on the 39th to 55th floor. Extra-large desks in each room are handy for business travelers, who can also plug in notebook computers readily. The pool and health club overlook Hong Kong Park. ⊠ *Supreme Court Rd., 2 Pacific Place, 88 Queensway,* ☎ *852/2877–3838 or 800/942–5050,* FAX *852/2521–8742. 565 rooms. 4 restaurants, bar, 4 no-smoking floors, pool, barbershop, beauty salon, health club, shops, business services. AE, DC, MC, V.*

$$$$ 🏨 **Mandarin Oriental.** The vast lobby, decorated with Asian antiques,
★ has a live band in the mezzanine Clipper Lounge early in the evening. Comfortable guest rooms have antique maps and prints and traditional wooden furnishings; the Eastern knick-knacks radiate a touch of Oriental flavor, with accents of black-and-gold glamour. The polite staff provides extremely efficient service. Standing beside the Star Ferry concourse, the Mandarin is rightfully the choice of many celebrities and VIPs. ⊠ *5 Connaught Rd.,* ☎ *852/2522—0111* FAX *852/2810–6190. 489 rooms, 58 suites. 4 restaurants, 3 bars, indoor pool, barbershop, beauty salon, health club, business services. AE, DC, MC, V.*

$$$$ 🏨 **Ritz-Carlton.** On the prime block between Chater and Connaught roads
★ the hotel has an elegant, refined atmosphere created by European antiques and reproductions mixed with Oriental accents. The large guest rooms, all with marble baths, honor bars, and colonial-style rosewood furniture, overlook either Victoria Harbor or Chater Garden. A special macrobiotic dining program is available in the coffee shop and on the room service menu. The Executive Business Center has Internet and e-mail access as well as computer workstations and color printer hookups.

☒ *Connaught Rd.,* ☎ *852/2877–6666,* FAX *852/2877–6778. 216 rooms and suites. 5 restaurants, bar, no-smoking floors, pool, health club, shops, business services. AE, DC, MC. V.*

Mid-Levels

$$ ⊞ **Bishop Lei International House.** Owned and operated by the Catholic diocese, this guest house is in a residential area of the Mid-levels. Rooms are clean and functional. The clientele tends to be church groups, academics, and students. ☒ *4 Robinson Rd.,* ☎ *852/2868–0828,* FAX *852/2868–1551. 205 rooms and suites. Restaurant, pool, exercise room, business services. AE, DC, MC, V.*

$ ⊞ **Garden View International House.** This attractive hotel, on a hill
★ overlooking the Botanical Gardens and harbor, is run by the YWCA. If you want to do your own cooking, ask for a suite with a kitchenette (with microwave oven). The coffee shop leaves much to be desired. Guests can use the swimming pool and gymnasium in the adjoining YWCA. Garden View is a five-minute drive (bus 12A or minibus 1A) from Central and just a few minutes from the Peak Tram station. ☒ *1 MacDonnell Rd.,* ☎ *852/2877–3737,* FAX *852/2845–6263. 130 rooms and suites. Coffee shop, pool, business services. AE, DC, MC, V.*

Wanchai

$$$$ ⊞ **Grand Hyatt.** No expense was spared in building this opulent,
★ black-marble-faced hotel, which adjoins the Hong Kong Convention Centre. The Art Deco lobby has a hand-painted ceiling by Italian artist Paola Dindo. The restaurants are popular with locals, who also line up to get into JJ's, the nightclub and disco. Seventy percent of the guest rooms have harbor views, while those remaining overlook the 11th-floor pool, garden, and vast recreation deck shared by the New World Harbour View (☞ *below*). The business center has an IBM room with IBM's latest technology and software; Reuters Business Briefing is available through the center computers. ☒ *1 Harbour Rd.,* ☎ *852/2588–1234,* FAX *852/2802–0677. 572 rooms and suites. 4 restaurants, bar, pool, beauty salon, driving range, 2 tennis courts, exercise room, nightclub. AE, DC, MC, V.*

$$$ ⊞ **New World Harbour View.** Sharing the Convention Centre complex with the Grand Hyatt (☞ *above*) is this more modest but equally attractive hotel. The moderate-size guest rooms have fax machines, modern decor, and plenty of beveled-glass mirrors. Amenities include excellent Chinese and Western restaurants, a cozy bar, jogging trails, and tennis courts. The free-form pool is Hong Kong's largest, complete with lagoons and an alfresco dining area. ☒ *1 Harbour Rd.,* ☎ *852/2802–8888 or 852/2731–3488,* FAX *852/2802–8833 or 852/2721–0741. 862 rooms and suites. 3 restaurants, 2 bars, 9 no-smoking floors, pool, barbershop, beauty salon, health club, shops, business services. AE, DC, MC, V.*

$$ ⊞ **The Wesley.** This 21-story, moderately (for Hong Kong) priced hotel is a short walk from the Convention Centre, the Academy for Performing Arts, and the MTR. The rooms are small but pleasantly furnished, and the corner "suites" have alcove work areas. A tram stop is outside the door, and Pacific Place is close by, as are the bars of Wanchai. ☒ *22 Hennessy Rd.,* ☎ *852/2866–6688,* FAX *852/2866–6613. 251 rooms. Restaurant, coffee shop. AE, DC, MC, V.*

Causeway Bay

$$$ ⊞ **The Excelsior.** Eighty percent of the rooms enjoy a splendid sea
★ view including the Hong Kong Yacht Club's neatly aligned yachts and boats, and the location is ideal for shopping and dining. At Talk Of The Town (TOTT), the top-floor restaurant-cum-bar-cum-nightclub, you can sample a creative East-meets-West cuisine to live music. The

fitness center includes rooftop tennis courts, and there is a jogging track in adjacent Victoria Park. The hotel sits on the first plot of land auctioned by the British Government when Hong Kong became a colony in 1841. ✉ *281 Gloucester Rd.,* ☎ *852/2894–8888,* FAX *852/2895–6459. 875 rooms, 22 suites. 4 restaurants, 2 bars, 5 no-smoking floors, beauty salon, 1 indoor tennis court, health club, shops, business services. AE, DC, MC, V.*

Kowloon

Tsim Sha Tsui

$$$$ 🏨 **Peninsula.** The 70-year-old Pen is one of the best and most famous
★ hotels in the world. Its taste and Old World style are in evidence everywhere: colonial architecture, a columned and gilt-corniced lobby where high tea is served (a prestigious rendezvous in town), a fleet of Rolls-Royces, attentive room valets, and luxurious bath accessories. All rooms are equipped with silent fax machines and the Pen's famous shoe box (staff will retrieve the shoes through the other opening from the corridor and have them cleaned). The superb spa houses a Roman-style pool, a sundeck, a jacuzzi, a sauna, and a steam bath to treat you like royalty. ✉ *Salisbury Rd., Tsim Sha Tsui,* ☎ *852/2366–6251,* FAX *852/ 2722–4170. 246 rooms, 54 suites. 7 restaurants, bar, pool, beauty salon, health club, shops, business services, helipad. AE, DC, MC, V.*

$$$$ 🏨 **The Regent.** The elegantly modern Regent on the southernmost tip
★ of Tsim Sha Tsui offers luxurious guest rooms and spectacular harbor views from the very edge of the waterfront. Rooms are spacious and bright, delicately decorated in a sophisticated and contemporary style. Take advantage of the hotel's jacuzzi and renowned spa and massage treatments. The hotel has the largest privately owned collection of Daimler limos outside the United Kingdom, as well as a fleet of Rolls Royce and Mercedes limos. You can be chauffeured in one of the three upon request. ✉ *18 Salisbury Rd., Tsim Sha Tsui,* ☎ *852/2721–1211,* FAX *852/2739–4546. 508 rooms, 94 suites. 5 restaurants, pool, health club, shops, business services. AE, DC, MC, V.*

$$$ 🏨 **Royal Garden.** An exquisite garden atrium with lush greenery and whispering running water rises from the ground floor to the hotel's rooftop. Guests especially appreciate Sabatini's restaurant and the rooftop state-of-the-art health club with an indoor-outdoor pool and spa services. ✉ *69 Mody Rd., Tsim Sha Tsui East,* ☎ *852/2721–5215,* FAX *852/2369–9976. 377 rooms, 45 suites. 6 restaurants, pub, no-smoking floor, indoor- outdoor pool, beauty salon, spa, health club, shops, dance club, business services. AE, DC, MC, V.*

$$ 🏨 **Kowloon.** The first hotel to install personalized Internet e-mail ad-
★ dresses in all rooms for guests' private use, the Kowloon has plans to include Internet access in the future. On the southern tip of Nathan Road's Golden Mile, it is just minutes from the Star Ferry and next door to the MTR. You are entitled to signing privileges in the Peninsula Hotel facilities. ✉ *19–21 Nathan Rd., Tsim Sha Tsui,* ☎ *852/2739–9811,* FAX *852/2739–9811. 736 rooms and suites. 3 restaurants, 4 no-smoking floors, beauty salon, shops, business services. AE, DC, MC, V.*

$ 🏨 **Salisbury YMCA.** If you can't afford the Pen, cross the street and
★ settle at this high-class Y, where you can enjoy the same magnificent harbor view at a fraction of the price. You can't compare the YMCAs in Hong Kong with the Y's in other parts of the world—in terms of either price tag or services. Rooms are clean, and you'll have superb recreational facilities. ✉ *41 Salisbury Rd., Tsim Sha Tsui,* ☎ *852/2369– 2211,* FAX *852/2739– 9315. 380 rooms and suites. 3 restaurants, 2 indoor pools, health club, squash, shops. AE, DC, MC, V.*

New Territories and the Outer Islands

New Territories

$$ ⊞ **Gold Coast.** Opened in 1994, this is Hong Kong's first conference resort. Its vast complex on the western harbor front of Kowloon is served by special ferries from Central, 30 minutes away, and there are shuttle buses to the MTR and the airport. The resort has a large marina, a water sports area, tennis courts, pitch-and-putt golf, an all-service spa, and even an archery range. It has gained a reputation among conference organizers for facilities that can accommodate up to 1,200 people. It is also the only hotel in Hong Kong with equipment for Outward Bound courses. ⊠ *1 Castle Peak Rd., Tuen Mun, New Territories,* ☎ *852/2452–8888,* ℻ *852/2440–7368. 443 rooms. 4 restaurants, 3 bars, pool, beauty salon, spa, 2 tennis courts, health club, squash, business services. AE, DC, MC, V.*

Cheung Chau Island

$ ⊞ **Cheung Chau Warwick.** Miles from the fast-paced city, this little gem on the beach aims to assure you a carefree and relaxed stay—no business services or executive floor, but a nice pool and a sandy beach. The six-story hotel only an hour by ferry from Hong Kong Island is a popular getaway for Hong Kong families. There are no cars on the leisurely island; the hotel is just a 10-minute walk from the pier. ⊠ *East Bay, Cheung Chau,* ☎ *852/2981–0081,* ℻ *852/2981–9174. 71 rooms. 2 restaurants, pool, beach. AE, DC, MC, V.*

Lantau Island

$ ⊞ **Silvermine Beach Hotel.** Lying along the bay, this resort in Mui Wo escapes the hyperactivity of Hong Kong. A ferry from Hong Kong Island will get you here in an hour, and the hotel is a five-minute walk from the pier. ⊠ *D.D.2 Lot 648 Silvermine Bay, Mui Wo, Lantau Island.* ☎ *852/2984–8295,* ℻ *852/2984–1907. 130 rooms. Restaurant, pool, exercise room, karaoke. AE, DC, MC, V.*

NIGHTLIFE AND THE ARTS

The Arts

The most comprehensive calendar of cultural events is *HK Magazine,* a free weekly newspaper distributed each Friday to many restaurants, stores, and bars.

City Hall (⊠ By Star Ferry, Hong Kong Island, ☎ 852/2921–2840) has posters and huge bulletin boards listing events and ticket availability. Tickets for cultural events held in government centers can be purchased in booths on the ground floor by the main entrance. **URBTIX** outlets are the easiest place to purchase tickets for most general performances. There are branches at City Hall and the Hong Kong Arts Centre (☎ 852/2734–9009 for bookings and information). The free monthly *City News* newspaper also lists events and is available at City Hall.

Chinese Opera

Cantonese Opera. There are 10 Cantonese opera troupes in Hong Kong, as well as many amateur singing groups. These groups perform "street opera," as in the Shanghai Street Night Market on Sunday, while others perform at temple fairs, in City Hall, or in playgrounds under the auspices of the Urban Council (☎ 852/2867–5125). Visitors unfamiliar with the form are sometimes alienated by the strange sounds of this highly complex and extremely sophisticated art form. Every gesture has its own meaning; in fact, there are 50 different gestures for the hand alone. It is best to have a local friend translate the gestures, as the stories are so complex that they make Wagner or Verdi librettos seem almost simplistic.

Peking Opera. A highly stylized musical performance, this type of opera employs higher-pitched voices than Cantonese opera. It is an older opera form and more respected for its classical traditions. Several troupes visit Hong Kong from the mainland each year, and their meticulous training is well regarded. They perform in City Hall or at special temple ceremonies. Call the Urban Council (☎ 852/2867–5125) for further information.

Dance
Hong Kong Dance Company (☎ 852/2853–2642). This company has been promoting the art of Chinese dance and choreographing new work with Chinese historical themes since 1981. The 30-odd members are experts in folk and classical dance. Sponsored by the Urban Council, they perform about three times a month throughout the territory.

Performance Halls
HONG KONG ISLAND
City Hall (✉ Edinburgh Pl., by Star Ferry, Central, ☎ 852/2921–2840). Classical music, theatrical performances, films, and art exhibitions are presented at this complex's large auditorium, recital hall, and theater.

Hong Kong Academy for Performing Arts (✉ 1 Gloucester Rd., Wanchai, ☎ 852/2584–8500). This arts school has two major theaters each seating 1,600 people, plus a 200-seat studio theater and 500-seat outdoor theater. Performances include local and international theater, modern and classical dance, and music concerts.

Hong Kong Arts Centre (✉ 2 Harbour Rd., Wanchai, ☎ 852/2582–0200). Several floors of auditoriums, rehearsal halls, and recital rooms welcome local and visiting groups to perform here. Some of the best independent, classic, and documentary films are shown, often with themes that focus on a particular country, period, or well-known director.

Hong Kong Fringe Club (✉ 2 Lower Albert Rd., Central, ☎ 852/2521–7251). This club hosts some of Hong Kong's most innovative visiting and local entertainment and art exhibitions. Shows range from the blatantly amateur to the dazzlingly professional. It also has good jazz, avant-garde drama, and many other events.

Queen Elizabeth Stadium (✉ 18 Oi Kwan Rd., Wanchai, ☎ 852/2591–1346). Although basically a sports stadium, this 3,500-seat venue frequently presents ballet and orchestral and pop concerts.

KOWLOON
Broadway Cinemathèque (✉ Prosperous Garden, 3 Public Square St., Yau Ma Tei, ☎ 852/2332–9000, ☎ 852/2384–6281 for ticket reservations). The train station-like design of this art house cinema is award-winning; foreign and independent films are announced on a departure board (local films are rare). A shop sells new and vintage film posters, and there's a coffee bar as well. Use the Temple Street exit at the Yau Ma Tei MTR to get here.

Hong Kong Coliseum (✉ 9 Cheong Wan Rd., Hunghom Railway Station, Hunghom, ☎ 852/2355–7234). This 12,000-plus seat stadium presents everything from basketball to ballet, skating polar bears to local and international pop stars.

Hong Kong Cultural Centre (✉ 10 Salisbury Rd., ☎ 852/2734–2009). This venue for shows and conferences contains the Grand Theatre, which seats 1,750, and a concert hall, which accommodates 2,100. The center is used by visiting and local artists, whose performances range from opera to ballet to orchestral music.

NEW TERRITORIES
Tsuen Wan Town Hall (✉ 72 Tai Ho Rd., Tsuen Wan, ☎ 852/2414–0144; take the MTR to Tsuen Wan Station). Although it's off the beaten track, this auditorium has a constant stream of local and international performers. Groups include everything from the Warsaw Philharmonic to troupes of Chinese acrobats. It has a seating capacity of 1,424 and probably the best acoustics of all the performance halls in Hong Kong.

Shatin Town Hall (✉ 1 Yuen Wo Rd., Shatin, ☎ 852/2694–2511). This impressive building, attached to New Town Plaza, an enormous shopping arcade, is a five-minute walk from the KCR station at Shatin. It hosts cultural events including dance, drama, and concert performances.

Performing-Arts Ensembles
Hong Kong Philharmonic Orchestra (☎ 852/2721–2320). Artists from Hong Kong, the United States, and Europe perform everything from classical to avant-garde to contemporary music by Chinese composers. World-class soloists visit regularly. Performances are usually held Friday and Saturday at 8 PM in City Hall or in recital halls in the New Territories (☎ 852/2721–2030 for ticket information).

Hong Kong Chinese Orchestra (☎ 852/2853–2622). Created in 1977 by the Urban Council, this group performs only Chinese works. The orchestra consists of strings, plucked instruments, wind, and percussion.

Nightlife

Hong Kong is a 24-hour city. There are night markets, a zillion restaurants (from haute cuisine to hole-in-the-wall), sophisticated piano bars, elegant lounges, superstrobed discos, cozy bars, smoky jazz dens, topless bars and hostess clubs, marble massage parlors, cabarets, and, of course, the karaoke (video sing-along) bars, oh so popular with locals.

Think twice before succumbing to the city's raunchier hideaways. If you stumble into one, check out cover and hostess charges *before* you get too comfortable. Pay for each round of drinks as it's served (by cash rather than credit card), and never sign any blank checks. As in every tourist destination, the art of the tourist rip-off is well-practiced. To be safest, visit spots that are sign-carrying members of the Hong Kong Tourist Association (HKTA). You can pick up its free membership listing (including approved restaurants and nightspots) at any HKTA Information Office.

Cabaret and Nightclubs
Club 97 (✉ 8–11 Lan Kwai Fong, Central, ☎ 852/2810–9333; ✉ HK$97) is a small, glitzy, often crowded nightclub for gatherings of the "beautiful people." The crowds don't arrive until well after midnight at **Propaganda** (✉ 1/F, 30-32 Wyndham St., Central, ☎ 852/2868–1316), the only gay club in the territory; the cavernous entrance leads to a dark, intimate disco with a comfy lounge area.

Cocktail and Piano Bars
High-altitude harbor-gazing is the main attraction at the Island Shangri-La's 56th-floor **Cyrano** music lounge (✉ 2 Pacific Place, 88 Queensway,

Hong Kong, ☎ 852/2820–8591). The Peninsula's **Felix Bar** (✉ Salisbury Rd., Tsim Sha Tsui, ☎ 852/2366–6251) not only has a brilliant view of the harbor, but the impressive bar and disco was designed by the visionary Philippe Starck. The Mandarin Oriental's mezzanine **Clipper Lounge** (✉ 5 Connaught Rd., Central, ☎ 852/2825–1935) is perfect for a relaxing drink after a long day of shopping or touring.

Dance Clubs

The perennial favorite nightspot is **JJ's** (✉ Grand Hyatt, 1 Harbour Rd., Hong Kong, ☎ 852/2588–1234), the Grand Hyatt's entertainment center. It contains a disco and a pizza lounge with a dart board and a bar screening major sporting events, but it is remembered most for its flashy disco lights, good house band in the music room, and the wall-to-wall suits and their escorts. The **Lost City** (✉ Chinachem Golden Plaza, 77 Mody Rd., Tsim Sha Tsui East, ☎ 852/2311–1111) is undoubtedly the most popular and thriving disco for young Chinese. It's a cross between a cheesy B-grade film set, Las Vegas camp glamour, and an over-the-top Broadway production. It contains a massive 100,000 sq ft of disco areas, karaoke rooms, a kitschy café, and plenty of zebra-striped sofas and chairs.

Hostess Clubs

Club BBoss is the grandest and most boisterous, in Tsim Sha Tsui East's Mandarin Plaza (☎ 852/2369–2883). Executives, mostly locals, entertain in this oddly named club, tended by a staff of more than 1,000. If your VIP room is too far from the entrance, you can hire an electrified vintage Rolls Royce and purr around an indoor roadway. Be warned that this is tycoon territory, where a bottle of brandy can cost HK$18,000. Along the harbor, in New World Centre, are **Club Cabaret** (☎ 852/2369–8431) and **Club Deluxe** (☎ 852/2721–0277), both luxurious dance lounges.

Jazz and Folk Clubs

The Jazz Club (✉ 2/F, California Entertainment Building, 34–36 D'Aguilar St., Central, ☎ 852/2845–8477) presents a wide selection of local jazz, R&B, and soul talent as well as top-notch international acts every month. There are many rousing evenings when Filipinos take on American country-and-western music in **Bar City** (✉ New World Centre, Tsim Sha Tsui, ☎ 852/2369–8571), particularly popular with young locals.

Pubs

Off-duty Central business folk flock to the pirate-galleon **Pier One** at Jardine House (✉ In front of Star Ferry Terminal, Central, ☎ 852/2526–3061) for an à-la-carte lunch or reasonably priced dinner buffet. Both branches of the Irish pub **Delaney's** (✉ G/F, Multifield Plaza, 3 Prat Ave., Kowloon, ☎ 852/2301–3980; ✉ 2/F One Capital Place, 18 Luard Rd., Wanchai, ☎ 852/2804–2880) have interiors that were "made in Ireland" and shipped to Hong Kong. There's Guinness and Delaney's ale (a specialty microbrew) on tap, private corner "snugs," and a menu of Irish specialties. A trendy place in Tsim Sha Tsui is an out-of-the-way strip called Knutsford Terrace, where a new breed of bars and restaurants have recently made their home. Tropical rhythms can be found at the Caribbean-inspired **Bahama Mama's** (✉ 4–5 Knutsford Terr., ☎ 852/2368–2121).

For Singles

The arts-minded mingle at the **Fringe Club** (✉ 2 Lower Albert Rd., Central, ☎ 852/2521–7251) in a historic redbrick building that also houses the members-only Foreign Correspondents Club. Solo business travelers can always find someone to talk to at hotel bars, frequented by both locals and expats. The Hyatt Regency's **Chin Chin** or **Nathan's** (⊠ 67 Nathan Rd., Tsim Sha Tsui, ☎ 852/2311–1234) are likely spots. The **Chinnery** in the Mandarin Oriental (⊠ 5 Connaught Rd.) has its appeal.

Topless Bars

With a few exceptions, most topless bars are scruffy dives. A beer may seem reasonably priced, at around HK$25, but the "champagne" the women drink is not. Charges for conversational companionship can also be an unexpected extra.

Bottoms Up (⊠ Basement, 14 Hankow Rd., Tsim Sha Tsui, ☎ 852/2721–4509) was immortalized by its use in the James Bond film *The Man with the Golden Gun.* Cozy circular bar counters are tended by topless women. This place is so respectable that visiting couples are welcomed. Over in Wanchai, the friendliest faces are those of off-duty Filipino amahs either working or lounging around the dance floors of spots such as the **San Francisco Bar** (⊠ 129 Lockhart Rd., ☎ 852/2527–0468). **Club Mermaid** (⊠ 96 Lockhart Rd., ☎ 852/2529–2113) has a similar atmosphere.

Wine Bars

For an intimate encounter, try **Le Tire Bouchon** (⊠ 9 Old Bailey St., Central, ☎ 852/2523–5459), which dispenses tasty bistro meals and fine wines by the glass.

OUTDOOR ACTIVITIES AND SPORTS

Participant Sports

Golf

Three Hong Kong golf clubs allow visitors with reciprocal privileges from a club at home to play their courses.

The **Clearwater Bay Golf and Country Club,** in the New Territories, has five outdoor and two indoor tennis courts, three indoor squash courts, and two indoor badminton courts, as well as an outdoor pool, a health spa, and an 18-hole golf course. Together with the Hong Kong Tourist Association (HKTA), the club sponsors a Sports and Recreation Tour, allowing visitors to tour the facilities and play golf. ⊠ *Clearwater Bay Rd., Saikung Peninsula,* ☎ *852/2719–1595, booking office 2335–3885 (HKTA tour,* ☎ *852/2801–7177).* ⊠ *Greens fees: HK$1,200 for 18 holes. Tour cost: HK$380, plus greens fees. Cart, club, and shoe rentals available; no lessons.*

The **Discovery Bay Golf Club** on Lantau Island has an 18-hole course that is open to visitors on weekdays. ⊠ *Take ferry from Star Ferry Pier in Central;* ☎ *852/2987–7271 or 2987–7273.* ⊠ *Greens fees HK$1,400, club rental HK$150, golf-cart rental HK$300, shoe rental HK$150. Lessons: HK$500–HK$600 per hr.*

The **Hong Kong Golf Club** (formerly the Royal Hong Kong Golf Club) allows visitors to play on its three 18-hole courses at Fanling, New Territories. ⊠ *Fanling,* ☎ *852/2670–1211 for bookings, 852/2670–0647 for club rentals (HK$250).* ⊠ *Greens fees: HK$1,400 for 18 holes. Deep Water Bay,* ☎ *852/2812–7070. Weekdays only.* ⊠ *Greens fees: HK$450 for 18 holes. Lessons at both locations for nonmembers on weekdays only: HK$250–HK$400 per half hour, HK$290–HK$1,270 for 18-hole coaching, depending on pro.*

The **Tuen Mun Golf Centre** is a public center with 100 golf driving bays and a practice green. ⊠ *Lung Mun Rd., Tuen Mun,* ☎ *852/2466–*

2600. ☞ *HK$11 per bay, HK$11 per club, and HK$11 per hour per 30 balls.* ۞ *Tues., Wed., and Fri.–Sun. 8 AM–10 PM, Mon. and Thurs. 1 PM–10 PM.*

Hiking

Hong Kong's well-kept and reasonably well-marked hiking trails, never more than a few hours away from civilization, are one of its best-kept secrets. Before you go, pick up trail maps at the Government Publications Centre (⊠ Pacific Place, Government Office, Ground Floor, 66 Queensway, Admiralty, ☎ 852/2537–1910; still providing materials at press time). Ask for the blueprints of the trails and the Countryside Series maps. The HM20C series is handsome four-color maps, but it's not very reliable.

The Hong Kong Trail, the most practical for first-time trailblazers, wends for approximately 48 km (30 mi) over Hong Kong Island from **Victoria Peak** to the beach community of **Shek O.** The full hike takes two days. The trail offers a panoramic view of the island with all of its history and splendor, passing through some dense forest untouched by development or fires. Follow the map to the starting point on the Peak (you can get there by tram or taxi), and take the trail down through **Pok Fu Lam.** Toward the end of the first day you'll reach **Wang Nai Cheung Gap,** where a road connects Happy Valley to the south side of the island. You can buy food at the grocery market at Parkview Apartments here and continue your hike, or take a bus or taxi back to your hotel. On the second day, hike through **Tai Tam Country Park,** then climb **Dragons Back Ridge** toward the northeastern part of the island. From here the trail takes you down to the unspoiled rural village at **Big Wave Bay.** Between here and Shek O you'll see lavish estates. From Shek O, you can take a bus or taxi home.

Kung Fu

The **Martial Arts School** (⊠ 446 Hennessey Rd., Causeway Bay, ☎ 852/2891–1044) of master Luk Chi Fu uses the "white crane" system of internal-strength training. This gentler version is said to be the forerunner of yoga. The technique relies on quick thinking, controlled breathing, and an instant grasp of the situation at hand. At the advanced level, a student can absorb blows and use spears and knives as if they were an extension of his or her body. Now run by the master's son, Luk Chung Mau, the school is open to visitors who are in Hong Kong for a few weeks. You can study the Lion Dance, kick-boxing, and uses of weaponry at the **South China Athletic Association** (⊠ Caroline Hill Rd., Causeway Bay, ☎ 852/2665–0834). Other schools offer courses that last from 10 days to a few months. For information contact C.S. Tang at the **Hong Kong Chinese Martial Arts Association** (☎ 852/2798–2763).

Social and Health Clubs

The following **social clubs** have reciprocal facilities. The **Hong Kong Jockey Club** offers free entry to the members' enclosure during racing season, but not use of club recreational facilities. Visitors with reciprocal privileges at the **Hong Kong Golf Club** are allowed 14 free rounds of golf each year. Other clubs with reciprocal policies are the **Hong Kong Yacht Club, Hong Kong Cricket Club, Kowloon Cricket Club, Hong Kong Football Club, Hong Kong Country Club, Kowloon Club, Hong Kong Club,** and **Ladies' Recreation Club.**

Two **health clubs** where you can pay by the day are the **Tom Turk Fitness Club** (⊠ Citibank Tower, Citibank Plaza, 3 Garden Rd., 3rd Floor, Central, ☎ 852/2521–4541; ⊠ International House, 8 Austin Rd., Tsim Sha Tsui, ☎ 852/2736–7188), which charges $115 for a day visit, $200 after 5 PM; and **California Fitness Center** (⊠ 1 Wellington

St., Central, ☎ 852/2522–5229), for HK$150 a day. The majority of first-class hotels have health clubs on their premises.

Water Sports

JUNKING

Junking—dining on the water aboard large junks that have been converted to pleasure craft—is unique to Hong Kong. You can rent a junk from **Simpson Marine Ltd.** (✉ Aberdeen Marina Tower, 8 Shun Wan Rd., Aberdeen, ☎ 852/2555–7349), whose junks, with crew, can hold 35 to 45 people. Costs start at HK$2,200 for an eight-hour day trip or four-hour night trip during the week, and HK$4,500 on summer weekends. The price goes up on holidays. **Jubilee International Tour Centre** (✉ Man Yee Bldg., 60 Des Voeux Rd., Room 302–303, Central, ☎ 852/2530–0530) also has charters. The **Boatique** (✉ Aberdeen Marina Club, Shop 10–11, Ground Floor, Aberdeen Marina Bldg., 8 Shum Wan Rd., Aberdeen, ☎ 852/2555–9355) pilot will take you to your choice of the following outer islands: Cheung Chau, Lamma, Lantau, Po Toi, or the islands in Sai Kung Harbour.

SAILING

B. Tours (☎ 852/2851–9601) operates pleasure cruises for private parties on its sailing junk, the Duk Ling. The vessel accommodates up to 35 people. To use the **Hong Kong Yacht Club** (☎ 852/2832–2817) you must belong to a club that has reciprocal privileges. Sometimes members need crews for weekend races, so experienced sailors can go to the club and check the "crew wanted" board in the Course Room.

Spectator Sports

Horse Racing

The Sport of Kings is run under a monopoly by the Hong Kong Jockey Club, one of the most politically powerful entities in the territory. Profits go to charity and community organizations. The season runs from September or October through May. Some 65 races are held at two race tracks—**Happy Valley** on Hong Kong Island and **Shatin** in the New Territories. Shatin's racecourse is one of the most modern in the world. Both courses have huge video screens at the finish line so that gamblers can see what is happening each foot of the way. You can view races from the Members' Stand at both tracks by showing your passport and paying HK$50 for a badge.

Rugby

One weekend every spring, Hong Kong hosts the international tournament of Sevens-a-Side teams at the Hong Kong Stadium, and the whole town goes rugby mad. In 1998, the tournament is scheduled for March 28–29, 1998. To avoid camping outside the stadium all night to buy tickets, you can purchase them in advance from an overseas agent. For a list of agents, contact Beth Coalter at the **Hong Kong Rugby Football Union** (✉ Sports House, 1 Stadium Path, Room 2003, So Kon Po, Causeway Bay, ☎ 852/2504–8300, FAX 852/2576–7237).

SHOPPING

Although Hong Kong is no longer the mercantile paradise it once was, many shopping aficionados still swear by it, returning year after year for such items as Chinese antiques, art from China and Southeast Asia, porcelain, tea and teaware, pearls, watches, cameras, eyeglasses, silk sheets and kimonos, tailor-made suits, and designer clothes found in off-the-beaten-path outlets. Hong Kong has also become an excellent place to buy sports gear, thanks to high volume and reasonable prices. The Hong Kong Tourist Association publishes a comprehensive guide called "Shopping In Hong Kong," which lists stores approved by the HKTA for their merchandise and service policies and can be picked up at HKTA information booths at Jardine House and Star Ferry, Kowloon.

Hong Kong Island

Art and Antiques

Hollywood Road is the place to look for Chinese antiques and collectibles.

Altfield Gallery (⊠ Prince's Bldg., Central, ☎ 852/2537–6370) carries furniture, fabrics, and collectibles from all over Asia. **C. L. Ma Antiques** (⊠ 43–55 Wyndham St., Central, ☎ 852/2525–4369) has Ming dynasty-style reproductions, especially large carved chests and tables made of unlacquered wood. **Eastern Dreams** (⊠ 47A Hollywood Rd., Central, ☎ 852/2544–2804; ⊠ 4 Shelley St., Central, ☎ 852/2524–4787) has antique and reproduction furniture, screens, and curios. **Galerie La Vong** (⊠ 1 Lan Kwai Fong, 13th floor, Central, ☎ 852/2869–6863) is the place to see the works of today's leading Vietnamese artists, many of whose creations reveal an intriguing combination of French Impressionist and traditional Chinese influences, as well as some purely contemporary styles. **Honeychurch Antiques** (⊠ 29 Hollywood Rd., Central, ☎ 852/2543–2433) is known especially for antique silver jewelry from Southeast Asia, China, and England. **Schoeni Fine Arts** (⊠ 27 Hollywood Rd., Central, ☎ 852/2542–3143) sells Japanese, Chinese, and Thai antiques; Chinese silverware, such as opium boxes; and rare Chinese pottery. **Teresa Coleman** (⊠ 79 Wyndham St., Central, ☎ 852/2526–2450) carries antique embroidered pieces and unusual Chinese collectibles.

Chinese Department Stores

Chinese Arts & Crafts (⊠ Prince's Bldg., Central; other locations around town, ☎ 852/2827–6667 for information) is a chain particularly good for fabrics, white porcelain, silk-embroidered clothing, jewelry, and carpets. Our favorite specialty item here is the large globe with blue lapis oceans and land masses inlaid in semi-precious stones, for a mere HK$70,000. **Shanghai Tang Department Store** (⊠ 12 Pedder St., ☎ 852/2525–7333), on the ground floor of the Pedder Building, is the current retro rage in Hong Kong, selling old-fashioned Mandarin suits for men and women, either custom-made or ready-to-wear, and Chinese memorabilia, including novelty watches depicting Mao Zedong and Deng Xiaoping. **Blanc de Chine** (⊠ 12 Pedder St., Central, ☎ 852/2524–7875) has beautiful Chinese clothes, in similar styles to those at the more famous Shanghai Tang (☞ *above*), but subtler colors, plus reproductions of antique snuffboxes and silver mirrors and picture frames.

Clothing Outlets

The Joyce Warehouse (⊠ 34 Horizon Plaza, 2 Lee Wing St., Ap Lei Chau, ☎ 852/2814–8313) has taken shopaholic locals by storm. This is the outlet for women's and men's fashions that are sold in the ritzy Joyce Boutiques in Central and Pacific Place, with labels by major designers. The **Pedder Building** (⊠ 12 Pedder St., Central), just a few feet from a Central MTR exit, contains five floors of small shops, most offering discounts of around 30% off retail. **Cascal** (☎ 852/2523–4999) has Celine, Dior, and Prada bags at about 20% off retail. **Ça Va** (☎ 852/2537–7174) has fabulous knitwear, along with suits and designer casual wear. **Shopper's World–Safari** (☎ 852/2523–1950) has more variety than most outlets and a small upstairs department with men's fashions. **Stanley Village Market** (Stanley Village; take Bus 6, 6A, or 260 from the Central Bus Terminus) is a popular haunt for designer sportswear, washable silk, and cashmere sweaters at factory outlet prices and in Western sizes. **China Town** (✉ 39 Stanley Main St.) has bargains on cashmere sweaters. **Sun and Moon Fashion Shop** (18A-B Stanley Main St.) sells casual wear, with good bargains on such familiar names as L.L. Bean, Yves St. Laurent, and Talbot's. The market is at its most enjoyable on weekdays, when it's less crowded.

Clothing—Tailor Made

A-Man Hing Cheong Co., Ltd. (✉ Mandarin Oriental Hotel, Central, ☎ 852/2522–3336) is known for European-cut men's suits and custom shirts and has its own list of distinguished clients. **Ascot Chang** (✉ Prince's Bldg., Central, ☎ 852/2523–3663; Peninsula Hotel, Tsim Sha Tsui, ☎ 852/2366–2398; Regent Hotel, Tsim Sha Tsui, ☎ 852/2367–8319) has specialized in making shirts for men since 1949. Clients have included George Bush and Andy Williams.

Jewelry

K. S. Sze & Sons (✉ Mandarin Oriental Hotel, ☎ 852/2524–2803) is known for its fair prices on one-of-a-kind pearl and gemstone creations. **Po Kwong** (✉ 82 Queen's Rd., Central, ☎ 852/2521–4686) is a good place to shop for South Sea Island pearls and other varieties.

Kung Fu Supplies

Kung Fu Supplies Co. (✉ 188 Johnston Rd., Wanchai, ☎ 852/2891–1912) is the most convenient place to buy your drum cymbal, leather boots, sword, whip, double dagger, studded wrist bracelet, Bruce Lee kempo gloves, and other kung-fu exotica.

Photographic Equipment

Photo Scientific Appliances (✉ 6 Stanley St., Central, ☎ 852/2522–1903) has excellent prices on a wide variety of cameras and other photographic equipment.

Tea

Fook Ming Tong Tea Shop (✉ Prince's Bldg., Central, ☎ 852/2521–0337; other branches at Mitsukoshi and Sogo stores in Causeway Bay and Ocean Terminal, Harbour Centre, Tsim Sha Tsui) is a mecca for the sophisticated tea shopper. You can get superb teas in beautifully designed tins or invest in some antique clay teaware.

Kowloon

Art and Antiques

Charlotte Horstmann and Gerald Godfrey (✉ Ocean Terminal, Tsim Sha Tsui, ☎ 852/2735–7167) is good for wood carvings, bronze ware, and antique furniture. **Eileen Kershaw** (✉ Peninsula Hotel, Tsim Sha Tsui, ☎ 852/2366– 4083) has fine Chinese porcelain and jade carvings.

Clothing—Tailor-Made

Tom Li at Leading Company (✉ Hyatt Regency Shopping Arcade, Nathan Rd., Tsim Sha Tsui, ☎ 852/2366–2737), recommended by locals, is a reasonably priced tailor who makes stylish suits for men and women. **W. W. Chan & Sons** (✉ Burlington House, 92–94 Nathan Rd., Tsim Sha Tsui, ☎ 852/2366–9738) is known for top-quality classic cuts and has bolts and bolts of fine European fabrics from which to choose. Chan will make alterations for the lifetime of the suit, which should be about 20 years. **Irene Fashions** (same address, ☎ 852/2367–5588) is the women's division of W. W. Chan.

Jewelry

Tsim Sha Tsui's **Jade House** (✉ 162 Ocean Terminal, Tsim Sha Tsui, ☎ 852/2736–1232) is a good place to shop for Hong Kong's most famous stone. The jade here, which comes both loose and in settings, ranges in color from green to shades of purple, orange, yellow, brown, white, and violet. Translucent, deep emerald-green Emperor's jade is the most expensive.

Outdoor Markets

The Flower Market (✉ Flower St., near Prince Edward MTR station) is a collection of street stalls offering cut flowers and potted plants, with a few outlets specializing in plastic plants and silk flowers. **The Jade Market** (✉ Kansu St., off Nathan Rd., Yau Ma Tei) displays jade in every form, color, shape, and size. The market is full of traders carrying out intriguing deals and keen-witted sellers trying to lure tourists. Some trinkets are reasonably priced, but unless you know a lot about jade, don't be tempted into buying expensive items. **The Ladies Market,** outside the Mong Kok MTR subway station along Mong Kok Road, has outdoor stalls full of women's clothes. If you rummage around enough, you might find a designer item or two at rock-bottom prices. **Temple Street** (✉ Kowloon, near Jordan MTR station) becomes an open-air market at night, filled with a colorful collection of clothes, handbags, electrical goods, gadgets, and all sorts of household items. By the light of lamps strung up between stalls, hawkers try to catch the eye of shoppers by flinging clothes up from their stalls; Cantonese opera competes with pop music, and there's the constant chatter of vendors' cries and shoppers' bargaining. The market stretches for almost a mile and is one of Hong Kong's liveliest nighttime shopping experiences.

SIDE TRIP TO MACAU

The Portuguese-administered enclave of 23.5 sq km (9 sq mi) on the South China coast lost any commercial or political significance a century and a half ago. It has survived mostly because of its casinos, which have provided Macau with much of its revenue since legal gambling was introduced in the 1840s in an attempt to compensate for the loss of entrepôt trade to newly founded Hong Kong. Although Portuguese is the official language, and Cantonese the most widely spoken, English is generally understood in places frequented by tourists.

Sights to See

Leal Senado (Loyal Senate). The legislature is the focal point of downtown and looks out on **Largo do Senado** (Senate Square), which is paved Portuguese-style with black and white tiles in a wave pattern and furnished with benches, plants, and a fountain in the shape of an armillary sphere. As vehicles are banned, the square is a pedestrian haven. The Leal Senado is a superb example of colonial architecture, constructed in the late 18th century to house the senate of leading citizens—at the time far more powerful than the governors, who usually served their appointed time and then returned to Portugal. Today the senate, with some elected and some appointed members, acts as the municipal government, with its president holding the same power as a mayor. Inside the building, a beautiful stone staircase leads to wrought-iron gates that open onto a charming garden. The foyer and garden are open during working hours, and there are frequent art and history exhibitions in the foyer and gallery. ✉ *Largo do Senado and Avenida Almeida Ribeiro.*

Macau Forum. This multi-purpose facility has a large stadium to seat 4,000 for sports events or pop concerts and an auditorium with 350 seats for operas and plays. The adjoining Tourism Activities Center, usually known by its Portuguese initials CAT, has two museums. The

Grand Prix Museum tells the story of the races that began here in 1953. It displays some of the cars and motorbikes that have raced here over the years, photos, videos, memorabilia, mock-ups of a pit stop and a rescue operation, plus two simulators, one interactive, in which you can experience the sensation of driving in the Grand Prix auto race. The **Wine Museum** concentrates on the history of wine making in photos, paintings, wine presses, and Portuguese wines. ⊠ *Rua Luis Gonzaga Gomes. Grand Prix Museum:* ☎ *853/798–4126.* 🎫 *10 patacas.* ☉ *Daily 10–6. Wine Museum:* ☎ *853/798–4108.* 🎫 *15 patacas.* ☉ *Daily 10–6.*

Museo Maritimo do Macao (Maritime Museum). This gem of a museum has been a favorite since its doors opened at the end of 1987. It is ideally located on a waterfront site on **Barra Square.** The four-story building resembling a sailing ship is among the foremost maritime museums in Asia. The adjacent dock was restored to provide a pier for a tug, a dragon boat, a sampan, and working replicas of a South China trading junk and a 19th-century, pirate-chasing *lorcha* (wooden sailing ship). Inside the museum are exhibits on the local fishing industry, models of historic vessels, light-box charts of great voyages by Portuguese and Chinese explorers, a relief model of 17th-century Macau, the story in lantern-show style of the A-Ma Temple, navigational aids such as an original paraffin lamp once used in the Guia lighthouse, and all manner of touch screens and videos. The museum also operates 30-minute pleasure junk trips around the Inner and Outer Harbors daily except Tuesday and the first Sunday of the month. ⊠ *Largo do Pagode da Barra, opposite A-Ma Temple,* ☎ *853/307–161.* 🎫 *Museum, 8 patacas; boat trip, 10 patacas.* ☉ *Wed.–Mon. 10–5:30.*

São Domingos. Possibly the most beautiful church in Macau, with a magnificent cream-and-white baroque altar of graceful columns, fine statues, and a forest of candles and flower vases, St. Dominic's was built in the 17th century by the Dominicans. It has had a stormy history: In 1644 a Portuguese officer was murdered at the altar by a mob during mass; in 1707 the church was besieged by the governor's troops when the Dominicans sided with the Pope against the Jesuits as to whether ancestor worship should be permitted among Chinese Christian converts. After three days, the soldiers broke down the doors and briefly imprisoned the priests. (At press time the church was closed for a total renovation, scheduled for completion in 1998.) ⊠ *Rua de São Domingos, at Largo do Senado.*

Dining

CATEGORY	COST*
$$$	over 150 patacas (over US$19)
$$	70 patacas–150 patacas (US$9–US$19)
$	under 70 patacas (under US$9)

per person including service but excluding wine.

$$$ ✕ **Bela Vista.** Atop a winding staircase in the landmark hotel of the
★ same name (☞ Lodging, *below*), this restaurant has it all—a nostalgically colonial setting, a romantic veranda, a cozy bar, friendly but efficient service, and a superb menu. The menu is regularly revamped with a balance between Macanese and Continental. Fish and seafood dishes are particularly good, and desserts—such as the rice pudding with cinnamon—are irresistible. ⊠ *8 Rua do Comendador Kou Ho Neng,* ☎ *853/965–333. Reservations essential. AE, DC, MC, V.*

$$$ ✕ **Os Gatos.** The setting would be reason enough to dine in the new restaurant of the traditional Portuguese inn, Pousada de São Tiago (☞ Lodging, *below*), which was built into a 17th-century fortress. Os

Gatos (The Cats) integrates the original bar, café, and large terrace into a casually smart restaurant with inside and outside sections separated by sliding glass doors. The outdoor area has huge linen umbrellas and patio furniture while indoors has hand-carved mahogany furniture, blue and white wall tiles, and terra-cotta tiled floors. The menu offers dishes from Portugal, Spain, Provence, Italy, and Greece. Specialties include paella, clams and pork, chicken *piri piri* (cooked with East African peppers), and duck in port wine. ⊠ *Av. da República,* ☎ *853/781– 111. AE, DC, MC, V.*

$$ × **A Lorcha.** This restaurant in a converted shop house near the Mar-
★ itime Museum is believed by many locals to serve the best Portuguese food in town. It is also one of the most attractive dining places, with stone archways, white stucco, and terra-cotta tile floors. Among the most popular dishes are seafood rice, bread-based casseroles, kidney beans, and codfish. Service is first-class, and prices are extremely reasonable. ⊠ *289 Rua do Almirante Sergio,* ☎ *853/313–193. Reservations essential. MC, V. Closed Tues.*

$$ × **Fernando's.** You have to search hard to find this great, country-style
★ Portuguese restaurant next to Hac Sa beach, because the entrance looks like that of a typical Chinese café (though local cabbies usually know how to find it). There's also an open-sided bar and courtyard in back overlooking a sandy beach. Clams in garlic are the best in town, and the *bacalhau* (codfish) is hard to beat. As the menu is only in Portuguese, you may need the aid of eccentric owner Fernando Gomes, who's always happy to translate and make suggestions. ⊠ *Hac Sa Beach 9, Coloane Island,* ☎ *853/882–264. No credit cards.*

Lodging

CATEGORY	COST*
$$$	over 800 patacas (over US$105)
$$	300 patacas–800 patacas (US$40–US$105)
$	under 300 patacas (under US$40)

Prices are for a standard double room, not including 10% service charge and 5% tax.

$$$ 🏨 **Bela Vista.** Originally built in the 1880s on a hill overlooking Praia
★ Grande Bay, this landmark hotel has been extensively renovated and upgraded by its new managers, Mandarin Oriental Hotels, and is now a deluxe inn with suites. The Bela Vista veranda has been famous among visitors to Macau for decades, and a marble-floored, open-air terrace is now available for private parties and barbecues. The clubby bar, with a working fireplace, is a great rendezvous. ⊠ *8 Rua do Comendador Kou Ho Neng,* ☎ *853/965–333,* FAX *853/965–588; in Hong Kong,* ☎ *852/2881–1688. 8 suites. Restaurant, bar. AE, DC, MC, V.*

$$$ 🏨 **Hyatt Regency and Taipa Island Resort.** Rooms here conform to Hyatt
★ Regency's high standards, with modern conveniences and attractive furnishings. The public areas were built in Macau from designs by Dale Keller, and they combine the best of Iberian architecture and Chinese decor. The Taipa Resort, which adjoins the hotel, has a complete health spa with various baths and massage and beauty treatments, a running track, a botanical garden, and the marvelous **Flamingo** Macanese veranda restaurant. The hotel is close to the racetrack and operates a shuttle-bus service to the wharf and to the Lisboa (☞ *below*). ⊠ *Taipa Island,* ☎ *853/831– 234,* FAX *853/830–195; in Hong Kong,* ☎ *852/2559–0168; in U.S.,* ☎ *800/233–1234. 365 rooms. 5 restaurants, 2 bars, pool, barbershop, beauty salon, 4 tennis courts, health club, squash, casino. AE, DC, MC, V.*

$$$ ☲ **Mandarin Oriental.** This beautiful hotel built on the site of the old
★   Pan Am seaplane terminal has marvelous views of the Pearl River and
islands. Its lobby is furnished with reproductions of Portuguese art and
antiques, and the **Café Girassol** could have been transported from the
Algarve. The **Bar da Guia** is probably the most elegant drinking spot
in town, and the casino is certainly the most exclusive. Recreation fa-
cilities overlook the outer harbor. Guest rooms have marble bathrooms
and teak furniture. ⊠ *Av. da Amizade,* ☎ *853/567–888,* ℻ *853/594–
589; in Hong Kong,* ☎ *852/2881–1688; in U.S.,* ☎ *800/526–6566. 438
rooms. 3 restaurants, bar, 2 outdoor pools, beauty salon, massage,
sauna, 2 tennis courts, exercise room, squash, casino. AE, DC, MC, V.*

$$ ☲ **Lisboa.** Rising above a two-story casino, with walls of mustard-color
tiles, frilly white window frames, and a roof shaped like a giant roulette
wheel, this utterly bizarre building is a local landmark. The main
tower of the Lisboa has, for better or worse, become one of the popular symbols of Macau. ⊠ *Av. da Amizade,* ☎ *853/377–666,* ℻ *853/
567–193; in Hong Kong,* ☎ *852/2546-6944. 1,050 rooms. 12 restaurants, 3 bars, pool, sauna, bowling, casino, dance club, theater, video
games. AE, DC, MC, V.*

$ ☲ **Grande.** A pre–World War II hotel geared for gamblers who frequent
nearby casinos, the Grande has a European atmosphere and good
restaurants. ⊠ *146 Av. Almeida Ribeiro,* ☎ *853/921–111,* ℻ *853/922–
397. 90 rooms. 4 restaurants, nightclub. AE, DC, MC, V.*

Nightlife

A major draw here are the casinos. Limitations on gambling are few
in Macau. No one under 18 is allowed in, but identity cards are not
checked. Although betting limits are posted, they do not discourage
high rollers. There are 24-hour money exchanges, and automatic teller
machines for drawing cash from Hong Kong banks. Bets are almost
always in Hong Kong dollars.

Of the six hotel casinos, that in the **Lisboa** (⊠ Av. da Amizade, ☎ 853/
377–666) has the busiest, in a two-story operation where the games are
roulette, blackjack, baccarat, pacapio, and the Chinese games fan-tan
and "big and small"; there are also hundreds of slot machines, which
the Chinese call "hungry tigers." The other five hotel casinos are in the
Mandarin Oriental (⊠ Av. da Amizade, ☎ 853/567–888); **New Century** (⊠ Est. Almirante Marques Esparteiro, Taipa Island, ☎ 853/831–
111); **Kingsway** (⊠ Rua Luis Gonzaga Gomes, ☎ 853/702–888); **Holiday Inn** (⊠ Rua de Pequim, ☎ 853/783–333); and **Hyatt Regency** (⊠
Taipa Island, ☎ 853/831–234). The non-hotel casinos are at the **Jai Alai
Stadium** (⊠ Terminal Maritimo do Porto Exterior, off Av. da Amizade);
the **Kam Pek** (⊠ Almeida Ribeiro), and the **Palacio de Macau,** (⊠ end
of Av. Almirante Sergio), usually known as the floating casino.

Macau A to Z

Arriving and Departing

BY BOAT

The majority of ships to Macau leave Hong Kong from the Macau Terminal in the **Shun Tak Centre** (⊠ 200 Connaught Rd.), a 10-minute
walk west of Central, which also houses the Macau Government
Tourist Office and offices for all shipping companies, most Macau hotels and travel agents, and excursions to mainland China. A fleet of
Boeing Jetfoils operated by the **Far East Jetfoil Company** (⊠ Shun Tak
Centre, ☎ 852/2516–1268) provides the most popular service between Hong Kong and Macau. In Macau, ships use the modern three-
story ferry terminal, which opened in 1994.

Jetfoil **fares** excluding tax for first-class are HK$110 on weekdays, HK$120 on weekends and public holidays, and HK$140 on the night service. Lower-deck fares are HK$97 weekdays, HK$108 weekends, and HK$126 at night. There is a **departure tax** of HK$26 from Hong Kong and 22 patacas from Macau, which is usually included in the price of the ticket.

BY HELICOPTER
Helicopter service is available from the Macau Terminal, with departures every 30 minutes, 9:30–5:30. The 20-minute flights cost HK$1,206 weekdays, and HK$1,310 weekends and holidays from Hong Kong, and HK$1,202 and HK$1,306 from Macau, including taxes. Book through the Shun Tak Centre (☎ 852/2859–3359) or the terminal in Macau (☎ 853/572–983).

Getting Around
Walking is the best method of getting around in the old parts of town and in shopping areas—the streets are narrow and crowded. You can rent a **bicycle** for about 10 patacas an hour at shops near the Taipa bus station. Public **buses** (2.30 patacas) are convenient. You can rent **mokes,** little jeeplike vehicles that are fun and ideal for touring (Happy Mokes, ☎ 853/831–212), as well as standard vehicles (Avis, ☎ 853/336–789). Tricycle-drawn two-seater **pedicabs** cluster at the ferry terminal and near hotels; be sure to bargain with the driver. Metered **taxis** (flag drop, 8 patacas; surcharge to other islands) cruise the streets and wait outside hotels.

Contacts and Resources
GUIDED TOURS
A number of licensed tour operators in Macau have offices in Hong Kong and specialize in English-speaking visitors: **Able Tours** (☎ 853/566–939, 852/2544–5656). **Estoril Tours** (☎ 853/710–461, 852/2540–8028). **International Tourism** (☎ 853/975–183, 852/2541–2011). **Macau Tours** (☎ 853/710–003, 852/2542–2338). **Sintra Tours** (☎ 853/710–361, 852/2540–8028).

VISITOR INFORMATION
Macau Department of Tourism (✉ Largo do Senado, ☎ 853/315–566). **Macau Tourist Bureau** (✉ Shun Tak Centre, 200 Connaught Rd., Central, Hong Kong, ☎ 852/2540–8180; Kai Tak Airport, Hong Kong, ☎ 852/2769–7970). **Macau Trade and Investment Promotion Institute** (✉ Luso Bank Bldg., 1–2 Rua Dr. Pedro Lobo, 7th and 8th floors, Macau, ☎ 853/712–660).

HONG KONG A TO Z

Arriving and Departing
By Plane
The major gateway to Hong Kong is **Hong Kong Kai Tak International Airport** (☎ 852/2769–7531). A new airport on Chek Lap Kok island, near Lantau, is scheduled to open in late spring, 1998. The new **Chek Lap Kok International Airport** will have an elaborate system of subways, buses and bridges connecting to Hong Kong Island and Kowloon.

Flying time to Hong Kong is between 17 and 20 hours from New York or Chicago, via Vancouver or Honolulu, and 13 hours direct from Los Angeles or San Francisco. Macau is a 20-minute flight from Hong Kong. Reconfirm your flights 72 hours before departure and arrive at the airport two hours before flight time. The airport policy is that passengers arriving 40 minutes or less before departure time are not allowed to board. The departure tax was HK$100 at press time but is subject to change.

Major international carriers between Hong Kong and North America are **Canadian Airlines International** (☎ 852/2868–3123), **Cathay Pacific Airways** (☎ 852/2747–1577), **China Airlines** (☎ 852/2868–2299), **Northwest** (☎ 852/2521–1083), **Singapore Airlines** (☎ 2529–6821), and **United Airlines** (☎ 852/2810–4888).

From the U.K., **British Airways** (☎ 852/2868–0303), **Cathay Pacific Airways** (☎ 852/2747–1577), and **Virgin Atlantic** (☎ 852/2532–3533) have daily flights from London Heathrow to Hong Kong.

Various Asian national airlines fly to Hong Kong via their capital cities, usually at reasonable rates.

BETWEEN THE AIRPORT AND CENTER CITY

The trip between Kai Tak Airport and Hong Kong Central takes about 30 minutes, longer in heavy traffic. Rush hours are generally 7:30 to 9:30 AM and 5 to 7:30 PM. A fast and efficient way to get to and from the airport is to use the **Airbus** (☎ 852/2745–4466), which runs every 10 to 20 minutes from 7 AM to midnight. Route A1 (HK$12) runs through the Kowloon tourist area and serves the Ambassador, Empress, Grand, Holiday Inn Golden Mile, Hyatt Regency, Imperial, International, Kowloon, Miramar, New World, Park, Peninsula, Regent, Shangri-La, and Sheraton hotels, plus the YMCA and the Star Ferry. Routes A2 and A3 (HK$19) go to Hong Kong Island. A2 serves the Harbour View International House, Furama, Hilton, Mandarin, and Victoria hotels. A3 serves the Causeway Bay hotels: Caravelle, Excelsior, and Park Lane Radisson.

If you have reservations at a hotel, follow signs to the area where **hotel limousines** wait. For normal **taxi** service, expect to pay HK$50 to HK$60 for Kowloon destinations and up to HK$120 for Hong Kong Island destinations, which includes the HK$20 fee for the Cross-Harbour Tunnel. Drivers will add a luggage-handling charge of HK$5 per piece.

From Chek Lap Kok: The ride to Central will be approximately 45 minutes. When the airport opens, transportation information booths in the arrival terminal will provide updated information about public transportation, taxis, and highway routes.

By Train

As Hong Kong is comprised mostly of islands, there is no surface transportation in and out, except by train to and from mainland China via the Kowloon Peninsula. The Kowloon-Canton Railway (KCR) has 13 commuter stops on its 34-km (21-mi) journey through urban Kowloon to Lo Wu, at the Chinese border. The main station is at **Kowloon Station** (⊠ Hong Chong Rd., Tsim Sha Tsui East, Kowloon). Fares range from HK$7.50 to HK$40. The trip takes about 40 minutes. The crossover point with the MTR is at Kowloon Tong Station (☎ 852/2602–7799).

Five express trains (🚄 HK$280 first class, HK$250 second class) depart daily to Guangzhou from Kowloon Station. The trip takes about 90 minutes. The last train back to Hong Kong leaves at 6 PM.

There are also direct trains (30 hours) to Beijing from Kowloon Station. In Hong Kong contact **China Travel Service** (CTS; ☎ 852/2853–3533) for reservations and information. New deluxe cabin service began in 1997 for this route.

Getting Around

By Bus

It is difficult to get bus operators on the phone and they don't usually speak English, but the HKTA information hotline (☎ 852/2801–7177) can be helpful. The HKTA Information Booths (☞ *locations, below*) have bus maps for every section of Hong Kong.

Minibuses, 14- to 16-seat yellow vehicles with single red stripes, travel all over Hong Kong and stop almost anywhere on request. They are slightly more expensive than ordinary buses. Their destination is written on the front, but the English-language characters are small. Wave the minibus down when you see the one you want. As fares are adjusted throughout the journey, you could pay as little as HK$2 or as much as HK$6.

Maxicabs look the same as minibuses but have single green stripes and run fixed routes. Rates run from HK$1.60 to HK$6.

By Car

The Hong Kong Tourist Association discourages self-driving for visitors, as the roads are tricky, traffic jams are common, and parking spaces are in short supply. Even post-handover, steering wheels are on the right-hand side and traffic flows British style, driving on the left. The only major car-rental company represented in Hong Kong is **Avis** (☎ 852/2890–6988). Chauffeured cars can be rented from **Fung Hing Hire Co.** (☎ 852/2572–0333).

By Ferry

The quickest and most romantic way to get between Central and Tsim Sha Tsui is by ferry. Fares are HK$2.20 for First Class, HK$1.90 for Second Class. The ferry runs from 6:30 AM to midnight daily.

There are ferries to all of the outlying islands from the Outlying Islands Ferry Pier just north of Exchange Square, Central Hong Kong. Obtain schedules at the pier from the booth for the island you wish to visit, or contact the **Hong Kong and Yaumatei Ferry Company** (☎ 852/2542–3081).

By Subway

The Mass Transit Railway (MTR) links Hong Kong Island to most of Kowloon and to parts of the New Territories. Extension lines are planned to connect the new airport with Kowloon and Central and should be installed by late spring of 1998. Trains run frequently, and are safe and easy to use. Color-coded maps to your destination are on prominent display in all stations. Station entrances are marked with a simple line symbol resembling a man with arms and legs outstretched. There are clearly marked ticket machines inside the station; change is available at the Hang Seng Bank counters inside the stations. Fares range from HK$4 to HK$11.

The special Tourist Ticket (HK$25) can save you money. If you plan to be using the MTR frequently for more than a week, purchase a Stored Value Ticket, which also provides access to the above-ground Kowloon Canton Railway (KCR). Tickets may be purchased at booths beside the Hang Seng Bank counters in every station for HK$70, HK$100, and HK$200.

For information and schedules, contact the **Mass Transit Railway** (MTR, ☎ 852/2750–0170).

By Taxi

Taxis are plentiful except in rain and rush hour traffic, and a bargain. Taxis in Hong Kong and Kowloon are usually red and have a roof sign that lights up when the taxi is available. Fares in the urban areas are

HK$14 for the first 2 km (1.2 mi) and HK$1.20 for each additional 0.20 km (.12 mi). There is a surcharge of HK$5 per large piece of baggage and a surcharge of HK$20 for driving through the Cross-Harbour Tunnel. Aberdeen Tunnel carries a surcharge of HK$5, and the Lion Rock Tunnel toll is HK$6. Taxis cannot pick up passengers where there is a solid yellow line painted on the road.

Most taxi drivers speak some English, but to avoid problems, get someone at your hotel to write out your destination in Chinese.

Outside the urban areas taxis are mainly green and white (blue on Lantau Island). New Territories taxis cost less than urban red taxis, with fares of HK$11.80 for the first 2 km (1.2 mi), and HK$1.10 every 0.20 km (.12 mi). Urban taxis may travel into rural zones, but rural taxis must not cross into the urban zones. There are no interchange facilities for these taxis, so do not try to reach the urban area using a green taxi.

By Tram
Trams run along Hong Kong Island's north shore from Kennedy Town in the west all the way through Central, Wanchai, Causeway Bay, North Point, and Quarry Bay, ending in the former fishing village of Shaukiwan. There is also a branch line that turns off in Wanchai toward Happy Valley. Destinations are marked on the front; the fare is HK$1.20. Avoid them at rush hours which are generally 7:30 to 9 AM and 5 to 7 PM, Monday through Friday.

Contacts and Resources

Consulates and Commissions
U.S. Consulate (✉ 26 Garden Rd., Hong Kong Island, ☎ 852/2523–9011, FAX 852/2845–0735). **Canadian Commission** (✉ Tower 1, Exchange Sq., 11th–14th Floors, 8 Connaught Pl., Hong Kong Island, ☎ 852/2810–4321, FAX 852/2810–8736). **U.K. Commission** (✉ Overseas Visa Section, Hong Kong Immigration Dept., Wanchai Tower, 7 Gloucester Rd., Hong Kong Island, ☎ 852/2824–6111, FAX 852/2724–2333).

Currency
Hong Kong continues to mint its own currency, apart from China. The units of currency in Hong Kong are the Hong Kong dollar ($) and the cent. (☞ Money Matters *in* the Gold Guide, *above*).

For the most favorable exchange rate, go to a bank. Most banks have foreign exchange counters and charge a commission of 5% to 10% for the transaction. There are 24-hour automated teller machines (ATMs) in banks all over Hong Kong, with Cirrus or Plus systems.

Emergencies
Police, fire, or **ambulance** (☎ 999). **Royal Hong Kong Police Visitor Hot Line** (☎ 852/2527–7177; English-speaking police wear a red shoulder tab). **Doctors and Hospitals:**

Queen Mary Hospital (✉ 102 Pok Fu Lam Rd., Hong Kong, ☎ 852/2855–3338), Queen Elizabeth Hospital (✉ 30 Gascoigne Rd., Kowloon, ☎ 852/2958–8888), Tang Shiu Kin Hospital (✉ 284 Queen's Rd. East, Hong Kong, ☎ 852/2831–6800), Princess Margaret Hospital (✉ 2-10 Princess Margaret Hospital Rd.; Laichikok, Kowloon, ☎ 852/2990–3200), Prince of Wales Hospital (✉ 30–32 Ngan Shing St., Shatin, New Territories, ☎ 852/2636–2211). **AIDS Hotline** (☎ 852/2780–2211).

Guided Tours
HKTA (☞ Visitor Information, *below*) offers the following:

The Kowloon and New Territories Tour, taking in sights as varied as a container terminal, a fishing village, a Taoist temple, and the Royal

Hong Kong Golf Club at Fanling; the six-hour "Land Between Tour," offering a glimpse of rural Hong Kong.

Harbour and Islands, Watertours of Hong Kong Ltd. (☎ 852/2739–3302 or 852/2724–2856) and the **Seaview Harbour Tour Co. Ltd.** (☎ 852/ 2561–5033) operate a variety of tours that cover the Inner Harbour and outer islands aboard junks and cruisers.

Mail
General Post Office (✉ next to Star Ferry Concourse, Central, ☎ 852/ 2921–2222; Hermes House, 100 Middle Rd., Kowloon, ☎ 852/2366– 4111 or 2843–9466). **American Express** (✉ 16–18 Queen's Rd., Central; Ground Floor, New World Tower, Central, ☎ 852/2844–0688; cardholders or traveler's check holders only).

Passports and Visas
Hong Kong's immigration laws function under the jurisdiction of the Special Administrative Region and are not the same as those in the rest of China. U.S., Canadian, and U.K. citizens need only a valid passport to enter and do not have to obtain a visa before entering. U.S. passport holders visiting Hong Kong as tourists may stay for up to 30 days, Canadians and EU passport holders (including U.K. citizens) may stay for up to 90 days. Special permission is needed from Hong Kong Immigration (☎ 852/2829–3163) to extend a tourist permit or work in Hong Kong.

Telephones
To make a local call from a pay phone, use the HK$1 coin. Dial 1081 for directory assistance from English-speaking operators. The code for Hong Kong is 852.

For long-distance calling, go to the **Hong Kong Telecom International** (✉ Century Sq., 1 D'Aguilar St., Central, ☎ 852/2810–0660, and TST Hermes House, Kowloon). Call 013 for international inquiries and for assistance with direct dialing. You can dial direct from specially marked silver-color phone booths that take phone cards (HK$25, $50, and $100), available from the Hong Kong Telephone Companies retail shops and Seven Eleven convenience stores throughout the island. Multilingual instructions are posted in the phone booths.

Tipping
Hotels and major restaurants add a 10% service charge. It is customary to leave an additional 10% tip in all restaurants, and in taxis and beauty salons.

Visitor Information
Hong Kong Tourist Authority (HKTA; multilingual telephone information service, ☎ 852/2801–7177; 24-hour facsimile information service, FAX 852/2177–1128).

9 West Central China

The character of West Central China, made up of Yunnan, Sichuan, Gansu, and Ningxia, depends on the fact that these provinces, and their history, are at the edge of the Chinese heartland.

WEST CENTRAL CHINA INCLUDES cities of several million inhabitants and destinations that are among the most beautiful in the country. Each of the provinces of Yunnan, Sichuan, Gansu, and Ningxia has a distinctive character and landscape. Sichuan is famous for its delicious, spicy cooking, its mountain landscapes, and the Yangzi River, as well as for being the principal home of the panda. In the province are the cities of Chengdu (gateway to Tibet) and Chongqing (a Yangzi River port), and the magnificent Buddha statue at Leshan. Much of Yunnan is sub-tropical China, a land of forests, non-Han minority peoples, the extraordinary Stone Forest, and the city of Kunming. Gansu, the arid corridor that is the beginning of the Silk Road, contains the oasis town of Dunhuang and its magnificent Buddhist grottoes. In remote Ningxia, accommodation is sparse and sights—as opposed to the inherent charms of the countryside—are thin on the ground.

By Christopher
Knowles

Curiously, although Ningxia appears to be the most peripheral of all the west central provinces, it is Yunnan, on the borders of Burma, Laos, Vietnam, and Tibet, that seems farthest from the popular idea of China. Kunming, its capital, is an attractive city, but rural Yunnan is the real attraction, for here, especially in the hot and humid southwest, is a languor and a cheerful charm that is far from the formal complexities of mainstream Han China.

Sichuan, though very obviously Chinese, has its own distinctive character. The capital, Chengdu, is a vibrant example of how the changes that have taken place in recent years have extended to the most distant reaches of the country. But here, too, it is the countryside of paddy fields and mountains that fascinates, and even the comparatively short journey from Chongqing to Dazu will take you through scenery typical of traditional China.

Gansu is the beginning of the Silk Road—the painted grottoes at Dunhuang speak for themselves, while the bleak desert landscape that surrounds them can, with a little imagination, evoke a time when these oasis towns were among the liveliest in the world.

Pleasures and Pastimes

Dining

In Ningxia and Gansu the food is unexceptional, but in Yunnan and, above all, in Sichuan, the food is excellent. Sichuanese-style cooking is hot, spicy, and strongly flavored, a more hearty version of traditional Chinese cooking. It is said that the use of peppers and spices, which abound in the province, came about to make people sweat in summer (in order to cool the eater in the great summer heat) and to warm them in winter. The adaptable Sichuan peppercorn, when mixed with other ingredients, can produce a whole range of flavors, such as "fishy" (fermented soya with garlic) or "peculiar" (vinegary and peppery, with a hint of sweetness).

A famous Sichuanese dish is *mapo doufu* (bean curd with minced pork, chili sauce, and hot peppers); its name comes from its supposed inventor, a certain Pockmarked Granny Chen, who owned a restaurant in Chengdu. Dumplings are very good in Sichuan, too—for example, *tangyuan*, which might consist of four separate dumplings, each stuffed with a different honeyed filling. In Chongqing, in particular, it is easy to sample the Sichuanese *huoguo* (hotpot), a simmering broth flavored with hot bean paste and fermented soya bean into which raw meat, vegetables, and noodles are dipped to cook. And then there is *gongbao jiding* (viceroy's chicken—diced chicken, peanuts, and green chilies quickly fried).

Lijiang, in Yunnan, is famous for its *baba* (pancakes), while the minority peoples in the subtropical part of the province are liberal with coconut, fish, lemon grass, bamboo, and peanuts. Fried river moss and Burmese-style food are delicacies in the border areas. In Kunming, try *guoqiao mixian* ("across-the-bridge-noodles"—a bowl of hot soup with a film of oil, into which you add raw pork or chicken, vegetables, and noodles to cook). The Muslim quarter has good food, too.

CATEGORY	PRICE*
$$$$	over $27
$$$	$21–$27
$$	$12–$21
$	under $12

Prices are per person for a five-course meal, excluding drinks, taxes, and tip.

Festivals

This is festival country. The most famous is probably the mid-April **Water Splashing Festival** in Xishuangbanna in deepest Yunnan, the purpose of which is to wash away the sorrow of the old year and refresh you for the new. At Hidden Lake, in the area of the Stone Forest near Kunming, the June 24 **Torch Festival** includes, apart from singing and dancing, bullfighting and wrestling. Dali has two festivals of note— the **Third Moon Fair,** from the 15th day to the 21st day of the third lunar month, in honor of Guanyin, Goddess of Mercy; and the **Three Temples Festival,** from the 23rd to the 25th day of the fourth lunar month. Lijiang has a **Fertility Festival** on the 13th day of the third lunar month. At Xiahe in Gansu, or more precisely, at the Labrang Monastery, the **Monlam** (Great Prayer Festival) takes place on the 13th, 14th, and 15th days of the first month of the Tibetan new year.

Hot Springs

Outside Chongqing in Sichuan are two—the **Northern and Southern Hot Springs.** Outside Kunming, Yunnan, are the **Anning Hot Springs,** where natural hot water is piped into rooms at hotels and guesthouses. At Tengchong, also in Yunnan in the mountainous west, is an area of volcanoes and hot springs with both indoor and outdoor facilities. In China, mixed bathing is not always encouraged.

Lodging

Price may have but a superficial bearing on quality. The $$$$ category includes the new generation of Chinese hotel, often built with foreign money, whose facilities are based on international standards. In the $$$ category are hotels with good facilities but with service and comfort that have been compromised in some way. The $$ category chiefly includes older hotels that have been modernized. In the final, $, category, facilities may be simple or even offer dormitory accommodation.

CATEGORY	PRICE*
$$$$	over $102
$$$	$78–$102
$$	$54–$78
$	under $54

Prices are for a standard double room with bath at peak season, excluding taxes and service charges.

Scenery

If Ningxia and Gansu have arid plains and desert, fringed with ancient denuded mountains, then eastern Sichuan and northern Yunnan are dominated by the majestic beginnings of the high Tibetan Plateau. If the mountains are high, the gorges are deep, including the Tiger Leaping Gorge in northern Yunnan, among the deepest in the world. The Yangzi River, the third-longest in the world, cuts through both Yunnan, where it is youthful and exuberant, and Sichuan, where it approaches adulthood, before a fearsome maturity sets in at the Three Gorges on the border with Hubei. Hills, dotted with villages unchanged for centuries, stretch to the farthest horizon beyond Lijiang in Yunnan, while scalloped terraces rise up the hills of Sichuan.

Walking, Hiking, and Trekking

In Yunnan you can spend a couple of days walking along the side of Tiger Leaping Gorge, to the north of Lijiang. In the southwest of Yunnan, you could try walking in the sub-tropical forest (CITS should be able to provide a guide). In Sichuan you can do the pilgrim climb up Emeishan, or hike around Qingcheng Shan, near Chengdu; in the north of the province, in the Aba Autonomous Region, you can go horse trekking in the mountains around Songpan. Beautiful Jiuzhaigou, also in the north of Sichuan, has excellent hiking trails.

Exploring West Central China

Sichuan is one of the largest provinces in the country and has the densest population. In the east of the province is the rural Chuanxi plain, while the mountainous border with Tibet lies in the west. Watered by the Yangzi, Sichuan is rich in natural resources.

Gansu is a long, slender province bending to the northwest from the center of the country. It is sparsely populated and, despite being watered by the Yellow River, is arid and barren, a mountainous corridor linking the desert areas of the old Silk Road (modern Xinjiang; ☞ Chapter 11) with the plains of China proper.

Yunnan, bordering Burma, Laos, and Vietnam, is the most southwesterly of the Chinese provinces. Home to about a third of China's ethnic minorities, it is also an area of considerable physical variety, from the rainforests of the deep southwest and the mountains in the north on the border with Tibet to the alpine plateaus around Kunming.

Ningxia, in the northern part of central China, all but surrounded by Inner Mongolia in the north and Gansu in the south, is the smallest of China's autonomous regions. Sparsely inhabited, it is mostly high, arid plateau, with some lowland plain, subject to harsh winters and dry, hot summers. It is watered by the Yellow River.

A visit to this region of China is a massive undertaking if you try to cover anything approaching all of it. You can visit the so-called highlights—Kunming, in Yunnan, known as "spring city" because of its year-round equable temperatures, with perhaps a day, or an overnight excursion to the Stone Forest; on the Yangzi, Chongqing, with an excursion to Dazu; and, in the remoter areas, Dunhuang and Xishuangbanna. It is in fact more rewarding to choose a particular area and go into it in as much depth as time, money, and tolerance allow.

From Kunming you can now fly to Dali, or Lijiang, areas that until recently meant long journeys by road. Beyond them, still comparatively difficult to get to, are the Tibetan villages and magnificent scenery of northern Yunnan. In Sichuan there is the holy mountain at Emeishan, and in Gansu the lesser-known grottoes at Maijiashan. Ningxia is interesting but lacks the aesthetic delights of the other areas in the region—it could be included in a tour of Mongolia (☞ Chapter 10) and Xinjiang (☞ Chapter 11).

Great Itineraries

Distances are vast and many places are time-consuming to reach. When planning a trip to this region, it is best to leave as little as possible to chance.

Numbers in the margin correspond to points of interest on the West Central China, Kunming, Chengdu, Chongqing, and Lanzhou maps.

IF YOU HAVE 4 DAYS

Fly to **Chongqing** in Sichuan. Have a brief look at the city and enjoy the local spicy food. Take a cruise along the Yangzi through the Three Gorges, as far as Wuhan (☞ Chapter 5) if time permits. In this way it is possible to see some magnificent scenery (before the gorges are much reduced by the construction of the giant new dam) and to glimpse the way of life in the Chinese rural heartland.

IF YOU HAVE 6 DAYS

After following the 4-day itinerary above, go to **Lanzhou** and make the long journey overland to visit the Labrang Monastery. Upon your return, go by train through **Gansu** to spend at least a day exploring the Buddhist Grottoes near **Dunhuang.**

IF YOU HAVE 10 DAYS

After following the 6-day itinerary above, go to **Chengdu** in Sichuan and stay long enough to visit both Emeishan Sacred Mountain and Leshan, where the largest Buddha in the world overlooks the river. Go by train to **Kunming** in Yunnan, from where you can visit Dali and Lijiang. Go to **Xishuangbanna** to see the minority peoples in a tropical setting.

When to Tour West Central China

In general, high summer is not the best time (the heat is intense and unrelenting, and the humidity is high)—unless you are visiting the mountainous areas, in which case the summer is the best time. Lowland Yunnan is at its best in winter; the rest of the region is most comfortable during either spring or autumn. A number of festivals take place throughout the year (☞ Pleasures and Pastimes, *above*).

YUNNAN

Yunnan has an area of 394,000 sq km (152,000 sq mi) and a population of approximately 38 million, including the Bai, Dai, Hani, Naxi, and Yi peoples. Geographically, it is characterized by high plateaus, with an average altitude of some 8,250 ft, which are part of the foothills of the Tibetan Plateau. In the northwest the average altitude reaches 16,500 ft. The climate is varied throughout the province—harsh and wintry in the north, sub-tropical in the south and southwest, and mild and vernal all year round in the area of Kunming. About one third of China's minorities live here, while half of the country's plant and animal species originated here.

Like other provinces in the south and west of China, Yunnan has always been an unwilling member of the Chinese empire. Originally the home of peoples that now form ethnic minority groups, Yunnan was first absorbed into China during the Qin dynasty, but long managed to maintain a determined, if uneasy, independence. By the 7th century, for example, the Bai people had established a considerable kingdom, Nanzhao, which by the 8th century had become sufficiently powerful to defeat the Tang armies. In the 10th century the Nanzhao was succeeded by the Dali kingdom; it was only during the Mongol Yuan dynasty that this area finally submitted directly to Beijing. Nonetheless, separatist movements persisted into the 20th century.

Bordering Burma, Laos, Vietnam and Tibet, as well as the Chinese provinces of Sichuan, Guizhou and Guangxi, Yunnan has absorbed influences from all of them. The result is a province that in many ways is the most fascinating in all China. Visits to Kunming and to Xishuang-banna can give an idea of the delights that remain to be discovered.

Kunming

400 km (250 mi) southwest of Guiyang; 650 km (400 mi) southwest of Chengdu; 1,200 km (750 mi) northwest of Hong Kong; 2,000 km (1,250 mi) southwest of Beijing.

Kunming, the capital of Yunnan, with a population of 1.5 million, is southwest China's answer to Chengdu—a large city, comparatively unknown, in a remote part of the world but with an atmosphere of some charm and an attractive liveliness about it that seduces rather than bludgeons. Like most cities in China, Kunming has lost much of its heritage, but here and there pockets remain. The equable climate has caused Kunming to be known as "the city of eternal spring." Both the city and the immediate area harbor places of interest. Kunming is also the jumping-off point for visits to other sites in the region.

Historically Kunming is a recent foundation by Chinese standards. During the 3rd century BC, the Eastern Zhou period, General Zhuang Qiao was forced to retreat to the shores of Lake Dianchi, where he founded Kunming. It became an important military base for subsequent dynasties and eventually became a capital of the Nanshao kingdom and a focal point of trade with India, Burma, Indochina, and central China. Later it briefly became the capital of the final vestige of the Ming empire when the last prince of the house of Ming took refuge here to rule over the Southern Ming kingdom, destroyed after eleven years in about 1660 by the invading Qing. The last prince was strangled here in 1662.

Kunming did not, however, lose its antipathy to subjugation; in 1855 the local Muslims (a couple of whose mosques still exist in the city), descended from the 13th-century Mongol conquerors, staged an uprising against the Manchurian rulers, a rebellion that was brutally put down. In 1863 a Muslim leader, Du Wenxiu, took the city and proclaimed a new kingdom. It lasted for a decade before the Qing reasserted themselves. By the turn of the 20th century the arrival of the railways turned Kunming into a modern city. Built by the French to link Kunming with Hanoi, the railway made possible the export of the region's copper and forestry resources. The process of modernization continued during the Second World War, when a number of industries were transferred here to protect them from the invading Japanese.

Kunming is lively but not exhausting. The center of the city is around Zhengyi Lu, Baoshan Jie, Nanping Lu, and Dongfeng Lu, in the vicinity of the Provincial Museum.

★ ❶ **Yuantong Si** (Yuantong Temple), the largest temple in the city, dates back some 1,000 years. It is composed of a series of pavilions and temples partially surrounded by water. There are plenty of vantage points from which to enjoy the busy and colorful comings and goings of the constant flow of worshipers and pilgrims, and there are frequently displays of flowers and miniature plants here. Among the temples is a recent addition housing a statue of Sakyamuni, a gift from the King of Thailand. ⊠ *Yuantong Jie.* ☜ *Y10.* ☉ *Daily 8–5.*

❷ The **Yunnansheng Bowuguan** (Yunnan Provincial Museum) is mostly devoted to the many ethnic minorities that live in the province. It is sometimes difficult to know what exactly you are looking at, but to a

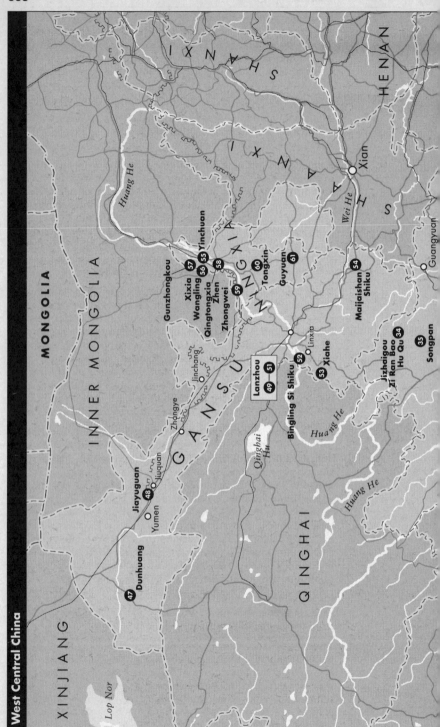

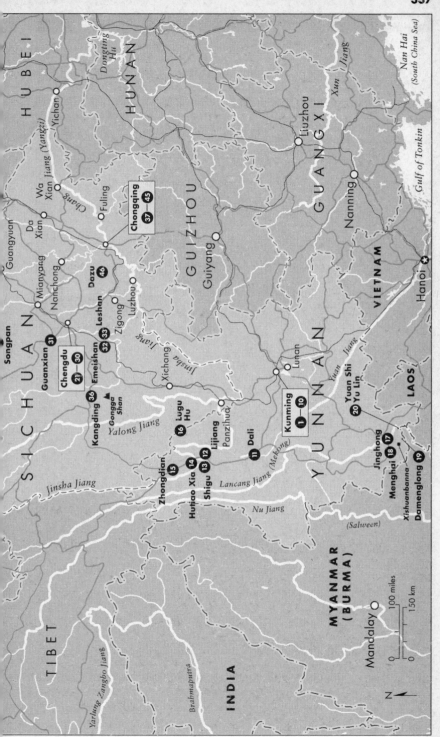

Kunming

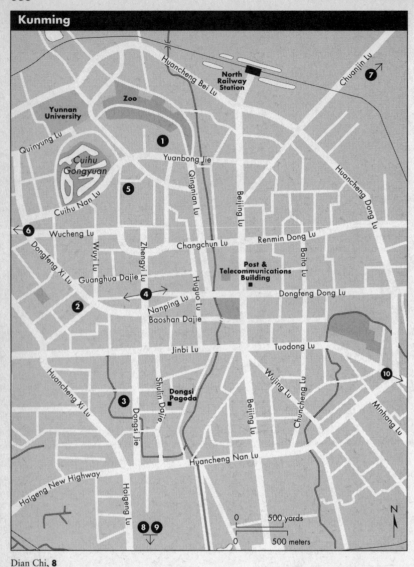

Zoo

Yunnan University

Quinyung Lu

Cuihu Gongyuan

Huancheng Bei Lu

North Railway Station

Chuanjin Lu

7

1

Yuanbong Jie

Qingnian Lu

Beijing Lu

Huancheng Dong Lu

5

Cuihu Nan Lu

Wucheng Lu

Changchun Lu

Renmin Dong Lu

Baita Lu

6

Dongfeng Xi Lu

Wuyi Lu

Zhengyi Lu

Guanghua Dajie

Post & Telecommunications Building

Dongfeng Dong Lu

4

Nanping Lu

Huguo Lu

Baoshan Dajie

2

Jinbi Lu

Tuodong Lu

Wujing Lu

Chunchen Lu

10

Huancheng Xi Lu

Shulin Dajie

Dongsi Pagoda

Dongsi Jie

3

Beijing Lu

Minhang Lu

Huancheng Nan Lu

Haigeng New Highway

Haigeng Lu

8 **9**

N

| 0 | 500 yards |
| 0 | 500 meters |

Dian Chi, **8**
Jindian Si, **7**
Muslim and market districts, **4**
Qiongzhu Si, **6**
Shilin, **10**
Stela, **5**
Xi Shan, **9**
Xi Ta, **3**
Yuantong Si, **1**
Yunnansheng Bowuguan, **2**

certain extent the exhibits speak for themselves, consisting of traditional costumes, photographs of the peoples in their native environment, and the tools and artifacts that they made and used. More than anything else it gives you an idea of the extraordinary ethnic diversity that once thrived in this region. These ways of life have gradually been eaten away by Beijing's version of modernization. ⊠ *Dongfeng Xi Lu.* 🖭 *Y10.* ⊘ *Mon–Thurs. 9–5, Fri. 9–2.*

❸ A stroll around the streets of the center is worthwhile. Here, the **Xi Ta** (West Pagoda; ⊠ Dongsi Jie) dates from the Tang dynasty and was once part of a temple. The old-fashioned lanes just north of Huashan Nan Lu seem all to have been razed, but several streets of traditional ar-
❹ chitecture still stand in the **Muslim and market districts** across the road from the Provincial Museum. But they, too, are under threat and
❺ after the year 2000 will probably remain no longer. The **stela** (⊠ Huashan Xi Lu) erected in 1912 is in memory of the last Ming prince strangled on the spot 250 years earlier.

Dining and Lodging

$$ ✕ **Beijing Restaurant.** Here the specialty is northern-style cooking, including seafood and duck. ⊠ *77 Xinxiangyun Lu, no phone. No credit cards.*

$$ ✕ **Dongfeng Hotel.** The unprepossessing exterior hides a dining room well known for steampot chicken and other local dishes. ⊠ *Wucheng Lu,* ☎ *0871/24808. V.*

$$ ✕ **Yiheyuan.** The fare at this central restaurant is generally very good Chinese food of all types. ⊠ *Zhengyi Lu, no phone. No credit cards.*

$–$$ ✕ **Baitadaiwei Canting** (Bai Ta Dai Restaurant). This is the place for
★ Dai minority food at very reasonable prices. ⊠ *Off Dongfeng Donglu, near Kunming Hotel, no phone. No credit cards.*

$–$$ ✕ **Yingjianglou Muslim Restaurant.** You can eat excellent food (much of which is suitable for vegetarians) here in simple surroundings at good prices. ⊠ *360 Changchun Lu, no phone. No credit cards.*

$ ✕ **Guoqiao Mixian.** This restaurant, simple to beyond minimalism in terms of decor, specializes in "across-the-bridge noodles." ⊠ *Nantong Jie, no phone. No credit cards.*

$$$$ 🏨 **Holiday Inn Kunming.** The best hotel in the city has a disco and a
★ bar with live music that serves as the meeting place for expatriates. The rooms are standard. ⊠ *Dongfeng Dong Lu, 650011,* ☎ *0871/316–5888,* FAX *0871/313–5189. 230 rooms. 2 restaurants, bar, air conditioning, dance club, shops, business services. AE, MC, V.*

$$$ 🏨 **Golden Dragon.** A joint venture with Hong Kong, this was the best before the appearance of the international chain hotels. It is still comfortable, if overpriced, and offers reasonable service. ⊠ *Beijing Lu, 650011,* ☎ *0871/313–2793,* FAX *0871/313–1082. 150 rooms. 2 restaurants, beauty salon, shops. MC, V.*

$$$ 🏨 **Green Lake Hotel.** In a pleasant part of town, just outside the center, it has old and new sections. The coffee shop is restful, and the rooms are comfortable. The hotel also has a clinic. ⊠ *6 Cuihu Nanlu, 650031,* ☎ *0871/515–7326,* FAX *0871/515–3286. 280 rooms. 4 restaurants, bar, shops. MC, V.*

$$$ 🏨 **Kunming Hotel.** The rooms at this central hotel are reasonably comfortable, with safes for valuables. ⊠ *145 Dongfeng Donglu, 650011,* ☎ *0871/316–2063,* FAX *0871/316–3784. 150 rooms. 2 restaurants, air conditioning, pool, health club. MC, V.*

Nightlife and the Arts

The main arts possibilities are minority dance performances or acrobatic displays. Check with CITS (☞ *below*) or at the Arts Theatre (⊠ Dongfeng Xilu).

There is a selection of karaoke bars around the city center.

The **Holiday Inn** (☞ *above*) has a good bar and disco. The **Bluebird** (✉ Dongfeng Donglu) is a café bar with a pleasant atmosphere. The **Golden Triangle** (✉ Dongfeng Donglu) is good café bar. **Wei's Place** (✉ Huancheng Nanlu) is popular with foreigners.

Outdoor Activities and Sports
Bicycles can be rented at the Kunming Hotel (✉ 145 Dongfeng Donglu). You can **jog** in Cuihu Gongyuan (Green Lake Park).

Shopping
Yunnan specialities include jade, batiks and other ethnic clothes and materials, embroidery, musical instruments, jewelry, marble, pottery, tea, and medicinal herbs. The main shopping streets are Zhengyi Lu, Dongfeng Donglu, Beijing Lu, and Jinbi Lu. The **Yunnan Wenwu Shangdian** (Yunnan Antique Store; ✉ Qingnian Lu) has objects from the region. The **Kunming Wenwu Shangdian** (Kunming Antiques and Handicrafts Shop; ✉ next to Holiday Inn) has items of interest. The **Flower and Bird Market** (✉ Tongdao Jie) is worth a visit for the atmosphere and for the array of antiques, fake and otherwise, and crafts on sale.

Side Trips from Kunming
6 Northwest of Kunming is the much-restored Tang-dynasty **Qiongzhu Si** (Bamboo Temple), the birthplace of Zen Buddhism in Yunnan. It is said that as two princes of the Kingdom of Dali were hunting, they came across a horned bull, which they pursued to the hill on which the temple stands. It disappeared in a cloud of smoke, through which the princes espied a monk whose staff sprouted to become a grove of bamboo. During its last major reconstruction, between 1883 and 1890, the abbot of the day employed a lay Buddhist, a master sculptor from Sichuan, to fashion 500 *arhats* or *lohans* (images of those freed from the materialist shackles of earthly existence) of particular vividness. ✉ *In hills, about 10 km (6 mi) northwest of city; take minibus from West bus station.* 🎫 *Y5.* ⊙ *Daily.*

7 The Taoist **Jindian Si** (Golden Temple) sits on a forested hill northeast of Kunming. Its current incarnation dates from the Ming dynasty, after which, during the early Qing, it was enlarged when it became the residence of Wu Sangui, a general sent here to deal with the recalcitrant locals. The most interesting construction is a pavilion, built on a vast slab of Dali marble and surrounded by a crenelated wall that is much decorated with cast bronze, from which the temple gets its name. The bronze work, which is used in many parts of the pavilion's construction, is meant to resemble timber work; the use of real timber has been kept to a minimum. Among the many trees in the temple are two camellias thought to date from the Ming period. There is also a large bronze bell cast in 1423. ✉ *About 10 km (6 mi) northeast of town; take bus 10 from North train station.* 🎫 *Y5.* ⊙ *Daily 8–5.*

8 **Dian Chi** (Lake Dian), with a shoreline of about 150 km (93 mi), lies just south of Kunming. As it is still exploited for fishing, junks with their traditional sail and rigging can be spotted at work here (it was the model for the Kunming Lake in the Summer Palace in Beijing). Away from the industrial areas, it is a pleasant place for its scenery and general rural atmosphere.

At the lake's northern tip **Daguan Gongyuan** (Daguan Park), which was first landscaped in 1682 for a Buddhist temple, offers rowing boats, pavilions, and the 1690 **Daguan Tower**, inscribed with a rhapsody by the Qing poet Sun Ranweng praising the lake's beauty. Boats can be taken from the park's dock to **Shan Yi Village** at the foot of the Western Hills (☞ Xi Shan, *below*).

Zheng He Gongyuan (Zheng He Park) lies near the southeastern point of the lake. It is dedicated to the admiral of the same name, a Muslim eunuch, who between 1405 and 1433 made a series of extraordinary sea voyages throughout Asia and Africa, leading to the establishment of trading links between China and large parts of the world. In a mausoleum here tablets record his life and achievements.

Near the lake's northeast end is **Haigeng Park,** a sort of living ethnographic display of the architecture and ways of life of the province's various minority peoples. ✉ *Buses from West bus station serve road around lake.*

★ ❾ Overlooking Lake Dian, the **Xi Shan** (Western Hills) hold a number of temples. It is possible either to drive to the various points of interest or to follow the footpaths from Gaoyao (where there is a bus station) or Shan Yi.

The **Huating Si** (Huating Temple), a relic from the Nanxia Kingdom dating from the 11th century, lies at the foot of the hills. Rebuilt in the 14th century, it was further embellished in the final two dynasties. Farther up is the pretty **Taihua Si** (Taihua Temple), from the Ming dynasty. A chair lift rises from the **tomb of Nie Er,** who was the composer of the Chinese national anthem. Close to the top is the Taoist **Sanqing Ge** (Sanqing Temple), formerly the residence of a Yuan (Mongol) dynasty prince. Finally you reach the **Long Men** (Dragon Gate), a network of narrow corridors, shrines, and grottoes dug out of the hillside by Taoist monks between 1781 and 1835. Tremendous views open out across the lake from up here, but the rock corridors are narrow and become crowded. ✉ *About 15 km (9 mi) south of Kunming; take bus No. 6 from Dongfeng Xi Lu to Gaoyao, and then minibus.* 🎫 *Y3–Y10 per attraction.* ☉ *Daily 8–5.*

★ ❿ One of the most popular trips from Kunming is to a geological phenomenon known as the **Shilin** (Stone Forest). It is composed of closely knit outcrops of dark gray limestone karst that have weathered into interesting shapes since their formation beneath a sea some 270 million years ago. The journey here takes you through hilly countryside dotted with the timber-framed architecture typical of the area.

You can take walks through the forest; you'll find plenty of Sani tribeswomen eager to act as guides and sell you their handicrafts. The area that most tourists go to has, inevitably, become rather commercialized, but there are other similar formations in what is in any case an interesting rural area.

At the small hotel close to the gate of the main site, sanitized but entertaining displays of traditional Sani dancing take place. ✉ *Lunan, 125 km (78 mi) southeast of Kunming; take tour through CITS or hotel, or take bus from long-distance bus station.* 🎫 *Y40.* ☉ *Daily 8–6.*

Dali

★ ⓫ *250 km (155 mi) northwest of Kunming; 140 km (87 mi) south of Lijiang.*

The charming town of **Dali** at the edge of the Erhai ("Ear Sea") has become something of a cult destination for independent travelers, like a miniature Katmandu. With the old gate towers still intact at either end of the town, it consists of little more than a long, single main street between them and side streets down to the lake on one side and up to the hills behind. Along these streets are some interesting shops and a whole variety of restaurants with quaint names that are largely aimed at the young foreigners passing through.

Dali is now the capital of the Bai Autonomous Region, a sop by the Beijing government to the independence aspirations of minority peoples. The Bai are a branch of the Yi people and settled this area some 3,000 years ago. The town was called Taihe when it was the capital of the Nanzhao Kingdom (AD 738–902), the result of the Bai's defeating the Tang dynasty army and exerting considerable influence throughout parts of Burma during the 9th century. During the Song dynasty, the independent Dali kingdom grew up before the region finally came under the heavy hand of Beijing during the Mongol period.

Following almost any street downward from the main street (Fuxing Lu) will bring you, after about half an hour, to the shore of **Erhai** (Ear Sea). Here, apart from the scenery, you may catch a glimpse of fishermen with their teams of cormorants tied to their boats awaiting the chance to go fishing. The birds are used in much the same way as they are in Guilin—with a sort of noose about their necks that prevents them from swallowing the fish once they have caught them.

Regular ferry crossings around various parts of the lake offer, in good weather, wonderful views of the lake and the surrounding mountains. There is also a temple on **Xia Putuo Dao** (Putuo Island). ⊠ *Boats leave from Zhoucheng.*

The most outstanding landmarks in Dali, the **San Ta** (Three Pagodas), are used as a symbol of the town and appear on just about every calendar of Chinese scenery. The largest, 215 ft high, dates from AD 824 and is decorated on each of its 16 stories with buddhas carved from the local marble. The other two pagodas, also rich in carved decoration, are smaller and more elegantly classical in style. In moments when the water is still, you can see their reflection in a nearby pool. ⊠ *Main road, just north of town—easy cycling distance, or 20-minute walk.* 🎟 *Y8.* ⊙ *Daily 8–5.*

Little more than a piece of local hokum, about 25 km (16 mi) north of Dali, **Hudiequan** (Butterfly Spring) is a beauty-spot. It consists of a pool surrounded by a marble balustrade, overhung by an ancient tree whose flowers are said to resemble butterflies. Alternatively, there is the tale that two lovers committed suicide here to escape the wrath of a cruel king and are among the butterflies that tend to congregate here every spring. ⊠ *North of town on Lijiang road.*

Three temples stand within reasonable distance of the town. No single one is especially spectacular, but because anything around Dali is located in wonderful scenery, a journey in any direction is worthwhile. **Gantong Si** (Gantong Temple; ⊠ Xiaguan Rd.) is close to the town of Guanyintang, about 5 km (3 mi) south of Dali. **Guanyin Tang Si** (Goddess of Mercy Temple; ⊠ Xiaguan Rd.), built on a rocky outcrop said to have been placed there by Guanyin herself to halt an invading army, is about 5 km (3 mi) south of Dali. Finally, the **Zhonghe Si** (Zhonghe Temple) is set splendidly among the hills right behind Dali. It is something of a steep climb (on foot) to get here, but the scenery in the vicinity is very attractive.

Dining and Lodging
Dali has numerous small restaurants aimed at foreign travelers. Most are around the intersection of Huguo Lu and Fuxing Lu; while the owners and the names come and go, these establishments all generally provide friendly service and a variety of local and foreign-inspired cooking, usually of a higher quality than that offered in the hotels.

$$ ☎ **Jinhua Hotel.** This new hotel with air-conditioning is the nearest thing
to luxury in Dali. ⊠ *Fuxing Lu, 671000,* ☎ *0872/267–3343,* FAX *0872/
267–3343. Restaurant, shops. V.*

$ ☎ **Old Dali Inn.** Attractively built around a courtyard, it's a basic but
★ comfortable hotel. The simple rooms are snug. ⊠ *Bo'ai Lu,* ☎ *0872/
267–0382. 40 rooms. Restaurant. No credit cards.*

Nightlife and the Arts

Although there is the occasional performance of traditional song and
dance, most of the entertainment on offer is aimed at backpackers and
comes in the form of small bars cum restaurants and cafés along
Huguo Lu. The occasional art exhibition also makes an appearance.

Outdoor Activities and Sports

There are plenty of opportunities for walking on the hills around Dali
and for cycling to all the other villages in the area.

Shopping

Local shops in Dali sell marble in various forms as well as batik (mostly
imported from elsewhere in China), jewelry, and local art. Clothes can
be made to measure. In the market at Shaping (☞ *below*) minority cloth-
ing is sold. Bargaining is expected everywhere.

Side Trips from Dali

A number of interesting villages or small towns lie fairly close to Dali.
The best known, on account of its Monday market (in action between
9 AM and 3 PM approximately), is **Shaping.** A visit here could be com-
bined with a look at the Butterfly Spring. The market, which deals in
local produce, including traditional Bai clothing, is a crowded, color-
ful affair. ⊠ *About 30 km (19 mi) north of Dali.*

Among the prettiest towns is **Xizhou,** which has managed to preserve
a fair amount of Bai traditional architecture. It has a daily morning
market. ⊠ *About 20 km (12 mi) north of Dali.*

The village of **Zhoucheng,** from which you can take a boat around the
lake, holds regular markets on the main square. The square also holds
a Qing dynasty stage once used by visiting opera troupes. ⊠ *About
30 km north of Dali.*

Lijiang

★ ⑫ *150 km (95 mi) northeast of Dali; 320 km (200 mi) northwest of Kun-
ming; 550 km (345 mi) southwest of Chengdu.*

Lijiang is the old capital of the Naxi people, kin of the Tibetans, who
are traditionally matriarchal and whose music and Dongba script are
unique to them. Badly damaged by an earthquake in early 1996, the
delightful town sits on a plain dominated by a snow-capped mountain.
You may have thoughts of Shangri-la when you are lost among the streets
and alleyways of the small old town, with its icy, fast-flowing stream
(the River Li) and charming bridges. The modern suburbs are unfor-
tunately composed of dreary streets lined with concrete apartment blocks.
Predictably, it was the old town that suffered most from the earthquake,
but a serious restoration project is under way.

The town is set amid beautiful scenery, including the 18,000-ft **Yulong
Xue Shan** (Jade Dragon Snow Mountain). In the town itself, the **Hei-
long Tan Gongyuan** (Black Dragon Pool Park) is home to the **Dongba
Research Institute Museum** and the Ming **Deyue Tian** (Deyue Pavil-
ion). ⊠ *Xinde Lu.* 🎫 *Y6.* 🕓 *Daily 7 AM–9 PM.*

One of the highlights of a visit to Lijiang is to attend a concert of Naxi music in the old town. Because of Lijiang's isolation the authentic sound of ancient Chinese music has survived here.

In the vicinity, you can visit monasteries with fine frescoes at **Fuguo**, **Longquan**, and **Baisha** (the former Naxi capital). Excellent views of Yulong Xue Shan can be had from a meadow halfway up its slopes, reached by chairlift.

⑬ **Shigu,** about 70 km (43 mi) west of Liijiang, is the site of the first bend
⑭ of the Yangzi. **Hutiao Xia** (Tiger Leaping Gorge), farther north, about 2½ hours' drive from Lijiang through an area of hills and unspoiled villages, is one of the deepest gorges in the world. It is possible to trek its length in one or two days; a rather precarious-looking road is also under construction.

⑮ **Zhongdian** is a village of Tibetan and Naxi people between the Sichuan
⑯ and Tibetan borders. **Lugu Hu** (Lugu Lake), on the border with Sichuan, is surrounded by colorful villages. All of the these places are served by long-distance buses from Lijiang. Shigu and Hutiao Xia could both be visited in a day by taxi.

Xishuangbanna

400 km (250 mi) southwest of Kunming; 425 km (265 mi) south of Dali.

The sub-tropical plateau and rainforest of Xishuangbanna Dai Autonomous Prefecture lies in the southern part of Yunnan, close to the borders of Burma and Laos. It is the home of the Dai people, Buddhists who are related to the Thais.

⑰ The main town, **Jinghong,** on the Lancang Jiang (Mekong River), has pleasant areas of traditional Dai houses. Also in town is the **Redaizuowu Kexue Yanjiusuo** (Tropical Plant Research Institute; ⊠ Jinghong Xi Lu). Xishuangbanna is well known for its **Water Splashing Festival** during the Dai New Year in mid-April.

Outside the town are a number of **minority villages**—Manjing Dai and
⑱ **Manluan Dian**, where weaving is a way of life, or **Menghai** and **Menghun**, which have Sunday markets. A number of interesting villages in the vicinity of the borders with neighboring countries have only recently opened to foreigners.

⑲ At **Damenglong** is the **Manfeilong** (White Pagoda), built in 1204 in honor of a footprint made by the Buddha himself.

Not far from Jinghong it is possible to go on walks in the **rain forest**
⑳ at **Mandian** or in the **Yuan Shi Yu Lin** (Primitive Rainforest Park).

Yunnan A to Z

Arriving and Departing

BY BUS

Kunming's long-distance bus station (⊠ Beijing Lu) is in the south of the city. Buses leave for Dali (11 hours), Lijiang (15 hours), Shiling (Stone Forest; 5 hours), Xishuangbanna (26 hours), and Guiyang.

BY PLANE

Yunnan is served by several branches of CAAC, Yunnan Airlines, Shanghai Airlines, and Dragonair, among other airlines.

Kunming is a busy air hub with flight links all over China, as well as to Dali (Xiaguan), Lijiang, and Xishuangbanna (Jinghong). There are also regular flights to Bangkok, Rangoon, Singapore, and Vientiane. The airport is about 20 minutes' drive from the center of town.

Direct service links **Kunming** with Guangzhou, Chengdu (24 hours), Chongqing, Emeishan (21 hours), Guilin, Guiyang, Beijing, and Shanghai (60 hours). The station is on the southern edge of the city.

Getting Around

Kunming has no shortage of taxis; the public bus system is comprehensive and cheap. To see things outside the town you can rent a bicycle or take a minibus from the Yunnan Hotel or from the railway stations.

The town of **Dali** can easily be explored on foot. You can go farther afield by bicycle; rentals are available locally.

Contacts and Resources

CAR RENTAL
Self-drive cars cannot be rented in **Kunming,** but cars with drivers can be hired through CITS. The same is true for **Dali.**

CONSULATES
Kunming: Burma (Myanmar; ✉ Camellia Hotel, ☎ 0871/312–6309). Laos (✉ Camellia Hotel, ☎ 0871/317–6623). Thailand (✉ Golden Dragon Hotel, ☎ 0871/3968916).

CURRENCY EXCHANGE
In **Kunming,** money can be changed in most of the hotels or at the Bank of China on Renmin Donglu.

In **Dali,** money can be exchanged at the Bank of China on Fuxing Lu.

EMERGENCIES
Kunming: PSB (✉ Beijing Lu). **Dali:** PSB (✉ Huguo Lu, Dali).

VISITOR INFORMATION AND GUIDED TOURS
Kunming: CITS (✉ 1–8 Wuyi Lu, 220 Huancheng Nanlu). **Jinhong:** CITS (✉ Galan Zhong Lu).

SICHUAN

This beautiful province (known to the Chinese as *tian fu zhi guo* or "heaven on earth"), with an area of 567,000 sq km (219,000 sq mi), is larger than France (though it forms only one seventeenth of the whole country) and is the most populous (109,000,000 people) in China. Essentially Han, it is also home to a large number of ethnic minorities—the Hui, Qiang, Miao, Tibetans, and Yi.

Geographically it is dominated by the Sichuan Basin, or Red Basin (because of the red sandstone that predominates here), in the east of the province, which accounts for almost half its area. On all sides it is surrounded by mountains, the Dabashan in the northeast, the Wushan in the east, the Qinghai Massif in the west, beneath which extends the fertile Chengdu Plain, and the Yunnan and Guizhou Plateau in the south.

Sichuan has a variable climate, influenced by the annual monsoons. The plains areas enjoy mild winters and long, hot summers. The mountain areas of the northwest are subject to harsh conditions year round, while the highlands of the southwest have moderately severe winters and temperate summers.

Although the civilization of Northern China reached Sichuan about 2500 BC, the province has always one way or another remained on the fringes of China. Kingdoms with a distinct culture ruled the area from 1600 BC to 300 BC approximately, but by 221 BC Sichuan became part of a united China. And yet its association was always somehow a loose one, its geographical position and its vastness encouraging an independent outlook.

After the founding of the first Republic of China in 1911, Sichuan fragmented into territories controlled by warlords and petty fiefdoms. Until the 1930s the province degenerated into poverty, massive debt, and corruption. The civil war, and the threat of Japanese invasion, threw the situation into relief. Many warlords sided with the Nationalists, although a large part of the Long March undertaken by the Communist troops passed through Sichuan. Then, when the Japanese took Nanking, Chongqing unexpectedly became the temporary capital of China.

Since Mao's death in 1976, Sichuan has gone from strength to strength, making the most of the economic reforms introduced by Deng Xiaoping, who came from Sichuan. Even now rumblings are to be heard on the subject of an independent Sichuan; but that seems remote. The vibrant city of Chengdu, the holy mountain of Emeishan, the giant Buddha at Leshan, and the river port of Chongqing on the Yangzi are among Sichuan's attractions.

Chengdu

240 km (150 mi) northwest of Chongqing; 1,450 km (900 mi) southwest of Beijing; 1,300 km (810 mi) northwest of Hong Kong.

Chengdu, a name that means little to anyone outside China, has become one of the most vibrant of Chinese cities. With a population of more than 2.5 million (4.5 when the outer suburbs are included), it has been the capital of the province of Sichuan since 1368 and has become the "gateway" to Tibet. In recent years it has seized the opportunity offered by a comparatively liberal government in Beijing to become a bustling, modern city where the tenets of Maoism have ceased to have any meaning, despite the statue of the Great Helmsman that still stands in the main square, gazing portentously along Renmin Lu. It is a city of tree-lined boulevards from which here and there radiate streets of traditional Chinese architecture that are soon likely to be razed as part of China's determination to modernize at all costs and certainly at the expense of its ancient civilization.

Within a reasonable distance from Chengdu are a number of places of interest that can be reached with comparative ease, including Emeishan, one of China's sacred mountains, and Leshan, home of the world's largest Buddha.

Chengdu has more than 2,500 years of recorded history. Until 316 BC it was capital of the Zhou Shu Kingdom, before the first unification of China under the short-lived Qin dynasty. In the centuries that followed, it never lost its importance, becoming the chief political, cultural, and economic center of southwest China. Indeed, because of its growing importance at the center of the silk industry, it quickly became known as "brocade city" (Jin Cheng, by which it is still sometimes known today). Its importance as a center of the arts was enhanced during the period known as the "Three Kingdoms" (AD 220–280), when it became capital of the state of Shu Han, its reputation for the production of brocade reaching its peak at this time. In the 8th century, during the Tang dynasty, perhaps the greatest period of Chinese history from the point of view of culture, the arts of lacquer ware and silver filigree were cultivated here as the city became a major center of trade and commerce. At the same time, it developed a reputation as a place outside the mainstream of Chinese life (partly, no doubt, due to its position in the far west of Han China), a refuge for poets and artists. Its reputation as a cultural center, in the academic sense, persists to this day—there are 14 colleges in Chengdu, including Sichuan University.

It is perhaps especially interesting as an example of a great city, obscurely located as far as the rest of the world is concerned, that reflects the pace of change, and the tensions that go with it, of modern China. It is also a great center for Sichuanese cooking, which many believe to be the best in China, and is also one of the last bastions in China of the art of tea drinking.

The main street is Renmin Lu, the main square at its northern end. The liveliest area is where Renmin Lu crosses the river.

㉑ **Du Fu Caotang** (Du Fu's Cottage) belonged to a famous poet of the Tang dynasty whose poetry continues to be read today. He came to Chengdu from Xian and built a cottage or hut overlooking the Huanhua River in AD 759, spending four years here and writing well over 200 poems. After his death the area became a garden; a temple was added during the Northern Song dynasty (960–1126). A replica of his cottage now stands among several other structures, all built during the Qing dynasty. Some of Du Fu's calligraphy and poems are on display here. ⌧ *Off Xi Yihuan.* 🚻 *Y15.* ⊘ *Daily 9–5.*

Another poet of the Tang dynasty who lived in Chengdu was Xue Tao. She was said to have spent time on the site of the current Wangjiang Lou Gongyuan (Riverview Pavilion Park), in the southeast of the city by the Fuhe (Fu River), from which she apparently drew water to make ㉒ paper for her poems. The four-story wooden **Wangjiang Lou** (Riverview Pavilion), dating from the Qing dynasty, offers splendid views of the river and the surrounding countryside. It stands amid more than 120 species of bamboo, a plant particularly revered by the poet. There are also several other pavilions to enjoy in the park. ⌧ *Wangjiang Lu.* 🚻 *Y3.* ⊘ *Daily 9–5.*

㉓ The **Wuhou Ci** (Temple of the Marquis of Wu), in Nanjiao Park in the southwest of the city, was built in the 6th century to commemorate the achievements of one Zhu Ge Liang (AD 181–234), a prime minister and military strategist of the Three Kingdoms era. Of the two pavilions here, one is dedicated to Zhu, the other to Liu Bei of the Kingdom of Shu, Emperor at the time of Zhu Ge Liang, whose tomb is close to the Liu temple. ⌧ *Wuhou Ci Dajie.* 🚻 *Y1.* ⊘ *Daily 9–12 and 2:30–5.*

In the northwest section of Chengdu stands the 49-ft-high, 262 ft in ㉔ diameter **Wang Jian Mu** (Tomb of Emperor Wang Jian), which honors a ruler of the Kingdom of Shu (AD 847–918). Made of red sandstone, it is distinguished by the male figures that support the platform for the coffin and the carvings of musicians, thought to be the best surviving record of a Tang dynasty musical troupe. ⌧ *Xian Lu.* 🚻 *Y1.* ⊘ *Daily 9–12 and 2:30–5.*

㉕ The **Sichuan Sheng Bowuguan** (Sichuan Provincial Museum) is in the far south of the city. There are two sections—historical on the ground floor and revolutionary on the upper floor. You can see pottery from the early Daxi settlements, bronzes from the Ba and Shu kingdoms, and some exceptionally interesting stone decoration and earthenware figures from Han tombs discovered around Chengdu. Also on display are Tang and Song porcelain and a magnificent 19th-century loom with examples of the brocade that would have been woven on it. ⌧ *Renmin nan lu just south of Yihuan Lu Nan San Duan (ring road).* 🚻 *Y2.* ⊘ *Tues.–Fri. 9–12 and 2–5.*

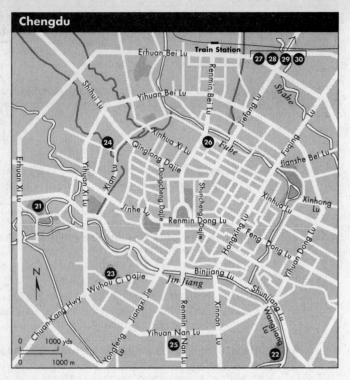

★ ㉖ **Wenshu Yuan** (Wenshu Monastery), the largest in Chengdu, is in the northern suburbs of the city. It dates back to the Tang dynasty, though the current incarnation was constructed in the Qing dynasty. Besides the small museum of calligraphy and paintings, the monastery has exquisite carving on some of the buildings. Worshipers come here in great numbers, creating the restful atmosphere special to Buddhist temples. The streets in the immediate vicinity are interesting, too, as much of the commerce is related to worship at the temple. ⌧ *Just off Renmin Zhonglu on Wenshu Yuan Jie.* 🚍 *Y5.* ⏱ *Daily 8:30–5.*

㉗ As Chinese zoos go, **Chengdu Dongwuyuan** (Chengdu Zoo) is not half bad—reasonably spacious and clean. Its main claim to fame is that it houses the largest number of captive giant pandas in the world, several of which have been successfully bred here. As well as the other animals that you expect to find in zoos, Chengdu exhibits rare animals native to China, including the eccentric-looking golden-haired monkey and the red panda. The best time to view is in the early morning. ⌧ *Northeastern suburbs; take bus No. 302 from near train station on Erhuan Lu.* 🚍 *Y3.* ⏱ *Daily 8–6.*

㉘ Next door to the zoo is the **Zhaojue Si** (Zhaojue Temple), recently restored, which dates from the Tang dynasty. ⌧ *Northeastern suburbs.* 🚍 *Y1.* ⏱ *Daily 8–6.*

★ ㉙ At the **Daxiongmao Bowuguan** (Giant Panda Breeding Research Base), recently opened to the public, about a dozen giant pandas live in luxurious conditions. There is a special breeding area and a small museum that explains the evolution and habits of pandas. As with the zoo, the best time to see the pandas in action is in the early morning. ⌧ *Jiefang Lu.* 🚍 *Expensive; visit may have to be arranged through travel agent or CITS.* ⏱ *Variable.*

③ Standing about 16 km (10 mi) north of the city, the **Baoguang** (Divine Light Monastery) was first built almost 2,000 years ago during the Eastern Han dynasty but has been rebuilt at least twice. It was last built by Emperor Kangxi during the early Qing period, but the 13-story, 98-ft-high pagoda dates from the Tang period. Among the five halls and 16 courtyards that make up this monastery, you can see the White Buddha from Burma, a granite Tibetan-style stupa, the 5th-century Thousand Buddha Tablet, and the spectacular Hall of Five Hundred Arhats, rows of life-size clay figures made in 1851. ⊠ *Xindu Town.* 🎫 *Y5.* ☉ *Daily 8–5.*

Dining and Lodging

Chengdu is one of the few places in China where restaurants exist that have established reputations.

$$$ ✕ **Chengdu Restaurant.** This unobtrusive restaurant is known for serv-
★ ing a good range of Sichuanese food. It has two sections, one with simpler food (for a fixed fee you can sample a number of specialties, such as marinated squid, and sweet and savory dumplings), the other with full meals. ⊠ *134 Shandong Dajie, no phone. AE, MC, V.*

$$–$$$ ✕ **Shufengyuan.** At this restaurant, where the dining rooms are arranged around a courtyard, the decor is handsome and the food excellent. ⊠ *153 Dong Dajie, no phone. AE, V.*

$$ ✕ **Banna Restaurant.** Here the food is Dai, so if you are not going to the Dai minority areas, this is your chance to at least sample their cooking. ⊠ *Hongxing Lu, no phone. No credit cards.*

$$ ✕ **Chen Mapo Doufu.** It has been famous for over 100 years because
★ of the consistently high quality of its cooking and in particular for the hot beancurd dish (doufu) named after the original proprietor. ⊠ *Jiefang Lu Erduan, no phone. MC, V.*

$$ ✕ **Yaohua Fandian.** Once visited by Mao, in 1958, the Yaohua serves Western dishes of varying quality as well as a full Chinese menu. ⊠ *22 Chunxi Lu, no phone. No credit cards.*

$$$ 🏨 **Jinjiang Hotel.** The original major hotel in Chengdu, in Soviet architectural style, has been modernized and has a good location. The rooms are a little shabby. It has a bank and a clinic. ⊠ *180 Renmin Nanlu, 610041,* ☎ *028/558–2222,* FAX *028/558–2223. 222 rooms. Air-conditioning, shops, disco. AE, MC, V.*

$$$ 🏨 **Minshan Hotel.** In a good location, this modern hotel with a grand
★ lobby where a string quartet plays has comfortable but overpriced rooms. ⊠ *Renmin Nanlu, 610041,* ☎ *028/558–3333,* FAX *028/558–2154. 150 rooms. 2 restaurants, bar, air-conditioning, shops. AE, MC, V.*

$$–$$$ 🏨 **Chengdu Grand.** Close to the railway station in the north of the city, this hotel has reasonably commodious, if overpriced, rooms. ⊠ *Bei Erhuan Lu, 610041,* ☎ *028/333–3888,* FAX *028/333–6818. 2 restaurants, shops. AE, MC, V.*

Nightlife and the Arts

Chengdu normally has something going on somewhere. Find out about local opera performances, visiting acrobatic troupes, art exhibitions, shadow puppet shows, and other events from CITS (☞ *below*), from your hotel, or from the Jinjiang Theater (⊠ *Huaxingzheng Jie*).

Tea-drinking in tea houses is a traditional pastime in Chengdu, and sometimes amateur opera performances take place in them. The best time to go is in the afternoon. Try the **Renmin Chaguan** (Renmin Park).

On the nightlife scene, as well as the usual karaoke parlors, there are private bars around Renmin Nanlu in the area of the Jinjiang Hotel. The major hotels have bars, and the Jinjiang has a disco as well.

Outdoor Activities and Sports

It is possible to rent **bicycles** in Chengdu—try the Traffic Hotel (✉ just off Renmin Nanlu south of river). For **jogging,** try the riverbank, Renmin Park, or perhaps the park of Du Fu's Cottage. There is a **swimming** pool at Mengzhuiwan (✉ off Xinhua Donglu, in east of city). For **walking,** try an ascent of Emeishan (☞ *below*).

Shopping

The main street for shopping is Chunxi Lu, to the east of the People's Square, where there are a number of shops selling interesting items, including the **Arts & Crafts Service Department Store.**

Guanxian

③ *55 km (34 mi) northwest of Chengdu.*

In this town, the **Dujiangyan** (Dujiangyan Irrigation System) has been in place for 2,200 years. In 256 BC the local governor, Li Bing, decided to harness the power of the Minjiang (Min River) to irrigate Chengdu Plain. The river was divided in two and then further divided to feed 6,500 sq km (2,500 sq mi) of canal. At the main site are the **Erwang Miao** (Two Princes Temple), dedicated to Li Bing and his son who saw his father's plan to fruition, and the suspension bridge that spans the so-called Outer and Inner rivers. There are buses to Guanxian from Chengdu. ✉ *Lidui Park.* 🎫 *Y5.* ⊙ *Daily.*

Emeishan

★ ③ *100 km (60 mi) southwest of Chengdu.*

One of China's holy mountains, the dwelling place of the Samantabhadra, the Buddhist Bodhisattva of Pervading Goodness, 10,000-ft-high Emeishan (Lofty Eyebrow Mountain) is in the south of Sichuan. On it are some 50 km (31 mi) of paths leading to the summit; the climb can be accomplished in two or three days. No mountaineering skills are required, but be prepared for sudden weather changes, which can produce mist or rain at a moment's notice. There are several temples (with accommodation) and places of interest en route. You can spend the night at the summit to see the famous sea of clouds and the sometimes spectacular sunrise. Solid footwear with a good grip is required, and a staff could be useful. The mountain is known for its monkeys, which have become rather spoiled and audacious, and should not be approached.

The pilgrimage can be made much easier if you use the minibus service up to Jieyin Dian at 7,800 ft, from where the climb to the top will take about two hours. If you want to avoid climbing altogether, there is a cable car to the summit from Jieyin Dian (though long queues can form for this).

There is a direct bus service from Chengdu to Baoguo, at the foot of the mountain (journey time four hours) and about 6 km (4 mi) from Emei Town. Trains from Chengdu to Emei Town take three hours.

Leshan

★ ③ *165 km (102 mi) south of Chengdu.*

In the small, swiftly changing town of Leshan a towering Buddha, carved from the rock face, sits inscrutably at the confluence of the Dadu and Min rivers. The Leshan **Dafo** (Grand Buddha) at 233 ft is among the tallest in the world. The big toes are each 28 ft in length. The construction of the Grand Buddha was started in AD 713 by a monk who wished to placate the river waters that habitually took local fishermen's lives. Although the project took more than 90 years to complete, it had no noticeable effect on the river waters. It is possible to clamber down, by means of a stairway, from the head to the platform where the feet rest; or you can take a boat ride to see it in all its grandeur from the river.

There are also several temples or pagodas in the vicinity, including **Wuyou Si** on Wuyou Shan (Wuyou Mountain), with its hall of recently restored arhats. ⊠ *Take boat from Leshan jetty and climb staircase.* ☎ *Y5.* ☉ *Daily.*

Leshan town is quite a lively place, with some interesting old streets—Dong Dajie and Xian Jie—and a good market.

Aba

350 km (220 mi) northwest of Leshan; 225 km (140 mi) northwest of Chengdu.

In northern Sichuan is the Aba Autonomous Prefecture, home to Qiang and Tibetan peoples. Reaching these places is a matter of long bus journeys on poor roads and simple accommodation at journey's end. The **③④** highlight of the area is **Jiuzhaigou Zi Ran Bao Hu Qu** (Jiuzhaigou Natural Preserve), which has scenery to rival Guilin's and some fine hik-**③⑤** ing trails. **Songpan** is an interesting market town in lovely scenery where horse trekking is popular.

Kangding

③⑥ *215km (135 mi) southwest of Chengdu.*

In western Sichuan, toward Tibet, is tougher terrain. You can see some magnificent scenery at Kangding. Just south of here, **Hailougou Glacier,** part of 24,790-ft Gongga Shan (Mount Gongga), is at the lowest altitude of any glacier in Asia. You can go hiking and pony trekking in the region.

Chongqing

240 km (150 mi) southeast of Chengdu; 1,800 km (1,120 mi) southwest of Beijing; 1,025 km (640 mi) northwest of Hong Kong.

Sichuan's first city in terms of population (a total of more than 6.5 million) is a busy river port in the eastern part of the province. Built on undulating hills at the point of confluence of the Yangzi with the Jialing River, it is one of the few cities in China where the bicycle is all but redundant (in fact it is sometimes referred to as "mountain city"). Chongqing is a major point of embarkation or disembarkation for the Yangzi cruise and it has its own atmosphere. The vicinity affords fine scenery and numerous day trips.

The recorded history of Chongqing ("Constant Celebrations," a name conferred by the first Song emperor to celebrate his conquest of the area) goes back some 3,000 years. During the 13th century BC, before the unification of China, it was the capital of the Kingdom of Ba. Its importance has always depended on trade, which in its turn has depended on the city's position on the river at the head of the Yangzi Gorges, through which the river flows to the ports of Wuhan and Shanghai. Before the arrival of the train and the airplane, nearly all of Sichuan's trade flowed through Chongqing, and yet it received the status of "city" only in 1927.

Once the Western powers established permanent footholds in China from the mid-to-late 19th century, they showed interest in exploiting the markets of Sichuan. The first westerners reached Chongqing by river in 1898, after the Chefoo Agreement of 1876 was amended in 1890 to allow the city to be opened to foreign trade. A regular steamer service began to ply the length of the river. By the first years of the 20th century a substantial foreign community had established itself, with offices of all the great trading companies of the day and with consulates to serve the residents.

When the Japanese took the Nationalist capital of Nanjing in 1938, the Chinese government moved to Chongqing, regarded as an impregnable fortress because of its location. The population grew quickly, particularly as it became home to the so-called united front, the temporary alliance between the Communists and the Nationalists against the Japanese. Chongqing's population swelled to 2 million, and it became a place of intrigue and desperation, where the misery of overcrowding and squalor was exacerbated by endless air raids by the Japanese, who were able to identify the city easily by following the Yangzi on moonlit nights.

What had been, at the turn of the century, an attractive town of temples within a city wall was largely destroyed by the end of the war. And yet the city still has something—there are sections where it is possible to grasp some idea of how the city must once have been. It has not lost that air of activity, of arrival and departure, that characterizes any port. The food, the excellent, spicy cooking of Sichuan, is good. It is an interesting city to stroll around—but not in high summer when it becomes unbearably hot, fully deserving of its reputation as one of the "furnaces" of China.

★ ③⑦ Two items almost unique to Chongqing are its **cable cars.** One links the north and south shores of the Jialing River, from Canbai Road to Jinsha Jie station. It is a worthwhile experience for the view of the docks, the city, and the confluence of the Jialing and Yangzi rivers. The other crosses the Yangzi itself and starts close to Xinhua Lu.

③⑧ There are also three **bridges** across the rivers—the oldest, built between 1963 and 1966, crosses the Jialing while the two newer bridges, built in 1981 and 1989 cross the Yangzi.

There are few areas more evocative than a port; and in a port few areas more evocative than the docks. Not, perhaps as busy and bustling as
③⑨ once upon a time, **Chaotianmen Matou** (Chaotianmen Docks) still offer an opportunity to glimpse something of China at work. ⊠ *Shaanxi Lu.*

④⓪ At 804 ft, **Pipa Shan** (Loquat Hill), until 1950 a private garden, is the highest point in the city. It is a good place from which to see the layout of the city and the activity on the river below, or, at night, the city lights. ⊠ *Zhongshan Lu.*

④① At the foot of the hill is the **Chongqing Bowuguan** (Chongqing Museum), in which the main items of interest are dinosaur remains discovered in the mid-1970s in different parts of Sichuan. Here, too, are some fine illustrated Han dynasty tomb bricks and exhibits of ethnographic interest, such as local puppets and woodblock prints. ⊠ *Foot of Pipa Shan.* 🎫 Y3. ⊙ *Daily 9–5:30.*

④② Originally built about 1,000 years ago (Song dynasty) and rebuilt in 1752 and again in 1945, the **Luohan Si** (Luohan Temple) is a popular and atmospheric place of worship. There is still a community of monks here (though not as many as there once were). The main attraction is the hall of 500 lifelike painted clay arhats, Buddhist disciples that

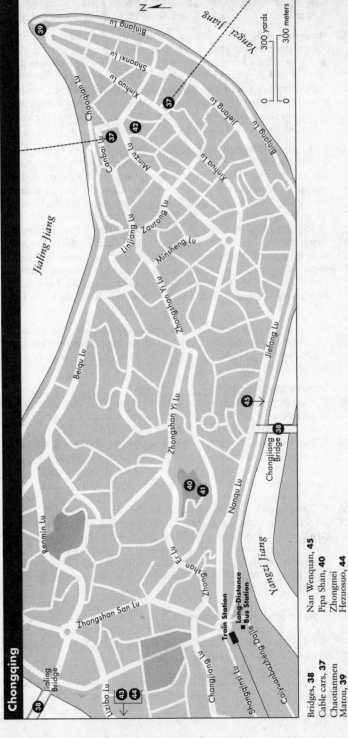

Chongqing

Bridges, **38**
Cable cars, **37**
Chaotianmen
Matou, **39**
Chongqing
Bowuguan, **41**
Hongyancun, **43**
Luohan Si, **42**

Nan Wenquan, **45**
Pipa Shan, **40**
Zhongmei
Hezuosuo, **44**

have succeeded in freeing themselves from the earthly chains of delusion and material greed. ⊠ *Minzu Lu.* 🚃 Y2. ⊙ *Daily 8:30–5:30.*

43 **Hongyancun** (Red Crag Village) is where Zhou Enlai, among other luminaries of the Chinese Communist Party, lived between 1938 and 1945 and where the Chongqing office of the Chinese Eighth Route Army was situated. A **geming bowuguan** (revolutionary history museum) has some interesting photographs of the personalities who played a significant role in the events of the time. There is, however, nothing written in English; you may perhaps find an English-speaking guide on the site. ⊠ *Hongyan Bus Terminus.* 🚃 Y6. ⊙ *Daily 8:30–5.*

44 In the name **Zhongmei Hezuosuo** (U.S.-Chiang Kai-shek Criminal Acts Exhibition Hall & SACO Prison), SACO stands for the Sino-American Cooperation Organization, a group developed through collaboration between Chiang Kai-shek and the United States government dedicated to the training and supervision of agents for the Guomindang. It was jointly run by the Chinese and the Americans, who built prisons outside Chongqing to house sympathizers of the Communist Party, with whom the Guomindang was technically allied during the struggle against the Japanese. The exhibition hall houses a few photographs and examples of the hardware used on the prisoners but with nothing in English. The prisons are a considerable walk from the exhibition hall. ⊠ *Foot of Gele Hill in northwest suburbs.* 🚃 Y5. ⊙ *Daily 8:30–5.*

45 To the south of the city is a set of hot springs set amid attractive scenery in **Nan Wenquan** (Southern Hot Springs). The springs produce sulphurous water at 38°C (100°F). ⊠ *20 km (12 mi) south of city.* 🚃 Y10. ⊙ *Daily 8:30–5.*

Dining and Lodging

$$–$$$ ✕ **Yizhishi Restaurant.** You can eat local snacks during the morning on one floor or full-scale local meals the rest of the day on the other floors. ⊠ *Zourong Lu,* ☎ *0811/384–2429. AE, MC, V.*

$$ ✕ **Lao Sichuan.** The best-known restaurant in Chongqing because it has been in existence for as long as anyone can remember, the "Old Sichuan" has interesting food (for example, chili-braised frogs) at reasonable prices. ⊠ *Bayi Lu.* ☎ *0811/384–1957. AE, MC, V.*

$$–$$$ ✕▥ **Chongqing (Chunking) Hotel.** In the center of town in an art-
★ deco-style building, the hotel is reasonably managed by a Hong Kong company. The rooms have television and minibar. The restaurant's generally very good food (local and regional) is served in pleasantly modernized surroundings. ⊠ *41–43 Xinhua Lu, 630011,* ☎ *0811/384–9301,* FAX *0811/384–3085. 74 rooms. Restaurant, bar, air-conditioning, shops. MC, V.*

$$$–$$$$ ▥ **Holiday Inn Yangzi Chongqing.** This international standard hotel is just outside the city center. ⊠ *Dianzi Ping, Nanping Xiang, 630060,* ☎ *0811/483380,* FAX *0811/483388. 2 restaurants, pool, health club, business services. AE, MC, V.*

$$$ ▥ **Renmin Guesthouse.** The original house was built in the 1950s in the image of the Temple of Heaven in Beijing. There is also a newer section, though the service is poor. ⊠ *175 Renmin Lu, 630015,* ☎ *0811/ 385–1421,* FAX *0811/385–2076. 140 rooms. Restaurant, bar, shops, disco. AE, MC, V.*

Nightlife and the Arts

There are often performances of Sichuan opera and acrobatics—ask CITS (☞ *below*) or at your hotel for information. It is worth trying to visit the **Huajia Zhi Cun** (Painters Village) at Hualongqiao. Established as a sort of collective in the 1950s, it has produced some interesting work. The **Sichuan Yi Shu Guan** (Sichuan Fine Arts Institute) in Huangjiaoping is also of interest.

Despite the fact that Chongqing is a port, it has even less in the way of nightlife than most other cities in China; beyond the karaoke parlors there is little.

Outdoor Activities and Sports

Chongqing is a hilly city—you will not find any bicycles for rent. Swimmers can try the pool at the Holiday Inn (☞ *above*), which also has a health club.

Shopping

The principal shopping area is in the vicinity of the Liberation Monument in the center of town. It is a lively area of shops and restaurants where you might pick up examples of lacquer ware, embroidery, and bamboo ware, as well as teas and local produce.

Side Trip from Chongqing

North of the city on **Jinyun Shan** (Jinyun Mountain) are some pretty views and a smattering of pavilions from the Ming and Qing periods. Three house imposing statues of the Giant Buddha, the Amitabha Buddha, and the famous general of the Three Kingdoms Period, Guan Yu, respectively. The park also has a set of **hot springs**, where it is possible to bathe in the 30°C (86°F) water, either in a swimming pool or in the privacy of cubicles with their own baths. ⊠ *Jinyun Shan, 50 km (30 mi) north of city.* 🎫 *Y5.* 🕒 *Daily 8:30–6.*

Dazu

★ **46**   *160 km (100 mi) northwest of Chongqing.*

At Dazu, a group of Buddhist cave sculptures that rival the ones at Datong, Dunhuang, and Luoyang is worth the effort to get to if you have the opportunity. The sculptures contain unusual domestic detail in addition to the purely religious work. There are two major sites at Dazu—Beishan and Baodingshan. Work at the caves began in the 9th century AD and continued for more than 250 years.

Baodingshan, where the carvings were completed according to a plan, is the more interesting site. Here you will find visions of Hell reminiscent of similar scenes from Medieval Europe; the Wheel of Life; and a magnificent 100-ft reclining Buddha. ⊠ *16km (10 mi) east of Dazu town; take minibus.* 🎫 *Y40.* 🕒 *Daily 8–5.*

Sichuan A to Z

Arriving and Departing

BY BOAT

You can either arrive in or depart from **Chongqing** by boat in order to pass through the Three Gorges of the Yangzi. "Tourist" boats offer air-conditioned cabins; ordinary passenger steamers used by most Chinese offer minimal comforts. Tickets can be arranged through CITS (☞ *below*).

It is possible to get to **Leshan** by boat from Chongqing.

BY BUS

There are three bus stations in **Chengdu** (⊠ main, off Xinnan Lu south of river; near railway station in north of the city; Ximen, off Shihui Jie in western part of city—serves Jiuzhaigou). There are frequent buses to Emeishan and Leshan and also to Chongqing. There is also service to Dazu and Kangding.

There are buses to **Leshan** from Chengdu (5 hours) and from Emeishan, only 31 km (19 mi) distant.

With one or two exceptions, arriving and departing **Chongqing** by bus is the least practical method because of its hilly location. However, the new bus station (✉ off Nanqu Lu in southwest of city, close to railway station) offers regular departures for Chengdu, Dazu (3 hours), Yibin, and Zigong. The **Kangfulai Passenger Transport Company** (✉ 223 Renmin Lu) runs air-conditioned buses to Chengdu, Dazu, Yibin, and Zigong.

BY PLANE
Chengdu has flights to and from all the major cities of China, including Guangzhou, Chongqing, Guilin, Guiyang, Hong Kong, Kunming, Lhasa (if you can get a visa), Nanking, and Shanghai. A bus service links the CAAC office (Renmin Lu) and the airport, which is 20 km (12 mi) west of the city.

There are daily or regular flights between **Chongqing** and all the major cities in China. The airport lies 25 km (16 mi) north of the city and CAAC (✉ Zhongshan Sanlu) runs shuttle buses between it and their office.

BY TRAIN
There are services from **Chengdu** to Chongqing (12 hours), Dazu (7 hours—trains stop at Youtingpu, about 30 km/19 mi from Dazu), Emeishan, Kunming (23 hours), and Xi'an. It is also possible to get to Guangzhou, Lanzhou, Beijing, Shanghai, and Ürümqi.

The train station in **Chongqing** (✉ off Nanqu Lu) is in the southwest of the city. Direct trains serve Guangzhou, Chengdu (11 hours), Kunming, Nanning, Beijing, Shanghai (2 days), and Xi'an.

Getting Around
There is comprehensive bus service around **Chengdu,** particularly along the main artery, Renmin Lu. Bus maps are available from CITS and the bus and railway stations.

Taxis are available outside the major hotels.

Because of its hilly nature, **Chongqing** has almost no bicycles and the buses are slow. The best way to get around is by taxis, which can be hailed in the street.

Contacts and Resources
CAR RENTAL
Self-drive cars cannot be hired in either **Chengdu** or **Chongqing,** but cars with drivers can be hired through CITS.

CONSULATE
United States (4 Lingshiguan Lu, Chengdu, ☎ 028/558–3992).

CURRENCY EXCHANGE
In **Chengdu,** money can be exchanged in the major hotels and at the Bank of China (✉ Renmin Nanlu, Renmin Donglu). You can change money in **Chongqing** in the hotels or at the Bank of China (Minzu Lu).

EMERGENCIES
Chengdu: PSB (✉ Wenwu Lu, part of Xinhua Donglu; 40 Wenmiaohou Lu). **Chongqing:** PSB (✉ Linjiang Lu).

VISITOR INFORMATION AND GUIDED TOURS
Chengdu: CITS (✉ Renmin Nanlu). Tibet Tourism Office (✉ 10 Renmin Beilu). **Chongqing:** CITS (✉ Renmin Hotel, Renmin Lu).

GANSU

Gansu is the long, narrow corridor province that links central China with the desert regions of the northwest. It has an area of 451,000 sq km (174,130 sq mi) and a population of 23 million, among whom are Hui, Mongol, Kazak, and Tibetan peoples.

Despite its length, the geography of Gansu is not as variable as you might expect. It has an average altitude of between 3,300 and 9,900 ft, with the highest peak reaching 19,000 ft. Although the eastern part of the province is a loess area through which flows the Yellow River, and much of the south and west is steppe land, the character of what was for long the poorest province in China is essentially rugged and barren. The climate is of the continental kind, with cold and dry winters and hot summers.

Historically Gansu has been a vital conduit between China and the western world, the beginning of the Silk Road along which merchants for centuries transported their wares until shifting power and maritime trade rendered it obsolete. Gansu first became part of China proper during the Qin dynasty (221–206 BC). Buddhism made its way into China through here as early as the first century BC. The oasis towns that were strung along the desert areas became the provision stations for pilgrim and merchant alike—as the merchants made their fortunes from silk and other luxuries, so the oasis towns became significant shrines.

Gansu became the edge of China, the last link with the Middle Kingdom and therefore with civilization. The Great Wall, the most solid representation of ancient Chinese opinion of the outside world, passed through Gansu to the great fortress at Jiayuguan, beyond which lay Dunhuang, and then perdition. And yet Gansu has never been the most compliant of provinces. The influence of Islam was considerable in Gansu. In the 19th century rebellions here were savagely put down. The decline of the Silk Road brought terrible suffering and poverty, from which the area has only very recently begun to recover as tourism boosts the local economy.

There has also been considerable industrial and mining expansion. Agriculture is important, but conditions are difficult, despite irrigation. Horses are reared here as well as sheep, pigs, and cattle; wheat, melons, cotton, and millet are important crops.

Ganzu's highlights include Dunhuang, side trips from Lanzhou, and Jiayuguan.

Dunhuang

47 *240 km (150 mi) northwest of Jiayuguan; 900 km (560 mi) northwest of Lanzhou; 1,800 km (1,100 mi) west of Beijing.*

Dunhuang, a small oasis town, is in many ways the most important destination on the Silk Road. Here you can see an extraordinary array of wall paintings in caves that form part of Mogao Ku, a massive and ancient Buddhist shrine just outside the town.

Dunhuang (Blazing Beacon) was made a prefecture in 117 BC, during the Han dynasty. At that time it was at the very edge of the Chinese empire, on the fringes of barbarian desert country. Its earthen "beacons" were a sort of extension of the Great Wall, used for sending signals between garrisons.

Buddhism entered China via the Silk Road at about the same time as Christianity was beginning to take hold in the Western world. As Dunhuang was the point of entry to the Chinese world, it was not long before a temple was established here. By AD 366 the first caves were being carved at the Mogao oasis. The carving continued until the 10th century; the works were subsequently left undisturbed for nearly a thousand years until adventurers from Europe and America began to plunder the area at the end of the 19th century. The paintings' and carvings' miraculous state of preservation is due to the dry desert conditions.

Many of the paintings were made using techniques that permitted the reproduction of endless, almost identical images. While such techniques were widely used, there were also plenty of opportunities for the input of eminent painters who came from afar, particularly during the period of peak creativity during the Tang dynasty.

Dunhuang remained an important center until the end of the Tang dynasty, after which the spread of Islam and the temporary decline of Chinese influence in the region brought an end to centuries of creative energy. Indeed, Dunhuang became known as Shazhou (Sand Town). But the paintings survived; even more astounding was the discovery by Sir Aurel Stein in 1907 of one cave, seemingly deliberately sealed by departing priests at this period of decline, that revealed a stack of early Buddhist sutras, including one written on paper and dated AD 406, many centuries before paper was in use elsewhere, and one of the earliest printed documents, the Diamond Sutra of 868, which is now in the British Museum. The discovered papers did not concern only religious matters; there were also many items relating to local administration. The Chinese took umbrage at the European Sinologists' depredations, with the result that there are next to no documents to be seen at Dunhuang. The murals and statuary are all still in place. Modern Dunhuang is still a dusty frontier town, although it has begun to change with the influx of tourists.

The surprisingly (given that Dunhuang is one of the prime historical sites in China) small **Dunhuang Xian Bowuguan** (Dunhuang Museum) has three sections. One deals with the items discovered in Cave 17 by Stein and his French colleague Pelliot. Another deals more in the practical items found in the region (silks and old textiles), while the third is devoted to sacrificial and funeral items. ✉ *Dong Dajie.* 💰 *Y10.* ☉ *Daily 9–12 and 2:30–5.*

South of Dunhuang, the oasis gives way to desert. Here, among the dunes, is **Yueyaquan** (Crescent Moon Lake), a crescent-shape pool of water that by some freak of the prevailing winds never silts up. The dunes, or *mingshashan* (singing sands), themselves are the main attraction. There are only a few, but they are huge. The climb to the summit is hard work but worth it for the views, particularly at sunset. Camel rides are available; the latest innovation is paragliding. ✉ *Take Dingzi Lu, continue about 5 km (3 mi) south of town.*

★ The Buddhist **Mogao Ku** (Mogao Grottoes) lie southeast of Dunhuang. At least 40 caves are open to the public (a flashlight is a useful item for your visit), the earliest dating from the Northern Wei period (AD 386–534: caves 246, 257, 259); followed by the Western Wei (AD 535–556: cave 249); the Sui (AD 581–618: caves 244, 420, 427); Tang (AD 618–907: caves 17, 96, 130, 148, 172, 209, 323, 329); and Five Dynasties (AD 907–960: caves 16, 98). These are just a selection of some of the most interesting—there are plenty of others. Which caves are open on a given day depends on the local authorities. If a particular cave is closed, you can request that it be opened; whether that will happen is another matter.

In creating the paintings, the artists plastered the surfaces of the cave walls first with mud and then with layers of dung, straw or hair, and still more mud. The final surface was prepared with china clay, and mineral paints were applied (to both walls and statues), the colors of which have changed as they oxidized over succeeding centuries. The monks who worshiped in these grottoes lived in small, unadorned caves in the cliff to the right of the painted caves as you look at them. The whole of the cliff was used up eventually, so several of the caves have been over-painted in later dynasties. ✉ *In direction of airport, 25 km (15 mi) southeast of town; take minibus.* 🎫 *Y80.* ☉ *Daily 8:30–11:30 and 2:30–4.*

Standing in the desert southwest of Dunhuang, **Dunhuang Gucheng** (Old City Movie Set) is the set left behind by the makers of the 1987 film *Dunhuang,* a collaborative effort between the Chinese and Japanese. It is a complete town as it may have looked at the time of the Song dynasty, with mud city walls more than 5 meters (16 ft) high. ✉ *20 km (12 mi) southwest of Dunhuang; take minibus from Dingzu Lu.* 🎫 *Y10.* ☉ *Daily.*

Southwest of Dunhuang are the **Xi Qianfodong** (Western Thousand Buddha Caves). Considered to be of less importance than those at Mogao, they do nonetheless contain paintings from the Northern Wei and Tang dynasties. ✉ *30 km (18 mi) southwest of town; take taxi.* ☉ *Daily 9–12 and 2–5.*

Dining and Lodging

The best food is probably to be found in the Dunhuang Hotel (Dunhuang Binguan) or the International Hotel. Enterprising individuals have started a few small restaurants around Dingzi Lu.

$$–$$$ ✕🏨 **Dunhuang Binguan.** The first hotel built to cater for the influx of foreigners after 1976, it provides reasonable comfort and facilities in a good location. ✉ *Dong Dajie,* ☎ *09473/22415,* ℻ *09473/22773. 60 rooms. Restaurant. MC, V.*

Nightlife and the Arts

Unless you can find a bar of some description along the main street, there is no nightlife in Dunhuang beyond the occasional performance of song or dance. Check with CITS (☞ *below*).

Outdoor Activities and Sports

The only option is to hire a bicycle, which is easily done from the several outlets around town.

Shopping

The sparse shopping is best done in your hotel. You may find some art work, and the translucent cups from Jiayuguan.

Side Trips from Dunhuang

The **Yumen** (Jade Gate) was the old starting point for caravans leaving China to head across the desert on the Silk Road's northern oasis route. The remains of Han beacons and the ruins of a Han town are haunting reminders of past times. ✉ *100 km (60 mi) northwest of Dunhuang.*

The **Yang Guan** (South Pass) began the southern oasis routes on the Silk Road. Here, too, the ruins in the desert have a haunting quality. ✉ *75 km (47 mi) southwest of Dunhuang.*

★ ⑱ The impressive old fort of **Jiayuguan,** 5 km (3 mi) outside the town of the same name, and some 280 km (175 mi) southeast of Dunhuang, stands in a dramatic spot guarding a pass between two mountain ranges. It was the westernmost point of the Great Wall during the Ming dynasty. The fort was built in 1372 with 33-ft-high walls and a circumference of well over 770 yds. In the vicinity of Jiayuguan you can visit parts of the Great Wall, rock paintings from the Warring States period, and tombs in the desert. ✉ *Gansu Lu.*

Lanzhou

900 km (560 mi) southeast of Dunhuang; 1,600 km (1,000 mi) south-east of Ürümqi; 450 km (280 mi) northwest of Xian; 1,150 km (710 mi) southwest of Beijing.

The capital of Gansu Province has a population of 1.5 million. Built on the banks of the Yellow River, Lanzhou spreads along a fairly narrow valley sandwiched between steep hills at a height of 5,000 ft. A city with a long history, it has been nearly ruined by rampant industrialization.

Founded over 2,000 years ago, it was already a substantial town by the middle of the Han dynasty, soon developing into one of the most important centers along the Silk Road. Following the decline of the Han, Lanzhou became capital of a series of tribal kingdoms. Its location, at the base of a narrow gorge through which all traffic heading northwest or southeast must pass, has continued to render it a town of considerable importance. After 1949 Lanzhou became the second-largest city in the region as the Chinese government turned it into an important industrial center. It is also a key railway junction linking the northwest with central, north, and northeastern China.

49 Wuquan Shan (Five Spring Mountain), named for the springs at its foot in the south of the city, rises to 5,250 ft. On it, from **Wuquanshan Gongyuan** (Five Spring Park) you can see wonderful views. In the park are a number of monuments. The **Chongqing** (Temple of Reverent Solemnity) dates from 1372. In it is a large bronze bell, 10 ft high and weighing 5 tons, that dates from 1202. A 16-ft bronze Buddha is from 1370. Behind Wuquanshan is Lanshan, reaching over 6,600 ft and accessible by chair lift. ⊠ *Take bus No. 8 from Jiuquan Lu in town centre.* 🎫 *Y5.* ⊗ *Daily 8–6.*

★ **50** The old-fashioned but nonetheless excellent **Sheng Bowuguan** (Provincial Museum) has some fine exhibits on three floors. Part of the museum's collection has been brought together under the heading "Cultural Relics of the Silk Road" to include 7,000-year-old pottery from the Dadiwan culture decorated with what are probably the earliest pictograms. There are also examples of decorated wares that prove there was contact between China and Rome at least as far back as 2,200 years ago, as well as early textiles and magnificent tri-colored Tang porcelain. The most famous item is the bronze "Flying Horse," found in an Eastern Han tomb at Wuwei. With its hoof delicately poised on the wings of a bird, its image is much used as a symbol of the area. Among the other items on display are collections of early Yangshao pottery, Zhou bronzes, fossil remains, and a Han dynasty tomb reconstruction. ⊠ *Xijin Xi Lu.* 🎫 *Y25.* ⊗ *Mon.–Fri., 9–12 and 2:30–5:30.*

51 The **Baitashan Gongyuan** (Mountain of the White Pagoda Park), a public park laid out in 1958, covers the slopes on the Yellow River's north bank close to the ancient crossing place used by merchants and travelers for centuries. The park is named for the white dagoba that was built at the summit of the hill during the Yuan dynasty (1271–1368) and rebuilt in the 15th century. In the pleasant park are some interesting pavilions and terraces. ⊠ *Zhongshan qiao.* 🎫 *Y2.* ⊗ *Daily 7–7.*

Dining and Lodging

The best restaurants in Lanzhou are in the hotels, particularly the Lanzhou Legend ($$$) and the Ningwozhuang Guesthouse. Otherwise, try Lanzhou's "Food Street" along Nongmin Xiang, lined with a variety of small restaurants behind the Jinsheng Hotel.

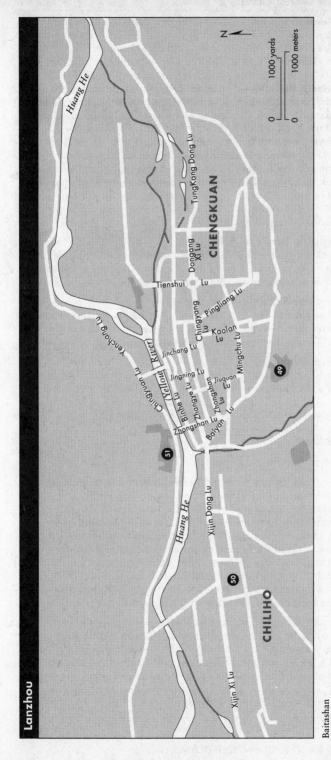

Lanzhou

Huang He

TungKang Dong Lu

CHENGKUAN

Dongang Xi Lu

Tienshui — Lu

Chingyang Lu

Pingliang Lu

Kaolan Lu

Yellow River

Jinchang Lu

Jingning Lu

Mingchu Lu

Jiuquan Lu

Binhe Lu

Zhangye Lu

Zhongshan Lu

Zhongshan Lu

Zhongshan Lu

Baiyan

Yenchang Lu

Chingyuan Lu

49

51

Huang He

Xijin Dong Lu

50

CHILIHO

Xijin Xi Lu

N

1000 yards

1000 meters

0

0

Baitashan
Gongyuan, **51**
Sheng Bowuguan, **50**
Wuquanshan
Gongyuan, **49**

$$$$ ⊞ **Lanzhou Legend.** The best of the new hotels, plush, expensive and unequivocally of an international standard, it has service to match the high prices. The rooms are well furnished. ⊠ *Panxuan Xi Lu, 730000,* ☎ *0931/888–2876,* FAX *0931/888–7876. 362 rooms, 22 suites. 3 restaurants, bar, air-conditioning, shops, business services. AE, MC, V.*

$$$ ⊞ **Huaiyi Hotel.** This refurbished hotel, originally built in the 1950s as the Friendship Hotel, is in the western part of the city opposite the provincial museum. The spacious rooms have been tastefully modernized. ⊠ *Xijin Xi Lu, 730000,* ☎ *0931/841–6321,* FAX *0931/841–6322. 150 rooms. 2 restaurants, bar, air-conditioning, shops. AE, MC, V.*

$$$ ⊞ **Ningwozhuang Guesthouse.** Before tourism took off, the best ac-
★   commodation in cities like Lanzhou was villa-style guesthouses set in beautiful gardens. This is one of those—old-fashioned but comfortable and secluded. Rooms are solidly furnished. ⊠ *Tianshui Lu, 730000,* ☎ *0931/841–6221,* FAX *0931/841–6223. 70 rooms. Restaurant, bar, air-conditioning, shops. MC, V.*

Nightlife and the Arts

Check with CITS (☞ *below*) or your hotel for what is available at the theater in the form of opera or acrobatics. There are a few karaoke parlors scattered around the center; the best bars are in the hotels.

Outdoor Activities and Sports

Unless you can find a bicycle to rent, the only possibility is to **walk** where you can on the hills surrounding Lanzhou. You can **jog** in the public parks, but they tend to be arranged in terraces up the hillside.

Shopping

Lanzhou is not a major shopping center, although you can find the same sort of crafts and souvenirs that you find all over China. However, carpets continue to be produced in Gansu, a province which is also noted for its brass ware.

Bingling Si Shiku

❺❷   *90 km (56 mi) west of Lanzhou.*

★   Near Yongjing, the **Thousand Buddha Temple and Caves,** filled with Buddhist wall paintings and statuary, are definitely worth the trip. They can be reached by bus or by a combination of bus and boat. The caves were first decorated in AD 420 though, as at Dunhuang, the best work was executed during the later dynasties, in this case the Song and Ming. It became a Tibetan monastery during the Yuan (Mongolian) dynasty. There are 34 caves, more than 700 statues (of which the largest is 89 ft high), and several hundred square yards of wall painting. A dam constructed in the late 1960s enables visitors to reach the caves by boat when the water level is high enough.

The site is magnificent, the caves having been carved out of the local porous stone cliffs on the northern bank of the Yellow River over a length of about 2 km (1 mi). The finest wall paintings are in Caves 3, 4, 11, 70, 82, and 114, where the largest Buddha (Maitreya, the Buddha of the Future) sits. ⊠ *CITS or private travel agent; or take local bus from Lanzhou's West bus station and then ferry.* ☑ *Travel and entrance, about Y150.* ☉ *Daily 8–5 (subject to water level).*

Xiahe

❺❸   *250 km (155 mi) southwest of Lanzhou.*

This is one of the most interesting excursions possible from Lanzhou.
★   In Xiahe, the **Laboleng Si** (Labrang Monastery) is among the most important of Tibetan institutions, a member of the Gelupka (Yellow Hat)

sect, and one of two great Lamaist temples outside Tibet (the other being the Ta'er Monastery in Qinghai). Founded in 1710, it once had as many as 4,000 monks, a number now much depleted. It is still a place of tremendous atmosphere, attracting large numbers of pilgrims who come swathed in their distinctive Tibetan costume.

Although partly gutted by fire in 1985, the temple looks much as it always has. It is divided into a number of institutes of learning (including law and medicine), as well as the **Gongtang baota** (Gongtang Pagoda), the **Qi Dao Tang** (Prayer Hall), and the **Ser Kung Si** (Golden Temple).

Apart from the religious festivals that take place during the Tibetan New Year and the month after, when pilgrims and nomads congregate by the thousand, a daily highlight (a feature of most Tibetan monasteries) is the gathering of monks outside for religious debate, when fine points of theology are discussed in the liveliest fashion. ✉ *1.5 km/1 mi west of long-distance bus station.* 🎫 *free; guided tours, about Y25.* 🕐 *Daily 8–7.*

Maijishan Shiku

54 *300 km (186 mi) southeast of Lanzhou.*

★ The **Maijishan Grottoes** (Corn Rick Mountain caves), among the four largest Buddhist caves in China, are best reached by taking the train to Tianshui and then a bus the remaining 30 km (19 mi). The site is a dramatic one, a steep outcrop of rock into which have been carved several dozen grottoes dating from the 4th century onward. The caves, between 100 and 230 ft above the foot of the mountain, are reached by wooden steps. An earthquake in the 8th century split the site in two, east and west. The western caves are the best preserved, having been left untouched since the Song dynasty. Early Western influences are seen in some of the work (for example in cave 100), while the finest work is generally considered to be that in cave 133, which has engravings dating from the Wei and Zhou periods. The eastern caves are less well preserved, but there is fine work here, too, most notably in caves 4, 7, 13, 102 and 191. A flashlight is essential; you should either join a tour or obtain a private guide in order to get the best out of the visit. ✉ *Due east of Tianshui; take minibus from train station.* 🎫 *Y31.* 🕐 *Daily 8–6.*

Gansu A to Z

Arriving and Departing

BY BUS

The long-distance bus station in **Dunhuang** (✉ Dingzi Lu) is in the south of the town. There are buses to Jiayuguan (7 hours) and other local destinations.

From **Lanzhou**'s East Bus Station (✉ Pingliang Lu) there are buses to Yinchuan (Ningxia) and Xian. From the West Bus Station (✉ Xijin Xilu) in the northwest part of the city, buses go to Jiayuguan and Xiahe.

BY PLANE

Dunhuang's airport is 13 km (8 mi) east of town. The CAAC office (✉ Dong Dajie) is in town. There are flights to Jiayuguan, Lanzhou, Beijing and Xian.

Lanzhou is linked by air to all of China's major destinations, including Guangzhou, Chengdu, Chongqing, Dunhuang, Hong Kong, Kunming, Beijing, Ürümqi, and Xian. The CAAC office (✉ Donggang Xilu) is close to the Lanzhou Hotel, from which several buses a day go to the airport. The airport is about 90 km (55 mi) north of the city.

BY TRAIN

The railway station serving **Dunhuang** is at Liuyuan, 130 km (80 mi) away. There are trains to Jiayuguan (6 hours) and Lanzhou (18 hours), as well as Chengdu, Beijing, Shanghai, Turfan, Ürümqi, and Xian. Buses leave regularly for Dunhuang (about 2 hours).

Lanzhou's train station is fairly central, toward the southwest of the city. Trains go northwest to Liuyuan (for Dunhuang), Turfan, and Ürümqi, and southeast to Xian, Chengdu, Beijing, and Shanghai.

Getting Around

For getting around in the immediate vicinity of **Dunhuang,** you should rent a bicycle. The alternative is to use minibuses, which leave when full for various places around and outside town. In **Lanzhou** taxis are readily available. Otherwise, the public bus system is good—maps can be had from CITS, from the railway and bus stations, and from bookshops.

Contacts and Resources

CAR RENTAL

It is not possible to rent self-drive cars in **Lanzhou** or **Dunhuang.** Cars with drivers can be rented through CITS.

CURRENCY EXCHANGE

In **Dunhuang** money can be changed in the major hotels or at the Bank of China (✉ Xi Daji). In **Lanzhou** money can be changed in the hotels or at the Bank of China (✉ Pingliang Lu).

EMERGENCIES

Dunhuang: PSB (✉ Xi Dajie). **Lanzhou:** PSB (✉ 38 Qingyang Lu).

VISITOR INFORMATION AND GUIDED TOURS

Dunhuang: CITS (✉ International Hotel or Dunhuang Hotel). **Lanzhou:** CITS (✉ Nongmin Xiang).

NINGXIA

The smallest of China's five autonomous regions is something of an enigma. With an area of 66,400 sq km (25,600 sq mi) and a population of a mere 5 million, it is surrounded by the provinces of Gansu and Shaanxi and the huge autonomous region of Inner Mongolia. It has a Hui (Muslim Han) population of just over a million, and significant numbers of Mongols and Manchurians.

An arid area traditionally inhabited by nomads, most of Ningxia is high, flat plateau, the rest being lowland plain along which the Yellow River flows, providing water for the network of canals that have been in use for many hundreds of years.

The climate of Ningxia is continental, characterized by very cold winters and warm summers that are rarely excessively hot. The annual rainfall is less than 8 inches.

With the exception of a couple of comparatively brief periods, the area has been under Chinese control since the Qin dynasty. Throughout this time Ningxia was part of various administrative regions until 1928, when it became a province. In 1958 the government turned the area into the Autonomous Region of Ningxia Huizu Zizhiqu.

Ningxia's capital, Yinchuan, is quite lively. The remoter areas offer an insight into the less-known aspects of Chinese life—ancient water wheels are still used for irrigation, and in some areas leather rafts continue in use.

Yinchuan

55 *350 km (220 mi) northeast of Lanzhou; 540 km (335 mi) southwest of Hohhot; 850 km (530 mi) southwest of Beijing.*

Once the capital of the 11th-century Western Xia dynasty, Yinchuan stands amid a network of irrigation canals thought to have been in constant use since the Han dynasty. It is close to the Yellow River to the east and the Helanshan mountains to the west. The town is actually divided in two, the New Town, where the railway station is located, and the Old Town, about 5 km (3 mi) southwest.

All ancient Chinese cities had their drum and bell towers, which were used to announce the beginning and end of the hours of curfew. Yinchuan's **Gulou** (Drum Tower), having survived the destructive phases of Chinese history, stands on the main street not far from the post office. ⊠ *Gulou Jie.* ☎ *Y3.* ⊙ *Daily 9–12 and 2:30–5.*

Close to the Drum Tower, the **Yuhuang Ge** (Yuhuang Pavilion) is a restored 400-year-old house containing a small museum with two mummified bodies removed from tombs found close to Yinchuan. ⊠ *Yuhuang Jie.* ☎ *Y3.* ⊙ *Daily 9–12 and 2:30–5.*

In the northern suburbs is a spot where there has been a pagoda since the 5th century. The current **Haibao** (Treasure) or **Haibao Ta** (North Pagoda) dates from 1771, when it replaced an earlier one destroyed by an earthquake in 1739. Forming part of a temple complex, it has 11 stories and is 177 ft high, offering fine views across the town to the Yellow River. Although actually rectangular in shape, it has niches placed to create the illusion that it is 12-sided. ⊠ *Jinning Jie.* ☎ *Y3.* ⊙ *Daily 9–12 and 2:30–5.*

In a former monastery, **Ningxia Bowuguan** (Ningxia Museum) houses materials illustrating the Hui Muslim culture and items dating back to the Western Xia and the Zhou dynasties. Of the monastery itself the most obvious remaining part is the pagoda, known as the **Xi Ta** (West Pagoda), with its glazed-tile roof. It was built in about 1050 during the Western Xia dynasty. ⊠ *Jinning Jie.* ☎ *Y20.* ⊙ *Daily 8–5.*

The modern, busy **Nanguan Si** (Nanguan Mosque) is interesting for its purely Arabian style of architecture. ⊠ *Just south of Nanguancheng Lu.* ⊙ *Daily 8–12 and 2–5.*

The restored **Nanmen** (South Gate), built in classical Chinese style, is all that remains of the city wall. ⊠ *Zhongshan Jie.*

Dining and Lodging

You can eat tolerably well in the hotel restaurants, but Yinchuan is a place where you are almost better off eating from the smaller places on the street, such as the Hanmin Canting, the Yinbinlou, or the Huanying. The local food is essentially Islamic, with lamb and beef dishes, dumplings and pastries, and blended teas.

$$–$$$ ☷ **Ningxia Hotel.** One of the better hotels in town, with modern furnishings, it has good facilities. ⊠ *3 Gongyuan Jie,* ☎ *0951/545131. 2 restaurants, air conditioning, shops. AE, MC, V.*

$$ ☷ **Ningfeng Hotel.** This good, new hotel has comfortable rooms and reasonable facilities. ⊠ *Jiefang Dongjie,* ☎ *0951/628898. Restaurant, bar, massage, shop. MC, V.*

Nightlife and the Arts

Check with CITS (☞ *below*) for occasional performances of local song and dance.

Outdoor Activities and Sports
Try the Zhongshan Park for **jogging.**

Shopping
Ningxia is well-known for its **carpets.** You can also buy the local **teas.** The main shopping street is Gulou Lu.

Side Trips from Yinchuan
Lying at the foot of the Helan Mountains 20 km (12 mi) west of Yinchuan, the **Xixia Wangling** (Western Xia Tombs) have a certain dramatic appeal. Because this dynasty (1038–1227), which lasted 189 years before being exterminated by the Mongols, was not included in the imperial annals, little is known about many aspects of it, including the occupants of the tombs. The founder of the dynasty, Li Yuanhao, is believed to have built 72 tombs for himself and his relatives. ⊠ *Take bus 17 from bus station to terminus and then taxi.* ☎ *Y10.* ☉ *Daily 8–5.*

⑤⑦ The village of **Gunzhongkou** is at a pass in the Helan Mountains some 15 km (9 mi) northwest of Yinchuan. It is a pleasant retreat from the heat in the summer and a good base for walks along the hills. Just to the north of the village are the **Baisikou Shuang Ta** (Baisikou Twin Pagodas), two pagodas that are not quite twins—the eastern one has 13 stories, the western 12—and yet they appear to be of the same height. ⊠ *Hire car or arrange tour with CITS.* ☎ *Y10.* ☉ *Daily 8–12 and 2–5.*

Qingtonxia Zhen
⑤⑧ *80 km (50 mi) south of Yinchuan.*

Qingtonxia Zhen (Old Qingtonxia) is an ancient town that contains one of the most famous sites in Ningxia, that of a group of **108 Dagobas.** Aligned in 12 rows forming a giant triangle on the shores of a lake in the middle of arid semi-desert, these Tibetan-style sacred pagodas were built in the Yuan (Mongol) dynasty. Nobody knows why they were placed here, unless it was in celebration of some great event or as thanks for the water of the lake; but they are an impressive sight nonetheless.

Zhongwei
⑤⑨ *70 km (43 mi) southwest of Yinchuan.*

A market town on the fringes of the desert, Zhongwei is close to the Yellow River. Here the **Gao Si** (Gao Temple) was originally built in the 15th century and has been rebuilt and expanded several times since. Essentially constructed of wood, it was designed to cater to all the main religions and beliefs of China, with chapels and shrines to Buddhism, Confucianism, and Taoism.

Outside the town it is possible to see relics of ancient ways of life. As in other parts of China, irrigation techniques using water wheels have been in operation since the Han dynasty. They have become obsolete, but examples can still be found close to the village of **Xiaheye** on the far side of the Yellow River. With luck you will be able to make the crossing using a leather raft, made from sheep or cow skin wrapped around a wooden frame, of a type that was used to transport goods over distances of up to 2,000 km (1,240 mi).

Tongxin
⑥⓪ *80 km (50 mi) southeast of Zhongwei; 160 km (100 mi) south of Yinchuan.*

This Hui town is well known for its **Qingzhen Dasi** (Great Mosque), which dates from the Ming dynasty and is the largest in Ningxia. Of wooden construction, it has a traditional Chinese basic design adorned with intricate Islamic fretwork. ✉ *Several km south of Tongxin bus station.* ☎ *Y5.* ◷ *Daily 8–12 and 2:30–5.*

Guyuan

⑥ *500 km (300 mi) south of Yinchuan.*

About 50 km (30 mi) northwest of Guyuan, at **Xumishan,** is a set of Buddhist grottoes. The 132 grottoes with their shrines and statuary date back some 1,400 years. Some of the statues reach 62 ft. Much of the art work, despite neglect, is in a surprisingly good state of preservation. ✉ *Hire minibus in Guyuan.*

Ningxia A to Z

Arriving and Departing

BY BUS

From **Yinchuan,** buses go to Lanzhou and Xian as well as to the other towns in the province. The bus station (✉ Zhongshan Jie) is in the south of town.

BY PLANE

Direct flights link **Yinchuan** with Guangzhou, Beijing, Shanghai, and Xi'an. The CAAC office (✉ Minzu Beijie) provides buses to the airport, which is 12 km (7 mi) outside the city.

BY TRAIN

Direct trains link **Yinchuan** with Datong, Hohhot, Lanzhou, and Beijing. The station is in the New City section.

Getting Around

Buses and minibuses around **Yinchuan** also link the old and new towns. Taxis are widely available.

Contacts and Resources

CAR RENTAL

Self-drive cars cannot be rented in **Yinchuan.** Cars with drivers can be rented through CITS (☞ *below*).

CURRENCY EXCHANGE

In **Yinchuan** you can change money in the major hotels or in the Bank of China on Jiefang Lu.

EMERGENCIES

PSB (✉ Jiefang Xijie, Yinchuan).

VISITOR INFORMATION AND GUIDED TOURS

CITS (✉ 150 Jiefang Xijie, Yinchuan).

10 The Mongolias

The Mongolias are a land of horses, sheep, and vast grasslands. Nights in yurts and days on horseback reveal the romance of the traditional nomadic culture. Most areas of the two Mongolias—the Inner Mongolia Autonomous Region of China and Mongolia, an independent country that used to be known as Outer Mongolia—are sparsely populated and little affected by the 20th century. From Hohhot and Ulaan Baatar, you can explore the legacy of Genghis Khan and the spiritual influence of Lamaism, a Tibetan branch of Buddhism with shamanist elements.

THE MONGOL EMPIRE once covered most of the Eurasian land mass, stretching from the Yellow Sea in the east to Budapest in the west and from Lake Baikal in the north to Burma in the south. Genghis Khan united the fierce tribes of the Mongolian steppes in the early 13th century. In Mongolia, Karakorum, the site of Genghis Khan's capital, attracts many visitors, though little remains of the original city.

By Bill Smith

Under Kublai Khan, Genghis Khan's grandson, the Mongols conquered most of China, establishing their Yuan dynasty capital in present-day Beijing in 1272. The Great Mongol Empire disintegrated after the Yuan dynasty collapsed in 1368.

In the 17th century, the Chinese Qing (Manchu) dynasty took control of Mongolia, separating it into Inner Mongolia and Outer Mongolia. The overthrow of the Qing in 1911 brought independence to Outer Mongolia, which became first a theocracy under a Living Buddha, then, from 1921, a communist state under strong Soviet influence. Inner Mongolia was occupied by the Japanese from 1931 to 1945. It became the Inner Mongolia Autonomous Region of China in 1947.

Both Mongolias were closed to the outside world for many years, leaving today's visitors with huge areas of countryside largely untouched by Western culture. Soviet and Chinese communism increased the differences between the two areas.

There are 2.4 million ethnic Mongolians in Mongolia and about 3 million in Inner Mongolia. In its cities and southern farming areas, Inner Mongolia is dominated by Han Chinese, who constitute 85% of the region's overall population of 20 million. Mongolia has more wildlife and is less developed, and the grasslands are generally less populated than those of Inner Mongolia. Its residents have a more traditional lifestyle.

The influx of Chinese people has made Chinese the main language of Inner Mongolia, although Mongolian and Chinese characters are found together on all official notices and street signs. In Mongolia, on the other hand, Cyrillic (Russian) script has largely replaced Mongolian characters, but everyone speaks Mongolian.

Wool, leather, meat, and dairy industries continue to form the mainstay of the rural economies. Inner Mongolia has large agriculture, coal, iron, and steel industries; Mongolia has some copper and coal.

In both Mongolias you can stay in *yurts* (circular felt tents called *gers* in Mongolian—the word yurt is of Turkic origin), eat mutton, drink *airag* (fermented mare's milk), and watch riders use *urgas* (pole-mounted lassos) to round up horses, sheep, goats, cows, and camels. Mid-summer Naadam fairs feature spectacular competitions in archery, Mongolian wrestling, and horseracing.

Pleasures and Pastimes

Dining

Mongolians traditionally subsist on mutton, beef, noodles, and dairy produce. The main specialties are "finger" mutton (hunks of boiled or roast mutton eaten from the bone), milk tea, cheese, and airag. Less common in the cities, this fare is usually served at grassland yurt sites. Mutton hotpot, thin slivers of meat plunged fondue-style into a circular trough of boiling water surrounding a miniature stove, is popular in Inner Mongolia. Served with bean curd, starch noodles, vegetables, and chili and sesame sauces, hotpot is ideal for a group to share. Two of Ulaan Baatar's most popular snacks are *buuz* (mutton-filled dumplings like Chinese *baozi*) and *horshoo* (mutton fritters). Hohhot and Ulaan Baatar have good Chinese, Korean, Muslim, and Russian-style dishes.

CATEGORY	PRICE*
$$$$	over $30
$$$	$20–$30
$$	$10–$20
$	under $10

Prices are per person for a 3-course meal, including tax but not tip.

Grassland Tours

The spectacle of a Mongolian rider chasing galloping horses across a lush green plain or steppe is something most visitors to the Mongolias want to see. Because of the great distances involved and lack of settlements and public transport, it is best to travel by minibus, jeep, horse or plane. Unless you are competent in Chinese or Mongolian, an English-speaking guide is essential. If you book a tour, check the itinerary carefully and make sure the price is agreed in advance. Horseback tours, day rides, or shorter trips all give an idea of how suited the small, sturdy Mongolian horse is to the high plains. There is no better way to see the grasslands, though long rides can be hard for novices. On some tours, yurts are carried with the group, providing a taste of real nomadic life. All tours of more than one day need to be booked in advance. Camel tours of desert areas can also be arranged. Many different tours are possible in both Mongolias, incorporating varied terrains—steppes, mountains, deserts, forests—ancient ruins, temples, traditional crafts, animal husbandry, and wildlife or hunting.

Lodging

Retiring to the comfort of a yurt after watching a vivid sunset over boundless grassland, you can open the roof-flap to reveal the clear, starry night sky. Yurts are warm but do not have toilets or showers; the latter are usually provided in separate blocks of circular wood, concrete, or tin buildings styled to blend with the yurts. Hohhot and Ulaan Baatar both have high-quality hotels. Rural hotels can be very basic, with few facilities in the rooms other than TV sets, so yurt accommodation is generally more enjoyable. Some tourist yurts in Inner Mongolia have smaller tin "yurts" attached, housing en suite toilets and washbasins. When entering a yurt, especially one belonging to a Mongolian family, avoid treading on the wooden threshold; many local people believe this represents stepping on the neck of the yurt's owner.

CATEGORY	PRICE*
$$$$	over $100
$$$	$50–$100
$$	$25–$50
$	under $25

Prices are for a double room at high season, including tax.

Naadam Fairs

Naadams were the annual gatherings of nomadic Mongol tribes for shamanist worship, trade, and courtship, along with archery, wrestling, equestrian, and drinking competitions. Although a few fairs are now staged mainly for tourists, the games and pageants are taken seriously by local people. Events, including evening song and dance performances, usually take place in a wide arena encircled by yurts, market stalls, and food tents. Naadam fairs start around July 11 in Mongolia and in late July or mid-August in Inner Mongolia. Exact dates vary each year.

Temples

With greater religious freedom in China and Mongolia, many Buddhist temples have revived. Temples in the Mongolias follow Lamaism, a Tibetan branch of Buddhism. Two of the best temples for Lamaist art, music, monks, and local devotees are Gandan Khiid in Ulaan Baatar and Xiletuzhao in Hohhot.

Exploring the Mongolias

Inner Mongolia is a crescent-shape region that stretches 2,400 km (1,500 mi) along China's northern and northeastern borders. The Gobi Desert straddles much of Inner Mongolia's long border with Mongolia to the north. Both Mongolias are landlocked, with Siberia to the north and east and China's Xinjiang Province and Kazakhstan to the west.

Officially, you must book a tour to obtain the separate visa required for travel to Mongolia, but hotels and small tour operators in Mongolia can issue confirmation of bookings for visa purposes. If you have sufficient time, it is worth mounting this extra hurdle. Border and visa regulations require foreign tourists to travel in both directions between Mongolia and China, including Inner Mongolia, by rail or air. So travel back and forth between rural areas of the two Mongolias is not possible. Customs and immigration formalities are conducted on the train, and there is a two-hour wait at the border while the bogies on the carriages are changed.

Access to grassland areas is easier to arrange for independent travelers in Inner Mongolia, especially if you are already in China. Hohhot is the main base for grassland tours. Many other cities in Inner Mongolia, including Baotou, the region's largest city, are full of 20th-century, multi-story concrete buildings and have little to attract tourists.

Great Itineraries

Numbers in the margin correspond to points of interest on the Mongolias, Hohhot, and Ulaan Baatar maps.

IF YOU HAVE 2–3 DAYS

Go to ▣ **Hohhot** to explore its temples, mosque, and old town. The next day travel 87 km (54 mi) to ▣ **Xilamuren** to tour the grassland, visit *aobaos* (hilltop shrines) and local people, and to try horse riding and Mongolian wrestling. Stay one or two nights in a yurt. Return to **Hohhot.**

IF YOU HAVE 5–6 DAYS

Take the train from Beijing to ▣ **Ulaan Baatar.** Spend the first day visiting the city, temples, and museums. Travel 360 km (223 mi) west across the grasslands by 4-wheel drive vehicle to ▣ **Karakorum.** Stay two or three nights in a yurt, spending the days touring the grassland, horse riding, visiting historical sites and Mongolian families, and watching horses, sheep, camels, and wildlife. Drive back to **Ulaan Baatar,** stopping to climb sand dunes. If time permits, add a day trip from **Ulaan Baatar** to **Manzshir Monastery.** Fly back to Beijing.

IF YOU HAVE 10 DAYS

Starting from **Hohhot,** drive 250 km (155 mi) to ▣ **Ejin Horo Qi,** site of the **Genghis Khan Mausoleum.** Stay in a yurt and return the next day to **Hohhot.** Spend a day visiting Hohhot's temples and old town. Drive 170 km (105 mi) to ▣ **Gegentala** for a taste of life in the grasslands; spend two nights in a yurt. Return to **Hohhot** before flying direct or via Beijing to ▣ **Ulaan Baatar.** Then visit ▣ **Karakorum** and **Manzshir Monastery** as above. Return from **Ulaan Baatar** to Beijing by train.

When to Tour the Mongolias

The dry, continental climate means May to September is the best time for temperatures and for greenery. Because most of the Mongolias occupy a plateau at an altitude of 3,250–4,900 ft, even summer evenings can be cool. Severe cold and wind make winter touring impractical.

Naadam fairs take place from mid-July to mid-August. As a result, this is peak tourist season when some tours and hotels may be fully booked.

For photographing temples or grassland scenery, early mornings and late afternoons give the best light. Ulaan Baatar's Gandan Khiid temple is especially interesting to visit when the monks and local worshippers arrive for early morning prayers.

INNER MONGOLIA

Inner Mongolia is a vast, crescent-shape area stretching across northern China. Its lengthy borders with Soviet-influenced Mongolia and eastern Siberia made it a sensitive region during the Sino-Soviet Cold War. Around 70% of Inner Mongolia is arid grassland sparsely occupied by herds of sheep, horses, goats, cattle, and camels. Open steppe complete with yurts, horses, and sheep can be readily found in most parts of the region. Short trips, even day trips, are possible from Hohhot.

Hohhot

410 km (254 mi) west of Beijing.

In Chinese-dominated Hohhot the only yurts you see are in restaurants and entertainment centers, though some of the modern white-tiled office blocks are topped by yurt-style domes. Hohhot, meaning Blue City in Mongolian, is the capital of the Inner Mongolia Autonomous Region. Hui Muslims are the most prominent minority in a population of 700,000. Mongolian, Ewenki, Daur, and other minorities live in the city but rarely wear traditional dress and are relatively invisible among the large Han Chinese majority.

A trip to Inner Mongolia must include a visit to the grassland, and Hohhot is the region's main base for grassland tours. The city itself has several interesting diversions, notably Xiletuzhao temple and the Inner Mongolia Museum.

Despite the rarity of real horses and camels, other than those used as photographers' props in Xinhua Square, the city's equine symbols are outlasting newer icons. Hohhot's Mao statue, which stood outside the railway station as many others still do across China, was felled in 1987 and replaced by a rearing silver horse. Another sign of China's reforms are the thriving mosques and Lamaist temples of Hohhot's old town.

Xinhua Square, dominated by a group of galloping horses, is fascinating in the early morning, when it is full of people practicing *qi gong* (breathing exercise), playing badminton, basketball, volleyball, or soccer, or just promenading. In the evening, children's rides and trampolines, food stalls, an English corner, fairy lights, photographers, and skateboarders take over. On the streets are kebab sellers, cigarette and yogurt stands, cyclists, yellow taxis, and tricycle carts carrying wardrobes and refrigerators. Restaurants are busy every evening and, as in Ulaan Baatar, many men drink heavily.

Do you know how to build a yurt or a birch-bark teepee? Or that Mongolians once used boomerangs to hunt hares, marmots, and other small

 animals from horseback? If not, visit the **Nei Mengu Bowuguan** (Inner Mongolia Museum), which also houses Asia's largest dinosaur skeleton. One section is devoted to fossilized remains of dinosaurs and other ancient animals. It includes a full mammoth skeleton, as well as a giant brontosaurus skeleton in its own room. On the other side of the museum are exhibitions of minority cultures, with items such as Mongolian bows and saddles and a yurt, a Daur shaman's costume, and an Oroqen teepee. On the second floor you can learn about the history of Inner Mongolia, though captions are only in Chinese and Mongolian. ⊠ *1 Xinhua Dajie,* ☎ *0471/664924.* ⊡ *Y8.* ☉ *Daily 10–5.*

★ ❷ Bare wood and subtle, faded shades of green and red make **Xiletuzhao Si** (Xiletuzhao Temple) more of a genuine throwback to the past than many of China's more garishly renovated temples. The current buildings date from the 19th century. It is an active temple where you can see monks and devotees in prayer and hear Lamaist chants and stirring, dissonant music played on traditional instruments. While the flapping turquoise, white, gold, and red prayer flags send their offerings skyward, you can visit the Tibetan Buddhist version of hell. Caverns under the temple contain graphic depictions of the various tortures awaiting sinners. ⊠ *Off Danan Lu.* ⊡ *Y3.* ☉ *Daily 9–5.*

❸ First built in the Ming dynasty, **Dazhao Si** (Dazhao Temple) is also known as Silver Buddha Temple after a statue of the Sakyamuni Buddha cast mainly from silver. The temple was rebuilt in 1640, and many of the existing structures and artifacts date from then. The 400-year-old Silver Buddha is housed in one of China's best-preserved Ming dynasty wooden halls. Close to the altar is an exquisite pair of carved dragon pillars. By the door to the hall are two cast iron lions, with cast iron incense burners in the courtyard outside. The temple also possesses some of China's most precious Tibetan scriptures. ⊠ *Off Danan Lu.* ⊡ *Y4.* ☉ *Daily 9–5.*

❹ Chinese architecture fails to disguise the **Qingzhen Dasi** (Great Mosque), readily identified by its crescent-topped minaret and Arabic script, and the bearded Muslim men who congregate outside. The mosque dates mainly from the Qing dynasty and is surrounded by *hutongs* (alleys) of Hui Muslim houses, shops, and restaurants. ⊠ *Tongdao Lu.* ⊡ *Free.* ☉ *Daily 10–4, except during prayer.*

❺ The Indian-style **Wuta Si** (Five Pagoda Temple) was built in 1733 as a stupa for relics. In the Qing dynasty the temple was part of a larger complex, but little else remains. Its square base tapers upward to five glazed pagodas decorated with Buddhas and Mongolian, Tibetan, and Sanskrit script. Behind the pagoda is a carved screen that includes a Mongolian astronomical chart. ⊠ *Gongyuan Dong Dajie.* ⊡ *Y2.* ☉ *Daily 9–5.*

❻ The **Zhaojun Mu** (Tomb of Wang Zhaojun), dedicated to a Han dynasty imperial concubine given as an appeasement to the chief of the Southern Hun tribe in 33 BC, is one of nine such tombs spread across Inner Mongolia. Wang Zhaojun's sacrifice, which led to 60 years of peace, is celebrated throughout the region. A pyramid-shape burial mound 98 ft high is topped by a small pavilion. There are good views over the surrounding park and farmland. One story says that only a pair of Wang Zhaojun's shoes was buried here. ⊠ *9 km (6 mi) south of Hohhot.* ⊡ *Y10.* ☉ *Daily 10–4.*

❼ Few tourists visit the **Baita** (White Pagoda), but it is one of the finest brick pagodas in northern China. The 138-ft-high octagonal structure has seven stories coated in chalk. Restored in the 1990s, the pagoda was first constructed in the Liao dynasty (916–1125) and was once a destination for pilgrims from all over Asia. Easy to get to by taxi or by a bicycle ride through flat farmland, the pagoda grounds make a

The Mongolias

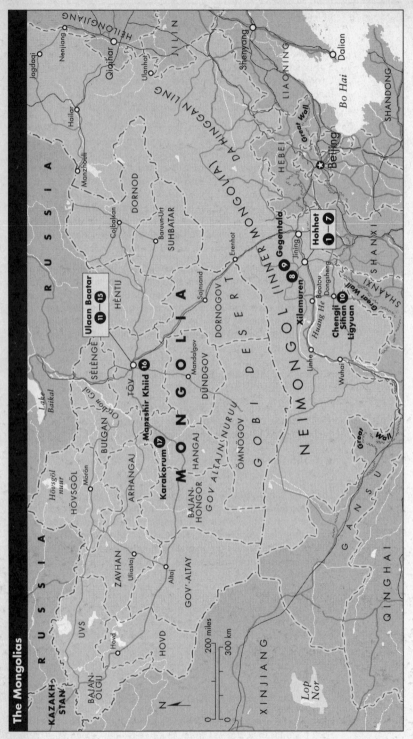

RUSSIA

KAZAKH-STAN

BAJAN-ÖLGIJ

UVS

HÖVSGÖL

ZAVHAN

GOV'-ALTAJ

HOVD

Uliastoj

Altaj

Hovd

Mörön

Lake Baikal

Hövsgöl nuur

BULGAN

Orhon Gol

ARHANGAJ

SELENGE

TÖV

Manzshir Khiid 17

Karakorum 17

HANGAJ

BAJAN-HONGOR

GOV' ALTAJ

ALTAJN NURUU

ÖMNÖGOV'

GOBI DESERT

DUNDGOV'

MANDALGOV'

Mandalgov'

DORNOGOV'

Sajnsand

HENTIJ

Ulaan Baatar 11—15

MONGOLIA

Baruun-Urt

SUHBATAR

Cojbalsan

DORNOD

Ulanhot

Manzhouli

Hailar

Jagdaqi

Nenjiang

Qiqihar

HEILONGJIANG

JILIN

DA HINGGANLING

NEI MONGOL (INNER MONGOL)

Erenhot

Xilamuren 8

Gegentala 9

Hohhot 1—7

Jining

Huang He

Linhe

Baotou

Dongsheng

Chengji Sihan 10

Ligyuan

Wuhai

Wuhai

Great Wall

Great Wall

Shenyang

LIAONING

Dalian

Bo Hai

SHANDONG

HEBEI

Beijing

SHANXI

SHAANXI

GANSU

QINGHAI

XINJIANG

Lop Nor

N

0   200 miles

0   300 km

good picnic spot. ⊠ *16 km (10 mi) east of Hohhot.* ☞ *Y5.* ☉ *Daily 9:30–5.*

Dining and Lodging

Hohhot's main specialty, Mongolian hotpot, is traditionally a group meal eaten from a large communal pot. Restaurants, other than those in the two leading hotels, do not usually have English-speaking staff or English menus. Casual, neat dress is acceptable.

$$ ✕ **Hanguo Shaokau** (Korean Barbecue Restaurant). Tastefully deco-
★ rated rooms seat single parties of up to 10. The lower walls have wood-effect panels, the upper are covered with white wallpaper. In the middle of each black rectangular table is a built-in gas grill on which a waitress, in traditional long black dress, barbecues tender chicken, beef, mutton, and vegetables. Pancakes, sauces, and lettuce accompany the grilled meat, and there is a wide selection of stir-fried dishes. The restaurant is immediately west of the Inner Mongolia Hotel, down a long driveway. ⊠ *Minority Village, Wulan Chabu Lu,* ☎ *0471/629–2288. AE, MC, V.*

$$ ✕ **Mao Lin Huoguo Cheng** (Mao Lin Hotpot City). A traditional Chi-
★ nese entrance, under a light-green, mock-tiled roof with upturned eaves, leads to pine-effect tables, a huge mirror, and ornamental pil-lars. A central area, where a chef fries and grills meat, divides the restau-rant into two large sections. In front of the chef is a beautifully presented selection of sauces, including red bean curd, sesame, chili, and coriander. Seafood, frogs legs, chicken, mutton, and starch noodles are among the choice of ingredients for the set-price individual hotpot. Self-ser-vice hot dishes include pancakes and *youmian* (buckwheat noodles). Mao Lin is opposite the Zhaojun Hotel. ⊠ *Xinhua Dajie,* ☎ *0471/ 696–6231. No credit cards.*

$$ ✕ **Tai Yang Huoguo Cheng** (Tai Yang Hotpot City). White lace curtains hide a large and lively restaurant specializing in individual combined hotpots and grills. Inside are white tablecloths and white walls with pictures of Mongolian scenes. You help yourself to whatever combi-nation of mutton, chicken, beef, noodles, bean curd, and vegetables you want to cook. A trolley service adds cold and stir-fried dishes. Tai Yang is close to the Hohhot railway station. ⊠ *Xilin Nan Lu,* ☎ *0471/628–1895. No credit cards. No toilet.*

$ ✕ **Yi Li Qing Zhen.** A blue front with Arabic script distinguishes this small, simple Muslim-run restaurant frequented mainly by locals. White plastic tablecloths, wooden stools, bare concrete floor, and white walls provide the backdrop to a typical selection of Hohhot dishes such as youmian, hotpot, and "finger" mutton (boiled and served on the bone). ⊠ *Dianying Yuan Lu. No credit cards. No toilet.*

$$$ ✕⊡ **Nei Menggu Fandian** (Inner Mongolia Hotel). A fountain and Mon-golian scenes on the walls greet visitors in a large, open lobby with a bar/coffee lounge at the center. The white and green tower block, with 20 floors, was the first hotel in Inner Mongolia to cater to foreign tourists and remains the most popular with tour groups. White and beige cur-tains and bedding, mahogany-colored furniture, and red carpets cre-ate a smart Western look for the guest rooms. Local dishes, such as roast mutton leg, are available in the Chinese-style restaurant. Mon-golian milk tea with millet and deep-fried steamed bread is an alter-native to the Western breakfast. ⊠ *Wulan Chabu Lu, 010010,* ☎ *0471/ 664233,* ℻ *0471/661479. 250 rooms. Restaurant, bar, dance club, travel services. AE, MC, V.*

$$$ ✕⊡ **Zhaojun Dajiudian** (Zhaojun Hotel). Beyond the sand-colored
★ tiles of the exterior, modern murals depicting Wang Zhaojun and grassland scenes, as well as a Genghis Khan tapestry rise above the re-

376

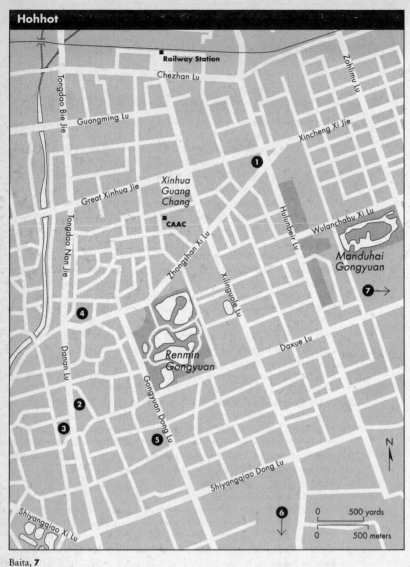

Hohhot

Baita, **7**
Dazhao Si, **3**
Nei Mengu
Bowuguan, **1**
Qingzhen Dasi, **4**
Wuta Si, **5**
Xiletuzhao Si, **2**
Zhaojun Mu, **6**

ception area of this Hong Kong joint venture. A staircase spirals down to a small shopping and games area. Opposite, a long corridor leads to a bank, travel center, and more shops. Beige carpets, some worn, cover the floors of the Western-style rooms. Pale yellow walls with framed prints contrast subtly with matching orange quilted bedspreads and patterned curtains. The hotel's main restaurant serves Cantonese dishes, such as sizzling "iron plate" beef and Singapore rice noodles, vegetable hotpot, snake, frog, and crab. ✉ *11 Xinhua Dajie, 010050,* ☎ *0471/ 662211,* FAX *0471/668825. 262 rooms, 15 suites. 3 restaurants, bar, beauty salon, dance club. AE, MC, V.*

$$ 🏨 **Yunzhong Dajiudian** (Yunzhong Hotel). Frequented by local business people, this busy hotel is in the middle of Hohhot's downtown shopping area. Guest rooms are a mixture of Chinese and Western styles. Plain fitted carpets, glass-topped coffee tables, and bedside lamps contrast with lacquer-look wooden chairs, desks, and cupboards. Yunzhong is behind the Minorities' Department Store. ✉ *Zhongshan Xilu, 010020,* ☎ *0471/696–8822. 130 rooms. Restaurant. No credit cards.*

$ 🏨 **Nei Menggu Tiwei Zhaodaisuo** (Inner Mongolia Sports Committee Hostel). A two-seater black vinyl settee, clocks, timetables, and local scenes fill the small lobby of this basic but clean hotel. Stairs lead to rooms furnished with functional wooden desks, beds, and chairs. The unpapered walls are painted white, cream, or pale green. The hostel is inside the Inner Mongolia Gymnasium complex. ✉ *Off Xinhua Dajie, 010050,* ☎ *0471/6967064. 90 rooms, 30 with bath/shower. Restaurant. No credit cards.*

$ 🏨 **Xincheng Binguan** (Xincheng Hotel). This 1950s Soviet-style former
★ sanatorium has long, red-carpeted corridors linking the various one-story buildings strung out in overgrown gardens. Hohhot's most popular hotel with backpackers, the Xincheng offers good value in relaxing surroundings, though in some rooms the plumbing and furniture are past their prime. ✉ *Hulunbei'er Nan Lu, 010010,* ☎ *0471/663322. 80 rooms, 60 with bath/shower. Restaurant, bicycles. No credit cards.*

Nightlife

The Zhaojun and Inner Mongolia hotels (☞ Nei Menggu Tiwei Zhaodaisuo, *above*) both have discos and karaoke bars. Many smaller hotels and restaurants offer similar entertainment.

Shopping

The **Minorities' Department Store** (✉ Hongshan Xi Lu) is the best place for cashmere clothing and souvenirs such as Mongolian robes and hats, hotpots, knives, and bowls. The large hotels sell similar items, but choice is more limited and prices higher. Dazhao and Xiletuzhao temples both have shops selling Buddhist and other souvenirs.

Side Trips to the Grassland

In Hohhot, tour companies compete fiercely for independent travelers to the grassland. Tourists are often assailed as soon as they arrive at the railway station. Some companies have stands at Beijing station. Most tours will give you a wonderful experience of the grassland, but it is best not to be rushed into booking. Check the itinerary and price carefully first, especially if you want to do some serious horseback riding. Standard packages usually allow little more than a few minutes on a horse. Major operators can all offer the following destinations.

❽ At **Xilamuren,** days are spent roaming across the carpet of green on foot or on horseback, trying Mongolian wrestling, and visiting local families, a temple, and aobaos. Nights involve folk songs and dancing, listening to the *matouqin* (horsehead fiddle), and eating roast mutton. Some people criticize tourist sites like Xilamuren as "not real," but the rolling grassland scenery, horses, sheep, temples, and aobaos are all authentic. Local people in this area mainly live in villages or isolated farmhouses, so yurts are restricted to seasonal use by herdspeople. Visitors can sleep in a traditionally constructed yurt with some modern facilities. If you're a first-time visitor to the grassland, you're likely to enjoy it, but if you've already been to Mongolia's grassland you may be disappointed. A Naadam fair is held for tourists in the second half of August. ⊠ *Rd. to Bayan Aobao, 87 km (55 mi) northwest of Hohhot.*

⑨ **Gegentala** offers scenery and activities similar to those at Xilamuren (☞ *above*) but is better during Naadam fair. Events at the tourist site merge with those of a larger fair nearby. Wrestling, archery, horseracing, and rodeo competitions at the tourist site are all attended enthusiastically by the locals. The men and women of the region are known for their wrestling skills; the Inner Mongolia regional team usually takes part in the local Naadam wrestling competitions. Over the hill to the south of the tourist camp, a tent-encircled Naadam arena is set up with food stalls, circus tents, and a stage for Mongolian song and dance. The lively fair lasts for about a week, immediately following the events at the tourist site. ⊠ *Siziwang Banner, 170 km (105 mi) northeast of Hohhot.*

⑩ A journey to the **Chengjisi Han Lingyuan** (Genghis Khan Mausoleum) involves crossing the Yellow River to the desert and grassland of the Ordos highland, where eventually you see the imposing navy-and-tan ceramic pleasure domes of the mausoleum. The tomb was built in 1954 and refurbished after the Cultural Revolution. In front of the central chamber stands a large golden censer between gigantic pikes topped with the nine-yak-tail banner of the Mongol armies. At the entrance, a white marble effigy of the all-conquering warrior greets visitors with a steely gaze. Rich murals decorate the interior walls, depicting the life story of Genghis Khan and details like the traditional Mongolian method of skinning a sheep. Mongolians place offerings of incense, liquor, cigarettes, sweets, and trinkets in front of a yellow silk yurt purported to contain the great khan's funeral bier. Near the mausoleum are re-constructions of a Yuan dynasty village and Genghis Khan's summer palace, built for a film set. From the buildings, you can see open grassland grazed by sheep, horses, goats, and camels. The Resonant Sand Gorge and Wudang Lamasery (Lamaist monastery) near Baotou can be combined with the mausoleum if you want a longer trip. ⊠ *25 km/15 mi from Ejin Horo Qi; 1½-hr bus ride from Dongsheng.* 🎫 *Y10.* ☉ *Daily 9–5.*

DINING AND LODGING

Xilamuren, Gegentala, and the Genghis Khan Mausoleum have yurt camps for tourists. All camps have dining halls and bathroom facilities, including basic showers that do not always have hot water, in communal blocks outside the yurts. The exception is Xilamuren, which has a tiny hut containing a toilet and washbasin attached to each yurt. At all sites, yurts are spaced out on concrete bases. They have traditional latticed frames with birch roof struts, wool felt walls covered with canvas, and thick rugs and low beds on the floor. Quilts, pillows, hot water flasks, and electric lights are standard. In summer, you are unlikely to be cold in a yurt, but at other times it is advisable to take warm clothes for sleeping in. Mutton dominates the set menus in the dining halls, accompanied by seasonal Chinese standards such as stir-fried chicken and chili, green beans, and egg-fried rice. Vegetarian and other special meals can be ordered.

Inner Mongolia A to Z

Arriving and Departing

BY BUS

Modern buses, many equipped with video, run daily to Datong and Beijing. These buses, some with sleepers, are quicker and cheaper than the train, but less comfortable. Hohhot Bus Station (✉ Chezhan Xi Lu) is right outside the railway station, to the west of the station square.

BY PLANE

Regular flights connect Hohhot with Beijing, Guangzhou, Xi'an, Shenzhen, Shanghai, and Wuhan. There are flights between Ulaan Baatar and Hohhot every Monday and Thursday. Hohhot Airport is 35 km (22 mi) east of the city center. Airport buses leave from the CAAC office (✉ Xilin Bei Lu, ☎ 0471/664103).

BY TRAIN

Daily trains run from Hohhot's train station (✉ Chezhan Jie) to Datong (6 hours), Yinchuan (12 hours), Lanzhou (22 hours), and Beijing (13 hours). If you already have a visa for Mongolia, you can travel to Ulaan Baatar via the rail junction of Jining or the border town of Erlianhot. Train tickets, especially sleepers, are hard to obtain; book through CITS, CTS, or hotel travel services.

Getting Around

BY BICYCLE

Hohhot is flat, and cycling is the best way to get around. Bicycles can be hired outside the Xincheng Hotel and from the Inner Mongolia Hotel. You will normally be asked to deposit some form of identification. If you are fit, you can ride to the White Pagoda or the Tomb of Wang Zhaojun. Traffic is much lighter than in Beijing and other larger cities, but take care. Watch the locals, then copy their (legal) moves.

BY BUS

City buses are crowded and relatively slow. They can be useful if you are just exploring the downtown shopping area.

BY TAXI

Taxis are plentiful and cheap. Average fares are Y10–Y20 within Hohhot. Taxis here have no meters, so try to agree on fares in advance.

Contacts and Resources

CURRENCY EXCHANGE

The main branch of the **Bank of China** (✉ Xinhua Dajie), opposite the Zhaojun Hotel, changes all major foreign-currency traveler's checks and cash. The Inner Mongolia and Zhaojun hotels both have foreign exchange services.

EMERGENCIES

There are no hospitals or clinics with English-speaking staff. If you need medical help, ask your hotel to assist. The large hotels have competent security staff and sometimes police officers on site.

TRAVEL AGENCIES

CITS (✉ outside railway station and in Zhaojun and Inner Mongolia hotels, Hohhot, ☎ 0471/624494; ✉ 28 Jianguomenwai Dajie, Beijing, ☎ 010/6515–8844). **CTS** (✉ in Inner Mongolia Hotel, Hohhot, ☎ 626774). **GMT** (✉ 2 Zhong Zhuan Dajie, ☎ /FAX 0471/452920). **Inner Mongolia Grassland Tour Travel Service** (✉ Dongfeng Dajie, ☎ /FAX 0471/492–4633).

In summer, CITS and CTS have stands inside the soft-seat waiting room of Beijing Railway Station. Other tour companies also have representatives at the station.

Little information is available other than tour company leaflets. Hotels and bookstores sell city maps in English and Chinese. The Foreign Languages Bookstore (✉ Xinhua Dajie) stocks an English-language guide to Inner Mongolia.

MONGOLIA

The independent nation of Mongolia, once known as Outer Mongolia, was a Soviet satellite state from the 1920s until the late 1980s. In the post-Communist era, Genghis Khan is once more a national hero, but Mongolia is still one of the world's least-developed countries. It is a paradise for wildlife enthusiasts, refugees from consumerism, and anyone who likes open spaces. The country is home to snow leopards, Gobi bears, wild camels, giant sheep, wolves, falcons, golden eagles, buzzards, marmots, deer, and gazelles. The horse and the yurt remain the mainstays of life on the steppes and even in Ulaan Baatar. Lamaism, a Tibetan form of Buddhism that incorporates many shamanistic elements, has resumed its position as the main religion.

Ulaan Baatar

850 km (527 mi) north of Hohhot, 1,120 km (694 mi) northwest of Beijing.

Grassland and forested hills surround Ulaan Baatar, adding to an atmosphere completely different from that of any Chinese city, including Hohhot. People often ride horses along the quiet streets, and cows graze outside the Mongolian parliament. *Dhels* (long robes tied at the waist and designed for horseback riding), knee-length boots, and felt or fur hats are common. Yurt neighborhoods outside the city center house up to 50% of the population.

In old Mongolia, even the capital was nomadic. It moved more than 20 times along the Orkhon, Selenge, and Tuul river valleys before an encampment was established in 1639 at Urga, now Ulaan Baatar. After several more moves and three changes of name, modern Ulaan Baatar was founded in 1924. It was named for the hero of the Mongolian Communist revolution, Sukhbaatar.

Today the city has a population of 600,000. As a result of the Communist government's promotion of population growth, 68% of Ulaan Baatar's residents are under 30. UNICEF is helping the city to deal with the problem of young children from the countryside begging on the main streets.

Open space, traditional Mongolian culture, and the Gandan Khiid monastery are the prime attractions. The Naadam fair, which begins around July 11, has the excitement of horseracing, archery and Mongolian wrestling.

★ ⑪ At **Gandan Khiid** (Gandan Monastery), golden roofs and Tibetan script; brilliant white walls; and red, green, and yellow painted woodwork provide a colorful backdrop as morning worshippers gather outside the temples. Monks dressed in red, gold, burgundy, violet, chocolate, and amber robes mingle with local people in suits, miniskirts, or traditional dhels. Built in 1840, Gandan Khiid is one of Mongolia's most important Lamaist, or Tibetan Buddhist, monasteries (or lamaseries). Most of the temple buildings were destroyed or ransacked in Mongolia's Stalinist purges and have been rebuilt.

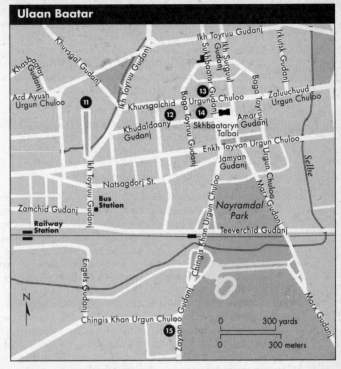

Sometimes shaven-headed young monks will offer to show visitors the prayer circuit around the temples, where Buddhists turn copper- and brass-covered prayer wheels, prostrate themselves on prayer stands in front of the monastery's central white stupa, and touch the sacred temple walls, prayer flag mast, and bronze censers. The current Dalai Lama, head of the Yellow Hat sect of Lamaism to which the monastery belongs, has visited several times. His picture is displayed in front of the altars. Photographs are not allowed inside the temples. ⊠ *Zanabazar Gudamj,* ☎ *01/360023.* 🎫 *Free.* ⊙ *Mon.–Sat. 9–11, Sun., 9–1.*

⑫ Buddhist art is the main treasure of the **Orligiin Muzei** (Fine Arts Museum). Tsam dancing masks, incense burners, and *tankas* (Tibetan-Mongolian Buddhist embroidered silk scroll pictures of deities) are the pick of the collection. Modern works are also displayed, many of them for sale. ⊠ *Khudaldaany Gudamj,* ☎ *01/327177.* 🎫 *Tg. 600.* ⊙ *Daily 10–5.*

⑬ Dinosaur skeletons and fossilized footprints enliven the **Baigaliin Muzei** (Museum of Natural History). In one of the world's richest countries for dinosaur fossils, many of them from the Gobi Desert area, the museum displays some of the best finds. Three floors of exhibits also show Mongolian steppe culture, wildlife, flora, and geology. ⊠ *Khuvsgalchid Urgun Chuloo and Sukhbaatar Gudamj,* ☎ *01/321716.* 🎫 *Tg. 300.* ⊙ *Tues.–Sun. 10–3, Mon. 10–4:30.*

⑭ Traditional decorations, ethnic clothing, jewelry, and handicrafts fill the **Tub Muzei** (Museum of Mongolian National History). A display section explains the rise of Genghis Khan and the Mongol empire. ⊠ *Khudaldaany Gudamj,* ☎ *01/325656.* 🎫 *Tg. 100.* ⊙ *Weekdays 10–4.30, Sat. 10–2.30; closed Sun.*

⑮ The **Bogd Khanny Vliin Ordon** (Winter Palace Museum of Bogd Khan) is the splendid Chinese-style residence of Bogd Khan, a Living Buddha who governed Ulaan Baatar's districts of monks, nobles, merchants, artisans, and Russians and Chinese until 1924. The museum is worth visiting just to walk around the courtyards and admire the faded glory of the architecture. Inside the palace's rooms are precious Buddhist artifacts and gorgeous ceremonial robes, plus Bogd Khan's winter coat made from 130 minks. ⊠ *Chingis Khan Urgun Chuloo,* ☎ *01/342195.* ▨ *Tg. 1,000; photo permit Tg. 1,800.* ☉ *Daily 10–5.*

Dining and Lodging

Many restaurants in Ulaan Baatar double as bars or discos, so they finish serving food between 6 and 9 PM. It is best to dine early, like the locals, as restaurants sometimes run out of food well before they close. Casual, neat dress is acceptable. Shorts and vest tops are rarely worn in Mongolia and are not advised.

$$$ ✕ **Buffet Restaurant Seoul.** This South Korean joint venture is inside
★ a park, in a white circular building reminiscent of the bridge of a ship. It serves set-price buffets only, with a wide choice of Korean, Japanese, Chinese, and western food. Korean chefs are on hand to pan-fry delicious marinated beef and sautéed potatoes. Eat as much as you like. There is a small bar area and a karaoke stage. Reservations are essential on summer weekends. ⊠ *Nayramdal Children's Park, across road from Bayan Gol Hotel,* ☎ *01/329709. AE, MC, V.*

$$ ✕ **Green Club.** "Indian food is our specialty," begins the extensive English menu of this compact restaurant with a bar in one corner. It is among the most popular social venues for foreign residents of Ulaan Baatar. In mutton-dominated Mongolia, the Green Club is a boon to vegetarian travelers. The Green Club Special is cheese and vegetable curry. Vegetarians can also try cauliflower curry, Indian snacks, and pizzas. Reservations are essential on Friday evenings. ⊠ *Rear of Peace and Friendship Centre, Enkh Tayvan Urgun Chuloo,* ☎ *01/311253. AE, MC, V.*

$ ✕ **Dulguun Tuya.** White plastic lounge chairs, neat tablecloths, and vases
★ of artificial flowers create a bar-meal atmosphere. The restaurant's standard fare includes beef with rice, cabbage, and fries; mutton and potato soup; and mutton burgers with fried egg, rice, and salad. In a pale green building behind the State Department Store it has a RESTAURANT, BAR, SHOP sign. ⊠ *Off Enkh Tayvan Urgun Chuloo,* ☎ *01/321404. No credit cards.*

$ ✕ **Elephant Restaurant.** Frequented by locals, this café-style restaurant has fast service, a limited range of Mongolian dishes, and functional decor with yellow tablecloths. From the English menu, the beef meal is a good-value filler—cubes of beef served with rice, red cabbage, fries, mashed potatoes, and gravy. It's 200 yds east of the State Department Store. ⊠ *Enkh Tayvan Urgun Chuloo. No credit cards.*

$ ✕ **Orgil Bar-Restaurant.** Western pop music classics and a relaxed
★ atmosphere attract mainly younger Mongolians to this popular small bar. Simple but tasty dishes from a limited menu include stir-fried shredded pancakes and mutton, and soup with cabbage, meatballs, and potatoes. The entrance is hidden behind kiosks on Enkh Tayvan Urgun Chuloo (Peace Ave.); the sign, in Cyrillic only, has pictures of a beer glass and a wok. ⊠ *Enkh Tayvan Urgun Chuloo and Ikh Toruu Gudamj. No English spoken. No credit cards.*

$ ✕ **Solo Café.** A part wood-paneled interior with a black, high-tech style bar, disco music, and a huge Cindy Crawford poster make this airy café a favorite with Ulaan Baatar's affluent younger crowd. Western dishes, such as beef steak and omelette, are the specialty. ⊠ *Khuvsgalchid Urgun Chuloo, opposite Victory Cinema. No credit cards.*

$$$$ ✕🏨 **Chinghis Khan Hotel.** A mirrored glass and red concrete tiered structure that backs onto a new conference center, the hotel has a huge foyer with a marble floor and glass walls. The Western-style rooms include a wooden desk, a lounge area, a minibar, IDD phone, and cable TV. A post office counter and a doctor are also available. On the fifth floor, a restaurant in the style of a giant yurt gives good views of the city and surrounding mountains while you dine. Dishes include carrot salad with cheese, caviar with lemon, borscht, spaghetti, and chicken breast with pineapple. ✉ *Khukh Tenger Gudamj, 49,* ☎ *01/313380,* 𝔽𝔸𝕏 *01/ 312788. 184 rooms. Restaurant, bar, exercise room, laundry service, travel services. AE, MC, V.*

$$$ ✕🏨 **Bayan Gol.** Each of the hotel's two towers has its own reception, but more services are housed in the north tower, nearer Sukhbaatar Square. Rooms have pristine decor and furnishings: cream walls and beige curtains and carpets. Many upper rooms have good views of Nayramdal Park or the mountains south of Ulaan Baatar. The hotel's main restaurant, flanked by the twin towers, has a good-value, four-course menu. Egg with caviar, cream of chicken soup, mutton goulash, and fruit salad is a typical selection. ✉ *Chinghis Khan Urgun Chuloo, 43,* ☎ *01/312255,* 𝔽𝔸𝕏 *01/326880. 209 rooms, 19 suites. 3 restaurants, 3 bars, beauty salon, business services, travel services. AE, DC, V.*

$$$ ✕🏨 **Flower Hotel.** Popular with Japanese tour groups, the hotel has standard rooms that use an understated blue-and-brown color scheme in carpets, curtains, bedding, and armchairs. There are floor lamps and subtly patterned white wallpaper. The hotel's Fuji Japanese restaurant offers chicken curry as well as ramen, sushi, and other Japanese standards. The Altai Restaurant has Western food such as beef with pineapple, fried fish, green salads, and potato salad. The large Chinese restaurant serves set-price buffets; get there early, as many dishes run out. ✉ *12 Khukh Tengerin Gudamj, 49,* ☎/𝔽𝔸𝕏 *01/358330. 200 rooms. 3 restaurants, sauna.*

$$$ ✕🏨 **Ulaan Baatar Hotel.** A plain, white concrete facade masks a small,
★ homey lobby with leather settees and red wool carpets leading up a double staircase. There is also a yurt reception room. All rooms have cable TV, IDD phone, minibar, and hair dryer. The first-floor restaurant serves both Mongolian and Western food and is popular with foreign travelers and expatriates. Meals include Mongolian dishes, Wiener schnitzel, and fried chicken. The room-service menu includes barbecued mutton and Mongolian milk tea. ✉ *Enkh Tayvan Urgun Chuloo, 46,* ☎ *01/320237. 150 rooms. 2 restaurants, beauty salon, sauna, billiards, business services. AE, DC, V.*

$$ 🏨 **Urge Hotel.** Just off Sukhbaatar Square in the heart of Ulaan Baatar, this small hotel on a quiet avenue occupies a whitewashed, four-story European-style house. Used mainly by Mongolians, the rooms have Chinese-style dark brown lacquered furniture, plain walls, and predominantly pale orange patterned curtains and bedding. ✉ *100 Khudaldaany Gudamj, 46,* ☎ *01/313772,* 𝔽𝔸𝕏 *01/312712. 15 rooms, 2 suites. Restaurant, bar, billiards, laundry service. AE, MC, V.*

$ 🏨 **Gegee.** In the middle of a housing estate 20 minutes' walk east of the city center, this hostel-style hotel is a current backpacker favorite. The rooms are converted flats, and some still have basic kitchen facilities. The functional, non-matching furniture and decor vary from room to room. There is an extra charge for showers. ✉ *Zalauuchuud Urgun Chuloo, 49, across from Flower Hotel, in five-story apartment block No. 10 (behind nine-story block No. 5);* ☎ *01/351438. 55 rooms without bath/shower. No credit cards.*

$ 🏨 **Mandukhai.** This Chinese-owned hotel has simply furnished, slightly
★ cramped rooms. The carpets in the corridors are worn, and other fa-

cilities, such as the showers and door locks, could benefit from maintenance, but the staff is friendly and the hotel offers good value. It is conveniently located but hidden behind apartment blocks on the north side of Peace Avenue, west of the State Department Store. ⊠ *Off Enkh Tayvan Urgun Chuloo, 42,* ☎ *01/322204. 65 rooms, 12 with bath/shower. 2 restaurants. No credit cards.*

Nightlife and the Arts

For traditional Mongolian song and dance, the main venue is the **Ulsyn Dramyn Teatr** (National Academic Drama Theater; ⊠ Chinghis Khan Urgun Chuloo and Natsagdorj Urgun Chuloo, ☎ 01/323490). The **Duur Bujgiin Balet Teatr** (State Opera and Ballet Theater; ⊠ Skhbaataryn Talbai/Sukhbaatar Sq., east side, ☎ 01/320357) performs Mongolian versions of classical ballets and operas.

Shopping

Knives, boots, traditional clothes, paintings of grassland scenes, and Buddhist art are among the items worth buying in Ulaan Baatar. Under Mongolian customs law, antiques must have an export certificate. Check that the shop can issue this before buying. The **Buriat Boot Factory** (⊠ Amar Gudamj, 2nd floor; in pink building next to Tuushin Hotel; entrance via external, covered stairway) hand-makes beautiful reindeer skin boots in the traditional style of the Buriat minority of northeastern Mongolia and Siberia. Kiosks outside the south and east gates of **Gandan Khiid** (⊠ Zanabazar Gudamj) stock incense burners, hand-painted Buddhas and *tankas* (painted cloth scrolls). The well-known local artist and newspaper cartoonist **Gulset** (⊠ Chinghis Khan Urgun Chuloo, small cabin in front of the Bayan Gol Hotel) sells watercolors, oils, copper teapots, brass Buddhas, tankas, and masks. Some of the paintings are his own work. The city's largest shop, the **Ikh Delgüür** (State Department Store; ⊠ Enkh Tayvan Urgun Chuloo, ☎ 01/324311), is good for leather boots, Mongolian dhels and headgear, and souvenirs, including Mongolian chess sets and miniature yurts. A large shop inside the gate of the Winter Palace Museum of Bogd Khan (⊠ Chingis Khan Urgun Chuloo, ☎ 01/342195; ☞ Bogd Khanny Vliin Ordon, *above*) has Mongolian teapots, knives, wool and cashmere, artwork, Buddhist items, and some antiques.

Manzshir Khiid

⑯ *46 km (29 mi) south of Ulaan Baatar.*

Manzshir Khiid is a unique combination of a ruined monastery, Mongolia's oldest nature reserve, and two small museums in a forested area among the Bogd Mountains. Founded at the site of a healing spring, the monastery still has one working temple. Late autumn Tsam mask dances, held to drive away evil spirits with some of the most fearsome faces you will ever see, reflect the shamanist roots of Tibetan Buddhism. Among the objects recovered from the lamasery is an enormous bronze cooking pot, cast in 1732, large enough to boil 10 sheep and 2 cows. Behind the temple, you can climb up to a hilltop shrine strewn with old money, much of it from Mongolia's communist era.

One museum, housed in a yurt, displays airag bags, butter churns, teapots, and traditional dress and furniture. The second has local flora and fauna, including stuffed deer, wolves, falcons, and other wildlife, and sculptures made from tree roots and dried plants. Nearby is a birchbark teepee. On the mountain slopes, you can ride horses or hike through deer forests. Manzshir is easily accessible on a day trip. If you want to stay overnight, there is yurt accommodation. ⊠ *Manazhir.* ✍

Monastery and museums Tg. 1,200; photo permit Tg. 1,800. ☉ May–Oct., daily 9–5.

Karakorum

⑰ *360 km (225 mi) southwest of Ulaan Baatar.*

Genghis Khan's 13th-century capital, Karakorum (Kharkhorin in Mongolian), was built on one of the ancient silk roads. Around the city's central fountain were canals and European-style architecture, with a thriving foreign merchants' sector. The area is Mongolia's richest historical site. After the demise of the Mongol empire the city was razed by the Chinese Ming dynasty. The new Karakorum is a small, modern town nearby.

In 1586 **Erdenezu Khiid** (Erdenezu Monastery) was built using the fallen stones of the city, leaving just a few tantalizing remains such as Turtle Rock, which marked one corner of the old city walls. Karakorum's main attraction and Mongolia's largest monastery, Erdenezu housed 1,000 monks in 60 temples at its height. It was closed and damaged during the Stalinist purges of the 1930s but now has seven active temples in the huge area inside its walls. Topped with 108 white stupas (bottle-shaped shrines), the walls are said to be a smaller replica of the original Karakorum city walls. The temples are a mixture of flat-roofed Tibetan style and Chinese-style wooden pillars, tiled roofs, and red walls. ⊠ *Outskirts of new Karakorum.* 🖃 *Tg. 1,800; photo permit Tg. 1,800 inside grounds, Tg. 6,000 inside temples. ☉ Daily 9–5.*

Accessible on day trips from Karakorum are the **ruins of an ancient Uighur Muslim kingdom,** several **Turkish monuments and inscriptions** dating back to the 8th and 9th centuries, and the **Orkhon waterfall,** legendary birthplace of the Mongolian people. The relics are interesting if unspectacular, but on the way to them you pass beautiful unspoiled grassland scenery with horsemen using their urgas, marmot hunters, camel herds, isolated yurts, falcons, and foxes. There are also wolves and snow leopards in the area, though you are unlikely to see them unless you go on a wildlife safari. Visits to local families and horse riding give you an even better idea of the traditional Mongolian way of life. You normally get to sample airag, cheese, and milk tea boiled on a dung-burning stove.

Dining and Lodging

$$ ✕ 🏔 **Karakorum Yurt Camp.** Set on open grassland within sight of old **★** and new Karakorum, the camp offers the chance to stay in a real yurt without having to rough it too much. The yurts are decorated in traditional style, with orange painted posts and roof slats, wool rugs on the floor, small but comfortable wooden beds, and a wood-burning stove that is kept going for you by attendants. Each yurt sleeps up to four people. Bathrooms and showers (not always hot) are in a separate block 100 yds away. A giant yurt makes an evocative dining room and venue for song and dance performances. The set meals include buuz, mutton stew, and other Mongolian standards. Vegetarian or other special dishes can be ordered. ⊠ *Karakorum. 12 yurts without bath/shower. Restaurant, horseback riding. No credit cards. Closed Nov.–Apr.*

Mongolia A to Z

Arriving and Departing

Although flying is much quicker, if you have time the 30-hour train journey from Beijing is worth making on one leg of your trip. On the way, you pass the Great Wall and open grassland scenery and meet mainly Mongolian, Russian, and Chinese fellow passengers. Both classes of sleeper offer ample comfort. At present, foreigners are not permitted to travel by bus between Inner Mongolia and Mongolia. Buses run up to the border on both sides, but there are no direct buses from Hohhot to Ulaan Baatar.

BY PLANE

The Mongolian airline, MIAT, and Air China run alternate-day Ulaan Baatar–Beijing flights. MIAT runs twice-weekly flights to Hohhot. There are also regular flights to and from Seoul, Osaka, Moscow, and Irkutsk. Buyant Uha Airport (☎ 008) charges a Tg. 4,704 departure tax. Aeroflot (☎ 01/20720), Air China (☎ 01/328838), Korean Airlines (☎ 01/311–1836), and MIAT (☎ 01/379968) have offices in Ulaan Baatar. In Beijing contact Air China (☎ 010/601–6667) or MIAT (☎ 010/6507–9727).

BY TRAIN

Mongolia has only one main railway line, the Beijing–Ulaan Baatar–Irkutsk section of the "Trans-Siberian" route. Trains run to and from Moscow and Beijing twice a week. Contact Ulaan Baatar Railway Authority (☎ 01/320332) or China International Travel Service, Beijing (☎ 010/6515–8844).

Getting Around

BY BUS

Several useful routes run along Peace Avenue and past Sukhbaatar Square, but buses can be crowded. Mongol Teever (☎ 01/326369), is the main operator. Regular buses run to Karakorum and Manzshir. The bus to Karakorum is much cheaper and slower than jeep travel and often provides more adventure.

BY TAXI

You can usually find a taxi quickly on the city's main streets. The standard rate is Tg. 180 per km (Tg. 110 per mi) for local and long-distance journeys. Try Jenko (☎ 01/332698), Hun (☎ 01/343251), Mongol (☎ 01/55322), or Zendemen (☎ 01/341795). Cars or 4-wheel drive vehicles with drivers can be hired for trips outside Ulaan Baatar. Drivers are unlikely to speak English, so you may need to hire a guide unless you book through a tour company.

Contacts and Resources

CURRENCY EXCHANGE

Major hotels all exchange U.S. dollars or traveler's checks. Most banks change only cash. The Trade and Development Bank (⊠ Khuldaany Jie, near Sukhbaatar Guangchang), accepts traveler's checks and credit cards (AE, MC, V).

EMBASSIES

United States (⊠ Ikh Toyruu Gudamj, ☎ 01/329095). **United Kingdom** (⊠ 18 Enkh Tayvan Urgun Chuloo, ☎ 01/327506).

EMERGENCIES

Police ☎ 102; Sukhbaatar district ☎ 01/3320341; Bayan Gol district ☎ 01/361734. **Hospitals:** Yonsei Friendship Hospital (☎ 01/310945). No. 2 Hospital (☎ 01/50295). Arono Dental Clinic (☎ 01/342609).

TELEPHONING

The country code for Mongolia is 976. Drop the initial 0 in the city code when phoning from outside Mongolia.

TRAVEL AGENCIES

In Mongolia's emerging tourism industry, at least 50 local operators are competing or co-operating with foreign tour companies. All offer tours, plane and train booking, and visa services.

Gana (✉ Box 1017, Ulaan Baatar 13, ☎ 01/367343). **Juulchin** (✉ Bayan Gol Hotel, Ulaan Baatar, ☎ 01/328428; ✉ Room 4015, International Hotel, Jianguomenwai, Beijing 10005, ☎ 010/6512–6688 ext. 4015). **Monkey Business** (✉ No. 1 Building, Yu Lin Li, Room 406, Youan-menwai, Beijing 100054, FAX 010/6329–2244, ext. 4406). **Stsoi** (✉ Door 25, Block 15, Sukhbaatar District, Ulaan Baatar, ☎ 01/328159).

VISAS

In China, the **Mongolian Embassy** (✉ 2 Xiushui Beidajie, Jain-guomenwai, Beijing, ☎ 010/6532–1203) issues visas seven days after application. You need an invitation letter or confirmation of hotel and/or tour booking.

VISITOR INFORMATION

Ulaan Baatar, a Survival Guide is a tourist publication with map and listings, produced each summer and sold by the main hotels. *The Mongol Messenger,* an English-language newspaper stocked by many kiosks and bookstalls along Enkh Tayvan (Peace) Urgun Chuloo and west of Sukhbaataryn Talbai, provides insights into contemporary life in Mongolia. The same shops also stock Mongolian phrasebooks.

11 Western China

Xinjiang, Qinghai

Can this really be China? The westernmost provinces constitute a different world, and indeed the borders have been in dispute throughout most of China's history. Western China in past centuries was Asia's most important trade route. The source of China's famous Huang He (Yellow River) is in the grasslands of eastern Qinghai. Both Qinghai and Xinjiang provinces are inhabited by large numbers of minority peoples; most of the Han Chinese are families of people who arrived after 1949 to help develop the outlying regions of the country.

By Jan
Alexander

QINGHAI SHARES A CULTURAL HISTORY with Tibet. Between 30% and 40% of the population are Tibetans, many of them semi-nomadic herders, and there are five so-called Tibetan Autonomous Prefectures. Close to half of Xinjiang's population are Uighurs, a Muslim Turkic people whose language and culture are closely related to those of their neighbors in the Central Asian republics.

Stretches of desert, rich with untapped oil reserves and other minerals, start in northwest Qinghai and continue on into Xinjiang, which was the hub of the fabled Silk Road that stretched from Chang'an, the ancient capital (now Xian), to the eastern shores of the Mediterranean. In the first century AD Buddhism came into China from India through what is now Kashgar. Islam also entered through Kashgar, in the 10th century, and spread through the western region for the next five centuries.

Today much of the western region is still remote. Ancient mosques and temples remain standing, some still in use, after centuries of wear and religious wars. Peasants pile their harvests onto carts pulled by donkeys and sell the goods in outdoor market stalls. There are vast snow-covered mountain ranges, forests that harbor wild yaks and the endangered snow leopard, deserts still best traversed on camelback, and lakes with water that is pure enough to drink.

Part of the dissension between the minority peoples who lay claim to the land and the Chinese is due to the Chinese government's efforts to bring in industry that will exploit the western region's many natural resources. The capital cities—Xining and Ürümqi—and even the small city of Yining in northwestern Xinjiang, are quickly catching up with modern China, with the attendant slapped-together buildings, traffic, and air pollution. However, the "wild west" of China, as many visitors like to call it, still has an exotic flavor that is deeply embedded in the lives of the long-term inhabitants.

Even in the cities, where many minority peoples have gone into business or professions, religion and tradition play crucial roles. Special festivals, ethnic music, traditional costumes, and indigenous cuisine, far from disappearing, have become a source of ethnic pride. Despite friction between the minority peoples and the Han Chinese, the gradual influx of outside visitors has given the government an incentive to encourage the practice of ethnic traditions instead of undermining them. Here is a world that is economically and spiritually far removed from China's rapidly industrializing provinces to the east, a paradise to travelers in search of the unspoiled and unfamiliar.

Pleasures and Pastimes

Dining

In Qinghai, the many Tibetan restaurants serve such traditional staples as yak butter tea, yak meat, and *stemba,* a dough made by combining yak butter, yak cheese, sugar, boiling water, and barley flour, and eaten with the fingers. Yak penis is a delicacy served when available.

Xinjiang's Uighur cuisine is a bit less exotic to the Western palate. Kabob stands grilling fresh lamb (the carcass is hanging over the grill) can be found in all the cities and small villages. Noodles, usually served with lamb and vegetables, are more common than rice in this part of China. Markets in Xinjiang sell a fresh-baked local bread, known as *nan,* and a variety of dried and fresh seasonal fruits. Look for Turpan grapes and Hami melon in summer, pomegranates and apples in the fall.

Restaurants in major cities serve Mongolian hotpot, normally in an all-you-can-eat buffet. The price is usually reasonable, and the buffet has ingredients to suit every palate: meat, seafood, chicken, bean curd, mushrooms, vegetables, and noodles. You pick the ingredients, boil them yourself in a chafing dish, and mix your own seasonings. You can make a satisfying meatless meal out of Mongolian hotpot; otherwise, it is difficult to stick to a vegetarian diet in western China. Traditional Chinese food is also available throughout the region.

Dress is casual everywhere except in the luxury hotel restaurants in Ürümqi. Unless otherwise indicated, reservations are not necessary.

CATEGORY	COST*
$$$	over $12
$$	$4–$12
$	under $4

Prices are per person for a standard meal, excluding drinks. Tipping is not necessary, although a 10% tip may be added in higher-priced restaurants. There is no sales tax.

Festivals

There are many ethnic festivals, especially during the summer, the high season for tourists. Traditional ethnic music and dancing take place, as well as special events, often including contests on horseback.

Dates for holidays based on the Muslim calendar vary slightly from year to year. The **Rozi Festival** (Feb.) ends the daytime fasts that are traditional in the month-long celebration of Ramadan, the Muslim new year. The Kazakh **Nawiriz Festival** (mid-Mar.) has special events on horseback—horse races, lamb-skin tussling, and contests in which young men chase young women on horseback. The **Korban Festival** (mid-Apr.; 70th day after the Rozi Festival on the Muslim calendar) is the Sacrifice Festival, to mark the time when Allah asked the prophet Abraham to sacrifice his son as a test of loyalty; every Muslim family slaughters a sheep and has a feast. The Mongolian **Naadam Fair** (July or Aug.) at Sayram Lake includes horse races, competitions in archery and wrestling, dancing, and music. At the height of the grape harvest season, the town of Turpan stages the **Grape Festival** (Aug.), with traditional Uighur music and dancing nightly around the city.

Lodging

Ürümqi has Xinjiang's only foreign-owned hotel, although there are other hotels in the city that are not far behind in terms of luxury and service.

Outside of Ürümqi, hotels in the western provinces are about two decades behind the rest of China. Most are fairly run-down, not as clean as westerners would like them to be, and subject to plumbing problems such as brown water, lack of hot water, or lack of any water. Even so, prices are no longer rock-bottom, unless you are willing to settle for a dorm room. The situation is gradually improving, however.

If you're staying in the mountains or near a lake between May and October, nomadic families may offer inexpensive accommodations in a yurt. There will be no plumbing but plenty of ambience. Expect to pay about Y20 per person per night, plus a few yuan extra for meals.

CATEGORY	COST*
$$$$	over $100
$$$	$70–$100
$$	$35–$70
$	under $35

Prices are for a standard double room with bath at peak season, unless otherwise stated.

Outdoor Adventures

This western region has the potential to be an athlete's paradise. CITS and a number of foreign travel outfitters now organize trips that involve trekking, mountain climbing, horseback riding in the lake areas, and riding camels through the desert. Some of the mountains have the potential to develop skiing trails, but there are no lifts as yet.

Exploring Western China

Great Itineraries

Western China is a long way from anywhere else, and most visitors like to spend two weeks at the very minimum. It's a pity to come this far and not see a range of sights, but even a few days can be a rewarding experience if you plan wisely.

Numbers in the margin correspond to points of interest on the Western China map.

IF YOU HAVE 3 DAYS

Day 1: Arrive in **Ürümqi**; visit the Xinjiang Autonomous Region Museum and Erdaoqiao Market. Day 2: Go to **Heavenly Lake** by bus or hired car. Ride around the lake on horseback and spend the night in a yurt. Day 3: Return to Ürümqi.

IF YOU HAVE 7 DAYS

On your first day in **Ürümqi,** visit the Xinjiang Autonomous Region Museum and Erdaoqiao Market. Go to **Turpan** the next day by bus or hired car; visit Jiaohe Ruins. On the third day visit the Flaming Mountains, Bezeklik Thousand Buddha Caves, Atsana Tombs, and Gaochang Ruins. Return to Ürümqi in the evening. Take a morning bus or hired car on the fourth day to **Heavenly Lake;** after a short hike around the lake, return in the afternoon and take the evening flight to **Kashgar.** Take a day to visit the Id Kah Mosque, the Kashgar Sunday Market, and the Tomb of Abakh Hoja. On day six, visit the Cave of the Three Immortals and the Mor Pagoda; return to Ürümqi on the evening flight. Leave Ürümqi on the seventh day.

IF YOU HAVE 15 OR MORE DAYS

Spend three to four days in **Xining,** starting with a visit to the Beishan Temple and a walking tour of the prison enterprises. On the second day, go to Qinghai Lake and Bird Island. The next day, go to the Ta'Er Monastery and the birthplace of the 14th Dalai Lama. On day four, fly to **Ürümqi.** Spend a day there visiting the museum and bazaar (☞ *above*). Go to **Heavenly Lake** the next day and spend the night. Spend three days in **Kashgar.** Take a day trip into the Pamir Mountains, via the Kharakoram Highway, and visit the local Kirghiz villages. Take a day trip to the Cave of the Three Immortals and the Mor Pagoda. Return to Ürümqi by plane or bus. Go to **Turpan.** Spend at least days 12 and 13 seeing the sights around Turpan—Jiaohe Ruins, Flaming Mountains, Bezeklik Thousand Buddha Caves, Atsana-Karakhoja Tombs, and Gaochang Ruins. Go next to ⏹ **Yining** and spend a day walking around the picturesque rural outskirts. Spend another day at Sayram Lake. If you have more time, look into an adventure trip (☞ *below*).

Adventure Trips

Many trips that take you hiking through mountains, horseback riding along Sayram Lake, bicycling through ancient Silk Road routes (you will have to bring your own bicycle), or seeing the Taklamakan Desert on camelback can be arranged through CITS (✉ 51 Xinjua Bei Lu, Ürümqi, Xinjiang 830002, ☎ 86/0991/282–1428, ☎ 0991/2810–0689) or Golden Bridge Travel (✉ Golden Bridge Hotel, 3–1 Tian Shan Lu, Ürümqi, 830002, ☎ 86/0991/282–6813, ☎ 0991/283–5767).

Most of these trips take off only in the high season—May to October. Prices vary according to the number of people in the group. Expect to spend approximately Y1,000 per person per day, including food, lodging, transport, and English-speaking guide.

15-DAY TRIP
Hike the snow-covered **Bogda Mountain** in the central Tian Shan (Heavenly Mountain) range, which has three peaks, the highest of which is 5½ km (3½ mi) above sea level. Hike down to the village of Da Ban Qian. From there a car picks you up and takes you to the Turpan basin, the hottest part of China. *July and Aug. only. Golden Bridge Travel.*

Ride by chartered bus from Ürümqi through the city of Korla to **Ruo-qiang county,** where you will see the huge nature reserve in the Altun Mountains. There are dozens of rare species of animals, including the Mongolian gazelle and the endangered snow leopard. *July to Oct. CITS Ürümqi.*

50-DAY TRIP
Take a camel trek from Dunhuang over Emin Pass along the ancient **Silk Road** route, across the Taklamakan Desert. The trip includes a visit to the ruins of Lou Lan, an ancient Silk Road trading center that mysteriously disappeared from records after several centuries. *Sept. to Oct. Golden Bridge Travel.*

When to Tour Western China
The best time is from early May to late October, when the weather is warm. This is the high tourist season, when many festivals take place and the land is in bloom with grasses and flowers.

XINJIANG

The vast Xinjiang Uighur Autonomous Region, covering more than 966,000 sq km (375,000 sq mi), is the largest province in China, and one of the most resource-rich and ethnically diversified. It borders Mongolia, CIS Central Asia, Afghanistan, Pakistan, and India. About 45% of Xinjiang's 15 million people are Han Chinese, about 50% are Uighur, and the remainder are Kirghis, Kazakhs, Tajiks, Uzbeks, Hui, Mongols, Heibei, Manchus, Tatars, Daur, and Russians.

Historians believe the area was first settled by nomadic Turkic tribes in the third century BC. In the 1980s, archaeologists discovered dozens of tombs in various parts of Xinjiang, with bodies that had been buried about 3,000 years before yet remained remarkably preserved, thanks to the arid desert climate. Many of the mummies, believed to be forefathers of the Uighurs, had European features, including fair hair and skin. The theory is that they intermarried with other peoples and gradually evolved into a tribe of mostly dark-haired people. Even today, fair coloring and blue or green eyes are not uncommon among Uighurs.

In the Qin and Han dynasties (221 BC–AD 220) Xinjiang was inhabited by a variety of tribes, with anywhere from 36 to 50 walled states. Genghis Khan's troops conquered part of the region in 1218. By the time the Qing dynasty came to power in 1644, the area was under constant dispute among four different Mongol tribes that roamed the areas north of the Tian Shan (Heavenly Mountains), while the areas south of the mountains were inhabited by the Uighur people, ruled by descendants of the Mongol khans. The Muslims declared independence during the Tang dynasty (AD 618–970) and held on to it until the 19th century.

Although territorial wars continued throughout most of Xinjiang's history, and climatic conditions on the vast desert were not always hospitable to travelers, the region nevertheless became the most important crossroad for trade between China, Europe, and the ancient Persian empire. Marco Polo named the various arteries of the trade route the Silk Road.

In this century, the Uighurs continued to resist Chinese rule. In 1933 they succeeded briefly, seizing power from a warlord governor and claiming the land as a separate republic, which they named East Turkistan. China tightened its grip after the revolution, however. Today the capital, Ürümqi, is about 73% Han, out of a population of 1.4 million. The Uighurs live mostly in the less industrialized areas, and many complain that business and government are dominated by the Chinese. Since the breakup of the Soviet Union, the Uighurs have seen their Muslim neighbors in CIS Central Asia gain independence and have renewed their own effort, only to be repressed in a series of crackdowns that resulted in arrests and executions.

While the territorial dispute may never be resolved, today much of Xinjiang is wide open to foreign visitors. The roads are bumpy, but the landscapes are magnificent. The Uighurs and other so-called minority groups are generally eager to introduce foreigners to their traditional music, cuisine, and celebrations.

One quirky side effect of China's rule is that Xinjiang is officially in the same time zone as Beijing. Clocks run on "Beijing time," so that the sun does not come up here until almost 9 AM in winter. Hours stated here are Beijing time.

Note also that in Xinjiang's cities, the main streets generally run on a north–south or east–west grid, and the names change according to the side of town. For example, People's East Road (Renmin Dong Lu) becomes People's West Road (Renmin Xi Lu).

Almost everyone in Xinjiang speaks Mandarin, but the predominant language is Uighur, a Turkic-derived language. Little English is spoken. A few Uighur words to remember: Hello: *Yahshimu siz* (yah-shee-moo siz). How much?: *Kanche pul?* (kan-che *poll*). Market: *Bazargha* (ba-*zaar*-ga). Thank you: *Rachmad* (rak-*mad*). Goodbye: *Heri hosh* (her-*ee* hosh).

Xinjiang has a desert climate, with very little rainfall. It gets very cold in winter and very hot in summer, especially in the Turpan basin, although the temperature can drop by as much as 20 degrees at night. Xinjiang's average annual rainfall is only six inches. Winter lasts from around November to April. The sun is strong all year, so pack sunglasses, sun hats, and sunscreen.

Ürümqi

❶ *1,530 km (950 mi) southwest of Ulaan Baatar; 2,250 km (1,400 mi) northwest of Beijing.*

The capital and largest city, Ürümqi has the distinction of being the most land-locked city in the world—the nearest sea is 1,400 mi away. It is a new city by Chinese standards, built on pasture land in 1763. Originally the city was little more than barracks for Qing dynasty troops. The Qing emperors called the city Dihua (Enlightening and Civilizing). In 1884, when the Chinese declared the region a province and named it Xinjiang (New Territories), Dihua became the capital. In 1954, five years after the Revolution, the city was renamed Ürümqi.

A sleepy and dusty trading post for light industrial goods and farm produce in the mid-1980s, Ürümqi has grown to a modern city, with new buildings constantly under construction. Nevertheless, the occasional peasant does walk a sheep along the street in downtown Ürümqi. About 3 km (2 mi) from the center of town is the Erdaoqiao district, a Uighur area where some residents still live in adobe huts and drive donkey carts.

The best way to get around Ürümqi is by taxi. Taxis are abundant and will take you 3 km (2 mi) for only Y10 (seatbelts, though useful, tend to be very dusty and may leave marks on clothing). For shorter distances, walking is fine, and the dry, sunny weather is almost always conducive to a stroll.

Start your tour of Ürümqi with a 15-minute walk up a stone path to the top of **Hong Shan** (Red Mountain), a hill about half a mile above sea level that offers a panoramic view of the city. At the top is the **Zhenlong Ta** (Zhenlong Pagoda), built by the emperor in 1788 to suppress an evil dragon. ⊠ *North end of Xinhua Bei Lu (45-min walk or 10-min taxi ride from Holiday Inn).*

South on Xinhua Lu, about 5 km (3 mi) from the center of town, near the intersection of Tuan Je Lu in the Uighur section of town, is the **Erdaoqiao Bazargha** (Erdaoqiao Market). Here, the streets are lined with adobe dwellings and full of donkey carts, flocks of sheep, men in embroidered skullcaps, and women in heavy brown wool veils and leggings. The main market is in a covered alleyway. You can bargain (cash only) for Uighur crafts, such as embroidered caps and vests and decorated knives. Farther down the passageway are several shops selling carpets. ⊠ *½ block north of Tuan Je Lu, between Xinhua Lu and Jie Fang Lu.*

At the **Xinjiang Bowuguan** (Xinjiang Museum), don't miss the exhibition of 3,000-year-old mummies, excavated from tombs in various parts of Xinjiang. Here you can see artifacts from the tombs and about a dozen mummies, identified in English. In addition, the museum has some fine examples of area costumes, crafts, musical instruments, and architecture, including a yurt. The museum shops have fairly good selections of carpets, Chinese jewelry, porcelain, and Uighur musical instruments (cash only). ⊠ *132 Xin Bei Lu,* ☎ *0991/481–1453.* ✉ *Y25.* ☉ *Tues.–Sun. 8–1 and 3–7.*

Dining and Lodging

Unless otherwise stated, restaurants are open noon to 3 and 6:30 to 9.

$$$ ✕ **Kashgari's.** Decorated with Uighur tapestries and other ornaments, this hotel restaurant has background music that evokes images of snake charmers. The Uighur cuisine is prepared with an imaginative flourish, using local ingredients such as Turpan raisins. ⊠ *Holiday Inn, ground floor, 168 Xinhua Bei Lu,* ☎ *0991/281–8788. AE, MC, V.*

$$$ ✕ **Pearl Palace.** A bit out of the way unless you are staying at the World Plaza, it's a Chinese seafood restaurant worth the trip, complete with tanks full of fresh catches that are flown in daily. Private rooms are available for large parties. Try the special fresh-baked *mianbao* (slightly sweet bread filled with a paste of nuts and mushrooms). ⊠ *Hotel World Plaza, 2 Beijing Nan Lu.* ☎ *0991/383–6400. Reservations essential. AE, MC, V.*

$$$ ✕ **Xi Wang Mu.** A memorable Chinese restaurant, it serves a number
 ★   of regional specialties from around the country. Try the Shanghai-style fish (a whole poached fish with ginger slivers) and chicken with Sichuan black bean sauce. There is also a delicious shark's fin soup.

✉ *Holiday Inn, 2nd floor, 168 Xinhua Bei Lu,* ☎ *0991/281–8788. Reservations essential. AE, MC, V.*

$$ ✗ **Shang Jian Jiu.** Instantly recognizable by the Jaeger Beer sign out front, this is a noisy, friendly place with an excellent all-you-can-eat Mongolian hotpot buffet for lunch and dinner. ✉ *Luoyang House, 18 Jianshe Lu,* ☎ *0991/481–5690. No credit cards.*

$$ ✗ **South Korea Restaurant.** An unpretentious little place, it is in the main shopping district. The specialty of the house is South Korean-style hotpot—even heavier on the seasonings than the Mongolian variety. ✉ *96 Zhongshan Lu, no phone. No credit cards.*

$ ✗ **Da Han San Guan.** At one of the cleaner choices on a little street known as Restaurant Alley, the noodles are tasty, and there are fresh-roasted sunflower seeds to munch on while you wait for your food. ✉ *33 Jian Shi Lu, no phone. No credit cards.*

$$$$ 🏨 **Holiday Inn.** The only foreign-owned hotel in all of Western China, it's the only one that measures up to Western standards. Silks, the disco, is popular among both visitors and locals, as is Unicorns, the lobby bar, which has live entertainment nightly. ✉ *168 Xinhua Bei Lu, 830002,* ☎ *0991/281–8788,* 🖷 *0991/281–7422. 383 rooms. 3 restaurants, bar, deli, air-conditioning, refrigerators, indoor pool, beauty salon, health club, shops, billiards, laundry service and dry cleaning, business services, meeting rooms, travel services, airport shuttle. AE, MC, V.*

$$$ 🏨 **Hotel World Plaza.** A huge high-rise hotel built near the airport in the early 1990s, the World Plaza looks more threadbare than its age warrants. Otherwise it's perfectly comfortable, with an eager-to-please staff. ✉ *2 Beijing Nan Lu, 830011,* ☎ *0991/383–6400. 600 rooms. 3 restaurants, air-conditioning, refrigerators, indoor pool, beauty salon, massage, health club, laundry service and dry cleaning, travel services, airport shuttle. AE, MC, V.*

$$ 🏨 **Silk Road Hotel.** This small, friendly hotel is at the south end of town, about 16 km (10 mi) from downtown Ürümqi, in a semi-rural area that has the feel of a Uighur village. The hotel itself is modern and clean. ✉ *52 Yia Nan Lu, 830001,* ☎ *0991/287–4999,* 🖷 *0991/287–1431. 53 rooms. 3 restaurants, bar, pool, business services. AE, MC, V.*

$ 🏨 **Golden Bridge Hotel.** Short on ambience, it is perhaps a level above the Hong Shan (☞ *below*); i.e., the showers always work and the rooms are cleaned daily. The Chinese restaurant in the basement level, popular among local business people, is very good. ✉ *3–1 Tian Shan Lu, 830002,* ☎ *0991/284–1111. 22 rooms. 2 restaurants, laundry service, travel services. No credit cards.*

$ 🏨 **Hong Shan Hotel.** A favorite among backpackers for its location in the center of town, it's just down the street from the Holiday Inn. Reservations are not accepted. ✉ *Xinhua Bei Lu at Guangmin Lu, 830002,* ☎ *0991/282–8025. 10 rooms. Travel services. No credit cards.*

Nightlife

Karaokes are the most popular form of nighttime entertainment in China's cities, and Ürümqi is no exception. They seem to come and go every few months, scattered all over the downtown district. At this writing, the karaoke at the Holiday Inn was still a local favorite. The action doesn't begin until after 10 PM.

Silks Disco (✉ Holiday Inn; ☞ *above*) starts jumping after about 10 PM, especially from Thursday to Sunday, with strobe lights and Western disco recordings. The **Rock & Roll Café** (✉ 1-108 Xinhua Bei Lu) plays rock music until the wee hours and tries to look like a Hard Rock Café.

Western China

KAZAKHSTAN

Lake Balkhash

Alakol

Karamay

④ **Sayram Hu**

③ **Yining**

Shihezi

Cha

Ysyk-Kol

Ürümqi ①

KYRGYZSTAN

Jiaohe
Gucheng

Aksu

Korla

Artux

Sugun

⑥

**Kashgar
(Kashi)** ⑤ ⑦

Mor Ta

X I N J I A N G

TADZHIKISTAN

Taxkorgan

⑧

AFGHANISTAN

Qiemo

Hotan

K
U
N
L
U
N
S

PAKISTAN

*Karakorum
Shankou*

HOH XIL

H
I
M
A
L
A
Y
A

X I Z A N G   Z I Z H I Q U
(TIBET AUTONOMOUS REGION)

INDIA

N

Q I N G S H A N   G A O Y U
(PLATEAU OF TIBET)

0   100 miles

0   150 km

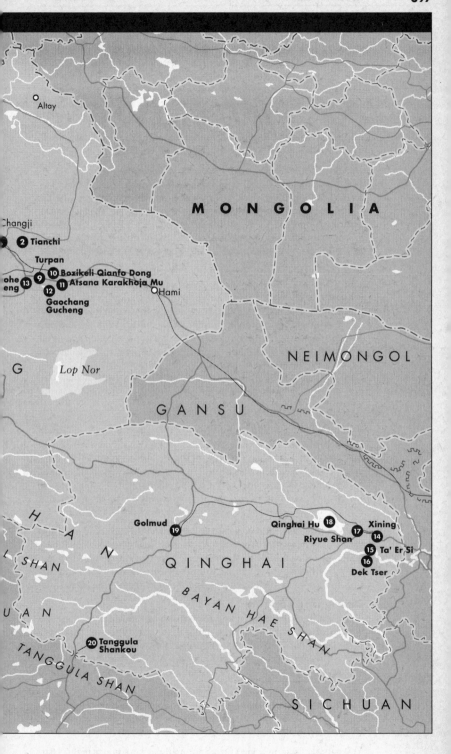

Altay

MONGOLIA

Changji
2 Tianchi
Turpan
10 Bozikeli Qianfo Dong
ohe
eng 13 9 11 Atsana Karakhoja Mu
12 Hami
Gaochang
Gucheng

NEIMONGOL

G
Lop Nor

GANSU

H
A
N
Golmud 19 Qinghai Hu 18 Xining
Riyue Shan 17 14
15 Ta' Er Si
L SHAN QINGHAI 16
UAN Dek Tser

BAYAN HAE SHAN

20 Tanggula
Shankou

TANGGULA SHAN

SICHUAN

Shopping

Stores are open 10 to 6 daily.

There is an extensive **outdoor food market,** selling local fruits, nuts, bread, and small cakes, along with handmade noodles and kabobs, in the alley beside the Xinjiang Jinxin Hotel (✉ Renmin Lu, east of Xinhua Nan Lu at Jie Fang Nan Lu), a lodging that doesn't admit foreigners.

Ürümqi is not known for its Uighur handicrafts in the way that Kashgar and Turpan are, but the **Erdaoqiao Market** (☞ Exploring Ürümqi, *above*) has a good selection of handicraft items, fruit (fresh and dried), and carpets brought in from other parts of Xinjiang.

Ürümqi does have a reasonable selection of **decorative arts** such as Chinese porcelain, cloisonné, jade, and embroidered items, and a small selection of Chinese jewelry, at lower prices than many other Chinese cities. Look for the decorative arts departments at the **Hongshan Department Store** (✉ Guangming Lu and Youhao Nan Lu), the **Xinbai Department Store** (✉ Zhongshan Lu), and the **Tianbai Department Store** (✉ Zhongshan Lu, just east of Xinhua Nan Lu). Only cash is accepted.

Ürümqi Carpet Factory (✉ 40 Jin Ger Lu) sells carpets made in the factory workshop, based on Central Asian patterns. You can walk in and request a tour of the factory any time during the day, after which a guide will usher you into the showroom and try to talk you into buying something. You can arrange shipment at an extra charge. **Xinjiang Antique Store** (✉ 325 Jie Fang Nan Lu) has a good selection of Uighur handicrafts and Chinese bric-a-brac, including jade, jewelry, carpets, ink brushes, bronze ware, and porcelain.

Tianchi

★ ❷ *115 km (72 mi) northeast of Ürümqi.*

About three hours' ride from Ürümqi is the not-to-be-missed Tianchi (Heavenly Lake), possibly the prettiest lake in China. The water is crystal clear, with a sapphire tint, untouched by boats, swimmers, or fishermen. Taiwanese tourists come here to commune with the Buddhist god of mercy. Others come for the hiking and horseback riding, or simply to spend a day enjoying nature. Around the lake are mountains covered by pine trees. In summer white flowers dot the hillsides.

Kazakh families set up yurts along the shores of Heavenly Lake from early May to late October, bringing their horses, sheep, and cashmere goats. The Kazakh people have a long history as horse breeders and are known as skilled riders. Most of the yurt dwellers are able to furnish horses—and a guide—for a day of riding around the lake.

Dining and Lodging

There are some excellent small **restaurants** without names along the western shore, near the hotels, that will prepare whatever they have on hand for lunch and dinner and produce a fresh and delicious array of stir-fried meat, vegetables, and noodles. Ask to move your table outside and you can enjoy the view while you eat. Prices for dinner for two will be Y30–Y50. Only cash is accepted.

There is a cluster of **hotels** (☞ *below*) at the western shore of the lake. You will not find any luxury accommodations here. Showers and toilet are shared, and some hotels have dorm beds only.

You can also stay in a **yurt** for about Y20 per person per night. Usually you pay a few yuan extra for meals (soup made mostly from flour, hard-as-rock sheep cheese, and tea with either salt or fried flour in it;

if you bring your own tea bags, your host will provide plain boiled water). The sleeping quarters are communal and there's no plumbing. However, you will have a rewarding glimpse into the way your Kazakh hosts live. Yurts are made from hides or canvas stretched over a wooden frame. The interior is colorfully decorated with handmade rugs and blankets, neatly hung along the walls and lining the floor. There is usually a wood-burning stove in the center, for cooking and keeping the yurt warm at night.

$ ✕ **Shui Xin Hotel.** Larger than the others, it has private guestrooms and a restaurant open for lunch and dinner. ✉ *Western shore of lake, near stop for bus from Ürümqi. 12 rooms with shared bath. Restaurant. No credit cards.*

Yining

❸ *700 km (435 mi) west of Urumqi.*

The city of Yining is the main stop in Ili Prefecture, a rich farming valley in northern Xinjiang near the border of Kazakhstan. Yining itself is too industrialized to be charming, but all around the city are the apple orchards for which Ili is famous, and in summer local Uighurs and Kazakhs perform traditional folk dances in the orchards. The countryside on the outskirts of Yining is a pleasant area to explore. Take a taxi to the Yili River bridge, 6 km (4 mi) from the town center, then walk or take a horse carriage over the bridge. Just across the river is a rustic village where the dirt roads are lined with birch trees. The houses have blue painted doors that open into courtyards filled with grapevines.

❹ From Yining, you can take a three-hour bus ride to **Sayram Hu** (Sayram Lake), in nearby Bole Prefecture. Sayram Lake's shore is active in the summer, especially in July or early August, when the **Naadam Fair** takes place.

At this time the area is full of Kazakhs, selling handicrafts, performing traditional music and dance, and staging a number of games and races on horseback. "Sheep polo" is a spectator sport that always draws a crowd. Here the men from the village slaughter and skin a sheep, then race around a ring on horseback, each contestant trying to grab the sheepskin from whoever has it, ride a complete circle around the ring with it. The game can go on for hours. In a politically incorrect version of the game, known as the "girl chase," young village men try to capture women on horseback.

In summer, you can circle the lake on horseback for about Y50 a day, with a guide. It is a pretty ride, with the grasslands in bloom and the snow-capped mountains in the distance.

Dining and Lodging

A yurt is the preferred place to stay at Lake Sayram. Yurts cost about Y20 a night per person, with accommodations about the same as at Heavenly Lake (☞ *above*).

$ ⌂ **Guozigou Hostel.** This bleak hotel on the shore of Lake Sayram has no plumbing. The restaurant serves uninspired and often greasy Chinese-style food for breakfast, lunch, and dinner. But it's the only option outside of a yurt. ✉ *North shore of Lake Sayram, no phone. 7 dorm rooms. Restaurant. No credit cards.*

$ ⌂ **Ili Bing Guan** (Ili Guest House). This simple hotel has rooms with bath and rooms with shared baths. There's nothing fancy here. ✉ *Center of Yining (tell taxi driver "Ili Bing Guan"). 12 rooms with bath, 15 with shared bath. No credit cards.*

$ ⊞ **Yining Bing Guan** (Yining Guest House). Usually you can get a room upon arrival. There are no amenities, but there are some rooms with private bath and some with shared. ⊠ *Center of Yining (tell taxi driver "Yining Bing Guan"). 12 rooms with bath, 20 with shared bath. No credit cards.*

Kashgar

➎ *675 km (420 mi) southwest of Yining; 1,175 km (730 mi) south of Ürümqi.*

The area that is now Kashgar (known as Kashi in Chinese) has a been a center for trade between China and the outside world for 2,000 years. A Buddhist kingdom was first established in Kashgar in the 1st century AD and thrived until Islam arrived and took hold in the 10th century. Today, Kashgar is a hub for merchants coming in on the fabled Karakoram Highway through the Kunjerab Pass from Pakistan and the Turogart Pass from Kirgiziya. When these two treacherous mountain passes are open, between May 1 and October 30, Kashgar becomes a particularly colorful city, abuzz with visitors.

The population—1.3 million in the town and surrounding area—is 93% Uighur. Kashgar sits on a fertile desert oasis; on the farmland that surrounds the town are fields of cotton and orchards. As the desert in this area is thought to be full of untapped oil reserves, as well as large deposits of precious stones and minerals, Chinese and foreign-driven industrial development is on the way. Yet Kashgar still has fine examples of traditional Uighur architecture. In the center of town are some old houses with ornately carved and painted balconies.

Start in the town square, which is filled with photographers with outdoor stands. The landmark in the square is the **Id Kah Emin** (Ai Ti Ga Er Qingzhen Si in Chinese), the largest mosque in China. The ornate structure of yellow bricks is the result of many extensions and renovations to the original mosque, which was built in 1442 as a prayer hall for Shakesirmirzha, the ruler of Kashgar. The main hall has a ceiling with fine wooden carvings and precisely 100 carved wooden columns. If it is not prayer time, you can go into the mosque.

Wander up Jiefang Bei Lu, which intersects the square near the mosque. Here are some of Kashgar's most intriguing **market stalls.** You'll find blacksmiths, coppersmiths, and other merchants selling jewelry, traditional Uighur instruments, knives and kitchen equipment, and brass sleigh bells for horses. Expect to dodge flocks of sheep as you stroll. Farther down the road is an area lined with small restaurants that specialize in steamed dumplings (filled with lamb meat).

During the high season (May–October), you can follow Jiefang Bei Lu northward to a small side street where signs point to the Qinibat Hotel and its newer neighbor, the Gilgit. Just outside the grounds of the Qinibat you'll find **makeshift cafés** where the frenetic interaction of traders from all over the region, black-market money changers, and police (who seem to be involved in the commerce) is a show in itself. Tea, beer, fresh baked nan, and kabobs are for sale in small stands, and the tables are up for grabs.

Take a taxi to the **Xiangfei Mu** (Tomb of Abakh Hoja), 5 km (3 mi) northeast of the city. The ornately tiled hall that houses the tomb—actually about two dozen tombs—is part of a massive complex of sacred Islamic structures, including a prayer hall. All were built around 1640. The Uighurs named the tomb and surrounding complex after Abakh Hoja, a 17th-century Islamic missionary who was believed to be a descendant of Mohammed, while the Chinese call it the Tomb of the Fragrant Concubine. Excavations of the glazed brick tombs indicate that the first occupant was Abakh Hoja's father, who is buried here along with Abakh Hoja and many of their descendants. As for Yiparhan, a.k.a. the Fragrant Concubine, one legend holds that she committed suicide rather than become a concubine of the Qing emperor Qianlong in Beijing, the other that she dutifully went to Beijing and spent 30 years in the emperor's palace, then asked to be buried in her homeland. Her alleged tomb was excavated in the 1980s—and found to be empty. Now the Fragrant Concubine is believed to be buried in Hebei Province. ⊠ *Izlati Lu.* ☉ *Daily, 8–6.*

In town, on Izlati Lu, turn left, going south, on Tauhuz Lu, then right on Renmin Dong Lu, and follow it about a mile to **Donghu Gongyuan** (East Lake Park). In this peaceful park, you can rent paddle boats on the lake. ⊠ *Renmin Dong Lu and Payinap Lu.* ☉ *Daily 10–8.*

The **Gong Anju Waishi Bangongshi** (Foreign Affairs Office of the Public Security Bureau), has a giant sculpture of Mao Zedong overlooking the city and the pool tables across the street—a stern reminder of what country this really is, although Kashgar looks little like China in any other way. ⊠ *Renmin Dong Lu between Jiefang Lu and Tianman Lu.*

Dining and Lodging

In these small towns in Western China, street numbers are not always used; the locals all know where certain hotels are. Reservations are not necessary or even possible to get in advance. If you want to be sure of having a room when you arrive in Kashgar or Turpan, ask CITS in Ürümqi (☞ Xinjiang A to Z, *below*) to phone and make a reservation for you. (Even so, you may get a puzzled look from the desk clerk when you say, "I have a reservation," and be asked the rote question: "You want a room?")

$$ ✕ **Kashgar Hotel Restaurant.** The cuisine is a mixture of Chinese and Uighur. You can order a barbecued sheep—the entire sheep, rolled out on a cart—a day in advance for special dinners. ⊠ *Kashgar Hotel (☞ below). No credit cards.*

$$ ✕ **Muslim Restaurant.** The dark restaurant serves a set breakfast, lunch, and dinner with Uighur dishes that keep on coming. Excellent bread and fair coffee are available at breakfast, and a welcome variety of Chinese greens, eggplant, and other vegetables, as well as meat and chicken, for lunch and dinner. ⊠ *Seman Hotel,* ☎ *0998/222–129. No credit cards.*

$ ✕ **John's Information & Café.** Young Western travelers gravitate to John's for information and conviviality. Maps and postcards are for sale. The clientele seems oblivious to the cooking, which combines the worst of Western and Chinese. Even the tea is weak and lukewarm. ⊠ *Xinmanolibag Lu, across from Seman Hotel,* ☎ *0998/224–186. No credit cards.*

$ ✕ **Limin Restaurant.** In season this is the closest thing Kashgar has to a Parisian sidewalk café, open from breakfast until the wee hours. It's full of young trendy European travelers, with an English-language menu that includes good coffee and toasted nan for breakfast, Chinese beer, and an array of Chinese dishes. Don't bother asking where the bathroom is; just slip back to the bushes behind the restaurant. ⊠ *398 Seman Lu, no phone. No credit cards. Closed Oct.–Apr.*

$$ 🏨 **Kashgar Hotel.** Formerly for government officials only, this sprawling hotel on the northeast edge of town recently opened to foreigners. One oddity is that the doors lock from the outside only. The floor attendants do keep a watchful eye, however. ⊠ *7 Ta Wu Gu Zi Lu, Kash-*

gar, Xinjiang 844000. ☎ *0998/222–367,* 🅵🅰🆇 *0998/224–679. 200 rooms.* ⊠ *3 restaurants, fans, shops, laundry service, meeting room. No credit cards.*

$ 🏨 **Gilgit International Friendship Hotel.** Completed in 1997, the hotel is a joint venture between the provincial government and a Pakistani company. It is barely distinguishable from the Qinibat (☞ *below*), next door, except that it is a few stories taller. Rooms have fans. ⊠ *Behind gates at intersection of Jiefang Bei Lu and Old Xinmalibag Lu,* ☎ *0998/ 222–103. 47 rooms. Restaurant, beauty salon, massage, laundry service, travel services. No credit cards.*

$ 🏨 **Qinibat Hotel.** The Qinibat is functional, but the hot water is not reliable and it is very noisy in high season. The hotel occupies the building that used to be the British Consulate, although most of the guest rooms are in a newer standard Chinese slapped-together high-rise extension. Rooms have fans. ⊠ *Behind gates at intersection of Jiefang Bei Lu and Old Xinmalibag Lu,* ☎ *0998/222–103. 39 rooms. Restaurant, laundry service, travel services. No credit cards.*

$ 🏨 **Seman Hotel.** In a sprawling building, the oldest part of which is the former Russian Consulate, the Seman is the most popular hotel in town among Western tourists, partly for its location, near a strip of sidewalk cafés. The showers work most of the time, and the staff are fairly friendly. ⊠ *Seman Lu and Xinmanolibag Lu, on west side of town,* ☎ *0998/222–129. 50 rooms. 2 restaurants, fans, beauty salon, massage, bicycles, shops, laundry service, travel services. No credit cards.*

Nightlife and the Arts

In the courtyard of the **Seman Hotel** traditional Uighur music and dance are performed frequently at night from May to October. There is a cover charge of Y20 per person.

Cafés and pool halls stay open past midnight Beijing time. There are about two dozen outdoor pool tables, as well as some open-air cafés, on Renmin Dong Lu, at Renmin Square, across from the giant Mao statue.

Shopping

Business is transacted on a cash basis here.

The **Sunday Market** actually is open every day, but the photo-opportunity-filled livestock market is here only on Sunday. You can bargain for fabrics, lace scarves, *dopas* (embroidered hats), handmade knives, dried fruit, children's toys, and most other non-food purchases. Go early for the best selections.

On the busy streets around the Id Kah mosque, **outdoor vendors** sell brass bells for horse-drawn carriages (the bells make nice Christmas ornaments), copper bowls and tea kettles, local gold jewelry, Chinese snuff bottles, and silver jewelry from Tibet and India.

The **Musical Instrument Shop** (⊠ 276 Kashgar Yusitang Buoyi Kasikhan Bazaar) has Kashgar's best selection of traditional Uighur string instruments, made in the workshop next door. **Kashgar Arts and Crafts Company** (⊠ 64 Jiefang Bei Lu, ☎ 0998/222–737), has reasonable prices on Uighur crafts produced in its workshops, such as quality embroidered caps and clothing, knives, pottery, and carpets.

Side Trips from Kashgar

Several kilometers northwest of Kashgar, you can visit the **Sanxian Dong** (Cave of the Three Immortals). According to legend, a Buddhist Kashgar king was told by a fortune teller that his three beloved daughters would all die, so he sequestered them in a cave to protect them. But the three princesses, fond of grapes, ordered their servants to bring great bunches. Bees followed the grapes inside, and sadly all three girls died of bee stings. Artists of the Buddhist period painted frescoes, now faded, inside the cave. You can climb in with a rope if you dare or view it from the outside, along with the surrounding desert and the snow-capped Tian Shan (Heavenly Mountains) in the distance. ⊠ *Hire taxi; or, by bicycle (about 1 ½ hrs each way), follow Jiefang Bei Lu north from Seman Hotel to outskirts of town; about 3 km (2 mi) from town, road divides into two highways; take highway leading west, toward Turogart Pass and Kirgiziya, 1 mile farther; cave on left.*

6 Some kilometers northeast of town stands the pretty and prosperous village of **Artux** (pronounced Ar-toosh), the capital of the ancient Shule state. Many of its houses have tiles or painted walls outside, with brass decorations on the doors. The roads are uncharacteristically smooth, funded by a native son who made a fortune in Turkey and then heeded the Muslim decree that says at least a fourteenth of one's earnings should be put back into one's birthplace.

7 The **Mor Ta** (Mor Pagoda) is about 29 km (18 mi) northeast of Kashgar. En route, you'll see the Heavenly Mountains, which continue into Kirgiziya. The pagoda, an ancient temple and tomb for Buddhist monks, is made of adobe and brick. Beyond the pagoda, reachable only by four-wheel-drive vehicle, are the crumbling adobe walls of the ancient city of **Hanoi,** believed to be 1,500 years old. ⊠ *Off Artux road.*

Pamir Mountains

305 km (190 mi) south of Kashgar.

8 The Karakoram Highway starts from Renmin Xi Lu in Kashgar and leads south for 2,100 km (1,300 mi), over the **Kunjerab Pass** into Pakistan. The pass is open only from early May to late October, but at any time of year you can charter a bus from CITS to the last stop in China, the town of **Taxkorgan,** a picturesque village in the Pamir Mountains. The area is inhabited by Kirgiz nomads.

There is also a lake, **Karakuri,** in the valley. In summer, you might see the nomadic men hold a "goatskin polo" match on the shores of the lake.

Turpan

9 *184 km (114 mi) southeast of Ürümqi.*

Turpan lies in a desert basin at the southern foot of the Heavenly Mountains. The basin, called the Turpan Depression, 328 ft below sea level, is the lowest spot in China and the second-lowest in the world. Temperatures have been known to soar over 110°F, and the sunshine is relentless.

The town of Turpan has a population of under 500,000—about 70% Uighur, 25% Han, and 5% Hui. It is surrounded by mountains and some of the richest farmland in Xinjiang. The area is known for its fruit orchards and vineyards. There are a few small wineries in and around Turpan. Late summer, when the grapes are ripe, is Turpan's busiest tourist season.

In summer, the heat discourages strolling around, but you can do it if you start early in the morning and stop frequently at the outdoor stands for cold drinks. Grapevine-covered canopies provide welcome shade over many of the city sidewalks. An option is to take a taxi, plenty of which cruise around town and many of which have air-conditioning.

From Lao Cheng Zhong Lu in the center of town, walk about 10 minutes west to the **bazaar,** behind an ornate green gate. Some crafts are available here, and plenty of local fruit, both fresh and dried. ✉ *Just past Bank of China on Lao Cheng Xi Lu near Gao Jiang Nan Lu.*

West on Lao Cheng stands the ancient **Qingzhen Si** (City Mosque) at the edge of town. Out here in a predominantly Uighur neighborhood are sod huts and donkey carts. Beyond the mosque are grape fields as far as the eye can see. ✉ *Lao Cheng Lu.* ⊙ *Non-prayer hours.*

From Qiu Nian Zhong Lu near where it intersects with Lao Cheng Zhong Lu take a taxi out to the **Emin Ta** (The Tower for Showing Gratitude to Eminhoja) at the southeast end of town, 1 km (½ mi) from the town center. The Emin Tower and adjoining **mosque** were built in 1778 in the Afghani style to commemorate a military commander who suppressed a rebellion by a group of aristocrats. The tower is built in the shape of a cone, with bricks arranged in 15 patterns. The keeper, who lives in the small building beside the mosque, can unlock the door for you to climb the 141-ft-high minaret. ✉ *From east end of Lao Cheng Dong Lu, turn right on last paved road before farmland, walk south to tower.* ⊙ *9–6.*

Dining and Lodging

$$ ✕ **Muslim Restaurant.** Like most hotel restaurants in the region, it is dark and lacks ambience, but it does offer a tasty and hearty variety of standard Uighur dishes—lamb, noodles, and vegetables. ✉ *Turpan Guesthouse, 8 Qiu Nian Nan Lu,* ☎ *0995/522–301. No credit cards.*

$ ✕ **Chipu Café.** The most popular of the little cafés that cater to foreigners on a strip around the junction of Qiu Nian Lu and Lao Cheng Lu serves a variety of Chinese dishes, posted on the outdoor blackboard in English. ✉ *Qiu Nian Lu above Lao Cheng Lu. No credit cards. Closed dinner.*

$$ ⌂ **Oasis Hotel.** Larger than the Turpan Guesthouse (☞ *below*), it has the same dingy grade of lobby and rooms. It's in a commercial part of town. The Turpan branch of CITS is on the grounds, next door to the hotel. ✉ *Qiu Nian Bei Lu,* ☎ *0995/522–478. 25 rooms.* ✉ *2 restaurants, air-conditioning, bicycles, laundry service, travel services. No credit cards.*

$$ ⌂ **Turpan Guesthouse.** In the grapevine-trellis covered courtyard, you can get fruit juices and beer during the summer. The rooms are as dingy as any others in Xinjiang, but the Muslim restaurant is quite good, and the gift shop is one exception to Turpan's status as a non-entity in the shopping category. ✉ *8 Qiu Nian Nan Lu,* ☎ *0995/522–301. 19 rooms. 2 restaurants, air-conditioning, shops, laundry service. No credit cards.*

$ ⌂ **Grain Trade Hotel.** Although it is spartan, dark inside, and crumbling in places, it is inexpensive and centrally located. ✉ *Lao Cheng Zhong Lu,* ☎ *0995/522–448. 20 rooms. Restaurant, air-conditioning, laundry service. No credit cards.*

Nightlife and the Arts

In summer evenings there are Uighur musical performances in the courtyard of the Turpan hotel, where you can sip fresh-squeezed fruit juices and beer.

The cafés in the center of town are open late, and much of the nightlife, Turpan style, consists of drinking beer and kicking back at the outdoor tables.

Side Trips from Turpan

About 47 km (29 mi) east of Turpan, in the middle of the Turpan Depression, the red clay **Huo Yan Shan** (Flaming Mountains), a branch range of the Heavenly Mountains, are named for the vibrant color and the way they seem to glow at sunset. The **Bozikeli Qianfo Dong** (Bezeklik Thousand Buddha Caves) are an ancient temple and monastery built into the side of the Flaming Mountains in the Mutou Valley area between the 5th and 9th centuries AD by slaves whose entire lives went into the construction. Many of the fine examples of Buddhist sculpture and wall frescoes were destroyed when Islam came to the area in the 13th century. Other sculptures and fragments of frescoes were taken by 20th-century archaeologists. The caves remain a feat of early engineering, and some of the 77 grottoes have partially restored frescoes. ⊠ *Northwestern side of Flaming Mts.* ⊗ 9–6.

⑪ The ancient **Atsana-Karakhoja Mu** (Atsana-Karakhoja Tombs) burial grounds southeast of Turpan have three tombs that are now open to visitors. The tomb of Minister Feng Changqing, a Tang dynasty governor, contains a fresco depicting the governor's life stages, from innocent child to wise Buddha-like old age. The tombs contain fairly well-preserved mummies. ⊠ *40 km (25 mi) southeast of Turpan; hire car from CITS (at Oasis Hotel) for about Y700/day for two passengers.*

⑫ The ruins of the ancient **Gaochang Gucheng** (City of Gaochang) lie in the valley south of the Flaming Mountains. At the entrance to the ancient city are donkey-driven carts to take you around the ruins. Legend has it that a group of soldiers stopped here in the 1st century BC on their way to Afghanistan, found that water was plentiful, and decided to stay. From the 8th to the 12th centuries Gaochang was a Buddhist city. In the 14th century Mongols conquered and destroyed the kingdom, leaving only the remains of walls and buildings that are here today. The walled **royal compound** was built of adobe. The **city walls** divided it into the inner city, the outer city, and the palace city. ⊠ *5 km (3 mi) southeast of Atsana-Karakhoja Tombs.* ⊗ 10–6.

⑬ The **Jiaohe Gucheng** (Jiaohe Ruins) lie in the Yarnaz Valley west of Turpan, on an island between two rivers. The city of Jiaohe was established as a garrison during the Han dynasty. It was built on a high plateau, protected by the natural fortification of cliffs rather than by walls. From the middle of the 8th century to the middle of the 9th century, the city was occupied by Tibetans. The buildings were devastated by Mongol hordes in the 13th century, but there are more fragments of actual streets and buildings here than at Gaochang (☞ *above*). ⊠ *8 km (5 mi) west of Turpan; hire car from CITS for about Y500 for two people or rent bicycles at Oasis Hotel.*

Xinjiang A to Z

Arriving and Departing

BY BUS

Daily buses link Kashgar (3 days), Turpan (5 hours), and Yining (5 hours, with a stop at Sayram Lake) with Ürümqi (Kashgar bus station, ⊠ Changjiang Lu, just east of railway station). The return bus schedules are sporadic and unreliable.

BY CAR

Contact CITS in Ürümqi (☎ 0991/282–6719; ☞ Visitor Information, *below*) for round-trip car transportation to **Yining** and/or Sayram Lake (✉ Y1500 for two people to stop at both destinations).

BY PLANE

Daily flights link **Ürümqi** with Beijing, Guangzhou, and Xian. Flights between Shanghai and Ürümqi run six days a week. There are also twice-weekly flights between Ürümqi and Alma Alta and Islamabad and weekly flights between Ürümqi and Moscow and Hong Kong.

Flights from Ürümqi to **Kashgar** depart every evening but Friday. There are no flights to **Turpan**. There are flights from Ürümqi to **Yining** six days a week. As with the buses, return flights are frequently delayed or canceled.

BY TRAIN

Daily trains run between **Ürümqi** and Beijing (4 days), Shanghai (5 days) and Xian (3 days). A train departs Ürümqi for **Turpan** (3 hrs) twice a day.

Getting Around

BY BICYCLE

Few people ride bicycles in **Ürümqi** due to the heavy traffic and dusty roads. Bicycles can be rented (✉ Y10–Y20 per day) at the Seman Hotel in **Kashgar.** The Oasis Hotel in **Turpan** has bike rentals. Present a photocopy of your passport to be held as identification.

BY BUS

In high season, friendly yurt owners hang around the China Youth Travel Services office at the Hongshan Hotel in Ürümqi. You can make an agreement with one and he will accompany you on the bus to **Heavenly Lake** (about 3 hours) and guide you to his yurt. Buses (✉ Y25 one way) leave daily from the Hongshan in season. They depart Heavenly Lake to return to Ürümqi every day at 11 AM and 4 PM.

City buses in **Ürümqi** (✉ Y1–Y3) are generally crowded, and there have been reports of pickpocketing, not to mention several bombings.

BY DONKEY CART

On the outskirts of Kashgar and Turpan you can hire a donkey cart (✉ Y2 per ½mi).

BY HIRED CAR

In Ürümqi and Kashgar, CITS (☞ *below*) can provide a car with driver at about Y200 per day for driving within the city. Trips outside the city can be arranged for higher fees.

BY TAXI

Taxis are widely available in Ürümqi, Kashgar, and Turpan (✉ Y10 for first mi). Ask your hotel desk attendant to write down your destination in Chinese for the driver, as well as the hotel's name for the return trip.

Contacts and Resources

BUSINESS HOURS

Airline, train and bus schedules, banks, offices, government departments, museums, and police stations run on Beijing time. Some local residents, however, set their watches by local time. When people make appointments, they make sure to establish the designated hour as local time or Beijing time. Government offices are open Monday through Saturday from between 8 and 9 until noon and from 2 until between 5 and 6. Restaurants and Uighur-run stores in Xinjiang generally operate on local time. This means that restaurants often serve meals late; for instance, lunch is typically served from 1 to 3 Beijing time, and dinner starts at 7 Beijing time.

Police: PSB (✉ Guangmin Lu, just northeast of Renmin Square, Ürümqi; ask hotel to phone PSB). **Hospital:** Chinese Medicine Hospital of Ürümqi (✉ 60 Youhau Nan Lu, ☎ 0991/242–0963). Kashgar and Turpan have large city hospitals.

Ürümqi: CITS (✉ Luyou Hotel, 51 Xinhua Bei Lu, ☎ 0991/281–4490); China Youth Travel Service (CYTS; Hongshan Hotel, 1st floor, ☎ 0991/281–6017. **Kashgar:** CITS (✉ Qinibat Hotel).

QINGHAI

A remote province on the northeast border of Tibet with sweeping grasslands locked in by mountain ranges, Qinghai is known to the rest of China mostly as a center for prisons and *laogais* (prison factories). Yet the province shares much of the majestic scenery of Xinjiang, combined with the rich legends and culture of Tibet. With the exception of the eastern area around Xining, Qinghai, formerly known as Amdo, was part of Tibet until the early 18th century. The mountains and forests of Qinghai are home to wild deer, wild yaks, and the endangered snow leopard.

The province is sparsely populated, with only 4.5 million people, not counting prisoners. About 60% of the population are Han Chinese and between 30% and 40% are Tibetan. The rest are Mongolian, Hui, and Salar (the two latter are Muslim ethnic minorities.) The 14th Dalai Lama himself was born in the northeastern part of Qinghai, in a mountainous peasant village a day-trip from Xining.

Xining

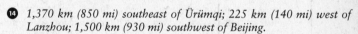 1,370 km (850 mi) southeast of Ürümqi; 225 km (140 mi) west of Lanzhou; 1,500 km (930 mi) southwest of Beijing.

Xining (Western Peace), the capital, started out as a remote Chinese military garrison in the 16th century, guarding the western borders. It was also an important center for trade between China and Tibet. A very small city by Chinese standards, with a population of 500,000, Xining today retains the flavor of a wild west outpost, in spite of the modern buildings that have begun to appear.

Xining lies on the Tibetan plateau at an altitude of nearly 7,000 ft above sea level. It's not high enough to cause serious altitude sickness, but you may feel light-headed during your first day or two here. Eating light and getting plenty of rest and water will help ease altitude discomfort.

The weather is moderate in the city, with cool summers and very little rainfall. In winter, the temperature averages around 30°F, with sunshine. The winter can be very cold in the surrounding mountains.

The city offers a study in contrasts. Start with a walk or taxi ride to the **Beishan Si** (North Mountain Temple) early in the morning, at the northwest end of town. The modern Buddhist temple, which is still in use, sits at the top of a hill and offers a sweeping view of town. ✉ *Just north of intersection of Qilian Lu and Changjian Lu.* ⊙ *Dawn–dusk.*

From Chanjiang Lu and Xi Jie you can stroll through the **market stalls** starting at Xi Jie, as it crosses the Nan Chuan (South River). Along a picturesque promenade beside the river vendors sell goldfish, parakeets, and birdcages.

On the western side of the river, Xi Jie crosses Huanghe Lu. Walk south about 15 minutes to the **Qinghai Bingguan** (Qinghai Guest House). There are a number of restaurants in and around the hotel where you can stop for lunch.

If you've ever wanted to see what a laogai looks like, here is your chance. Follow Nanshan Lu east to Nantan Jiedao (South Beach District). After about 300 yards watch for a road turning to the right. You will see two grim-looking compounds on the left, both laogai. Pass the gate of the second one, **Qinghai Pimao Beifu Chang** (Qinghai Hide and Garment Factory). Right next door to the entrance gate is another door leading to the factory shop, where the goods made by inmates of this prison are displayed for sale. The complete story of Qinghai's laogais is told in the book *New Ghosts, Old Ghosts: China's Prisons and Labor Reform Camps* (by James D. Seymour and Richard Anderson, M.E. Sharpe, Inc. 1997, available in the U.S.). You can walk or take a taxi back along Nanshan Lu to the Qinghai Hotel.

Dining and Lodging

$$ ✕ **The Cafe.** A huge hall with large round tables, Chinese style, it has an excellent Mongolian hotpot buffet, all you can eat, for Y35. ✉ *Xining Hotel, 215 Qi Yi Lu,* ☎ *0971/823–8701. No credit cards.*

$$ ✕ **Shang Yi Da Xia.** This popular Muslim restaurant is in downtown Xining, a few doors east of the Bank of China tower. It has a small, crowded dining room, but excellent hotpot and kabobs. ✉ *190 Dongguan Lu, no phone. No credit cards.*

$$ ✕ **Tibetan Restaurant.** The aroma of yak butter permeates this small place with Tibetan crafts on the walls. It is just down the street from the Xining Hotel (☞ *below*). ✉ *348-29 Qi Yi Lu. No credit cards.*

$$ ✕ **Xining Cinema Restaurant.** The restaurant, on the northwest end of town next to the Xining Cinema, has an all-you-can-eat mutton buffet. As the night wears on, customers, fueled with beer and the 60-proof clear potion known in Western China as *bai jiu* (white liquor) begin dancing around the tables. ✉ *33 Qi Lian Lu,* ☎ *0971/814–9770. Reservations essential. No credit cards.*

$$$ 🏨 **Qinghai Hotel.** Large and somewhat impersonal, it has rooms that are more expensive than those at the Xining (☞ *below*), but no cleaner or more comfortable. The hotel has a shopping arcade, a small Bank of China branch, and a CITS office. ✉ *20 Huanghe Lu,* ☎ *0971/614–4888,* FAX *0971/614–4145. 58 rooms. 3 restaurants, beauty salon, massage, health club, laundry service, meeting rooms, travel services. MC, V.*

$$ 🏨 **Xining Hotel.** At the smaller of the two main hotels in town the desk clerks speak better English than those at the Qinghai (☞ *above*). The lobby bar is a pleasant meeting place, although it is rarely open for actual service. ✉ *215 Qi Yi Lu,* ☎ *0971/823–8701,* FAX *0971/823–8798. 25 rooms. ✉ 4 restaurants, health club, laundry service, business services. No credit cards.*

Shopping

Xining is a good place to find Tibetan and Chinese crafts at reasonable prices. **Native Arts and Crafts** (✉ Qinghai Hotel, 2nd floor arcade, 20 Huanghe Lu), has vests, hats, and toys in designs using the techniques of traditional Tibetan folk embroidery; brass gongs; jewelry; and some Chinese jade and porcelain objects. **Ba Chang Ge** (✉ 30 Bei Da Lu) has Chinese antique porcelain, jade figurines from the region, and Tibetan folk embroidery.

Side Trips from Xining

Trips can be arranged through CITS (☞ Visitor Information, *below*) at the Qinghai Hotel. The government travel agency has something of a monopoly on transportation of tourists to the scenic spots outside Xining. The surest way to get around without being turned away by the police for entering an area without clearance seems to be through CITS.

⑮ Ta'Er Si (Ta'Er Monastery) is southeast of Xining. Built in 1560, it is one of the world's major centers of the Buddhist sect known as Yellow Lamaism. With a dozen different prayer halls, an exhibition hall, and the monks' quarters, the complex covers nearly a quarter of a square mile. The **Kumbum Festival,** a religious fair at which monks perform 500-year-old songs and activities including the Devil Dance to purge bad spirits, is held five times a year at the monastery, in February, May, July, November, and December. Shops right outside the main gate of the monastery sell beads, prayer scarves, brass gongs, and even some sacrificial yak skulls. ⊠ *Huangzhong, 26 km (16 mi) southeast of Xining.*

⑯ Dek Tser, a peasant village in Ping'an County, is the birthplace of the 14th Dalai Lama, the exiled spiritual leader of Tibetan Buddhism. The long, winding, and rocky road up to the high mountain village is not for the faint-hearted. Behind the wooden door next to the old Hong Ya School (which is still marked in Chinese characters) live two great-nieces of the Dalai Lama. One teaches at the school. Across the road a few feet farther uphill, a wall encloses a temple painted in bright colors. If you knock on the great-nieces' door, they will let you in to see the temple, past a yard filled with pigs, chickens, donkeys, sheep, and cows. ⊠ *32 km (20 mi) south of Ta'Er Si.*

⑰ Riyue Shan (Sun Moon Mountain) in Huangyuan County has two pagodas—the Sun and the Moon—on adjoining peaks, each with friezes depicting the story of a 7th-century Chinese princess, Wen Cheng, who married the Tibetan emperor against her will thanks to the wiles of Ludong Zan, the Tibetan prime minister. ⊠ *11 km (7 mi) west of Xining.*

⑱ Qinghai Hu (Blue Sea Lake) lies between the Hainan and Haibei Tibetan Autonomous Prefectures. Its 360-km (224-mi) circumference is surrounded by four mountain ranges. From late spring to early fall, the grasslands and rolling hills surrounding the lake are green and covered with yellow rapeseed flowers. Wild yaks roam here. Beyond the hills, the area is ringed with snowcapped mountains. The main entrance to the lake is behind the **Qinghai Lake Tent Hotel** in Jiangxigou Township, along the main road. At a long dock you can charter a motor boat in summer to take a two-hour boat ride to **Niao Dao** (Bird Island), a sanctuary for hundreds of species of birds, including egrets, cranes, gulls, swans, and wild geese. ⊠ *24 km (15 mi) west of Xining.*

DINING AND LODGING

Several small restaurants line the main road beside the lake, just west of the Qinghai Lake Tent Hotel. The restaurants serve Qinghai Lake's only fish—the so-called naked carp—yak meat, and other local delicacies. Lunch will cost about Y25–Y30 per person.

$ 🏨 Qinghai Lake Tent Hotel. The hotel is a rustic resort: not actually tents, but cabins in which the plumbing doesn't necessarily work. ⊠ *Jiangxigou Township, Gonghe, Qinghai, 81306,* 🕿 *0974/3520. 10 cabins. Restaurant. No credit cards. Closed Oct.–Apr.*

Golmud

⑲ *675 km (420 mi) west of Xining.*

Golmud, in central Qinghai province, is the largest metropolitan area in the world, covering nearly 49,000 sq mi. That's not much less than ½ sq mi of space per person, as the population is a mere 120,000. It lies on a dry, windy plateau. On the horizon is a long stretch of dry earth with mud craters that look like those of the moon. The plateau is inhospitably cold in winter and desolate all year. Although the area has a number of famous landscapes nearby, including pasture lands, glaciers, and the Tanggula Mountain Pass (☞ Side Trips, *below*), most trips require a permit.

Dining and Lodging

$ ✕ **Xining Peace Restaurant.** Here you'll find good Sichuan food amid dusty surroundings. ⊠ *Next to Golmud Hotel. No credit cards.*

$ ⌂ **Golmud Hotel.** This is the only hotel that admits foreigners. ⊠ *160 Kunlun Lu,* ☎ *0979/412–817. 23 rooms. Restaurant, laundry service. No credit cards.*

Side Trips from Golmud

❷⓿ The chief reason to visit Golmud is to travel over the **Tanggula Shankou** (Tanggula Mountain Pass) (June to September) into Tibet.

Qinghai A to Z

Arriving and Departing

BY BUS

The daily bus between Golmud and **Xining** takes about 20 hours. Buses leave Xining from the main bus station, opposite the train station. Purchase bus tickets for Lhasa from CITS (⊠ Golmud Hotel) in **Golmud**; the buses (30–35 hrs) run several times a week when the pass is clear, departing from the Tibet bus station (⊠ Xizang Lu).

BY PLANE

Twice-weekly flights link **Xining** and Beijing, Guangzhou, Xian, and Ürümqi. The airport, southeast of town, takes about an hour to reach by taxi. A weekly flight from Xining to **Golmud** and back departs on Sundays.

BY TRAIN

Trains run at least twice weekly between **Xining** and Beijing, Shanghai, Qingdao, and Xian. Tickets can be purchased from CITS (☞ *below*) or at the railway station (⊠ east of town just beyond Qilian Lu). Daily trains run between Xining and **Golmud** (express, 18 hrs).

Getting Around

The best way to get around both Xining and Golmud is on foot or by taxi. For day trips, catch a taxi in town and negotiate the fare to your destination in advance, or hire a car and driver from CITS.

Contacts and Resources

EMERGENCIES

Police: PSB (Public Security Bureau; Bei Da Lu, just south of Xining Hotel, Xining; in Golmud Hotel, Golmud). **Hospitals:** Qinghai People's Hospital (⊠ Gonghe Lu, east side of Xining); Xining Number 2 People's Hospital (⊠ Qilian Lu, at northwest end of Xining).

VISITOR INFORMATION

CITS (⊠ Qinghai Hotel, 20 Huanghe Lu, Xining, ☎ 0971/614–4888, ext. 2471).

12 Side Trip to Tibet

Whether it is the altitude or the cultural purity of Buddhist Tibet, every traveler feels a little light-headed in this country perched on the roof of the world. So long isolated from the West, the Tibetan peoples reached the 20th century with a unique, sophisticated medieval culture that, despite the shock waves of the Chinese Cultural Revolution, still prevails. Monasteries, though severely damaged by the invading Chinese, fill the countryside, and in Lhasa the great Buddhist institutions display outstanding works of Tibetan art.

By Nigel Fisher

TIBET LIES ON A VAST PLATEAU as large as Western Europe, sandwiched between two Himalayan ridges whose peaks reach 5 mi high. The plateau is the source for all the major rivers in South and East Asia: the Indus, Sutlej, and Brahmaputra from the far western highlands; the Mekong, Salween, Yangzi, Yalong, Gyrong, Yellow, Minjiang, and Jialing from the eastern region. Under the People's Republic of China the western half of the plateau has been designated the Tibet Autonomous Region, comprising the traditional Tibetan provinces of Ü (capital, Lhasa), Tsang (capital, Zhigatse), and Ngari (sometimes called Western Tibet). The remainder has been swallowed up by the Chinese provinces of Sichuan and Qinghai.

Until 1707, when Jesuit missionaries established themselves in Lhasa, the West had no serious contact with Tibet. Before then the Roof of the World, as this Himalayan nation is poetically called, was isolated. Long, long ago, so one story goes, an ogress, Sinmo, and a monkey, Avalokiteshvara, were the only living creatures on the Tibetan plateau. In her loneliness, Sinmo lured the meditating monkey into her cave, where their combined efforts produced six offspring. These were to become the ancestors of the country's six main tribes.

Tibet did not become a nation until the 7th century, when a chieftain, Songsten Gampo, consolidated his rule by subjugating the ancient kingdom of Zhangzhung in the west. Songsten became the first true king of the unified Tibetan Empire, making Rasa (later renamed Lhasa) the capital.

For two centuries, the Tibetan Empire prospered, establishing advantageous treaties with its neighbors. Trade and knowledge were exchanged. The teachings of Buddha were brought to Tibet and received with enthusiasm by the ruling class. Elements of the shamanistic Bon faith, which the Tibetans had previously embraced, were incorporated into Buddhism. Riven by political and religious differences, the empire broke up in the 9th century. The influence of Buddhism diminished, and Tibet subsided into isolation for the next four centuries. When the Mongols swept through Central Asia in the 13th century, Buddhism had a rebirth in Tibet, as it did all over east Asia, and it became the country's official religion.

Tibet emerged again as an autonomous nation state in the 15th century when the monk Tsongkhapa rose as both a spiritual and a political leader. He established a new Buddhist doctrine, which emphasized moral and philosophical rigors rather than mysticism, and, in 1409, he renovated and enlarged the Jokhang temple and brought the Great Prayer Festival to Lhasa. He also founded three great monasteries: Ganden, Drepung, and Sera. This building frenzy was supported by the widening acceptance of Tsongkhapa's doctrine, which later was embodied in the Gelugpa order, or order of the Virtuous Ones.

Though political power lay in the hands of the kings of Tsang, a Tibetan tribe who ruled out of Zhigatse, the country's second-largest city, the spiritual power now rested with the head lama of the Gelugpa order. This leader was (and still is) chosen from among newborn infants on the death of the previous head lama in the belief that the latter's spirit had entered the newborn. Eventually the division between the spiritual lamas and the temporal kings of Tsang became untenable. The Mongols sided with the lamas, defeating the king of Tsang and paving the way for Dalai Lama V (1617–82) to become both spiritual and temporal head of state. Lhasa was once again securely positioned as the nation's capital and a theocracy was established.

As the next Dalai Lama was ineffectual, the declining influence of the Mongols gave the Manchu Qing dynasty (1644–1912) its opportunity. Chinese troops moved into Lhasa, and the Chinese emperor Kang Xi declared Tibet a protectorate. Chinese control, sometimes manifest, sometimes latent, lasted until 1912.

In 1904 the British sent an expeditionary force into Tibet to combat the Chinese influence and guard against possible Russian encroachment, which could threaten British interests in India. At the fall of the Manchu dynasty in 1912, Tibet, with British support, gladly expelled all Chinese and declared the country's total independence. The withdrawal of the British from India in 1947 made Tibet again vulnerable, and in 1950, 30,000 veteran troops of the new People's Republic of China attacked a defending force of 4,000 ill-equipped soldiers. The result was slaughter on a gigantic scale, culminating in the death of 1.2 million Tibetans and the destruction of virtually every historic structure. Tibet became a vassal state of China.

In 1959, to quell a massive popular uprising in Lhasa, the Chinese ruthlessly shelled Norbulingka Palace and the crowds surrounding it, as well as the Potala (palace of the Dalai Lamas) and the Sera Monastery. When a crowd of 10,000 sought sanctuary in the Jokhang, the Chinese bombarded that, too, and after three days of gunfire in the capital, some 10,000 to 15,000 Tibetan corpses littered the streets. Dalai Lama XIV, three days before the massacre, had sought asylum in India, where he later set up a government-in-exile in Dharamsala. China then formally incorporated Tibet into the People's Republic, began a process of dissolving the monasteries and stripping Tibetans of their culture, and in 1965 renamed the country the Xizang Zizhiqu (Xizang Autonomous Region; TAR).

In 1966 the Chinese Cultural Revolution reached Tibet. Virtually every sacred and cultural monument was damaged if not destroyed outright. Monks and Tibetan loyalists were jailed and tortured or simply killed. Not until the death of Mao did the havoc abate, and by then some 6,250 monasteries and convents had been destroyed or severely damaged, thousands of Tibetans tortured and killed, and another 100,000 put in labor camps. The rest of the world virtually turned a blind eye. Eventually, in 1980, Deng Xiaoping's era of tolerance began. Some religious institutions have been restored and religious practices are now permitted. Massive numbers of Han Chinese, encouraged with incentives, are moving into Tibet, changing the face of this country, particularly in Lhasa, where probably half the population is Chinese. In some provinces the percentage is even higher.

Demonstrations still take place, and the call for Tibetan freedom is still heard. In 1988, 1989, and 1993, bloody uprisings inspired by the monks challenged Chinese rule. Martial law was temporarily instituted. Discontent with the Chinese "invasion" continues, and the possibility of more demonstrations is always present. But, at the slightest hint of public protest, the Chinese make a few more Tibetans disappear and deny foreigners permission to enter the TAR. Tibet may not seem to the casual observer to be a police state, but it is.

Not all of Tibet is open to foreigners. Certain "closed" regions may be visited with a special permit, sometimes granted on request from the Public Security Bureau in Lhasa. Travel may be suspended without notice, which you'll only discover on being denied an entry permit or by finding that the flights to Lhasa are "fully booked." This is likely to occur at politically sensitive times such as the Tibetan New Year, the anniversary of the 1959 uprising on March 10, the anniversary of the 1989 demonstration in June, and International Human Rights Day in December.

On the Roof of the World the people live at altitudes that average between 11,500 and 16,400 ft. At the higher elevations vegetation is sparse. Wild grasses in the mountain wilderness are covered by a blanket of snow in winter. Narrow gorges make passes between sky-scraping peaks. A few valleys are open to cultivation, and fresh-water lakes reflect the sun's brightness through the rarified air. Ignore the Chinese intrusion, the ugly modern buildings and open-pit mines around the towns, and you'll journey along the top of the world knocking at the doors of the deities' heavens.

Pleasures and Pastimes

Architecture

Monasteries, some small, some vast, usually follow a similar layout: Entrance is through a portico. Murals depict the Four Guardian Kings (four directions of the compass), who display their prowess in martial arts. The Wheel of Rebirth is also represented. Then often there are the two gatekeepers, Vajarapani on the east side and Hayagriya on the west side. The murals on the inner wall of the portals portray protector deities of the town or of that particular monastery. Through the portico is the central hall, whose size is determined by the number of columns. The rows of seats are for lamas attending ritual ceremonies— the elevated seats are for the head lamas. Clockwise around the hall you usually find a series of murals telling the story of the Lord Buddha's life or that of other critical historical figures. Facing the entrance and at the back of the elevated seats are the rows of sacred images and scriptures. In major temples, there is usually an inner sanctum: the treasure house where the most revered images are kept. Also within the monastery complex are *klangtsens* (residential units) with their own chapels and assembly halls. In the larger monasteries the complex will have *tratsangs* (colleges), where various aspects of Buddhist precepts are taught.

The most common sight in Tibet is the Buddhist stupa, called a *chörten*. A chörten is built both as an act of merit and to serve as a reliquary for the ashes of a religious leader. The Potala has the most celebrated ones, which contain the ashes of past Dalai Lamas. Everything about the chörten has religious significance. In its totality, it embodies the Buddhist concept of true reality, in which the bonds of temporal and physical needs are dissolved. The chörten has a square base, a rounded dome, an oblong slab, a tiered triangular spire, and a small ornament. These five elements represent fire, earth, water, air, and space. Motifs tell the principal events in the life of Buddha.

On the domestic front, private houses have flat roofs and slightly inward-leaning walls built of brick. More picturesque are the homes of the nomads who follow their flocks of sheep and herds of yak on the mountain slopes. These yak-hair tents are large enough for a whole family to sleep, eat, and cook in. A hole in the roof over the firepit in the tent's center acts as a chimney, but because there's no exhaust fan the smell of yak-butter permeates the whole tent.

Art

With a history of 13 centuries of Buddhist influence, Tibet is an extraordinary repository of religious art, especially illuminations, murals, and *tankas* (painted cloth scrolls). Sculpted images of deities and historic figures are mostly in metal, clay, or stucco, though a few are of wood or stone. Despite destruction by the Chinese and the persecution of artists since 1950, an abundance of Tibet's art treasure still remains. In the new era of tolerance, Tibetans are relearning their art and are actively restoring the masterpieces of their past.

Buddhism and all of its art forms arrived in Tibet from India at a time when Buddhism was on the wane there, and soon Nepalese art began to influence the Tibetan style. Chinese influence came much later, in the 16th century, and was limited principally to the development of the landscape background in portraits of historic figures.

Tibetan art in general, and images in particular, are not meant to serve as accurate representations or portraits, but rather to express states of the Buddha-mind and to assist in reaching higher levels of (Buddhist) consciousness. Art is intended to represent purity of spirit and to nurture meditation—most images are to guide the meditator in his communication with a particular deity, with the goal of assimilating the deity's attributes and taking the next spiritual step to nothingness/completeness. Deities and historic figures have been sculpted or painted by artists from the 7th century onward in various postures expressing myriad spiritual attributes. In the 1,000 rooms of the Potala alone there are more than 200,000 images.

Dining
Tibetan cooking is simple; the staple is *tsampa* (roasted barley flour) washed down by bowls of *soja* (butter tea). You are likely to eat it more than once only if panic hunger strikes. A more enjoyable dish is *momo,* a steamed meat dumpling, often served with *then-thuk* (noodles). Other dishes include *lasha* (lamb with radish), *gyuma* (black pudding), *thu* (cheese cake), and *dresi* (sweet rice). If you are invited to a Tibetan banquet, you'll have these and more—18 dishes in all. Outside Lhasa, Tibetan fare is tsampa, tsampa, and tsampa, with the occasional splurge of yak meat and mutton along with yogurt. Local cheese is often rock hard; moisten it in the mouth before chewing to avoid breaking teeth. Fussy eaters should order a picnic from their Lhasa hotel before going off for trips into the countryside. Beer (Lhasa piju) is available nearly everywhere. The local drink is *chang* (a fortified barley ale). Bring your own imported spirits, even if just to brush your teeth. Local water is not potable; it must be boiled or treated with iodine before it passes your lips.

CATEGORY	PRICE*
$$$$	over $27
$$$	$21–$27
$$	$12–$21
$	under $12

Prices are per person for a three-course meal, excluding drinks, taxes, and tip.

Festivals
The most colorful times to visit Lhasa are during festivals, when pilgrims come into town and banners fly, adding to the gaiety. Festivals occur according to the Tibetan lunar calendar, and so the dates vary every year. The following times, therefore, are approximate. **Losar,** the Tibetan New Year Festival (February), is Tibet's most colorful celebration, with performances of Tibetan drama. During **Mönum** (the Great Prayer Festival; February) the image of Maitreya is paraded from the Jokhang around Barkhor. At the **Lantern Festival** (the Day of Offerings; February) huge sculptures made of yak butter are placed on the Barkhor pilgrimage route. **Buddha's Enlightenment Day** (May/June) draws many pilgrims, and there are outdoor opera performances. **Drepung Zöton**

(Yogurt Festival; August) takes place at the monastery, with the hanging of a monumental tanka and dances by the monks. **Zöton** (August—two days after Drepung Zöton) is known as the popular Yogurt Festival; it starts at the Drepung Monastery and moves to Norbulingka, where operas and dances are held. **Labab Düchen** (October/November) commemorates the deities' coming to earth and attracts numbers of pilgrims. **Paldren Lhamo** (November) honors the protective deity of Jokhang, whose image is paraded around the Barkhor.

Lodging

There are no luxury hotels in Tibet. The best that can be found are moderately modern hotels in Lhasa. Outside Lhasa in the major towns, there are bland Chinese hotels, about half of which have hot running water. You may prefer to seek a Tibetan guest house, many of which are quite clean, where the hospitality is warm and welcoming, but be forewarned that the shared bathing facilities in these guest houses are primitive.

CATEGORY	PRICE*
$$$$	over $102
$$$	$78–$102
$$	$54–$78
$	under $54

Prices are for a standard double room with bath at peak season, excluding tax and service charges.

Photography

Place Tibet's unique art, architecture, dress, and behaviors against the backdrop of the majestic Himalayas, studded with 6,000 monasteries, and you have a photographer's heaven. Take your film with you. Print film is available, at a price, in Lhasa; slide film is well nigh impossible to buy. Do not photograph Tibetans without their permission—it's rude and an affront to their culture.

Shopping

The bazaars are fun and the Tibetans love to bargain. They respect you for doing so, too. The best buys are traditional jewelry, metalwork, carpets, woodwork, and textiles. Appliquéd tankas make superb wall hangings to take home. Antiques, according to government regulations, require a permit to export.

Trekking

Not all of Tibet is accessible by road, which makes trekking all the more thrilling. The scenery is staggering and the discoveries enthralling. In many places you feel as if you are the first person to tread here. The best months for clambering over the Roof of the World are April through June and September through November, though the summer rainy season often is not that wet. Self-sufficiency is important, as once out of Lhasa, not much is available. On the other hand, the high altitude respects those who pack with a minimum of weight. Trekking agencies are not very experienced, so you will likely be blazing a trail along with them.

Exploring Tibet

Lhasa lies in Central Tibet and in the fertile Kyi-chu Valley, which extends north to its glacial origins in the Nyenchen Tanglha range. This region is the most heavily populated within the TAR. South of Lhasa and Central Tibet are the Lower Brahmaputra valleys that pass into Assam (India) and Bhutan. Western Tibet is the region of the Upper Brahmaputra Valley, whose main city is Zhigatse. Through the central part of Southern Tibet, you can make the land trip from Nepal crossing the border at Podari/Dram and up to Tsongdu and Zhigatse en route to Lhasa. The southern county of Dingri is traditionally known as the highland region of Tibet and is bordered on the south by the high Himalayan range that includes Mt. Everest and the popluar trekking routes around the Everest base camp. Far Western Tibet has only recently been opened to foreigners and is one of the least populated parts of the country. Eastern Tibet, some 1,200 km (750 mi) east of Lhasa, is characterized by rugged mountains with steep rocky slopes often topped with glaciers and broken by deep gorges. Less than half of this region is in the Tibetan Autonomous Region (TAR). Northern Tibet, Jangtang, is a vast lakeland wilderness with elevations ranging from 14,760 ft to 16,400 ft and rarely visited by outsiders.

Great Itineraries
Numbers in the text correspond to numbers in the margin and on the Tibet and Lhasa maps.

IF YOU HAVE 3 DAYS
Take it easy on your first day in Lhasa, adjusting to the altitude. Keep your sightseeing to the heart of the old city, around **Barkhor Square.** Off the square is **Jokhang Temple,** the most sacred temple in Lhasa. If your are up to it, you can also visit the **Temple of Meru Nyingba** (adjoining the east wall of Jokhang) and the **Ani Tshamkung Nunnery** southeast of Jokhang on Waling Lam. In the morning of the second day go up to the **Potala.** Spend the afternoon exploring the religious cave paintings and carvings on the hill of **Chagpo Ri,** being sure to visit Chogyel Zimuk. On the third day, go out to **Drepung Monastery,** inspect the monastery, and then make the pilgrimage along the Drepung Lingkor. Return to Lhasa for an afternoon at the **Norbulingka Palace,** the summer palace of the Dalai Lamas. At the end of the day, you can do some final shopping around the Barkhor or visit the **Ramoche Monastery.**

IF YOU HAVE 10 DAYS
Enter Tibet by land from Katmandu, Nepal, and take two or three days to reach **Lhasa.** Give yourself three or four days visiting the sights in the capital city (☞ *above*). During this time, arrange to go on a trekking tour, climbing into the **Himalayas** on the Nepalese border, visiting off-the-beaten track monasteries, hiking to the **lakes,** or discovering the attractions of the **gorges.**

When to Tour Tibet
Tibet is a land of extremes. In winter temperatures can sink to −23°C (−10°F), but in summer the thin mountain air permits the sun to penetrate, to heat the days to 30°C (high 80°s F). The optimal time for a visit is mid-April through June. It rains a little in the summer, so if you can't make the spring, go in September but leave before the weather turns freezing in mid-November.

LHASA

Lhasa, with a population of a little over 160,000, is remarkably small considering its long history. Its major sights, both historically and architecturally, fall into three eras: First, the 7th- to 9th-century building boom, which produced the first Potala Palace on Mt. Marpori (AD 637) and the Buddhist-influenced Jokhang temple (641). Second, the 15th century, when Tsongkhapa renovated and enlarged the Jokhang temple (1409) and founded the three great monasteries: Ganden, Drepung, and Sera. Third, when Lhasa again became the capital, Dalai Lama V (1617–82) rebuilt (and expanded) the Potala on the foundations of the original. Over the next three centuries the lamas constructed the great Gelugpa monasteries and palaces, of which the Norbulingka Palace is the most notable.

The city today, nearly 50 years after the Chinese invasion, still contains a generous amount of Tibetan architecture, art, and culture. The area known as Barkhor, which encompasses the Jokhang Temple, remains a Tibetan enclave.

A Good Route

The high altitude of Lhasa will tax your stamina on your first day, so take it easy. Go down to the **Barkhor** ① for lunch and then spend the afternoon in the **Jokhang** ② temple. It will take at least a couple of hours. If there is time, you can visit the **Ani Tshamkung** ③ nunnery, just south of the Jokhang, and the temple of **Meru Nyingba** ⑤ (adjoining the east wall of the Jokhang). Nearby is the **Gyel Lakhang** ④, Lhasa's mosque. Or, if you've had enough of sacred matters, wander the streets of Barkhor checking out the smells and sounds. North of Dekyi Shar Lam is the 15th-century **Ramoche** ⑥.

The **Potala** ⑦ palace, which beckons you to visit from the moment you arrive in Lhasa, should be your first stop on the second day. It will take the full morning to cover both the White and Red palaces. Spend the afternoon exploring the religious cave paintings and carvings on Chakpo-Ri, being sure to visit **Chogyel Zimuki** ⑧.

On the third day, go out to the **Drepung** ⑨. Give yourself at least an hour and a half inspecting the monastery and then make the Drepung Linghor, the 90-minute pilgrimage walk around the monastery. The next stop is the **Nechung** ⑩ monastery, just southeast of Drepung. Then return to old Lhasa and shop around the Barkhor.

For the fourth day, go out to **Sera Thekchenling** ⑪ northeast of Lhasa. Return to spend an afternoon at the **Norbulingka** ⑫ complex. If you have more than four days in Tibet, you can head out of town, possibly to visit the enormous **Ganden** ⑬ monastery, 40 km (25 mi) from Lhasa, or simply to get the feel of rural Tibet.

Sights to See

❸ **Ani Tshamkung.** The main temple at this nunnery was built in the early 14th century; a second story was added in the early 20th century. Before the Chinese invasion of Tibet, the nuns were responsible for lighting the butter lamps in the Jokhang. Considerable damage occurred during the Cultural Revolution, but the nunnery was restored in 1984 and now has more than 80 nuns in residence. The chief pilgrimage site is the Tsamkung (meditation hollow) where Songsten Gampo concentrated his spiritul focus on preventing the flood of the Kyi-chu River. ⌧ *Waling Lam, southeast of Jokhang.* ◷ *Daily 9:30–4:30.*

❶ **Barkhor.** This plaza around the Jokhang temple, the spiritual and commercial hub of old Lhasa, is now the only part of the city that has not been overrun by the migrating Chinese. Properly speaking, the Barkhor is only the intermediary circumambulation surrounding the Jokhang, but the name is commonly used to refer to the heart of Lhasa. Off the Barkhor walkway are market places and more temples. Join the pilgrims making the Barkhor circuit and you will step back into the "Forbidden City," passing monks sitting before their alms bowls, chanting mantras. The circuit is crammed with stalls where vendors sell trinkets, carpets, hats, prayer shawls, and just about anything you might not know that you want. The streets running north off the Barkhor walkway to Dekyi Shar Lam are shopping streets (☞ *Shopping, below*).

Along the north wall of the Jokhang is the **Nangtseshak**, a two-story former prison that had more than its share of notoriety in the past.

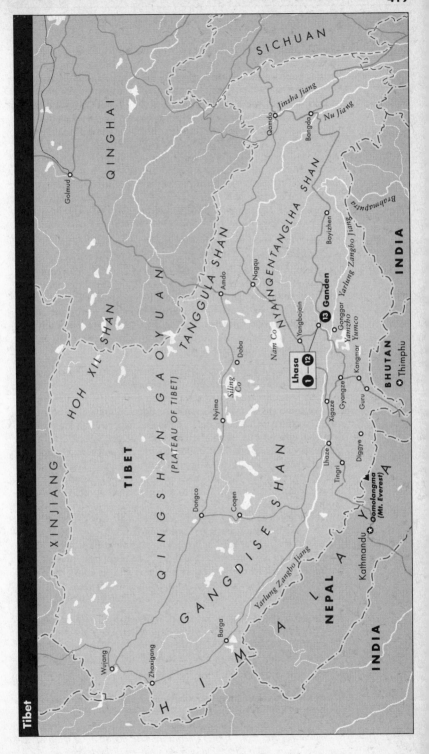

Tibet

SICHUAN

QINGHAI

Jinsha Jiang

Qamdo

Nu Jiang

Bangda

Golmud

Bayizhen

INDIA

HOH XIL SHAN

TANGGULA SHAN

NYAINQENTANGLHA SHAN

Yarlung Zangbo Jiang

Brahmaputra

Nagqu

QINGHAI GAOYUAN

Amdo

Yangbajain

Gonggar

13 Ganden

XINJIANG

(PLATEAU OF TIBET)

Doba

Yamzho Yumco

Nam Co

Lhasa 1 — 12

TIBET

Siling Co

Kangmar

BHUTAN

Thimphu

Nyima

Gyangze

Guru

Xigaze

Dongco

Coqen

Lhaze

Diggye

Tingri

QINGSHAN

Oomolangma (Mt. Everest)

GANGDISE SHAN

Barga

Yarlung Zangbo Jiang

HIMALAYA

NEPAL

Kathmandu

Wujang

Zhoxigang

INDIA

South of the Barkhor plaza are several notable buildings, many of them former residences of important advisors to Dalai Lama XIV.

❽ Chogyel Zimuki. In caves scattered over Chakpo-Ri, a hill opposite and to the southwest of the Potala, are as many as 5,000 religious rock-carvings and paintings. How old they are is uncertain, but arguably they were made in Songsten Gampo's time—the 7th century; some are of later vintage. The best and most interesting are at Chogyel Zimuki, sometimes called Dragla Lugug, a grotto-style temple in which the inner sanctum is a cave. Beyond the temple's gate is a monastic building from which you can mount the steps of the two-story grotto chapel. From the second floor on the right is the entrance into the spherical cave, which has a central rock column. Inside, three of the walls and the column bear 71 sculptures carved on the sheer granite. They are considered to be the work of Nepalese artists in the 7th to 9th centuries. ✉ *Follow Mirik Lam south from Lhasa Fandian (former Holiday Inn) to dirt road along base of Chakpo-Ri facing Marpo Ri, hill on which Potala stands, to Chogyel Zimuki.* 🎟 *Free.* ☉ *Daily sunrise–sunset.*

❾ Drepung. The largest of the Gelugpa monasteries was the residence for lesser lamas. Founded in 1416, it was enlarged in the 16th century by the Dalai Lama II to become the effective center of political power in Tibet before the Potala was completed. By the era of the Dalai Lama V (1617–82) it had become the largest monastic institution in the world, with 10,000 residents. During the Cultural Revolution it suffered only minimally; the most important chapels were left intact. Now about 500 monks live here.

The Drepung complex comprises the Tshomchen, the four main trat-sangs—institutions for teaching, often translated as colleges—and the Ganden Potrang, where Tibet was ruled before the Potala existed. Each of these has its own *klangstens* (residential units). The layout of each is a courtyard, a large hall, and inner chapels. Each klangsten is arranged on a slope, with the courtyard at the lowest level. The monastery's most important building is the Tshomchen. The roof of its vast assembly hall (the **Dukhang**) is supported by 183 columns. The hall is 164 ft by 118 ft, with the central portion of the ceiling raised for an atrium effect. Banners add to the ceremonial pomp. On this, the ground floor, are several chapels. More chapels populate the second and third floors as well as the roof. Visit them all. Look especially for the two-story **Düsum Sangye Lhakhang** (Buddhas of Three Ages Chapel) at the rear of the Dukhang on the ground floor. Here in the large illuminated room each of the three Buddhas of past, present, and future is guarded by two bodhisattvas. Other statues adorn the room; along the western side are images of the four spiritual sons of the Buddha. Smaller statues represent past kings and their consorts.

To set out on a pilgrimage around the monastery, the **Drepung Linghor,** leave from the upper left corner of the parking lot. The walk takes about 90 minutes. The path winds west of the perimeter wall and uphill in the direction of Gephel Ritrö and then descends in the direction of Nechung. You can also walk 3½ hours up to the **retreat of Gephel Ritrö.** The retreat (now restored) was founded in the 14th century where monks tended yak herds. The summit, **Gephel Ütse,** is another 2½ hours of steep climbing. ✉ *Off Dekyi Num Lam, 7 km (4 mi) west of Lhasa center; take bus that passes Lhasa Fandian (former Holiday Inn), get off at base of Gephel Ri, and walk 1 km (1/2 mi) north; or hire a car or minibus taxi from town.* 🎟 *Y25.* ☉ *Daily, 9–4; some chapels close noon–2.*

❹ Gyel Lakhang. In perhaps the most Buddhist of cities, Gyel Lhakhang is a bit of an anomaly. It is Lhasa's largest mosque, for the approxi-

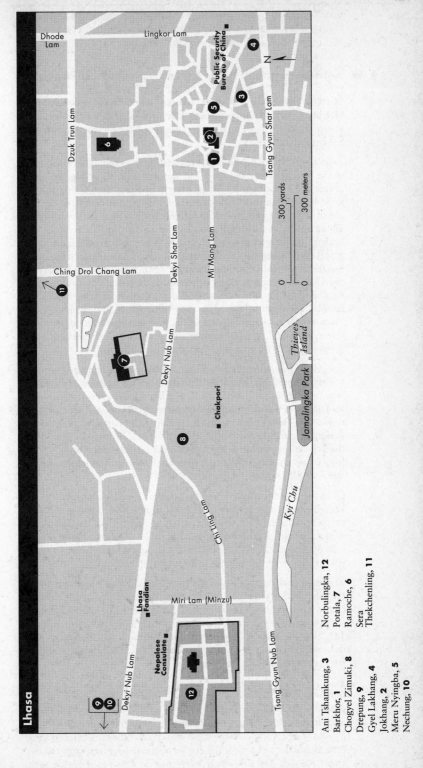

Lhasa

Dhode Lam

Lingkor Lam

Public Security Bureau of China

N

Dzuk Trun Lam

Tsang Gyun Shar Lam

300 yards

300 meters

0

0

Ching Drol Chang Lam

Dekyi Shar Lam

Mi Mang Lam

Dekyi Nub Lam

Thieves Island

Jamalingka Park

Chakpori

Kyi Chu

Chi Ling Lam

Lhasa Fandian

Miri Lam (Minzu)

Nepalese Consulate

Dekyi Nub Lam

Tsang Gyun Nub Lam

Ani Tshamkung, 3
Barkhor, 1
Chogyel Zimuki, 8
Drepung, 9
Gyel Lakhang, 4
Jokhang, 2
Meru Nyingba, 5
Nechung, 10

Norbulingka, 12
Potala, 7
Ramoche, 6
Sera
Thekchenling, 11

mately 2,000 Muslims resident in the city. It was built in 1716 for the
immigrants who arrived in the 17th century from Kashmir and Ladakh.
⊠ *Linghor Lho Lam (near East Linghor Lam).* ⌧ *Daily 8–5, except
during prayers Fri.* AM.

★ ❷ **Jokhang.** Believed to be the country's first significant Buddhist-in-
spired temple, this is the most sacred building not only in Lhasa but
in all of Tibet. Day and night, Tibetans pay homage and, during the
pilgrimage season, long queues of devotees shuffle toward the inner
sanctum, where they touch their foreheads on the sacred image of Jowo
Sakyamuni (Buddha).

Built probably in 647, during Songtsen Gampo's reign, Jokhang stands
in the heart of the old town. The site was selected as the geomantic
center of Tibet by Queen Wengcheng, a princess from China brought
to Songtsen Gampo as his second wife. Her site selection, in the middle of Othang Lake, posed an elementary problem that was eventually solved by thousands of goats carrying loads of earth to fill the lake.
Perhaps unfairly after so much goatly effort, the original name of the
city, Rasa (Place of the Goats), was changed to Lhasa (Place of the Deity).
But the building of the temple was further delayed. Queen Wengcheng
also divined that before the completion of the temple the demon ogress
needed to be pacified. This required the construction of 12 outlying
temples geomantically sited so as to be positioned on the body of the
"supine ogress." Through divination, temples were built on her thighs,
knees, and so on, to pin her down; this, conveniently, formed three successive rings of four around the location of Jokhang.

Songtsen's first wife, Princess Bhrikuti from Nepal, financed the building of Jokhang. (She had already undertaken the building of the Potala
when she arrived in Lhasa in 632 and kept active even after Songsten
took Princess Wengcheng as his second wife.) In honor of her and recognition of Tibet's strong reliance on Nepal, Jokhang's main gate was
designed to face west, that is, toward Nepal. Among the few bits of
the 7th-century construction that remain are the door frames of the
four inner chapels, dedicated to Mahakarunika, Amitabha, Sakyamuni, and Maitreya.

Over the centuries, several renovations have enlarged the Jokhang to
keep it the premier temple of Tibet. It came close to losing this position when, in the 1950s, the Chinese Army shelled it and the Red Guards
of the Cultural Revolution ransacked it. At one time during this period of sacrilege, parts of it were used as a guest house and as a pigsty.
About a third of the damage has since been repaired.

The Inner Jokhang consists of three stories and forms a square enclosing
the inner hall, Kyilkhor Thil. Encircling the Inner Jokhang is the inner
circumambulation, known as the Nangkhor. The Outer Jokhang,
sometimes referred to as the western extension and constructed in
1409, contains the lesser chapels, storerooms, kitchens, and residential units. The whole complex is circled by the Barkhor walkway,
fringed by the old city of Lhasa.

Start your visit in the Barkhor (☞ *above*), a wide plaza in front of the
Outer Jokhang. Look for the two willows of recent vintage flanking
the stump of a willow tree planted by Queen Wengcheng. A wall now
gives it some protection. Enter the temple through the portico supported
by six fluted columns. At the small threshold courtyard, pilgrims prostrate themselves and, over the course of centuries, have worn the flag-
stones smooth. The side murals of the portico depict the Four Guardian
Kings and the Four Harmonious Brethren. Within the main courtyard
is the assembly hall that Tsongkhapa had constructed for the Great Prayer

Festival in 1409—which, incidentally, greatly enhanced Lhasa's claims as the spiritual capital of Tibet. Along the outer walls are 19th-century murals, and in the inner hall are murals dating from 1648. On the north side is the residence of the Dalai Lamas.

Before entering the Inner Jokhang, you should walk the Nangkhor (Inner Circumambulation) in a clockwise direction. It's lined with prayer wheels and murals on the east side, which is also known for its series of Buddhist images. On the north side are several chapels of minor consequence. Outside the wall on the south side is the debating courtyard, renovated in 1986, which contains the platform where thrones for Tsongkhapa and other dignitaries were set up for the Great Prayer Festival. Enter by the **Zhung-go** (Main Gate), which has finely carved door frames from the early Tibetan period. Left of the door is a painting of the future Buddha; on the right a painting of the past Buddha. A footprint of the Dalai Lama XIII is enshrined in a small niche. Continue on through to the large Entrance Hall, whose inner chapels have murals depicting the wrathful deities responsible for protecting the temple and the city of Lhasa. Straight ahead is the inner sanctum, the three-story **Kyilkhor Thil,** some of whose many columns probably date from the 7th century, particularly those with short bases and round shafts.

The chapels on the ground floor of the Kyilkhor Thil are the most rewarding. In the West Wing be sure to see the **Je Rinpoche Dakpa Namgye Lhakhang,** a chapel whose central image is Tsongkhapa flanked by his eight pure retainers. In the North Wing, in the chapel **Mahakarunika Lhakhang,** whose entrance has a heavy metal chain curtain, is a reproduction of the image of the deity Mahakarunika. The chapel also contained Buddha relics from Bodha Gaya, but some of the sacred treasure was smuggled out during the Cultural Revolution, and some was destroyed. The most revered chapel of the inner hall is **Jowo Sakyamuni Lhakhang** in the middle of the East Wing, opposite the entrance. Here is the 5-ft image of Jowo Rinpoche, representing the Buddha at the age of 12. It was brought to Tibet by Queen Wengcheng and somehow has survived, despite an exciting history of being plastered up, buried in sand, and lasting through the Cultural Revolution. ⊠ *Barkhor.* 🎫 *Free.* ⊘ *Daily sunrise–sunset.*

❺ Meru Nyingba. The original temple, built soon after the Jokhang, is where the Tibetan alphabet was finalized by the scholar Tonmi Sambhota. Within this 20th-century reconstruction are murals portraying many of the forms taken by Pehar, the chief guardian of the Gelugpa Budddhist sect. ⊠ *Eastern wall of Jokhang off northern arc of Barkhor.* ⊘ *Sunrise–Sunset.*

❿ Nechung. This monastery is dedicated to Pehar, a deity that protects Tibet. From its construction in the 12th century, the temple has been home to important oracles whose advice on political appointments and future events has been sought regularly. The Lhasa government made no major decisions without first consulting the oracle; even today, the current oracle resides in Dharamsala as an adviser to the Dalai Lama and his Tibetan government-in-exile. Except for the gilded roofs and their embellishments, Nechung buildings largely survived the Cultural Revolution. The three-story temple building at the north end of the courtyard is approached by steps flanked by lions. The murals on the portico depict Pehar and his retinue. In the assembly hall murals show the *Deities of the Eight Transmitted Precepts,* and in the Jordungkhang chapel on the western side, you'll find more images of Pehar. Also in this chapel is the tree trunk where, as a dove, Pehar landed after making his successful escape from imprisonment in a casket thrown into the Kyi-chu River. There are two other chapels on the ground floor, two on the second floor, and a single chapel on the third floor. You can also visit the residence of the Nechung Oracle, located behind the main building. ⊠ *Dekyi Num Lam, 8 km/5 mi west of Lhasa center, 1 km/½ mi southeast of Drepung Monastery.* 🎟 *Y20.* ☉ *Daily 9–noon, 2–4:30.*

⑫ Norbulingka. The Dalai Lama VII, a frail man, chose to build a palace on this particular site because of its medicinal spring. In 1755, not content just to have a summer home for himself, the Dalai Lama enlarged the palace with the construction of the **Kelzang Podrang** to the southeast, a three-story palace whose ground floor is dominated by his throne, and had his whole government move down to the palace from the Potala. The next Dalai Lama expanded the property, adding a debating courtyard, the **Tsokyil Podrang** in the center, to mark the site of the medicinal spring, the Lukhang Lho pavilion, and the Druzing Podrang to serve as a library and retreat. The gardens were landscaped by Dalai Lama XIII (1876–1933), who later (1930) oversaw the construction of a new complex, **Chensel Lingka Podrang** to the northwest, containing three small palaces. The last addition was **Takten Migyur Podrang** to the north, an ornate two-story building notable for Buddha images on the ground floor and the impressive Europeanstyle reception room on the floor above, by Dalai Lama XIV in 1954–56, three years before he fled to India. In fact, it was from here that the Dalai Lama, disguised as a soldier, made his escape on March 17, 1959, three days before the Chinese massacred the Tibetans and fired artillery shells into every Norbulingka building. Only when the Chinese searched through the corpses did they recognize that the Dalai Lama had escaped.

The work done to repair the damage in the aftermath of the March 1959 uprising is not of high caliber. The palace's 80 acres are divided into three areas: the opera grounds (where Tibetan operatic performances are held during the Yogurt Festival), government buildings, and the palaces. The palaces are in four complexes and are visited by pilgrims in the following sequence: Kelzang Podrang to the southeast, Takten Migyur Podrang to the north, Tsokyil Podrang in the center, and Chensel Lingka Podrang to the northwest. ⊠ *Mirk Lam.* 🎟 *Y25.* ☉ *Daily, sunrise–sunset.*

★ ⑦ Potala. Virtually nothing remains of the original 11-story Potala Palace built in 637 by King Songtsen. What you see today is a 17th-century replacement. The Dalai Lama V, anxious to re-establish the importance of Lhasa as the Tibetan capital, employed 7,000 workers and 1,500 artisans to resurrect the Potala Palace on the 7th-century foundation, using the original palace as its prototype. After eight years, the White Palace was completed in 1653. The Red Palace, the central upper part, was not completed until 1694, 12 years after the Dalai Lama's death, but his death was kept a secret by the regent Desi Sangye Gyatso in order not to interrupt the construction. The Potala has been enlarged since then, mostly in the 18th century, with continual renovations, including stabilizing and strengthening the structural walls in 1991. The vast Potala, once the spiritual and political headquarters of Tibet's theocracy, is now a museum.

The Potala was the world's tallest building before the advent of 20thcentury skyscrapers. Towering above the city from the slopes of Mt. Marpori, the structure is 387 ft high; its 1,000 rooms house some 200,000 images. The outer section, the White Palace, was the seat of government and the winter residence of the Dalai Lama until 1951. The inner section, the Red Palace, contains the temples and the reliquary tombs of the Dalai Lamas. The Eastern Gatehouse is the main entrance used by pilgrims, who climb up from Zhol Square below. Other visitors usually reach the Potala at the rear drive-in entrance on the north side so as to avoid the steep climb. By coming in from the north and entering directly into the White Palace, you miss the ancillary buildings, including two printing presses dating from the 17th century.

Between the White and Red Palaces is a yellow building that houses the Tanka Rooms, in which are kept huge tankas. Once used in the celebration of the Yogurt Festival, they are no longer displayed, although one was unfurled in 1994. In the White Palace you can pass through the Spartan quarters of the Dalai Lama. On either side of the palace are the former secular apartments and offices of the government. The Red Palace, looming up from the White Palace, is the spiritual part of the Potala. Murals chronicle Buddhist folklore and ancient Tibetan life. Within the four stories that make up the functional part of the Red Palace are dozens of small chapels, where often a human skull and thigh bone are the only decoration. Interspersed among the chapels are eight golden chörten containing the embalmed remains of Dalai Lama V and Dalai Lamas VII–XIII.

Underneath the 13-story, 1,000-room fortress are the dungeons. Past justice was rough—as it still tends to be today, though under different masters—and refusal to pay taxes, displaying anger, or insulting a monk meant torture and jail. The worst place to be sent was the Cave of Scorpions, where prisoners became target practice for the stinging tails. ⊠ *Zhol.* 🚌 *Y55.* 🕙 *Mon.–Sat. 9–4.*

❻ Ramoche. On the northern side of Dekyi Shar Lam, this temple was founded by Queen Wengcheng at the same time as the Jokhang. The temple's present three-story structure dates from the 15th century. Despite restorations in the 1980s, it lost much of its former glory after the Chinese used it to house the Communist Labor Training Committee during the Cultural Revolution.

Ramoche was to be the home of the most revered statue of Jowo Rinpoche. A threat of a Chinese invasion in the 7th century induced Queen Wengcheng to hide the image in a secret chamber in the Jokhang. Some 50 years later it was rediscovered and placed within the main chapel of Jokhang. As a substitute, Jokhang reciprocated with a statue of Jowo Mikyo Dorje, which had been brought from Nepal and represented Buddha as an eight-year-old. It was decapitated during the Cultural Revolution and its torso "lost" in Beijing, but both head and body were later found, put back together again, and placed in a small chapel at the back of Ramoche's Tsangkhang (Inner Sanctum). ⊠ *Ramoche Lam, off Dekyi Shar Lam, north of Tromzikhang Market.* 🚌 *Y20* 🕙 *Daily 9–noon, 2–4:30.*

⓫ Sera Thekchenling. This important Gelug monastery, founded in 1419 on 24 acres, contains numerous chapels, with splendid murals and icons. Originally it was a hermitage for Tsongkhapa and his top students. Within a couple of hundred years, the community numbered 5,000 to 6,000 monks. The complex comprises the tsokchen (great assembly hall), three tratsangs, and 30 klangstens.

On the clockwise pilgrimage route, start at the two buildings that will take most of your visit. **Sera Me Tratsang** (founded in 1419), which promotes elementary studies, has a dukhang rebuilt in 1761 with murals depicting Buddha's life. Among its numerous chapels, the most interesting are the five along the dukhang's north wall: the Ta-og Lhakhang is hard to forget as it's a little macabre, with skeletons and skulls adorning its exterior. The three-story college for tantric studies, **Ngagpa Tratsang,** is the complex's oldest surviving structure (1419), where the dukhang is supported by 42 short and four tall columns. Here you find statues of famous lamas and murals depicting paradise.

Continue to **Sera Je Tratsang** (the largest of the three colleges, with four stories), where you can take time out in the shaded courtyard, once the site for philosophical debates; today pilgrims come here to offer scarves and talismans. Other sites on the pilgrimage route are **Hamdong Khangtsang** (a principal residential unit), the **Tsokchen** (covering 2,000 sq m, with 89 tall columns and 36 short columns), and Tsongkhapa's **hermitage** on Mt. Phurbuchok, which has a two-story chapel. ⊠ *5 km (3 mi) north of Lhasa at base of Mt. Purbuchok.* ☎ *Y20.* ⊙ *Daily 9–noon, 2–4:30.*

Dining and Lodging

Dining is expensive in Lhasa and somewhat limited. The larger hotels offer a full meal plan (breakfast, lunch, and dinner). The Lhasa Fandian's, for example, costs $55, while a breakfast purchased separately is $16. Though these plans can save money, they do restrict you from trying local restaurants and various ethnic fare. Except for the Fandian, most hotels offer only one type of fare—usually Chinese.

$$$$ ✕ **Grand Highland Palace.** For the best multinational cuisine, it is worth paying a bit extra to come here. Most of the specialties are Nepalese, but there is some good spicy Thai food and a few European dishes. The ambience is smart and rich for Lhasa, and to add to the mood, Indian and Nepalese dances are performed. ⊠ *3/F Luga Market, near CAAC,* ☎ *0891/633–9391. No credit cards.*

$$$$ ✕ **Lhasa Fandian.** The most reliable fare is here. At its Himalayan Restaurant you can try Tibetan cooking that will include momo and thukpa as well as Nepalese dishes. Chinese cuisine is in its Sichuan restaurant and, would you believe it, Western meals are served in the Hard Yak Café. If you're just hankering after a sundae, you can get that here, too. ⊠ *1 Minzu Lam,* ☎ *0891/632–2221,* FAX *0891/632–25796. No credit cards.*

$$$ ✕ **Sonam Dokhang.** Some of the best Tibetan food is prepared here. Decor is minimal, but the staff is friendly and helpful. Also, you'll find savvy travelers dining here who can bring you up to date on what's happening in Tibet. ⊠ *Dekyi Nub Lam, near Himalaya Hotel,* ☎ *0891/633–2985. No credit cards.*

$$ ✕ **Crazy Yak.** This local restaurant offers well-prepared Tibetan and Chinese food that is reasonably priced. The interior uses Tibetan artifacts for atmosphere, made all the more pleasant by Tibetan operatic and folk dance performances. ⊠ *Dekyi Shar Lam, near Yak Hotel,* ☎ *0891/633–6845. No credit cards.*

$$$–$$$$ 🏨 **Lhasa Fandian.** This, the former Holiday Inn, is the best that Lhasa has to offer; it's equivalent to a middle-range hotel in Hong Kong or Beijing. The more expensive tour groups stay here. Though it lacks any Tibetan atmosphere, it is the cleanest and most efficient hotel in Tibet. In two of its three buildings, "S" and "C," the rooms have piped oxygen, which can be important for getting your energy back. "H" building does not have the oxygen, and its rooms are priced 30% less. All rooms have a private bathroom. Other advantages of staying here are the five acceptable restaurants, car hire services, and fax services. There's even a karaoke bar and a health clinic. ⊠ *1 Minzu Lam, Lhasa 850001,* ☎ *0891/632–2221,* FAX *0891/632–25796. 450 rooms. 5 restaurants, pool, beauty salon. No credit cards.*

$$ 🏨 **Tibet Hotel.** Down a notch from the Lhasa Fandian (☞ *above*) in price and distance from town, the Tibet Hotel has well-worn, but clean rooms, each with a bathroom. There is the attempt here to give some Tibetan ambience in the furnishings. A full meal plan is offered for $35 (breakfast is $9). An in-house travel agency can arrange tours and a car. A small discotheque is the evening entertainment. ⊠ *Dekyi Nub Lam, Lhasa 850001,* ☎ *0891/632–4554. 80 rooms. Restaurant, dance club, travel services. No credit cards.*

$ 🖫 **Himalaya Hotel.** All rooms, clean and sparsely furnished, have their own bathroom. Two restaurants, one Chinese and the other Tibetan, serve reasonable fare (a full meal plan is $22). The location is near the Kyi River and a 10-minute walk from the Barkhor. *9 Linghor Lam, Lhasa 850001,* ☎ *0891/633–4082,* ℻ *0891/633–4855. 116 rooms. 2 restaurants, business services, travel services. No credit cards.*

$ 🖫 **Snowlands.** Most of the backpackers choose hotels in the Barkhor area. The locals are friendly and, because fellow backpackers are here, it's the best place to swap travel information. Rooms, mostly doubles or four-bed dorms, face the inner courtyard. Washing facilities are spartan, and water rarely runs in the winter months but guests and staff remain good-natured. There is a Sichuan restaurant. ⊠ *Mentsikhang Lam, Lhasa 850001,* ☎ *0891/632–3687. 30 rooms without bath. Restaurant. No credit cards.*

$ 🖫 **Yak Hotel.** Often the first choice for travelers on a tight budget wanting to be in the Barkhor area, the Yak offers a range of accommodation from doubles with a toilet, some even with a shower, to five-bed dorms with shared toilet and washing facilities. Inspect the rooms before accepting, as they vary widely, from rather depressing to light and fresh. ⊠ *36 Delyi Shar Lam, Lhasa 850001,* ☎ *0891/632–3496. 12 doubles, 170 beds with shared toilets and showers. No credit cards.*

Nightlife and the Arts

Tibetan operas are performed at the **TAR Kyormolung Operatic Company** and the **Lhasa City Academy of Performing Arts.** Traditional Tibetan music is played at the **Himalayan Restaurant** (☞ Lhasa Fandian *in* Dining, *above*).

Shopping

The **Tromsikkhang** (⊠ alley northeast from Barkhor) market is worth popping into, if only to look at all the yak-butter you'll ever want to see or smell. In the **traditional market** extending all around the Jokhang and the Barkhor you will find such Tibetan handicrafts as textiles and carpets, as well as religious artifacts and paintings. The **Friendship Store** (⊠ Yutok Lam) also has traditional artifacts.

Side Trip to Ganden Namgyeling

★ ⑬ *45 km (28 mi) southeast of Lhasa.*

Established by Tsongkhapa, the founder of the Gelugpa sect, in 1409, this enormous monastery became the foremost center of the sect. Unlike other monasteries, where abbots were often selected on the basis of heredity, this one was supervised by an abbot chosen on the basis of his worthiness who served a term of seven years.

Of the six great Gelugpa monasteries, **Ganden** was the most seriously desecrated and damaged by Chinese using artillery and dynamite during the Cultural Revolution. Since the early 1980s, Tibetans have put tremendous effort into rebuilding the complex. Some 300 monks are now in residence; the Ganden community once numbered around 3,000 monks. Pilgrims come daily from Lhasa (trucks leave the Jokhang at 7:30 AM) to pay homage to the sacred sites and relics.

The monastery comprises eight major buildings on either side of the dirt road. The most impressive structure is the **Serdhung Lhakhang** (Gold Tomb of Tsongkhapa) in the heart of the complex, easily recognized by the recently built white chörten before the red building. On the second floor is the chapel of **Yangchen Khang,** with the new golden chörten of Tsongkhapa. The original (1629), made of silver, later gilded, was the most sacred object in the land. The Chinese in 1959 destroyed it, though brave monks saved some of the holy relics of Tsongkhapa—which are now in the new gold-covered chörten.

If necessary, cut short your visit to the buildings of the complex so as to make the **Ganden Linghor,** a splendid pilgrimage walk that takes about an hour to complete. Start at the prayer flags and pass the shrines on the way to the spot where Tsongkhapa meditated and decided upon the locations of the six great Gelugpa monasteries. Go on to the rock known as the Gauge of Sin, where you may want to test yourself by squeezing through the narrow cleft. It is believed that the pilgrim who becomes stuck is too full of sin. ⊠ *36 km (22 mi) southeast on main Tibet–Sichuan highway, then right onto winding road 9 km (5½ mi).* ☺ *Daily, sunrise to sunset.*

TIBET A TO Z

Cautions

Don't openly talk politics with Tibetans. It can put them on the spot as they may wish to explain their feelings about China's occupation, but they can be charged with treason and receive a 20-year jail term. Do not photograph the people without first asking their permission.

Your companion for the first few days will be a green oxygen bag. At the 12,000-ft altitude, shortness of breath is a constant companion. You may have to pause when mounting steps and experience some mild discomfort—perhaps a headache or minor chest pains. These can be managed by an aspirin or two; not by cigarettes or alcohol. The simple remedy is to avoid exertion and drink plenty of non-alcoholic fluids. Severe altitude sickness should be brought to the attention of a physician—immediately. If you have high blood pressure, heart ailments, or respiratory problems, you may want to reconsider your route.

Arriving and Departing

A visa valid for the People's Republic of China is required. The PRC embassy in Kathmandu will not issue these visas: you need to obtain one elsewhere—New Delhi, Bangkok, or your home country, for example. That's standard; after that, requirements for entry into Tibet are always in a state of flux. Access for groups (a minimum of four usually makes a group) normally poses no problem, and the travel agent takes care of the details. Access for individuals is more difficult.

Public Security Bureau (PSB) personnel are everywhere, sometimes in uniform and sometimes in civilian clothes with dark glasses, reading a newspaper upside down and watching you. The PSB monitor civil unrest, visa extensions, crime, and traffic. Beware of the charming Tibetan who may be a secret policeman happy to entrap you into giving him a photograph of the Dalai Lama. Offices are in all towns and many of the smaller townships. However, visa extensions are possible only in Lhasa, Zhigatse, Tsetang, Kermo, and Ziling. These offices can also issue Alien Registration Permits for the "closed" areas.

For travel to some regions of Tibet, you need a special "Alien Travel Permit" from the local PSB Aliens Exit and Entry Division. Sometimes they give it; sometimes they don't.

Whenever there is a whiff of unrest, individual travelers are prevented from entering Tibet. The Chinese government considers individual tourists harder to monitor and keeps them from fraternizing with local Tibetans. Journalists, for example, are officially denied the right to go to Tibet. However, individuals do get in with perseverance.

By Plane

The easiest direct route is **from Hong Kong** with a change of plane in Chengdu. China Southwest Airline has twice-weekly non-stop flights **from Kathmandu** (with fantastic views of the Himalayas, including Everest) to Lhasa and daily flights from Chengdu. Both cost about $200 one way. Individual travelers cannot buy the airline ticket before reaching Kathmandu or Chengdu. Sometimes, even then you will not be given a ticket, in which case, you can hook up with others and have a Kathmandu or Chengdu travel agent book you as a group.

By Road

By road **from Kathmandu** you can (usually) cross the border at Kodari. Sometimes the Tibetan border guards deny entry, but they often let individuals through and more often they will permit a group. The 900-km (560-mi) route from Kathmandu to Lhasa takes two or more days, traversing passes as high as 4,900 m (16,400 ft). Overnight stops are in Zhangmu and Shigatse. Usually you have to walk the 8 km (5 mi) between the two border posts—Kodari in Nepal and Zhangmu in Tibet—but porters are available (usually) to assist. The cost from Zhangmu to Lhasa is about $55 in a minibus. Hiring your own 4-wheel drive vehicle costs about $160. Exiting Tibet from Lhasa to Kathmandu is easier. The police do not stop you; the Nepalese frontier is always open and a Nepalese visa is granted at the border.

By road **from China** into Tibet is tough. The inexpensive way that is most likely to meet with success is to cross the frontier by bus from Golmud, a sprawling town in Qinghai at the end of the railway line from Xining. The distance by bus is 1,115 km (691 mi) and the trip takes anywhere from 30 to 50 hours by bus (cost: Y85); it can get very bleak and cold at night. Private buses also make the run, but there is more likelihood that police will turn individual westerners back.

Festivals and Holidays

Tibet has two sets of holidays: events observed by the People's Republic of China, which shut down businesses and government offices, and Tibetan Buddhist festivals, which are often shut down by the government. The lunar calendar determines the timing of many events.

Getting Around

By Car

Foreigners are not permitted to drive in Tibet. All cars are hired with driver. Rates depend on mileage, with a daily charge if the mileage is low. Rates start at $55 for a Landcruiser, but they vary from agent to agent. Try the Lhasa Fandian (☞ Dining and Lodging, *above*) and the CITS across from the Fandian to check on their rates and service.

By Taxi

Minibuses ply a fixed route.

Time Zone

Tibet observes Beijing standard time, which is eight hours ahead of Greenwich mean time and 13 hours ahead of U.S. eastern standard time.

Contacts and Resources

Consulates
Nepalese Consulate (⊠ 13 Norbulingka Lu, Lhasa, ☎ 0891/632–2881).

Currency Exchange
The official exchange bureaus are at the Lhasa Hotel and the Bank of China (⊠ Dekyi Linghor Lam). You can also change traveler's checks at the Bank of China branches in Zhigatse, Zhangmu, and Shiquanbe.

Emergencies
Lhasa Fandian Clinic (☞ Dining and Lodging, *above*). **People's Hospital** (⊠ Linghor Lam, ☎ 0891/632–2200).

Guided Tours
Beware of guides, especially in a group tour, whose descriptions and explanations of things Tibetan reflect the Chinese party line. Try to find a Tibetan, not a Chinese guide. Typically the cost of an organized tour for a week based out of Lhasa runs $1,000 plus airfares.

Travel Agencies
Travel agencies in Hong Kong know the ropes and can handle efficiently the travel arrangements (hotels, papers, and flights) for a group of four or more travelers. **Mera Travels** (☎ 0852/391–6892, Hong Kong) is experienced in adventure travels for Tibet. **Tibet Tourist Corporation** (TTC) is part of the nationally run China International Travel Service (CITS) ⊠ Dekyi Nub Lam, Lhasa, ☎ 0891/633–6626. **Tibet International Sports Travel** (TIST; Himalaya Hotel, Shar Linghor Lam, Lhasa, ☎ 0891/633–4082) is a fairly helpful and knowledgeable agency.

Visitor Information
Tibet Tourism Bureau (⊠ Yuanlin Lam, Lhasa, ☎ 0891/633–4315).

13 Portraits of China

China at a Glance: A Chronology

Doing Business in China

Books and Films

CHINA AT A GLANCE: A CHRONOLOGY

400,000–200,000 years ago	Early Paleolithic age: Fossil remains date Peking Man, which exhibits characteristics of modern Mongoloids.
8000–5000 BC	Neolithic age: Beginnings of agriculture.
2205–1766 BC	Xia dynasty.
1766 BC–1122 BC	**Shang** dynasty: Beginnings of concept of "mandate of heaven," emphasizing good conduct of government and right of the populace to rebel against wicked leaders. Noted for highly developed bronze castings, carved jade ritual objects, and oracle bones.
1027 BC–770 BC	**Zhou** dynasty establishes capital near present-day Xian. Development of the feudal system.
551 BC–479 BC	Lifetime of Kung Fu-tzu (Confucius), teacher of moral principles of conduct and princely rule. Beginnings of iron age.
476–221 BC	Warring States period.
372 BC–289 BC	Lifetime of Meng-Tzu (Mencius), proponent of living in proper relationships based on duty defined in social terms.
220 BC–206 BC	**Qin** Shihuang unites China, establishes capital at Xian. Work begun on Great Wall. Civil service exams instituted. Script and weights and measures are standardized. Confucian scholars are persecuted. Beginning of overland trade with Roman Empire.
206 BC–AD 220	**Han** dynasty: Beginnings of papermaking. Territorial expansion to Central Asia, Korea, Southwest China, and Vietnam. Collapse of Han dynasty and dissolution of the empire.
AD 25–AD 220	Introduction of Buddhism. Silk Route developed.
AD 265–420	Xin dynasty.
AD 420–589	Northern and Southern dynasties.
AD 589–618	Empire reunified under the **Sui** dynasty. Grand Canal constructed. Development of gentry class. Reinstatement of civil service exams.
AD 618–AD 907	**Tang** dynasty. Great flowering of the arts and sciences. Rise of scholar-officials. Expansion of Buddhism and Confucian ethics.
AD 907–960	Five Dynasties and Ten Kingdoms period: Empire collapses and barbarians invade north China. Beginnings of urban life and neo-Confucianism. Paper money and a primitive printing press are introduced, as well as the foot binding of women. First military use of gunpowder.
AD 960–1280	Sung dynasty.
1260	Mongol leader Kublai Khan establishes Peking as his capital.
1279–1368	Mongol conquest of all of China and founding of **Yuan** dynasty under "foreign" rule. Marco Polo visits China.
1368–1644	**Ming** dynasty is marked by consolidation of power and institutional foundations of Chinese state. Peking is capital.
1550	Europeans come to China seeking trade and Christian converts.
1644	Manchu conquest and founding of **Qing** dynasty. Pigtail forced on Chinese as sign of submission.

1662–1722 Kangxi Emperor, strong supporter of Confucian morality, consolidates the dynasty militarily.

1736–96 Qianlong Emperor presides over glorious period of pre-modern history.

1794 First American ship arrives at Chinese port. Beginnings of Sino-American trade.

1839 Opium War against British drug trade in Canton.

1842 Treaty of Nanjing ends Opium War.

1843 Treaty ports, allowing the growth of Western commerce and culture and legal extraterritoriality for foreigners, begin at first 5, and eventually 80 sites. Hong Kong is ceded to Great Britain and China is opened to Christian missionaries.

1851 Heavenly Kingdom of Great Peace is proclaimed by the Taipings, a peasant organization embracing a mystical Christian ideology.

1853 Taipings take Nanjing and declare it their capital.

1858 After second Opium War, the Treaty of Tianjin opens additional ports to foreign traders and grants extraterritorial privileges to foreigners.

1860 Anglo-French troops enter Peking and destroy the Old Summer Palace.

1862 Foreign forces enter continuing war against Taipings.

1864 Final defeat of Taipings by combined Chinese and European forces.

1877 First batch of Chinese students sent to Europe to study.

1893 Birth of Mao Zedong.

1894–5 China loses Korea, Taiwan, and Pescadores Islands in Sino-Japanese War.

1898 Hundred Days Reform seeks to remake the examination system, the administration, and government institutions in order to inaugurate a system of modern government.

1900–01 Eight-Power allied invasion to suppress the Boxer rebellion, which is led by fanatical peasant secret societies. The Empress Dowager is forced to flee, and the palace is occupied. Russia invades Manchuria.

1901–11 Qing reforms: new school system, modern government departments, and the abolition of the old examination system.

1908 Death of Empress Dowager Cixi.

1911 Republican revolution led by Sun Yat-sen leads to fall of the Qing dynasty.

1912 Nationalist party (Guomindang; GMD) is formed. Yuan Shikai becomes president of the Republic and Beijing is declared capital.

1916 Death of Yuan Shikai. Beginnings of warlord era.

1917 China declares war on Germany.

1919 China refuses to sign the Treaty of Versailles, which cedes former German territories in Shandong province to Japan. Anti-imperialist sentiments give way to the May Fourth Movement, ushering in new ideas of science and democracy ringing with patriotism.

1921 Chinese Communist Party (CCP) founded in Shanghai.

1925 May 30th Movement is marked by anti-imperialist student demonstrations in Shanghai.

1926 GMD armies in the Northern Expedition, from Guangzhou to the Yangzi valley, defeat warlord forces in south China.

1927 GMD turns against CCP. Chiang Kai-shek establishes GMD capital in Nanjing.

1928 U.S. recognizes government of Chiang Kai-shek in Nanjing.

1931 Japan occupies Manchuria.

1934 Communists driven out of their base in Jiangxi province by the GMD and begin the Long March, arriving in Yanan, Shaanxi province, some 6,000 miles and one year later.

1935 Mao Zedong becomes chairman and undisputed leader of the CCP at the Zunyi Conference.

1936 Chiang Kai-shek is kidnaped by one of his generals during the Xian Incident and is released only when the GMD agrees to cooperate with the Communists against the Japanese.

1937–45 Sino-Japanese War.

1945 U.S. General George Marshall arrives in China to try to put together a coalition government between the Communists and the Nationalists.

1946 Full-scale civil war between GMD and CCP breaks out.

1949 People's Republic of China is established under Mao Zedong in Beijing. Nationalists flee to Taiwan.

1950 China enters Korean War against the U.S. Marriage and agrarian reform laws passed. Sino-Soviet Treaty of Friendship, Alliance, and Mutual Assistance is signed.

1951–52 Three Antis Campaign against corruption, waste, and bureaucratism and the Five Antis Campaign against bribery, tax evasion, theft of state assets, cheating, and stealing of economic intelligence.

1952 Land Reform completed. Violent measures against landlords and local despots.

1953 Korean armistice. Beginning of First Five-Year Plan inaugurating transition to socialism by subordinating agriculture to industry.

1954 First National People's Congress adopts PRC state constitution. U.S. signs Mutual Defense Treaty with Nationalist government on Taiwan.

1955 Setting up of agricultural producers' cooperatives begins, in which peasants cultivate land together and share a common product in proportion to their pooled contributions.

1956 Mao Zedong makes Hundred Flowers speech inviting criticisms of cadres and the bureaucracy.

1957 Anti-Rightist Campaign purging erstwhile critics of the regime who dared to speak out during the Hundred Flowers period.

1958 Commune system established by amalgamating the former agricultural producers' cooperatives. Great Leap Forward aimed at economic transformation in industry and agriculture. Chinese shell Nationalist offshore islands of Quemoy and Matsu.

1959   Revolt in Tibet suppressed. Dalai Lama flees to India. Chinese Defense Minister is dismissed for speaking out against the Great Leap Forward.

1960   Soviet withdrawal of experts. Overambitious and misguided industrial targets of the Great Leap result in devastating famine with an estimated 30 million deaths.

1960–62   Three years of natural disasters.

1962   Sino-Indian border war.

1964   China's first nuclear explosion.

1965   First signs of the Cultural Revolution erupt in the literary sphere in nationwide criticism of the play, *Hai Rui Dismissed from Office*.

1966   Eleventh Plenum of Eleventh Central Committee formalizes the Cultural Revolution in move against Mao's critics, which leads to the ousting of the head of state Liu Shaoqi and general secretary of the party Deng Xiaoping. Reign of terror and massive destruction ensue.

1967   Military is called in to restore order.

1968   Millions of urban youth sent to the countryside to learn from the peasants.

1969   Border clashes with the Soviet Union. Ninth Party Congress names Defense Minister Lin Biao as Mao Zedong's closest comrade-in-arms and successor.

1971   Head of a powerful military faction, Lin Biao dies in a mysterious plane crash over Mongolia. U.S. State Department abolishes travel restrictions to China, and U.S. table tennis team visits Beijing. Taiwan is expelled from the UN, and China takes its seat on the UN Security Council.

1972   President Nixon and Prime Minister Tanaka of Japan visit China. Shanghai communiqué is signed beginning the process of normalization of relations between China and the U.S.

1975   Premier Zhou Enlai outlines program of four modernizations in agriculture, industry, science and technology, and national defense. Death of Chiang Kai-shek in Taiwan.

1976   Death of Zhou Enlai. First Tiananmen demonstrations against the radical political line of the Cultural Revolution. A severe earthquake measuring 7.5 devastates the city of Tangshan. Death of Mao Zedong is followed by the arrest of the Cultural Revolution protagonists, the "Gang of Four," led by Mao's wife.

1977   Deng Xiaoping returns to power.

1978   Sino-Japanese Treaty of Peace and Friendship is signed. Third Plenum of the Eleventh Central Committee inaugurates socialist modernization and liberalized agricultural policies.

1978–79   Wall poster movement attacking the Cultural Revolution and Mao Zedong evolves into the Democracy Wall Movement.

1979   Resumption of formal diplomatic relations with the United States. Deng Xiaoping visits the United States. Sino-Vietnamese war. Democracy Wall is closed down and leading dissident Wei Jingsheng is arrested and sentenced to 15 years' imprisonment.

1980   Trial of the "Gang of Four" and former military figures associated with Lin Biao. Opening of four special economic zones.

1981 Campaign against spiritual pollution and Western influences.

1983 Anti-crime campaign resulting in thousands of executions and deportations to the countryside.

1984 Third Plenum of the Twelfth Central Committee endorses broad economic and urban reforms.

1986 Student demonstrations begin in Hefei, Anhui province, and spread to Shanghai, Beijing, and 17 other cities.

1987 Party General Secretary Hu Yaobang is dismissed for failure to crack down on the students. Anti-bourgeois liberalization campaign ensues against Western values and institutions.

1989 Death of Hu Yaobang leads to massive demonstrations in Beijing on Tiananmen Square for six weeks. Declaration of martial law does not quell the crowds in the Square. The military is brought in on June 4, resulting in hundreds of deaths. General Secretary Zhao Ziyang is dismissed from office.

1992 Fourteenth Party Congress endorses concept of a socialist market economy.

1995 Chinese test-fire missiles off northern coast of Taiwan.

1997 Paramount leader Deng Xiaoping dies. Upon expiration of 99-year lease, sovereignty over Hong Kong reverts to China.

— By Nancy Hearst

DOING BUSINESS IN CHINA

IF YOU'RE A BUSINESS TRAVELER in China, you probably still feel like a pioneer, even though it has been almost 20 years since Deng Xiaoping launched the "open door" policy and started inviting foreign investment into the previously isolated country. "We are learning how to compete in the market economy, and we need foreign expertise," a Chinese official or enterprise manager might tell you. But don't be misled into believing that you can come in with a plan this week and sign a contract next week, or that Western-style efficiency will be welcome in a joint venture with a Chinese company.

The Chinese, as every foreign business traveler quickly learns, have an elaborate, unwritten code of rules that apply to every aspect of business, from negotiating the contract to selling the product. A good way to prepare yourself is to read Sun Tze's *The Art of War*. The true author of this Chinese classic is unknown, but the best guess is that it was written by a brilliant military strategist who lived sometime around the 4th century BC. Sun Tze's basic principle held that moral strength and intellectual faculty were the decisive factors in battle, and today, these are the guiding factors in negotiating business deals. Not that you're dealing with adversaries—not exactly. But from the days when the first foreign firms began to eye China's vast potential market of 1.2 billion consumers, the Chinese quickly realized that they had something the world wanted, so why not assure themselves a share in the capital that foreign ventures were sure to generate?

In recent years, a number of major Western companies have played hardball with Chinese officials and held their own. Take the time the city government of Beijing tried to evict McDonald's. One of Hong Kong's wealthiest businessmen, Li Kai Shing, who was born in a Chinese village and knew how Sun Tze's war strategies could help him achieve the impossible, spent years donating money to various projects in China, mostly schools. Li was collecting bargaining chips, and in 1994 he was ready to cash in. He wanted to build an office tower that would face Beijing's version of the Champs-Elysées, the area of Chang An Avenue Avenue and Wangfujing, including the most valuable tract, which was the corner across from the Beijing Hotel that was occupied by McDonald's. He allegedly told the Beijing Municipal Government that if he couldn't have the corner he wouldn't invest in China at all. Li had cast a brick to attract a jade; i.e., used a bait to catch something big. However, McDonald's, too, knew it had something the Chinese people really wanted. "Know the terrain," Sun Tze wrote. And keep the opponent under strain to wear him down. McDonald's employed the latter maneuver by resisting the order to move for two years, until the Beijing government finally agreed to compensation in the form of the right to open at least two more outlets along an adjacent street.

The Disney Company was pressured in quite a different way. In 1996, Disney was in discussions with the central government about distributing movies, selling merchandise, and building theme parks in China when Liu Jianzhong, director of the Film Bureau in the Ministry of Radio, Film and Television, warned that there might be no final approval for these projects if a Disney subsidiary went ahead with production of a film about the Dalai Lama, the Tibetan spiritual leader who is considered an enemy by the Chinese government. Disney refused to stop the film from being made. At this writing, the mayor of Shanghai had been talking to Disney executives privately about business ventures, so it didn't seem that the company was blacklisted all over China. Disney had also contracted none other than Henry Kissinger to put his diplomatic skills to work for the company in China. According to *The Art of War,* you sometimes have to yield a city or give up ground in order to gain a more valuable objective. Although it might seem a good idea in the short run to bow to ideological pressure from China, it is probably best for a company's long-term goals and international image to hold out. Sun Tze also said, "Loot a burning house. Capitalize on an opportunity at the expense of your adversary's chaotic situation." There has been dissension within the ranks of China's government and there could be more, so attempts to appease local or central authorities who make demands today may backfire if they fall out of favor domestically, or if America's political relations with China deteriorate.

Furthermore, though the Chinese authorities may insist that their politics are none of our business, the lack of a clear rule of law in China can work against conducting business here. On a number of occasions business people have found themselves arrested and detained on trumped-up or nonexistent charges following a disagreement with a local partner or government authority over terms. Often the disagreement has to do with a city or provincial ministry's wanting an unreasonable share in the company. It is to the advantage of all foreigners living or spending time in China to push for political reforms that would incorporate due process of law.

This is all part of pioneering. If you think of how the settlers who crossed America's wild west in 1850 changed the face of the country, you'll have a fair analogy, except that modern technology is bringing a faster rate of change in China. In a country that had almost no modern roads 20 years ago, there are now more than 20 expressways and new ones coming up. According to World Bank figures, China's economy is one of the fastest-growing in the world, with an annual average rate of 9.2% since 1978, though this was showing signs of leveling off in late 1997. From being a country with virtually no capital, it has moved to among the top six nations in the world in terms of foreign exchange reserves. The people wear designer fashions, and there are construction cranes on almost every city street.

Some observers think that as the market economy grows, a measure of democratic reform will come. The Chinese people themselves are likely to demand a freer flow of information, if only to help them make financial decisions. In early 1997, there was talk in China of a desperate need for the domestic news media to report responsibly and independently on the wild gyrations of the Shenzhen and Shanghai stock markets, so that the 21 million Chinese who

own corporate equities can monitor their investments. Thomas Friedman, writing in *The New York Times,* suggested that the U.S. send a delegation led by the head of the Securities Exchange Commission and some major business editors to talk to Chinese officials about how to answer internal pressures for a freer press. Pointing out that the nuclear meltdown at Chernobyl helped hasten the collapse of the Soviet Union partly because "without a responsible free press, rumors ran wild and devastated what little confidence was left in the regime," Friedman wrote, adding, "I hope it won't take a meltdown of the Shanghai stock market to spur a free press in China."

Of course, if you are trying to sell your product to the consumer market or set up a production facility utilizing China's abundant labor pool, you aren't going in to change the country single-handedly, although you may be part of a cumulative effect. Most likely, you will have to go in and do business the way the Chinese do. In spite of the economic reforms, this is still a centrally planned system called "socialism with Chinese characteristics." It is still a society with a thousand years of practice at handling foreign traders. Here are some fundamentals you should know before you go:

Your Team: If you're new to the place, retain the services of a China consultant who knows the language and has a strong track record. The nonprofit U.S. China Business Council (1818 N St. NW, Suite 200, Washington, D.C. 20036, tel. 202/429–0340, fax 202/775–2476, with additional offices in Hong Kong, Beijing, and Shanghai) is a good source for consulting services, referrals, and other information. If you don't speak Mandarin fluently you will also need to have a translator accompanying you on the trip. Choose your own translator who will be looking out for your interests.

Know who you'll be meeting with in China, and send people with corresponding titles. The Chinese are very hierarchical and will be offended if you send a low-level manager to meet a minister. All of this ties into the all-important and intricate concept of "face," which can best be explained as the need to preserve dignity and standing.

Don't bring your spouse on the trip, unless he or she is involved in the business.

Otherwise the Chinese will think your trip is really a vacation.

Attitudes Toward Women: The Chinese will take a woman seriously if she has an elevated title and acts serious. Women will find themselves under less pressure than men to hang out at the karaoke until the wee hours. This is partly because the party list might include prostitutes. A business woman will also avoid the trap that Chinese local partners sometimes lay to get rid of an out-of-favor foreign manager. They'll have a prostitute pick him up, then get the police to catch him so that he can be banished from the country for a sexual offense.

Business Cards: Bring more than you ever thought you'd need. Consult a translator before you go and have cards made with your name and the name of your company in Chinese characters on the reverse side.

The Greeting: When you are introduced to someone in China, immediately bow your head slightly and offer your business card, with two hands. In the same ceremonious fashion accept your colleague's business card, which will likely be turned up to show an Anglicized name.

Be there on time. The Chinese are very punctual. When you are hosting a banquet, arrive at the restaurant at least 30 minutes before your guests.

The Meeting: Don't make plans for the rest of the day, or evening, or tomorrow or the next day. And don't be in a rush to get home. Meetings can go on for days, weeks, whatever it takes to win concessions. Meetings will continue over a lavish lunch, a lavish dinner that includes many toasts with mao tai, and a long night at a karaoke, consuming XO cognac from a showy bottle. To keep in shape for the lengthy meetings, learn the art of throwing a shot of mao tai onto the floor behind you instead of drinking it down when your host says "ganbei." (Chances are he is not really drinking either.)

Gifts and Bribes: Yes, a local official might ask you to get his child into a foreign university or buy your venture partner a fleet of BMWs. A few years ago a survey by the Independent Commission Against Corruption in Hong Kong found that corrupt business practices may represent 3%–5% of the cost of doing business in China,

a factor that respondents (Hong Kong firms) claimed was bearable and not a disincentive. However, the Chinese government has been campaigning against corruption and business fraud. American companies have the added constraint of the Foreign Corrupt Practices Act, which prohibits offering or making payments to officials of foreign countries. The law can be a good excuse for not paying bribes. However, you may find yourself faced with a great many arbitrary fees to be paid to the city and county for everything from your business license to garbage collection. It is hard to avoid paying these.

The U.S. has capitulated somewhat to so-called tied aid, in which matching sums of aid are given to an emerging country when it grants a major capital project contract to a U.S. firm. The Europeans and Japanese have been offering tied aid for years, and the U.S. saw this as unfair competition. Though the U.S. Export-Import Bank officially opposes tied aid and does not initiate the offers, it now has some funds available to help U.S. companies compete for large infrastructure projects.

To win friends in a small but legal way, you should hand out small gifts to the people you meet. Bring a shipment of such items as pens, paperweights, and T-shirts emblazoned with your company logo. And, before you leave town, host a banquet for all of the people who have entertained you. The banquet is not merely a way to reciprocate hospitality; as the host, you can use the occasion to make your demands for the business venture heard. The best time to have your banquet is when the parties concerned are almost ready to sign the contract.

Communication: Gestures that seem insignificant on the surface will help make or break your efforts to gain entry into China. Escort a departing visitor to the elevator as a way of giving him face, for example. To make a visitor feel particularly esteemed, walk him all the way to the front door of the building. And don't "have other plans" when your Chinese associates invite you out. As in many Asian countries, personal relationships are more important than the contract. The people you are dealing with may not tell you what they really want from a partnership with you until you're out eating and drinking.

There are many ways of saying "no," and some may sound like "yes" to foreigners. If you hear that your proposal "is under study" or has arrived at "an inconvenient time," start preparing a new one.

A manager of a local factory in search of a foreign venture partner might tell you that the deal can be done, but that doesn't mean it will be. Make sure you meet with the officials in charge of your sector in the city, those who have the authority to approve the deal. If someone says he has to get the boss's approval, you should have a hearing with the boss—even if it means getting your boss there on the next flight to meet with his counterpart.

Early on you may be asked to sign a "letter of intent." This document is not legally binding; it serves more as an expression of seriousness. But the principles in the letter, which look like ritual statements to the Westerner because they lack specific detail, may be invoked later if your Chinese partner has a grudge against you. He'll say you have not lived up to the spirit of mutual cooperation and benefit initially agreed upon.

How to Get Your Way: You will have to give your Chinese partner something he wants. He might, for instance, want your capital to go into lines of business other than what you had in mind. You might have to agree to this if establishing a presence in China is important to your business. Take the example of John C. Portman III, vice chairman of the Atlanta-based architecture firm John Portman & Associates. Portman spent the early 1980s courting the Shanghai government. Besides volunteering suggestions for redeveloping the city, he set up a trading company that brought an exhibition of goods from Shanghai to Atlanta. Not his usual line of business, but in the end the friendships he'd cultivated netted his company the coveted contract to design and develop the $200-million Shanghai Centre, which houses the Portman Shangri-La Hotel, and China now accounts for about half of the company's total business.

Know when to be flexible, but for important details such as who actually has control of the venture and its operations, hold out, even if it takes a year or more. There are ways to make sure of who is really in charge of a joint venture, even though for matters of face and power the Chinese partner will probably want to provide the person with the loftiest title. You will also want to own the controlling share, because it means quality control, profitability, and decision-making power over matters for which your company is legally liable. Often an inside deal is worked out, whereby the foreign party provides the general manager, who actually is in charge of day-to-day operations, while the Chinese partner brings in the chairman, who works with a board of directors and has authority only over broad policy issues.

Don't go to China and tell your prospective partner you want to start production by a certain date. Expect your Chinese associates to drive their hardest bargain just when you thought it was safe to go home. They know that once rumors of a concluded negotiation become public, you will not be able to back down from the deal without having to make difficult explanations to your investors and headquarters.

Demand that your contract include an arbitration clause, which stipulates that if a dispute arises the matter will be tried by an arbitrator, preferably either in the U.S. or in a third country. However, even in China, there are arbitration centers that comply with international standards and are well ahead of the court system.

Being There: Saddled with 50 employees from the state-owned enterprise and you don't even have a customer in China? That's the way things have been done. You will have to make changes slowly and be prepared to train people for new skills. Profits may be equally slow to roll in, but remember the corporate axiom that has become the main China strategy circa 1990s: We're in it for the long haul.

If you're trying to break into the China market with a product or service, learn more about the consumers you're targeting through a focus study. These have become popular among prospective consumers, who have proved willing to sit through sessions lasting as long as three hours. (Focus panels generally last only 40 minutes in the United States.) You might find you have to change your advertising message drastically. Coffee manufacturers, for example, don't win Chinese customers with a "wake up" message because coffee is considered an after-dinner beverage. Test the name in different cities, because meaning can vary according to the local language. As the *Economist Intelligence Unit* reported recently, one company had a name for a butter product that meant "yellow oil" in one city, "engine oil" in another, and "cow fat" in a third.

Will Feng Shui Help Your Prospects? The 7,000-year-old art of placing objects in harmony with the environment and the elements is virtually mandatory in Hong Kong and Taiwan—it always had a stronger influence in southern China. On mainland China it's officially considered feudalist superstitious nonsense, but of course, if it facilitates business. . . . If there's any doubt in your mind, by all means call a geomancer.

While China speeds along toward overtaking the United States as the world's largest economy—the World Bank forecasts that will happen in the year 2020—any number of factors may make or break your efforts to reap some of the benefits of this dizzying growth. Barring serious political upheaval, you'll probably want to stay here and make constant—i.e., day-to-day—adaptations to the changing demands of the market. Like armies, companies in China have to figure out when to advance their presence, when to scale back, when to retreat to another location. And with each new strategy, be prepared to negotiate, feast, and sing karaoke songs.

— By Jan Alexander

BOOKS AND FILMS

Books

For general overviews of Chinese history from the 1600s to the present, start with *The Search for Modern China* (Jonathan Spence, Norton, New York, 1990) or *The Rise of Modern China* (Immanuel Hsu, Oxford University Press, New York, 4th edition, 1990). To explore deeper roots, with essays on specific cultural topics, read *An Introduction to Chinese Civilization* (John Meskill, ed., D.C. Heath, Boston, 1973). The story of Hong Kong is presented in *A Borrowed Place: The History of Hong Kong* (Frank Welsh, Kodansha, New York, 1994). A number of memoirs have been published in recent years that provide not only personal stories, but also intimate windows on China's vast socio-economic changes. *Wild Swans: Three Daughters of China* (Chang Jung, Simon & Schuster, New York, 1991) covers much of the 20th century in its look at the author's family. *A Single Tear* (Ningkun Wu, Atlantic Monthly Press, New York, 1993) traces the travails of a patriotic, U.S.-trained scholar who returns to China in 1950. *The Private Life of Mao Zedong: The Memoirs of Mao's Personal Physician* (Zhisui Li, with Anne Thurston, Random House, New York, 1994) combines the doctor's personal history and an intimate, controversial focus on the PRC's founding father.

The United States and China (John K. Fairbank, Harvard University Press, Cambridge, MA, 4th ed., 1983) is a good primer for bilateral relations, while *The Great Wall and the Empty Fortress: China's Search for Security* (Andrew Nathan and Robert Ross, Norton, New York, 1997) is a solid analysis of China's foreign policy concerns. A thoughtful collection of essays on current U.S.–China relations can be found in *Living with China: U.S.–China Relations in the Twenty-First Century* (Ezra Vogel, ed., Norton, New York, 1997). Among the scores of excellent books on Chinese politics are *Politics of China* (Roderick MacFarquhar, ed., Cambridge University Press, New York, 2nd ed., 1993), and *Sowing the Seeds of Democracy in China: Political Reform in the Deng Xiaoping Era* (Merle Goldman, Harvard University Press, Cambridge, MA, 1994).

At the juncture of politics and the economy is *China's Second Revolution: Reform After Mao* (Harry Harding, Brookings Institution, Washington, DC, 1987). *One Step Ahead in China: Guangdong Under Reform* (Ezra Vogel, Harvard University Press, Cambridge, MA, 1989) probes deeply into the changes in southern China since 1978.

One of the best windows into contemporary Chinese society is by the Chinese journalists Sang Ye and Zhang Xinxin, titled *Chinese Lives: An Oral History of Contemporary China* (ed. by W.J.F. Jenner and Delia Davin, Pantheon, New York, 1987). Western journalist Orville Schell has written several books that track China since the mid-1970s, the latest being *Mandate of Heaven: The Legacy of Tiananmen Square and the Next Generation* (Simon & Schuster, New York, 1995). *China Pop* (Jianying Jha, The New Press, New York, 1995) is a superb look at popular culture in the PRC today. For the bottom line on dissident expression, including art, culture, and politics, see *New Ghosts, Old Dreams: Chinese Rebel Voices* (Geremie Barme and Linda Jaivin, Times Books, New York, 1992).

For a taste of historical Chinese literature, spend some time with *Story of the Stone*; it's also known as *Dream of the Red Chamber* (Xueqin Cao, trans. by David Hawkes, Penguin, New York, 1973). Any book or essay by author Lu Xun will give you a taste of China's painful path from dynastic rule through early Communist rule; try *Diary of a Madman and Other Stories* (trans. by William Lyell, University of Hawaii Press, Honolulu, 1990). *Bolshevik Salute* (Meng Wang, University of Washington Press, Seattle, 1989) is one of China's first modern novels translated into English. Of the collections of Chinese literature and poetry both ancient and modern, check out *An Anthology of Chinese Literature: Beginnings to 1911* (Stephen Owen, ed. and trans., Norton, New York, 1996) and *From May Fourth to June Fourth: Twentieth Century Chinese Fiction and Film* (David D.W. Wang and Ellen Widmer, eds., Cambridge University Press, New York, 1993).

Films

Among Chinese directors, Chen Kaige captures the beauty of the Chinese countryside in his mysterious, striking *Life on a String* (1991). He also directed an epic story of the artistic and personal commitment of two Peking opera stars, *Farewell, My Concubine* (1993); and *Temptress Moon* (1997). Tian Zhuangzhuang directed *The Blue Kite* (1994), a story of the travails of a young schoolteacher under communism in the 1950s and '60s. The outstanding films of director Zhang Yimou, such as *Red Sorghum* (1987), *Ju-Dou* (1990), *Raise the Red Lantern* (1991), *Shanghai Triad* (1995), *The Story of Qiu Ju* (1992), and *To Live* (1994) all star the excellent actress Gong Li, whose roles range from a glamorous mob mistress in 1930s Shanghai to a rural worker.

An American filmmaker of Chinese descent, Peter Wang, looks wryly at contemporary China in *A Great Wall* (1986). Director Ann Hui's *Song of the Exile* (1990) follows a young woman returning home to Hong Kong after graduating from a British university.

A Western take on Chinese history is presented in Bernardo Bertolucci's *The Last Emperor,* filmed in China. Three documentary films by Ambrica Productions (New York), *China in Revolution 1911–1949* (1989), *The Mao Years 1949–1976* (1994), and *Born under the Red Flag 1976–1997* (1997), depict the political and social upheavals that followed the death of the last emperor. They are available from Zeitgeist Films (☎ 800/255–9424). The Long Bow Group (Boston) has produced *The Gate of Heavenly Peace* (1996), a documentary film about the Tiananmen Square protests; it is available from Naata (☎ 415/552–9550).

— By Colin B. Cowles

CHINESE VOCABULARY

Many of the pronunciations for the *pinyin* below appear to have two syllables. Actually, there are two separate sounds, but they move smoothly from one into the other and make but a single sound when said correctly. For example, the *pinyin* "dian" is pronounced "dee-**en**," with a slight emphasis on the second part of the word: this should be a single sound, as opposed to what you would hear if you said separately the letters "D" and "N." Below, only the words with hyphens in them are pronounced this way. All other "spelled sounds" (a literal translation of the word *pinyin*) should be pronounced as indicated.

English	Pinyin	Pronunciation
Basics		
Yes/there is/to have	you	yoh
No/there isn't/ to not have	mei you	**may** yoh
Please	qing	ching
Thank you	xie xie	**shay** shay
Excuse me	ma fan ni	mah fahn nee
Sorry	dui bu qi	**dway** boo chee
Good/bad	hao/bu hao	how/**boo** how
Goodbye	zai jian	dzy jee-**en** (y as in why)
Mr. (Sir)	xiansheng	shee-**en** shung
Mrs. (Ma'am)	nu shi	**nyoo** shuh
Miss	xiao jie	shee-**ao** jee-**ay**
Days of the Week, Time Expressions		
Sunday	xing qi ri/	shing chee **dz**/
	xing qi tian	shing chee tee-**en**
Monday	xing qi yi	shing chee **ee**
Tuesday	xing qi er	shing chee **ahr**
Wednesday	xing qi san	shing chee **sahn**
Thursday	xing qi si	shing chee **sih**
Friday	xing qi wu	shing chee **woo**
Saturday	sing qi liu	shing chee **lee**-o
Week	xing qi	shing chee
Month/moon	yue	yway
Year	nian	nee-**en**
When	shen me shi hou?	shun muh shur ho?
Night/evening	wan shang	wahn **shahng**
Yesterday	zuo tian	zwo tee-**en**
Today	jin tian	jeen tee-**en**
Tomorrow	ming tian	ming tee-**en**
Numbers		
1	yi	ee
2	er (used as a numeral)	ahr
2 of . . .	liang	lee-**ahng**
3	san	sahn
4	si	sih
5	wu	woo

6	liu	**lee**-o
7	qi	chee
8	ba	bah
9	jiu	jee-**o**
10	shi	shur
11	shi yi (10 + 1)	shur **ee**
15	shi wu	**shur** woo
20	er shi (2 10)	**ahr** shur
21	er shi yi (2 x 10 + 1)	**ahr** shur **ee**
30	san shi	**sahn** shur
50	wu shi	woo shur
100	(yi) bai	(ee) by
200	er bai/liang bai	**ahr** by
500	wu bai	woo by
1,000	(yi) qian	(ee) chee-**en**
first/second/third . . .	di yi/di er/di san . . .	dee ee/dee ahr/dee **sahn**

Useful Phrases

Hello/How are you	ni hao/ni hao ma?	**nee** how/nee how mah?
Do you speak . . .	ni hui shuo . . .	nee **hway** shwo
. . . English?	. . . ying wen ma	**yeeng** wen mah?
I don't understand.	wo bu dong	woh **boo** dohng
I don't know.	wo bu zhi dao	woh **boo** jer dow
I am lost.	wo mi lu le	woh mee loo luh
What is this?	zhe shi shen me	juh shur **shun**-muh
Where is . . .	. . . zai nar?	. . . **dzy** nahr?
the train station?	huo che zhan jahn . . .	who-**oh** chuh (zai nar?)
the subway station	di tie zhan . . .	dee tee-**ay** jahn . . .
the post office	you ju . . .	yoh jew . . .
the bank	ying hang . . .	**yeeng** hahng . . .
the hospital	yi yuan . . .	yee yoo-en
my hotel	wo de bing guan . . .	woh duh **beeng** gwahn . . .
I am American	wo shi mei guo ren	wo **shur** may gworen
British	ying guo ren	**yeeng** gwo ren
Australian	ao da li ya ren	ow dah lee **yah** ren
Canadian	jia na da ren	jee-**ah** nah **dah** ren
Where are the . . . rest rooms?	ce suo zai nar?	**tsuh** swoh zy nahr?
Left (side)	zuo (bian)	zwoh (bee-**en**)
Right (side)	you (bian)	yoh (bee-**en**)
In the middle	zai zhong jian	zy johng jee-**en**
I'd like a room	wo xiang yao yi ge fang jian	woh shee-ahng yow ee guh **fong** jee-en
I'd like to buy . . .	wo xiang mai . . .	woh shee-angh my
How much is that?	na duo shao qian?	nah **dwoh** shao chee-**en**?

A little	yi dian	ee dee-**en**
A lot	hen duo	hun **dwoh**
More	duo	**dwoh**
Less	shao	shao
I feel ill	wo bu shu fu	woh boo **shoo** foo
I need a doctor	wo bi xu kan yi sheng	woh **bee** shoo kahn **ee** shung
I have a problem	wo you yi ge wenti	woh yoh ee guh **wen** tee

Dining Out

Do you have	ni you ying wen	nee yoh **yeeng** wen
an English menu?	cai dan ma?	tsy **dahn** mah?
a bottle of . . .	yi ping . . .	ee peeng . . .
Bill/check	mai dan/suan zhang	my **dahn**/swahn **jahng**
Bread	mian bao	mee-**en** bao
House specialty	ben jia te cai	bun jee-**ah** tuh **tsy**
I do not eat meat	wo bu chi rou	woh **boo** chur **roh**
I'd like to order.	wo xiang dian cai	woh shee-ahng dee-**en** tsy
Is service/ the tip included?	zhe bao kuo xiao fei ma?	juh bao kwoh shee-**ao** fay mah?
Menu	cai dan	tsy **dahn**
Fork	cha zi	**chah** zuh
Please give me . . .	qing gei wo . . .	ching **gay** woh . . .
boiled water	kai shui	**ky** shway
tea	cha	chah

INDEX

NOTES

NOTES

NOTES

NOTES

Fodor's Travel Publications

Available at bookstores everywhere, or call 1–800–533–6478, 24 hours a day.

Gold Guides

U.S.

Alaska	Florida	New Orleans	Seattle & Vancouver
Arizona	Hawai'i	New York City	The South
Boston	Las Vegas, Reno, Tahoe	Pacific North Coast	U.S. & British Virgin Islands
California	Los Angeles	Philadelphia & the Pennsylvania Dutch Country	USA
Cape Cod, Martha's Vineyard, Nantucket	Maine, Vermont, New Hampshire	The Rockies	Virginia & Maryland
The Carolinas & Georgia	Maui & Lāna'i	San Diego	Walt Disney World, Universal Studios and Orlando
Chicago	Miami & the Keys	San Francisco	Washington, D.C.
Colorado	New England	Santa Fe, Taos, Albuquerque	

Foreign

Australia	Europe	Montréal & Québec City	Scotland
Austria	Florence, Tuscany & Umbria	Moscow, St. Petersburg, Kiev	Singapore
The Bahamas	France	The Netherlands, Belgium & Luxembourg	South Africa
Belize & Guatemala	Germany	New Zealand	South America
Bermuda	Great Britain	Norway	Southeast Asia
Canada	Greece	Nova Scotia, New Brunswick, Prince Edward Island	Spain
Cancún, Cozumel, Yucatán Peninsula	Hong Kong	Paris	Sweden
Caribbean	India	Portugal	Switzerland
China	Ireland	Provence & the Riviera	Thailand
Costa Rica	Israel	Scandinavia	Toronto
Cuba	Italy		Turkey
The Czech Republic & Slovakia	Japan		Vienna & the Danube Valley
Eastern & Central Europe	London		
	Madrid & Barcelona		
	Mexico		

Special-Interest Guides

Adventures to Imagine	Fodor's Gay Guide to the USA	Halliday's New Orleans Food Explorer	Rock & Roll Traveler USA
Alaska Ports of Call	Fodor's How to Pack	Healthy Escapes	Sunday in San Francisco
Ballpark Vacations	Great American Learning Vacations	Kodak Guide to Shooting Great Travel Pictures	Walt Disney World for Adults
Caribbean Ports of Call	Great American Sports & Adventure Vacations	National Parks and Seashores of the East	Weekends in New York
The Complete Guide to America's National Parks	Great American Vacations	National Parks of the West	Wendy Perrin's Secrets Every Smart Traveler Should Know
Disney Like a Pro	Great American Vacations for Travelers with Disabilities	Nights to Imagine	Worldwide Cruises and Ports of Call
Europe Ports of Call		Rock & Roll Traveler Great Britain and Ireland	
Family Adventures			

Fodor's Special Series

Fodor's Best Bed & Breakfasts

America
California
The Mid-Atlantic
New England
The Pacific Northwest
The South
The Southwest
The Upper Great Lakes

Compass American Guides

Alaska
Arizona
Boston
Chicago
Colorado
Hawaii
Idaho
Hollywood
Las Vegas
Maine
Manhattan
Minnesota
Montana
New Mexico
New Orleans
Oregon
Pacific Northwest
San Francisco
Santa Fe
South Carolina
South Dakota
Southwest
Texas
Utah
Virginia
Washington
Wine Country
Wisconsin
Wyoming

Citypacks

Amsterdam
Atlanta
Berlin
Chicago
Florence
Hong Kong
London
Los Angeles
Montréal
New York City

Paris
Prague
Rome
San Francisco
Tokyo
Venice
Washington, D.C.

Exploring Guides

Australia
Boston & New England
Britain
California
Canada
Caribbean
China
Costa Rica
Egypt
Florence & Tuscany
Florida
France
Germany
Greek Islands
Hawaii
Ireland
Israel
Italy
Japan
London
Mexico
Moscow & St. Petersburg
New York City
Paris
Prague
Provence
Rome
San Francisco
Scotland
Singapore & Malaysia
South Africa
Spain
Thailand
Turkey
Venice

Flashmaps

Boston
New York
San Francisco
Washington, D.C.

Fodor's Gay Guides

Los Angeles & Southern California
New York City
Pacific Northwest
San Francisco and the Bay Area
South Florida
USA

Pocket Guides

Acapulco
Aruba
Atlanta
Barbados
Budapest
Jamaica
London
New York City
Paris
Prague
Puerto Rico
Rome
San Francisco
Washington, D.C.

Languages for Travelers (Cassette & Phrasebook)

French
German
Italian
Spanish

Mobil Travel Guides

America's Best Hotels & Restaurants
California and the West
Major Cities
Great Lakes
Mid-Atlantic
Northeast
Northwest and Great Plains
Southeast
Southwest and South Central

Rivages Guides

Bed and Breakfasts of Character and Charm in France
Hotels and Country Inns of Character and Charm in France
Hotels and Country Inns of Character and Charm in Italy
Hotels and Country Inns of Character and Charm in Paris

Hotels and Country Inns of Character and Charm in Portugal
Hotels and Country Inns of Character and Charm in Spain

Short Escapes

Britain
France
New England
Near New York City

Fodor's Sports

Golf Digest's Places to Play
Skiing USA
USA Today The Complete Four Sport Stadium Guide

WHEREVER YOU TRAVEL, *H*ELP IS NEVER FAR AWAY.

From planning your trip to providing travel assistance along the way, American Express® Travel Service Offices are always there to help you do more.

China

American Express Int'l., Inc.
L1 15D CWTC Shpg Arcade, CWTC
1 Jian Guo Men Wai Ave.
Beijing
10/6505-2888

China International Travel Service (R)
Rm. 417 4/F Cits Bldg.
103 Fuxingmennei Ave.
Beijing
10/6601-1122 x417

China International Travel Service (R)
Lobby, Guanming Bldg.
2 Jinling Rd. (East)
Shanghai
21/6323-8750

China International Travel Service (R)
14 North Ronghu Road
Guilin
773/282-2648

China International Travel Service (R)
Sheraton Hotel
Bing Jiang Nan Road
Guilin
773/282-5588 x8234

China International Travel Service (R)
Sheraton Hotel
12 Feng Gao Road
Xian
29/426-1888 x1000

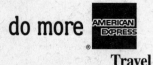

do more AMERICAN EXPRESS
®
Travel

http://www.americanexpress.com/travel

American Express Travel Service Offices are located throughout China.